WHY CRIME?

WHY CRIME?

An Interdisciplinary Approach to Explaining Criminal Behavior

Second Edition

Matthew B. Robinson
APPALACHIAN STATE UNIVERSITY

Kevin M. Beaver
FLORIDA STATE UNIVERSITY

CAROLINA ACADEMIC PRESS

Durham, North Carolina

Library of Congress Cataloging-in-Publication Data

Robinson, Matthew B.
  Why crime? : an interdisciplinary approach to explaining criminal behavior /
Matthew B. Robinson, Kevin M. Beaver.
    p. cm.
  Includes bibliographical references and index.
  ISBN 978-1-59460-707-3 (alk. paper)
  1. Criminology. 2. Criminal behavior. 3. Antisocial personality disorders.
I. Beaver, Kevin M. II. Title.

  HV6001.R63 2009
  364.2--dc22

                                    2009027273

CAROLINA ACADEMIC PRESS
700 Kent Street
Durham, North Carolina 27701
Telephone (919) 489-7486
Fax (919) 493-5668
www.cap-press.com

Printed in the United States of America

*This work is dedicated to
Professors C. Ray Jeffery and Frederic L. Faust of
The Florida State University, each of whom
laid the foundation for this book.*

Contents

Preface

Why Crime? An Interdisciplinary Approach to Explaining Criminal Behavior is about (as you might guess) why crime happens. Yet, the book is meant to serve as more than just an introduction to criminological theory. Instead of rehashing the same old material in the same old way, we discuss individual criminological theories only to the degree that they are supported by scientific evidence. From the evidence presented, we ultimately put forth a new theory of antisocial behavior and criminality. *Why Crime?* advances the state of knowledge in criminological theory by integrating current theories into an integrated, interdisciplinary theory of antisocial behavior and criminality.

Why Crime? is different from any other criminological theory text on the market in several ways. Before we point out the differences, let us first characterize the typical criminological theory text. Traditionally, theory texts organize the materials in the same general fashion. First, they normally summarize individual theories of crime by academic discipline—for example, sociological theories (which are typically broken down into social structure and social process theories), psychological theories, biological theories, and so on. This approach is not acceptable for the mere fact that there are no real dividing lines in knowledge. Criminal behaviors cannot adequately be explained by any one theory in existence, nor by any one academic discipline for that matter. Thus, in this book we deemphasize the academic disciplines from which theories arose by intentionally *not* discussing any one theory or academic discipline in any greater depth than another.

Instead, we focus on the factors that either produce or reduce criminality, delinquency, and other maladaptive, aggressive, violent, and antisocial behaviors that have been identified by various theories across numerous academic disciplines. This approach is widely pursued by the biological sciences and by environmental psychologists, among others. Yet, sociology and other social sciences, including criminology, are really only now beginning to use this approach for the study of behavior. As such, our book advances the field of knowledge. Unfortunately, Criminology still seems to be a discipline stuck in its past.

Second, most texts give biological factors brief or no coverage, as if these factors are unimportant. In fact, the biological sciences have made more progress in advancing our understanding about behavior in the past 10 years than sociology has made in the past 50 years. This is a controversial statement to be sure, but it is one that can be supported with evidence. For example, it took 50 years for Robert Merton's theory of structural strain to be broadened into a general strain theory by Robert Agnew. There are some texts on the market that adequately summarize biological factors, most notably Adrian Raine's (1993) *The Psychopathology of Crime*, Dianne Fishbein's (2001) *Biobehavioral Perspectives in Criminology*, Anthony Walsh's (2002) *Biosocial Criminology*, Kevin Beaver's *Biosocial Criminology: A Primer* (2008), and Anthony Walsh's *Biology and Criminology: The Biosocial Synthesis* (2009). Each of these texts is intended to provide more coverage of biological factors as they relate to criminal behavior. Such books offer examples of how different factors are interrelated, but none of these texts offers a theory of antisocial behavior or criminality that integrates biological factors with nonbiological factors. *Why Crime?* offers an integrated theory, one that combines biological, sociological, psychological, anthropological, economic, and other factors.

The notable differences about *Why Crime?* are numerous. First, we use a perspective (or way of looking at the world) known as the *integrated systems perspective* to organize the material-factors that increase or decrease the risk of antisocial behavior are placed into one of six levels of analysis, from cell to society. This is a perspective the primary author learned about in graduate school under the tutelage of Professors C. Ray Jeffery and Frederic L. Faust. Second, our goal is not really to explain only crime or criminality but rather to develop a theory for why people commit antisocial behaviors in general, which include criminality, delinquency, and other maladaptive, aggressive, and violent, behaviors. This theory advances our understanding of such behaviors beyond current knowledge. Third, we draw out the important criminogenic and crime preventive factors from theories of crime and leave the theories and theorists themselves behind. This serves to place emphasis on where it belongs—the knowledge rather than the people who have created it. Fourth, we state relationships between these factors and antisocial behavior in a testable format. We provide nominal and operational definitions of key concepts for the purposes of theory testing. Fifth, after summarizing the main findings of tests of traditional theories of crime, we offer a new theory of antisocial behavior and criminality in the final chapter, one based on the integrated systems perspective, one that is integrated and developmental in nature. *Why Crime?* meaningfully integrates theoretical contributions from not only sociology—the field that currently dominates criminological thinking and theorizing—but also biology, psychology, human development, and other fields that are ignored relative to sociology.

The organization of *Why Crime?* is perhaps the most unique feature. The book is not organized around the traditional categories of crime theories. For example, we do not organize the material based on the academic disciplines that created the theories—thus biological theories are not separated from psychological theories merely because they originated from separate disciplines. We argue vehemently in the book that this serves to reinforce artificial boundaries in knowledge about crime and to create *disciplinary myopia* which limits our understanding of it. Additionally, we do not spend a lot of time assessing the merits of one particular theory of crime versus another theory of crime, which tends to create divisions within the general disciplines of criminology and criminal justice.

Throughout the book, we illustrate that so-called competing theories of crime actually end up making similar predictions about crime and that many produce the same criminal justice and crime prevention policy implications. Thus, we discuss significant overlap between distinct theories of crime. We accomplish this by organizing the tremendous material about theories of crime into chapters based on which level of analysis they fit into in the integrated systems perspective. This perspective suggests that antisocial and criminal behavior results when factors at six levels of analysis interact in the environment. While some factors may end up having greater influence on behavior than others, we do not simply create a multifactor theory that places disproportionate emphasis on any one academic discipline. Rather, we suggest that all academic disciplines can make meaningful contributions to our understanding of the etiology of antisocial and criminal behavior and that the tools and methodologies of each discipline are needed to fully account for it.

Chapter by Chapter

The book is comprised of 10 chapters. The first chapter discusses the nature of criminality, delinquency, and antisocial behaviors. The second chapter introduces the reader to purposes of theory and lays out important terms for the rest of the book. The third chapter discusses different theoretical perspectives in criminological theory and introduces the integrated systems perspective.

Each subsequent chapter is organized around one level of analysis, starting with the cell level (chapter 4), moving to the organ level (chapter 5), then to the organism level (chapter 6), group level (chapter 7), community and organization level (chapter 8), and society level (chapter 9). Key concepts from theories of crime are placed into their respective level of analysis—for example, genetic studies into cellular level explanations, brain dysfunction studies into organ level explanations, personality theories into organism level explanations, learning theories into group level explanations, and so on. We attempt to cull the important crime-related factors from criminological theories so that we can conclude (chapter 10) with an integrated, interdisciplinary theory of antisocial behavior which combines the various criminogenic factors into an explanatory model.

We conclude the book with this integrated theory and a call for testing of the theory. We also seek to develop more rational and theory-informed policy implications for American criminal justice. *Why Crime?* is the only book on the market that takes such an approach.

This second edition presents a newly modified version of our theory—the Integrated Systems Theory of antisocial behavior that's been so well-received by criminologists. The theory is more parsimonious in order to make it easier to test.

Acknowledgments

Matthew Robinson would like to acknowledge his amazing wife, Holly, and his special children, Bella and Marley, for all you do, including letting me work on this book when I could have been outside playing with you.

Kevin Beaver would like to acknowledge his beautiful wife, Shonna, and his two adorable children, Brooke and Jackson, for their patience while writing this book.

Both authors would like to acknowledge all the people at Carolina Academic Press who recognized the importance of this work and who worked behind the scenes to make this book a reality.

WHY CRIME?

1

What Is Crime?

Introduction

What is crime? We hear about crime all the time, especially in the news. What types of behaviors does crime encompass? How is crime similar to and different from related words such as criminality, delinquency, aggression, deviance, and antisocial behavior? When you hear the word *crime,* what comes to mind? If you are like most people, you probably have a pretty good idea of what is meant by the term. Although there is a straightforward legal definition of crime, most of us equate crimes with *any* behaviors that are done intentionally and that produce some physical or financial harm to another person. Crime as a *natural* concept is any act that is seen as "fundamentally wrong, strongly disapproved, and deserving of punishment," regardless of whether it is legal or not (Gottfredson, 1999, p. 47).

The *natural definition* of crime refers to acts that break the *natural law* or law from a higher source. For many people, natural law refers to rules of behavior from their religion, such as the ten commandments. For others, it simply refers to the belief that some acts are just "naturally" wrong regardless of their legal or illegal status. In the criminal law, such behaviors are referred to as *mala in se* offenses, behaviors that are wrong in and of themselves (e.g., rape, murder).

Legally, a crime does not occur unless some act violates the criminal law. Clearly, there are scores of intentional behaviors that result in death, physical injury, and property loss that are not against the criminal law. Such acts would *not*

3

legally be considered crime, even if we all thought that the act was wrong, immoral, deviant, or bad. What makes the act a crime is if it is defined as a crime by the government by the passage of a criminal law.

Legal Definition of Crime

Legally, a crime occurs when an *act* (or behavior) is committed that is in violation of the criminal law. The *legal definition of crime* consists of acts that break the criminal law that are committed intentionally or with culpability, that cause harm, and that are done without justification or valid defense.

Culpable means "meriting condemnation or blame especially as wrong or harmful especially as wrong or harmful" (*Merriam-Webster's Collegiate Dictionary*, 2009). Culpable acts include those behaviors that are committed negligently, recklessly, and knowingly. *Negligence* refers to behaviors that are committed as a result of a failure to meet normal or recognized expectations. An example is failing to follow safety regulations meant to protect human life which results in death. *Recklessness* refers to behaviors that are committed without due caution for human life or property. An example is forcing employees to work in dangerous conditions. Acts committed *knowingly* refer to behaviors committed with knowledge that an outcome is likely. An example is continuing to manufacture a product after product testing reveals a high likelihood of a deadly defect.

The term *crime* is the label we apply to certain behaviors that violate the law. The key point is that crimes are created by the criminal law, which is made by people. This means crime does not exist in nature; it is invented by people. This is not to say that aggressive and harmful behaviors do not occur in nature. The point is that when they do, they are not automatically crimes. In fact, no behavior is inherently criminal and any behavior can be made a crime at any time (Robinson, 2002). Box 1.1 contains some examples that prove the latter point.

Box 1.1 Loony Laws and Silly Statutes

- In Vermont, it is against the law to jump from a plane unless it is a true emergency.
- In Maine, it is a crime to walk down the sidewalk with your shoelaces untied.
- In Washington, it is against the law to pretend that your parents are rich.
- In Kentucky, it is a crime to use a reptile as part of a religious service.
- In Massachusetts, it is against the law to eat peanuts while in church.
- In New Jersey, it is a crime to slurp soup.

- In Indiana, it is against the law to shoot open a can of soup.
- In Rhode Island, it is a crime to throw pickle juice on a trolley.
- In Minnesota, it is against the law to dance in public places.
- In Kentucky, it is a crime to remarry the same man four times.
- In Colorado, it is against the law to throw shoes at a wedding.
- In Missouri, it is a crime to carry a bear down the highway unless it is caged.
- In Washington, it is against the law to punch a bull in the nose.
- In Texas, it is against the law to milk someone else's cow.
- In Ohio, it is a crime to fish with explosives.

Source: Lindsell-Roberts, S. (1994). *Loony laws and silly statutes.* New York: Sterling Publications.

You may be wondering, how can such acts be crimes? It is likely that at some time in history, these acts were considered problematic, probably because some people actually engaged in these acts and others thought they caused harm. Every state has such loony laws and silly statutes on the books, even though they are not likely being widely enforced (if at all).

Because crime is a human invention, there is some disagreement among the people who study crime for a living about what behaviors should constitute crime. Henry and Lanier (2001) discussed a dozen different viewpoints on what crime is or should be before offering an integrated definition. The summary definition offered by Henry and Lanier includes "crimes of the powerless," "social deviance," and "crimes of the powerful" (p. 230). Most criminologists and criminal justice scholars use theory to try to explain and/or predict *crime;* thus, they tend to limit their studies to behaviors that violate the criminal law. A very large share of those study only so-called *serious crimes* or *street crimes* such as homicide, forcible rape, aggravated assault, robbery, theft, burglary, motor vehicle theft, and arson (what Henry and Lanier defined as "crimes of the powerless"). These serious crimes included in the U.S. government's *Uniform Crime Reports* are defined in box 1.2. These acts were defined by our government as serious because they were claimed to be the most harmful, pervasive, and frequently occurring types of crimes in the United States (Robinson, 2002). These are also the crimes that most criminologists and criminal justice scholars try to explain.

Box 1.2 American Street Crimes

- *Criminal homicide.* Includes murder and nonnegligent manslaughter: the willful (nonnegligent) killing of one human being by another.

Deaths caused by negligence, attempts to kill, suicides, and accidental deaths are excluded. Justifiable homicides are classified separately and traffic fatalities are excluded.

- *Forcible rape.* The carnal knowledge of a female forcibly and against her will. Rapes by force and attempts or assaults to rape regardless of the age of the victim are included. Statutory offenses (where no force is used but the victim is under the legal age of consent) are excluded.
- *Robbery.* The taking or attempting to take anything of value from the care, custody, or control of a person or persons by force or threat of force or violence and/or by putting the victim in fear.
- *Aggravated assault.* An unlawful attack by one person upon another for the purpose of inflicting severe or aggravated bodily injury, which usually is accompanied by the use of a weapon or by means likely to produce death or great bodily harm. Simple assaults are excluded.
- *Burglary.* The unlawful entering of a structure to commit a felony or a theft. Attempted forcible entry is included.
- *Larceny-theft.* The unlawful taking, carrying, leading, or riding away of property from the possession or constructive possession of another. Examples are thefts of bicycles or automobile accessories, shoplifting, pocket-picking, or the stealing of any property or article which is not taken by force and violence or by fraud. Attempted thefts are included. Embezzlement, confidence games, forgery, worthless checks, and so on are excluded.
- *Motor vehicle theft.* The theft or attempted theft of a motor vehicle. A motor vehicle is self-propelled and runs on the surface and not on rails. Motorboats, construction equipment, airplanes, and farming equipment are specifically excluded from this category.
- *Arson.* Any willful or malicious burning or attempt to burn, with or without intent to defraud, a dwelling house, public building, motor vehicle or aircraft, or personal property of another.

Source: Crime in the United States, 2007: Uniform crime reports. Washington, DC: U.S. Department of Justice, Federal Bureau of Investigation.

Other Conceptions of Crime

Elite deviance is a term put forth by Simon (2007) in his book by the same name. Elite deviance includes not only criminal acts, but also unethical acts, civil and regulatory violations, and other harmful acts that are committed intentionally, recklessly, negligently, or knowingly. Elite deviance is a term that encompasses *white-collar crime* (Sutherland, 1977a, 1977b), *corporate crime* (Clinard & Yeager, 2005) *corporate violence, occupational crime* (Blount, 2002), *governmental deviance* (Erman & Lundman, 2001), *crimes of the state* (Michalowski & Kramer, 2006), *crimes of privilege* (Shover & Wright, 2000), *profit without honor* (Rosoff, Pontell, & Tillman, 2006), and those *crimes by any other name* (Reiman, 2006), committed by our *trusted criminals* (Friedrichs, 2006). These are acts that cause tremendous physical, financial, and moral harms to Americans but are either not vigorously pursued by the criminal justice system or are not actually against the criminal law.

As explained by Kappeler, Blumberg, and Potter (2000, p. 122) "all the violent crime, all the property crime, all the crime that we concentrate our energy and resources on combating is less of a threat to society" than deviance committed by corporations, governments, and elites in society. Speaking of corporate crime, Mokhiber (2007) says it "inflicts far more damage on society than all street crime combined. Whether in bodies or injuries or dollars lost, corporate crime and violence wins by a landslide." Similarly, Cullen and colleagues (2006) claim: "The violent or 'physical' costs—the toll in lives lost, injuries inflicted, and illnesses suffered—are perhaps the gravest and certainly the most neglected of the damages that corporate lawlessness imposes on the American people."

Is this possible? And if so, what are the implications for criminological theory? In the following section, we compare relative harms of street crimes and elite deviance and discuss why this issue is relevant for criminological theory.

Comparative Harms of Crime and Noncrime

What is defined as crime is *not* a function of what is most harmful to society. If you believe that you are more likely to be victimized by street crime than acts of elite deviance committed by wealthy individuals or corporations, you are wrong (Robinson, 2002). The belief that elite deviance is less harmful than street crime is a myth (Kappeler et al., 2000).

There is considerable evidence that elite deviance causes more physical and property damage than all eight serious crimes combined. Kappeler et al. (2000) estimated that economic losses from corporate crime alone cost somewhere between 17 to 31 times as much as street crime. Reiman (2006), using the sparse data available on white-collar and corporate crime shows that it costs us at least $404 billion in losses every year. More recently, Robinson and Murphy (2008) document more than $1 trillion in losses caused by elite deviance, including the following documented costs:

- Defective products—$700 billion per year
- Health care fraud—$80 billion per year
- Insurance fraud—$80 billion per year
- Computer fraud—$67 billion per year
- Securities and commodities fraud—$40 billion per year
- Telemarketing fraud—$40 billion per year
- Automotive repair fraud—$22 billion per year
- Check fraud—$10 billion

Recently, numerous corporations engaged in widespread acts of elite deviance that led to hundreds of billions of dollars of losses and serious damage to the stock market. For example, the Enron Corporation, an energy rights trading company, declared bankruptcy in December 2001, with debts of more than $31 billion. Enron allegedly hid its indebtedness by treating loans as if they were revenue, by creating false subsidiary corporations so they could attribute losses to those corporations, and by encouraging shareholders to buy more Enron stock while corporate executives sold their stock. According to Reiman and Leighton (2002), as many as 20,000 employees lost their retirement money although company executives made hundreds of millions of dollars. Enron investors lost about $60 billion, employees lost more than $2 billion in pension plans, and 5,600 people lost their jobs. To make matters worse, Enron CEO Kenneth Lay sold off $103 million of his company stock while discouraging and even forbidding his employees from selling theirs, even as the value of the stock plummeted from $80 per share to only 30 cents per share. Roughly 20,000 employees thus lost their retirement accounts. Enron also intentionally manipulated California's power crisis for financial gain, something that ultimately led to the recall of the state's governor and the subsequent election of Arnold Schwarzenegger to the position of governor.

Similarly, WorldCom's stock fell from a high of $64 per share to only nine cents per share. WorldCom's fraud was in the amount of $11 billion, and caused losses in the area of $180 billion as well as 30,000 lost jobs. After WorldCom was high with a record fine for its fraud, the company changed its name and remains in business today.

Such corporations were assisted in their wrongdoings by consulting firms such as Arthur Anderson, who helped the companies hide their debts by first being their accountants and then by destroying evidence during the subsequent investigations. Interestingly, Arthur Anderson also had long ago been involved in the failing of perhaps the most infamous savings and loan (S&L) failure—Charles Keating's Lincoln Savings and Loan.

The corporations were also assisted by major banks including J.P. Morgan Chase and Citigroup. The *Wall Street Journal* called the banks "Enron Enables" and wrote: "They appear to have behaved in a guileful way and helped their corporate clients undertake unsavory practices. And they appear to have had an entire divisions that, among other things, helped corporations avoid taxes and manipulate their balance sheets through something called structured finance, which is a huge profit center for each bank." Further, brokerage firms such as Merrill Lynch saw their employees knowingly promoting the nearly worthless stocks of these corporations.

Other major corporations also engaged in similar activity. For example, Aldelphia was charged by the Security and Exchange Commission (SEC) with "fraudulently excluding $2.3 billion in debt from its earnings report. AES, AOL-Time Warner, Cedent, Halliburton, K-Mart, Lucent Technologies, Micro-Strategy, Rite Aid, and Waste Management are all said to have misstated revenues in different ways at more than $100 million in each case."

The total combined harms of the above corporate crimes are unknown, but estimates are in the hundreds of billions of dollars if not more. David Simon (2007, p. 117) asserts that: "Collectively, the 2002–2003 scandals helped cause a $5 trillion loss in stock market values, and cost the public at least $200 billion and one million jobs."

And this says nothing about the lives lost because of corporate crime. One example proves this point. Tobacco use kills many more people each year (more than 400,000) than murderers (less than 20,000) and causes more financial losses each year (approximately $100 billion in direct health care costs) than all street crime combined (approximately $20 billion) (Robinson and Murphy, 2008). While murder by definition is intentional, manufacturing and promoting the use of tobacco is not intended to kill people. Yet, lawsuits against the tobacco industry show that the tobacco industry's recklessness and negligence have produced hundreds of thousands of deaths each year. In essence, tobacco executives know their products lead to many deaths, yet they use advertising to downplay the risks associated with smoking and to encourage people to smoke. Further, they mislead the public about the addictive nature and dangers association with smoking, even creating bogus research on these topics to confuse the public; such behaviors went on for decades. They also targeted children, knowing that people do not generally start smoking as adults, and that without new users (youth), they could not sustain their business. Thus, some scholars claim that we should have laws that criminalize any act which causes harm to others, if the act is done intentionally, negligently, recklessly, or knowingly (so that a person or persons can be held responsible for the resulting harms due to their culpability).

Other harms associated with legal acts and/or crimes which are not considered serious or as worthy of criminal justice attention demonstrate that the label of "crime" is not reserved for the most harmful acts in society. Numerous scholars have documented harms caused by elite deviance. For example, Robinson and Murphy (2008) report the following numbers with regard to deaths produced by elite deviance:

- Tobacco use   438,000
- Obesity   112,000
- Hospital error   100,000
- Occupational disease and injury   55,000
- Unsafe and defective merchandise   30,000

Many of these deaths result from the negligent, reckless, and knowing behaviors of elites—corporate executives, food companies, doctors, employers, and manufacturers; therefore, they are good examples of culpable killings. Although it is true that acts committed with intent (such as murder) are generally considered more serious than those committed negligently, recklessly, or knowingly, people killed by big tobacco, food companies, as well as reckless and negligent doctors, employers, and product manufacturers are just as dead as those murdered. This is why many view those killed by such behaviors as victims (Friedrichs, 2006; Reiman, 2006; Rosoff, Pontell, & Tillman, 2006; Simon, 2007).

Although surveys of Americans show they have historically viewed street crimes as the most serious crimes, Robinson (2009) argues this is because we are all raised by informal sources of social control such as our parents and heavily influenced by mass media images of crime to believe in the criminal law. There is some evidence that when the public are aware of the harms caused by acts of elite deviance, they are likely to rank such acts as even more serious than street crime. A survey of more than 1,100 people by the White Collar Crime Survey, for example, found that in four of six cases, the respondents thought the white-collar offenses were more serious than the similar street crimes (e.g., when a bank teller embezzled $100, versus when someone stole $100 from a handbag; knowingly sending bad meat to a grocery store which is sold making a person ill, versus robbing someone on the street causing serious injury; a doctor lies on an insurance form to receive more money, versus a patient lies on an insurance form to receive more money; and an insurance company denies a valid claim to save money, versus a patient files a false claim to save money). Further, about two-thirds of respondents thought more resources should be devoted to apprehending white-collar offenders (Piquero, Carmichael, and Piquero, 2008).

Why does it matter for criminological theories that serious street crime really is not as harmful as elite deviance? If criminology and criminal justice scholars want to be able to explain and predict *harmful* behaviors, they ought to be able to explain and predict those acts that are actually the *most harmful*. Since the criminal label is applied to behaviors by human beings, if criminologists and criminal justice scholars limit their studies *only* to *criminal* behaviors, their subject matter will be determined by legislators (lawmakers). American lawmakers tend to be wealthier, older, white males (Robinson, 2009). This is problematic for several reasons:

- Harmful acts committed by individuals like them (i.e., wealthier, older, white males) may not be called crimes.
- Harmful acts committed by their financial backers (e.g., major corporations) may not be labeled crimes.
- Many relatively harmless acts will be labeled crimes (as illustrated in box 1.1).

If the ultimate goal of theorists is to have their research used to prevent *harmful* acts (whether they be illegal or not), then limiting one's studies to *only* crimes would mean that most harmful behaviors would not be prevented because they would not be widely studied by criminologists and criminal justice scholars. Additionally, the factors that produce elite deviance may be different than those that produce common street crimes. Given the harms associated with elite deviance, the factors that produce it are no less important to understand.

Acts of elite deviance and white-collar offenders must also be carefully studied by criminologists and criminal justice scholars so that they, too, can be explained and predicted. This is another way of saying that a theory's *scope* is broader if it can explain more harms rather than fewer harms (the issue of scope is discussed in chapter 2). Historically, most theories of crime have been aimed at explaining or predicting street crimes committed by poor people. Throughout this book, we will discuss the scope or explanatory power of various theories; in doing so, we will discuss how well they explain and/or predict not only typical street crimes but also acts of elite deviance.

Crime versus Criminality, Delinquency, and Other Important Terms

As explained earlier, a crime is an act that violates the criminal law. Many criminologists and criminal justice scholars use the term *crime* interchangeably with other terms such as criminality, delinquency, antisocial behavior, deviance, and aggression. Although these terms are related, they do not mean the same thing. Therefore, it is important to understand the main distinctions between them.

Criminality (or criminal behavior) is an act that is in violation of the criminal law. It includes acts, failures to act, attempts to act, and agreements to act. Consider this example for clarification: When one commits the crime of murder, *murder* is the crime because it is the term we use to describe a particular type of killing. Killing another person is the *criminal behavior.* There are many ways a person can legally be killed by another (e.g., self-defense, in the line of duty as a police officer, and so forth). So, the *behavior* of killing (i.e., taking the life of another human being) is not always a *crime.* It is only a crime under certain circumstances. As noted, crimes also include failures to act (e.g., not paying your taxes, not paying child support), attempts to act (e.g., trying to break into someone's home), and agreements to act (e.g., a conspiracy where two people enter into a written or verbal agreement to break the law).

Criminologists and criminal justice scholars who use theory to examine harmful human behaviors must decide precisely what they want to be able to explain and predict. Do we want to explain *only* why people commit *murder* (a crime) or do we want to explain why people *kill others* under any circumstances (human behavior)? Do we want to explain *only* why people steal each other's property (the crime of *theft*) or do we want to explain why people *take each other's property* generally (human behavior)? The more types of human behaviors we can explain, the wider or broader the scope of our theories, and the more useful our theories will be for developing policies to prevent harms in society.

There are other terms that are often (incorrectly) used interchangeably with crime and criminal behavior. For example, *delinquency* consists of acts committed by juveniles that, if committed by adults, would be considered crimes by the criminal justice system. Technically, juveniles do not commit crimes, only adults commit them. Since different states have a different maximum age for juvenile status, an act committed by a 16-year-old in one state may be called juvenile delinquency, while in another it would be called a crime. This makes the distinction between crime and delinquency ambiguous when studying harmful human behaviors across jurisdictions. Logically, many of the factors that produce criminality in adults will produce acts of delinquency in juveniles. In fact, the conditions that result in harmful behavior will result in delinquency first since criminality is only committed by adults.

Antisocial behavior is a term that is broader than crime or delinquency because it includes any behaviors that conflict with the prevailing norms of society. *Norms* are expectations for behavior—they set forth acceptable and unacceptable behaviors for people living in a society. So, antisocial behaviors, or violations of norms, are typically viewed as abnormal. This means the term is synonymous with *deviance,* which is basically any behavior that deviates from the norms of a society. Social deviance is made up of "any thought feeling, or behavior viewed as objectionable by a group of people" ... something is deviant if it "violates the social norms that the group members share regarding how a person should behave" (Simons, Simons, & Wallace, 2004, p. 4).

Crime is a legal concept, a label invented by humans and applied to some antisocial behaviors but not others. According to Lee and Coccaro (2001), many crimes can be found in the *Diagnostic and Statistical Manual of Mental Disorders, Fourth Edition (DSM-IV)* under the categories of adult antisocial behavior, antisocial personality disorder, and intermittent explosive disorder, among others. Yet, even though "certain psychiatric conditions are associated with increased criminality and an increased risk of committing a crime, no current DSM-IV diagnosis uses the commission of a crime as the sole criterion. The presence or absence of a medical or psychiatric disorder does not categorically define the behavior of a person as criminal or noncriminal, just as a criminal act does not necessarily reflect the underlying psychopathology" (Lee & Coccaro, 2001, p. 35).

Generally, antisocial behaviors not only violate norms, but also can be considered *maladaptive,* which means they interfere with someone's ability to fully develop, mature, or experience their full potential. Many criminal acts can be viewed as adaptive strategies because they make life better for those who commit them. For example, people often steal to get money to buy things such as food, drugs, and so forth.

The key criteria for determining whether any behavior would be considered antisocial are contained in box 1.3. The criteria come from the American Psychiatric Association's *DSM-IV-TR.* Antisocial behaviors are either actually or potentially harmful to the people who engage in them or to others.

Box 1.3 Criteria for Antisocial Behaviors

A. There is a pervasive pattern of disregard for and violation of the rights of others occurring since age 15 years, as indicated by three (or more) of the following:

   (1) failure to conform to social norms with respect to lawful behaviors as indicated by repeatedly performing acts that are grounds for arrest

(2) deceitfulness, as indicated by repeated lying, use of aliases, or conning others for personal profit or pleasure

(3) impulsivity or failure to plan ahead

(4) irritability and aggressiveness, as indicated by repeated physical fights or assaults

(5) reckless disregard for safety of self or others

(6) consistent irresponsibility, as indicated by repeated failure to sustain consistent work behavior or honor financial obligations

(7) lack of remorse, as indicated by being indifferent to or rationalizing having hurt, mistreated, or stolen from another

B. The individual is at least age 18 years.

C. There is evidence of Conduct Disorder with onset before age 15 years.

D. The occurrence of antisocial behavior is not exclusively during the course of Schizophrenia or a Manic Episode.

Source: American Psychiatric Association. (1994). *Diagnostic and statistical manual of mental disorders* (4th ed., text revision). Washington, DC: Author.

Figure 1.1 Criminal and Antisocial Behaviors

Criminal Behavior	Antisocial Behavior
Not required to be offensive to most people	Is perceived as being offensive to most people
Would include victimless crime	Would not include victimless crime
Always violates criminal law	Sometimes violates criminal law
Can be normal and adaptive in nature	Is not normal and is maladaptive in nature

Source: Adapted from Fishbein (2001, p. 10)

Figure 1.1 compares criminal behavior with antisocial behavior. Sometimes behaviors can be both antisocial and criminal. But, the vast majority of antisocial behaviors are not illegal. Take another look at box 1.3 and try to think of some behaviors that would be considered antisocial but not criminal.

Finally, the term *aggression* is probably the broadest category of all behaviors that are studied by criminologists and criminal justice scholars. Aggression is "a forceful action or procedure (as an unprovoked attack) especially when intended to dominate or master"; "hostile, injurious, or destructive behavior or outlook especially when caused by frustration" (*Merriam-Webster's Collegiate Dictionary*, 2009). It is synonymous with other terms such as attack, assault, and assail. It is the broadest category because it includes virtually every behavior committed by one person against another, including many that are legal, normal, and even celebrated (such as the sack of a quarterback in football).

Of all these behaviors, the one that is viewed as most "normal" is aggression, depending on the situation or context. For example, it is widely acknowledged that all children will normally commit aggressive acts early in life. The American Academy of Pediatrics (AAP, 1998) claims that all humans have "feelings of anger and aggression ... These impulses are normal and healthy" (p. 507). According to AAP, defiant behavior in children starts as early as the second year.

The American Academy of Child & Adolescent Psychiatry (AACAP) concurs, writing: "Rudiments of aggression ... are ... apparent shortly after birth" (Pruitt, 1998, p. 102). For example: "Many children hit, bite, and scratch at some point ... Some children act aggressively with other children" (Pruitt, 1998, p. 63), especially in the second year of life (p. 164). AACAP (2008) says that hitting, biting, and scratching are "fairly common and often appear by the child's first birthday." Additionally, since children are naturally selfish, between the ages of three and four, they may take pleasure in cruel acts against animals or other people.

AAP and AACAP agree that while aggressive behavior is normal for children who have not yet developed enough *self-control* to control their behavior, when such behavior is recurrent, persistent, and interferes with the functioning of the child, his or her family and/or school, the behavior is probably not normal and may require intervention. This is an important lesson for students of criminological theory—aggression is not a matter of black or white but rather should be viewed as shades of gray—all children are aggressive, but some children will be more aggressive than others.

What This Book Is Aimed at Explaining

The theories identified and discussed in this book will be aimed at explaining and predicting a wide variety of behaviors. These include criminal behaviors, delinquent behaviors, and other harmful and aggressive antisocial, deviant, or maladaptive behaviors that are not necessarily illegal.

This book is at odds with the majority of criminological theory texts that focus exclusively on crimes and/or delinquent acts. It is evident that a great deal of crime is normal rather than abnormal. It is also apparent that much criminality is adaptive rather than maladaptive. Do we really need theories and scientific studies to understand why these crimes are committed? Consider these real-life examples of relatively mundane crimes:

- A person steals a cellular phone from another person.
- A person steals a bottle of vitamins from a grocery store.
- A person steals a package of chuck steak from a grocery store.
- A person steals a carton of cigarettes from a convenience store.
- A homeless person whose only possession is a bicycle steals a $2 bicycle lock.

Such crimes are relatively easy to explain; they are committed by poor and/or young people to advance their standing in life, even if the advancement is only temporary. Some steal for the thrill of it, some steal for food when they are hungry, and still others steal to support or sustain drug habits. Many such acts committed by young people are normal, as adolescents often learn the rules by breaking them; in a sense, they experiment with lawbreaking to establish their own boundaries. Despite these facts, each of the descriptions in the preceding list resulted in a prison sentence of at least 25 years to life as each was a third offense in a "three strike" state (Robinson, 2002). The most significant thing that made these acts maladaptive was that they led to severe punishments!

American criminology has traditionally focused on explaining such criminal and delinquent acts committed by low-income, poorly educated, underemployed citizens (as if it is some great mystery why they steal to obtain more property). This is true even though the majority of criminality is relatively harmless; as we demonstrated earlier, relative to other forms of harms, criminality does less damage to society. In fact, some crimes are considered *victimless* because they are engaged in by willing participants (e.g., prostitution, drug use). Perhaps the questions of why some people are willing to pay money for sex and others need to alter their brain chemistry by using drugs to fit in or to have fun in social situations are worthy of pursuit. But, do we really need to explain why one person steals food from a grocery store? Do we need theories to account for why a drug addict robs another? Do we need the scientific method to help us explain why such acts occur?

We believe most crimes are normal and easy to understand. Experts suggest that although criminal behavior is relatively normal, very few people commit serious crimes, particularly repetitive violent crimes: "Millions of teens and young adults, most of them male, commit delinquent acts. However, only a fraction of this group—around 5 percent—exhibit chronic, severe antisocial behavior" (*Crime-Times*, 2001, p. 1). A large body of research illustrates that chronic antisocial behavior is committed by people who start out as children with behavioral problems and then go on to commit delinquency as juveniles and crimes as adults.

This book is not *only* about why the law gets violated. The answer to the question posed by the book's title, *Why Crime?*, is really a simple one—crime happens because of the criminal law. We can explain *all* crime by the fact that the criminal law exists; without the criminal law there would be no crime. And thus, *all* crime can be prevented by eliminating the criminal law.

This book is really about why people engage in behaviors that are harmful to others and to themselves, whether or not the acts are illegal. The focus is on human behavior generally and maladaptive behaviors in particular, rather than those behaviors proscribed by law. We also focus on the risk factors that occur early in life, in childhood and adolescence, which are thought to be predictive of adult antisocial behaviors. This is because behavior across the life course tends to be stable. Box 1.4 includes a discussion about the relative stability of antisocial behavior across the life course.

Box 1.4 The Stability of Antisocial Behaviors

According to Lee and Coccaro (2001), many acts that are aggressive and impulsive are related to one's temperament, which is inherited and thus can be recognized early in life. Aggressive and impulsive acts are relatively stable through life, are expressed early in life, and are associated with certain characteristics of individuals and their environments. As noted by Simons, Simons, & Wallace (2004, p. 16), "antisocial tendencies tend to become manifest during childhood. The roots of an adult antisocial lifestyle appear to be planted during the person's formative years."

The American Academy of Pediatrics (AAP) agrees: "The ease with which a child adjusts to his environment is strongly influenced by his temperament—adaptability and emotional style. For the most part, temperament is an innate quality of the child, one with which he is born ... By the time a child has reached the school years, his temperament is well defined ... It is not something that is likely to change much in the future" (Schor, 1999, p. 124). *Temperament* includes *activity level* (i.e., the level of daily activities), *rythmicity/regularity* (i.e., the regularity of important functions like eating and sleeping), *approach/withdrawal* (i.e., how well a person initially responds to a new stimulus), *adaptability* (i.e., how easily a person responds to a new situation), *intensity* (i.e., the energy level with which a person responds to a new situation), and *mood* (i.e., positive or negative emotions and behaviors).

Children are then often categorized as either *easy, slow to warm up or shy,* and *difficult*. Parents of difficult children—who are negative in mood, intense in emotion, adapt poorly to new situations, and challenge his or her parents—are much more likely to become frustrated and withdrawal from their children. The American Academy of Child & Adolescent Psychiatry (AACAP) also calls temperament inborn which predisposes children to respond in certain ways to the world around them (Pruitt, 1998, p. 14).

Many studies show evidence of stability of antisocial behavior. For example, a study of children at three different time periods (6–11 years old, 12–17 years old, and 20–25 years old) by Donker et al (2003) found a high level of stability of antisocial behavior from childhood to adulthood especially when young people committed early status and/or antisocial behaviors in childhood. *Status offenses* are behaviors that are only considered wrong when committed by and which are only applied to children (e.g., running away, incorrigibility, and so forth).

Many studies examine the effects of personality traits on behavior over the life course, concluding that behavioral and emotional traits unique to individuals are fairly constant over one's life and explain the stability of behavior. For example, Raine et al. (1998) studied more than one thousand male and female Indian and Creole children from the island of Mauritius and found that behavioral measures of stimulation seeking and fearlessness at age 3 years were moderately related to measures of aggression at age 11 years. The study measured aggression using a survey of parents—known as the Child Behavior Checklist—that assessed involvement in both physical and verbal aggression of children (e.g., fighting, attacking, showing cruelty, threatening, destroying property, arguing, swearing, screaming, having bad tempers). Antisocial behavior was measured using a scale of nonaggressive acts (e.g., being disobedient at school, being disobedient at home, keeping bad friends, lying, talking excessively, cheating, being moody, sulking, running away from home, teasing).

Citing a tremendous amount of research (Caspi & Silva, 1995; Caspi et al., 1995; Farrington, 1989; Henry, Caspi, Moffitt, & Silva, 1996; Lahey & Loeber, 1994; Loeber et al., 1993; Moffitt, 1993; Raine et al., 1997; Sanson et al., 1993; Tremblay et al., 1994), Raine et al. stated: "Because aggression in early childhood is capable of predicting aggression in adulthood, some of the foundations for later aggressive and violent behavior are probably set in the first few years of life." Typically research examines relationships between early difficult temperament and later involvement in aggressive and antisocial behaviors. For example, a study by Tremblay et al. (1994) of a group of boys from kindergarten through age 13 years showed that early, highly delinquent behavior in the boys was best predicted by the personality characteristic *impulsivity* at a very young age. *Impulsivity* is a term that suggests short-sightedness—that a person acts without much thought for potential long-term consequences of behavior.

In another study of 31 hyperactive teenagers and 32 controls, Taylor et al. (1996) found that childhood hyperactivity predicted adolescent violent behavior, poor relationships with peers, a lack of involvement in social activities, and poor academic performance. *Hyperactivity* refers to a very active person, one with an inability to sit still. Lynam (1996) suggests that such research provides evidence for the link between childhood hyperactivity and adult pathological behavior, and may explain why 5% to 6% of offenders commit more than half of the street crime each year. According to Fishbein (2001, p. 12): "Even though there are many ways to characterize these individuals, there appears to be a subgroup of offenders that is known to persistently engage in impulsive … antisocial behavior (see e.g., Nagin & Farrington, 1992). Their behavior is potentially violent (resulting in physical injury) and is not simply understood by knowing the behavioral outcome. Instead, they can be characterized by relatively stable personality and temperamental traits, including impulsivity, negative affect, and cognitive deficits."

Another study by Lyman, Leukefeld, and Clayton (2003) tested the ability of the "Five Factor Model (FFM)" to explain the stability of antisocial behavior including substance use and abuse. The study of 481 adults found that personality traits such as agreeableness, intelligence, conscientiousness, extraversion, and neuroticism accounted for a large portion of antisocial behavior and substance use and abuse over the course of the subjects' lives. *Agreeableness* generally refers to one's willingness to get along with others. *Intelligence* refers to one's ability to solve problems. *Conscientiousness* refers to being careful and following one's conscience. *Extraversion* refers to being outgoing. Finally, *neuroticism* refers to the tendency to experience negative emotional states such as anxiety.

Another study (Allesio et al, 2008) probed for a relationship between depressive symptoms and antisocial behavior in a sample of 107 Italian youth. Over a ten-month period, depression and antisocial behavior were stable.

Obrvadovic (2008) examined the effects of *interpersonal callousness* (IC) in persistent antisocial behavior. Using both parent and teacher reports of *IC* behaviors among 506 inner-city boys assessed every year from ages 8 to 16 years, the author found evidence of stability in IC which could help account for stability of antisocial behavior across a nine year period (during later childhood and adolescence).

Another study of 626 twin pairs during late adolescence and early adulthood in Minnesota (Burt et al, 2007) found that genetic factors were largely responsible for the stability of antisocial behavior from late adolescence until adulthood. Environmental influences were largely responsible for change from antisocial to prosocial behaviors. Similarly, MacMillan, McMorris, and Kruttschnitt (2004) looked at the effects of stability and change in maternal circumstance on developmental trajectories of antisocial behavior in children ages 4 to 7 years based on a national sample of young mothers. The authors found that escape from poverty lessons antisocial behavior across the life course, whereas remaining in poverty intensifies antisocial behavior.

For both biological and social reasons, a small group of offenders thus appear to be distinguishable from the great bulk of antisocial populations. They are different not only in their biology (e.g., genetic traits) but also their social environments (e.g., parenting). Their behaviors also differ, including both their propensities for antisocial behavior as well as when their antisocial behavior emerges over the life course. Patterson, DeBaryshe, and Ramsey (1989) and Patterson, Crosby, and Vuchinich (1992) contrasted *early starter* offenders with *late starters;* the former engage in antisocial behavior earlier in life and engage in far more serious antisocial behavior across the life course. Moffit (1993) suggests the early starters likely experience neuropsychological deficits such as cognitive deficiencies which put them on a trajectory toward a life of crime. When combined with later environmental conditions such as abusive or inadequate parenting, early starters may become life-course persistent offenders (Piquero & Benson, 2004). *Life-course persistent* offenders have different personality traits and family experiences that make them more susceptible to recurrent rather than occasional criminality and antisocial behavior. *Adolescent-limited* are more "normal" in terms of their biological and environmental influences.

A parallel characterization is made by Park et al (2008) of *high starter, incremental,* and *steady* offenders. Other longitudinal research on young people reveals at least six groups of delinquent populations: high-level; chronic low-level; decreasing high-level; decreasing low-level; rare; and nonoffenders (Wiesner & Capaldi, 2003), but these categories are based on both level of offending behavior (high or low) as well as trajectories of offending behavior (increasing or decreasing) (Wiesner & Capaldi, 2003).

Given the tremendous evidence cited here, it appears that antisocial behaviors and behavioral propensities in childhood can be used as fairly good predictors of later criminal and antisocial behaviors. That is, there is strong evidence in criminology of persistent criminality across the life course (Haapanen, Britton, & Croisdale, 2007). According to Fishbein (2001, p. 61), antisocial behavior is a developmental trait that appears early in life as a result of an inability to develop fully. It manifests itself in "difficult temperament, impulsivity, social adjustment problems, physical fighting, poor academic achievement, distractibility, and oftentimes, depressed or negative mood." Environmental stressors such as parental rejection, ineffective socialization, inconsistent discipline, abuse victimization, negative peer influences, negative academic experiences, and poverty can all increase the likelihood of antisocial behavior. While behavioral propensities may be stable across the life course, these environmental factors are not, meaning that their influence on behavior will change over time (Elliott, 1994; Farrington, 1995; Kelley et al., 1997; Loeber & LeBlanc, 1991; Loeber & Stouthamer-Loeber, 1998).

Of all the antisocial behaviors subject to study by criminologists, we would argue that of most importance are violent behaviors, behaviors that cause physical harm to other people. Many forms of violent behavior begin early in life and warning signs for future violent behavior can be identified early in life, as well. Once the predictors of violent behavior are discovered and understood, we ought to be able to do a better job of preventing violence in our communities and country. Ultimately, if we can explain why these behaviors occur and can accurately predict when and where they occur, prevention should be made much easier.

In order to prevent behavior, we must first develop a full understanding of it. As you will see in chapter 2, the role of *theory* is to explain and predict behavior. American criminologists have now spent more than a century developing theories of crime. Before we move on to the issue of what is theory and to the numerous theories that have been put forth over the years, examine box 1.5, which contains some basic facts about crime. These come from Braithwaite (1995, p. 44), who offered "the strongest and most consistently supported associations in empirical criminology" regarding criminal behavior. Braithwaite claimed: "Any credible theory would at least have to be consistent with these findings, and preferably would offer an explanation for most of them."

Box 1.5 Braithwaite's Facts about Crime

1. Crime is committed disproportionately by males.
2. Crime is committed disproportionately by 15- to 25-year-olds.
3. Crime is committed disproportionately by unmarried people.
4. Crime is committed disproportionately by people living in large cities.
5. Crime is committed disproportionately by people who have experienced high residential mobility and who live in areas characterized by high levels of residential mobility.
6. Young people who are strongly attached to their schools are less likely to engage in crime.
7. Young people who have high educational and occupational aspirations are less likely to engage in crime.
8. Young people who do poorly at school are more likely to engage in crime.
9. Young people who are strongly attached to their parents are less likely to engage in crime.

10. Young people who have friendships with criminals are more likely to engage in crime themselves.
11. People who believe strongly in the importance of complying with the law are less likely to violate the law.
12. For both women and men, being at the bottom of the class structure, whether measured by socioeconomic status, socioeconomic status of the area in which the person lives, being unemployed, or being a member of an oppressed racial minority (e.g., blacks in the United States), increases rates of offending for all types of crime apart from those for which opportunities are systematically unavailable to the poor (i.e., white-collar crime).
13. Crime rates have been increasing since World War II in most countries, developed and developing. The only country that has been clearly shown to have had a falling crime rate in this period is Japan.

Source: Braithwaite, J. (1995). *Crime, shame, and reintegration* (chap. 3). New York: Cambridge University Press.

It is clear that these "facts" of crime apply to the street crimes listed in box 1.2. But, how well do these facts fit elite deviance? The facts in box 1.5 fit many forms of criminality, but most of them do not fit elite deviance very well, nor do they fit well with many other forms of antisocial behavior. For example, Piquero & Benson (2004: 161) note: "In a number of ways, white-collar crime is different from ordinary street crime. Involvement in it occurs at a different point in the life course. It has a dramatically different opportunity structure. Those who participate in it are drawn from a different sector of the American social structure. Finally, it may have significantly different motivations from those who engage in street crime."

Those facts that seem to hold true for most forms of criminality include points 1, 10, and 11. Without doubt, crimes of all types are committed disproportionately by members of the male gender. This is likely explained by biological *and* social factors. Having friendships with criminals is associated with criminal behavior, but these friendships may be the result of common interests and may not explain criminal behaviors engaged in by groups. Virtually all criminal behavior (and antisocial behavior for that matter) is committed in the context of groups. Finally, for all types of behaviors, it seems that believing a behavior is wrong makes it less likely generally that a person will engage in it (Vold, Bernard, & Snipes, 1998).

The remaining points seem to hold true for street crime but are less important for other forms of antisocial behaviors. For example, while street crime is in fact committed disproportionately by young males (criminologists often say crime is a young male phenomenon) the most harmful behaviors committed in the United States (i.e., elite deviance) are actually committed by much older people, usually in the course of their normal occupations. Piquero & Benson (2004, p. 158) write that white-collar offenders tend to "have a brief flirtation with delinquency during adolescence that ends in the late teens or early 20s. However, after a period of conformity during their 20s and 30s, they begin to offend again later in life by committing white-collar crimes." The authors reason this is due to increased opportunity to commit crimes associated with their work positions. In terms of corporate criminals, Robinson and Murphy (2008) assert that much of their criminality is due to opportunities that present themselves in the context of working for corporations, as well as a corporate culture that emphasizes attaining wealth by any means (including greedy corporate crimes).

Similarly, while street crime is committed disproportionately by unmarried people, this is likely not true for acts of elite deviance. Most white-collar and corporate criminals, for example, are older, married men.

The belief that crime is committed disproportionately by people living in large cities holds true for street crimes such as murder, but not for most intentional killings and other forms of harms. Because this assertion is not true with regard to elite deviance, the notion that crime is committed disproportionately by people who have experienced high residential mobility and who live in areas characterized by high levels of residential mobility also does not apply to other forms of harmful behaviors. Most white-collar and corporate criminals, for example, are wealthy enough to be able to avoid moving frequently and to avoid residing in areas of high residential mobility.

The points that assert that attachment to schools and families reduces the likelihood that people will engage in crime do not appear to be relevant for many forms of antisocial behavior committed by people who seem to fit in and seem to conform to society's expectations for behaviors. For example, many teenagers from two-parent families, who are doing well in school and working at jobs, occasionally engage in deviant acts such as vandalism, spray-painting buildings and garbage cans, and so forth. These behaviors are often referred to as "boys being boys." The same can be said for the claims that high educational and occupational aspirations are related to low amounts of criminal behavior and that poor performance in school is related to high amounts of criminal behavior. Although logic suggests that white-collar and corporate criminals would be highly educated and intelligent, this is not necessarily true, and even when people do well in school, this does not mean they earned it. So, it is possible that many people who commit harmful behaviors, even intentionally, do not have high educational and occupational aspirations.

Attachment to parents can protect people from the criminal element unless one is attached to criminal parents; in this case, attachment to parents would increase the risk of criminality. Many white-collar and corporate criminals come from very respectable families to whom they were likely closely attached. So, a close attachment to parents may not reduce one's risk of antisocial behavior, as Braithwaite claims.

The claim that being at the bottom of the class structure increases rates of offending for crime is simply a class-biased assumption. Street criminals tend to be less well off financially than the general population as a whole, but these are not the most dangerous people in the country (Robinson, 2002). Piquero and Benson (2004, p. 160) concur, saying even though "white-collar offenders often have acquired some level of material, occupational, and social success" and thus they have something to lose, "these trappings of success and achievement" do not "promote conformity" for white-collar offenders.

To the degree that the theory we develop in this book is to be applied to street crimes, the theory logically must be able to account for the facts presented by Braithwaite. Alternatively, to the degree the theory ought to explain other forms of antisocial behaviors and forms of criminality, these "facts" become less important.

Summary

In this chapter, you learned about different conceptions of crime, including the natural definition and legal definition of crime. The natural definition of crime suggests acts should be illegal if they violate natural law, i.e., if they are inherently wrong. The legal definition of crime requires that acts actually violate the criminal law to be illegal. Generally, acts have to be committed with culpability in order to be illegal, meaning they must be committed intentionally, negligently, recklessly, or knowingly.

Since crime does not exist in nature but instead is invented by people through the criminal law, this means anything can be a crime, nothing is automatically a crime, and people disagree about what behaviors should be crimes. This is problematic because criminologists tend to limit their studies to street crimes rather than acts of elite deviance such as white-collar and corporate crime. Elite deviance is more costly than street crime in terms of lives lost, injuries suffered, as well as property losses caused. Criminological theories ought to be able to be able to explain the most harmful behaviors, thus, they should be able to explain acts of elite deviance. Studying only those acts called crimes by law-makers would lead criminologists to ignore the most harmful acts, including harmful acts committed by people like them and their financial backers, as well as to study several relatively harmless acts.

Criminologists have discovered facts of crime that generally hold true for street crime, including that most crime is committed by men, young people, unmarried people, people living in large cities, peoples living in conditions of residential mobility, people who are not strongly attached to their parents or schools, people who have low educational and occupational aspirations, people who have friendships with criminals, and people who do not believe in complying with the law. Yet, these facts are mostly inconsistent with acts of elite deviance. A major flaw in criminological theory is that it cannot explain acts of elite deviance.

Although criminality is related to terms such as delinquency, antisocial behavior, deviance, and aggression, each means something different. Of most interest to us in this book are violent forms of antisocial and criminal behavior, as well as acts of abnormal aggression that start early in childhood. Although antisocial behavior is fairly stable across the lifespan and virtually everyone will commit delinquent or criminal acts at some point in their lives, early starters to antisocial behavior tend to persist across the life course and engage in more serious forms of antisocial behavior than late starters and adolescent limited offenders. Temperamental traits such simulation seeking, fearlessness, hyperactivity, negative affect, impulsivity, extraversion, depression, neuroticism, and interpersonal callousness tend to be found in early starters and life course persistent offenders and are indicative of more serious delinquency and criminality.

Discussion Questions

1. What is crime?
2. What does it mean that crime is invented by people?
3. Compare the legal definition of crime with a natural definition of crime.
4. What is meant by the term *serious crime*?
5. List and define the serious crimes in the United States.
6. What is elite deviance?
7. Which causes more harm in the United States, serious crime or elite deviance?
8. Why is it problematic that criminologists focus most on serious crime as opposed to other forms of harmful behaviors such as elite deviance?
9. What are the main differences between criminality, delinquency, antisocial behavior, deviance, and aggression?
10. How is antisocial behavior stable across the life course?
11. Which of Braithwaite's facts of crime apply well to elite deviance?

2

What Is Theory?

- Introduction
- Theory defined
- Functions of theory: Explanation and prediction
- Parts of theory: Propositions, concepts, and definitions of concepts
- Types of major theories in criminology
- How people use theory every day
- Theory versus philosophy
- Policy implications of theory
- How to evaluate theory
- Summary

Introduction

What is theory? Do you see it as something that is important for the study of crime? Or is theory just some useless abstract thing? Most people probably could not define the word *theory* if asked to do so. Those who have a rudimentary understanding of theory still are likely to believe that theory has no place in the real world; instead, it is something that is for the classroom. We hold a different view. We believe that theory is crucial to the understanding and prevention of the types of antisocial behaviors discussed in chapter 1.

Theory Defined

Here are some definitions of *theory* from notable scholars:

- "an explanation ... a sensible relating of some particular phenomenon to the whole field of information, beliefs, and attitudes that make up the intellectual atmosphere of a people at a particular place and time" (Vold, Bernard, & Snipes, 1998, p. 2)

- "a statement about the relationships between observable phenomena" (Stinchcombe, 1968, pp. 3–5)
- "an explanation ... telling why or how things are related to each other" (Bohm, 2001, p. 1)
- "a generalization of a sort which explains how two or more events are related and the conditions under which that relationship takes place" (Williams & McShane, 1994, p. 2)
- "a systematic collection of concepts and statements purporting to explain behavior ... an attempt to make sense out of observations" (Shoemaker, 1996, p. 7)
- "a set of interconnected statements or propositions that explain how two or more events or factors are related to one another" (Curran & Renzetti, 1994, p. 2)
- "a view on why something occurs" (Lilly, Cullen, & Ball, 1959, p. 3)
- "a statement about actual events, about what is and a prediction about what will be" (Akers, 1997, p. 2)
- "explanation ... an attempt to make sense and order of events that are otherwise unexplainable" (Miller, Schreck, and Tewksbury, 2006: pp. 5–6).

Each of these definitions discusses part of what theories do. If we were to combine the definitions into one, we would arrive at a more complete definition of theory. Our definition of theory is "a statement of a relationship between two or more propositions and concepts that explains and predicts some behavior." This definition will be expanded on below.

Functions of Theory:
Explanation and Prediction

Some of the most important words from the preceding definitions of theory include relationship, explanation, prediction, propositions, and concepts. A *relationship* exists when two or more things vary or change together. For example, there may be a relationship between the weather and criminality. When it gets hot, people tend to get cranky and frustrated and may become aggressive. When it gets cold, people are more likely to stay inside and avoid contact with others. Additionally, there are more opportunities for crime in warmer climates, so crime rates tend to be higher in warmer places (Rotton & Cohn, 2004). Because weather and criminality change together, there is a relationship between them. But, a relationship is not the same thing as cause and effect. Box 2.1 discusses the necessary conditions for causality.

Box 2.1 Criteria for Causality

1. *Correlation/association.* Two concepts or variables must be related to one another. That is, as one changes, so must the other. For example, if a scientist asserted that exposure to pornography causes rape, he or she must first demonstrate that amounts of exposure to pornography and amounts of rape vary together. If a group's exposure to pornography varied but their rape behaviors did not, there is no relationship between the two concepts.

2. *Time-order sequence.* The cause must occur before the effect. For example, in the proposition that exposure to pornography causes rape, the exposure to pornography must occur before the rape. If a man rapes a woman before he ever watches a pornographic video, then being exposed to pornography could not have caused the rape.

3. *Lack of spuriousness.* No other factor must act upon the presumed cause and the presumed effect, making it look like a relationship exists when one does not really exist. That is, the relationship cannot be false. For example, in order to prove the proposition that exposure to pornography causes rape, it must be demonstrated that no other factor actually caused the person to watch pornography and commit rape. Other possible causes of watching pornography and committing rape include a desire for power and sex, a hatred of women, unusually high levels of testosterone, and so forth. These factors might increase one's exposure to pornography and rape, making it look like pornography causes rape.

As shown in the box, one must demonstrate three conditions to establish causality. First, you must show that there is a relationship between two things. This is easily done, for if one thing changes and so does another, a relationship has been established. Second, you must demonstrate that the presumed cause comes before the effect, or else it cannot be said to be the cause of the other event. This too can be established. However, the final criterion—a lack of spuriousness—cannot be established in studies of human behavior. The reason is that you would have to rule out every other possible factor (known and possibly unknown) that contributes to behavior before you can assert confidently that you have identified the cause of it. This is simply impossible to do.

An *explanation* is a statement about why something occurs. For example, some criminologists claim that criminal behavior is increased by drug abuse, that when one becomes addicted to drugs and suffers withdrawal from some substance, he or she is more likely to commit a crime in order to get the drugs needed to produce the desired high (chapter 6 discusses relationships between drugs and crime). A *prediction* is a statement about when or where something is likely to occur. For example, criminologists predict that someone is more likely to become a crime victim when he or she hangs out late at night in places where alcohol is served (chapter 6 discusses relationships between victim lifestyles and criminal victimization). This is a prediction about when and where criminal victimization is likely to occur. Some theories are aimed at telling us why something happens (explanation), whereas others tell us when and where something will happen (prediction).

Ultimately, if theories can tell us why crime occurs, and when and where it is most likely to occur, we ought to be able to use the knowledge generated by the theories to prevent crime. For example, research has consistently related some forms of criminal behavior, most notably highly aggressive forms of violent crime, to traumatic injuries to certain areas of the human brain (chapter 5 discusses relationships between head injury and criminality). Given this research, we can derive policies aimed at reducing head injuries that ought to ultimately result in less violent crime. The issue of policy implications of theories is discussed later in this chapter.

Parts of Theory: Propositions, Concepts, and Definitions of Concepts

Propositions are the key sentences of the theory. For example, social control theories suggest that crime will occur when individuals are not bonded to society. Box 2.2 lists the main propositions of Hirschi's (1969) *social bonding theory*. Note how it contains four propositions that specify how one's level of the social bond is related to criminality. We use Hirschi's theory as an example because research shows it is the most accepted theory among criminologists (Walsh & Ellis, 1999). *Concepts* are the key words that are found in the propositions of the theory. For example, in social bonding theory, some key concepts are attachment, commitment, involvement, beliefs, and delinquency.

Box 2.2 Social Bonding Theory

1. The greater one's attachment to parents, the less likely one is to commit acts of delinquency in childhood and adolescence.
2. The greater one's commitment to succeeding through conventional means such as school and work, the less likely one is to commit acts of delinquency in childhood and adolescence.

3. The greater one's involvement in legitimate activities such as recreation, the less likely one is to commit acts of delinquency in childhood and adolescence.
4. The more one's beliefs are consistent with the criminal law, the less likely one is to commit acts of delinquency in childhood and adolescence.

Each of these concepts must be defined by scholars so that they can be understood by others and tested in the real world. Concepts are defined in two ways, nominally and operationally. Thus, there are nominal definitions of concepts and operational definitions of concepts. *Nominal definitions* are simply dictionary definitions of the concepts. They tell us what the concepts mean. *Operational definitions* are more technical and specific. They are also ways of defining concepts, but they specifically tell us how the concepts will be measured in a study. For example, consider this proposition: Brain injury increases aggression. The main concepts in this proposition are brain injury and aggression (because they are the main things in the proposition that are related to one another). A scholar who wanted to test this proposition to see if it would be supported or refuted with empirical evidence would have to define these concepts nominally and operationally.

Brain injury could be defined as "trauma to the head that resulted in a loss of brain function." This would be the nominal definition. A nominal definition for aggression could be "violent actions that are hostile and unprovoked." These definitions simply tell the reader what the concepts mean. Remember that the concepts also need to be operationalized, or defined, so that they can be measured in a study. So, how would one measure head injury and aggression? Head injury could be operationalized as "the number of times a person sustained any blow to the head that required medical attention." Criminologists could then access medical records from hospitals to verify whether an individual was exposed to some type of brain injury. Examples of useful tools to assess head injury include neurological evaluations by doctors and brain scans. An operational definition of aggression could be "the number of times a person attacks another person without being provoked." Criminologists could ask individuals to self-report their own aggressive acts, or could ask their potential victims, or could even rely on official police and courts statistics. Regardless of the measure chosen, for it to be an operational definition of the concept, it must be defined in such a way that it can be measured (or counted).

Returning to the social bonding theory outlined in box 2.2, criminologists have defined these concepts both nominally and operationally. Hirschi and Gottfredson (2001, p. 83) provided nominal definitions of these attachments. Attachment is "the bond of respect, love, or affection"; commitment is "the bond of aspiration, investment, or ambition"; involvement is "the restriction of opportunity to commit delinquent acts by engaging in conventional activities"; and belief is "the bond to conformity created by the view that criminal and delinquent acts are morally wrong." These concepts are typically measured using surveys of parents and children to examine the strength of the bond between family members. Some examples of operational definitions of attachment are: "How many nights per week do you have dinner with your parents/children?" and "How many times per week do you read a story to your children?" Such measures would be attempts to assess how close parents are to children. Children who are closer to their parents (more attached) are generally thought to be less likely to commit delinquency (see Chapter 7). As defined in chapter 1, delinquency refers to criminal acts committed by juveniles. It can be operationalized in many ways. For example, an operational definition is "the number of times a juvenile self-reports a criminal act" or "the number of times a juvenile gets taken into custody by police for allegedly committing a crime." The significance of operational definitions is that they allow for theories to be tested and either supported or refuted by empirical evidence in the real world. In the case of social bonding theory, you'll see in chapter 7 that there is much evidence that factors like attachment are indeed important for understanding antisocial behavior, especially by children and adolescents.

How People Use Theory Every Day

There are literally thousands of theories about all kinds of behaviors. Box 2.3 provides some interesting examples. The key features of these theories is that they can be tested to see if they are supported or refuted by empirical evidence.

Box 2.3 Some Interesting Theories

- *Theory of acquired characteristics (Chevalier de Lamarck, 1744–1829).* Changes occur in organisms as a result of environmental influences rather than genetics. For example, the long necks of giraffes evolved over time because generations of giraffes learned to stretch up to the trees to feed on leaves.
- *Beer's law (chemistry).* Absorption of any substance into another substance is proportional to the number of absorbing molecules in the absorbing substance. For example, a larger sponge with more molecules can absorb more spilled liquid than a smaller sponge.

- *Game theory (politics, economics, psychology).* Individuals and groups pursue their own self-interests by rationally calculating not only what would likely be advantageous to them but also what may be disadvantageous to their opponents. For example, one gang may calculate the potential rewards of entering the illicit drug market and also consider the strategies of rival gangs who seek to benefit from the drug trade.
- *Romeo and Juliet effect (psychology).* Two individuals who are kept apart from one another by their families may become more attracted to each other. For example, the father of a young lady refuses to let her date a rugged-looking young man in the neighborhood. Because the daughter is not allowed to date him, her attraction to the young man increases.

Source: Bothamley, J. (1993). *Dictionary of theories.* London: Gale Research International.

For criminologists and criminal justice scholars who want to know why crime occurs and who want to know where and when it is most likely to occur, theory is very useful. Yet, perhaps you do not see theory as relevant for the real world. Williams and McShane (1994, p. 1) claimed: "Most people immediately rebel when threatened with their first exposure to theory ... because they think of theory as something abstract and not really applicable to the 'real world.' What they don't understand is that we all use theory; theory is part of everyday life." Akers (1997, p. 1) wrote: "To many students, criminal justice practitioners, and other people, theory has a bad name. In their minds, the word 'theory' means an irrelevant antonym of 'fact.' Facts are real, while theories ... are just fanciful ideas that have little to do with what truly motivates real people." According to Shoemaker (1996, p. 7): "To the layperson, a theory often suggests a wild speculation, or set of speculations, an unproved or perhaps false assumption, or even a fact concerning an event or type of behavior, based on little, if any, actual data."

You may think that crime is easy to understand without theory. According to Lilly et al. (1995, p. 1): "Often commentators ... suggest that using good common sense is enough to explain why citizens shoot or rob one another and, in turn, to inform us as to what to do about such lawlessness." Maybe your common sense tells you that crime is caused by greed, laziness, or bad morals or that criminals are just bad people. If you have already made up your mind that these are the key causes of crime, theory is useless. You may ask, why do we need theory to explain crime when we already know what causes it? We argued in chapter 1 that there are some crimes whose causes are obvious, like when a hungry person with no money steals food from a grocery store or when a drug addict robs a person to obtain money to purchase drugs.

While some street crime may be easy to understand, some commonly held beliefs about why most forms of antisocial behavior occur are probably dead wrong, as you will see throughout this book. We need theory to explain and predict crime because human behavior (including criminality) is much more complex than you might believe. As noted by Lilly et al.: "Crime is a complex phenomenon, and it is a demanding, if intriguing, challenge to explain its many sides ... the search for answers to the crime problem is not so easy" (p. 1).

Why do you think crime happens? Make a list of all the factors that you think are important for understanding crime. In doing this, you can create propositions that state relationships between the things in your list and crime. The things in your sentences would be the concepts. If you string together a few of your related propositions, you are essentially creating a theory of crime, that is, as long as the concepts in your propositions can be measured in the real world.

Perhaps you still do not think theory is important. Paternoster and Bachman (2001, p. 1) claim that "for too many students [theory] is simply irrelevant, and irrelevant things are difficult to focus on. Students often believe that ... theory has nothing to do with the 'real world.'" In fact, all of us actually use theory every day. Miller, Schreck and Tewksbury (2006: 5–6) assert: "Too often, theory is erroneously thought of as philosophy or logic that has little relevance for real-world situations. In reality, theory is part of everyday life, an attempt to make sense and order events that are otherwise unexplainable."

For example, do you consider the weather in deciding what to wear each day? If so, why? Most likely if it is supposed to be hot, you will want to wear as few clothes as possible. If it is supposed to snow, you will probably want to have on many layers of warm clothing. If it is going to rain, you will want to bring an umbrella or put on a rain jacket.

Where do you get information about the weather? Do you look outside? If so, what do you look for? The sun? Clouds? To feel the temperature, do you stick your hand outside the door? Do you put your fingers up against your windows? Or do you just check a thermometer? Perhaps you simply tune in to the Weather Channel on your television or on the Internet to get your local forecast.

Regardless of which source(s) you consult to get the weather forecast before you get dressed, you are using theory to influence your behavior. You are relying on scientific information to decide what to wear. Some of the observations are visual (e.g., the sight of the sun or of clouds), some are tactile (e.g., feeling cold or heat), and some are based on precise measurements (e.g., temperature, barometer, and wind flow). And so, theory is in fact useful in the real world.

Theory versus Philosophy

All of these observations and measurements are scientific, and that is what makes them theoretical. When explanations (telling why something happens) or predictions (telling when or where something will happen) are based on real-world observations using the human senses (i.e., sight, hearing, touch, smell, and taste), they can be considered theories. When explanations or predictions are not based on science, they are not theories. Instead, they can better be understood as philosophies.

This is an important distinction. Both theories and philosophies attempt to explain and predict behavior. The former make propositions that are testable. The latter do not. That is, theories can be tested by gathering observations in the real world, while philosophies cannot be tested empirically. In other words, if theories are false, they can be disproven. If philosophies are false, they cannot be disproven. Philosophies are basically suppositions that are not testable by empirical evidence; philosophers often do not require supportive empirical evidence to be convinced that their ideas are right.

Box 2.4 contains an example of a theory and a philosophy. Notice that the theory can be tested to see if it is false. The philosophy cannot be shown to be true or false, because its key concept cannot be measured with the empirical senses.

Box 2.4 Theory versus Philosophy

- *Theory.* Abnormal levels of neurotransmitters (normally occurring brain chemicals) in the brain can lead to aggressive behaviors. These neurotransmitter levels are affected by one's genetic code, as well as by diet, drug use, and other environmental factors.
- *Philosophy.* Possession by evil spirits causes aggression. When people are possessed by demons, they may act very strangely and even commit acts of violence.

The difference between the theory and philosophy in box 2.4 is that the theory can be tested with empirical evidence. Neurotransmitter levels can be measured and related to aggressive behaviors, whereas possession by demons cannot be measured and thus cannot be related to aggressive behaviors (neurotransmitter levels are discussed in chapter 5).

Since philosophies cannot be subjected to empirical testing, they are not *falsifiable*. That is, if they are false, they cannot be shown to be false. Theories are falsifiable; if they are wrong, they can be proven wrong. You may ask, why would a theorist want to show that a theory is false? Well, we can learn just as much from being wrong as we can from being right. For example, humankind used to believe that the Earth was flat and that the Earth was the center of the universe. We now know that both of these assertions are wrong. Thus, each has been falsified (or disproven). Because each assertion about the Earth has been disproven through scientific tests, we have learned something about the Earth and our universe.

Box 2.5 contains some theoretical propositions about crime that have been falsified. Because they were theoretical, they were testable. Scholars tested these propositions against evidence from the real world and generally found them to be false. Even though many of them may sound absurd to you, remember that they still helped us learn about criminal behavior. We learned that these are not true statements about criminal behavior.

Box 2.5 Some Falsified Theories

- *Phrenology (Franz Joseph Gall, 1758–1828).* Configurations of the brain dictate an individual's personalities and abilities. Thus, skull topography (e.g., bumps on the head) can be related to human behavior.
- *Somatotypes (Ernst Kretschmer, 1888–1964; William Hebert Sheldon, 1898–1970).* Body type (e.g., degree of muscularity) is a good predictor of human behavior, including aggression.
- *XYY Supermale.* Men with an extra Y chromosome will have higher levels of male hormones (e.g., testosterone) and thus commit more aggression.

Many ancient explanations of various phenomena were not based on science and thus were not theoretical. Technically, they can never be disproven. Yet, we know now that thunder is not caused by angry gods in the sky. Think back to what it must have been like to live as an early human, not knowing anything about the effects of air masses, temperatures, pressure gradients, cold/warm fronts, jet streams, humidity, and winds on the weather. Thunder must have been very frightening. Today, scientists tell us that thunder is one of the consequences resulting from lightning. Lightning is caused by a buildup and discharge of electrical energy between positively and negatively charged particles. The rapid heating and cooling of air near the lightning causes a shock wave that results in thunder. So, science has taught us that ancient philosophies about thunder are probably wrong.

We now know that influenza (the flu) is not a sickness influenced by the stars. Instead, it is caused by viruses that are transmitted by inhaling droplets in the air that contain viruses, or by handling items contaminated by an infected person. There are three general categories of the flu virus, including types A,

B, and C. Type A influenza mutates constantly, yielding new strains of the virus every few years. It is responsible for major epidemics every several years. Types B and C are less common and result in local outbreaks and milder cases. Again, science has taught us that ancient philosophies about the flu are probably wrong.

One of the examples in box 2.4 is demonology, the belief that criminal behavior comes from possession by evil spirits. Have you ever seen the movie *The Exorcist?* Although this is a good example of what demon possession might look like, we cannot really experience demons with any human sense—that is, they cannot be seen, heard, touched, tasted, or smelled. Thus, even if demon possession causes criminal behavior, we cannot prove it. Similarly, if demons do not cause criminal behavior, we can never disprove it. Thus, it is not testable, not falsifiable, and not theoretical. As a result, we cannot learn from this philosophy.

Even so, ancient cultures carried out *exorcisms* (where demons were forced out of the body by a religious ceremony) and practiced *trephining* (where holes were drilled into the skull to let the demons out) based on the belief that these demons were responsible for the seven deadly sins:

- Lucifer caused pride;
- Mammon caused avarice;
- Asmodeus caused lust;
- Satan caused anger;
- Beelzebub caused gluttony;
- Leviathan caused envy; and
- Belphegor caused vanity and sloth (McAdam, 2000).

Imagine believing that strange and aggressive behaviors were caused by evil spirits. With the birth of the scientific method, we can now look back and suggest that many of the strange and aggressive behaviors attributed to demons were probably caused by severe brain disorders (i.e., mental illnesses) and other medical conditions like epilepsy (mental illnesses are discussed in chapter 6).

The main benefit of theory is that humans can advance their knowledge about behaviors (e.g., criminal behavior) by constructing and testing theories. Even if theories turn out to be disproven, humankind still learns something about human behavior. Philosophies, which oftentimes are posited by powerful people (e.g., politicians) based on nothing more than conjecture and opinion, are not useful for advancing our knowledge. Keep your ears open ... it is likely that as you make your way through this book, a major politician is promoting philosophical ideas about crime that cannot be subjected to direct empirical testing.

Policy Implications of Theory

Speaking of politicians, all criminal justice policies are rooted in ideas about why crime happens. That is, everything we do to reduce crime is based on our beliefs about why crime occurs. Many of our criminal justice policies are based on philosophies, while some are based on theories of crime. Each of the main forms of punishment in the United States uses some degree of punitiveness (i.e., punishment) to attempt to reduce recidivism (i.e., repeat offending). So, if the United States uses forms of punishment to try to make people not want to commit crime, what do we assume causes criminal behavior? In other words, if we assume that pains associated with the administration of punishment will reduce criminal behavior in the future, what must we believe motivated the offenders' past criminal behaviors?

Most American criminal punishments are rooted in the assumptions that offenders are *rational* (i.e., deliberate and planning) and *hedonistic* (i.e., pleasure seeking), and that offenders can freely choose to commit crime. Logically, then, if offenders are rational and freely choose to commit crimes, we ought to be able to make them not want to choose to commit crime by causing fear in them through punishment. This is called *deterrence* (deterrence is discussed further in chapter 8). Box 2.6 describes how each of the main forms of punishment used in the United States supposedly creates fear in offenders.

Box 2.6 Major Forms of Punishment in the United States

- *Probation.* Offenders on probation are supervised by their probation officer and must follow many rules that they would not have to follow even in prison. Thus, they should be deterred from committing future crimes for fear that they might be put on probation again.
- *Incarceration.* Prisons and jails are horribly violent and repressive places. Any criminal who is incarcerated ought to be afraid to come back. Additionally, all of society should fear suffering the pains of incarceration. This is supposed to stop people from committing crimes.
- *Intermediate sanctions (e.g., boot camps).* Juvenile offenders are forced to go to classes, work, and train through various physical fitness activities. It is hoped that juveniles will fear being forced to undergo such strenuous conditions again in the future, thereby deterring juvenile delinquency.
- *Death penalty.* Not only does the death penalty incapacitate the offender, it sends a message out to all of society that anyone who com-

mits murder can be executed for his or her offense. It is hoped that this will prevent people from committing murders.

Source: Robinson, M. (2009). *Justice blind? Ideals and realities of American criminal justice* (3rd Ed.).

The American criminal justice system basically dismisses the possibility that human behaviors such as criminality are caused by factors beyond the offender's control. Theories that assume a causal relationship between some factor and criminal behavior are considered *deterministic* because they assert that crime is determined by factors beyond the control of offenders. Our criminal justice system operates on the philosophical assumption that humans are freewilled and therefore completely responsible for their actions.

Some explanations of crime are classified as *rational choice theories* (Clarke & Cornish, 2001). These explanations claim that crime is freely chosen by rational offenders to maximize pleasure and minimize pain. Rational choice theorists examine offender decision making and the factors that affect it, such as assessments of risks and rewards and the morality of various behaviors (Clarke, 1983, p. 232). The balance between likely risks and rewards influences offenders' target selection, as does the offender's view of whether it is right or wrong to hurt another person or take his or her property. The level of risk is one of the factors that makes a potential target good or bad (Brantingham & Brantingham, 1984). Offenders plan to reduce the level of risk associated with committing criminal offenses by selecting the most suitable targets.

According to Taylor and Harrell (1996, p. 2), offenders often behave in a rational fashion, since they choose to commit crimes that require little effort, provide high rewards, and pose a low risk of painful consequences. As noted by Hickey (1991) and Wright and Rossi (1983), even violent criminals are selective in their choices of targets. Serial killers rarely choose weight lifters or martial arts experts as victims. Other violent criminals rarely choose armed victims; they pose too much of a risk (Siegel, 1995). The mere fact that victims are not chosen at random suggests a rational offender (Fattah, 1993).

Although these assertions are logical and make sense, there is a major problem associated with explanations of crime based on rational choice. When scholars conclude that offenders are rational based on their behaviors and then use the concept of rationality to explain the same behaviors, this constitutes *circular reasoning* (Akers, 1994, p. 8). As noted by Jeffery and Zahm (1993, p. 339), the concept of choice "is neither empirical nor observable, and the investigator can only know when an individual has made a choice when he behaves in a given way. From the observed behavior, the investigator inputs a cause (such as ra-

Figure 2.1 The Rock and the Man

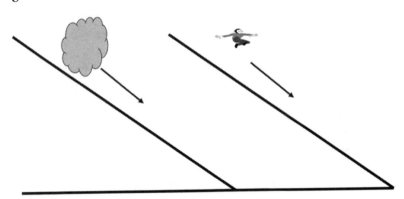

Source: Figure created by author.

tional choice ...)." Because the heart of the rational choice model is focused on "an analysis of the thought or cognitive means by which individuals process information from the environment," it is not possible to test the theory directly (Jeffery & Zahm, 1993, p. 337). Thoughts cannot be studied directly; they can only be verbalized by offenders. Verbal statements constitute verbal behavior, not the thought processes they are portrayed to represent by rational choice theorists. These problems with rational choice theory make interpretations of findings within such a framework questionable. This is why we consider so-called rational choice theories not really theories but instead philosophies (because the key concept of rational choice cannot be tested directly with empirical evidence).

Take a look at figure 2.1, which depicts a rock rolling down a hill and a man walking down another hill. What causes the rock to roll down the hill? Gravity? Probably, but why did the rock begin to roll down the hill? You would never say that the rock chose to begin rolling, would you? At the same time, what makes the man walk down the hill? Is his walking caused by something, or did he choose to walk down the hill? Now think of the man walking down the hill as an analogy for a man progressing through his life. Do people choose to commit crimes as children? As teenagers? As adults? Do we decide, from birth, whether we will end up as criminals or as noncriminals?

You probably think all people can choose to walk or not, where to walk and when to walk there, and even whether or not to commit crimes and become criminals. Remember that in order for an explanation to be considered theoretical, it must be testable. Can we test the proposition that humans choose to behave? Think about the man walking down the hill, for example. Can you think of a way to show with empirical evidence that the man chose to walk down the hill? According to many criminologists, this is impossible to do.

Since most criminal justice policies are based on such beliefs about rational humans, they are not based on scientific understanding of behavior produced by criminological theories, but instead are based on philosophical assumptions about human behavior. The administration of the death penalty, for example, is not based on scientific evidence showing a deterrent effect on crime. Instead, it is used against a very small percentage of murderers mostly to gain revenge and to make it impossible for the offenders to offend again. There is no valid evidence that would-be murderers are deterred from committing murder based on their fear of being executed (Robinson, 2008). Indeed, much research has concluded the exact opposite, that most murders are very irrational and impulsive, committed in the heat of the moment between people who know each other (Bohm, 2007). For example, consider a man who comes home to find his wife in bed with another man. If the couple argues, and one of the two picks up a gun, will he or she likely think of the death penalty before pulling the trigger? What about in a bar fight between two young men? If one picks up a bar stool and maliciously begins beating the other about the head, is the offender going to stop because he may get the death penalty? Not likely. The death penalty is based on assumptions about the crime of murder and philosophical guesswork regarding human behavior.

Some criminal justice policies are based on *theories* about human behavior. One example of a policy that has recently been proposed and even passed in some states is the castration of repeat sexual offenders (e.g., child molesters). As intrusive and alarming as this sounds, and as much as it raises concerns about individual rights of offenders, it is based on sound theoretical propositions. Research has shown that castration, whether by actual removal of the testes or by administering certain chemicals, results in a reduction of testosterone levels in the bloodstream. To the degree that aggression generally, and sexual aggression in particular, is caused by high levels of testosterone, we might expect castration to result in lower levels of aggressive behaviors (the effects of testosterone and other hormones are discussed in chapter 5). We are neither suggesting that this type of approach will be effective at reducing violent behavior nor arguing in favor of it; we are simply using it as an example of a criminal justice policy that is rooted in a theoretical proposition ("higher levels of testosterone produce higher levels of aggression"). Even if they are ineffective and morally reprehensible, castration policies are at least rooted in theories of crime that suggest that hormones are related to behavior (hormones are discussed in chapter 6).

According to Paternoster and Bachman (2001, p. 2), "all theories of crime contain within them suggestions of implications for criminal justice policy." That is, we can derive policy implications for reducing crime from any theory of crime. Theories of crime suggest both what should be done to reduce crime and what should not be done to reduce crime. Each theory of crime posits a cause of criminal behavior; if these causes are found to be important for explaining crime, then these causes can be eliminated in order to reduce crime; if they are not found to be important for explaining crime, then steps need not be taken to eliminate the suspected causes. Of the plethora of theories that have been put forth by criminologists over the decades, which explanations of crime have most influenced criminal justice policy?

The rational choice perspective is the dominant perspective influencing criminal justice policy in the United States today; thus we can logically assume that most theories of crime are seen as irrelevant for explaining crime. After all, if other theories were thought to explain crime well, our efforts to reduce crime ought to be informed by knowledge generated by tests of theories of crime. Since most theories of crime are seen as irrelevant for explaining crime, policies already in place based on retribution (getting even with offenders) and deterrence (creating fear in offenders) become reinforced.

How to Evaluate Theory

There are dozens of theories of criminality. Each of these theories attempts to explain and/or predict criminal behavior. So, which one should you believe? That is, how can you tell which one is right?

There are several criteria that can be used to judge the relative merits of all theories. The most important criterion for evaluating each theory is empirical validity. The word *valid* means true, correct, accurate, or right. *Empirical validity* refers to how much evidence supports the theory. Generally, the more evidence that shows a theory is valid the better. The more studies that support a theory the better. A theory that has been tested and shown to be false (falsified) is not useful for helping us explain or predict criminality. This is the most important criterion to decide which theories are the best at explaining and/or predicting criminality.

Theories should not be accepted as true or rejected as false simply because someone says so. Instead, they should be judged based on the degree of support with evidence generated from studies by scholars. Virtually every theory will have some degree of support, however, because studies will ultimately be conducted somewhere at some time that find evidence that the theory is true.

When this occurs, the relative merits of studies are assessed to ensure that their findings can be considered valid. Let's say a study finds that a sample of prison inmates in one state have lower IQs than the general population of that state. Is this support for the proposition that lower intelligence is related to criminality? To a degree. But, being that IQ may not be a valid measure of intelligence and that the sample was a group of people who had been apprehended and caught by the criminal justice system, the findings of this study may not be generalizable (or applied) to all criminals. This finding may not be obtained in similar studies from other states, and/or results from studies of nonincarcerated offenders may find that they generally do not have lower IQs than people in the general population. For example, would you expect white-collar criminals to have lower IQs? The relationship between intelligence and antisocial behavior is discussed in chapter 6.

Many theories of criminality are considered valid by criminologists. So, how can you tell which ones are true? You can use the following three criteria to assess theories: the scope of the theory, conceptual clarity, and logical adequacy of the propositions.

First, the *scope* of the theory is how much antisocial behavior can be explained by the theory. For example, how many different types of crime can be explained by the theory? Generally, the more types of behaviors that can be explained by the theory, the better, because a wider scope is considered more useful than a narrow scope. *Low self-control theory*, also known as a *general theory of crime*, supposedly explains all types of crimes at all times (Gottfredson & Hirschi, 1990). Self-control theorists assert that poor parenting skills lead to impulsivity and low self-control in children, which produces various forms of shortsighted, stupid, and risky behaviors (low self-control is discussed in chapter 7). The theory has wide scope because it supposedly explains all forms of crimes, as well as many legal but harmful behaviors (e.g., smoking cigarettes, engaging in unprotected sex, and so on). A theory that could only explain one type of crime (e.g., burglary) would be considered less useful, generally, because it could not be used to prevent a lot of different types of crimes. A theory of burglary, for example, would not be useful for explaining, predicting, and preventing violent crimes. If low self-control theory is true, then a policy implication of improving parenting skills could reduce a lot of harms, including a lot of criminality and noncriminality.

Recall that the theory developed in this book is aimed at explaining harmful and maladaptive antisocial behaviors. Ideally, the theory will have broad scope or the ability to explain a lot of behavior.

Second, *conceptual clarity* refers to the degree that the concepts of a theory are clearly defined. Consistent with the two types of definitions of concepts discussed earlier, a theory's concepts need to be defined so that people can understand them (i.e., the nominal definitions must be clearly defined) and so that they can be measured in the real world (i.e., the operational definitions must be clearly defined). If people cannot understand the concepts of the theory, then the theory's concepts are not clearly defined. Additionally, if the concepts cannot be defined so that they can be measured in the real world, then the theory's concepts are not clearly defined. Take the low self-control example discussed earlier. In order for this theory's concepts to be clearly defined, low self-control, the main concept in the theory, must be defined so that it can be understood and measured. In chapter 7, we will show the various difficulties associated with attempting to measure low self-control without engaging in *circular reasoning*, which is a flaw in logic that amounts to labeling someone's behaviors and then using that label to explain the behaviors you've labeled. When a person behaves impulsively, without much thought for the consequences of his or her actions, we can label that person as having a low level of self-control. To then turn around and use the label of low self-control to explain why the person behaves in an impulsive way would be circular reasoning.

Finally, better theories will state their propositions in a logical fashion. This is the criterion we call *logical adequacy of the propositions*. It refers to at least two things. First, theories that contain complex technical jargon may be less understandable and thus less useful. Second, and more problematic, theories that are *tautological* lead to circular reasoning and thus are not logically stated. A theory is tautological if it is true by definition. Some theories discussed in this book are considered tautological because the concepts they use to explain criminality are verified when a person commits a crime. For example, the theory of low self-control discussed in chapter 7 asserts that people commit crime because they are unable to control their impulses and act without considering the negative long-term consequences of their crimes. The presence of low self-control cannot be verified apart from the behaviors it is supposed to explain. This makes the theory tautological. How do you know if a theory is tautological? Ask yourself this: Can the theory's key concepts be measured separately from the behaviors it is supposed to explain? If the answer is no, then the theory is tautological. Since the presence of low self-control cannot be verified except when a person behaves in a certain way, the theory is tautological.

There are many other criteria that can be used to evaluate theories of antisocial behavior and criminality, but empirical validity and scope are the most important. A theory with lots of supportive evidence that can explain lots of behaviors would be worth using to derive policy implications to prevent those behaviors. Of course, a theory with narrow scope that only explains one type of behavior can still be highly useful for preventing that type of behavior, as long as the theory has been verified by empirical evidence. To the degree that different types of antisocial behavior are explained by different factors, we should not expect any one theory to explain all types of behaviors. Therefore, we might expect a lot of theories with narrow scope to be useful in the derivation of policies to prevent various types of crimes.

In chapter 3, we will put forth a perspective to explain crime based on the *integrated systems perspective,* which posits that antisocial behavior generally can best be explained and predicted when numerous factors interact. Using this perspective allows scholars to identify the constellation or group of factors that are important for antisocial behavior and criminality.

Summary

In this chapter, you learned about theory. A theory is a statement between two or more concepts (things) which helps us understand the world by explaining why something occurs. Criminological theories tend to suggest causes of criminality, but demonstrating a cause and effect relationship between some factor and criminal behavior is impossible since scholars cannot demonstrate a lack of spuriousness. This is because it is impossible to rule out the influence of other variables that may be the real cause. Theories are also aimed at predicting when and where things like crime occur.

If we know why crime occurs and when and where it will occur, it ought to be easier to prevent. Every theory has policy implications, which suggest what we should do to prevent criminality as a result of the theory's main explanations and predictions. Most criminal justice policies assume that people have free will and are therefore responsible for their actions. This is philosophical rather than theoretical. Philosophies cannot be tested with empirical evidence. Instead they are often tautological, or true by definition, and thus lead to circular reasoning. Circular reasoning occurs when scholars label a behavior and then use that label to explain the behavior, without any independent evidence that verifies the relationship.

Theories are made up of propositions, which are sentences that state a relationship between things, and concepts, which are the real world things in the sentences. The concepts are defined in two ways, nominally and operationally. Nominal definitions tell us what the concepts mean whereas operational definitions define the concepts so that they can be measured in a study.

Theory is relevant for the real world because it helps us understand it. We can test theories to see if they are correct or false and therefore we can learn about what produces human behavior by testing theories. However, philosophies cannot be tested and are therefore not falsifiable or useful for learning about the world.

Theories are evaluated with various criteria, including empirical validity (i.e., how much evidence supports the theory), scope (i.e., how much crime is explained by the theory), logical adequacy (i.e., how complete are the propositions and do they make sense), and conceptual clarity (i.e., how clearly are the concepts defined and can they be measured). The best theories consist of logically stated, sensible propositions made up of clearly defined, measurable concepts, are supported by a lot of empirical evidence, and can explain a lot of crime.

Discussion Questions

1. What is theory?
2. What are the main functions of theory?
3. Identify and define the main parts of a theory.
4. Create a theory by writing out one or two sentences that explain why crime happens. Then, identify the main propositions and concepts, and provide nominal and operational definitions of the key concepts.
5. How is theory used in the real world? How might it be used by society to prevent or reduce crime?
6. What is the main difference between theory and philosophy?
7. Are criminals rational and hedonistic? Do they freely choose to commit crimes or is their behavior caused by factors beyond their control? Explain.
8. How are real-world policies derived from theories?
9. Identify and define the main criteria used to evaluate a theory.

3

Perspectives in Criminological Theory

Introduction

What is your basic view of crime? What do you think causes crime? Is it something inside of some people that makes them more likely to commit crimes? Or is it something in society that causes crime? Perhaps it is both, or something else entirely? Your answers to these questions depend on your *perspective*. By this point in your life, regardless of your age, your perspective is probably well established and affects all that you see and the way you see it. It also likely prevents you from seeing everything you need to see.

What Is a Perspective?

All distinct theories of crime are based on some *perspective*. A perspective can be understood as a fundamental conceptual approach and all the activities that emanate from it (Faust, 1995). Stated differently, a perspective is a way of looking at the world, a way of thinking about problems. For criminologists and criminal justice scholars, their perspective determines how they set out to study criminal behavior.

Understanding one's perspective is important because it can have effects on the following:

- How criminologists and criminal justice scholars define the problem
- The methods they use to study the problem
- How they interpret the evidence
- The policies that result from studies

Consider the difference in perspectives of biologists who study crime and sociologists who study crime. A biologist studies humans, their biological makeup (cells, organs, etc.), and their resulting behaviors. A sociologist studies society and its social makeup (peer groups, families, etc.), and behaviors that result from social interactions.

Biologists define crime as a biological problem with its roots in one's biological structures and processes. For example, crime may be caused by flawed genes, a muscular body build, or brain injury. Biologists would then use their own methods to study crime, including genetic screening mechanisms, brain scans, and similar methods. When interpreting the evidence from their studies, they would consider and discuss the implications of their findings for a person's biological makeup. Finally, biologists would derive policy implications aimed at reducing criminality; these policies would be aimed at changing the criminal's biology.

Sociologists define crime as a social problem with its roots in society. For example, crime may be caused by demands imposed on individuals within a competitive economic society, by hanging out with deviant peers, or by being raised by ineffective parents. Sociologists would then use their own methods to study crime, including interviews, surveys, and participant observation techniques. When interpreting the evidence from their studies, they would consider and discuss the implications of their findings for society. Finally, sociologists would derive policy implications aimed at reducing criminality; these policies would be aimed at changing the features of society that produce crime.

Major Types of Perspectives in Criminological Theory

Classical versus Positivistic and Probabilistic Perspectives

There are several different perspectives within criminology. Historically, criminology texts have compared the classical and positivistic perspectives. The *classical perspective*, also referred to as *classicism* or the *Classical School of Criminology*, was developed in the 1700s in Europe. Its founders posited that all human behavior resulted from a rational calculation of potential rewards and punishments. Classical scholars saw mankind as *hedonistic* (pleasure seeking and wanting to avoid pain) and *rational* (able to consider potential pleasures and pains prior to engaging in behaviors). Essentially, all human behavior was motivated by pleasure-seeking and pain avoidance considerations (for excellent summaries of this perspective, see Einstadter & Henry, 2006; Lilly, Cullen, & Ball, 2007; Miller, Schrek, & Tewksbury, 2006; Walsh & Ellis, 2007). These assumptions form the basis for theories of *deterrence* by criminal justice punishment. These theories assert that punishment can be effectively used to prevent crime by causing fear in would-be offenders (see chapter 8).

Associated with classicism is the notion that human beings possess *free will*, or the ability to exercise complete control over one's life and choices. Nearly a hundred years later, also in Europe, scholars challenged the notion that people have free will by putting forth a new perspective commonly referred to as *positivism* or the *Positive School of Criminology*. This perspective denies that humans have free will, and instead posits that all human behavior is determined by the impact of biological and environmental factors on us. This argument is commonly called *determinism*, and *hard determinists* believe that human behavior is caused by such factors, which are beyond the control of human beings to change (for excellent summaries of this perspective, see Einstadter & Henry, 2006; Lilly, Cullen, & Ball, 2007; Miller, Schrek, & Tewksbury, 2006; Walsh & Ellis, 2007).

Which do you believe makes more sense? Is human behavior including antisocial and criminal behavior caused by factors beyond our control? Or do we have complete control over what we do? A middle ground approach is commonly referred to as *soft determinism*. This perspective assumes that humans can make choices, but that our choices are not free choices; thus free will does not exist. Instead, our choices are shaped by factors beyond our control, due to the influence of both biological and environmental factors. According to this perspective, humans still have a choice to engage in certain behaviors, but certain people may be more likely to make certain choices given their biological makeup as well as the environment in which they live.

Consistent with soft determinism is a relatively newer way of thinking about human behavior which posits a *probabilistic* perspective rather than a classical or deterministic perspective. Probabilists assert that human behavior should be viewed like other phenomena, in that it is made more or less likely under certain circumstances. Thus, there is no free will and there are also no causes of crime. Instead, antisocial and criminal behaviors are more probable or likely to occur when people experience certain conditions. If someone asked you what conditions would make crime more likely, what would you say? If someone asked you what conditions would make crime less likely, what would you say?

Disciplinary versus Multidisciplinary and Interdisciplinary Perspectives

Positivistic and probabilistic perspectives can be either disciplinary, multidisciplinary, or interdisciplinary in nature. According to retired criminologist Frederic L. Faust, there are essentially three types of perspectives in criminology and criminal justice:

- *Disciplinary perspectives* involve a concentration in a discretely defined subject area having an organized body of accumulated thought and information and an established general approach to the conduct of inquiry and practice. Disciplinary perspectives result in scholars looking at the world from only one academic discipline or field of study.
- *Multidisciplinary perspectives* involve the selective aggregation of distinct and separate contributions from several disciplines concerning a subject area of common interest. Multidisciplinary perspectives result in scholars looking at the world from more than one academic discipline or field of study, by selectively combining two or more of them because of their common focus.
- *Interdisciplinary perspectives* involve a synthesis or integration of contributions from all disciplines about interactions among all categories of analysis associated with a specific range of phenomena. Interdisciplinary perspectives result in scholars looking at the world from all useful academic disciplines or fields of study, by integrating or synthesizing knowledge from virtually all fields of study.

Box 3.1 clarifies these types of perspectives through an example.

Box 3.1 Perspectives within Criminological Theory

Here is a useful exercise for being able to understand the differences between disciplinary, multidisciplinary, and interdisciplinary perspectives. Remember, disciplinary perspectives try to explain behavior from only one academic discipline or field of study, multidisciplinary perspectives try to explain behavior from more than one academic discipline or field of study by selectively combining two or more of them because of their common focus, and interdisciplinary perspectives try to explain behavior from all useful academic disciplines or fields of study by integrating or synthesizing knowledge from virtually all fields of study.

Imagine that you have a large glass bowl and several eggs. With a marker, label one egg with a B. This egg represents all the knowledge that has been generated within the academic discipline of biology. Label another egg with a P. This egg represents all the knowledge that has been generated within the academic discipline of psychology. Label another with an S for sociology, another with an A for anthropology, another with an E for economics, and so on.

Now, imagine that the bowl is antisocial behavior or criminality, that which you wish to explain. If you were an expert in biology, having been trained in all the theories and methods of a biologist, you would use all your tools and expertise to try to explain antisocial behavior. So, put the B egg in the bowl. If you were an expert in psychology, having been trained in all the methods of a psychologist, you would use all your tools and expertise to try to explain antisocial behavior. In this case, you would put the P egg in the bowl. If you put only the B *or* the P egg in the bowl, your explanation would be disciplinary in nature, because it would be based on only one academic discipline. If you put both the B *and* the P eggs into the bowl, your explanation would be psychobiological or biopsychological in nature and thus would be multidisciplinary.

If you put all the eggs you labeled into the bowl, one for each academic discipline, and then whipped them up as if you were going to scramble them, your explanation would be interdisciplinary. Since you have integrated the knowledge of numerous disciplines, you can no longer really tell where the biological egg is, where the psychological egg is, where the sociological egg is, and so on. They have all been mixed together.

Think of how this metaphor applies to explaining antisocial behavior. If scholars want to best explain why behavior occurs, they will have to use the knowledge from all available academic disciplines, not just one or two, because many disciplines have useful things to add and non has a corner on the truth. Otherwise, their explanations will be limited and not complete.

Most early theories of crime were based on a disciplinary perspective, because they examined the separate effects of biological, psychological, and social factors on criminal behavior. Originally, there were separate biological theories of crime, psychological theories of crime, sociological theories of crime, and so forth. Most criminology books still are organized along these lines, with separate chapters on biological, psychological, and sociological theories. Since criminology developed as a subdiscipline of sociology, most early theories of crime were sociological in nature; they posited social causes of crime (e.g., immigration, industrialization, urbanization, poverty). Even today, most theories of crime are sociological in nature (Bohm, 2001), giving little attention to biological factors (Raine, 1993). Barak (1998) called the originators of such theories *sociological traditionalists*. They claim that sociological explanations of crime are the most or even the only valid explanations of crime.

Later, multidisciplinary theories of crime were developed as other academic disciplines began to examine the effects of nonsocial factors on crime (e.g., self-concept, ego, personality). Scholars combined knowledge being generated within two or three academic disciplines and created theories of crime that were social-psychological in nature, sociobiological or biosocial in nature, and so on. Multidisciplinary theories are now the most common type of criminological theories. Barak (1998) called originators of these theories *multidisciplinary specialists*. Their theories highlight the importance of their own disciplines but at least acknowledge that other disciplines are also important to studying crime, but usually less so. Box 3.2 shows the major multidisciplinary perspectives in criminological theory.

Box 3.2 Multidisciplinary Perspectives within Criminological Theory

Individual Trait Theories
Criminals differ from noncriminals on a number of biological and psychological traits. These traits, in interaction with the social environment, produce criminality.

Social Disorganization
Disorganized communities produce crime through weakened informal social controls such as families. They lack collective efficacy to fight crime and disorder.

Social Learning
Crime is learned through associations with criminals who generally approve of crime and that neutralize or justify crime under certain circumstances. Interacting with antisocial peers is a major cause of crime and criminal behavior will be repeated if reinforced.

Anomie/Institutional Anomie

Not being able to achieve the American Dream (i.e., economic success) due to limited opportunities for success creates structural strain and criminality. When the goal of the American Dream takes precedence over the legitimate means to achieve the goal of economic success, criminality is likely. When social institutions such as the family are weak relative to economic institutions, crime rates will be high since these institutions will be unable to effectively exert informal social control.

Strain/General Strain

When individuals cannot obtain success goals legally, they experience strain. Under certain conditions, they are likely to respond to this strain through innovation or crime. Goal blockage or any negative experiences can produce aggression due to increasing negative emotions. Crime is a more likely response to strain when it results in negative affect such as anger and frustration.

Social Control/Self-Control

Criminal motivation is assumed to be widespread. Criminality is likely in the absence of social controls. These controls are rooted in social relationships in the form of social bonds and are also internal to individuals in the form of self-control.

Labeling/Reintegrative Shaming

People become stabilized in criminal roles when they are labeled as criminal and stigmatized, as well as when they develop criminal identities by either formal or informal labeling processes. Reintegrative responses that permit reconnections with society after punishment are less likely to create defiance and a commitment to crime.

Critical

Inequality in power and material well-being create conditions that lead to street crime and corporate crime. Capitalism and its market economy are especially criminogenic because they create vast inequality that impoverishes many and provides opportunities for exploitation for the powerful.

Peacemaking

Crime is caused by suffering, which is linked to injustice rooted in inequality and daily personal acts of harm. Making "war on crime" will not work. Making peace is the solution to crime.

Feminism

Crime cannot be understood without considering gender. Patriarchy is a broad structure that shapes gender-related experiences and power. Men may use crime to exert control over women and to demonstrate masculinity—that is, to show that they are "men" in a way consistent with societal ideals of masculinity.

Developmental/Life Course

Criminality is a developmental process that starts before birth and continues throughout the life course. Individual factors interact with social factors to determine the onset, length, and end of criminal careers. They key theoretical issues involve continuity and change in crime.

Integrated

These theories use components from other theories—usually strain, control, and social learning—to create a new theory that explains crime. They often are life-course theories, arguing that causes of crime occur in a sequence across time.

Adapted from: Cullen & Agnew (2002). *Criminological theory: Past to present.* Los Angeles, CA: Roxbury.

Theories of crime based on a multidisciplinary perspective are logically more complete than theories based on only one academic discipline, because criminal behavior is produced by biological, psychological, social, economic, and other factors. Yet, multidisciplinary theories often neglect vital concepts that have been shown to be related to criminal behavior. They also reinforce artificial boundaries between academic disciplines. Each of these problems is discussed in this chapter.

In the latter part of the 20th century, a few criminologists began to try to develop interdisciplinary theories of crime. Barak (1998) called these theorists *interdisciplinary generalists.* They are open to knowledge being generated in other academic disciplines. This development has been hindered by academic specialization within American colleges and universities. Criminological theories have been reductionist, for they reduce criminal behavior down to one discipline (usually sociology). Other disciplines are disregarded. Why does this occur?

Traditionally, when one develops extensive education and training in an academic discipline, the scholar does not gain much knowledge about other disciplines, except for those that are intimately related to the one being studied. Rather than being exposed to the universe of knowledge about human behavior that has been generated in all academic disciplines (hence the term *university*), students in undergraduate and graduate programs across the country typically develop expertise only within their academic discipline of study (and perhaps a related field). For example, students of sociology will learn about theories of crime that have been created by sociologists (and perhaps psychologists). Students in psychology may learn about psychological theories, sociological theories, and perhaps biological theories (to the degree they are related to psychology). In a select few academic departments in the United States, students are taught by faculty with backgrounds diverse enough that they gain familiarity with knowledge about human behavior being generated within many different academic disciplines. If this knowledge can be meaningfully combined and integrated, these students can look at the world from an interdisciplinary perspective.

Those who study behavior from an interdisciplinary perspective try to identify the relevant factors from all useful academic disciplines for explaining and predicting antisocial behavior. These scholars thus borrow knowledge from any academic discipline whose concepts are testable, falsifiable, and thus can be used to advance our knowledge about human behavior, including antisocial behavior and criminality. According to Fishbein (2001, p. 1): "The only way to eventually stimulate a comprehensive and accurate understanding of antisocial behavior is through the integration of various disciplines." Similarly, Raine (1993, p. xvii) claimed that "if we are to fully understand criminal behavior we need to be fully aware of *all* influences that bear on it." Box 3.3 clarifies through an example why integration generally is important for being able to fully explain and predict criminality.

Box 3.3 How Disciplinary Perspectives Prevent Us from Seeing the Whole Truth

An ancient Indian story illustrates how limited perspectives can keep people from seeing the truth. Imagine that six blind men encountered a "thing." Each man had to rely on his other senses to describe the thing and decide what it was.

One man thought the thing was a wall, because it was hard, rough, and incredibly broad. Another man thought the thing was a tree, because it was hard and rough, but taller and more narrow than a wall. And leaves were on the ground all around this thing, so it must be a tree. The third man also felt that the thing was hard, but he concluded that it had to be a spear because it was smooth, narrow, and sharp.

So, the first three men agreed that the thing was hard but only two thought it was rough while the other said it was smooth. And all the three men disagreed about the relative size of the thing. Their conclusions reflected the differences in their own unique experiences.

The fourth and fifth men described the thing in a completely different manner than the first two. The fourth man thought the thing was a rope, because it was skinny and flimsy, and swayed in the wind. The fifth man thought the thing was a live snake, because it was thin but firm and moved on its own.

So, the fourth and fifth men agreed that the thing could not be a wall, tree, or spear, because it was thin and it moved. Yet, they disagreed about whether the thing was alive or not. Their conclusions reflected their different experiences.

The sixth man also agreed that the thing could not be a wall, tree, or spear, but also said it was nothing like a rope or snake. Rather, it was wide, smooth, and shaped like the kind of fan you hold in your hand on a hot day. Thus, he concluded it must be a fan.

Believe it or not, each man was describing the same thing. Yet, none of them could accurately describe the thing because they could not "see" the whole truth. This is because each was only seeing a small part of the whole truth.

The whole truth is that the thing was an elephant. The first man (who thought it was a wall) was feeling the elephant's body, while the second man (who thought it was a tree) was feeling one of its legs. The third man (who thought it was a spear) was feeling the elephant's tusk. The fourth man (who thought it was a rope) was feeling the elephant's tail, and the fifth man (who thought it was a snake) was feeling the elephant's trunk. Finally, the sixth man (who thought it was fan) was feeling one of the elephant's ears.

Had the elephant triumphantly bellowed through its trunk, perhaps the men would have known what the thing really was. Or, had the sixth men combined their limited experiences, they would have been more likely to figure out that the thing was an elephant. In the story, only a wise man could tell the six men that the thing each was describing was an elephant. And he told them that had all of the men put their heads together and combined their perspectives they would have been able to conclude that it was an elephant.

Think of how this metaphor applies to explaining crime. If scholars want to be able to best explain why crime happens, they will have to be sure that their perspectives are not so limited to be incomplete. Specifically, in order to fully understand human behaviors like antisocial behavior and criminality, the perspectives of scholars in numerous academic disciplines—like biology, psychology, sociology, and so forth—must be combined.

Source: Adapted from Quigley, Lillian (1959). *The Blind Men and the Elephant*. New York: Charles Scribner's Sons.

Historically, biology has received very little attention in criminological theories. This is ironic given the state of scientific evidence. According to Moir and Jessel (1995, p. 10), "the evidence that biology is a central factor in crime, interacting with cultural, social, and economic factors, is so strong ... that to ignore it is perverse." Criminology, to the degree it only includes social factors in its explanations, is both scientifically and ideologically blind (Horowitz,

1993). Recently, biological factors have been incorporated into multidisciplinary examinations of crime (Beaver, 2008; Walsh, 2009; Walsh & Beaver, 2008). In fact, has been an explosion of biosocial articles published in some of the top journals in the discipline of criminology (Beaver, 2008; Beaver, Wright, & DeLisi, 2008; Beaver et al, 2008; Boutwell & Beaver, 2008; Cauffman, Steinberg, & Piquero, 2005; DeLisi et al., 2008; Heide & Solomon, 2006).

At the very least, biologists recognize what many social scientists do not, that it is *individuals* who behave; thus, a focus on individuals is required to explain behavior. This is especially true given that environmental factors operate differently on all individuals, presumably because no two individuals share the same genes and the same brain (Walsh, 2002). None of this suggests that the individual level is the only level of study, just that it is an important level of study.

According to Walsh (2002, p. 13): "Academics appear to have a significant psychological investment in ideas that were painfully assimilated in graduate school" which leaves them in a form of "internalized coziness" (Rock & Holdaway, 1998, p. 6). A survey of American criminologists by Walsh and Ellis (1999) found that they listed at least 23 different theories when asked which one enjoys the most empirical support. Furthermore, social control theories are the number one theory identified by criminologists, even though they really enjoy little empirical support (social control theories are discussed in chapter 7). Biological theories ranked low in the survey of criminologists. Much has changed since the survey was conducted, but it is a safe bet that most criminologists are unaware of the importance of biological factors for understanding behavior. For example, recent evidence from an analysis of doctoral students studying criminology shows that they are being miseducated about the impact of biology on antisocial behavior (Wright et al, 2008).

This book contains many propositions and findings generated in the biological sciences. The reason is simple: "Biology's role in behavior is obvious because all behavior is controlled by the brain and the nervous system. Genes choreograph the development of the brain through transcription and translation of DNA into proteins ... genes affect the molecular structure of the brain at every level, including brain anatomy, neurotransmitter levels and receptors, and the processes that control the development of interconnections among neurons" (Bloom et al., 2000, p. 20). The effects of genes on human behavior are discussed in chapter 4, and the relationship between the brain and behavior is discussed in chapter 5. Given the state of the evidence, there is no legitimate excuse for ignoring such factors.

Other academic fields also tend to be ignored within criminology. For example, Simons, Simons, & Wallace (2004, p. xi) assert that "delinquency and criminology textbooks give scant attention to theoretical developments and research findings from family sociology and developmental psychology" even though the "theory and research has much to say about the validity of criminological frameworks and be used to elaborate and extend those theories." In this book, research generated by such fields will be examined in order to better understand criminal and antisocial behavior, particularly as it relates to normal human and moral development.

An Example: Integrated Systems

An example of an interdisciplinary perspective used to examine human behavior is the *integrated systems perspective*. This perspective is also probabilistic in nature, meaning it does not assert that humans have free will but it also explicitly rejects causality. Instead, it assumes that behavior is made more or less probable to occur given the circumstances.

The integrated systems perspective examines factors at various levels of analysis, including the cell level, the organ level, the organism level, the group level, the organization/community level, and the society level (see figure 3.1). The integrated systems perspective allows various factors which have been identified by numerous academic disciplines to be discussed and meaningfully integrated or synthesized into a coherent theoretical explanation of behavior without reinforcing disciplinary boundaries. Such a perspective assumes that "everything ... affects everything else, and ... these effects are continuously changing over time" (Barak, 1998, p. 188; also see Thornberry, 1987; Vila, 1994; Henry & Milovanovic, 1996).

Figure 3.1 Integrated Systems

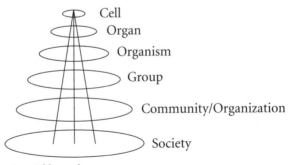

Source: Figure created by author.

The integrated systems perspective was developed by scholars such as White-head (1925), Lewin (1935), Murray (1938), and Miller (1978). Systems think-ing has been applied recently to environmental toxicology (Yu, 2001), biophysical processes (Saradhi, 2001), family function (Schwab, Gray-Ice, & Prentice, 2000), group psychotherapy (Durkin, 1996), marketing (Covington, 1997), business architecture (Gharajedaghi, 1999), business dynamics (Sterman, 2000), and living human systems (Capra, 1996; Cramer, 1993; Agazarian & Gantt, 2000; Laszlo, 1996). Only once that we are aware of has this idea been specifically ap-plied to criminological theory (Jeffery, 1990). Faust (1995) and several of his students have further developed this perspective (e.g., Kelley & Nute, 2000).

Lewin's model of human behavior was: $B = f(p,e)$; behavior was consid-ered a function of both the person and the environment. That behavior re-sults from factors unique to individuals and their unique environments appeals to our common sense, despite the continuing *nature versus nurture* debate within criminology.

The integrated systems perspective is based on the belief that every behav-ior is a "person-environment event" (Goldstein, 1994, p. 3). Called the *inter-actional model* by Goldstein, this model assumes that the sources for behavior come from the continuous interactions between people and their environ-mental conditions. An individual's behavior is influenced by factors in the en-vironment and simultaneously the person's behavior affects these same environmental conditions. The reciprocal influence of person factors on en-vironmental factors and environmental factors on behavior operates continu-ously (also see Endler & Magnusson, 1976, p. 960).

The integrated systems perspective does not use simple additive logic; it does not view human behavior as a product of the person plus the environment. Rather, the model uses interactive logic; it divorces itself from the notion of causal-ity and asserts that all occurrences in the physical environment simultaneously affect each other. Therefore, the critical concept in the systems perspective is *interaction* rather than causation. According to Jeffery (1990, p. 25), this forces the investigator to "think in terms of the mutual interdependence of variables rather than in terms of linear causation and influence."

As noted by Walsh & Beaver (2009, p. 9): "*Any* trait, characteristic, or behav-ior of *any* living thing is *always* the result of biological factors interacting with environmental factors." Thus, examining the separate influences of biological and environmental factors on behavior is illogical. Walsh & Beaver (2009, p. 33) pro-vide this example: "Genes and environments are separate entities as are hydrogen and oxygen, and can be analyzed as such, but when they have worked their magic and produced a phenotype [e.g., a human being] they are no more separable than hydrogen and oxygen are when talking about the water they produce."

The integrated systems model specified by Jeffery (1990) is based on the assumption that behavior results from the continuous, mutual influence of changing systems of organisms and the environment at many levels of analysis. These include the cell, organ, organism, group, organization/community, and society levels. Individual factors that may increase (risk factors) or decrease (protective factors) the likelihood of behavior can be organized around these levels of analysis.

Each of these levels of analysis represents a system, made up of smaller systems and making up larger systems (see Buckley, 1968; Klir, 1972; Kuhn, 1974, 1975; Boulding, 1978; Miller, 1978). Miller (1978, p. 25), in his book *Living Systems*, explained that the "universe contains a hierarchy of systems, each more advanced or 'higher' *level* made up of systems of lower levels ... *Cells* are composed of atoms, molecules, and multimolecular organelles; *organs* are composed of cells aggregated into *tissues; organisms*, of organs; *groups*, of organisms; *organizations*, of groups (and sometimes individual organisms); *societies*, of organizations, groups, and organisms; and *supranational systems*, of societies and organizations." Miller defined the levels this way:

- "A cell is a minute, unitary mass of intricately organized protoplasm. All living systems either are free-living cells or have cells as their least complex living components ... Free-living cells are ordinarily totipotential, while cells that are aggregated into the tissues of organs, organisms, or higher levels of systems are usually specialized for certain processes, partipotential, and therefore dependent upon other systems for some critical processes" (p. 203).
- "Organs ... are the subsystems of organisms [and are] all the components which carry out the processes of a given subsystem or an organism ... a part of the body having a special function." The organs of an organism are formed from tissues, which are collections of "adjacent cells of like origin and structure which carry out similar, specialized processes" (p. 315).
- Organisms, of course, are individual living things (p. 361).
- Groups are "a set of single organisms, commonly called *members*, which, over a period of time or multiple interrupted periods, relate to one another face-to-face, processing matter-energy and information" (p. 515).
- "Organizations are systems ... whose components and subsystems may be subsidiary organizations, groups, and (uncommonly) single persons ... Organizations are subsystems, components, or subcomponents of societies, sometimes of more than one society" (p. 595).
- "A society is a large, living, concrete system with organizations and lower levels of living systems as subsystems and components" (p. 747).

Miller did not explicitly define *community* because he conceptualized it at the same level as an organization. In this book, we treat community as synonymous with neighborhood, and we also treat community and organization factors within the same level of analysis because both are made up of smaller groups.

According to Miller, these levels "are derived from a long scientific tradition of empirical observation of the entire gamut of living systems. This extensive experience of the community of scientific observers has led to a consensus that there are certain fundamental forms of organization of living matter-energy" (p. 25). A human being is a system in itself. Human beings are systems made up of smaller subsystems (such as organs and cells) and are parts of larger supersystems (such as groups, communities, organizations, and societies). Logically, since levels above are made of levels below, a change in one level will produce changes in all levels.

Each of the systems in a living system constantly interacts with other systems above and below. Cells interact in and with a physical environment to form organs. For example, genes interact with an environment to produce the human brain. Organs interact in and with a physical environment to form organisms. For example, human beings result from the interaction of human organs. Organisms interact in a physical environment with other organisms to form groups. For example, peer groups develop when individual persons come together and form bonds. Factors at each level affect and are affected by factors at other levels of analysis.

The integrated systems approach assumes that behavior results from these interactions. Criminal behaviors can then be related to a constellation of risk factors which can best be organized around the six levels of analysis in the integrated systems perspective (cell, organ, organism, group, organization/community, and society). The *constellation of risk factors* refers to the group of things that are known to produce antisocial behavior and criminality in people. Separate theorists have posited that such risk factors contribute to crime, one at a time. It does not make much sense to discuss theories individually, especially if they make complementary predictions about criminal behavior or can be meaningfully integrated to gain a more complete understanding of the behavior that is to be explained.

Here is an example of interaction between variables. In a study of pollution and crime, Masters, Hone, and Doshi (1997) suggested that "environmental pollution interacts with poverty, poor diet, alcohol or [illicit] drug use, and social stress to put some individuals at risk for subclinical toxicity, leading to a loss of impulse control and increased violent crime." All these factors interact to increase one's risk of committing violent criminality. We discuss the effects of pollution in chapter 5 (organ level explanations), diet and drug use in chapter 6 (organism level explanations), and loss of impulse control (commonly called low self-control) in chapter 7 (group level explanations of crime). Masters et al. (1997) asserted that being exposed to toxins in the environment such as lead, copper, cadmium, or manganese can lead to brain damage, learning disorders, and attention deficits. Lead can damage glia cells in the brain, copper can lead to abnormal development of the hippocampus in the brain, and manganese can reduce levels of serotonin and dopamine, two naturally occurring brain chemicals (discussed in chapter 5). The effects of these chemicals on an individual are worsened by nutritional deficiencies, including a diet low in calcium. They are also magnified by drug use, including alcohol. The concept of interaction allows us to fully illustrate how different factors affect one another and ultimately result in criminality.

Members of academic disciplines should not study criminality in isolation from other academic disciplines. As explained by Miller (1978): "At each of the levels of living systems, the variables and indicators are derived from more than one academic discipline. The general systems approach is necessarily interdisciplinary, even antidisciplinary. No traditional academic discipline prepares a scientist to deal with all the relevant variables of a living system" (p. 1043). While all scientists, including criminologists, "have a right to select their own parameters and variables, to limit their thought as they deem best [it should be recognized that] limits exclude the rest of the world" (p. 1051). Figure 3.2 identifies some of the key disciplines that are involved in an integrated systems explanation of criminality (and there are undoubtedly others).

Figure 3.2 Disciplines Included in an Integrated Systems Explanation

Cell	Biology, Behavioral Genetics
Organ	Biology, Neurology, Psychology, Psychiatry
Organism	Biology, Psychology, Nutritional Studies, Pharmacology/Medicine, Education, Counseling
Group	Sociology, Criminology, Psychology, Psychiatry, Education, Counseling
Community/Organization	Sociology, Criminology, Criminal Justice, Geography, Anthropology, Psychology, Education, Victimology, Economics
Society	Sociology, Criminology, Criminal Justice, Education, Economics, Anthropology

Source: Figure created by author.

How Integrated Systems Is Different from Traditional Criminological Theory

The integrated systems perspective is, in essence, a way of looking at crime that is largely different from any other approach in criminology. Walsh (2002, p. viii) described traditional criminological theories as "not wrong [but] merely incomplete," asserting that "the causes of criminal behavior can be sought at many levels as long as each level is part of a coherent and mutually reinforcing whole." This belief lies at the heart of the integrated systems perspective. There is no one cause of antisocial behavior; there are many sources of behavior and each has effects on the others.

The integrated systems perspective is similar to what Bernard (2001, p. 337) called the *risk factor approach,* whereby "risk factors associated with an increased or decreased likelihood of crime" are identified. Since there "are many such risk factors," every academic discipline can potentially add something to our understanding of the etiology of human behavior, including antisocial behavior. With the goal of theorists to identify the risk factors that increase or decrease the probability of criminality, "the competition among theories does not result in the falsification of some theories and the verification of others. Instead, the competition among theories is empirical: it is about whether particular risk factors associated with particular theories explain a lot or a little of the variation in crime." This approach assumes that:

- *Some people are more likely than others to engage in crime, regardless of the situation they are in*; and
- *Some situations are more likely to have higher crime rates regardless of the characteristics of the people who are in them.* (Bernard, 2001, p. 341)

The first assumption is simply another way of asserting that there are factors at the cell, organ, and organism levels that make some individual people more likely to behave in ways that produce harms to others. The second assumption is another way of saying that there are factors at the group, organization/community, and society level that increase criminality in people. It is the interaction of these factors that produces human behavior, for all factors simultaneously affect each other to produce human behavior. Bernard (2001, p. 342) acknowledged this when he wrote that multiple factors "interact with each other to produce a greater effect than one would expect from simply adding the two separate effects together."

With this integrated systems approach, then, scholars aim to identify the factors at all levels of analysis, from cell to society, that come together, interact, and produce antisocial behavior and criminality. In other words, we attempt to identify the *constellation of risk factors* related to particular types of crime. As Bernard (2001, p. 343) put it: "The essential questions should be: which variables are related to crime, and in which ways?" Some factors may have greater effects on behavior, while others may be of less importance. More specifically, the effect of each factor on behavior will depend upon how much exposure a person has with the factor, how regularly one has exposure with the factor, how early in life one has exposure with the factor, and how strong the factor is. Logically, the more times a person interacts with a factor (*frequency*), the more likely it will influence his or her behavior. The more regular the exposure to the factor, the more likely it will influence his or her behavior (*regularity*). The earlier in life one has exposure to a factor, the more likely it will influence his or her behavior (*priority*). And, the stronger the influence of the factor on the person, the more likely it will influence his or her behavior (*intensity*). The modalities of exposure to risk factors (frequency, regularity, priority, and intensity) are derived from Sutherland's (1947) differential association theory, discussed in chapter 7.

Miller (1978), in essence, predicted that a systems explanation of behavior would "select, from among different and sometimes opposing viewpoints, fundamental ideas already worked out by others, and fit them into a mosaic, an organized picture of previously unrelated areas" (p. 1). That is the goal of this book, to build a theory of antisocial behavior using what we already know.

For example, what are the risk factors for violent behavior? Box 3.4 summarizes some important risk factors for violence in children and adolescents. Although these factors are not meant to represent an exhaustive list, scholars across many academic disciplines agree they are important for understanding violence.

Box 3.4 Risk Factors for Violent Behavior in Children and Adolescents

There are undoubtedly scores of factors associated with violent behaviors. According to the American Academy of Child & Adolescent Psychiatry (AACAP): "Numerous research studies have concluded that a complex interaction or combination of factors leads to an increased risk of violent behavior in children and adolescents." These factors include:

- Previous aggressive or violent behavior;
- Being the victim of physical abuse and/or sexual abuse;
- Exposure to violence in the home and/or community;
- Genetic (family heredity) factors;

- Exposure to violence in the media (TV, movies, etc.);
- Use of drugs (including alcohol);
- Presence of firearms in the home;
- A combination of stressful family socioeconomic factors (poverty, severe deprivation, marital breakup, single parenting, unemployment, loss of support from extended family); and
- Brain damage from head injury.

When children have been exposed to such risk factors, particularly several of these risk factors, there is a risk of antisocial and criminal behavior, especially when children are frequently angry, have temper tantrums or violent outbursts, are extremely irritable and impulsive, and are easily frustrated. Keep in mind that occasional violent behavior in children is normal and is not the same as sustained or repeated violent criminality in adults. Yet, as shown in chapter 1, early antisocial behavior can be a good predictor of adult criminality. In children, violent behavior can include "explosive temper tantrums, physical aggression, fighting, threats or attempts to hurt others (including homicidal thoughts), use of weapons, cruelty toward animals, fire setting, [and] intentional destruction of property and vandalism."

Source: American Academy of Child & Adolescent Psychiatry. (2002). Understanding violent behavior in children and adolescents. Retrieved from: *www.aacap.org/publications/factsfam/behavior.htm.*

Each of these risk factors from box 3.4 can be placed into the appropriate level of analysis of the integrated systems perspective to show that this perspective is already being used in the real world. Previous aggressive or violent behavior is at the organism level, since it is the individual person who behaves. Being victimized by physical and/or sexual abuse is at the group level of analysis, since victimization tends to occur in the context of close groups such as families (discussed in chapter 7). Exposure to violence can be placed at the group level (when it occurs in the home), at the community level (when it occurs in the neighborhood) and at the organization level (when it occurs in the media) (discussed in chapters 7 and 8). Genetic factors are at the cell level of analysis (discussed in chapter 4). Use of drugs is an organism level factor, since it is the individual who ingests the drugs (discussed in chapter 6). Presence of guns in the home is at the group level of analysis. Guns are not discussed in this book based on the ambiguous nature of the research. Stressful family conditions are at the group level of analysis, including marital breakup and single parenting (discussed in chapter 7). We discuss poverty, unemployment, and deprivation at the society level of analysis in chapter 9, since we view their causes at the largest level of analysis. Finally, brain damage from head injury is at the organ level of analysis (discussed in chapter 5). The AACAP has thus identified some very important risk factors for violent behavior, including some at the cell level, organ level, organism level, group level, community level, organization level, and society level of analysis.

Assumptions of Integrated Systems

There are several major assumptions underlying the integrated systems approach. They include:

- There is no such thing as free will.
- Humans can still choose how to behave or not.
- The ability to choose is influenced by factors beyond the control of individuals.
- Some of these factors are internal to the individual, such as his or her biological makeup (e.g., genetics, personality characteristics, structure and functioning of the brain).
- Some of the factors are external to the individual, such as opportunities for legitimate success (e.g., access to school and work).

Figure 3.3 illustrates the logic of how factors inside the individual and factors outside the individual can influence a person's behavior. The integrated systems perspective asserts that each individual is essentially the product of factors within the individual and in the individual's various environments (family, peer groups, schools, etc.). Humans, because of the strength of the frontal lobes of their brains, are able to choose between two paths—social or antisocial, criminal or not criminal—but these choices are greatly constrained by factors beyond their control. Choice cannot be used to explain human behaviors, because choice *is* human behavior, as explained in chapter 2. The relevant question is what makes a person choose one path over another.

These assumptions pit the integrated systems approach against the two leading historical perspectives discussed earlier—the classical school of criminology and the positive school of criminology. Figure 3.4 compares these two leading perspectives and concludes with the major weaknesses of each.

The *equality fallacy* refers to the belief that since all people have free will, they are equal in terms of their abilities and drawbacks. This is false. Integrated systems asserts that some people have more advantages and disadvantages than others, and these affect how people behave. Integrated systems suggests that in-

Figure 3.3 The Logic of Integrated Systems

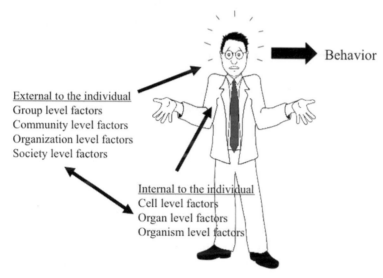

External to the individual
Group level factors
Community level factors
Organization level factors
Society level factors

Behavior

Internal to the individual
Cell level factors
Organ level factors
Organism level factors

Source: Figure created by author.

Figure 3.4 Integrated Systems versus Classicism and Positivism

	Classicism	Positivism	Integrated Systems
Mechanism	Probabilism	Choice	Causality
Behavior Is …	Freely chosen based on hedonism pain avoidance	Determined by factors beyond one's control	Made more likely when various factors come together
Main Problems	Equality fallacy (All people are born with equal abilities)	Dualistic fallacy (People are either criminal or non-criminal)	Integrated systems does not assume all people are born with the same abilities or that there are non-criminals
	Choice cannot be empirically verified or falsified	Impossible to demonstrate causality	Integrated systems does not assume that people freely choose to commit crime or that crime is caused

Source: Figure created by author.

dividuals experience variations in *protective factors* (things that decrease the likelihood of behaving in an antisocial way) and *risk factors* (things that increase the likelihood of behaving in an antisocial way). This means individuals are not "equal" in terms of the advantages and disadvantages they face and are not "equal" in terms of inborn abilities; neither are they simply "criminal or noncriminal" since everyone violates the law.

The *dualistic fallacy* refers to the belief that there are two classes of people, criminals and non criminals, and that what makes the two groups different is that the former have been exposed to *causes* of crime whereas the latter have not. This is false. Integrated systems asserts that all of us criminals; some start earlier than others and some commit more serious crimes than others, but there is no such thing as a non criminal, nor a cause of crime.

Finally, integrated systems suggests that behavior is neither freely chosen nor caused by factors beyond the control of the individual. Rather, antisocial behavior is made more or less likely based on exposure to protective and risk factors.

This book is about the risk factors that increase the likelihood of antisocial behavior. Obviously, protective factors are important in themselves. Yet, they are not widely discussed in this book for the following reasons: (1) protective factors are usually the opposite of risk factors (e.g., experiencing stress because of negative encounters is a risk factor for depression; not experiencing stress because of positive encounters is a protective factor against depression); (2) the depth of the research into risk factors is voluminous and cannot be reviewed adequately without giving each risk factor careful consideration. One of the goals of this book is to identify the most important risk factors for antisocial behavior.

This is not to say that protective factors are not important. Behavior results from interactions between risk factors and protective factors; the more exposure one has to risk factors the greater the likelihood of antisocial behavior, and the more exposure one has to protective factors the lower the likelihood of antisocial behavior. In the interest of space, many protective factors are not discussed in this book. One example is religion. A large body of research suggests that religion is a protective factor against antisocial behavior, although some of the research concludes the relationship is spurious or false (e.g., Baier, 2001; Benda, 1995, 1997; Benda & Corwin, 1997; Benda, Pope & Kelleher, 2006; Clear et al., 2000; Cochran, Wood, & Arneklev, 1994; Evans et al., 1995; Giordano et al, 2008; Petterson, 1991; Ross, 1996). We do not deny the findings that suggest religion can be a protective factor, we simply assert that such factors are less important for understanding the etiology of antisocial behavior and are more important for understanding why antisocial behavior is not manifested in people predisposed to it.

Advantages of Integrated Approaches

There are at least four advantages of integrated theories of behavior, like the integrated systems theory developed in this book. First, since human behavior (including antisocial and criminal behavior) cannot be explained by any single theory currently in existence, approaches that allow scholars to incorporate multiple factors into an explanatory model are superior. Barak (1998, p. 4) claimed, for example, that the fragmented nature of criminological theory "diminishes the field's ability to consolidate the various bodies of knowledge and to impact public policy." According to Bernard (2001, p. 340), no theory can ever really be falsified because every theory will enjoy some degree of support, however small: "Falsification requires an 'all or nothing' conclusion (the theory is either verified or falsified) based on competitive testing and statistical significance" while the risk factor approach and the integrated systems approach both allow "a graduated conclusion (a theory may explain a little or a lot of the variance) based on location of independent variation and direction of causation."

Second, integration allows scholars to break away from the traditional disciplinary nature of criminological theory, which is myopic and simplistic. Criminological theorists tend to have limited vision—referred to as disciplinary myopia—with respect to knowledge being generated outside of their own academic discipline and even outside of their own specializations. Myopia is a medical term that refers to near-sightedness. In layman's terms, it is used to refer to describe a lack of foresight or discernment, or a narrow view of something. *Disciplinary myopia* refers to not being able to see outside of your own academic discipline. This is troubling, because behavior is produced by many factors at all levels of analysis that have been discovered by numerous scholars in numerous academic disciplines. No academic discipline can claim complete jurisdiction over behavior.

In his presidential address to the American Society of Criminology, John Laub (2006) asserted that a paradigm for criminology should not be tied to any particular discipline. He said that "disciplinary positivism and disciplinary hegemony are serious threats to criminology. Moreover, if one starts with a theory or a discipline ... one can become blind to facts or, even worse, compelled to reject them" (p. 240). When discussing the "dangers of disciplinary blinders," Laub pointed out: "When criminology looks to single disciplines such as sociology, psychology, or economics, the field does not advance in large part because those disciplines seek to establish institutional hegemony by imposing their research agenda on the field of criminology" (p. 248).

Sociology is the dominant field within criminological theory, primarily because criminological theory grew out of sociology. Wright et al. (2009) write that "many sociological theories of crime require a fundamental belief about the nature of human action. Behavior, assume most social theories of crime, is the product of *external* socializing influences, such as parental efforts, peer groups, and neighborhoods.... virtually all social theories of human misbehavior seek to exclude and to vilify bodies of knowledge that challenge basic sociological tenets." Sociological explanations of criminality ignore other factors, including *internal* influences such as genetics and brain function.

The following example shows how ignoring biological factors in favor of focusing exclusively on sociological variables can be problematic. The fact that street crime peaks in the late teenage to early adulthood years is something that cannot be explained sufficiently by sociological criminology. Walsh (2009) explains that young people tend to commit more aggressive and violent acts during the ages of 15 to 25 years due to higher levels of the hormone testosterone and the excitatory neurotransmitters dopamine and glutamate, as well as lower levels of the calming neurotransmitters serotonin and GABA, in addition to other brain differences that lead them to be more impulsive and emotional, as well as more subjected to the influence of peers. Theoretical integration allows us to better explain such realities.

Third, with integration, learning about theories is made less arduous. Rather than learning about each theory individually, because of the fragmented nature of criminological theory (Barak, 1998), students can take a more holistic approach to understanding behavior that allows them to see the connections between factors from different levels of analysis. In essence, the theories themselves are left behind and the factors that are contained within the original theories are what is left.

Consider this example: *Mesomorphy* (muscular body build) has been used by biologists as a predictor of violent and aggressive behaviors such as street crimes (one such theory has been called *somatotype or body type theory*, see Bohm, 2001). Low social status has also been linked by sociologists to some forms of violent and aggressive behaviors (one such theory is called strain theory, discussed in chapter 9). Since mesomorphy and body build generally can be affected by one's social status, it makes more sense to discuss mesomorphy and social status together rather than separately as they interact to produce aggression and violence (Raine, 1993). Each of these factors is also affected by factors from other levels of analysis, such as neurotransmitter levels, diet and nutrition, and economic structure. Integrated approaches allow for specific interrelationships between such factors at different levels of analysis to be synthesized into a single theory, which is more accurate and complete than separate theories that contain only a few concepts.

A final advantage of integration is that there is no need to classify individual theories. There are many ways to classify the scores of theories of crime that have been posited over the years. The most traditional way, as noted earlier, is by academic discipline. Most criminological theory texts present the theories according to their academic discipline, so they have chapters on biological theories, psychological theories, sociological theories, and so on. As noted by Jeffery (1990), there are no real barriers or dividing lines in knowledge, so organizing theories of human behavior by academic discipline makes little sense. Others organize the theories chronologically, from the earliest developed to the latest. This can be useful, but many of the older theories are disciplinary in nature and thus have the same flaws. According to Williams and McShane (1994, p. vi): "Classification of the theories into the various sections is a rather arbitrary process. Different texts and instructors classify the theories differently, depending on their assumptions, chronological order, relationships with other theories, and so forth." In the foreword to Vold, Bernard, and Snipes's *Theoretical Criminology* (1998), Bernard wrote that progress on the book was hindered by the "increasingly complex and interrelated nature of criminology theory" which makes classifying the theories difficult.

With integration, scholars can cull out and integrate factors from individual theories, leaving behind what is not testable and is, therefore, useless for the advancement of knowledge about antisocial and criminal behavior, as well as that which has been falsified or disproven. The alternative is to continue doing what we criminologists and criminal justice scholars have done for decades—teaching the same material in the same manner, either by academic discipline or chronologically. According to Bernard (1998), this is responsible for the astounding lack of progress with regard to theories of crime, which makes it difficult to determine what material has been falsified and thus is in need of exclusion from criminological theory texts and courses. Given the tremendously diverse nature of the numerous theories, and that many of them make sense, are highly believable, and enjoy some degree of empirical support, falsifying distinct theories is nearly impossible. A refreshing alternative is theoretical integration.

Interesting debates regarding theoretical integration have occurred between notable criminologists. D. Wayne Osgood (1998) discussed the advantages of interdisciplinary integration in a paper where he advocated "building criminology by stealing from our friends"—that is, our theories of crime should be informed by research in other, especially related, disciplines. He suggested that we should "make a regular practice of academic thievery by keeping our eyes on sister disciplines to see what ideas would be useful to take for ourselves" (p. 1). Because we are "an inherently interdisciplinary field" there should be "no limit to the list of disciplinary perspectives from which one could study crime and the social institutions that address crime." The downfall of criminology will come about if our theories are not interdisciplinary: "If we do not bring the work by others into criminology, then we run the risk that our own work will become irrelevant and that policy makers and funding sources will not see criminology as having anything to say on the topic" (p. 41).

Barriers to Achieving Integration

As logical as an interdisciplinary perspective may seem, there are significant barriers that must be overcome to achieve an integrated theory of criminal behavior. As discussed by Tittle (1997), theoretical integration "is no panacea" (p. 2). The barriers discussed by Tittle include a lack of creativity and tradition, the former referring to the inability to create and/or understand integrated theories and the latter to the history of criminology. "Because we have a history and pattern of honoring scholars by preserving their works as inviolate entities, many people are reluctant to try integration for fear of offending somebody whose theory is being transformed. And, of course, they have a good basis for their concern since some of our leading theorists have been known to object to the 'desecration' presumably involved in integration" (p. 8). As explained by Tittle,

> the most difficult part of integration is that theorists must make decisions as to which concepts, variables, or processes will be conditional, and which ones will be part of externally-based input streams to specific concepts ... some decisions must be made about causal priority—which process will go first or which will be subsumed by another concept. Integration can never involve "whole hog" merger of pre-existing theories; the integrationist must be willing to disassemble theories, divorce them from their makers, and reconstruct through some new paradigm ... as long as disassembly and divorce fly in the face of cultural norms, we cannot freely use integration as a toll and we will suffer for it (p. 9).

Another barrier to integration is that each academic discipline uses its own terminology and techniques to study behavior. It is impossible for any one person to develop expertise in every academic discipline. Fishbein (2001) suggested that we make efforts to familiarize ourselves with the studies of other academic disciplines, so we can at least understand and even "borrow" their findings as they are relevant for explaining crime.

Finally, there is much resistance to integration. "There remains unfamiliarity with and resistance to interdisciplinary perspectives, and there has been a lack of communication among various branches of investigation" (Fishbein, 2001, p. 5). Some criminologists, for example, simply reject integration as useless and/or impossible. Part of this owes itself to *disciplinary myopia*, not being able to see outside of one's own discipline.

Scholars have argued that theories with different assumptions about human nature should not be integrated. Consider social learning theories and social control theories as an example (discussed in chapter 7). Social learning theories assume that humans are naturally born good and therefore need to learn to commit antisocial behavior and criminality—both the justifications that make criminality acceptable and the techniques needed to commit it. Alternatively, social control theories assume that humans are naturally born selfish and thus need to learn to be concerned with the consequences of their behaviors for others. Tittle (1997) successfully illustrated how differing assumptions do not necessarily mean that two theories cannot be integrated; it depends on if those assumptions actually conflict and if they are really fundamental to the theories rather than convenient for the theorists. We show in chapter 7 that the assumptions of social control and social learning theories do not make integration impossible. Stated simply, both sets of these theories assert that learning is highly involved in criminality. Social control theories assume that people must learn to abide by the law and to conform to society's rules and norms whereas social learning theories assume that people must learn to commit crime and justify it in given contexts.

Interestingly, virtually all theories of crime make the same basic prediction about criminal behavior: People with more reasons to commit antisocial behavior and crime than reasons not to commit antisocial behavior and crime are more likely to commit antisocial behavior and crime. The difference between theories, then, tends to be the way in which each states this same prediction. Each uses different concepts unique to the academic discipline from which it arose.

The invention of each proposition is akin to reinventing the wheel again and again. Scholars in one academic discipline suggest something "new" even though the ideas have already been promoted by scholars in other disciplines. As explained earlier, the reasons for committing crime are called *risk factors* and the reasons for not committing crime are called *protective factors*. Whether one commits crime, then, is a result of exposure to risk factors and protective factors. Exposure to risk factors increases the likelihood of committing crime; exposure to protective factors decreases the likelihood of committing crime.

Summary

In this chapter, you learned about a perspective and the various kinds of perspectives in criminological theory. A perspective is a way of looking at the world, it is how you see things. Perspectives are developed by life experiences including one's education and it has effects on how scholars define problems, the methods they use to study it, how they interpret the evidence, and the policies that result from their studies.

The most well-known perspectives including the Classical School of Criminology, which posited that crime resulted from choices of people pursuing pleasure over pain, and the Positive School of Criminology, which suggested that factors beyond the control of people caused their behavior. The Positive School contains both hard deterministic and soft deterministic arguments. Hard determinists posit causal relationships between various factors and behavior, suggesting no room for choice. Soft determinists assert that people choose to behave but that their choices are affected by factors beyond their control. This is consistent with the notion of probabilism, which suggests that behavior is more or less likely in the presence of certain conditions.

Perspectives within criminological theory include disciplinary, multidisciplinary, and interdisciplinary perspectives. Disciplinary perspectives examine criminal behavior from only one academic discipline, typically sociology. Multidisciplinary perspectives examine criminal behavior from more than one academic discipline by selecting combing them. Interdisciplinary perspectives examine criminal behavior from all academic disciplines and therefore are logically more complete and likely to discover more of the truth with regard to sources of behavior. The academic discipline that is most ignored in criminology is biology, although recent efforts have successfully integrated biological factors into multidisciplinary theoretical perspectives.

The integrated systems perspective is organized around six different living systems, the cell, organ, organism, group, community/organization, and society. Each lower level is part of the next level above it, and each level above is made up of the levels below it. Thus, a change at one level leads to a change at all levels. The integrated systems perspective suggests that factors at each level of analysis interact to produce behavior. Antisocial and criminal behavior is produced by a constellation or group of risk factors from various levels of analysis. Antisocial and criminal behavior is more likely to occur when one is exposed to risk factors, especially when exposure to risk factors occurs frequently, regularly, early in life, and when the risk factors are intense.

The integrated systems perspective is superior to the Classical School because it is not plagued by the equality fallacy—the false belief that all people are equal in terms of their advantages and disadvantages. Further, it does not posit that people have free will, something that is not testable. It is superior to the Positive School because it is not plagued by the dualistic fallacy—the false belief that there are only two classes of people, criminals and noncriminals. Further, it does not posit that behavior is caused by factors beyond our control, something that cannot be empirically demonstrated.

There are several advantages and disadvantages associated with integrated theoretical approaches such as the integrated systems approach. The main advantage is that it helps s overcome disciplinary myopia, the inability to see and understand research being done outside our academic discipline.

Discussion Questions

1. What is a perspective?
2. What does one's perspective affect?
3. How is a biologist's perspective different from a sociologist's perspective?
4. Identify and define three main types of perspectives in criminology.
5. Why do scholars develop limited perspectives from their own academic disciplines?
6. What is the integrated systems perspective? Identify and define the main levels of analysis in this perspective.
7. What produces human behavior according to the integrated systems perspective?
8. List the key risk factors for violent behavior according to the AACAP.
9. Discuss the assumptions of the integrated systems perspective.
10. Contrast the integrated systems perspective with classicism and positivism.
11. What are the main advantages to integrated theories of crime?
12. What are some of the barriers to achieving theoretical integration?

4

Cellular Level Explanations of Crime

- Introduction
- Behavior in the context of cells
- Genetics
- Other cellular level factors
- Summary

Introduction

When you were conceived, your parents passed along a legacy to you; your father passed along half of his genetic material and your mother passed along half of hers. As a result, you are, genetically speaking, half your father's child and half your mother's child. Even if you were raised by only one of your parents, or adopted and raised by others, chances are you will end up behaving like both of your biological parents, at least to some degree. This observation has led some to believe that genetic factors may be instrumental in shaping behaviors, personality traits, and other human characteristics.

Behavior in the Context of Cells

Genes are located on cells, which are the smallest level of analysis in an integrated systems analysis of antisocial behavior and criminality. Cells are the basic units of which all living things are composed. Some single cells are complete organisms (e.g., bacteria) and actually behave for their own survival. Other cells coordinate specialized functions and become the building blocks of multicellular organisms (e.g., humans). Certain cells work together to create organs, such as the brain, which is created from hundreds of billions of neurons (i.e., brain cells). (In chapter 5 you will be exposed to research revealing how the brain is involved in all types of human behaviors, including criminality.) Since organs are created by cells, factors at the cellular level of analysis produce effects at the organ level of analysis. For instance, genetic factors affect the structure and the function of the brain as Bloom cogently captures in the following quote: "the structures in the brain and nervous system derive from particular gene products and all voluntary and involuntary behaviors originate or are mediated in these structures" (Bloom et al., 2000, p. 42). Because the brain can be considered *the* organ of behavior, its structure and its ability to function properly are important for understanding how any organism (e.g., humans) behaves. Using this logic, then, cell level factors are important for understanding human behavior because in many ways antisocial behavior begins at this level of analysis.

Genetics

The main area of research at the cellular level concerns the effects of genetic factors on personality traits, behaviors, and other measurable features. In the most basic terms, genes are the biochemical parts of cells that determine what cells will become. It is your genes that determine whether you become a mouse, a cat, a dog, or a human.

The human body is made up of approximately 100 trillion cells (although no one has ever actually counted them all!). Every cell except red blood cells contains the entire *human genome*, essentially a blueprint containing all the necessary information to build a person. In the center or nucleus of these cells is the human genome, which "consists of tightly coiled threads of deoxyribonucleic acid (DNA) and associated protein molecules, organized into structures called chromosomes" (U.S. Department of Energy, 2001, p. 1). It is believed that there are 6 feet of DNA strands packed into each human cell. Genes occupy a fixed position on the 46 human chromosomes within the nucleus of cells. Each chromosome contains thousands of genes, which are the units of heredity.

Genes achieve their effects by directing the synthesis of proteins, which are complex molecules made of amino acids. "Each DNA molecule contains many genes—the basic physical and functional units of heredity. A gene is a specific sequence of nucleotide bases whose sequences carry the information required for constructing proteins, which provide the structural components of cells and tissues as well as enzymes for essential biochemical reactions" (U.S. Department of Energy, 2001, p. 2). DNA is made up of two chains of nucleotides

Figure 4.1 Human DNA and Genes

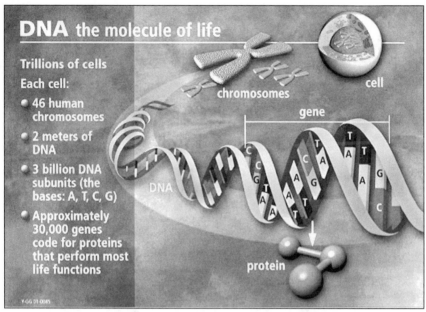

Source: U.S. Department of Energy Human Genome Project (2001). Retrieved from *http:// www.ornl.gov/hgmis*

that wind around each other like a twisted ladder. The steps of the ladder are made up of bonded pairs of nitrogenous bases (called *base pairs*)—adenine (A) and thymine (T) which bond together, and cytosine (C) and guanine (G) which also bond together. The order of these chemicals determines what you are (see figure 4.1).

In the human genome, there are approximately 25,000 genes (although it was originally believed that there were as many as 100,000 genes) and 3 billion base pairs. Sequencing the order of these base pairs was the goal of the *Human Genome Project,* which "began officially in 1990 as a $3-billion, 15-year program to find ... human genes and determine the sequence of the 3 billion DNA building blocks that underlie all human biology and its diversity" (U.S. Department of Energy, 2001, p. 3). Ideally, the functions of all human genes will be discovered, including the role that they play in human diseases and behaviors. Figure 4.2 illustrates how genes direct cells to become a human being.

The primary responsibility of a gene is to code for the production of proteins." These proteins determine, among other things, how the organism looks, how well the body metabolizes food or fights infections, and *sometimes even*

Figure 4.2 From Genes to Human

Source: U.S. Department of Energy Human Genome Project (2001). Retrieved from *http://www.ornl.gov/hgmis*

how it behaves" (Human Genome Management Information System, 2001, emphasis added). While it is widely accepted that our genes determine *what* we are, a more controversial issue is whether genes determine *who* we are. That is, do they determine our intelligence levels, personalities, and behaviors? The short answer is *no*, genes do not *determine* medical and behavioral conditions. Rather, genes increase or decrease the likelihood that certain phenotypes will surface and, just as importantly, genetic effects can be moderated by certain environments. For example, you may have genes that increase the odds that you will develop some type of cancer, but you may never actually develop cancer, especially if you limit your exposure to the environmental conditions that are known to increase your risk of cancer (e.g., UV rays, cigarette smoke, bad diet, pollution, etc.). Likewise, you may also have inherited genes from your parents that make it more likely that you will be tall, but you may not actually grow to be very tall if you do not consume the essential nutrients needed to grow.

Genetic factors thus predispose people to a whole range of medical conditions and behavioral problems, where *probabilistic* rather than *deterministic*— genes can increase the probability or likelihood that a person will behave in a way that will get him or her into trouble with the law. As Walsh (2002, p. 18) explained: "There are no genes 'for' crime, but there are genes that lead to particular traits (e.g., low levels of empathy, IQ, self-control, fear, conscientiousness, and high levels of sensation-seeking, egoism, negative emotionality, and aggression) that increase the probability of criminal behavior, more so in some environments than in others." According to Fishbein (2001, pp. 27–29), other conditions are partially heritable, including drug abuse, impulsivity, antisocial personality disorders, extroversion, and psychiatric disorders related to anxiety and misconduct.

Fishbein, a leading biosocial criminologist, added to this view when she accurately noted that "genetic or acquired biological traits are thought to contribute to biochemical and physiological conditions which may predispose individuals to a combination of particular behavioral and psychological outcomes that may occur, or be suppressed, in various environmental settings" (2001, p. 3). This is another way of saying that we are who we are because the genes we inherit from our parents play a large role in deciding not only what we become, but also who we become.

According to the U.S. Department of Energy (2001, p. 3): "Researchers in the field of behavioral genetics have asserted claims for a genetic basis of numerous physical behaviors, including homosexuality, aggression, impulsivity, and nurturing." Notice that some of these behaviors have a good deal to do with criminality. First, engaging in homosexual acts is actually a crime in many states, although such laws are no longer enforced after the US Supreme Court struck down Texas' sodomy law in the case of *Lawrence v. Texas* (2003). Second, many criminal acts involve aggression against others. Third, impulsivity has historically been related to official measures of delinquency and criminality (discussed in chapter 6), as has nurturing style of parents (discussed in chapter 7). This knowledge base points to the very real possibility that genetic factors may be intertwined with the development of antisocial behavior and thus may have tremendous significance for criminological theory.

This is not the same as saying that our genes cause us to become criminal or not. Such a deterministic viewpoint is completely unfounded as are a series of other criticisms leveled against genetic explanations of antisocial behaviors. Box 4.1 reports on some of the major misconceptions of genetics-related research. As will become strikingly obvious when reading this box is that genes are not the sole *cause* of criminality; studies examining the effects of genes on behavior suggest that environmental factors also influence behavior. Genes only express themselves through behaviors *if* environmental conditions allow it. Many environmental factors can thus be identified as important for triggering genes to be expressed.

Box 4.1 Misconceptions about Genetics

1. *A gene is directly responsible for criminal behavior.*

    There is no crime gene and all genetic researchers realize that genes do not directly *cause* any behavior, but rather create higher or lower levels of proteins, enzymes, and other chemicals in the body that increase or decrease the likelihood of antisocial behavior. For example, genes may affect the probability that a person acts impulsively or aggressively. This does not mean that a person who possesses the genetic predispositions for impulsivity or aggression will commit crimes. A genetic predisposition to aggressiveness may result in a person becoming a successful businessperson or perhaps a top athlete; how genes are expressed depends on environmental conditions such as opportunities for legitimate success. Whether or not the person becomes a career criminal—one who devotes his or her life to criminality—depends not only on his or her genetic makeup, but also on numerous environmental factors.

2. *Since genes influence behavior, environmental factors do not matter.*

    As noted earlier, both biological factors (such as genetics) and environmental factors (such as social class, opportunities for crime, and so on) are important for explaining all human behavior. No geneticists claim that *only* genes matter; in fact, their research has revealed that genetic factors predispose individuals to behave in certain ways, while environmental factors trigger genes (that is, make them more likely to be expressed). The debate in criminology, aimed at determining whether crime is caused by biological *or* environmental factors is a spurious debate: human behavior is always a function of both nature *and* nurture.

3. *Since criminal behavior is influenced by genetics, it is impossible to change a criminal.*

    Genetics research does not suggest that crime is a person's destiny. Although genetic makeup is determined at the moment of conception, a person does not and cannot behave until after birth. Human behavior, including antisocial behavior and criminality, requires an environment. If a person is identified as *predisposed* to behave in a given way, that person's environment can be altered (even before birth) so that the genes are less likely to be expressed. Changing the environment can thus change the effects that certain genes have on behaviors.

4. *Genetics research is evil because it will be used to ha[...]* *most often being controlled by the criminal justice system.* The United States has a long and sordid history with the misu[...] logical explanations of behavior. Claims of genetic inferiority have[...] used in this country to forcibly sterilize those who were considered to [...] feebleminded or low in intelligence. Supreme Court Justice Oliver Wen- dell Holmes justified forced sterilization of the feebleminded in the case *Buck v. Bell* (1927) by writing that "three generations of imbeciles are enough." Holmes was referring to Carrie Buck, her mother Emma Buck, and Carrie's infant child, all of whom were misdiagnosed as "feeble- minded" by scientists attempting to prove the merits of sterilization by illustrating what can happen when defective genes were allowed to be passed over three generations of one family. There is no doubt that ge- netics research could be used in harmful ways; however, this should not be used as a reason to ignore genetic effects. Rather, knowledge is power and with a greater understanding of the influence of genetics on human behavior, the better equipped we will be to rehabilitate criminals.

5. *Changes in crime rates cannot be accounted for by genetic factors.* A certain amount of criminality may be expected at any time given the presence of individuals with genetic conditions that predispose them to behave in ways that will get them recognized by the "powers that be" (i.e., the criminal justice system). Changes in crime rates can probably best be explained by changes in environmental conditions that act as triggers for underlying genetic conditions.

Source: Adapted from Raine, A. (1993). *The psychopathology of crime: Crimi- nal behavior as a clinical disorder.* San Diego, CA: Academic Press.

Walsh (2002, pp. 24–25) also discussed misconceptions of genes and be- havior, where he pointed out that at the one extreme is the notion that genes are destiny and at the other extreme is the notion that genes are irrelevant. As the following quote makes clear, he concluded that both are wrong: "Genes do not code for any kind of behavior, feeling, or emotion ... they *facilitate* our behavior and our feelings" by creating hormones, neurotransmitters, and pro- teins (naturally occurring substances in the body and brain discussed in chap- ter 5) which "produce tendencies or dispositions to respond to the environment in one way rather than in another." The importance of the environment is probably best stated later by Walsh: "Seeds from a prize-winning rose are very likely to realize their maximum genetic potential in a Virginia garden but are unlikely to thrive at all if planted in the Nevada desert" (p. 29).

vironment, and Human Behavior: "Inter-
sible phenotypic variation among organ-
ernal forces, the environment, mold the
ally proposed variations." A *phenotype* is
acteristics of an organism including the or-
s the total genetic inheritance of an organ-
behaviors can change throughout life not
nvironment, but also because of genetic ef-
urse. The phenomenon of *neoteny*, the pro-
wth and development, accounts for why
environmental iac... ence people differently at different stages of
their lives. Genetic effects also change over the life course; some genes play a
role in the early development of the brain and then turn themselves off, whereas
others act later.

As should have been made clear by now, genes and the environment both
contribute to human behavior. Some human traits are largely genetic and are
influenced little by environmental factors (e.g., eye color), while all complex
behaviors are *polygenic*, meaning that they are influenced by many genes. To
the degree that aggression, violence, and antisocial behaviors are influenced
by genetic factors, it is certain that hundreds or more genes are implicated.

Main Propositions of Genetic Studies

Given the preceding discussion, a main proposition at the cell level of
analysis is that genetic makeup predisposes an individual to behave in ways
that make criminal behavior more or less likely to occur. This proposition has
generally been tested using three methodologies: family studies, twin studies, and adoption studies. Each of these studies is a form of genetic epidemiology or "the study of the clustering of specific traits in families and
populations" (Bloom et al., 2000, p. 23). More recently, molecular genetic
studies have attempted to locate the specific genes involved in behavioral
conditions.

Family studies are conducted by examining how people behave within families. Early studies traced the family trees of individuals and compared the degree of criminality among family members. Family studies are used to test the
following proposition: *Criminal behavior will run in families.* Box 4.2 discusses
some early family studies and outlines why they are not very useful in isolat-
ing the role that genes play in human behaviors.

Box 4.2 Family studies of Criminality

According to criminologists and criminal justice scholars, there is little question that crime tends to run in families. The question is, why? Think of all the things that families share—not only genes, but also similar environments. Logically, if families share genes and are exposed to the same environmental conditions, we should expect family members to be similar in terms of their behaviors.

Early studies examining the clustering of crime in families appeared to reveal that mental characteristics such as "feeblemindedness" were entirely heritable. Consider, for example, Richard Dugdale, who was asked in 1874 by the Prison Association in New York to inspect county jails. Dugdale became intrigued by the high incidence of kinship among inmates. He thus used his own funds to conduct an extended investigation of one large kin group living in and around Ulster County, New York, whom he dubbed "the Jukes." Dugdale eventually uncovered a family of some 709 tawdry individuals who were descendants of a Dutch immigrant named Max.

In 1875, Dugdale reported his findings to the Prison Association and eventually wrote *"The Jukes": A Study in Crime, Pauperism, Disease, and Heredity*. Dugdale located six members of the "Jukes" family in a county jail and traced the genealogy of the family back over 200 years. In so doing, he discovered that a large number of the family members were poor, ill, involved in prostitution, and had illegitimate children.

Vold, Bernard, and Snipes (1998, p. 53) wrote that Dugdale's study "had a striking impact on the thinking at the time, despite the fact that it was based on unreliable, incomplete, and obscure information and was filled with value judgments and unsupported conclusions." Indeed, many interpret the Jukes study as an effort to convince society that poverty and crime are inevitable results of bad stock. In fact, Dugdale was a public health reformer who wrote in support of treatment for physiological disorders to cure social ills rather than removal or death for imbeciles. Nevertheless, many used Dugdale's findings to support a *eugenics* movement, aimed at improving society through restrictions on immigration and forced sterilization (Robinson, 2003).

"Kallikak" is a fictitious name given to another family studied by American psychologist Henry Goddard. Goddard collected data for a longitudinal study that contrasted the descendants of one "upstanding man" and his upstanding Quaker wife with the descendants of the same man and an illicit "tavern wench." Kallikak is a pseudonym that comes from two Greek words, *kallos* (good) and *kakos* (bad). Goddard assigned this name to the family to help illustrate the effects of moronic breeding (*moron* was a term used to describe people with a mental age between 8 and 12 years).

Previous to his study of the Kallikaks, Goddard and his assistants had worked with the staff at Ellis Island in identifying morons attempting to immigrate to the United States. Their work at Ellis Island had supposedly given them sufficient expertise to classify morons by sight!

Goddard located the descendants of the upstanding man and the "tavern wench" (*kakos*) living in poverty and compared these folks to the "legitimate" descendants of the married couple (*kallos*). Goddard described one Kallikak woman, Deborah, this way: "This is a typical illustration of the mentality of a high-grade feeble-minded person, the moron, the delinquent, the kind of girl or woman that fills our reformatories. They are wayward, they get into all sorts of trouble and difficulties, sexually and otherwise, and yet we have been accustomed to account for their defects on the basis of viciousness, environment, or ignorance."

As Goddard expected, the results of the study confirmed that the kakos line were much more likely to be troubled or in trouble as compared to the kallos line. As noted by Vold et al. (1998, p. 57): "Of 480 descendants of this union [with the barmaid] ... 143 were feebleminded, 36 illegitimate, 33 sexually immoral, 24 confirmed alcoholics, 3 epileptics, 3 criminals, and 8 keepers of houses of prostitution ... [versus] 496 'normal' descendants [with his wife] who 'married into the best families of their state.'" Goddard published the results of his study in *The Kallikak Family* (1912). Allegations have even been advanced suggesting that Goddard doctored photos of the kakos line to give the individuals a more depraved and sinister appearance, for example by painting dark circles under the eyes of small children.

The Kallikak study was a landmark event for the eugenics movement, which led to compulsory sterilization of 60,000 "feebleminded" people in 33 states. The U.S. Supreme Court upheld the practice of mandatory sterilization for the feebleminded. The first state to enact the sterilization law was Indiana in 1907. This was when America was experiencing an influx of immigrants from Europe into its large cities, leading to the Immigration Restriction Act in the 1920s. Forced sterilizations were legal in California until the 1970s!

Many criminological theories were also developed during this time, including the theory of social disorganization (discussed in chapter 8), which described and explained juvenile delinquency and crime in the city of Chicago in the early 1900s. Since American criminology largely grew out of the Chicago School of Criminology, this is one reason why criminological theories tend to be class biased and focused almost exclusively on explaining street crime. This point is addressed more fully in chapter 9.

While family studies such as these can demonstrate that crime runs in families, they do not prove that this is attributable to genetics. Since family members also share similar environments, criminologists cannot rule out the possibility that crime runs in families because of shared environmental conditions—for example, parents may teach their children to commit crime; thus crime might be learned (social learning theories are discussed in chapter 7). Remember that geneticists do not claim that human behaviors are inherited from parents, but instead claim that predispositions to behave are heritable. These predispositions only become behaviors in the presence of certain environmental conditions.

Sources: Dugdale, R. (1877). *The Jukes: A study in crime, pauperism and heredity.* Putnam, NY: Arno; *Eugenics, or you can't keep a good idiot down.* Retrieved 2002 from *http://www.historyhouse.com*; Goddard, H. (1973). *The Kallikak family: A study in the heredity of feeble-mindedness.* New York: MacMillan; Smith, J.D. (1985). *Minds made feeble: The myth and legacy of the Kallikaks.* Rockville, MD: Aspen Publication; Vold, G., Bernard, T., & Snipes, J. (1998). *Theoretical criminology* (4th ed.). New York: Oxford University Press.

The most widely used methodology to examine genetic effects on phenotypes is the twin research design. Twin studies compare the degree of criminality between monozygotic (identical) twins and dizygotic (fraternal) twins. All humans share between 90 and 99% of their DNA. The 1 to 10% of variation in genes is what accounts for phenotypic differences (differences in observable characteristics such as behavior). Monozygotic (MZ) twins share 100% of their genetic makeup, while dizygotic (DZ) twins share about half of their dissenting DNA (i.e., the DNA that differs from person to person). Since MZ twins are more genetically similar than DZ twins, it is possible to explore the relative effects of genes and the environment on a phenotype. More specifically, if genes play a role in behavior, we would expect that MZ twins would be more behaviorally alike than DZ twins. Scholars compare the concordance rates between DZ and MZ twins, where concordance occurs when both twins have committed criminal acts. Twin studies test the following proposition: *If genes are influential on criminal behavior, then MZ twins will have higher concordance rates than DZ twins.*

Adoption studies can also be used to examine the genetic origins of human behaviors. In adoption studies, adopted children are compared to their biological parents and to their adopted parents on some form of antisocial behavior. If the biological parents were antisocial, then the child would be genetically predisposed to engage in crime. If the adopted parents were antisocial, then the child would be environmentally predisposed to engage in crime. It logically follows that genetic influences are detected in twin studies if the child resembles their biological parents on antisocial behaviors. Adoption studies test the following proposition: *If genetic factors influence antisocial behaviors, then a*

Key Concepts of Genetic Studies

Recall from chapter 2 that concepts are the key words that are found in propositions. Propositions typically state relationships between concepts. From the propositions stated in the preceding section, the following concepts can be isolated and defined:

- Criminal behavior
- Families
- MZ twins
- DZ twins
- Concordance rates
- Adopted children
- Criminal parents
- Noncriminal parents

Definitions of Concepts of Genetic Studies

Recall from chapter 2 that when scholars test propositions of theories, the key concepts of the propositions must be defined so that they can be understood by others and tested. Concepts are defined in two ways, nominally and operationally. Nominal definitions are dictionary definitions of the concepts. They tell us what the concepts mean. Operational definitions are more technical and specific. They tell us how the concepts will be measured in a study. Box 4.3 defines the key concepts of genetic studies. Scholars have used these definitions to test the propositions laid out earlier. The findings of these tests are discussed later in this chapter.

Box 4.3 Key Concepts of Genetic Studies

- *Criminal behavior. Nominal*—committing any act that violates the criminal law. *Operational*—the number of convictions in court for a violation of the criminal law.
- *Family. Nominal*—a group of people sharing a common bloodline who live in close conjunction to one another. *Operational*—a group of people sharing the same last name, where genealogy is verified by blood tests or self-reported claims of relations.

- *MZ twins. Nominal*—identical twins who originate from one egg and one sperm during conception. *Operational*—two siblings who share 100% of genetic makeup, as determined from blood samples, questionnaires, and/or physical resemblance.
- *DZ twins. Nominal*—fraternal twins who originate from two eggs and two sperm during conception. *Operational*—two siblings who share approximately 50% of their dissenting DNA, as determined from blood samples, questionnaires, and/or physical resemblance.
- *Concordance rates. Nominal*—the degree to which two siblings are behaviorally similar. *Operational*—the likelihood that if one sibling is criminal, the other sibling will be criminal, as expressed in a percentage.
- *Adopted children. Nominal*—children who were put up for adoption by their biological parents and raised by adoptive parents. *Operational*—children who were put up for adoption by their biological parents and raised by adoptive parents, as measured by adoption records and/or questionnaires.
- *Criminal parents. Nominal*—biological parents who have violated the criminal law. *Operational*—biological parents who have been convicted in court for violating the criminal law.
- *Noncriminal parents. Nominal*—biological parents who have not violated the criminal law. *Operational*—biological parents who have not been convicted in court for violating the criminal law.

Evaluation of Genetic Studies

Recall from chapter 2 that a theory can be evaluated with numerous criteria. We argued that the most important evaluative criteria for any theory are empirical validity and scope. In the following sections we discuss the empirical validity and scope of genetic studies, and then assess the logical adequacy of the propositions and the clarity of the key concepts.

Empirical Results from Twin and Adoption Studies

A wealth of empirical based research has been conducted that analyze samples of twin pairs to estimate the influence that genes and the environment have on a range of antisocial outcomes. Some of these studies have compared the concordance rates of criminality for MZ twins and DZ twins. The results of these studies have provided compelling evidence indicating that criminality is influenced by genetic factors. To illustrate, Raine (1993, p. 55) reviewed 13 studies of twins reared together and found that "all 13 show greater concordance rates for criminality in MZ as opposed to DZ twins." After acknowledging the limitations of these studies, Raine averaged the concordance rates across all studies and found that overall the concordance rates were 51.5% for MZ twins compared with 20.6% for DZ twins. Theoretically, if any trait was determined entirely by a gene or genes, there would be a 100% concordance rate for identical twins. Of course, behaviors are not determined entirely by genetics, so we expect to find lower concordance rates than 100%. Raine concluded from these studies that "it is difficult to escape from the conclusion that they indicate some degree of genetic predisposition for crime" (p. 57).

Twin-based studies also examine whether other types of antisocial behaviors—besides criminal arrests—are also influenced by genetic factors. In these types of studies, antisocial behavior is often measured through standardized scales designed to tap individual variation in violent, aggressive and delinquent acts that are either not criminal or that have not been detected by the criminal justice system. The results of these studies have been quite compelling in showing that antisocial behaviors are strongly influenced by genetic factors. For instance, four meta-analyses have been published that examine the relative effects on genetic and environmental factors on various forms of antisocial behaviors (Ferguson, in press; Mason & Frick, 1994; Miles & Carey, 1997; Rhee & Waldman, 2002). The results garnered from these meta-analyses have been strikingly consistent in showing that genetic factors explain about 50% percent of the variance in antisocial behaviors, while the environment explains the other 50%. Large literature reviews have also pointed to the same conclusion—mainly, that antisocial phenotypes are strongly influenced by genetic factors (Moffitt, 2005). Importantly, heritability estimates are probably lower for behavior than for personality traits because parents are more able to change their children's behaviors than to change their personality traits.

Although the evidence presented above appears to point to the inescapable conclusion that genes are involved in the etiology of antisocial behaviors, there are a number of limitations with studies of twins raised together. Perhaps the most important of these limitations is that MZ twins may be reared in environments that are more similar than the environments of DZ twins. If this is the case, then twin studies would artificially inflate genetic influences while simultaneously underestimating environmental effects. A different research design is needed to determine whether this shortcoming is biasing the results of twin-based studies.

Studies of MZ twins who have been reared in separate environments overcome the main limitation of traditional twin studies—that is, that environments account for higher concordance rates in MZ twins than in DZ twins. Of the studies that have been conducted with identical twins reared apart and the individual case studies that have been conducted on MZ twins reared apart, each shows that concordance rates are higher in MZ twins than DZ twins. It is possible that twins separated at birth are raised in similar environments but certainly they are not exposed to identical environmental conditions.

In addition to twin studies, adoption studies can also be employed as a way of estimating genetic and environmental effects on antisocial behaviors. Adoption studies overcome some of the problems with twin studies (e.g., MZ twins having more similar environments than DZ twins). Perhaps the most widely known adoption study, at least in relation to criminal involvement, was conducted by Mednick and his colleagues (1984). In this study, criminal behavior was examined in a sample of 14,427 adoptees, their adoptive parents, and their biological parents. The analysis revealed that adoptees whose biological parents (i.e., genetic risk) and adoptive parents (i.e., environmental risk) had been convicted of a property crime were most likely to be involved in crime.

In another adoption study, Cadoret et al. (1995) examined the genetic and environmental influences on aggression and conduct disorders. To do so, they analyzed a sample of adoptees whose biological parents had a history of alcoholism or antisocial personality disorder (i.e., genetic risk). These adoptees were compared to a control group of adoptees whose biological parents did not have a history of antisocial behaviors (i.e., no genetic risk). Environmental risk was measured by examining the adoptive home environment, where families that had marital problems, legal problems, and other signs of antisocial behavior were considered high-risk families. The results of their statistical analyses indicated that adoptees who were genetically at-risk for antisocial behaviors (i.e., their parents were antisocial) and who were reared in a risky environment were the most apt to display aggression and conduct disorders. These findings underscore the importance of both genetics and the environment in the development of antisocial behaviors.

More evidence linking genes to criminal behavior was uncovered in Raine's (1993) review of 15 adoption studies in which he drew four main conclusions. First, 14 of the 15 studies reported at least some heritability for criminality. Second, these studies were conducted by independent research groups. Third, the studies were conducted in three different countries. Fourth, the studies that examined violent and property crimes separately found relationships for property crimes but not violent crimes. Adoption studies usually "show that being raised in an environment more advantageous than which could be provided by biological parents or adoptees can have beneficial effects on personality and cognitive traits" (Walsh, 2002, p. 37). This better specifies the meaning of the findings that adoptive children tend to be more like their biological parents in personality and cognitive measures.

The twin and adoption studies reviewed above provide strong empirical support for perspectives linking genes to criminal outcomes. However, there are also mounds of research showing that other types of antisocial behaviors—beyond crime and delinquency—are also strongly influenced by genetic factors. To illustrate, studies have found genetic bases for a whole range of behavioral conditions that have relevance from criminological theory. For example, *conduct disorder* is considered a precursor to antisocial personality disorder in adults (discussed in chapter 5) and is characterized by chronic stealing, truancy, lying, bullying, fighting, aggressiveness, cruelty to animals, and other forms of delinquency and status offenses in juveniles. *Oppositional defiant disorder* is less serious and consists of a pattern of defiant behavior. It is characterized by temper loss, frequent arguments, defiance of rules, being easily annoyed, and anger. Research from a twin study of 2,682 adult twin pairs found a large genetic influence on the development of conduct disorder (Slutske et al., 1997) and smaller studies of twins showed a heritable influence on cognitive ability and troublesome behaviors (McGuffin & Thapar, 1997).

There is also evidence that one of the strongest correlates to crime—substance use and abuse—is under substantial genetic control. Of course this should not be interpreted to mean that *polygenic*, or influenced by numerous genes that affect levels of neurotransmitters in the brain. According to Blum and Payne (1991), brain functioning of alcoholics may be different because of genetic differences, such that alcoholics more easily experience negative emotions and/or do not experience positive emotions as easily without altering their brain chemistry through drug use. This could owe itself to diminished opioid activity in the brain (Wand et al., 1998) and/or abnormalities in serotonin function, another naturally occurring brain chemical (Lappalainen et al., 1998). Lower sensitivity to alcohol has also been found to be related to alcoholism, as measured by lower levels of brain waves in electroencephalograms (EEGs) (Schuckit & Smith, 1996; Volavka et al., 1996).

One twin study examining alcoholism and less serious drinking behaviors among 3,516 identical and fraternal male twins found that genetic factors explained at least 50% of alcoholism and drinking (Prescott & Kendler, 1999). Interestingly, alcoholics also tend to have greater cravings for sweets, especially when coupled with the personality traits of novelty-seeking and harm avoidance and the psychiatric condition bipolar affective disorder (Kampov-Polevoy, Garbutt, & Jonowsky, 1997, 1999; Kampov-Polevoy et al. 1998). In addition, DeMott (1999) reported findings from a study by Coolidge et al. of 70 identical and 42 fraternal twins between the ages of 4 and 15 years where approximately 68% of conduct disorder was estimated to be heritable, as was 63% of antisocial behavior.

Genetic links to use of other drugs, both legal and illegal (e.g., nicotine and heroin), have also been identified. Consider, for example, research suggesting that genes may help explain why some people start smoking cigarettes and why some find quitting more difficult. Being born with a predisposition to some personality and behavioral traits (e.g., anxiety and restlessness) makes it more likely that a person will begin smoking, probably because nicotine in cigarettes alters chemicals in the brain such as dopamine (Clarke, 1998; Spitz & Shi, 1998). Carmelli et al. (1992) reported that concordance rates for smoking were higher in identical twins than fraternal twins, as were concordance rates for quitting smoking and not smoking. Spitz and Shi (1998) found that individuals with a particular genotype were more likely to be smokers. A national comorbidity study found that 57% of nicotine dependent smokers had one or more symptoms of mood disorders before they began smoking, and another study reported that depression is more common in smokers than nonsmokers (Breslau, Kilbey, & Andreski, 1993). These findings suggest that nicotine may act as an antidepressant by releasing the neurotransmitters dopamine, norepinephrine, and serotonin. At the same time, genetic makeup may also make it less likely that a person will continue smoking if he or she tries a cigarette. According to Vastag (1998), a gene on chromosome 19 regulates the production of an enzyme that metabolizes nicotine in the bloodstream; when this gene is defective, only about half of the enzyme is produced and thus when these people smoke, they suffer more nausea, dizziness, and other negative side effects.

Box 4.4 summarizes the findings of the Minnesota Twin Study, a major study examining the effects of genetics on behaviors. It is important to note that after reporting on this study, Konner and Kunz (1990, p. 62) claimed: "Our genetic inheritance plays at least as large a role in determining our personalities as the way we are raised or the education we received."

Box 4.4 Findings from the Minnesota Twin Study

Jim Lewis and Jim Springer were 40-year-old MZ twins who were separated at birth and adopted into different families. Even despite being reared in different families, they were eerily similar. "Both had taken law enforcement training. Both had blueprinting, drafting, and carpentry as hobbies. Lewis had been married three times, Springer twice. Both first wives were named Linda; both second wives, Betty. Each named his first son James Allan. Each had a dog named Toy. Of their first meeting, Lewis said, 'It was like looking in a mirror'" (Konner & Kunz, 1990).

Researchers at the University of Minnesota have directed a large-scale study to examine the genetic and environmental influences on virtually every imaginable phenotype. Data have been collected from 402 pairs of twins; 261 of them were identical and 44 of these were reared apart. Another 141 were fraternal twins, of which 27 were reared apart. "Subjects responded to questions charting their feelings of well-being, attitudes toward achievement, social closeness, alienation, aggression, and even traditionalism." Subjects were categorized into one of three personality types: *positive emotionality* (active, pleasurable, effective in interactions with surroundings); *negative emotionality* (being involved in life in a negative way with frequent stress, anxiety, and anger); and *constraint* (restrained, cautious, deferential, and avoiding danger and impulsive thrill-seeking behaviors). The scholars found a 40% genetic contribution for positive emotionality, a 55% genetic contribution for negative emotionality, and a 58% genetic contribution for constraint. Thus, "about 50 percent of measured personality diversity can be attributed to genetic diversity." Konner and Kunz (1990, p. 66) concluded: "We need to recognize that to no small extent we are who we are when we are conceived."

Personality characteristics are discussed in greater detail in chapter 6. Keep in mind when you read this chapter that personalities have strong genetic underpinnings.

Source: Konner, M., & Kunz, A. (1990). Under the influence. *Omni, 12* (4), 62–66.

Empirical Results from Molecular Genetic Studies

Although adoption and twin studies represent a very important first step in determining the genetic and environmental foundations to antisocial behaviors, they are host to at least one main drawback—namely, they are unable to reveal which genes are implicated in the etiology of antisocial behaviors. Stated differently, adoption and twin studies provide estimates of the relative influence of genetic and environmental factors but reveal absolutely nothing about the specific genes that may be associated with antisocial outcomes. Relatively recently, researchers have begun to genotype people and examine whether specific DNA markers are related to a range of antisocial behaviors and personality traits. These studies, while still in their infancy, have identified a number of genetic polymorphisms that are likely to contribute to the development of maladaptive and antisocial outcomes.

Most of the genes that have been found to relate to antisocial behaviors are involved in *neurotransmission* (Morley & Hall, 2003; Rowe, 2002). These are genes that assist in sending neurotransmitters from one nerve cell in the brain to another. *Neurotransmitters* are naturally occurring brain chemicals such as dopamine and serotonin that are released by one nerve cell in the brain and received by the next; neurotransmitters underlie all human thought and behavior. Dopaminergic genes, serotonergic genes, and genes that code for the production of enzymes that breakdown neurotransmitters are all hypothesized to be associated with violence and criminality. There is emerging research testing this possibility, and the results of these studies have been promising. For instance, researchers have examined the effects of a polymorphism in the dopamine transporter (DAT1) gene. The DAT1 gene, which codes for a protein that is involved in the transportation of dopamine, has been mapped to chromosome 5 and has a variable number of tandem repeats (VNTR) in the 3' untranslated region of the gene. A number of studies have found that certain alleles of this polymorphism are associated with violence and delinquency in adolescents and young adults (Beaver, Wright, & Walsh, 2009; Guo, Roettger, & Shih, 2007). An *allele* is an alternative form a gene.

There are also a number of dopaminergic receptor genes that have been linked to antisocial phenotypes. Dopaminergic receptor genes facilitate the post-synaptic detection of dopamine. Two dopamine receptor genes in particular—the dopamine D2 receptor gene (DRD2) and the dopamine D4 receptor gene (DRD4)—have been the focus of a growing amount of research. DRD2, which codes for the production of the D2 receptor protein, has been mapped to chromosome 11 and has a polymorphism that consists of two alleles: the A1 allele and the A2 allele. The available empirical evidence indicates that the A1 allele is the risk allele that increases the odds of a range of antisocial phenotypes. For instance, the A1 allele has been found to confer an increased risk of victimization (Beaver et al., 2007a), alcoholism (Connor et al., 2002), and pathological gambling (Comings et al., 2001). Of particular importance is that a handful of studies have found that the A1 allele of DRD2 increases involvement in acts of violence and aggression (Beaver et al., 2007b; Guo, Roettger, & Shih, 2007). Taken together, the limited evidence seems to suggest that the A1 allele of DRD2 is related to a number of antisocial phenotypes, including criminal and violent behaviors.

Another dopamine receptor gene—DRD4—has also been studied in relation to criminal outcomes. DRD4, which is partially responsible for the production of a receptor protein that is involved in the post-synaptic binding of dopamine, is located on chromosome 11 and has a polymorphism, where a 48 base pair sequence can be repeated between 2 and 11 times. Research has indicated that the 7-repeat (7R) allele is the risk allele for a range of antisocial phenotypes. For instance, this polymorphism has been linked to ADHD

(Faraone, Doyle, Mick, & Biederman, 2001), conduct disorder (Rowe et al., 2001), and pathological gambling (Comings et al., 2001). Given that these phenotypes covary significantly with criminal involvement, it is quite possible that the 7-repeat allele may also be related to aggression and violence. Research conducted by Schmidt et al. (2002) seems to provide some support for this conclusion. In this study, the researchers reported an association between the 7R allele of DRD4 and maternal reports of aggression in a sample of young children. Additional research has also provided some documentation of a link between the 7R allele and violence and aggression (Beaver et al., 2007b).

In addition to dopaminergic polymorphisms, there is also some research examining whether serotonergic genes, especially the serotonin transporter gene (5HTT) might be associated with antisocial outcomes. 5HTT has been mapped to chromosome 17 and has a polymorphism (5HTTLPR) that consists of two different groups of alleles: low expressing alleles and high expressing alleles. The low expressing alleles are the alleles that are thought to increase the odds of maladaptive behaviors. A line of research has tested this proposition, the results of which have been relatively supportive. To illustrate, the low expressing alleles have been linked to ADHD symptoms (Cadoret et al., 2003), alcohol consumption (Herman, Philbeck, Vasilopoulos, & Depetrillo, 2003), and conduct disorder (Cadoret et al., 2003). There is also some research indicating that carriers of the low expressing alleles are more likely to engage in violence as children (Beitchman et al., 2006; Haberstick, Smolen, & Hewitt, 2006). Additionally, researchers have found the low expressing alleles to be more common in samples of violent offenders when compared to samples of nonviolent offenders (Liao et al., 2004; Retz et al., 2004). Collectively, these studies seem to converge on the conclusion that the 5HTTLPR polymorphism is implicated—at least to some degree—in the etiology of antisocial conduct.

Two genes that are involved in the metabolism of neurotransmitters have also been linked to a number of antisocial and criminal outcomes. The first gene—the COMT gene—is located on chromosome 22 and is involved in the production of the COMT enzyme, which breaks down neurotransmitters, including dopamine. COMT has a single nucleotide polymorphism that results in the production of two different amino acids. The first allele, known as the Met allele, codes for the production of the amino acid of methionine, while the other allele, known as the Val allele, codes for the production of the amino acid valine. The extant genetic research suggests that possession of the Met allele increases the risk of developing certain psychopathologies as well as antisocial phenotypes (Volavka, Bilder, & Nolan, 2004).

A growing body of research has provided empirical support upholding the proposed association between the Met allele and violence, aggression, and aggressive personality traits (Rujesco et al., 2003). For example, Lachman et al. (1998) examined whether the Met allele had an effect on aggressive behaviors in a sample of schizophrenics. The results of their study indicated that schizophrenics who had a long history of serious violence were more likely to possess two Met alleles when compared with schizophrenics without a history of violence. Additional studies of schizophrenics have provided strikingly similar results tying the Met allele to violence (Kotler et al., 1999; Strous et al., 1997). Interestingly, one team of researchers actually found that the Val allele, not the Met allele, was associated with increased violent behaviors among schizophrenics (Jones et al., 2001). Although the results of the available studies are very promising, much more research needs to be undertaken to determine the precise role that the COMT gene plays in the etiology of violence and aggression.

The second gene that is involved in the metabolism of neurotransmitters that has been found to be related to antisocial phenotypes is the MAOA gene. The MAOA gene is located on the X chromosome and, as a result, males have only one copy of this gene, while females have two copies. Similar to COMT, the MAOA gene is responsible for coding for the production of the MAOA enzyme. Similar to COMT, this enzyme is involved in the metabolism of certain neurotransmitters, including dopamine and serotonin. The MAOA gene has a 30 base pair VNTR polymorphism in the promoter region of the gene. The alleles for this polymorphism are typically grouped into two categories: one category of alleles corresponds to low MAOA activity and the other category of alleles corresponds to high MAOA activity. A line of research has provided consistent evidence linking the low MAOA activity alleles to antisocial phenotypes.

In a groundbreaking study, Caspi et al. (2002) examined the effects of the MAOA genotype and childhood maltreatment on antisocial behavior in a sample of males from the Dunedin Multidisciplinary Health and Development Study. They hypothesized that the low MAOA activity alleles would only have an effect on antisocial phenotypes for males who had been maltreated as children. Analysis of the data substantiated their propositions—specifically, the low MAOA activity alleles were unrelated to antisocial behavior for the full sample. However, when this association was examined in greater detail, the data revealed that the low MAOA activity alleles were strongly related to antisocial behavior among males who were maltreated as children. The effect size for this finding was quite impressive: although only about 12 percent of the sample had been maltreated and possessed the low MAOA activity alleles, they accounted for 44 percent of all violent convictions. The importance of this study was that a measured gene (i.e., MAOA) was found to interact with a putative environmental risk factor (i.e., childhood maltreatment) to predict a behavioral phenotype (i.e., antisocial behavior). Once again, these results draw attention to the fact that antisocial behaviors are created by genetic factors and environmental factors working interactively. Importantly, a recent meta-analysis confirmed that the low MAOA activity alleles work in tandem with adverse environments to produce maladaptive outcomes (Kim-Cohen et al., 2006).

Scope

Recall that the scope of a theory identifies what types of behaviors are to be explained by the theory. Raine's (1993) review of twin and adoptive studies suggested a larger heritability for nonviolent crimes than violent crimes. Yet, genes likely play a role in violent and aggressive behaviors, too. Genetic makeup may predispose a person to react in certain situations with violence rather than nonviolently. There is evidence, for example, that some people react to perceived conflict physically rather than verbally as most people would. It is hypothesized that brain dysfunction increases the odds that some antisocial populations will respond aggressively in the face of conflicts that would not trigger violence in most. This research is discussed in chapter 5.

Very little research has been conducted with regard to the role of genetics in elite deviance, which as you saw in chapter 1 is far more dangerous than street criminality. Is there any evidence that violent and/or property white-collar deviants can be explained by genetics? Although not directly examining the genetic basis to white-collar crime, there is one study that examined the genetic basis to credit card and check fraud (Beaver and Holtfreter, 2009). The results of this study revealed that the MAOA gene interacted with delinquent peers to predict involvement in fraudulent behaviors. Whether these findings would apply to more traditional types of white-collar crimes remains an open empirical question. However, the traits that increase success in the business world are certainly influenced by genetics, as traits that are likely to increase antisocial behavior are also necessary for business success in a competitive capitalistic marketplace (e.g., aggressiveness, egoism or selfishness). Given that research has revealed that all behaviors are genetically influenced, explanations for white-collar criminality should not ignore the role of genetic factors.

Conceptual Clarity

Recall that a theory's concepts need to be defined so that people can understand them (i.e., the nominal definitions must be clearly defined) and so that they can be measured in the real world (i.e., the operational definitions must be clearly defined). The nominal definitions of the concepts used in genetic studies are clearly defined and thus easy to understand. There are some issues with the operational definitions, however. Specifically, oftentimes researchers do not directly measure the behaviors that they are interested in studying; instead they use attitudinal measures about how subjects say they feel about particular behaviors. And when measuring attitudes and behaviors, researchers often rely on different scales. According to Fishbein (2000, p. 82): "While one study may use the Barratt Impulsiveness Scale to measure impulsivity, another study may use the Eysenck Scale or a behavioral measure." Whether these scales measure the same thing is not certain.

Frequently studies assessing behavioral traits or attitudes rely on self-report measures, which may limit the validity of the findings since people lie, exaggerate, forget, and so on when trying to recall their own past.

Logical Adequacy of Propositions

Recall that propositions of a theory should be stated in a logical manner, meaning that they can be understood and that nothing important is omitted. Additionally, theories that are tautological or that engage in circular reasoning cannot be considered logically stated. The propositions of genetic studies are stated in a logical fashion and are easy to understand. They also are not tautological because scholars define the key concepts of study in a manner that allows them to be measured separately from the behaviors that are to be explained. The main advantage of propositions stating relationships between genes and behavior is that they allow scholars to take into account both genetic and environmental factors in assessing the influence they have on behavior.

Other Cellular Level Factors

There are other cellular level factors beyond genetics that have effects on human behavior, including neurotransmitters, hormones, and enzymes. (Importantly, all of these chemicals are controlled, in part, by genetic factors.) Neurotransmitters are naturally occurring brain chemicals that are allow neurons to communicate with each other. Some enzymes are also found in the brain and are partially responsible for synthesizing and breaking down neurotransmitters. Hormones are biochemical substances that are secreted into the bloodstream by endocrine glands located throughout the body. We discuss the relationship between these factors and behavior in greater detail in chapter 5.

Summary

In this chapter, we discussed factors at the smallest level of analysis in the integrated systems perspective, the cell level. More specifically, we examined the relationships between genetics and antisocial behaviors. Genes are the biochemical part of a cell that determines what the cell becomes; genes are located on chromosomes and are essentially a segment of DNA. Genes work primarily by constructing proteins that serve various functions in the body. Genes are not deterministic but instead are probabilistic. Genes rely on the environment to express themselves, suggesting that behavior is always the result of genetic-environmental interactions. Further, complex behaviors such as criminality are polygenic, meaning more than one gene is involved.

A wealth of behavioral genetic research has examined samples of twin pairs to estimate the genetic and environmental influences on antisocial phenotypes. The results of these studies have revealed that approximately half of the variance in antisocial phenotypes is due to genetic factors, with the other half attributable to the environment. Genes have been implicated in numerous behavioral outcomes, including conduct disorder (CD), attention deficit hyperactivity disorder (ADHD), substance abuse, and violence. In response to these findings, recently there has been an emerging line of research examining the specific genetic polymorphisms that might be related to antisocial behaviors. As a result, we reviewed evidence bearing on the effects that dopaminergic genes, serotonergic genes, MAOA, and COMT had on antisocial phenotypes. This line of research revealed support for the likelihood that these genes are associated with criminality and antisocial behaviors. Moreover, we also dispelled antiquated myths about genes and argued that all human behaviors, including antisocial behaviors, are the result of genetic and environmental factors working independently and interactively. The evidence presented also indicated that the majority of our genes affect brain structure and that certain of these genes influence brain chemistry by affecting levels of neurotransmitters in the brain. As a result, the effect that genes have on antisocial phenotypes likely operates indirectly by affecting brain structure and brain function (see chapter 5). In addition, genes also have their effects on behavior by affecting personality traits (see chapter 6). Collectively, this line of reasoning stresses the importance of examining the indirect pathways from genes to antisocial phenotypes.

Discussion Questions

1. What is a cell?
2. What is a gene? What is the human genome?
3. Do genes determine behavior? Explain.
4. Discuss the main misconceptions of genetics and human behavior.
5. List and discuss the main propositions about genes and behavior.
6. Identify and discuss the main methods of studying the relationships between genes and behavior.
7. What is a concordance rate? What do findings showing that monozygotic twins have higher concordance rates than dizygotic twins mean?
8. Can the findings of the Minnesota Twin Study be explained away by nongenetic factors or coincidence? Explain.
9. What types of behaviors appear to have a genetic component?
10. Are the concepts of cellular level explanations of crime clearly defined? Explain.
11. What is the logical adequacy of cellular level explanations of crime?
12. What is the scope of cellular level explanations of crime?

5

Organ Level
Explanations of Crime

Introduction

The organ level of analysis is the next level of analysis in an integrated systems explanation of antisocial behavior and criminality. Organs are comprised of cells, which were discussed in the previous chapter. An example of an organ is the brain, which is part of the *central nervous system*, and which is made up of hundreds of billions of *neurons*. In this chapter you will see how the brain is involved in all types of human behaviors, including criminal and antisocial behaviors. Since the brain is *the* organ of behavior, its structure and its ability to function properly are important for understanding how any organism, including humans, behaves. Several years ago, Robinson (1998) wrote a paper titled, "It's All in Your Head: Integrating Neurological Factors into Criminological Theory" where he argued that everything must affect the brain before it affects behavior. In this paper, Robinson also stressed that any theory of behavior, including antisocial behavior and criminality, is logically incomplete if it does not discuss the role of the brain. Walsh (2002, p. 75) reinforced this view when he argued: "Whether a behavior-motivating stimulus arises from within the person or from the environment, it is necessarily mediated by the brain, arguably the most immensely complicated structure in the universe ... Because the brain is the executor of all that we do and think, the basics of neuroscience must be part of the criminologist's repertoire of knowledge."

Behavior in the Context of the Central Nervous System

The brain and the spinal cord make up the *central nervous system*. The brain weighs about 3 pounds, with the consistency of set yogurt. At 1,300 to 1,400 grams, the human brain is much smaller than that of an elephant (6,000 g), but is much larger than that of a chimpanzee (420 g), a cat (30 g), and other animals that are not as able as humans to think and plan for the future. When considering behavior, the brain is the most important organ in the body, for it is literally the organ of behavior—without the brain there is no behavior (Greenfield, 1996).

Many criminological theories include concepts that are not directly testable and are, therefore, nonfalsifiable. Many of these concepts are *mentalistic* because they refer to crime-producing factors which supposedly reside in the *minds* of offenders. Such mentalistic phenomena cannot be empirically verified. An offender's thought processes are under control of the brain, making them physical and not mental. Although the existence of mentalistic phenomena cannot be empirically disproven, neither can they be empirically demonstrated. This means they are not useful for the advancement of scientific knowledge about behavior. Since the brain is testable and can be observed during behavior, it is useful for advancing knowledge about criminal behavior.

The first pictures of the living brain were taken with X-rays in 1917, but this was limited mostly to structural images of the brain. Almost a half-century later, computerized tomography (CT) scans were used to capture soft tissues but could not chart brain functioning. As discussed in box 5.1, brain functioning can now be observed using techniques that permit researchers to observe metabolic activity each millisecond. For example, positron emission tomography (PET) scans are used to examine brain activity while people are reading, hearing, or thinking about words and speaking them. As a result, it is possible to locate areas of the brain that are tied to various types of behaviors. Electroencephalographic (EEG) technology allows researchers to detect nerve impulses when stimulated by outside stimuli.

Box 5.1 Methods Used to Measure Brain Structure and Function

- *Angiography* detects dye injected into the blood of the patient to provide images of blood vessels in the brain.
- *Electroencephalography* (EEG) uses electrodes placed on the scalp of
  the patient to detect electrical activity of the brain.
- *Computerized tomography* (CT) sends X-ray beams through one side
  of the brain more than 100 times to create three-dimensional cross-
  sectional images of the brain's structures; the radiation not absorbed
  by the brain is picked up by radiation sensors on the other side and
  pictures are assembled.
- *Positron emission tomography* (PET) detects radioactive materials injected into the blood of the patient; picks up blood flow, glucose levels, and oxygen levels being used by the brain; and detects gamma
  rays when radioactive materials break down.
- *Magnetic resonance imaging* (MRI) detects radio frequency signals sent
  into a magnetic field around the patient's head to produce anatomical views of the brain.
- *Functional magnetic resonance imaging* (fMRI) detects changes in blood
  flow during task performance to provide anatomical and functional views
  of the brain.

Sources: Chudler, E. (2001). *Brain imaging.* Retrieved from *http://faculty.wash
ington.edu/chudler/image.html*; Mathias, R. (1996). *The basics of brain imaging.* Retrieved from *www.nida.nih.gov/Nida_Notes/NNVol11N5/Basics.html*;
Raine, A. (1993). *The psychopathology of crime.* San Diego, CA: Academic
Press.

All environmental influences must be received via the senses, perceived, and
processed by the brain before a person can behave. Everything we smell, see,
hear, taste, or touch is experienced in our brains (see figure 5.1). No behavior
occurs without sensory information being relayed to the brain. As explained
by Fishbein (2001, p. 35): "It is the function of our brains that gives rise to
our emotions, moods, drives, memories, intelligence, personality, and much
more. Accordingly, there is no way to study the complexities of human behavior without including the central role of the brain."

The brain acts like a puppeteer pulling strings of the body while the muscles of the body are like the puppets controlled by the brain (Greenfield, 1996).
The brain sends instructions in the form of electrical-chemical messages to the
body telling each muscle what to do so that behavior can occur. Twelve pairs

Figure 5.1 The Brain and Behavior

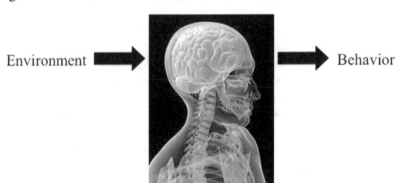

Source: Figure created by author.

of nerves in the brain enable organisms to receive and respond to stimuli in the environment.

The human brain is a product of gene-environment interaction, meaning that the developing human brain is influenced by both genetic and environmental factors (Jeffery, 1990; Siegel, 1999; Kotulak, 1996). The human genome provides the instructions for the development of the human body. Shore (1997) estimated that more than 50% of our genes are involved in brain development. Genes specify how the brain will be structured, how cells will be built, and how neurotransmitters and enzymes will be produced (Dowling, 1998; Kotulak, 1996; Walsh, 2002; Wright, Tibbetts, & Daigle, 2008). Genes specify a great bit of how the brain will wire itself—that is, how it will make connections between its brain cells. Because individuals are unique with regard to their genes (except for monozygotic twins) and thus also have unique brains, "no two individuals are alike and no two individuals will respond to environmental cues in the same way" (Jeffery, 1996, p. 7).

Our experiences help form brain connections and actually reinforce connections specified by genes. With every experience, the brain wires itself, or makes connections between neurons (Depue & Collins, 1999). The brain is plastic, or able to make connections, early in childhood, continues to be plastic in adolescence, and becomes less plastic as we age. In fact, the brain dies as we age, as connections between neurons are lost when we do not use them. More stimulation of the brain means a greater likelihood that neural connections will survive (Levine, 1993). Against this backdrop it is probably not too surprising to learn that research has revealed that children reared in enrich environments (e.g., where they spend a lot of time with loved ones engaged in play) tend to have greater cognitive abilities (Noble, Norman, & Farah, 2005).

For the brain to continue to work throughout life, it must have two things—glucose or blood sugar from foods consumed, and oxygen from the lungs. The brain requires about 10 times as much glucose as the rest of the body's organs, and uses about 20% of the body's oxygen intake even though it only weighs about 2% of total body weight. This is because the brain is extremely active, even when we are not, since it regulates all of our internal autonomic behaviors such as breathing, body temperature, heartbeat, and so on (Dennet, 1993; England & Wakely, 1991; Fitzgerald, 1985; Glees, 1988; Greenfield, 1996; Levitan & Kaczmarek, 1991; Pinchot, 1994; Steinberg, 1995). Logically, then, what we eat and the condition of the oxygen we breathe can affect our brains and our behaviors. For example, low blood sugar, or hypoglycemia, can produce aggressiveness, loss of self-control, and hallucinations and delusions (Robinson & Kelley, 1998). The effects of diet on behavior are discussed in chapter 6.

Brain Structure and Function

The brain can be divided into different parts or sections, each of which has its own functions and roles in human behavior. At a broad level, MacLean (1990) specified three brain types, including the *reptilian* (brain stem), *paleomammalian* (limbic system), and *neomammalian* (cerebrum). As humans evolved, the brain evolved to become more complex. Evolutionary psychologists assert that the neomammalian brain, when developed, provides control over the impulses of the paleomammalian brain. If the neomammalian brain is underdeveloped, or if the paleomammalian brain is too strong, impulses generated within primitive brain structures may result in antisocial behavior (Walsh, 2002).

In terms of the modern human brain, Raine (1993, p. 105) wrote: "The brain can crudely be divided into two areas—cortex and subcortex. The cerebral cortex makes up the outer aspects of the brain and is of relatively recent origin in evolutionary terms, while phylogenetically older structures below this level make up the subcortex." Humans share the ancient brain structures of the reptilian brain that create impulses to aggression and violence with lesser evolved organisms. In this light, aggression and violence can be viewed as normal in the context of evolution.

The largest portion of the brain is the cerebrum. The cerebrum is the wrinkled mass of the brain, divided into two hemispheres. The left hemisphere controls the right side of the body while the right hemisphere controls the left side of the body. Both sides are connected and communicate via the *corpus callosum*, which is made up of hundreds of millions of nerve fibers. Certain functions can be isolated to one side of the brain; for example, language, logic, math, and generating ideas tend to be housed in the left side of the brain, while vision, perspective, insight, spatial matters, music, and emotion are primarily generated on the right side of the brain (Greenfield, 1996; Jeffery, 1990). According to Walsh (2002, p. 77): "It is generally accepted that the right hemisphere is specialized for perception and the expression of emotion (particularly negative emotions), and that the left hemisphere is specialized for language and analytical thinking." Figure 5.2 shows the main divisions of the human brain.

The cerebrum contains the axons of neurons which carry electrical-chemical signals throughout the brain. The thin outer layer of the cerebrum is the *cerebral cortex*, also known as the gray matter, loaded with the soma or cell bodies of neurons and their connections. The cortex is the part of the brain where higher functions such as association, planning, and reasoning take place. Regions of the cortex are connected by fibers and tracts which allow the brain's parts to communicate with one another. The inner portion of the cortex is the white matter and contains nerve cell axons covered by myelin that carry information from the brain to the spinal cord. Included in the brain stem is the

Figure 5.2 The Human Brain

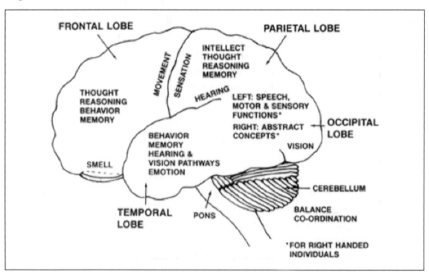

Source: Harvard Neurosurgery [On-line]. Available: *http://neurosurgery.mgh.harvard.edu/abta/primer.htm*

reticular activating system (RAS) which filters information and helps determine the arousal level of an individual (Walsh, 2002). The RAS and the autonomic nervous system (ANS), which is controlled by the hypothalamus, are believed to determine the normal degree of arousal of an individual. The research concerning the RAS and the ANS is discussed in chapter 6.

There are four lobes found in the two brain hemispheres, each named after the bones of the skull under which they are located: the frontal lobe, the parietal lobe, the occipital lobe, and the temporal lobe (Dennet, 1993; England & Wakely, 1991; Fitzgerald, 1985; Glees, 1988; Levitan & Kaczmarek, 1991; Pinchot, 1984; Steinberg, 1995). The entire brain is surrounded by membranes and flooded with fluid. The two areas of the brain that are the most relevant to the study of aggression and violence are the frontal and temporal lobes. The *frontal lobes* of the brain are responsible for higher intelligence, rationality, planning, behavioral inhibition, and the regulation of emotion and affect. Structures of the limbic system (including the hippocampus and amygdala), along with the hypothalamus and thalamus, are found in the *temporal lobes*. The hippocampus is involved with emotional behavior, learning, motivation, and memory. The amygdala coordinates autonomic and hormonal responses during emotional states and also is involved with emotion. The hypothalamus controls autonomic functions, such as body temperature and heart rate, and also works with the pituitary gland to control hormonal levels. The pituitary gland is the size of a pea but also plays an important role in emotion.

Complex brain functions such as decision-making involve a coordinated effort between brain cells from numerous areas of the brain. While some brain functions can be specified to one particular region of the brain, others are spread across numerous regions. For example, automatic behaviors such as reflexes are specific to the hypothalamus, while thought and planning are spread across the parts of the cerebral cortex. The hypothalamus, weighing only about 0.3% of the brain's total weight, coordinates behavior and emotion. The pituitary gland hangs by a stalk from the hypothalamus, and controls the body's hormonal processes. The thalamus, located in the center of the temporal lobes, is the sensory gatekeeper of the brain, sorting out and processing the millions of nerve signals that pour into the brain every second from the outside world (Greenfield, 1996).

Not only are parts of the frontal lobe involved with motor functions and behavioral movements, but they are also heavily involved in higher-order intellectual functioning, planning, and complex cognitive processes. The frontal lobe also plays a role in emotion, mood, and voluntary behavior generally. At the base of the frontal lobe, parts of the brain inhibit or control emotions generating from more primitive areas of the brain. The *parietal lobe* receives and interprets senses, and is involved in the sensations of touch, pain, and temperature. The *occipital lobe* deals with vision and processes incoming environmental signals to help form perceptions of the outside world. The *temporal lobe* is involved in the forming of complex memories, in the processing of language and hearing, in smelling, and in the forming of emotions. It also adds emotional meaning to sensory information (Greenfield, 1996; Jeffery, 1990).

In general, the larger the cortex relative to body size, the more intelligent the species. Although other species have larger brains than humans, their bodies are also much larger. This may be what has led some philosophers to assert that humans are superior to other species, and it may be responsible for the belief held by many criminologists that humans can choose to commit crime rationally (e.g., see Nagin & Paternoster, 1993; Piquero & Tibbetts, 2001). The human brain also dedicates less of its areas to sensory functions, meaning that a lower proportion of it is used for seeing, hearing, smelling, and so forth, while more of it can be used for association, learning, or higher processes of thought.

The wrinkles of the cerebrum, or convolutions, increase the surface area of the brain. They allow the brain to be much smaller than it would be if the brain was flat. The *cerebellum*, or little brain, is located at the base of the hindbrain, attached to the brain stem. It serves a role in the planning and execution of movement, balance, and eye movements. In humans, this part of the brain controls involuntary behaviors less than it does in other species that have a larger cerebellum relative to their cortex. Some involuntary behaviors such as breathing, heartbeat, and so on are controlled in humans by the medulla oblongata.

Normal Brain Function: Neurons and Neurotransmitter Levels

The human body and brain contain more than 1,000 times as many cells as there are stars in the Milky Way galaxy. There are hundreds of different kinds of cells in humans, specialized by function for our benefit. One type of cell relevant for human behavior, including antisocial behavior, is the nerve cell, known as a *neuron*. Neurons are the basic cells of the nervous system and are the driving force of all thought in the brain. The nerve cell is specialized in its spidery shape and its excitable nature, meaning it can generate and convey electrical impulses. Connections between brain cells are made when neurons communicate with one another, much like a computer. Since there are over 100 billion neurons in the brain, each with potentially thousands of connections to other neurons, the brain is an amazingly powerful organ. Neuronal connections underlie all thoughts, feelings, emotions, and behaviors (Walsh, 2002).

Other brain cells, known as *glia,* are even more prevalent than neurons. Glia cells assist the neurons in important ways. For example, some glia provide needed support for neurons by transporting nutrients to neurons, cleaning up debris, and holding them in place. The primary function of glia cells is thought to be providing insulation or myelin for the protection of neurons.

Neurons can conduct an astounding 300 electrical-chemical signals per second. The cell body, or *soma,* is only 1/1,000 of an inch across, and the control center—the nucleus of the brain cell—is located here. Its two special features include its plasma membrane, which is the source of the electrical impulse, and its neurites or connecting fibers, which link one neuron to another. Neurites include the *axon* (usually one per neuron), which is long, and *dendrites,* which are shorter and branched. These make up the vast majority of the overall surface area of the neuron. Axons send signals to other neurons while dendrites receive the information. The overall shape of the neurites helps determine the physical shape of the neuron and the connections it establishes with other neurons, which then determines its primary role in brain function. Figure 5.3 shows an image of a single neuron.

Figure 5.3 A Neuron

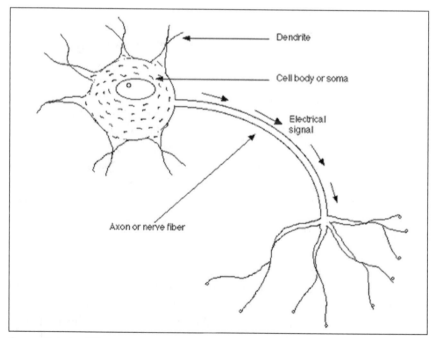

Source: Katerina Velanova

A *sensory neuron* is a nerve cell that transmits impulses from a receptor such as those in the eye or ear to a more central location in the nervous system. A *motor neuron* is a nerve cell that transmits impulses from a central area of the nervous system to an effector such as a muscle. Neurons carry information across the brain and to other parts of the body by means of an electrical impulse created by the natural exchange of potassium, sodium, calcium, and chloride. When a neuron is not sending a signal, it is at rest, meaning that each of the chemicals is balanced (this is called the *resting potential*). At rest, there tend to be more sodium ions outside the neuron and more potassium ions inside the neuron. The exchange of sodium and potassium in a neuron after a stimulus is presented causes an *action potential* or a firing of a neuron, which results in an electrical impulse that will pulse across a neuron. This electrical impulse travels from one neuron to another by crossing over the structures of the nerve cells in the brain and spinal cord.

The branching fibers (dendrites) of neurons bring information to the cell body of neurons while axons take information away from neurons. Bundles of fibers from neurons are held together by connective tissue and form nerves. The space between neurons is known as the *synapse*. As the electrical impulse passes over a neuron, chemicals known as *neurotransmitters* are released from one neuron (at the presynaptic nerve terminal) into the synapse and then received by another neuron (at the postsynaptic receptor). Neurotransmitters are released from vesicles when triggered by the electrical impulse.

At the synapse of a neuron receiving an electrical impulse, neurotransmitters can be received from the sending neuron. The synapse is a fluid-filled space about 1/600th the width of a human hair. There may be as many as 1 quadrillion synapses (that's 1,000,000,000,000,000) in the brain (Chudler, 2001). The electric signal cannot leap from one cell to another, and so neurotransmitters are released and received from one neuron to another to bridge the synapse. Electrical signals can travel as fast as 120 meters per second (268 miles per hour) (Chudler, 2001). Neurotransmitters fit into specific receptor sites at other neurons, much like a key into a lock or a baseball into a glove (Greenfield, 1996). The shape and size of a neurotransmitter molecule are fitted to a particular type of receptor.

The effects of neurotransmitters on behavior depend on several factors, including the type of neurotransmitter received, the amount of neurotransmitter received, the presence of other neurotransmitters, and the condition and numbers of receptors within the cell receiving the electrical impulse. Two basic types of synapses are excitatory and inhibitory, the former of which generate cell firing and the latter of which prevent it. The design, structure, and position of synapses affect how nerve signals are transmitted and received. For example, messages sent have greater effects when sent shorter distances because signals fade with distance and time. Neurotransmitters may be received by another cell, they may leak away into the nerve cell's fluid, they may be broken down by enzymes in the brain, or they may be reabsorbed by the sending cell (Dennet, 1993; England & Wakely, 1991; Fitzgerald, 1985; Glees, 1988; Levitan & Kaczmarek, 1991; Pinchot, 1984; Steinberg, 1995).

Neurotransmitters tend to either excite (also known as *depolarization*) or inhibit (also known as *hyperpolarization*) brain activity—that is, increase or decrease brain function. According to the Society for Neuroscience (1996, p. 1), neurotransmitters

> attach to a slot on the surface of the receiving neuron—a protein called a receptor site. Many scientists compare the union to a key fitting in a lock. Once attached, different neurotransmitters either trigger "go" signals that allow the message to be passed to the next neuron in the communication line or produce "stop" signals that prevent the message from being forwarded. The signals are in the form of charged particles or ions. A large concentration of positively-charged particles entering a receiving neuron tells it to pass on the message ... a large concentration of negatively-charged particles entering the neuron will inhibit it from passing on the message.

For a chemical to be considered a neurotransmitter, it must meet the conditions outlined in box 5.2. A range of neurotransmitters has been identified. According to Chudler (2001), they include the "small molecule neurotransmitters" such as acetylcholine (ACh), serotonin (5-HT), dopamine (DA), norepinephrine (NE), histamine; "amino acids" such as gamma-aminobutyric acid (GABA), glycine, glutamate, aspartate; and "neuroactive peptides" such as gastrin, secretin, oxytocin, beta-endorphin, enkephalin, somatostatin, prolactin, thyrotropin, insulin, and glucagon.

Box 5.2 Criteria for a Chemical to Be a Neurotransmitter

- The chemical must be produced within a neuron.
- The chemical must be found within a neuron.
- Upon stimulation, a neuron must release the chemical.
- After release, the chemical must act on a receptor of another neuron and cause an effect.
- After release, the effect of the chemical must be inactivated by reuptake or enzyme.

- If the chemical is applied to the postsynaptic membrane, it should have the same effect as when released by a neuron.

Source: Adapted from Chudler, E. (2001). *Neuroscience.* Retrieved from *http://faculty.washington.edu/chudler/neurok.html*

Neurotransmitters are believed to underlie literally *all* perceptions, thoughts, and forms of behavior, including learning, memory, and movement. According to Fishbein (2001, p. 36): "neurotransmitters regulate emotion, mood, hunger, thirst, sleep, and a host of other behavioral and psychological processes." And, as will be discussed later in this chapter, there is also evidence indicating that the amount of neurotransmitters in the brain is also related to aggressiveness.

Neurotransmitter levels are partially determined by the genes we inherit from our parents. "Too few or too many receptors, or a deviation in the way they function, can alter neurotransmitter activity levels in the brain. Thus, levels of neurotransmitter activity and metabolism are to a great extent genetically determined," (Fishbein, 2001, p. 30). Neurotransmitter levels are also affected by environmental conditions such as stress, social status, diet, drug use, and neurotoxins (Dinan, 1996; Graeff et al., 1996; Petty et al., 1996; Stokes, 1995). They are built by the brain from other chemical substances in the blood known as *precursors* and are converted from precursors to neurotransmitters by enzymes. For example, the neurotransmitter acetylcholine (ACh) is a combination of choline and an enzyme. The catecholamines include dopamine (DA), norepinephrine (NE), and epinephrine, each of which is made of various enzymes. Serotonin (5-HT) consists of tryptophan and other chemicals.

Main Propositions of Neurotransmitter Studies

At least five or six dozen neurotransmitters have been discovered. Some are excitatory, meaning they increase brain activity, while others are inherently inhibitory, meaning they decrease brain activity. Scholars have attempted to relate only a handful of neurotransmitters to antisocial behaviors. This line of research has tested the following propositions:

- High levels of the neurotransmitter dopamine are related to antisocial behavior.
- Low levels of the neurotransmitter serotonin are related to antisocial behavior.
- Low levels of the neurotransmitter norepinephrine are related to antisocial behavior.

Key Concepts of Neurotransmitter Studies

From the preceding propositions, the following concepts can be isolated and defined:

- Neurotransmitter
- Dopamine
- Serotonin
- Norepinephrine
- Antisocial behavior

Box 5.3 defines the key concepts of neurotransmitter studies. Scholars have used these definitions to test the main propositions of neurotransmitter studies. The findings of these tests are discussed in the following section.

Box 5.3 Definitions of Key Concepts of Neurotransmitter Studies

- *Neurotransmitter. Nominal*—naturally occurring brain chemicals produced within a neuron, found within a neuron, which act on the receptor of another neuron and cause an effect when released by other neurons. *Operational*—levels of neurotransmitters are typically measured in the cerebrospinal fluid of individuals, but can also be measured in whole blood or urine of individuals; other measures include levels of amino acid precursors that are synthesized into the neurotransmitter, enzymes that convert the precursor into the neurotransmitter, or metabolites formed when the neurotransmitters are broken down.
- *Dopamine. Nominal*—an excitatory neurotransmitter involved in arousal, sleep, and basic motor activity. *Operational*—the levels of dopamine measured through the preceding techniques.
- *Serotonin. Nominal*—a neurotransmitter within inhibitory properties that is important in behavioral regulation and impulse control. *Operational*—the levels of serotonin measured through the preceding techniques.
- *Norepinephrine. Nominal*—an excitatory and inhibitory neurotransmitter involved in arousal and basic body functions. *Operational*—the levels of norepinephrine measured through the preceding techniques.
- *Antisocial behavior. Nominal*—any behaviors that conflict with the prevailing norms of society and/or that are viewed as abnormal. *Operational*—any form of behavior defined as antisocial, measured by official crime reports, self-reported behaviors, or evaluations from others.

Empirical Validity of Neurotransmitter Studies

Raine (1993) reviewed 29 studies that examined the effects that eight different neurotransmitters had on antisocial behaviors and concluded that serotonin and dopamine are the two neurotransmitters that are most likely involved in the etiology of various aggressive, antisocial, and violent behaviors. Serotonin, in particular, has produced the most consistent results, with low levels of serotonin being linked to a range of antisocial phenotypes. Beginning in the mid-1970s, researchers began to examine whether variations in serotonin levels were associated with different forms of violence. In some of the earliest research examining this issue, Asberg et al. (1976) reported a relationship between relatively low levels of serotonin and increased suicidal behaviors. In light of these findings, researchers hypothesized that if serotonin was associated with self-directed violence, then its effects might extend outward to other, more traditional types of serious physical violence.

Brown and colleagues (Brown et al., 1979; Brown et al., 1982) explored this possibility in a number of studies that were carried out in the late 1970s and early 1980s. In these studies, Brown et al. found an inverse relationship between serotonin levels and acts of aggression among males. Importantly, these studies analyzed data drawn from two independent studies, thereby decreasing the likelihood that the results were a methodological or statistical artifact. Since the publication of these studies, a wave of research has tested the association between serotonin levels and other antisocial phenotypes. The results from these studies have revealed an inverse association between serotonin levels and aggressive and violent behaviors in adults (Limson et al., 1991) as well as in children (Kruesi et al., 1990). These statistically significant findings should, however, be tempered by the fact that some studies have failed to detect any association between serotonin levels and antisocial behaviors (Gardner, Lucas, & Cowdry, 1990; Simeon et al., 1992; Lidberg et al., 1985).

There is some reason to suspect that serotonin may only have effects on certain types of antisocial behaviors—namely, acts that are impulsive and unplanned. Evidence in support of this view comes from a study carried out by Linnoila et al. (1983) where they examined serotonin levels in a sample of offenders. They found that low serotonin levels were disproportionately found among offenders who committed acts of impulsive violence in comparison with offenders who engaged in planned and premeditated crimes. As a result, studies that pool together all types of antisocial behaviors (i.e., impulsive acts and premeditated acts) may fail to detect a serotonin effect.

Moore, Scarpa, and Raine (2002) examined the possibility that serotonin levels may only relate to impulsive aggression in a meta-analysis of 20 studies.

The results of this meta-analysis revealed two broad findings. First, across studies there was a statistically significant and inverse association between serotonin levels and violent behaviors. Second, this association was not confined only to impulsive acts—that is, low levels of serotonin appeared to have effects on impulsive and premeditated antisocial phenotypes.

Since serotonin cannot pass the blood-brain barrier, it is not possible (without risking brain damage) to directly measure serotonin levels in the brain. As a result, indirect ways of measuring serotonin are used. The serotonin studies discussed above all measured serotonin via a serotonin metabolite, 5-hydroxindoleacetic acid (5-HIAA). However, there are a number of studies that have measured serotonin levels through blood platelet levels. Interestingly, the studies that have examined the effects of blood serotonin levels on antisocial behaviors have, in general, found a positive relationship (Mann et al., 1992; Pliszka et al., 1988; Unis et al., 1997) To illustrate, Moffitt and her colleagues (1998) found that violence was more frequently employed by subjects with higher blood serotonin levels.

So why do 5-HIAA studies report negative associations between serotonin and antisocial behaviors, while blood platelet studies report positive associations between serotonin and antisocial behaviors? Although the precise reason(s) for these seemingly counterintuitive findings are not fully known, Rowe (2002, p. 77) provides a reasonable explanation:

> …the studies of spinal fluid measure the amount of metabolite after serotonin has been released into the synapse between nerve cells and then used. If the metabolite is low, it means that less serotonin has been available for communicating between nerve cells. The platelet serotonin studies measure the amount of serotonin still stored inside the platelet—the amount that has not yet been released for communication. Thus, if communication between cells is poor, this effect would theoretically result in *high* concentrations of serotonin stored (in neurones or platelet cells) and *low* concentrations released to be converted into a serotonin metabolite (by synapse or muscle), conceptually resolving the opposite direction of the associations found with the two assays.

Nonetheless, the findings from both 5-HIAA studies and blood platelet studies point to the very real possibility that serotonin is involved to some degree in the development of antisocial phenotypes.

A recent study also highlighted the importance of serotonin to antisocial behaviors (Crockett et al., 2008). In this study, twenty subjects were asked to fast overnight. They were then provided with drinks that contained tryptophan—a precursor to serotonin. After consuming the drink, the subjects were asked to play a game that involved splitting pots of money with another person. The next day this same process was repeated except that the subjects were administered drinks that did not contain tryptophan. On the first day, subjects rejected 67% of unfair offers, while on the second day, when they did not receive tryptophan (and presumably their serotonin levels were lower), they rejected 82% of unfair offers. These findings appear to provide some credence to hypotheses linking serotonin levels to behavioral reactions.

In addition to serotonin, dopamine is another neurotransmitter that has been linked to antisocial behaviors. Dopamine is thought to be positively related to violence, aggression, and crime. A body of research has tested this proposition and the results of these studies have produced mixed findings. Results culled from rodent studies have indicated that high levels of dopamine are associated with increased rates of physical violence. Studies employing human samples, however, have not consistently found a relationship between dopamine levels and violence. For instance, studies have found that patients who use antipsychotic drugs that are known to reduce dopamine also tend to have reductions in their violent behaviors (Brizer, 1988; Yudofsky, Silver, & Schneider, 1987). However, a meta-analysis conducted by Raine (1993) did not find evidence supporting the nexus between dopamine levels (as measured by dopamine metabolites) and aggression. Taken together, the available evidence seems to suggest that dopamine levels are only minimally related to antisocial phenotypes.

Normal Brain Function: Enzyme and Hormone Levels

Brain functioning is greatly affected by brain chemistry, including not only neurotransmitter levels, but also enzyme levels and hormone levels (Fishbein, 2001). As a result, we next review the associations between various enzymes, hormones, and human behavior.

One enzyme that has been studied quite extensively in relation to antisocial behaviors is monoamine oxidase (MAO), which is responsible for there are two main categories of hormones: sex hormones and stress hormones. The main *sex hormones* are called androgens, which are responsible for the growth and development of the male reproductive system. According to Raine (1993, p. 83): "Hormones represent biochemical substances that are secreted into the bloodstream by endocrine organs located throughout the body, including the testes (testosterone), ovary (progesterone), and pancreas (insulin)."

The predominant androgen is testosterone, produced by the male testes. The other androgens are produced mainly by the adrenal cortex (the outer substance of the adrenal glands). The ovaries, which normally secrete estrogen (a female hormone), also produce minute amounts of androgens, which necessarily results in women being exposed to much lower levels of androgens than men. *Stress hormones* include cortisol and dehydroepiaridrosterone (DHEA), both of which are produced by the adrenal glands. These stress hormones are secreted in response to stressful and life-threatening situations and they allow for reactions that increase the chances of survival.

Main Propositions of Enzyme and Hormone Studies

The following propositions concerning enzymes and hormones and aggression have been subjected to empirical testing. Scholars have posited that:

- Low levels of the MAO enzyme are related to antisocial behavior.
- High levels of androgens such as testosterone are related to antisocial behavior.
- Low levels of stress hormones such as cortisol are related to antisocial behavior.

Key Concepts of Enzyme and Hormone Studies

From the preceding propositions, the following concepts can be isolated and defined:

- Enzyme
- MAO
- Hormone
- Androgen
- Testosterone
- Stress hormone
- Cortisol

Box 5.4 defines the key concepts of enzyme and hormone studies. Scholars have used these definitions to test the main propositions of enzyme and hormone studies. The findings of these tests are discussed in the following section.

Box 5.4 Definitions of Key Concepts of Enzyme and Hormone Studies

- *Enzyme. Nominal*—chemicals that convert precursors into neurotransmitters and help break down neurotransmitters. *Operational*—

the levels of enzymes found in the brain, measured using the same techniques that are used to assess neurotransmitter levels.

- *MAO. Nominal*—an enzyme responsible for metabolizing serotonin, dopamine, and norepinephrine in the brain. *Operational*—the levels of the MAO enzyme found in the brain or in blood platelets.
- *Hormone. Nominal*—biochemical substances that are secreted into the bloodstream by endocrine organs located throughout the body. *Operational*—concentrations of hormones as measured in the blood and saliva.
- *Androgen. Nominal*—a steroid hormone that is responsible for providing the body with energy, bone density, sex drive, and so forth. *Operational*—concentrations of androgen hormones as measured in the blood and saliva.
- *Testosterone. Nominal*—a steroid hormone that is responsible for providing the body with energy, bone density, sex drive, and so forth. *Operational*—concentrations of testosterone as measured in the blood and saliva.
- *Stress hormone. Nominal*—hormones produced by the adrenal glands that are involved in stress response, allowing us to react to stressful situations in a healthy way. *Operational*—concentrations of stress hormones as measured in the blood and saliva.
- *Cortisol. Nominal*—a hormone that is secreted in response to stressful stimuli. *Operational*—concentrations of cortisol as measured in the blood and saliva.

Empirical Validity of Enzyme and Hormone Studies

One of the more established associations in the biosocial criminological literature is the inverse relationship between MAO levels and antisocial behavior (Ellis, 1991). Some of the strongest evidence indicating that MAO was involved in violence and aggression in humans came from a study conducted by Brunner et al. (1993). In this study, Brunner and his colleagues identified a Dutch kindred with 14 male family members who had a genetic mutation that prevented the production of MAO. These males acted aggressively, were physically violent, and had severe mental deficits. Through genetic analyses, Brunner et al. determined that the lack of MAO was largely responsible for the antisocial phenotypes displayed by these males. This genetic mutation is rare and thus whether the association between MAO and antisocial behaviors is generalizable to the larger population could not be answered with this single study.

A body of research has used subjects drawn from the general population to examine whether MAO levels are associated with various types of imprudent behaviors. The results of these studies have provided consistent evidence linking low MAO levels to increased involvement in misconduct. To illustrate, Alm et al. (1996) reported lower levels of the MAO enzyme in juvenile delinquents. More specifically, adolescent delinquents with low levels were nearly four times as likely to persist with their criminality into adulthood when compared to delinquents with high levels of MAO. Perhaps the strongest evidence of an association between MAO and antisocial phenotypes comes from a literature review conducted by Ellis (1991). In this review, Ellis reported that the existing studies indicated strong associations between low MAO levels and criminality, impulsivity, hyperactivity, sensation seeking, drug and alcohol use, and psychopathy. Of all the biological criminogenic risk factors, low MAO levels appears to be one of the most potent.

Unlike MAO which is an enzyme, *testosterone* is a hormone that has been tied to violence, aggression, and dominance. A commonly advanced proposition is that high levels of testosterone are thought to increase antisocial behaviors. A good deal of research has accrued to support this proposition. To illustrate, research conducted on inmates has shown that they have elevated levels of testosterone, and those inmates with higher testosterone levels tend to be the ones serving time for violent and sex crimes rather than for property crimes (e.g., Dabbs et al., 1995). Even female inmates with higher levels of testosterone have been shown to be the most aggressive (Dabbs & Hargrove, 1997). Since these findings cannot necessarily be generalized from incarcerated prisoners to the rest of the population, the research conducted on non-inmates needs to be discussed.

There is a vast amount of research that has been conducted on the general population showing an association between testosterone levels and antisocial phenotypes. In general the results of these studies have indicated that high testosterone levels early in life are related to behavioral problems. For example, Sanchez-Martin et al. (2000) studied 28 male and 20 female preschoolers and found that higher levels of testosterone in the boys were related to more aggressive play and interactions with other children. Raine et al. (1998) studied 1,130 male and female children from Mauritius (an island country in the Indian Ocean) and found that taller and heavier children at age three years were more aggressive at age 11 than shorter and smaller children. These authors speculate that taller and heavier youngsters may have higher levels of testosterone, which would account for their body size differences and for some of their aggressiveness.

Banks and Dabbs (1996) found that 29 delinquents who engaged in fighting, weapons use, and drug use had higher levels of testosterone than a con-

trol group of 36 college students. Another study of 54 men from low socioeconomic backgrounds showed a relationship between high testosterone levels and self-reported verbal and physical acts of aggression directed at their
female partners (Soler, Vinayak, & Quadagno, 2000). Testosterone levels have
been found to be related to violent crime, violations of prison rules, spouse
abuse, marital disruption, difficulties in job performance, and substance
abuse (Mazur & Booth, 1998). Not all studies of humans find relationships
between testosterone levels and aggression; some find no association (Fishbein, 2001).

In light of these findings, it should be pointed out that a recent meta-analysis reported a relatively small (mean weighted r = .14), yet statistically significant, association between testosterone levels and antisocial behaviors (Book,
Starzyk, & Quinsey, 2001). It is quite possible, however, that this effect size is
somewhat attenuated. According to Mazur and Booth (1998), testosterone
should only be related to dominance-related behaviors, not with all types of violence and aggression. Since most testosterone studies do not make the distinction between dominance and non-dominance behaviors, the true effect
size for testosterone could be artificially deflated.

Another hormone that has been found to be related to antisocial behaviors
is the *stress hormone*, cortisol. The general consensus is that since cortisol is a
stress hormone low levels should be related to increased involvement in antisocial behaviors. Low levels of cortisol would be an indicator of under arousal,
a biological marker for antisocial behaviors. There is some research supporting this hypothesis. For example, McBurnett et al. (2000) studied 38 boys between the ages of 7 and 12 years who were referred to a clinic for problem
behaviors. Low levels of salivary cortisol were related to higher amounts of aggression as determined by the parents, teachers, and peers of the children.
Studies carried out by Tennes and colleagues (Tennes & Krey, 1985; Tennes et
al., 1986) also revealed that lower levels of cortisol were associated with more
aggressive behavior directed at peers and teachers. Cortisol levels have also been
found to be inversely correlated with conduct disorder (McBurnett et al., 2000;
Pajer et al., 2001). Other studies discussed by Raine (1993) also found this link,
including studies of habitually violent incarcerated offenders (Virkkunen, 1985),
adolescents with conduct problems (Kagan, Reznick & Snidman, 1987), and
disinhibited children (Kagan, et al., 1987; McBurnett et al. 2000). Van Goozen
(2005) provides an excellent overview of the literature on the association between cortisol and antisocial behaviors and concludes that the evidence is mixed
on whether cortisol is indeed a causal contributor to antisocial behaviors. Much
more research is thus needed before any definitive conclusions can be drawn
about the true effect that cortisol has on antisocial phenotypes.

Brain Dysfunction: Abnormal Influences

At birth, even though the infant human brain is much smaller than it will be during adulthood, the structure of the brain is completely formed by around four months after conception. More specifically, at birth, the human brain only weighs about 350 to 400 grams, roughly one third of its adult weight (Chudler, 2001). The first parts of the brain to develop are the structures of the old, primitive reptilian brain, which are responsible for basic survival behaviors. The more complex regions of the brain develop later in pregnancy and some even continue to develop long after birth.

Interactions between the human brain and the environment begin almost immediately at the moment of conception. Between eight to 16 weeks after conception, over 1 million neurons grow in the brain of a fetus every five minutes. Exposure to toxins, such as alcohol, cigarettes, and other drugs, can negatively affect brain development in utero (DeCristofaro & LaGamma, 1995; Harvey & Kosofsky, 1998; Piquero & Tibbetts, 2001; Risemberg, 1989). Maternal diet and maternal exposure to stressful situations have also been shown to impede the development of the fetal brain (Muhajarine, 1996; Nehig & Debry, 1994; Lin, 1991; Phillips, Henderson, & Schenker, 1989; Saugstad, 1997).

Brain dysfunction is a term that is used to indicate some interference of normal brain functioning. Although normal brain function can lead to aggressive behavior, such as when children learn to solve their problems with aggression, brain dysfunction is likely to lead to more serious types of antisocial behavior because it represents impairments in cognition and problem solving (Moffitt, 1990, 1993, 1996; Pennington & Bennetto, 1993; Seguin et al., 1995). Problems with impulsivity, attention and concentration, problem solving, and planning for the future have all been linked to some form of brain dysfunction (Mirsky & Siegel, 1994; Robinson & Kelley, 1998). Part of the reason that brain dysfunction has been tied to antisocial phenotypes is because people with brain dysfunction likely misperceive threats or hostility when confronted with normal daily interactions, a condition known as *hostile attributional bias* (e.g., see Giancola, 1995; Hare, 1999, 2000).

Raine (1993, p. 120) added to this view when he argued that poorer comprehension and communication skills (both of which are indicators of brain dysfunction) could lead to

> misinterpretation of events and motives in an interpersonal encounter, which in turn could precipitate violence. Similarly, a child with poor linguistic skills may be less able to talk himself/herself out of trouble with parents or peers. Poor verbal abilities and communication skills

per se could contribute to peer rejection in childhood, which, in combination with other later social and situational factors, could predispose to alienation and violence. Alternatively, linguistic abnormalities
could result in verbal deficits that lead to school failure, which in turn
could predispose to later alienation and violence.

Brain dysfunction can be traced to specific locations of the brain by recognizing an individual's behavioral responses (Yeudall, 1977; Volavka, 1995). As
noted by Raine (1993, p. 108): "there are differences in the quality of functioning of different parts of the brain, that such dysfunction is in part measured
by neuropsychological tests, and that such differences may potentially predispose an individual to commit criminal and antisocial acts." For example, damage to the frontal lobe can result in reduced abilities to formulate plans, reduced
intellectual functioning involving reasoning and recognizing consequences of
actions, reduced ability to sustain concentration and focus for long-term goals,
reduced amounts of self-control, and impairments in formation of language
to regulate behavior in terms of foresight (Raine et al., 1994). Frontal lobe damage may lead to distractibility, impulsivity, irritability, lack of guilt or shame,
periodic affective disorder, and sensitivity to alcohol (Robinson & Kelley, 1999).
Those who develop *frontal lobe syndrome* will be argumentative, violent, and aggressive (Raine, 1993). Prefrontal dysfunction is also related to reduced fear
and anxiety (Raine, 1997) and other cognitive deficits (Reiss et al., 1996).

Dysfunction of the left temporal lobe is associated with disturbances in the
comprehension of written or spoken words; difficulty with language activities
such as reading, writing, spelling, and arithmetic; and problems with logical
and analytical thinking involving sequential processing of information. It is
also associated with hallucinations secondary to verbal processing abnormal-
ity. Epilepsy is also often associated with brain dysfunction. Woermann et al.
(2000) reported findings of reduced gray matter in the left frontal lobes of
some epileptics who engaged in acts of unprovoked aggression. Other research
has found that deficits in prefrontal cortex activity are related to unprovoked
violence and *antisocial personality disorder* (APD), which is characterized by de-
ceit, recklessness, irresponsibility, and a lack of remorse and empathy for others (Davidson, Putnam, & Larson, 2000; Raine et al., 1994).

If brain dysfunction is associated with antisocial phenotypes, then the main
question becomes, what factors cause the development of brain dysfunctions?
A rich line of literature has examined this issue and, as a result, numerous factors have been identified as potential causes to brain dysfunction. Although
far from exhaustive, there are at least three main sources. First, brain dysfunctions can be the result of genetic factors. Second, prenatal exposure to

toxins, especially drugs ingested by pregnant women, are likely causes of brain dysfunction. Third, postnatal head injuries (e.g., accidents) are known to produce brain dysfunctions. Collectively, the sources of brain dysfunction are multifaceted, with many of them originating from environmental stimuli.

Main Propositions of Brain Dysfunction Studies

The following propositions concerning brain dysfunction and aggression have been subjected to empirical testing. Scholars have posited that

- Brain dysfunction is associated with an increased risk of antisocial behaviors.
- Maternal drug use during pregnancy is a source of brain dysfunction.
- Exposure to environmental toxins is a source of brain dysfunction.
- Head injury is a source of brain dysfunction and antisocial behaviors.

Key Concepts of Brain Dysfunction Studies

From the preceding propositions, the following concepts can be isolated and defined:

- Brain dysfunction
- Maternal drug use during pregnancy
- Exposure to environmental toxins
- Head injury

Box 5.5 defines the key concepts of brain dysfunction studies. Scholars have used these definitions to test the main propositions of brain dysfunction studies. The findings of these tests are discussed in the following section.

Box 5.5 Definitions of Key Concepts of Brain Dysfunction Studies

- *Brain dysfunction*. *Nominal*—some interference or impairment in normal brain functioning, such as in cognition and problem solving. *Operational*—any signs of less normal brain functioning or abnormal brain functioning, as measured through angiography, EEG, CT, PET, MRI, or fMRI.
- *Maternal drug use during pregnancy*. *Nominal*—any consumption by a pregnant woman of a legal or illegal substance that can cause or create significant psychological and/or physiological changes in the body, and/or cause addiction, habituation, or a marked change in consciousness. *Operational*—any indications of drug use by a pregnant

mother, including blood tests, medical records, official reports, and
self-report studies.

- *Exposure to environmental toxins. Nominal*—being exposed to any harmful substance in the environment. *Operational*—the degree or amount
of exposure to harmful substances in the environment, as measured by
self-reports, medical records, and/or levels of environmental contami-
nants found in the blood, hair, and bones of individuals.
- *Head injury. Nominal*—any trauma to the brain. *Operational*—any
signs of less normal brain functioning or abnormal brain functioning caused by head injury, as measured through angiography, EEG,
CT, PET, MRI, fMRI, hospital records, and self-report studies.

Empirical Validity of Brain Dysfunction Studies

A large body of research has examined the association between brain functioning or brain structure and various antisocial phenotypes using the brain-
imaging techniques discussed in box 5.1. The results of these studies—most
of which have been carried out by the renowned scientist, Adrian Raine—have
provided compelling evidence linking brain structure and brain functioning
to violent, aggressive, and criminal acts. In one of the first studies to use brain-
imaging techniques to examine violent criminals, Raine and his colleagues
(1994) scanned the brains of 22 murderers and 22 matched controls who had
not committed murder. Using PET scans, they found that, in comparison with
non-murderers, the murderers had reduced activity in the prefrontal cortex. Raine
and his colleagues (1997) also conducted another study to analyze potential
differences in brain structure and brain function in 41 murderers and 41
matched controls who had not committed murder. The results of the PET
scans revealed again that the murderers had lower activity not only in the prefrontal cortex, but also in the corpus callosum and regions of the brain that are
involved in the modulation of behaviors. In addition, this study also revealed
structural brain differences between murderers and non-murderers in the
amygdala, thalamus, and medial temporal lobe.

In another landmark study, Raine et al. (1998) scanned the brains of 15
predatory murderers, nine affective murderers, and 41 non-murderers. Predatory murderers identify their murder victims, stalk them, and murder in cold
blood. Contrast this with affective murderers who murder in response to some
type of provocation. Affective murderers are often characterized as hot-tem-
pered and impulsive. Raine and his associates hypothesized that the brains of
affective murders, when compared to the brains of predatory murderers, would

have an overactive limbic system and an under-active prefrontal cortex. These brain differences would lead to intense feelings of anger and hostility (generated from the limbic system) and yet their prefrontal cortex would not be equipped to control and curtail these impulses. It takes no stretch of the imagination to realize that this scenario would be a recipe for murder. Predatory murders, however, would not have these brain abnormalities because their murders require forethought, planning, and coordination—all of which depend on the prefrontal cortex. Raine et al.'s study provided strong empirical support for their hypotheses: the brains of affective murderers had lower prefrontal cortex activity and higher limbic system activity when compared to the brains of predatory murderers.

There are also a number of studies that have found evidence of brain dysfunction in samples of psychopaths. For instance, in yet another study conducted by Raine et al. (2000), psychopaths, in comparison with non-psychopaths, were found to have an 11 percent reduction in the gray matter of the prefrontal cortex. Yang et al. (2005) also examined brain structure in a sample of 16 unsuccessful psychopaths, 13 successful psychopaths, and 23 non-psychopaths. Unsuccessful psychopaths were psychopaths who had been caught and convicted of a crime, while successful psychopaths were psychopaths who had not been caught for their criminal involvement. MRIs were used to measure the volume of gray matter in the prefrontal cortex. The results revealed that there were not any differences in gray matter between successful psychopaths and the sample of non-psychopaths. The study authors concluded that successful psychopaths had the cognitive abilities to escape detection. Other studies have found structural differences in the corpus callosum of psychopaths (Raine et al., 2003), as well as functional differences in the amygdala and hippocampus (Kiehl et al., 2001; Raine et al., 2004). Collectively, these studies provide compelling evidence that antisocial behaviors—especially those committed by habitual offenders—are partially the result of brain abnormalities.

Toxins and Brain Dysfunction

A wealth of research has examined whether exposure to certain toxins is associated with subsequent brain dysfunction. Out of this research, a number of toxins have been identified as likely being a contributor to brain dysfunction. The most commonly identified toxins are those that affect the fetus in utero. For instance, prenatal exposure to cigarette smoke, alcohol, and other drugs have been linked to brain dysfunction and, in some studies, to antisocial behaviors as well. To illustrate, Brennan, Grekin, & Mednick (1999) found that maternal smoking during the third trimester of pregnancy was associated with an increased risk of arrests in adulthood for persistent nonviolent and violent criminality (also see Chan, Keane, & Robinson, 2001; Fergusson & Horwood, 1995; Orlebeke et al.; Rasanen et al., 1999). Exposure to cigarettes in the womb has also been associated with an increased risk of conduct disorder and other behavioral problems such as drug abuse (Weissman et al., 1999). Cigarettes also contain nicotine, a stimulant that has been linked to hyperactivity in children of mothers who smoked during pregnancy (Thomas et al., 2000). Research has revealed that prenatal exposure to tobacco smoke is related to greater immaturity, impulsivity, oppositional behaviors, emotional instability, physical aggression, and early onset of criminal behavior, even after controlling for numerous criminogenic influences (Day et al., 2000; Gibson & Tibbetts, 1999). In addition, alcohol use can cause *fetal alcohol syndrome* in children and increases the likelihood of developing numerous criminogenic risk factors such as cognitive impairments, lower mental abilities, learning disabilities, and attention deficits.

Maternal drug use during pregnancy has been linked not only to low birth weight, but also to reductions in the amount of oxygen the fetus receives, perhaps leading to brain dysfunction (Holmes, 1992; also see Farrington, Ohlin, & Wilson, 1986; Hawkins, 1996; Jeffery, 1998a, 1998b; Kelley, 1997; Pallone, 1991; Pallone & Hennessy, 1993; Reiss & Ross, 1993; Tonry & Farrington, 1995; Tonry, Ohlin, & Farrington, 1991). Evidence supporting this view has mounted. For instance, prenatal exposure to cocaine has been linked to infant brain size and to problems in cognitive and behavioral development (Bateman & Chiriboga, 2000). However, since pregnant mothers who use cocaine also tend to use other substances (e.g., tobacco), it is difficult to isolate the effect of cocaine from the effects of these other substances.

Substances found in the external environment and that are not intentionally introduced via the mother (e.g., maternal cigarette smoke during pregnancy) can also affect brain functioning (Fishbein, 1998). Exposure to neurotoxins such as lead can cause neurological brain dysfunction. Every year, 3 million to 4 million preschool children suffer from lead poisoning. Most of these live in poor, inner-city neighborhoods. Because lead primarily enters the body through oral absorption, environmental contamination can occur when water pipes in older homes are allowed to corrode. Absorption of lead is also a function of diet (Lucas, Sexton, & Langenberg, 1996). Specifically, people who eat higher fat and high-calorie diets will absorb more lead. This makes children especially vulnerable to lead poisoning.

Studies indicate that lead levels in the environment are related to cognitive, learning, and attention problems in children (Loeber, 1990; Rutter & Giller, 1983), all of which are risk factors for antisocial behavior and criminality. Lead exposure has also been linked to low IQ, poor school performance, hyperactivity, impulsivity, and a low tolerance for frustration (Needleman et al., 1990). Tuthill (1996) examined hair samples from 277 first graders and found that children with the highest levels of lead were the most likely to demonstrate symptoms of ADHD as reported by teachers and doctors. Needleman et al. (1996) used X-ray fluorescence to study total lead accumulation in the bone density of 212 boys between the ages of 7 and 11 years and found that higher levels of lead accumulation were related to teacher and parent evaluations of aggression, as well as self-reported acts of delinquency. Controlling for socioeconomic status and child rearing practices, the children with higher lead levels showed more signs of anxiety, depression, and attention deficits. Another study (Needleman, 2000) reported higher bone lead levels in 216 delinquents than in 201 controls.

Thee association between lead and antisocial behaviors has also been detected at aggregate levels of analysis. To illustrate, Masters (1997) found that high levels of lead and manganese pollution were highly related to crime rates throughout the United States. Finally, in another study, Nevin (2000) correlated declining lead levels in the United States with improving IQ levels and declining rates of murder and unwed pregnancies.

But perhaps the most compelling evidence linking lead to antisocial behaviors comes from a recent study conducted by Wright and his colleagues (2008). This team of researchers measured prenatal lead levels in a sample of 250 pregnant females. The children of these mothers were then followed longitudinally and information about their criminal involvement was tracked. Once the children were young adults, Wright et al. tested to see if there was an association between prenatal lead levels and criminal arrests. The results of this study indicated that prenatal lead levels were significantly associated with total number of arrests, even after controlling for other environmental variables, such as poverty.

In addition to lead, another potential environmental source of brain dysfunction is pollution emitted by corporations and pesticides. According to the Boston Physicians for Social Responsibility (2000), approximately 1 billion pounds of pollution are released by U.S. industry annually. One pollutant found in gas is MMT (an additive containing manganese). Higher levels of manganese have been found in the hair of violent criminals (Masters, Hone, & Doshi, 1997). Exposure to pesticides is another major source of brain dysfunction, as nearly 100,000 children are poisoned per year. Exposure produces disruption of hormones and brain damage (Weiss, 1997) and can lead to conditions such as irritability and learning problems (Porter, Jaeger, & Carlson, 1999). Some organophosphate chemicals are found in higher levels in housing facilities in the nation's inner cities and can affect children even before they are born (Landrigan et al., 1999).

Traumatic Brain Injury and Brain Dysfunction

In some instances, traumatic brain injury (TBI) can produce brain dysfunction and TBI has also been tied to antisocial behaviors. According to the Center for Disease Control, 1.4 million US residents sustain traumatic brain injuries each year; 50,000 of them die, 235,000 are admitted to the hospital, and 1.1 million are treated and released from the emergency room. TBI arises from numerous sources including vehicular accidents, falls, acts of violence, and sports injuries, and is most common in males aged 15 to 24 years.

There is a logical link between TBI and antisocial behavior:

> Although TBI may result in physical impairment, the more problematic consequences involve the individual's cognition, emotional functioning, and behavior, which can affect interpersonal relationships, school, and work ... consequences of TBI often influence human functions along a continuum from altered physiological functions of cells through neurological and psychological impairments, to medical problems and disabilities that affect the individual with TBI, as well as the family, friends, community, and society in general. (AMA, 1999)

This statement, crafted by scores of scientists after reviewing thousands of contemporary research studies on TBI, provides strength to the assertion of the integrated systems approach. In this case, TBI has effects on all levels of analysis, from cell to society.

The AMA also links numerous other problems to TBI, including

> a myriad of functioning problems ... memory impairment and difficulties in attention and concentration ... [and] (d)eficits in language use and visual perception. Frontal lobe functions, such as the executive skills of problem solving, abstract reasoning, insight, judgment, planning, information processing, and organization, are vulnerable to TBI ... Common behavioral deficits include decreased ability to initiate responses, verbal and physical aggression, agitation, learning disabilities, shallow self-awareness, altered sexual functioning, impulsivity, and social disinhibition. Mood disorders, personality changes, altered emotional control, depression, and anxiety are also prevalent after TBI.

Consider these tremendous consequences in the context of human brain development. The human brain continually adapts even after birth, in essence remaking itself with new experiences. By age 2, the brain weighs over three fourths of its adult weight (Chudler, 2001). Although human infants have their neurons in place at birth, baby brains are immature since the connections between neurons are not fully established. Brain damage to adults is traumatic and severe because once an adult brain cell is killed, it does not regenerate.

Brain damage in children is different since the branching fibers of children (axons and dendrites) continue to grow and make new connections with new experiences. As estimated by Luiselli et al. (2000), more than 15,000 children suffer TBI annually in the United States. Injury to infants and children can lead to difficulty in learning. It has been related to behavior impairments, impulsivity, and nonresponsiveness to punishment (Anderson et al., 1999). Children with head injuries tend to have a here-and-now orientation and often have problems learning or understanding the future consequences of their actions (Bechara et al., 1999). Varga-Khadem, Cowan, & Mishkin (2000) found that childhood head injury was associated with reductions in intelligence, attention, and cognition. TBI can also lead to relationship problems, including difficulties making and sustaining friendship networks.

It is also important to point out that there is a close nexus between alcohol and drug use and TBI, as roughly 50% of TBIs are associated with alcohol use. Another 20% are caused by violence-related incidents, half of which involve firearms. In the very young, physical abuse and assaults contribute to TBI. These research findings illustrate a two-way relationship—TBI contributes to violent behavior and violent behavior leads to further TBI.

One of the most widely known case studies involving TBI, brain dysfunction, and antisocial behavior is that of Phineas Gage (Harlow, 1848), who was a dynamite worker for the Great Western Railway. Gage experienced an accident in which an iron tamping rod was blown through his lower cheek and upper forehead. Gage survived this accident but suffered devastating personality changes. Prior to the accident Gage was a responsible worker and family man without a history of antisocial behavior. After the accident he became very impulsive, profane, and antisocial. Remarkably, Gage's skull was preserved and thus contemporary researchers have been able to identify the precise regions of the brain that were affected (see figure 5.4). Specifically, the left frontal lobe of the brain was severely damaged, an area of the brain that has specifically been linked to violent and aggressive behavior (Carlson, 1994; Damasio et al., 1990; Jeffery, 1990; Raine, 1993; Robinson & Kelley, 1999).

Figure 5.4 The Skull of Phineas Gage

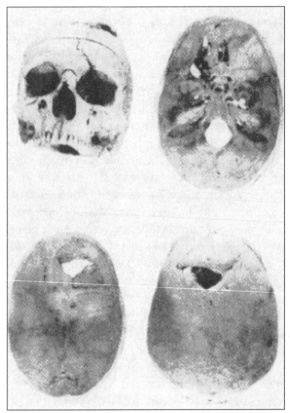

Source: "The Amazing Case of Phineas Gage" [On-line]. Available: *http://www.epub.org. br/cm/no2/historia/phineas.htm*

Evaluation of Organ Level Explanations

In the following sections, we discuss important criteria for evaluating research on the brain, including the scope of the research, the clarity of concepts, and the logical adequacy of the propositions. The relative empirical validity of each area of brain research was discussed earlier.

Scope

The research reviewed above seems to point to the conclusion that serious, violent criminal acts are tied to abnormal neurotransmitter, enzyme, and hormone levels, and to brain dysfunction. As noted by Raine (1993, p. 124), the "general belief in the literature [is] that neuropsychological dysfunction may be more associated with more serious violent offending." Specifically, studies have verified that conduct-disordered behaviors of children, delinquent acts of adolescents, and violent repetitive criminal acts of adults are all explained by these biological risk factors. Left hemisphere brain dysfunction may also lead to impairments in verbal IQ, while right hemisphere dysfunction may lead to performance IQ deficits. Brain imaging studies also suggest that frontal dysfunction is related to violent offending, while temporal dysfunction is related to sexual offending of pedophiles and violent sexual assaulters.

Very little research has been conducted with regard to the role of the brain in white-collar and corporate crimes. In fact, we are aware of no studies that have directly assessed this issue. Although purely speculative, it is possible that brain dysfunction is not associated with white-collar and corporate crime because people who suffer from TBI tend to be at a significant disadvantage when it comes to succeeding through legitimate means such as work (which is where a great deal of white-collar and corporate crime occurs). However, it is likely that there are many people in positions of power who commit various types of antisocial behaviors that are influenced by neurotransmitter systems. But, because of their positions of power, they are far less likely to come to the attention of the justice system.

Conceptual Clarity

Although the concepts of brain studies are easy to understand, differences among neurotransmitters, hormones, enzymes, and other chemicals in the brain and body are frequently difficult to comprehend. Similarly, operational definitions are not always easy to understand, in part because the major factors at the organ level of analysis are measured in various ways.

Propositions

Despite claims from some scholars that biology has no place in theoretical criminology, the organ level propositions are some of the most testable theoretical predictions. Although they may be technical and require some expertise in the biological sciences, they are not tautological and they do not lead to circular reasoning. As with propositions dealing with genes and behavior, organ level propositions allow—in fact require—scholars to take into account environmental factors. Scholars who conduct brain imaging studies often couch their findings in an integrated model such as the one that is being advocated in this book. To illustrate, Raine (1993, p. 153) advised his readers to view findings from brain studies from a "heuristic standpoint," one that sees brain function and dysfunction only as predispositions that require "other environmental, psychological, and social factors to enhance or diminish this biological predisposition ... it is [also] important to emphasize that the cause of [brain] dysfunction could be environmental as well as biological or genetic." Criminologists should begin to think from an interdisciplinary perspective so that *all* relevant criminogenic factors can be identified and studied in unison as opposed to in isolation (Fishbein, 2001, p. 85).

As argued in this chapter, many of the sources of brain dysfunction come from normal, daily life. Fishbein (2001, p. 64) captured environmental effects on the brain when she stated that "Social, economic and physical deprivation, poverty, traumatic stress, family dysfunction, prenatal drug exposures, and other negative childhood experiences and environmental conditions all have a profound impact on brain function." For example, levels of neurotransmitters such as serotonin are affected by environmental factors such as stress, socioeconomic status, and parenting styles (Field et al., 1998; Pine et al., 1996, 1997). In chapter 7, we discuss the importance of groups for determining behavior, including the role of the family in early childhood development.

Some people, by way of their race and class at birth, are more likely to be exposed to the harmful conditions that produce brain dysfunction. Criminological theories such as social disorganization or differential social organization (discussed in chapter 8), plus cultural deviance or subcultural theories (discussed in chapter 9), would be strengthened if they accounted for how social and physical environmental conditions affected the brains of individuals living there.

Other Organ Level Factors

There are other factors aside from brain function and dysfunction that may be placed at the organ level of analysis. For example, there is growing evidence that heart rate and skin conductance measures are related to antisocial behavior. Since heart rate and skin conductance are indicators of autonomic nervous system (ANS) activity, we discuss these factors in chapter 6 (organism level of analysis)

Summary

In this chapter, we examined relationships between organ level factors and antisocial behavior. The brain is the main organ of behavior. It is part of the central nervous system and is responsible for all emotion and behavior. All environmental factors pass through the brain prior to impacting behavior. The main advantage of the brain is that is measurable and therefore non-mentalistic. The brain results from genetic-environmental interaction, meaning genetics and environmental factors are important for understanding brain function and dysfunction.

The main lobes of the brain are the frontal, parietal, occipital and temporal lobes, each with its own unique functions. The frontal and temporal lobes are the most important for understanding criminality. Underactive frontal and overactive temporal lobes tend to produce aggressive behavior.

Neurons are nerve cells located in the central nervous system. They conduct electrical impulses that cause the release of neurotransmitters in the brain. Such neurotransmitters are related to various outcomes, including impulsivity, hyperactivity, depression, suicide, violence, and criminality.

Evidence also shows that enzymes and hormones affect antisocial behaviors. For example, higher levels of testosterone are associated with an increased risk of aggression and dominating behaviors, as well as violence, sex crimes, and drug abuse. Lower levels of cortisol are related to an increased risk of impulsivity, hyperactivity, sensation-seeking, psychopathy, drug abuse, juvenile delinquency, and criminality. Research presented in this chapter also indicate that genes influence neurotransmitter levels, but so do environmental conditions such as stress, diet, drug use and abuse, and pollution. Enzymes, especially MAO, which are responsible for cleaning up neurotransmitters in the brain, also affect neurotransmitter levels. Drug use and abuse, poor diet/nutrition, abuse/neglect, head injuries, exposure to environmental pollution, and exposure to toxins in utero are all known contributors to brain dysfunction. Exposure to toxins such as lead produces attention deficits, lowered IQs, learning disabilities, and personality changes. The many effects of brain dysfunction include learning disabilities and cognitive deficits, school failure, attention deficits, personality changes, unemployment and poverty, drug use and abuse, and antisocial behavior, including serious violence.

Discussion Questions

1. What is an organ?
2. What is the brain? How do scientists measure the brain?
3. What does it mean that all of our experiences are perceived in the brain?
4. Identify the four lobes of the human brain. What are the main functions attributed to each lobe of the brain?

5. What is a neuron?
6. What is a neurotransmitter?
7. The effects of neurotransmitters on behavior depend on what factors?
8. What factors have effects on neurotransmitter levels in the brain?
9. List and discuss the main propositions about neurotransmitters and behavior.
10. What types of behaviors appear to be affected by neurotransmitter levels?
11. What are enzymes?
12. What are hormones?
13. List and discuss the main propositions about enzymes, hormones, and behavior.
14. What types of behaviors appear to be affected by levels of enzymes and hormones?
15. Discuss the condition of conduct disorder. Can this disorder explain why children misbehave? Explain.
16. What is brain dysfunction? Identify and discuss its main causes.
17. List and discuss the main propositions about brain dysfunction and behavior.
18. What types of behaviors appear to be affected by brain dysfunction?
19. Discuss the case of Phineas Gage. Were his behavioral changes caused by his brain injury? Explain.
20. Are the concepts of organ level explanations of crime clearly defined? Explain.
21. What is the logical adequacy of organ level explanations of crime?
22. What is the scope of organ level explanations of crime?

6

Organism Level Explanations of Crime

Introduction

This chapter deals with factors at the individual-level that have been found to be related to antisocial behaviors. Individuals are made up of cells (chapter 4) and organs (chapter 5), and comprise groups (chapter 7), communities and organizations (chapter 8), and societies (chapter 9). Factors at the individual-level of analysis include things that are unique to individual people, such as personality traits, intelligence levels, mental illness, diet and nutrition, and drug consumption. With respect to personality, we examine the claim that there are certain personality types that are associated with the odds of breaking the law. We review the evidence that intelligence is related to behavior and we also review the research bearing on whether there is an association between mental illness and antisocial behavior and criminality. Finally, we explore relationships between behavior and diet/nutrition and drug use/abuse.

Behavior in the Context of the Individual

Every living thing on this planet is an organism or individual. According to *Merriam-Webster's Collegiate Dictionary* (2009), an organism is "a complex structure of interdependent and subordinate elements whose relations and properties are largely determined by their function in the whole; an *individual* constituted to carry on the activities of life by means of organs separate in function but mutually dependent [or] a living being" (emphasis added). From this definition, it is clear that the term *organism* is synonymous with *individual*. As discussed in chapter 3, an individual is a living organism that is comprised of organs, which are made up of cells. The definition of individual, according to *Merriam-Webster's*, is: "of, relating to, or distinctively associated with an individual; being an individual or existing as an indivisible whole; existing as a distinct entity; having marked individuality." The term *individuality* means the "total character peculiar to and distinguishing an individual from others [or] personality." In this chapter, we show how individual characteristics are related to the development of antisocial behaviors. Given the weight of the evidence, we begin with the effects of personality on behavior.

Personality Traits

Merriam-Webster's Collegiate Dictionary (2009) defines *personality* as "the quality or state of being a person; the complex of characteristics that distinguishes an individual or a nation or group; especially the totality of an individual's behavioral and emotional characteristics." It is closely related to disposition, temperament, temper, and character: "personality means the dominant quality or qualities distinguishing a person or group" whereas *disposition* "implies [one's] customary moods and attitude toward the life around one." The term *temperament* "implies a pattern of innate characteristics associated with one's specific physical and nervous organization" whereas *temper* is "the qualities acquired through experience that determine how a person or group meets difficulties or handles situations." *Character* is "the aggregate of moral qualities by which a person is judged apart from intelligence, competence, or special talents."

If we combine these definitions into one, personality can be thought of as the "aggregate of qualities that distinguish one as a person." According to Vold, Bernard, and Snipes (1998, p. 88), personality is "the complex set of emotional and behavioral attributes that tend to remain relatively constant as the individual moves from situation to situation." So, for the purposes of this chapter, personality can be conceptualized to include disposition or temperament (which is mostly innate or inborn) and character (which is acquired primarily through culture and through learning). In this chapter, personality research will be divided into two main areas: personality inventories which chronicle the existence of certain personality traits (e.g., impulsivity), and antisocial personality disorder.

Personality Inventories

Some criminologists assert that personality traits (such as low self-control) explain antisocial, criminal, and delinquent behavior (e.g., see Caspi et al., 1994). Perhaps the most widely known personality inventory is the one set forth by Eysenck (1977) that highlighted the traits of *extroversion, neuroticism,* and *psychoticism.* An *extroverted* person tends to be outgoing, adept in social situations, and willing to take risks. A *neurotic* person suffers from chronic anxiety and worry. Finally, a *psychotic* person may be suffering from delusions and may be angry and violent. Similar to Gottfredson and Hirschi's (1990) notion of low self-control, Zuckerman (1987) proposed the personality trait *P-Imp-USS,* characterized by impulsivity, aggressiveness, and lack of social responsibility. These personality traits have consistently been claimed to be important sources of criminality, along with many others posited by psychologists and criminologists, including but not limited to *antisocial personality, psychopathy, negative emotionality, lack of social perspective taking, low empathy, impulsivity, thrill seeking, egoism or selfishness, weak constraint or low self-control, machismo, negative self-feelings, anxiety, anger, hostility, irritability, anger or bad temper, amorality, lack of social responsibility, narcissism, sadism,* and so on. The research is clear that antisocial populations typically are characterized by multiple, co-occurring personality traits, a phenomenon known as *comorbidity* (e.g., Rasmussen, Storsaeter, & Levander, 1999).

Antisocial Personality Disorder

Antisocial personality disorder (APD) is a condition identified by the American Psychological Association (APA) in its *Diagnostic and Statistical Manual of Mental Disorders* (DSM-IV-TR). The APA defines the disorder as a "pervasive pattern of disregard for, and violation of, the rights of others that begins in childhood or early adolescence and comes into adulthood" (p. 645). It is thought to be present when a person shows three or more of the following symptoms:

- Repeated violations of the law that are grounds for arrest
- Repeated lying, use of aliases, or conning others for personal profit or pleasure

- Impulsivity or failure to plan ahead
- Repeated physical fights or assaults
- Repeated failure to sustain consistent work behavior or honor financial obligations
- Lack of remorse

To be diagnosed with APD, the conditions must not only be present, they must be persistent and maladaptive, and cause major impairment. As we will discuss later, these personality traits have been strongly linked to antisocial behaviors. At this point, however, it is also important to point out that the way an individual behaves is not only due to personality traits, but also to the state of the nervous systems, a fact that is usually ignored by criminologists.

Box 6.1 The Autonomic Nervous System

According to the *Gale Encyclopedia of Psychology* (2001), the human nervous system consists of two main structures: the central nervous system (CNS) and the peripheral nervous system (PNS). The CNS includes the brain and the spinal cord, while the PNS includes the sense organs and the nerves linking theses sense organs, muscles, and glands to the CNS. The PNS is further subdivided into the autonomic nervous system (ANS), which controls automatic bodily processes, and the somatic nervous system (SNS), which is responsible for intentional movement of the muscles. According to Chudler (2001), the ANS is part of the larger PNS. It regulates the insides of the body, including the heart, stomach, and intestines, as well as other organs and muscles. The ANS functions in an involuntary, reflexive manner, meaning that it operates automatically without our influence. The ANS is critically important in two situations: (1) those emergency situations that cause stress and require us to *fight* or take *flight*; and (2) those nonemergency situations that allow us to *rest* and *digest*.

The ANS controls muscles in the skin, in the eye, in the stomach, in the intestines and bladder, and in the heart and it also regulates glands. There are three parts of the ANS: (1) the sympathetic nervous system, (2) the parasympathetic nervous system, and (3) the enteric nervous system. The sympathetic nervous system initiates the "fight or flight" response when a person is confronted with a stressful situation, causing heart rate and blood pressure to increase. The parasympathetic nervous system allows the body to save energy when relaxing—for example, when you have eaten a large meal and are sitting in front of the television letting your food digest. The enteric nervous system regulates the normal activity of the digestive system and prepares it for the future.

As explained by Streeten (2001), the somatic part of the nervous system works by conveying messages from our sensory organs to the sensory portions of our brains, where impulses reach our awareness. The motor components of the brain then transmit impulses to the skeletal muscles that permit voluntary control of movements. The ANS sends sensory impulses from the blood vessels, the heart, and other organs through nerves to other parts of the brain (mainly the medulla, pons, and hypothalamus). These impulses control automatic or reflex responses through the efferent autonomic nerves, creating reactions of our organs to the outside world.

ANS nerves send messages to the organs by releasing transmitter substances. According to Streeten (2001), the most important of these transmitters are acetylcholine (ACh) and norepinephrine (NE), each of which was discussed in chapter 5:

> Situations such as emotional excitement, fear, apprehension, psychic distress, panic reactions, sexual activity and fight-or-flight stimuli probably activate many parts of the sympathetic nervous systems ... It is evident, therefore, that while we are not constantly aware of the activity of the autonomic nervous system as we are of unusual sensory and motor events, the normal functioning of the autonomic nervous system day and night, from heart-beat to heart-beat, plays a largely unconscious but vital role in our livelihood.

How does the ANS relate to behavior of individuals, especially with regard to antisocial behaviors? Some criminologists reason that how the ANS reacts to stress explains why some individuals are more likely to commit antisocial behaviors. According to McEwen and Krahn (1999), experiences of stress activate adaptive responses, meaning that the body responds to stress normally through the ANS to help overcome it:

> Stress can prematurely age us and leave us chronically fatigued or depressed. When exposure to stress—whether from a traumatic event to just the daily hassle of rush hour traffic or too much email—disrupts the body's internal balance (homeostasis), it can go one of three general ways: the body can regain its normal equilibrium once the stress has passed or it can become stuck in an over- or under-aroused state. How a person copes with stress—by reaching for a beer or cigarette as opposed to heading to the gym—also plays a big role in the impact stress will have on our bodies.

Criminality is also a potential response to stress, as posited by other theories including general strain theory (discussed in chapter 9).

Stress activates the ANS, which stimulates the output of two hormones, cortisol from the adrenal cortex and adrenaline from the adrenal medulla (the brain is discussed in chapter 5). Humans cope with stress with the assistance of these two hormones and the activity of the ANS. According to McEwen and Krahn (1999)

> the ANS and the adrenalin keep us alert by increasing our heart rate and blood pressure and quickly mobilizing energy reserves. In contrast, cortisol works more slowly, helps replenish energy supplies and, at the same time, helps us to remember important things ... The elevation of ANS activity, combined with hyperglycemia and too much insulin can result in heart disease and other harms. Chronic stress is believed to interfere with our ability to remember information by impairing and killing nerve cells in the hippocampus, a region of the brain that is important for spatial and verbal memory ... Individuals may differ in their health and well being because they differ in behavioral and neuroendocrine adaptive mechanisms, that is, the ways in which their hormone and nervous systems react. You might, compared to a friend, have higher or lower allostatic load, not only because you are subjected to different degrees of life stressors but because you are "wired" differently and have had different life experiences that make you react in different ways.

This is where the criminological literature is lacking. Science shows that the ANS is always active, working to maintain normal internal functioning; studies suggest that individuals with an underactive ANS (suggesting a state of hypoarousal) are more prone to antisocial behavior (Raine, 1993). Because the ANS is involved in conditioning—for example, anticipating punishment when considering committing crimes—findings of an underactive ANS would suggest a lower level of conditioning among offenders. If present in childhood, this would make parenting more difficult as it would be harder to socialize a child (Eysenck, 1964; Mednick & Christiansen, 1977). Studies of social learning and social control (discussed in chapter 7) do not consider such individual level factors as ANS functioning. Later in the chapter, we discuss in detail studies testing the effects of the ANS on behavior.

Key Propositions of Tests of Personality

From the earlier discussion of personality and crime, the following propositions have been tested:

- Certain personality traits are more likely to characterize people who commit antisocial behaviors, including crime and delinquency.

- Antisocial populations tend to exhibit slow ANS activity.

Key Concepts of Tests of Personality

From the preceding propositions, the following concepts can be isolated and defined:

- Personality traits
- Slow ANS activity
- Delinquency
- Criminality
- Antisocial behavior
- Antisocial populations

Box 6.2 defines the key concepts of personality studies. Scholars have used these definitions to test the key propositions of tests of personality. The findings of these tests are discussed in the following section.

Box 6.2 Definitions of Key Concepts of Personality Studies

- *Personality traits. Nominal*—the way an individual normally feels, thinks, and behaves. *Operational*—indicators of the way an individual reports he or she normally feels, thinks, and behaves. Typically measured using a number of personality tests that assess traits such as impulsivity, negative emotionality, the ability to empathize, and others.
- *Slow ANS activity. Nominal*—an underactive autonomic nervous system. *Operational*—evidence of an underactive autonomic nervous system, inferred from low skin conductance (SC) activity, low heart rate (HR) activity, and/or low event-related potential (ERP) activity.
- *Delinquency. Nominal*—acts committed by juveniles that, if committed by adults, would be considered crimes by the criminal justice system. *Operational*—usually measured by official indicators such as arrests and adjudication of guilt in a court, also measured by self-report data and reports of observations of behaviors by parents and teachers.
- *Criminality. Nominal*—committing any act that violates the criminal law. *Operational*—the number of times a person is arrested, is convicted in court for a violation of the criminal law, and/or self-reports violating the law.
- *Antisocial behavior. Nominal*—any behaviors that conflict with the prevailing norms of society and/or that are viewed as abnormal. *Op-*

erational—any form of behavior defined as antisocial, measured by official crime reports, self-reported behaviors, or evaluations from others.

- *Antisocial populations. Nominal*—a group of people that engage in behaviors considered to be abnormal or deviant. *Operational*—a group of people that engage in behaviors considered to be abnormal or deviant, typically identified through official data sources such as courts, correctional facilities, or treatment centers.

Empirical Validity of Tests of Personality

A wealth of research has examined the association between myriad personality traits and different measures of antisocial phenotypes. The results of these studies have provided strong empirical evidence linking certain personality traits to violence, aggression, crime, and delinquency. The main problem with summarizing this line of research—at least exhaustively—is that there are literally mounds of personality traits that have been identified as contributing to antisocial phenotypes. As a result, we focus on those personality traits that have been the most consistently associated with antisocial phenotypes. Again, we want to underscore the point that the following review of the research is not meant to be exhaustive, but rather will highlight those personality traits that are robust and powerful predictors of antisocial behaviors.

Some of the earliest criminological research exploring the nexus between personality and antisocial behavior came from research carried out by Sheldon and Eleanor Glueck. Their studies compared 500 officially recognized delinquents with 500 non-delinquents. The results of their research were highly influential in showing that a range of personality traits were more prevalent in the delinquents than in the non-delinquents. For example, the Glueck's (1950, p. 275) summarized their research by stating

> On the whole, delinquents are more extroverted, vivacious, impulsive, and less self-controlled than the non-delinquents. They are more hostile, resentful, defiant, suspicious, and destructive. They are less fearful of failure or defeat than the non-delinquents. They are less concerned about meeting conventional expectations, and are more ambivalent toward or far less submissive to authority. They are, as a group, more socially assertive. To a greater extent than the control group, they express feelings of not being recognized or appreciated. (p. 275)

Since the publication of the Glueck's book in the 1950s, criminologists and psychologists have identified other personality traits that are thought to be causally related to criminal and offending behaviors. Of all the personality traits examined, those relating to *self-regulation*, such as *impulsivity* and *low self-control*, have been found to be among the most predictive of criminal involvement (Farrington, 1993; Pratt & Cullen, 2000). These types of personality traits refer to behaving without considering potential future consequences; they are motivated mainly by concerns of pleasure and reward and discount or lack of consideration for the ramifications of their behaviors.

Impulsive individuals are typically not controlled by families or peers or any other societal influences (in chapter 7 we examine the association between impulsivity and social groups). For example, Pratt and Cullen (2000) conducted a meta-analysis of studies that had examined the association between levels of self-control and antisocial behaviors. The results of this meta-analysis revealed that one of the strongest predictors of crime was low levels of self-control. Similarly, another meta-analysis indicated a consistent association between attention deficit hyperactivity disorder (ADHD)—a disorder that overlaps considerably with self-control—and crime and delinquency (Pratt et al., 2002). And still another meta-analysis indicated that problems with self-regulation were significant predictors of persistent sexual offending (Hanson & Morton-Bourgon, 2005). Collectively, the results of these meta-analyses, along with those generated from other studies, point to the inescapable conclusion that problems with self-regulation are very potent predictors of antisocial conduct (Agnew, Brezina, Wright, & Cullen, 2002; Ratchford & Beaver, 2009).

There is also an abundance of research showing that people who commit acts of antisocial behavior regularly exhibit other personality traits besides those associated with poor self-regulation. Some of the richest information about these personality traits comes from a meta-analysis carried out by Miller and Lynam (2001). In this meta-analysis, the authors analyzed fifty studies that had tested for an association between a wealth of personality traits and antisocial behaviors. The results of their study indicated that the following personality traits were significantly associated with antisocial behavior: *neuroticism, agreeableness, conscientiousness, psychoticism, negative emotionality, constraint, novelty seeking, reward dependence, self-directedness, and cooperativeness.* Clearly, personality traits are highly implicated in the etiology of crime and delinquency; unfortunately, most mainstream criminological theories fail to take into account these different personality traits.

One important personality characteristic in the development of antisocial behaviors is *empathy.* Broadly speaking, empathy refers to a person's ability to relate and understand another person's situation. It seems rather common-sensical to think that persons who lack empathy would be more criminal. And, a line or research has found strong empirical evidence to support this hypothesis. Jolliffe and Farrington (2004), for instance, conducted a meta-analysis of studies that had examined the association between empathy and offending behaviors. After analyzing the results of 35 studies, they found that there was a relatively strong and statistically significant association between cognitive empathy and antisocial behavior. Moreover, they reported that the effect of empathy was strong for violent offenders, but much weaker for sexual offenders. The evidence garnered from this meta-analysis thus points to the likelihood that empathy is related to certain types of offenses and certain types of offenders.

Another personality factor that seems to be related to criminal involvement is what might be called *promiscuity*. Ellis and Walsh (2000) reviewed dozens of studies and found a positive relationship between number of sexual partners and criminality and antisocial behavior. Additionally, early sexual activity tends to be associated with greater involvement in antisocial and criminal behavior. It is possible that active and early sexual behavior is generated by the same traits that produce antisocial behavior and criminality—impulsiveness, deceitfulness, hedonism, machismo, and so forth. A recent genetic study also suggests that the covariation between sexual promiscuity and criminal involvement may be the result of shared genetic factors (Beaver, Wright, & Walsh, 2008). More specifically, there is some evidence that a polymorphism in the DAT gene (see chapter 4) may explain variation in antisocial behaviors and in sexual involvement. If that is the case, then part of the reason for the strong association between the promiscuity and crime might be because they share a common origin—that is, shared genetic factors.

A clinical diagnosis of *antisocial personality disorder* has also been shown to have a strong association with criminal and delinquent involvement. For example, in a comprehensive review of the major crime correlates, Andrews and Bonta (2006) identified antisocial personality disorder as one of the most robust and consistent predictors of antisocial behaviors. Additionally, a meta-analysis indicated that antisocial personality disorder is a significant predictor of persistent sexual offending (Hanson & Morton-Bourgon, 2005), while another meta-analysis found that antisocial personality disorder was one of the strongest predictors of delinquent involvement for females (Hubbard & Pratt, 2002). That the effect of antisocial personality disorder is found for males and females as well as various types of offender is testimony of the importance that role that it plays in the etiology of antisocial behaviors.

One of the most exhaustive and methodologically rigorous tests of the association between crime and personality traits was conducted by Caspi et al.

(1994). They assessed personality traits in a cohort of 1,037 individuals born in Dunedin, New Zealand, between April 1, 1972, and March 31, 1973, and 508 randomly selected fourth-grade boys in public schools in Pittsburgh, Pennsylvania. Box 6.3 outlines the measures used in each study and contains the main findings.

Box 6.3 A Test of Personality Traits and Crime

Dunedin Sample (n = 1,037)

Measures (Independent Variables)
  Multidimensional Personality Questionnaire (self-report personality instrument with 177 items and yielding 10 scales)
  Scales—(definitions are for people who score high on the scale)
  Traditionalism—Desires conservative social environment, endorses high moral standards.
  Harm avoidance—Avoids excitement and danger; prefers safe activities even if tedious.
  Control—Reflective, cautious, careful, rational, planning.
  Aggression—Hurts others for own advantage, will frighten and cause discomfort in others.
  Alienation—Feels mistreated, victimized, betrayed, and the target of false rumors.
  Stress reaction—Nervous, vulnerable, sensitive, prone to worry.
  Achievement—Works hard, enjoys demanding projects and working long hours.
  Social potency—Forceful and decisive, fond of influencing others, leadership roles.
  Well-being—Has a happy, cheerful disposition, feels good about self and sees a bright future.
  Social closeness—Sociable, likes people and turns to others for comfort.
  Higher Order Scales—Combines previous scales into new categories.
  Constraint—Combination of traditionalism, harm avoidance, and control scales (high constraint individuals endorse conventional social norms, avoid thrills, and act cautiously).
  Negative emotionality—Combination of aggression, alienation, and stress reaction scales (high negative emotionality individuals more easily experience negative emotions such as fear, anxiety, and anger, and break down under stress).
  Positive emotionality—Combination of achievement, social potency, well-being, and social closeness scales (high positive emotionality in-

dividuals more easily experience positive emotions, more easily become engaged in social groups and work, and view life as pleasurable).

Key Findings Aggression, alienation, stress reaction, and social potency scales are positively related, and traditionalism, harm avoidance, and control scales are negatively related to self-reported delinquency over past 12 months.

In either boys or girls, aggression, alienation, and stress reaction scales are positively related, and traditionalism and control scales are negatively related to informant reports of delinquency during past 12 months (at age 18 years).

In either boys or girls, aggression and alienation scales are positively related, and traditionalism and control scales are negatively related to official crime reports of delinquency between ages 10 and 16 years (police contacts) and up until age 18 years (court convictions).

Pittsburgh sample (n = 430 boys)

Measures (Independent Variables)

Child Behavior Checklist and supplemental delinquency inventory (self-report personality instrument)

"Common language version" of *California Child Q-sort* (contains 100 statements describing range of personality attributes, administered to teachers and primary caregivers).

Parents completed the "Parent Report Form" and teachers completed the "Teacher Report Form" (both are complementary versions of the Child Behavior Checklist).

Researchers constructed personality variables and used criterion scoring approach to assess differences in *constraint, negative emotionality,* and *positive emotionality* between boys across six levels of offending.

Key Findings Across all three data sources, negative emotionality is positively correlated with delinquency among African American and Caucasian boys over past 6 months and constraint is negatively correlated with delinquency among African American and Caucasian boys over past 6 months.

Source: Caspi, A., Moffitt, T., Silva, P., & Krueger, R. (1994). Are some people crime-prone? Replications of the personality-crime relationship across countries, genders, races, and methods. *Criminology, 32*(2): 55–68.

From this research, Caspi et al. (1994, p. 185) concluded that "individual differences in personality are correlated consistently with delinquency ... the same pattern of personality correlations was repeated consistently." Caspi et al. (1994, p. 186) also concluded that some criminological theories (such as the theory of low self-control discussed in chapter 7) are simplistic because: "Crime-proneness is defined not by a single tendency (such as low self-control or impulsivity) but by multiple psychological components" such as "high negative emotionality and by low constraint." If this is true, it means that more serious delinquents would tend to be characterized by "aversive affective states such as anger, anxiety, and irritability." They would tend to "construe events in a biased way, perceiving threat in the acts of others and menace in the vicissitudes of everyday life." Juveniles with weak constraint—that is "great difficulty in modulating impulses"—would be most likely to commit acts of delinquency because of aversive affective states.

One of the more significant issues for Caspi et al. and for other researchers exploring the effects of personality centers on the causes of personality factors. In general, there are two different perspectives. On the one hand, dominant theories, such as Gottfredson and Hirschi's (1990) theory, focuses on social factors, especially family environments, as the main force involved in sculpting personality. These theories simultaneously reject the possibility that biological factors have any effect on the development of personality. On the other hand, theories from outside of criminology argue that genetic factors are critically important in the formation of personality traits. Importantly, these theories typically acknowledge that the environment—although not always the family environment—may also be involved in structuring personality traits (Harris, 1998). Empirical research pitting these two perspectives against each other has found virtually no support for the idea that only environmental factors are important; in fact, the overwhelming majority of research shows that genes explain at least half of the variance in personality traits with the other half being explained by environmental factors, such as peers (Harris, 1998). This line of research thus indicates that genetic factors tend to have their effects on antisocial behaviors indirectly by affecting personality traits.

Empirical Validity of Tests of ANS

A good deal of research has also examined whether ANS activity is linked to various forms of antisocial behavior. Recall that the ANS directly relates to how an individual will behave in given environments. Individuals with a hyperaroused ANS are easily conditionable and generally well behaved. Individuals with a hypoaroused ANS are less conditionable and generally more likely to seek sensation through any means (Brennan et al., 1997). As a result, the general hypothesis is that antisocial persons will tend to display various markers of under arousal. The results from a rich body of research tend to provide some evidence in favor of this proposition. For instance, Ellis and Walsh (2000) reviewed 40 studies that had examined the association between ANS activity and antisocial phenotypes. They found that almost all of the studies revealed low ANS activity was related to a greater likelihood of engaging in antisocial behaviors.

In addition, the evidence also tends to show that antisocial populations tend to be characterized by reduced skin conductance orienting responses (SCOR). This means that when confronted with new situations or experiences, samples of offenders exhibit relatively low levels of SC, a measure of ANS arousal. Yet, there is weak evidence of reduced SC response when antisocial individuals are presented with a negative stimulus (Raine, 1993). This same research illustrates that antisocial populations tend to be characterized by deficient conditioning, which means they have difficulty associating punishment with bad behavior. This is especially true with regard to antisocial individuals from better social backgrounds (Raine, 1997). Yaralian and Raine (2001) reviewed the research bearing on the nexus between ANS and antisocial behaviors. Their review indicated that various antisocial populations are characterized by reduced skin conductance (SC) activity, including psychopathic criminals, nonpsychopathic criminals, and conduct disordered children.

Measures of resting heart rate—another marker of ANS activity—have also been shown to relate to antisocial behaviors. Lower resting heart rates are expected in antisocial populations because they are indicative of less anxiety and fearlessness. Thus, children who have lower heart rates also tend to show less anxiety and fearlessness (Scarpa et al., 1997). Normally, when an individual experiences a neutral situation, his or her heart will slow down (decelerate), and in conditions of stress, the heart will speed up (accelerate); thus "larger deceleratory responses indicate greater attentional processing and orienting than shutting out environmental events" (Yaralian & Raine, 2001, p. 60). Research shows that psychopathic offenders tend to be characterized by larger anticipatory heart rate acceleratory responses followed by lower SC responses to aversive stimuli. Lower heart rate at age 15 years also predicts criminality at age 24 years (Raine, Venables, & Williams, 1990a, 1990b). Yaralian and Raine (2001; p. 61) suggested: "Reduced fear is thought to predispose to violence because fearless individuals are less concerned about negative consequences of fighting (e.g., injury or punishment)." Such individuals may actively seek out new and exciting and even risky activities in order to increase their arousal level.

The most compelling empirical evidence linking low resting heart rate to antisocial behaviors comes from a meta-analysis conducted by Ortiz and Raine (2004). This meta-analysis analyzed 40 studies that consisted of children and adolescents. The results of their meta-analysis indicated a strong, consistent, and statistically significant effect of resting heart rate ($d = -.44$) and heart rate in the presence of stressful stimuli ($d = -.76$) on antisocial behavior. Stated differently, relatively low heart rate levels were associated with increased involvement in antisocial behaviors. In light of this evidence, Ortiz and Raine concluded that a low heart rate appears to be one of the strongest biological risk factors for antisocial phenotypes. A more recent meta-analysis also revealed that low resting heart rate was associated with psychopathy and conduct problems (Lorber, 2004).

Additional evidence linking ANS activity to antisocial phenotypes comes from studies analyzing electroencephalography (EEG), which measures electrical activity of the brain. In general, this line of research reveals lower levels of cortical activity among antisocial populations. Researchers have estimated that 25% to 50% of offenders suffer from EEG abnormalities (Raine, 1993). Such abnormalities tend to be located in the temporal and frontal lobes of the brain, two areas important for aggression and violence (discussed in chapter 5), particularly for murderers and violent recidivists (Volavka, 1995; Raine, 1997).

Longitudinal studies (studies conducted over a period of time) of 101 male schoolchildren (Raine, Venables, & Williams, 1990a, 1990b) recorded electrodermal, cardiovascular, and cortical measures of ANS activity at age 15 years and showed a relationship between these measures and the likelihood of having criminal records at age 24 years. The study was limited to property taking and wounding behaviors (e.g., theft and assault). Consistent with a developmental approach, a reanalysis of these data showed that adolescents with higher heart rate levels, higher SC arousal, and better SC conditioning were less likely to become criminals by age 29 years (Raine, Venables, & Williams, 1995, 1996). Other research (Brennan et al., 1997) has suggested that heightened ANS activity can be considered a protective factor for antisocial behavior.

Integrated thought is very important to interpret the meaning of these results. For example, there is evidence of reduced frontal brain area in individuals with low ANS arousal. This would suggest that brain damage to the prefrontal cortex could promote slower ANS arousal. According to Yaralian and Raine (2001, p. 65): "Prefrontal dysfunction may also explain previously reviewed arousal and orienting deficits among antisocials ... the area of the prefrontal cortex is positively correlated with a number of SC orienting responses ... Several other brain-imaging and neurological studies suggest that the source of orienting deficits in antisocials may be dysfunction of the prefrontal cortex (Hazlett et al., 1993; Tranel & Damasio, 1994)." In addition, a study of murderers showed evidence of reduced glucose metabolism in the prefrontal cortex and other regions of the brain, consistent with the evidence presented in chapter 5 about brain dysfunction and violence (Raine, Brennan, & Medrick, 1994; Raine, Buchsbaum, & LaCasse, 1997). Again, these findings appear to be most relevant for violent offenders without social disadvantages (Raine et al., 1998).

Intelligence

There has been longstanding interest in the possible association between intelligence and antisocial behaviors. According to *Merriam-Webster's Collegiate Dictionary* (2009), *intelligence* refers to "the ability to learn or understand or to deal with new or trying situations: reason [or] the skilled use of reason; the ability to apply knowledge to manipulate one's environment or to think abstractly as measured by objective criteria (as tests); mental acuteness [or] shrewdness; the act of understanding [or] comprehension." Typically, intelligence is measured with one of many tests that assess *Intelligence Quotient* (IQ), which is "a number used to express the apparent relative intelligence of a person that is the ratio multiplied by 100 of the mental age as reported on a standardized test to the chronological age." With a measure of IQ, it is possible to determine the relative degree of intelligence. For example, relative to the average person of a particular age (whose IQ would be 100), an IQ of 80 would be 20 points lower than average and 120 would be 20 points above average.

Historically, the relationship between low intelligence and criminality was merely assumed. Vold et al. (1998) suggested that intelligence became the factor of supposed inferiority in criminals after theories related to physical appearance fell out of favor. Early on, low intelligence was thought to be indicative of an evolutionary throwback. This led to the family inheritance studies of "feeblemindedness" by scholars such as Dugdale and eventually many of the harmful eugenics policies (discussed in chapter 4). IQ tests were developed by psychologists and were initially designed to be used for positive social outcomes, such as assisting the educationally challenged to perform well in school. Low IQ is, however, still viewed as a risk factor for antisocial behavior.

Key Proposition of Tests of Intelligence

From the preceding discussion of intelligence and crime, the following proposition has been tested:

- Individuals with lower intelligence levels are more likely to commit acts of delinquency and criminality.

Key Concepts of Tests of Intelligence

From the preceding proposition, the following concepts can be isolated and defined:

- Intelligence
- Delinquency
- Criminality

Box 6.4 defines the key concepts of intelligence studies. Scholars have used these definitions to test the key proposition of tests of intelligence. The findings of these tests are discussed in the following section.

Box 6.4 Definitions of Key Concepts of Intelligence Studies

- *Intelligence. Nominal*—the ability to learn or understand or to deal with new or trying situations or to reason and apply knowledge to manipulate one's environment or to think abstractly as measured by objective criteria. *Operational*—one's relative degree of intelligence, as measured through IQ tests, which produce a number that expresses the relative intelligence of a person that is the ratio multiplied by 100 of the mental age as reported on a standardized test to the chronological age.
- *Delinquency. Nominal*—acts committed by juveniles that, if committed by adults, would be considered crimes by the criminal justice system. *Operational*—usually measured by official indicators such as arrests and adjudication of guilt in a court, also measured by self-report data and reports of observations of behaviors by parents and teachers.
- *Criminality. Nominal*—committing any act that violates the criminal law. *Operational*—the number of times a person is arrested, is convicted in court for a violation of the criminal law, and/or self-reports violating the law.

Empirical Validity of Tests of Intelligence

Although testing the association between IQ and criminality is a political minefield, an impressive line of research has emerged showing that delinquents tend to have IQs that are 8 to 10 points lower than non-delinquents. The literature testing the IQ-crime nexus has a long tradition and according to Vold et al.

(1998, p. 52) early tests examining the relationship between intelligence and criminality were supportive (e.g., see Gordon, 1976; Jensen, 1969). Yet, most of the research was conducted on inmates incarcerated in prisons and juveniles officially adjudicated by courts as delinquent; this means prisoners and delinquents generally were found to have lower IQs than nonprisoners and nondelinquents. Given that the criminal and juvenile justice systems may be more likely to apprehend, try, and convict or adjudicate individuals with lower IQs than those with higher IQs, the meaning of these findings was called into question. Moffitt and Silva (1988) tested to see whether this "differential detection" hypothesis would be able to account for the association between IQ and delinquent involvement. To do so, they examined IQ scores in a sample of delinquents who were apprehended by the police and a matched sample of delinquents who were not apprehended by the police. The results of their analysis indicated the two groups had IQ scores that were not significantly different. These findings provide strong empirical evidence indicating that the association between IQ and delinquency cannot be explained away in terms of differential detection.

Most research reviews assessing the relationship between IQ and delinquency or criminality tend to support the notion that low IQ scores are more prevalent among delinquent and criminal populations (Hirschi & Hindelang, 1977; Wilson & Herrnstein, 1985; Quay, 1985). For example, Hirschi and Hindelang (1977) suggested that IQ is at least as good a predictor of official involvement in delinquency as social class or race (also see Gordon, 1987). Some studies have found that lower IQs are more prevalent among more serious offenders (Blumstein, Farrington, & Moitra, 1985; Denno, 1990) and that low IQ scores measured early in childhood are associated with a greater likelihood of offending in adolescence and adulthood (Lipsitt, Buka, & Lipsitt, 1990). Even more evidence of the role of IQ in the etiology of violence comes from a study showing that sexual offenders have lower IQs when compared to nonsexual violent offenders (Guay, Ouimet, & Proulx, 2005).

In a classic test of the association between IQ and delinquency, Lynam and his colleagues (1993) explored the possibility that the effect of IQ on delinquency may be confounded by socioeconomic status, race, test motivation, school failure, and self-control. They also examined the possibility that delinquent involvement causes lower IQ (i.e., from injuries incurred from antisocial behaviors). Analysis of data drawn from the Pittsburgh Youth Study revealed that even after controlling for a host of potential confounders, the association between IQ and delinquency remained statistically significant. Additional analyses revealed evidence indicating that low IQ predates delinquency rather than delinquency predating a low IQ. The results of this study provided some of the strongest findings implicating IQ as a potential causal contributor to delin-quency and other forms of antisocial behaviors.

Contemporary research, however, has also shown that the relationship be-tween IQ and antisocial behavior is more complex than previously suggested. To be more specific, studies examining the effects of intelligence on criminal involvement use standardized IQ tests such as the Wechsler Adult Intelligence Scale-Revised (WAIS-R). The WAIS-R includes 11 different subtests that assess different aspects of intelligence (e.g., verbal versus performance IQ). Delin-quents, in comparison with non-delinquents, tend to score lower on the ver-bal component, but they do not score lower on the performance component (Herrnstein, 1995). *Low verbal IQ* signifies "poor abstract reasoning, poor judgment, poor school performance, impulsiveness, and low empathy" (Walsh, 2002, p. 110), all of which can interfere with occupational success and can en-courage antisocial behavior (Farrington, 1996). Several studies have demon-strated that low IQ scores in childhood precede delinquency and criminality (e.g., see Lipsitt et al., 1990). For example, a study of inmates showed evi-dence of lower verbal IQs in impulsive inmates (Myers & Ellis, 1992). Another study linked early language development at ages 6, 18, and 24 months and child's speech abilities at ages 3 to 5 years to criminality later in life (Stattin & Klackenberg-Larsson, 1993). The effects of IQ tend to be the most profound on life course persistent offenders (Stattin & Klackenberg-Larsson, 1993), on offenders who start early and who continue on with deviance into adulthood (Moffitt, 1993) and on offenders who commit the most crimes (Caspi et al., 1995b; Farrington, 1996).

Some researchers have argued that low verbal IQ is an indicator of neu-ropsychological deficits, deficits that affect various regions of the brain such as the prefrontal cortex (Moffitt, 1990; Ratchford & Beaver, 2009). Because brain dysfunctions are associated with antisocial phenotypes (see chapter 5), it takes no stretch of the imagination to see why verbal IQ would be related to crimi-nal behaviors. Regardless of whether IQ measures brain dysfunction or some other factor, the available evidence, indicates a robust association.

Mental Illness

According to the National Alliance for the Mentally Ill (NAMI), *mental ill-nesses* are brain disorders that interfere with normal thinking, feeling, and be-having. Mental illnesses are biological disorders and are should not be equated with insanity. *Insanity* is a legal term that is typically reserved for the court-of-law. Insanity usually implies that a person does not know right from wrong or cannot adjust his or her behavior accordingly. It is rarely used as a defense, even for murder, and is rarely successful. Since this book is about why crime happens, the legal condition of insanity is not relevant here.

As defined by Zimbardo (1992, p. 618), mental disorders are "disruptions in emotional, behavioral, or thought processes that lead to personality distress or that block one's ability to achieve important goals." People with mental illnesses often have diminished capacities to think and reason clearly, to solve problems, and to communicate and interact with others. Indicators of mental illness include, but are not limited to, the following:

- Personal distress or anxiety
- Maladaptive behavior
- Irrational behavior
- Unpredictable behavior
- Antisocial behavior

Some of the most common mental illnesses include depression, manic depression (or bipolar disorder), and schizophrenia. Box 6.5 defines these conditions and discusses their causes.

Box 6.5 Major Mental Illnesses

According to NAMI, the most significant mental illnesses, include major depression, bipolar disorder, and schizophrenia.

Major Depression

Major depression (also known as clinical depression or unipolar depression) affects nearly 15 million American adults every year, which translates into about 7% of the adult population. Major depression, the leading cause of disability in the United States, is persistent and significantly interferes with thoughts, behavior, mood, activity, and physical health. Although depression can occur at any age and among any ethnic or racial group, it is about twice as common in women as in men.

Other depressive disorders include dysthymia and bipolar disorder, or manic depression. Dysthymia is a less severe form of depression. Bipolar disorder is a form of depression that is accompanied by periods of mania, which indicates abnormal elevated mood or irritability, self-esteem, and excessive energy, thoughts, and behavior.

According to NAMI, symptoms of major depression include: "profoundly sad or irritable mood; pronounced changes in sleep, appetite, and energy; difficulty thinking, concentrating, and remembering physical slowing or agitation; lack of interest in or pleasure from activities that were once enjoyed;

feelings of guilt, worthlessness, hopelessness, and emptiness; recurrent thoughts of death or suicide; and persistent physical symptoms that do not respond to treatment, such as headaches, digestive disorders, and chronic pain."

According to NAMI, numerous psychological, biological, and environmental factors contribute to the development of depression. Three neurotransmitters discussed in chapter 5—norepinephrine, serotonin, and dopamine—are thought to be involved with major depression. Antidepressant medications can be very effective because they work by altering levels of neurotransmitters in the brain. Depression also runs in families and is thought to have a genetic basis. As discussed in chapter 4, environmental events, such as stressful life events, likely trigger the genetic propensity to depression (Kendler & Prescott, 2006).

Bipolar Disorder

Bipolar disorder, also known as manic depression, affects almost 6 million adult Americans, representing nearly 3% of the adult population. Bipolar disorder is most common in adolescence and young adulthood and is characterized by extreme shifts in mood, energy, and functioning and by episodes of both mania and depression that can last anywhere from days to months. According to NAMI, the symptoms of mania include: "either an elated, happy mood or an irritable, angry, unpleasant mood; increased activity or energy; more thoughts and faster thinking than normal; increased talking, more rapid speech than normal; ambitious, often grandiose, plans; increased sexual interest and activity; and decreased sleep and decreased need for sleep." The symptoms of depression, the other phase of bipolar disorder, are listed above.

It is possible that people with bipolar will experience a "mixed state," which occurs when symptoms of mania and depression co-occur. This state is characterized by depressed mood accompanied by mania, which produces agitation, sleep problems, appetite change, psychosis, and even suicidal thinking. Similar to major depression, bipolar disorder is thought to result from chemical imbalances in the brain. Bipolar disorder also runs in families is strongly influenced by genetic factors. As with depression, environmental stressors tend to trigger episodes of bipolar disorder, perhaps explaining why the illness usually first emerges during the late teens and early 20s.

Schizophrenia

Schizophrenia affects almost exactly the same number of American adults as bipolar disorder, more than 2 million, or just over 1% of the adult population. According to NAMI, schizophrenia can interfere "with a person's ability to think clearly, manage emotions, make decisions, and relate to others." Like bipolar disorder, schizophrenia tends to emerge in adolescence and early adulthood. Treatment of schizophrenia is less successful than with depression and bipolar disorder and, as a result, people diagnosed with schizophrenia usually suffer from it throughout their lives.

As explained by NAMI, there is no one symptom that positively identifies schizophrenia. Instead, the symptoms of schizophrenia are typically found in other brain disorders. For example, psychosis is also comorbid with bipolar disorder. The symptoms of schizophrenia include positive, disorganized, and negative symptoms. Positive symptoms describe experiences of psychosis, delusions, and hallucinations. Disorganized symptoms suggest confused thinking and speech, and nonsensical behavior. Negative symptoms suggest emotional flatness, disruptions in daily activities, and depressed mood.

The causes of schizophrenia are not known, but NAMI reports that the brains of people with schizophrenia are different, as a group, from the brains of people without the illness: "Schizophrenia seems to be caused by a combination of problems including genetic vulnerability and environmental factors that occur during a person's development."

Source: National Alliance for the Mentally Ill. (2007). Mental illness. Available: *www.nami.org/illness.*

According to NAMI and the National Institute of Mental Health (NIMH), treatments for mental illnesses have become much more effective over the past 25 years. Typically, treatment consists of a combination of medication and counseling, and most forms of mental illness are highly treatable.

Empirical Validity of Mental Illness

There is little question that most people with mental illnesses, or brain disorders, are not violent. In fact, NAMI asserts that people with major mental illnesses commit no more than their fair share of violent criminality.

Out of the many studies of mental illness and crime (e.g., Backlar, 1998; Blackburn, 1998; Davis, 1991; Haapasalo & Virtanen, 1999; Palermo, Gumz, & Liska, 1992; Steury & Choinski, 1995; Sullivan & Spritzer, 1997; Torrey, 1994; Wessely, 1997), a clear consensus has emerged suggesting that although there is a statistically significant association between mental illness and violence, the relationship is relatively weak to modest (Monahan, 1997). Mental illnesses are most likely to result in violence when the following conditions prevail:

- The person is suffering from paranoia and is experiencing delusions.
- The person is not being formally treated.
- The person is self-medicating (i.e., using or abusing drugs).

It is not surprising, then, that the mental illness most likely to result in violence is schizophrenia (Prins, 2001). Those suffering from schizophrenia are also most likely to be diagnosed with APD (Hodgins, Lapalme, & Toupin, 1999). It is also not surprising that research shows that untreated mentally ill people tend to be at high risk for drug abuse (including alcohol and tobacco). Other research suggests that childhood mental illnesses, along with antisocial behavior, predict adult criminality (Elander et al., 1997). But perhaps the most convincing evidence of a link between violence and schizophrenia comes from a large review of the literature conducted by Walsh and her colleagues (2002). They found that across studies there was a statistically significant association between violent behaviors and schizophrenia. Importantly, this effect was relatively small, with schizophrenics accounting for less than 10% of all violent behaviors.

Even though the relationship between mental illness and crime is modest, there is little question that people with mental illnesses are overrepresented in the nation's criminal justice system. It is estimated that roughly one in 10 of the nation's prisoners is mentally ill (Robinson, 2002, p. 298), although some suggest that it may be closer to four out of 10 (Torrey et al., 1992). NAMI and the Public Citizen's Health Resource Group published the book *Criminalizing the Seriously Mentally Ill: The Abuse of Jails as Mental Hospitals*, where they reported that most mentally ill people who are incarcerated committed very minor crimes. Since the publication of NAMI's report, the overrepresentation of mentally ill in prison may have even increased. A U.S. Department of Justice study (Ditton, 1999) found that 16% of all inmates in state and federal jails and prisons are known to be suffering from schizophrenia, manic depression, depression, or another severe mental illness. There are now at least 300,000 people with major mental illnesses incarcerated in the United States.

From such statistics, the logical conclusion appears to be that people with mental illnesses are generally more dangerous than people without mental illnesses. In fact, many scholars conclude that mental illness is related to criminality, although this type of conclusion is typically based on studies that analyzed samples of inmates. For example, a study by Modestin, Hug, & Ammann (1997) reported higher incidents of criminality among patients being treated for affective disorders when compared to a matched control group. Overall, 42% of patients had criminal records versus 31% of nonpatients.

One of the main problems with studies that examine criminal involvement among the mentally ill is that the data they used may not be appropriate when studying the criminogenic effects of mental illness. To illustrate, Belfrage (1998) examined official criminal records of 1,056 individuals 10 years after they were released from mental hospitals in Stockholm, Sweden, where they had received treatment for schizophrenia, affective psychoses, or paranoia. He found that nearly

40% had criminal records. All of the violent crimes committed in the sample were committed by people with schizophrenia. Most notably, the majority of crimes committed by the sample were very minor crimes, such as shoplifting.

The conclusion reached by Belfrage was that mentally ill patients were more criminal than the general population. This conclusion, however, was possibly false given that the data analyzed were official crime data. A finding suggesting that people with mental illnesses are more likely to be officially recognized as criminals does not mean they are actually committing more crimes. Another possible interpretation is that the mentally ill are more likely to be convicted and sentenced when compared to the non-mentally ill. This could be especially true given that the latter are more likely to have stable work histories, strong contacts in the community, and better legal representation in the justice system.

Studies that do not rely exclusively on official crime records have found some support for the mental illness and crime connection, but the relationships are generally weak. At least one study found a relationship between depression and attacks generated by anger and hostility (Fava et al., 1996). In light of this evidence, the following conclusions can be drawn regarding the association between mental illness and crime:

- Most mentally ill people are not dangerous and do not commit serious criminality.
- Mentally ill people are more likely to become violent and commit crime when they are suffering from paranoia and experiencing delusions, when they are not being treated by doctors, and when they are using or abusing drugs.
- Much (if not most) of the crime committed by people with mental illnesses is attributable to a lack of quality treatment in the nation's communities, as well as follow-up treatment upon release from mental institutions and hospitals (e.g., see Lurigio, 2001).

Diet and Nutrition

The research that examines the association between diet/nutrition and behavior attempt to answer the following questions: Can diet affect human behavior? If so, how does diet affect human behavior? More specifically, does what you eat affect your risk of committing crime? Although not much mainstream criminological research has examined this possibility, for reasons to be detailed momentarily, the logical answer would be "yes." For example, the brain is the product of interactions that occur between genes and environmental influences (as discussed in chapter 5). At the most simple level, this means:

- No genes = no brain
- No environment = no brain
- No diet = no brain
- No brain = no behavior
- No behavior = no antisocial behavior or criminality

Since our brains are sustained by nutrients, it seems somewhat reasonable to posit that different diets may actually be related to different phenotypes.

Although the importance of a healthy diet is widely recognized, Americans, as a whole, do not eat well. The typical diet of children looks startlingly similar to those of adults by the age of two years. Toddlers, older children, and even adults have the same basic problems with their nutritional intake: too many calories; too much fat and saturated fat; too many calories from fat; too much sugar, too much salt; not enough fruits and vegetables; not enough vitamins and minerals; not enough whole grains. The recommended diet for most people is contained in figure 6.1.

Figure 6.1 The Food Pyramid

Source: U.S. Department of Agriculture and the U.S. Department of Health and Human Services (2009)

Our understanding of the influence of diet on behavior is rather limited in large part because there has historically been relatively little research dedicated to examining the effects that diets have on antisocial behaviors. This gap in the research, however, may be a serious oversight because according to Bryce-Smith: "Unfortunately, the idea that ... crime [is] essentially the result of adverse social factors is so deeply embedded in human society that those seeking to conduct studies of non-social factors such as defective diets usually find that they face an uphill task" (quoted in *Crime-Times*, 1998, Vol. 4, No. 1, p. 1).

Before turning to the findings of studies that test for associations between diet and nutrition and behavior, it is important to keep in mind that the effects of nutrition begin to take hold even before the birth of a child. The foods that a pregnant woman eats cross the placenta and are absorbed by the developing fetus. The health benefits of eating a nutritious diet are well known; for example, premature birth is much less likely among pregnant women who eat diets high fortified with folic acid (Scholl et al., 1996). Premature babies can suffer significant neurological damage and develop learning disabilities and brain disorders (Meis et al., 1995). This finding hints at the possibility that diet and nutrition, both prenatally and postnatally, should be examined in greater detail by criminologists.

Key Proposition of Tests of Diet and Nutrition

From the preceding discussion of diet and nutrition and crime, the following proposition has been tested:

• Nutritional intake is related to antisocial behavior.

Key Concepts of Tests of Diet and Nutrition

Based on the previous proposition, the following concepts can be isolated and defined:

• Nutritional intake
• Antisocial behavior

Box 6.6 defines the key concepts of studies of diet and nutrition. Scholars have used these definitions in testing the link between diet and nutrition and behaviors. The findings of these tests are discussed in the following section.

Box 6.6 Definitions of Key Concepts of Studies of Diet and Nutrition

- *Nutritional intake. Nominal*—any food, drink, and nutritional supplements consumed by an individual. *Operational*—total consumption of nutritional products, as measured by self-report surveys and/or observations by trained staff and/or purposeful supplementation and dietary modification for the purposes of observing changes in behavior.
- *Antisocial behavior. Nominal*—any behaviors that conflict with the prevailing norms of society and/or that are viewed as abnormal. *Operational*—any form of behavior defined as antisocial, measured by official crime reports, self-reported behaviors, or evaluations from others.

Empirical Validity of Studies of Diet and Nutrition

The foods we eat contain the vitamins, minerals, and other essential nutrients that work to keep the body and brain functioning and they are also implicated in the regulation of neurotransmitter levels. A number of studies have shown that improper diet can lead to aggressive and antisocial behaviors, as well as to drug abuse (DeFrance et al., 1997). In a review of studies published between 1985 and 1995, Breakey (1997) reported that results showed a clear relationship between diet and the moods and behavior of children. Similar conclusions have been reached by other comprehensive reviews of the literature (Richardson, 2006). Specifically, studies have found evidence that behavior is negatively affected by vitamin deficiencies, including iron, thiamine, tryptophan, niacin, vitamin B6, vitamin C, and magnesium (Ortega et al., 1994; Smith, Fairburn, & Cowen, 1997; Werbach, 1995). Also, research has shown diets low in folic acid are associated with depression (Alpert & Fava, 1997), while other research has even revealed that babies fed formula rich in fatty acids perform better on IQ tests as children than babies fed formulas without such fatty acids (Birch et al., 2000).

Just as importantly is that research has indicated that the weight of the evidence indicates that dietary intervention can decrease irritability and problem behaviors including aggression and violence. For example, *hypoglycemia*, or low blood sugar/glucose that impairs brain function, is associated with symptoms such as disinhibition, confusion, loss of coordination, hallucinations, and aggression. A line of studies has indicated that reduced sugar intake can affect behavior (Schoenthaler, 1991). One study, for example, illustrated that a one-month carbohydrate-free diet reduced symptoms of bipolar affective disorder (Fishbein & Thatcher, 1982).

Case studies indicate that an effective way of reducing troublesome behaviors among juveniles is through dietary therapy. For example, a study that examined the effectiveness of dietary intervention found improvements in moods and concentration as well as better control of temper and an increase in empathy through regulation of iron levels of two teenagers (Tu, Shafey, & Van-Dewetering, 1994). Increases in selenium also have been found to increase mood and decrease anxiety in people (Benton & Cook, 1991; Hawkes & Hornbostel, 1996). Similarly, administration of omega-3 fatty acids (found in fish, leafy green vegetables, nuts, and some oils) may be successful at controlling some aggression, attention deficits, mental disorders, and other behavioral problems (Hamazaki et al., 1996; Hibbeln & Salem, 1995; Hibbeln et al., 1998a and 1998b; Stevens, Zentall, Abate, et al., 1995; Stevens, Zentall, and Deck, et al., 1995). Although the association between omega-3 fatty acids and behaviors is not entirely clear, it is important to note that omega-3 fatty acids increases serotonin levels. And, since serotonin is related to antisocial behaviors, then the effect of omega-3 fatty acids may indirectly affect behavior by affecting serotonin levels. Evidence supporting this possibility comes from a laboratory experiment conducted showing that deficiencies of tryptophan, an amino acid used to manufacture serotonin, were related to aggression (Bjork et al., 1999).

Research by Schoenthaler and Bier (2000) and Schoenthaler et al. (2000) examined the association between vitamin intake and disciplinary school infractions. Their analysis centered on studies in a predominantly Hispanic elementary school. The results of their study revealed that vitamin supplements were able to reduce problem behaviors by as much as 50%. Moreover, the effects tended to be strongest among the worst behaved students.

Perhaps the most compelling evidence linking *malnutrition* to behavioral problems comes from a study conducted by Liu and colleagues (2004). In this study, the examined the effects that malnutrition at age 3 had on externalizing behavioral problems at ages 8, 11, and 17 years of age. The results of this study were staggering. Malnutrition at age 3 predicted aggression and hyperactivity at age 8, externalizing behavioral problems at age 11, and conduct disorder at age 17. Additional analyses indicated that the effect of malnutrition on behavior operated indirectly by affecting neuropsychological development.

Other studies have reported similar results where nutritional intake is related to ADHD and behavioral problems (Babinski, Hartsough, & Lambert, 1999; Jacobson & Schardt, 1999). The possibility that diets could affect ADHD is critically important because the ADHD-crime relationship is well established (Fishbein, 1990; Pratt et al., 2002). What this means is that treatment for

ADHD could begin with dietary therapy as opposed to medicine, which is precisely what The Center for Science in the Public Interest recommends.

One significant point illustrated by the research is that the effects of diets have some of their most potent effects in utero. For instance, the results of one study of more than 100,000 Dutch men born in the 1940s indicated that pregnant mothers who experienced severe malnutrition (because of a famine) during the first and second trimesters of pregnancy were more likely to have children who grew up with an increased risk for antisocial personality disorder (Neugebauer, Hoek, & Susser, 1999). In another study, Franzek et al. (2008) examined the effects that this same famine had on drug use. What they found was that children who were exposed to the famine during the first trimester were at-risk for becoming addicted to drugs during adulthood.

The research examining the effects of diet and nutrition on behaviors is relevant for the main argument of this book—mainly, that antisocial behavior is attributable to a wide range of integrated factors. As discussed in chapter 5, research has revealed that reductions in exposures to lead can also increase IQ (Ruff et al., 1993). Furthermore, diets high in fats are believed to cause increased bile secretions, which allow more lead to be absorbed into the bloodstream. This means that more fat in the diet will likely lead to greater effects of lead poisoning in people exposed to lead (Lucas et al., 1998). At the same time, high-fat foods increase cholesterol; a review of 32 studies showed a link between low cholesterol and violence (Golomb, 1998). Yet, a diet high in fat may reduce tryptophan (Steegmans et al., 1996) and serotonin activity (Moffit & Silva, 1988), both of which are related to aggression (Smith et al., 1997).

Drug Consumption

As defined by Liska (2000, p. 4), a drug is "any absorbed substance that changes or enhances any physical or psychological function in the body." Drugs include both legally ingested substances (e.g., alcohol and tobacco) and illegally ingested substances (e.g., marijuana, cocaine, heroin, and so forth). The definition of a drug in *Merriam-Webster's New Collegiate Dictionary* (2009) includes "often an illegal substance that causes addiction, habituation, or a marked change in consciousness."

Drugs tend to have their effects on mood and behavior primarily by altering brain chemistry (Fishbein & Pease, 1996). All drugs, whether legal or illegal, have been found to affect the brain by interacting with naturally occurring brain chemicals known as neurotransmitters (e.g., dopamine). "The major drugs of abuse—e.g., narcotics like heroin or stimulants like cocaine—mimic the structure of neurotransmitters, the most powerful mind-altering drugs the human body creates" (Lynam & Potter, 1998, pp. 60–61). The effects of any drug depend on numerous factors, including the type of drug used, its potency and quantity, the method in which the drug is ingested, the setting in which the drug is ingested, the frequency of use, the mood of the user, and the user's biological and psychological makeup (Gaines & Kraska, 1997; Lynam & Potter, 1998). As the preceding sentence makes clear, the relationship between drugs and behavior is highly complex.

Keep in mind a clear distinction with regard to drug use versus drug abuse. Drug use is generally viewed as any consumption of a drug, including recreational or occasional use. Drug abuse, in contrast, implies a frequent amount of use and a dependence on drugs. According to Lynam and Potter (1998, p. 60), drug abuse is "illicit drug use that results in social, economic, psychological or legal problems for the drug user." The Bureau of Justice Statistics (2001) defines drug abuse as "the use of prescription-type psychotherapeutic drugs for nonmedical purposes or the use of illegal drugs." Only a small portion of drug users, ranging between 7 to 20% depending on the type of drug, actually become drug abusers (Kraska, 1990). The Office of National Drug Control Policy (ONDCP) puts the risk at between 10 percent and 33 percent, depending on the drug (Robinson & Scherlen, 2007).

Lynam and Potter (1998, p. 62) listed outcomes of drug abuse, including:

- **Physical dependence**—Characterized by a growing tolerance of a drug's effects. Increased amounts are needed to prevent withdrawal symptoms.
- **Psychological dependence**—Craving for or compulsive need to use drugs because they provide the user with a feeling of well-being and satisfaction.
- **Tolerance**—The user continues regular use of a drug and must administer progressively larger doses to attain the desired effect, thereby reinforcing the compulsive behavior known as drug dependence.
- **Withdrawal**—The physical reaction of bodily functions that, when a body is deprived of an addictive drug, causes increased excitability of the bodily functions that have been depressed by the drug's habitual use.

These outcomes suggest that drug abuse can be maladaptive.

The major types of drugs can be categorized according to their major effects on brain function and human behavior (Fishbein & Pease, 1996). General categories of drugs include *stimulants, depressants, hallucinogens, and narcotics/ opiates* (Inciardi & McElrath, 1998; Liska, 2000). Lynam and Potter (1998) also added *inhalants* (drugs that are drawn into the body by breathing in) as a separate category because of their use among young people. Inciardi and McElrath (1998) added *analgesics* (pain killers), *sedatives* (which produce calm and relaxation), and *hypnotics* (depressants that produce sleep). Such drugs are referred to as *psychotherapeutics* by ONDCP (Robinson & Scherlen, 2007).

As defined by Inciardi and McElrath (1998, pp. xii–xiii), the key substances are:

- **Stimulants**—Drugs that stimulate the CNS and increase the activity of the brain and spinal cord.
- **Depressants**—Drugs that act on and lessen the activity of the CNS, diminishing or stopping vital functions.
- **Hallucinogens**—Drugs that act on the CNS, producing mood and perceptual changes varying from sensory illusions to hallucinations.
- **Narcotics**—Drugs that dull the senses, relieve pain, and cause sleep.

Drug use in the United States is measured using two primary sources, the *National Survey of Drug Use and Health* (a survey of people twelve years and older) and *Monitoring the Future* (a survey of 8th, 10th, and 12th graders (Robinson & Scherlen, 2007). Data from these surveys shows that nearly 20 million Americans admitted to using an illicit substance in the past month in 2007; such people are referred to as "current users." The main drug of use is marijuana, followed by psychotherapeutic (prescription) drugs. Lifetime use of illicit drugs was much higher at 46 percent in 2007. As for young people, more than 21 percent of 12th graders, 17 percent of tenth graders, and 7 percent of 8th graders were current users of an illicit substance in 2007. The main illicit drug of use among young people was marijuana. Lifetime use of illicit drugs was much higher at 47 percent, 36 percent, and 19 percent for 12th, 10th, and 8th graders, respectively.

Use of alcohol and tobacco is much more prevalent. For example, more than half of Americans (51 percent) aged 12 or older reported being current drinkers of alcohol in 2007. More than one fifth (23 percent) of persons aged 12 or older participated in binge drinking (five or more drinks on the same occasion at least once in the past month). Also, 7 percent of the population aged 12 or older were heavy drinkers (five or more drinks on the same occasion on each of 5 or more days in the past month). In 2007, more than 28 percent of Americans aged 12 or older were current users of a tobacco product, including 24 percent who were current cigarette smokers.

Key Proposition of Tests of Drugs and Behavior

From the preceding discussion of drugs, the following proposition has been tested:

- Drug use and drug abuse is associated with increases in antisocial behavior.

Key Concepts of Tests of Drugs and Behavior

From the preceding proposition, the following concepts can be isolated and defined:

- Drug use
- Drug abuse
- Antisocial behavior

Box 6.7 defines the key concepts of studies of drugs and behavior. Scholars have used these definitions to test the key proposition of tests of drugs and behavior. The findings of these tests are discussed in the following section.

Box 6.7 Definitions of Key Concepts of Studies of Drugs and Behavior

- *Drug use. Nominal*—any consumption, such as recreational or occasional use, of a substance that alters brain chemistry, including legal and illegal drugs. *Operational*—any consumption of a drug, verified by self-report measures, drugs tests, or medical records.
- *Drug abuse. Nominal*—a high degree of consumption of substances that alter brain chemistry, including legal and illegal drugs, that is suggestive of some problem level of use, or overuse that results in social, economic, psychological, or legal problems for the drug user. *Operational*—a high level of drug consumption that leads to physical dependence, psychological dependence, tolerance, or withdrawal, verified by self-report measures or medical records.
- *Antisocial behavior. Nominal*—any behaviors that conflict with the prevailing norms of society and/or that are viewed as abnormal. *Operational*—any form of behavior defined as antisocial, measured by official crime reports, self-reported behaviors, or evaluations from others.

Empirical Validity of Tests of Drugs and Behavior

Do drugs lead to antisocial behavior and criminality? Keep in mind that, by definition, use or abuse of any illegal substance is illegal. Thus, to some degree the relationship between drugs and crime exists because drugs are illegal.

According to Nurco, Kinlock, and Hanlon (1998, p. 221) "Evidence of criminal activity among narcotics users is longstanding and abundant; however, it is apparent that relationships among the important variables involved are much more complex than were initially believed." Prevalence and diversity of criminality among narcotics users seem to be high, but most crime committed by drug users is non-violent; only a relatively small portion of crime committed by drug users is violent (Goldstein, 1988; Nurco et al., 1998).

According to ONDCP (2000), there are three relationships between drugs and crime:

- **Drug-defined offenses**—These are violations of drug laws such as possessing, using, or growing drugs.
- **Drug-related offenses**—These are offenses attributable to pharmacological effects of the drugs on the brain and offenses committed for the purposes of obtaining money to support drug use.
- **Offenses related to a drug-using lifestyle**—These include committing crimes that result from interactions with people also in the drug use lifestyle.

Drug-defined offenses are thus created by the criminal law and could be eliminated if drugs were not illegal, as could the drug-related offenses committed to obtain drugs. The other drug crimes result from the actual effects of drug use on the brain and from extended drug use.

The drug most relevant for a psychopharmacological violence effect is a legal drug: alcohol (Robinson & Scherlen, 2007). Other drugs that may promote violent behavior include stimulants, barbiturates, and PCP (e.g., see Asnis & Smith, 1978; d'Orban, 1976; Ellingswood, 1971; Feldman, Agar, & Beschner, 1979; Gerson & Preston, 1979; Glaser, 1974; Tinklenberg, 1973; Virkunnen, 1974). The suspected and sometimes asserted link between opiates and marijuana and violence may, according to some researchers, be nonexistent (e.g., see Finestone, 1967; Greenberg & Adler, 1974; Inciardi & Chambers, 1972; Kozel, Dupont, & Brown, 1972; Kramer, 1976; Schatzman, 1975). These drugs may actually "ameliorate violent tendencies. In such cases, persons who are prone to acting violently may engage in self-medication, in order to control their violent tendencies" (Goldstein, 1998, p. 245). Furthermore, other researchers have found that heroin users will refrain from committing violent crimes to acquire money to buy their drug if alternatives exist (e.g., see Cushman, 1974; Goldstein & Duchaine, 1980; Goldstein, 1979; Gould, 1974; Johnson et al., 1985; Preble & Casey, 1969; Swezey, 1973).

A large percentage of offenders claim they were on drugs at the time of their crimes. Additionally, a sizable portion of jail inmates reported committing crime to obtain money for drugs. Finally, arrest statistics reported in the Arrestees Drug Abuse Monitoring (ADAM) Program show that approximately two thirds adult arrestees in the United States test positive for at least one drug (usually marijuana or cocaine).

This does not mean that the pharmacological effects of drugs *caused* these people to commit crimes. Instead, another interpretation is that these people either committed crimes to further their drug habits or that the drugs were not related to the offenses.

Another factor that has been linked with drug use is childhood physical disorders (Horner & Scheibe, 1997; Robinson & Kelley, 2000; Walker, Fisher, & Gaerin, 1997). This type of research suggests that some drug use and abuse may be a form of self-medication aimed at alleviating symptoms of physical illnesses.

One of the more pressing questions is: How do these drugs ultimately affect behavior? The answer to this question is obviously complex, but a line of studies has shown relationships between neurotransmitter levels (discussed in chapter 5) and alcoholism (see Fishbein & Pease, 1996), and some have found structural differences in areas of the brain, including the amygdala (Hill et al., 2001). Similar findings have been reported for gamblers, suggesting that many addictive behaviors are under the influence of the brain (Slutske et al., 2001). In this light, craving for drugs can be understood as a result of a deficient brain (Ruden, 1997). When the neurotransmitters dopamine (which is involved in goal-directed behavior) and serotonin (which inhibits such behavior) are in equilibrium, a person will be unlikely to crave drugs (Depue & Collins, 1999). However, when dopamine levels are high or when serotonin levels are low, addiction is much more likely to ensue (Ruden & Byalick, 1997). Hormone levels (discussed in chapter 5) have also been linked to some forms of drug abuse. For example, Stalenheim et al. (1998) found that high concentrations of total testosterone were related to Type II alcoholism (a form of alcoholism that occurs early in life, mostly in males, and that has a strong genetic component), as well as antisocial personality disorder and deviant behavior.

As with diet, the effects of drug use on individuals begin before birth. A sobering statistic is that among pregnant women aged 15 to 44 years nearly 20 percent in any given years admit to smoking cigarettes while pregnant, more than 10 percent admitted to using alcohol, and about 3 percent report using illegal drugs (Robinson & Scherlen, 2007). Rates of drug use during pregnancy tend to be higher among the nation's disadvantaged women. The effects of *fetal alcohol syndrome* include low IQ, learning disabilities, physical abnormalities, delinquency, and ultimately criminality (Roebuck, Mattson, & Riley, 1999). Exposure to alcohol in the womb may also lead to impulsivity, conduct disorder, and brain dysfunction, all of which are related to or comprised of antisocial behavior (Sood et al., 2001). One study even shows that being exposed to alcohol in the womb is associated with an increased likelihood of drinking in adolescence (Baer et al., 1998).

There is increased attention being paid to the effects of cigarette smoking on children. Exposure to nicotine in the womb can lead to low birth weight babies who are cognitively impaired. Nicotine also increases the risk of spontaneous abortion. Most relevant to this book, however, is the research indicating that children who were exposed to nicotine in the womb are at increased risk for impulsivity and antisocial behavior in childhood, adolescence, and adulthood (Brennan, Grekin, & Mednick, 1999; Day et al., 2000; Fergusson, Woodward, & Horwood, 1998; Fried, Watkinson, & Gray, 1998; Gibson & Tibbetts, 1999; Orlebeke, Knol, & Verhulst, 1997). In terms of risk for future criminality, some believe the increased likelihood of antisocial behavior among those born to mothers who smoke while pregnant is due to an increased risk for substance abuse and psychiatric disorders (Moolchan & Robinson, 2001; Weissman et al., 1999). Some research also shows that prenatal marijuana exposure is linked to hyperactivity, inattention, and impulsivity (Day et al., 1994; Goldschmidt, Day, & Richardson, 2000; Fried et al., 1998).

It should be noted, however, that the association between prenatal exposure to drugs and later life behavioral problems may be spurious (Wakschlag et al., 2002). More specifically, it is quite possible that mothers who use more drugs and alcohol during their pregnancy are more antisocial than mothers who refrain from using these substances. Since antisocial tendencies are highly heritable, the association between maternal drug use and offspring antisocial behavior may be confounded by genetic factors. There is a line of research that is beginning to emerge testing this possibility and the results have revealed that genetic factors may be driving this association—that is, the relationship between prenatal exposure to drugs and alcohol and antisocial behavior is spurious (Boutwell, Beaver, & Gibson, 2009; Maughan, Taylor, Caspi, & Moffitt, 2004).

Evaluation of Organism Level Explanations

In the following sections, we discuss the scope of organism level explanations of crime and we also generally assess clarity of the key concepts and the logical adequacy of the key propositions.

Scope

Most of these studies, including those of personality, intelligence, diet/ nutrition, drug use/abuse, and mental illness, assess the effects of organism level factors on violence. Yet, the studies of drug use/abuse and mental illness tend to suggest that drug abusers and the mentally ill are not any more violent, but instead are more likely to commit acts of property crimes aimed at feeding addictions and/or surviving. In a similar vein, there are few studies of organism level factors on acts of elite deviance, but it is likely that some of the factors discussed in this chapter are relevant for understanding many crimes in the business world. Efforts have been made to apply personality inventories to white-collar offenders (Collins & Schmidt, 1993; Robinson & Scherlen, 2007). Some of the personality traits discussed in this chapter are likely prevalent in the upper management of major corporations. Traits such as *extroversion, risk taking, negative emotionality,* and *lack of social perspective taking* would make one well suited for success in the cutthroat world of big business. Thus, the scope of organism level factors may not be limited only to street level criminality (Babiak & Hare, 2006).

As with most risk factors, there are always exceptions to the general pattern of results. The question, then, is whether the findings for this single study represent a significant challenge to the existing studies or are the findings simply a fluke. For example, at least one study found that individuals with high IQs also commit crime. This study of patterns of offending among 1,750 intellectual elites found that even some "angels are rebels"—that is, even people with high IQs freely admitted to committing various types of crimes (Oleson, 1997). "Official statistics and self-report studies traditionally support the claim that the average offender has a slightly subnormal IQ score, but because social researchers usually study vulnerable groups such as juveniles or prison inmates, very little is known about elite offenders with superior intellectual abilities" (p. 1). Unfortunately, the research was conducted on high IQ inmates in the United States and the United Kingdom (UK), meaning it was partly biased in its sample to incarcerated people. However, the sample also included university students and members of the International Society for Philosophical Enquiry, a high IQ society in the UK. The findings of this study, as well as those of other studies showing counter-intuitive findings, should be tackled head on and not simply ignored. As a result, much more research needs to be conducted to determine with greater precision whether the organism level factors presented in this chapter will be associated with antisocial behaviors in replication studies.

Conceptual Clarity

Although research tends to support personality theories, many of the concepts of personality theories are tautological. This means that the presence of many personality traits is verified by the fact that people behave in a delinquent, criminal, or aggressive and antisocial manner (Geiss, 2000). Thus, the theories, when applied to criminality, are true by definition. This leads to the problem of circular reasoning. Equally troubling, personality traits are sometimes poorly defined, but more often they overlap. Thus, the cluster of traits becomes more important than any single characteristic.

In addition, IQ as a concept is also plagued by significant problems. For example, what do IQ tests actually measure? Can IQ tests tell us where intelligence comes from? Is it inborn, from genetics, or is it learned through life experiences and culture? From the review presented, there is obviously unresolved debate about some of these issues. Most troubling is that sometimes it is difficult to understand the concept of IQ and IQ tests do not all necessarily measure the same dimension of intelligence. With that said, there is a strong knowledge base linking IQ to antisocial phenotypes.

The concepts relating to diet/nutrition are clearly defined, they are easy to understand, and they are testable. Unfortunately, scholars must often rely on self-report measures of the foods and drugs that people consume, meaning that the results are potentially biased. To the degree that self-report measures are validated with direct observational measures, this is less problematic. Statistical techniques allow scholars to hold stable other factors that may influence findings of crime, but it is not possible to hold constant all other criminogenic factors. Therefore, the precise effect that malnutrition and diet has on antisocial behaviors is not well understood.

Definitions of various mental illnesses are problematic. Research suggests that mental illnesses consist of traits, behaviors, emotions, and thought processes that exist as shades of gray—that is, it is not a black and white issue whether a person has a particular mental illness. As a result, diagnoses of mental illnesses are somewhat unreliable. If this is true, then it is difficult to identify the true association between mental illness and antisocial behavior. Nonetheless, serious mental illnesses, under the conditions of delusions, no treatment, and drug abuse, can be considered a risk factor for violence at the street level. More problematic for studies of mental illness, however, is the overreliance on official measures of criminality. People with mental illnesses are more likely to be recognized as criminal or delinquent, but this does not necessarily mean they commit more acts of crime and delinquency. The empirical validity of such studies would be increased if these results were substantiated by studies using self-reports or independent observer rating of antisocial behaviors.

Logical Adequacy of Propositions

The organism level propositions discussed in this chapter are often treated in other criminological theory texts as *biological theories.* The propositions laid out in this chapter should generally be considered logical in that they imply environmental effects on the behavior of organisms and also are more likely to be tested on representative samples of people in the population. Organism level factors generally, and biological factors in particular, almost always *only* provide a potential for behavior; the effects, however, are contingent on the presence of certain environmental factors. It is also widely suggested that organism level and biological factors cannot account for crime changes over time (crime trends) nor crime rate differentials between places and times (Taylor, Walton, & Young, 1974). Neither is true (Walsh, 2002) because environmental factors can trigger biological conditions and affect crime trends and rates. As explained by Bohm (2001, pp. 40–41):

> There probably are no positivistic criminologists today who would argue that a biological imperative for crime exists. Nor, for that matter, are there many criminologists today, of any ideological persuasion, who would deny that biology has some influence on criminal behavior. Thus, the position held by most criminologists today is that criminal behavior is the product of a complex interaction between biology and environmental or social conditions.

This means organism level factors cannot, in isolation, account for why crime occurs.

As noted earlier, the most significant weakness of personality theories of crime is that they are at-risk for being tautological. Consider this statement by Walsh (2002, p. 133) as a prime example: "Among the neuropsychological and temperamental deficits that can lead to a lifetime of antisocial behavior are the separate but often linked syndromes of *attention deficit with hyperactivity disorder* (ADHD), *oppositional defiant disorder* (ODD), and *conduct disorder* (CD)." Ellis and Walsh (2000) reported 99 studies showing a positive relationship between ADHD and delinquency. Given that these syndromes typically require delinquency for diagnosis, the disorders and the delinquency are the same thing. Lynam (1996, p. 211) defined conduct disorder as "the persistent display of serious antisocial actions that are extreme given the child's developmental level and have a significant impact on the rights of others." ODD is a less severe form of CD that often develops into it; it is characterized by behaviors such as frequent temper tantrums, lying, and so forth. According to Walsh (2002, p. 135), symptoms of ADHD usually appear first, followed by ODD, and then CD. In other words, these syndromes are just labels used to describe where a child is in terms of his or her aggressive behaviors.

Two examples of questions that illustrate the tautological nature of personality theories are provided by Caspi et al. (1994, p. 166) from the Minnesota Multiphasic Personality Inventory (MMPI) and the California Personality Inventory (CPI):

- "I have never been in trouble with the law."
- "Sometimes when I was young I stole things."

People who say no to the first question and yes to the second may be labeled with a certain personality trait, such as *poorly socialized*. Then, these personality traits are used to explain why certain individuals commit delinquent acts or crimes. This is circular reasoning, where individuals are labeled on the basis of their behaviors and then the label is used to explain the same behaviors. If it is true that delinquents can be differentiated from nondelinquents, and criminals from noncriminals (or more accurately, if serious, career criminals can be differentiated from nonserious and first-time offenders) by personality traits, it is still not appropriate to use those personality characteristics as explanatory factors. Why not?—Because personality traits are merely descriptors of behaviors.

How can propositions regarding personality be improved? Since the role of the brain must be incorporated to fully explain behavior, so too must it be to understand personality: "Our personalities, ethics, temperament, and our social traits—including asocial traits such as violence as an extreme manifestation—are all products of our brain, just as much as our ability to walk, talk, memorize, and listen to music. But even educated people will say, 'it's not your brain, it's your personality,' as if personality were an extracranial phenomena" (Goldberg, 2001). This quote clearly demonstrates that personality traits originate from the functioning of the brain. Given that the brain is programmed by genes (discussed in chapter 5), it is not surprising that genes play a major role in troublesome behaviors.

The notion that street criminals are characterized by lower levels of intelligence is logical and makes sense. However, it is illogical to assert that low intelligence is the cause of all crimes. For example, white-collar and corporate offenders are not cognitively impaired and may even have relatively high IQs.

Finally, the propositions pertaining to the diet-behavior link are logically stated. The results from these studies posit at least a three-stage model of antisocial behavior: first, a person consumes food or a drug; second, his or her brain chemistry is changed as neurotransmitter levels increase or decrease; and third, behavior changes as a result of changed brain function. Although this may seem logical, keep in mind that this three-stage model ignores the state of the brain before consumption of the food or drug. Our brain chemistry increases or decreases the likelihood that we will eat a poor diet and use drugs in the first place.

Other Organism Level Factors

There are other individual level risk factors not mentioned in this chapter. Many psychologists, for example, would assert a whole range of personality traits that are relevant for understanding antisocial behavior. As we argued in this chapter, these are merely descriptions of how a person behaves, says he or she behaves, feels like behaving, or prefers to behave. Yet, other organism level factors that have not received widespread attention certainly affect individual behavior. Many of these can be conceptualized as group level factors, such as peer influences and family socialization, and thus will be discussed in the next chapter.

Summary

In this chapter, we examined the effects of organism level factors on antisocial behavior. We argued that genes influence temperament, a key part of personality and behavior, and that learning also plays a role in the development of character, another part of personality and behavior. Furthermore, we reviewed research that personality traits such as impulsivity, low self-control, negative emotionality and antisocial personality disorder increase the risk of antisocial behavior. Studies also show the following personality traits to be important for understanding antisocial behavior: neuroticism, agreeableness, conscientiousness, psychoticism, negative emotionality, constraint, novelty seeking, reward dependence, self-directedness, and cooperativeness.

We also discussed research suggesting that personality traits such as negative emotionality are influenced by lower level factors such as neurotransmitters in the brain and genes, and by larger level factors such as family environment and parenting style. At the same time, we suggested that the child's temperament also influences family conditions such as parenting style and use of discipline so that there is a reciprocal relationship between parenting and children's personalities. We also presented evidence indicating that low levels of autonomic nervous system (ANS) arousal, known as hypoarousal, are related to an increased risk for antisocial behavior. Studies of intelligence show that low verbal IQ is related to an increased risk of antisocial behavior and to occupational problems. Mental illness and the potential for drug use and abuse are influenced by neurotransmitter levels, which are partially determined by genetics. Drug use and abuse also can alter neurotransmitter levels and perhaps even trigger mental illnesses. Improper diet/nutrition (i.e., vitamin deficiencies) and conditions such as low blood sugar or hypoglycemia also influence neurotransmitter levels and can increase the risk of poor mood, hyperactivity, conduct disorder (CD), attention deficit hyperactivity disorder (ADHD), drug abuse, aggression, and antisocial behavior. Finally, we showed in this chapter that maternal drug use during pregnancy may result in neuropsychological deficits. As for drug use itself, the drug most important for understanding violence and other antisocial behavior is alcohol.

Discussion Questions

1. What is an individual?
2. What is meant by the term *personality?*
3. Why is it that any theory can be interpreted as a personality theory?
4. What is psychoanalysis? Can it be used to help us understand antisocial behavior? Explain.
5. What does it mean that personality is behavior?
6. What are the main elements of antisocial personality disorder? Can it be used to explain antisocial behavior? Explain.
7. List and discuss the main propositions about personality and behavior.
8. What types of behaviors appear to be affected by personality?
9. Contrast the central nervous system (CNS) with the autonomic nervous system (ANS).
10. List and discuss the ways that scientists measure ANS activity. How is the ANS related to antisocial behavior?
11. According to the evidence presented, from where does personality appear to emerge?
12. What is executive cognitive function (ECF)? How is it related to antisocial behavior?
13. What is intelligence?
14. List and discuss the main propositions about intelligence and behavior.
15. What types of behaviors appear to be affected by intelligence levels?
16. What is the meaning of IQ? How is IQ measured?
17. Is IQ a valid measure of intelligence? Explain.
18. What problems is a person with a low IQ more likely to encounter?
19. Contrast verbal IQ with performance IQ.
20. What is mental illness?

21. List and discuss the main propositions about mental illness and behavior.
22. What types of behaviors appear to be affected by mental illness?
23. Contrast the term *mental illness* with *insanity*.
24. Briefly discuss the main types of mental illness, including their symptoms and their prevalence in the United States.
25. When is a person with a major mental illness most likely to commit violence?
26. Why are people with mental illnesses overrepresented in criminal justice populations?
27. What is diet and nutrition?
28. List and discuss the main propositions about diet/nutrition and behavior.
29. What types of behaviors appear to be affected by diet/nutrition?
30. Why is it logical to assume that you truly are what you eat?
31. What is a drug?
32. List and discuss the main propositions about drug consumption and behavior.
33. What types of behaviors appear to be affected by drug consumption?
34. What are the most commonly used drugs in the United States?
35. The effects of any drug on a person depend on what factors?
36. Contrast drug use with drug abuse.
37. List and define the main categories of drugs.
38. Which drug is most important for helping us understand antisocial behavior?
39. What is the relationship between genetics and drug use and abuse?
40. Why do mental illness and drug abuse co-occur?
41. Are the concepts of organism level explanations of crime clearly defined? Explain.
42. What is the logical adequacy of organism level explanations of crime?
43. What is the scope of organism level explanations of crime?

7

Group Level
Explanations of Crime

Introduction

Recall from chapter 3 that groups are simply a collective of organisms or individuals. *Merriam-Webster's Collegiate Dictionary* (2008) defines a group as "a number of individuals assembled together or having some unifying relationship"; "an assemblage of objects regarded as a unit"; and "an assemblage of related organisms." Groups include families, peers, and so on. Groups are made up of organisms (chapter 6) and they comprise communities and organizations (chapter 8) and ultimately societies (chapter 9). Factors at the group level of analysis include, but are not limited to, influences of family members, peer groups, religious groups, and schools. We discuss the influence of schools within peer group influence given that most school level factors pertain to peer groups; religion is discussed in chapter 8 as it relates to other community level factors. When reading this chapter, be aware that the two most relevant theories of antisocial behavior and criminality at the group level of analysis are *social learning theories* and *social control theories;* these theories are based on different assumptions about human nature (some even claim their assumptions conflict and thus the theories cannot be integrated). In this chapter, we examine the evidence from empirical tests of social learning and social control theories in order to summarize the influences of families and peers, two primary socializing groups that can serve as risk factors of protective factors.

Behavior in the Context of Groups

Recall the brief discussion from chapter 1 that some theories are based on different assumptions about human nature generally and human behavior in particular. Two sets of theories relevant for the group level of analysis stand out as excellent examples. Social learning theories and social control theories each explain deviance using group level factors, yet they posit two different causal pathways to behavior. *Social control theories* assert that criminality, deviant behavior, and antisocial behaviors are normal and expected in the absence of controls that are imposed on individuals by the groups and communities to which they belong. To the degree that people do not have a "stake in conformity" (Toby, 1957), they are free to deviate; to the degree that people have developed self-restraint and learned to control their impulses, they will not deviate. Conformity is achieved when people are adequately bonded to society, attached to other people, committed to law-abiding behavior, and involved in legitimate activities (Hirschi, 1969). These theories assume that people should be expected to commit criminal acts unless society stops them from doing so. In fact, Emile Durkheim (1897), one of the earliest social control theorists, speculated that humans may have unlimited appetites with no natural inborn controls.

Social learning theories assume the exact opposite about human behavior; these theories see humans as *not* naturally inclined to criminality, deviant behavior, and antisocial behavior. Social learning theories assert that criminality is learned in a process of communication between individuals, that people learn both how to commit crime and how to justify their illegal acts. In the absence of exposure to deviant influences, people will not commit criminal acts; that is, if people did not learn to be bad, they would not be bad. Learning can be thought of as the accumulation of information stored in the brain from life experiences. Vold, Bernard, and Snipes (1998, p. 180) defined learning as "habits and knowledge that develop as a result of the individual entering and adjusting to the environment."

Social learning theories suggest that antisocial and criminal behaviors are learned. Although peers are the group most responsible for teaching children how to commit crime and that crime is acceptable, social learning theorists would suggest that the family, too, is criminogenic. Social control theories suggest that antisocial and criminal behavior is normal in conditions of weak bonds to society. The group most relevant for establishing strong bonds to society is the family; peers also help bond a person to society. So, the two schools of thought agree that peers and families are important to understand the etiology of crime.

In essence, social control theories suggest that peers and family members are important for explaining why people do *not* commit crimes, whereas social learning theories suggest that peers and family members are important for explaining why people *do* commit crimes. Using the key terminology in this book, the former assume that peers and families are *protective factors* from criminality, while the latter assume that peers and families are *risk factors* for criminality. It is interesting to note that both sets of theories see learning as important to understanding criminal behavior. Social learning theories assert that it is criminal behavior that must be learned, whereas social control theories assert that it is conformity must be learned.

The evidence suggests that both sets of assumptions are partially correct. Peer and family influences can direct people toward criminal and antisocial behavior and away from criminal and antisocial behavior. What determines whether group level factors produce crime or prevent it depends on the nature of the exposure to the peers and family members.

Akers (2001, pp. 194–195) identified which groups are important for understanding individual behavior:

> The most important ... groups are the primary ones of family and friends, though they may also be secondary and reference groups. Neighbors, churches, school teachers, physicians, the law and authority figures, and other individuals and groups in the community (as well as mass media and other more remote sources of attitudes and models) have varying degrees of effect on the individual's propensity to commit criminal and delinquent behavior.

Similarly, Jang (1999, p. 645) claims:

> The family, school, and peers are the three most important social environments for the adolescent. Adolescents spend most of their time in those environments and their development takes place primarily through the development of relationships with people associated with those environments ... Thus it is not surprising to see major theories of delinquency focus on how the adolescent's relationships with immediate environments influence his or her behaviors.

In the rest of the chapter, we outline and discuss the two theories that pertain most to groups—social learning and social control theories. Later in the chapter, specific findings related to peer influences and family influences are discussed.

Social Learning Theories

Social Learning Theories

Imitation

Social learning theories go at least as far back as Gabriel Tarde's (1890) *theory of imitation*. Imitation theory posits that people learn to behave simply by watching others, particularly when inferiors imitate the behaviors of superiors. A simple example of this would be a child watching a parent drink out of a glass and then drinking out of the glass after the parent. Tarde asserted that it is more likely that people will imitate each other when they spend a lot of time together (such as a child and a parent). The American Academy of Pediatrics (1998) asserts that children imitate their parents, and the American Academy of Child & Adolescent Psychiatry suggests that older children also imitate their parents, highlighting the importance of good behaviors by parents.

Differential Association

Decades later, between 1934 and 1947, Edwin Sutherland developed the theory of *differential association*. In 1939, Sutherland put forth seven propositions of differential association. In 1947, he offered nine. They include the following:

1. Criminal behavior is learned.
2. Criminal behavior is learned in interaction with other persons in a process of communication.
3. The principal part of the learning of criminal behavior occurs within intimate personal groups.
4. When criminal behavior is learned, the learning includes techniques of committing the crime, which are sometimes very complicated and sometimes simple, and the specific direction of motives, drives, rationalizations, and attitudes.
5. The specific direction of motives and drives is learned from definitions of the legal codes as favorable or unfavorable.
6. A person becomes delinquent because of an excess of definitions favorable to violation of law over definitions unfavorable to violation of the law.
7. Differential associations may vary in frequency, duration, priority, and intensity.
8. The process of learning criminal behavior by association with criminal and anticriminal patterns involves all of the mechanisms that are involved in any other learning.

9. While criminal behavior is an expression of general needs and values, it is not explained by those general needs and values, since noncriminal behavior is an expression of the same needs and values (Paternoster & Bachman, 2001).

After reading these nine propositions, you should get the sense that Sutherland believed that criminal behavior and noncriminal behavior are both learned in the same way. People learn to commit crime much the same way they learn to ride a bike, tie their shoes, and so on. In fact, Sutherland (1947, p. 4) wrote that "criminal behavior is part of human behavior ... and [so it] must be explained within the same general framework as any other human behavior." This is the same assertion made by the integrated systems perspective discussed in chapter 3. As explained by Sutherland (1939, p. 4): "The processes which result in systematic criminal behavior are fundamentally the same in form as the processes which result in systematic lawful behavior ... Criminal behavior differs from lawful behavior in the standards by which it is judged but not in the principles of the [causal] processes."

Differential association explains that the content of learning includes not only the techniques for committing crimes (the how-to part of learning) but also the motives, drives, rationalizations, and attitudes that produce crime (the why part of learning). In other words, it explains that people learn how to commit crime and why crime is acceptable and even desirable behavior.

The theory also explains that the process of learning occurs through associations with deviant peers. Sutherland viewed learning through interpersonal communication as the most important type of learning. Although he did not explicitly ignore the effects of the mass media on behavior, Sutherland suggested that it was associations with peers (and thus differential associations) that best account for individual behavior (Sutherland & Cressey, 1974). The importance of differential associations depends on the number of times a person is exposed (*frequency*), the length of the exposure (*duration*), how strong the definition is (*intensity*), and whether the exposure is experienced early in life or later (*priority*). Recall from chapter 3 that these contingencies were modified for use in the integrated systems perspective used in this book.

Sutherland did point out that the way a community is organized (which includes its degree of conflict between different cultures) would determine whether criminal associations would be promoted or prevented. This means his theory is sensitive to larger level phenomena, including *social disorganization* (discussed in chapter 8) and *culture conflict* (discussed in chapter 9). Sutherland asserted that some groups in communities inevitably come to value criminal behavior. *Subcultural theories* test propositions related to the belief that some groups hold values that are different than the mainstream and that members learn these values from one another; thus, some see subcultural theories as learning theories (discussed in chapter 9).

Differential Identification

Daniel Glaser (1956) later modified Sutherland's theory and called it *differential identification.* His version of social learning theory suggests that one need not actually hang out with criminal peers to be affected by them; instead, one could be negatively affected merely by identifying with criminal peers, directly or indirectly. For example, a young person may identify with a subculture, such as a gang, without actually belonging to it. If an individual thinks that gangs commit crimes such as selling drugs, the person may commit crimes to feel like he or she belongs. If differential identification is true, this suggests that media broadcasts of criminal acts could produce more criminality as people who felt any connection to the offenders would be more likely to commit crimes themselves. For example, the term *Columbine effect* has been used to describe the ripple effect of the 1998 massacre at Columbine High School on school violence elsewhere in the country (Robinson, 2001). Dozens of organizations, such as the Center for Media and Public Affairs, the National Coalition on Television Violence, the Media Awareness Network, and the Center for Media Literacy, have published research showing the harmful effects of violence in television and the movies on child and adolescent behavior. Box 7.1 shows major conclusions from the impact of media violence on behavior.

Box 7.1 Media Violence and Behavior

Studies of the impact of media on violence are crystal clear in their findings and implications for society. The National Institute on Media and the Family (2008) reports the following statistics and findings about media and violence:

- By the time a child is eighteen years old, he or she will witness on television (with average viewing time) 200,000 acts of violence including 40,000 murders.
- Children, ages 8 to 18, spend more time (44½ hours per week—6½ hours daily) in front of computer, television, and game screens than any other activity in their lives except sleeping.
- Since the 1950s, more than 1,000 studies have been done on the effects of violence in television and movies. The majority of these studies conclude that children who watch significant amounts of television

and movie violence are more likely to exhibit aggressive behavior, attitudes and values.

- The American Medical Association, American Academy of Pediatrics, American Psychological Association, American Academy of Family Physicians, and American Academy of Child & Adolescent Psychiatry all agree that violence in the media influences the behavior of children, especially younger children who are more impressionable, less able to distinguish between fantasy and reality, less able to discern motives for violence, and more likely to learn by observing and imitating.
- Children who watch more TV and play more video games are not only exposed to more media violence, but are more likely to act more aggressively with peers, to assume the worst in their interactions with peers, to become less sensitive to violence and those who suffer from violence, to seek out additional violence in entertainment, to see the world as violent and mean, and to see violence as an acceptable way of solving problems.

The American Academy of Pediatrics (1998, p. 512) claims the main messages children learn from television violence are: 1) violence is an acceptable way to deal with problems; and 2) violence does no real harm (since people on television reappear even after being hurt or killed, or simply vanish from the scene). This encourages violence in children who see it. The American Academy of Child & Adolescent Psychiatry (AACAP) states that "80 percent of the programs that children watch contain violence. There is widespread agreement that children who are allowed to see violence on television show more aggressive behavior than those who don't" (Pruitt, 1998, p. 154).

Differential Reinforcement

Although propositions by early learning theorists seem logical, they are very difficult to test because of their reliance on concepts such as Sutherland's "definitions favorable to the violation of the law" and "definitions unfavorable to the violation of the law." In an effort to make propositions about learning directly testable, Robert Burgess and Ronald Akers (1968) and C. Ray Jeffery (1965) utilized the logic of classical conditioning found in the works of Ivan Pavlov and operant conditioning from B. F. Skinner to develop the theory of *differential reinforcement* (Vold et al., 1998). This theory suggests that when criminal behavior is rewarded (reinforced), it is likely to be repeated, whereas when it leads to pain (punishment), it is not likely to be repeated. Operant conditioning utilizes consequences to change voluntary behavior.

The following are the main propositions of differential reinforcement:

1. Criminal behavior is learned according to the principles of operant conditioning.
2. Criminal behavior is learned both in nonsocial situations that are reinforcing or discriminative and through social interaction in which the behavior of other persons is reinforcing or discriminative for criminal behavior.
3. The principal part of learning of criminal behavior occurs in those groups that comprise the individual's major source of reinforcement.
4. The learning of criminal behavior, including specific techniques, attitudes, and avoidance procedures, is a function of the effective and available, and the rules or norms by which these reinforcers are applied.
5. The specific class of behaviors that are learned and their frequency of occurrence are a function of the reinforcers that are effective and available, and the rules or norms by which these reinforcers are applied.
6. Criminal behavior is a function of norms that are discriminative for criminal behavior, the learning of which takes place when such behavior is more highly reinforced than noncriminal behavior.
7. The strength of criminal behavior is a direct function of the amount, frequency, and probability of its reinforcement (Paternoster & Bachman, 2001).

Observational Learning Theory

In 1973 and 1977, Albert Bandura (1973, 1977) developed his own social learning theory. Bandura's theory is similar in nature to those above, and it asserts that learning occurs through observation. Bandura (1977) noted: "Learning would be exceedingly laborious, not to mention hazardous, if people had to rely solely on the effects of their own actions to inform them what to do. Fortunately, most human behavior is learned observationally through modeling: from observing others one forms an idea of how new behaviors are performed, and on later occasions this coded information serves as a guide for action." (p. 22).

Bandura's theory assumes that after individuals observe the behavior of others, they organize and rehearse the behavior symbolically and then overtly. Behavior is modeled into words or images which helps retaining the information. Individuals are more prone to repeat an observed behavior if it results in some outcome that rewards or reinforces the behavior, and if it is engaged in by someone looked up to, similar to Tarde's assertions about imitation. When applied to aggression, Bandura showed that children were more likely to copy the behavior of an adult beating up a doll if the behavior was rewarded rather than punished. And when children were shown a film of an adult beating up a live clown, they tended to copy that behavior themselves when brought into a room and introduced to a live clown!

Social Structural Learning Theory

Ronald Akers's (1999) version of the theory, called *social structural learning theory*, is considered the best known and most complete social learning theory. His theory is based in part on Albert Bandura's (1969) assertions that behavior can be learned by watching others without directly experiencing pleasure or pain.

Akers' theory combines elements of imitation, differential association, differential reinforcement, as well as social structural elements to explain how crime is learned; because of the structural elements, Akers calls it *social structural learning theory*. Akers's social learning theory rests on the assertions that the main concepts are testable, so he offers definitions for imitation, differential associations, and differential reinforcement, as well as definitions favorable and unfavorable to law violation. As explained by Akers (2001, p. 195), "definitions favorable and unfavorable to criminal and delinquent behavior are developed through imitation and differential reinforcement." Imitation is "engagement in behavior after the observation of similar behavior in others" (p. 196). Differential reinforcement is "the balance of anticipated or actual rewards and punishments that follow or are consequences of behavior" including "past, present, and anticipated future rewards and punishments" (p. 195). It includes positive reinforcement (i.e., getting something pleasurable from your behavior), negative reinforcement (i.e., escaping or avoiding pain through behavior), positive punishment (i.e., experiencing pain as a result of behavior), and negative punishment (i.e., losing something pleasant because of behavior), each of which varies in terms of amount, frequency, and probability.

The causal logic suggested by Akers maintains that criminal behavior originates in the context of associations with criminals who hold definitions favorable to violating the law, when observers imitate the behavior of these people. Criminal behaviors are continued when reinforced either directly by reward or pleasure, or when an individual observes others being rewarded for criminal behavior. Structural conditions such as income inequality, poverty, and so forth increase the likelihood that one will associate with criminal or delinquent peers (these factors are discussed in chapter 9).

In 1998, Akers (p. 50) summarized his theory this way:

> The probability that persons will engage in criminal and deviant behavior is increased and the probability of their conforming to the norm is decreased when they differentially associate with others who commit criminal behavior and espouse definitions favorable to it, are relatively more exposed in-person or symbolically to salient criminal/deviant models, define it as desirable or justified in a situation discriminative for the behavior, and have received in the past and anticipate in the current or future situation relatively greater reward than punishment for the behavior.

According to the causal logic put forth by Akers, imitation of behavior becomes less important as a person gets reinforced for his or her behavior. His theory is developmental in the sense that he views deviance as a process rather than an event, one that develops over time mostly in the group environment.

As posited by Akers (2001, pp. 198–199), structural factors indirectly affect antisocial and criminal behavior: "The society and community provide the general learning contexts for individuals. The family, peer groups, schools, churches, and other groups provide the more immediate contexts that promote or discourage the criminal or conforming behavior of the individual ... Social learning is hypothesized as the behavioral process by which social disorganization, group/culture conflict or other social structural variables ... induce or retard criminal actions in individuals." This assumption related to the role of larger level factors is also made by proponents of the integrated systems perspective (discussed in chapter 3).

Summary of Social Learning Theories

Although there are numerous social learning theories, they all make essentially the same assertion, that in the absence of deviant influences, antisocial and criminal behaviors would be far less likely. That is, it is association with deviant and violent peers, role models, images, and so forth that produce deviant and violent behavior in those exposed. In spite of the fact that the major social learning theories were developed by different theorists over decades and that each used different terminology and concepts in the theories, they all essentially make the same assertion that antisocial behavior and criminality should be expected when people learn to be deviant and violent from others.

Main Propositions of Social Learning Theories

Given the predictions made by social learning theories, the following propositions have been tested:

- Antisocial behavior, delinquent behavior, and criminality are learned from peers and families through the processes of imitation, differential association, and differential reinforcement.

Key Concepts of Social Learning Theories

From the preceding propositions, the following concepts can be isolated and defined:

- Peers
- Families
- Imitation
- Differential association
- Differential reinforcement
- Delinquent behavior
- Antisocial behavior
- Criminality

Box 7.2 defines the key concepts of social learning theories. Scholars have used these definitions to test the main propositions of studies related to peer and family influences. The findings of these tests are discussed in the following section.

Box 7.2 Definitions of Key Concepts of Social Learning Theories

- *Imitation. Nominal*—engagement in behavior after the observation of similar behavior in others. *Operational*—copying behavior after observing it in person or via media outlets.
- *Differential association. Nominal*—the process by which a person is exposed to normative definitions that are relatively more or less favorable to violating the law. *Operational*—the number of deviant peers one considers friends, the amount of time a person spends with deviant peers, how frequently one hangs out with deviant peers, and other such indicators usually measured through self-reports or parental estimates.
- *Differential reinforcement. Nominal*—the balance of anticipated or actual rewards and punishments that follow or are consequences of behavior including past, present, and anticipated future rewards and punishments. *Operational*—behavior committed after positive reinforcement

(i.e., getting something pleasurable from your behavior) or negative reinforcement (i.e., escaping or avoiding pain through behavior), or behavior prevented by positive punishment (i.e., experiencing pain as a result of behavior) or negative punishment (i.e., losing something pleasant because of behavior), as measured by self-report studies.

- *Peers. Nominal*—people who are close to a person; friends. *Operational*—friends identified by individuals in self-report surveys or surveys of parents and teachers.
- *Family. Nominal*—a group of people sharing a common bloodline who live in close conjunction to one another. *Operational*—a group of people sharing the same last name and same genealogy, who claim to be related to one another.
- *Delinquency. Nominal*—acts committed by juveniles that, if committed by adults, would be considered crimes by the criminal justice system. *Operational*—usually measured by official indicators such as arrests and adjudication of guilt in a court, also measured by self-report data and reports of observations of behaviors by parents and teachers.
- *Antisocial behavior. Nominal*—any behaviors that conflict with the prevailing norms of society and/or that are viewed as abnormal. *Operational*—any form of behavior defined as antisocial, measured by official crime reports, self-reported behaviors, or evaluations from others.
- *Criminality. Nominal*—committing any act that violates the criminal law. *Operational*—the number of times a person is arrested, is convicted in court for a violation of the criminal law, and/or self-reports violating the law.

Evaluation of Social Learning Theories

In the following sections, we address social learning theories. We assess the empirical validity of the theories, discuss the scope of the research, as well as address the conceptual clarity and the logical adequacy of the propositions.

Empirical Validity of Social Learning Theories

Most learning theories of antisocial behavior and criminality enjoy a large amount of support (Akers, 1994), whereas others are not directly testable against empirical evidence. Warr (2001, p. 186) summarized the support enjoyed by social learning theories as follows: "No characteristic of individuals known to criminologists is a better predictor of criminal behavior than the number of delinquent friends an individual has [for another good review of the evidence, see Matsueda & Anderson, 1998; Warr, 1996].... Few, if any, empirical regularities in criminology have been documented as often or for as long as the association between delinquency and delinquent friends."

Spending Time with Friends

Generally, spending more time with deviant peers is associated with a higher likelihood of offending, especially among adolescents (Regnerus, 2002). A study of 8,838 respondents of an in-school survey, and two in-home interviews found that having highly delinquent friends and spending a great deal of time in unstructured socializing with friends were related to increased delinquency (Hainey & Osgood, 2005). Those who associate most with deviant peers tend to be among those classes of offenders committing the largest numbers of delinquent acts among adolescents (Wiesner & Capaldi, 2003). Interestingly, friendships with girls are found to reduce the likelihood of delinquent behaviors, especially for female school age girls (McCarthy, Felmlee, & Hagan, 2004).

As noted by Warr, however, the meaning of the association between peers and deviance is still debated. As you will see, scholars disagree about which comes first, associations with deviant peers or deviant behavior.

Additionally, according to a growing number of scholars, "differential association and social learning are not enough to account for the high levels of antisocial behavior we observe among adolescents. People are drawn to each other on the basis of similarity, and they become more similar because of their associations" (Walsh, 2002, p. 225).

One problem with social learning theories is that associations with delinquent, deviant, and/or criminal peers usually occur *after* a person begins to engage in delinquent, deviant, and criminal behaviors (Lanier & Henry, 1998). The saying "birds of a feather flock together" is appropriate here, as associations with other delinquents, deviants, and criminals do not explain why a person begins his or her career with antisocial behavior (Glueck & Glueck, 1950). The evidence suggests that other factors account for the etiology of behavior, while associations with others engaged in the same behaviors reinforce the likelihood of continued behaviors.

Consider the following question:

Does the fact that our behavior is strongly related to that of our close associations mean that we learned those behaviors from them, and that they influenced our own conduct, as differential association theory would predict? Or does it mean that we simply select those people as friends whose attitudes and behaviors closely resemble ours ...?

We believe there is no real consensus in the field about this issue, although [it is likely] that both processes are at work. Our friends do influence us in subtle and not-so-subtle ways, and we tend to select as companions those who are most like ourselves. (Paternoster & Bachman, 2001, p. 178)

Studies show support for the "notion that a delinquent attracts the attention of peers, that audience members take note of this phenomenon, and that they therefore increase their delinquency in proportion to their own desire for peer attention" (Rebellon, 2006: 403). In other words, delinquency prompts peers to spend more time with delinquents.

According to Akers (2001, p. 197), "associations with peers and others are most often formed initially around attractions, friendships, and circumstances, such as neighborhood proximity, that have little to do directly with coinvolvement in some deviant behavior." After deviant individuals commit acts in group situations and receive reinforcement from their peers, they may very well seek out other deviants. This is not inconsistent with Akers's social learning theory. Still, Akers does recognize that deviant behavior can develop independent of peer associations; it is because delinquent behavior increases after associations with delinquent peers that Akers claims the theory is supported.

Matsueda and Anderson (1998) claim there is a two-way relationship between peer associations and delinquency, because each factor affects the other, and delinquency predicts delinquent associations better than delinquent associations predict delinquency. A study by Thornberry et al. (1994, p. 62) also reported a two-way relationship between peers and delinquency. The debate between those who propose that delinquent associations precede delinquency and those who claim that delinquency precedes delinquent associations "may have unnecessarily occupied the time of theoretical criminology ... It is time for criminological theories to reflect the complexity of interrelationships observed in the everyday world." Such findings are consistent with Thornberry's *interactional theory*, which proposes reciprocal relationships between various factors and behavior (discussed in chapter 10) and the integrated systems perspective used in this book (discussed in chapter 3).

Reed and Rose (1998) suggested three possible relationships between peers and behavior. First, the *socialization hypothesis* suggests that peers influence deviant behavior. Second, the *social selection hypothesis* suggests that deviant behavior influences peer selection. Third, the *rationalization process* suggests that delinquents form their pro-delinquency attitudes after engaging in delinquency, whether with peers or not. In their study of serious theft, Reed and Rose reported evidence in support of the socialization model and the social selection hypothesis. This finding is consistent with other longitudinal tests of social learning theories (Agnew, 1992; Thornberry et al., 1994). Finally, Reed and Rose found that associations with delinquent peers are associated with greater theft and that committing theft is associated with greater associations with delinquent peers. The key process does not involve a change in attitudes, beliefs, or what Sutherland called definitions, however.

The causal order of peer influences may depend on the type of offender being examined. For life course persistent (LCP) offenders, relatively stable antisocial personality characteristics tend to precede associations with delinquent peers, while for adolescent limited (AL) offenders, peer associations tend to precede antisocial behavior. In life course persistent offenders, "*stable* antisocial characteristics precede associations with delinquent peers." In adolescent limited offenders, "association with delinquent peers precedes the development of *temporary* antisocial characteristics" (Walsh, 2009, p. 169). The antisocial behavior of AL offenders is temporary and situational in nature, whereas for LCP offenders it is persistent and occurs before peer influences (Walsh, 2002, pp. 136–137).

Spending Time in Groups

Another fact about antisocial behaviors that is consistent with social learning theories is that acts of delinquency by juveniles and crimes by adults tend to be committed in group situations. Warr (2001) writes: "The group nature of delinquency is one of the most solidly established features of delinquent behavior and has been repeatedly noted by criminological researchers since the 1930s (Reiss, 1986; Warr, 1996). The fact that most offenders commit offenses with companions rather than alone can be construed as evidence that individuals acquire the motivation and knowledge to engage in crime through interaction with others." The importance of peers to young people peaks in the middle to late teenage years, meaning that this is when delinquency would be most likely in peer situations (Warr, 1993). A more detailed analysis of longitudinal data from the National Youth Survey (NYS) showed that the effects of peers and attachment to school on delinquency generally increase from early to middle adolescence (Jang, 1999). The influence of peers was found to peak at age 13 years and then decline thereafter, while the influence of attachment to school was found to peak at age 15 years and then decline. This study also found that the effect of the family on delinquency tends to fluctuate, but is generally weak and becomes insignificant once effects of schools and peers are considered. Delinquency tends to be highest in middle adolescence.

Even with these findings, it is not clear that young people commit acts of which they believe their friends will approve. Much research suggests that what really matters in peer interactions is what one's friends do, not what they say they do or what they appear to support (e.g., see Matsueda & Anderson, 1998). If this is true, then imitation of peer behavior and reinforcement of behavior may explain behavior better than differential association. At least one study, however, found that juvenile reports of having delinquent peers could actually be a measure of their own delinquency (Zhang & Messner, 2000). In this study, youth with more delinquent peer associations (as reported by their parents) reported higher rates of delinquency. Given that the parental measure of peer influences yielded different results than the measure of peer influences by the youth, it is possible that diverging results of social learning theories are at least partly attributable to the ways in which peer influences are measured.

Scope of Social Learning Theories

On the one hand, the scope of learning theories seems small, as typically tests of these theories are limited to relatively minor acts of delinquency and criminality, including those by its founders such as Akers. Akers's tests of social learning theory have focused on crimes such as substance abuse, smoking, drinking, and rape and sexual coercion among college males (Akers, 1992, 1998; Akers et al., 1979; Akers, 1985; Akers & Cochran, 1985; Akers & Lee, 1996; Boeringer et al., 1991). The only serious crime in these studies is sex crimes. Other studies have found support for effects of definitions favorable to deviance and having deviant friends on academic dishonesty among college students (Lersch, 1999) and computer crime among college students (Skinner & Fream, 1997).

On the other hand, many scholars suggest that learning plays a major role in acts of white-collar and corporate crime, as well (e.g., see Friedrichs, 1996; Robinson & Murphy, 2008; Rosoff, Pontell, & Tillman, 2002; Simon & Hagan, 1999; Simon 2002). To the degree that white-collar and corporate crimes are learned and promoted on the job, the scope of social learning theory would be much wider. Without question, the mechanisms of reinforcement are important for understanding the continuation of any behavior.

According to Vold et al. (1998, p. 187), most tests of the original differential association theory have been conducted on juveniles. Thus, it best accounts for delinquency rather than adult criminality. This may not be so problematic if one's goal is to explain the origination of abnormal behavior—as suggested in chapter 1, the etiology of adult criminality begins in childhood and adolescence.

Conceptual Clarity of Social Learning Theories

The concepts of most social learning theories, including imitation and differential association, are not defined operationally so that they can be directly measured. As explained by Akers (2001, p. 195): "Definitions are one's own attitudes or meanings that one attaches to given behavior. That is, they are orientations, rationalizations, definitions of the situation, and other evaluative and moral attitudes that define the commission of an act as right or wrong, good or bad, desirable or undesirable, justified or unjustified." These definitions are general or specific, and positive or neutralizing. General definitions refer to those that are normally held by a person, while specific definitions are only espoused in certain situations. Positive definitions specifically justify criminal behavior, while neutralizing definitions merely allow one to justify deviance.

How can such things be measured? Akers continues: "Cognitively, [definitions] provide a mind-set that makes one more willing to commit the act when the opportunity occurs. Behaviorally, they affect the commission of deviant or criminal behavior by acting as internal discriminative stimuli. Discriminative stimuli operate as cues or signals to the individual as to what responses are appropriate or expected in a given situation" (Akers, 2001, p. 195). How can a scientist measure one's mind-set and the cues or signals sent to an individual as to how he or she should behave?

Some claim differential association theory is not directly testable because its key concepts (definitions favorable and unfavorable to the violation of the law) cannot be empirically verified or refuted (Curran & Renzetti, 1994). Its nonfalsifiable status should not be surprising given that differential association is based on George Herbert Mead's *symbolic interactionism*, which asserted that human beings act toward things on the basis of the meanings that the things have for them (Blumer, 1969, pp. 2–3). Thus, "the key factor determining whether people violate the law is the meaning they give to the social conditions they experience, rather than the conditions themselves. Ultimately, whether a person obeys or violates the law depends on how they *define* their situations" (Vold et al., 1998, p. 186). Ask yourself, how could a scientist measure how individuals define the situations they find themselves in, whether these situations are viewed as favorable to the violation of the law or not?

Although some scholars such as Akers maintain that differential association can be measured and thus continue to include it in their theoretical models of criminality (e.g., Akers, 1999), even if the proposition was testable, it is not possible to tell if a person has more definitions favorable to violation of the law than unfavorable to violation of the law (Sampson, 1999). Scholars must be able to measure something before they can count it. Donald Cressey (1960), Sutherland's coauthor, agreed that differential association is not directly testable.

Indirect tests can be made of differential association. For example, Matsueda (1988) claimed that juveniles who have more delinquent friends also report committing more delinquent acts and that adherence to beliefs in law violations increases the risks of engaging in delinquency. Matsueda cited numerous studies that indirectly tested the main proposition that hanging out with deviants increases one's risk of deviance. The problem is that self-reported delinquent peers may actually be a measure of self-reported delinquency on the part of respondents, as noted earlier.

As with all other single factor and multifactor theories, social learning theories are plagued with the problem of overprediction; given the exposure to all of the deviant peers, family members, and criminogenic images in the media, logic would suggest that a lot more deviance would occur than we are aware (Bohm, 2001, p. 89). This means we should expect a lot more delinquency and crime among people who live in environmental conditions described by theorists.

The modalities of differential association (frequency, duration, priority, and intensity) were also never clearly defined by anyone (Warr, 2001, p. 185), although criminologists have an understanding of what they mean. As discussed earlier, frequency of association denotes the amount of exposures a person has with people. Duration is how long associations last. Priority refers to the fact that earlier exposures are supposed to have more influence on behavior than latter exposures. Intensity refers to the strength of exposures. The modalities of exposure are adapted for the integrated systems theory of antisocial behavior put forth in chapter 10 (see chapter 3 for a discussion of how these modalities apply to the model).

Logical Adequacy of Social Learning Theories

Generally, the propositions of social learning theories are logically stated— that is, they make sense. Learning clearly plays a role in all human behavior; children not only learn how to behave (e.g., how to ride a bike, how to walk, how to commit crimes, and so on), but also learn from others justifications for behaviors (e.g., riding a bike is fun, walking is an important form of transportation, crime is acceptable). One problem that plagues learning theories, however, is that they do not take into account the role of the human brain in learning. Stated as clearly as possible, the brain is the organ of learning (discussed in chapter 5); without the brain, there is no learning.

As with all other social theories, learning theories thus tend to ignore individual differences, especially in terms of how people learn (Beirne & Messerschmidt, 2000). Since no two people (other than identical twins) share the same genes, and since no two people (including identical twins) share the same environmental experiences, no two people have the same brain. As discussed in chapter 5, all brains are the same in terms of structure and all essentially function the same way; nevertheless, no two people learn the same way. Numerous learning styles have been identified; these are not taken into account by learning theories of crime.

Akers (2001, p. 196) acknowledged the possible role of biological factors in behavior, but ultimately dismissed them:

> There may be a physiological basis for the tendency of some individuals (such as those prone to sensation-seeking) more than others to find certain forms of deviant behavior intrinsically rewarding (Wood et al., 1995). However, the theory proposes that most of the learning in criminal and deviant behavior is the result of social exchange in which the words, responses, presence, and behavior of other persons directly reinforce behavior, provide the setting for reinforcement (discriminative stimuli), or serve as the conduit through which other social rewards and punishers are delivered or made available.

It is possible that Akers did not give credence to biological factors simply because he was not trained in the discipline; to the degree this is true, it suggests social learning theories are plagued by disciplinary myopia.

Differential association theory, in particular, serves as an example of disciplinary myopia. Vold et al. (1998, p. 198, note 61) pointed out that when Sutherland was finalizing his theory at the University of Indiana, in a nearby building B.F. Skinner was conducting experiments on learning that would lead to the behaviorist school of thought. Either Sutherland was not aware of Skinner's work or saw it as irrelevant for the role of learning crime. Either way, had Sutherland and Skinner teamed up during this time, learning theory would undoubtedly have progressed faster.

It is quite odd that Sutherland's assertions about the etiology of crime evolved the way they did. Paternoster and Bachman (2001, pp. 175–176) pointed out, for example, the following historical discussion of Sutherland's progression:

> In his first edition of his textbook on crime, *Criminology* ... Sutherland (1924) set forth a theory of crime at the individual level, implied that there were important differences between offenders and nonoffenders, and attributed criminality to multiple causal factors ... At least in Sutherland's early foray into criminological theory, then, he laid the causes of crime on the doorstep of such factors as dysfunctional

personalities, poor family socialization, low intelligence, and the biological deficiencies of criminals. Sutherland's original theory of crime,
then, was both individual-centered and multi-factored.

This is ironic given Sutherland's more parsimonious and simplistic theory of
differential association. Some might say then that differential association theory
hindered the development of the field of knowledge about criminality. As explained
by Warr (2001), Sutherland's original ideas about crime were influenced by several events in American sociology (and what would become criminology), most
notably the so-called Chicago School of Criminology (discussed in chapter 8).

Learning theories also generally posit a very simplistic version of learning
(Bohm, 2001, p. 86), although Akers's (1999) social learning theory takes into
account peer influences, familial influences, the influence of the mass media,
as well as social structural elements. Evidence in favor of imitation and differential reinforcement is very weak (Sampson, 1999).

Research shows that reinforcement of behavior is not only a social process
but also a biological process. A study of habitual criminals conducted by Wood
et al. (1997) suggested that when crimes are committed, they lead to pleasure
through symbolic meanings of the acts as well as neurophysiological highs, presumably through alterations of neurotransmitter levels in the brain. This is consistent with Katz's (1995) theory related to the many seductions of crime and to
Ellis's (1987, 1991, 1996) arousal theory. As behavior is rewarded, it is reinforced and thus likely to be repeated. When something feels good to a person,
it affects levels of dopamine in the brain; this counteracts the negative effects of
stress on an individual. When a person feels better, he or she is more likely to
repeat the behavior, especially when other forms of socially acceptable stimulating
behaviors are not available. Social learning theories tend to ignore this.

Biological factors not only play a role in learning (because of the way information is learned in the brain), but also help us understand why people
make the associations they do. In other words, differences in individuals help
us understand why people hang out with the people they hang out with. Thus,
it may be the individual differences that explain not only why people are more
likely to engage in antisocial behavior and criminality, but also why they are
more likely to hang out with criminal friends. According to Walsh (2002, p. 125):
"Association with delinquent peers acts more like a catalyst, speeding up and
enhancing antisocial conduct among the predisposed, than as a stimulator of
uncharacteristic behavior among the innocent." This would explain why behavior usually precedes definitions or attitudes favorable for behaviors (Bagozzi
& Warshaw, 1992). In some neighborhoods, associations with delinquent peers
may be sufficient to produce delinquency; in others it is not necessary.

Social learning theories also tend to ignore gender differences. Some studies have found differential effects for males and females. For example, Mears, Ploeger, and Warr (1998) reported that the factor of exposure to delinquency peers affects men and women differently. This study proposed that women in general possess something, presumably from learning through our culture, that protects them more from the effects of delinquent peers. Women, according to Gilligan (1982), are socialized to be more concerned with the care of others, while males are socialized to pursue their own self-interest. Mears et al. (1998) also cited evidence that there are qualitative differences in the moral reasoning of men and women. Their evidence suggested that women are more sensitive and empathetic to others, which may imply that they are more drawn to similar people and less affected by negative peer influences. Their findings also showed that females spend less time, on average, than males with their peers on weekdays and that males have more delinquent peers than females. Finally, the protective factor of moral evaluation learned by females can be neutralized if females are exposed to male delinquents.

Social Control Theories

Anomie Theory

Social control theories go at least as far back as Emile Durkheim's (1893, 1897) *theory of anomie* (discussed in chapter 9 as a society level factor). Durkheim claimed that as societies became larger and more advanced, institutions like the family would be less able to regulate (or control) its members' behaviors. Furthermore, labor would be less specialized in larger societies, and there would be many more people with no specialized skills to offer to the labor force. Thus, they would have little stake in conformity—little reason to conform to society's rules and expectations.

Social control theories, based on Durkheim's theory of anomie, view deviance as the norm; thus conformity is what they seek to explain. The most important question they ask is, why don't people commit crimes given all the reasons to do so?

Failure of Personal and Social Controls

One of the earliest social control theories was that of Albert Reiss (1951), who put forth what has been called *failure of personal and social controls.* Reiss studied more than 1,000 white male youth probationers and found that probation revocation was most common among the juveniles who were diagnosed as having what he called poor personal control over their behaviors and who were least affected by social controls. In his study, this meant that the juveniles did not regularly attend school and were described as behaviorally problematic by school personnel. Restraints to delinquency (or controls) are found in the family, neighborhood or community, school, and within the self (Paternoster & Bachman, 2001).

Stake in Conformity

Later in the same decade, Jackson Toby (1957) put forth the concept *stake in conformity,* which is central to all control theories. Although all young people have reasons to break the law, those most likely to do so are juveniles with little to lose by not conforming. This means young people who could lose face at school and in their families, or lose something else of value, would be least likely to commit acts of delinquency. He also noted that support or reinforcement for delinquency by peers is more likely in neighborhoods where lots of young people have a low stake in conformity, suggesting a link between social control and social learning theories.

Multiple Control Factors

The next year, Ivan Nye (1958) put forth his theory of *multiple control factors,* which postulates that delinquency results from weak social controls including *direct controls* (i.e., threat of punishment and informal sanctions), *indirect controls* (i.e., attachments to noncriminal role models), and *internal controls* (i.e., strong moral conscience). Many important control mechanisms occur within the family. Surveying nearly 800 high school students, Nye compared various measures of social controls to some very minor acts of delinquency. Vold et al. (1998, p. 204) wrote: "In all, Nye tested 313 relationships between youths and their parents. He found that 139 of those were consistent with his control theory, 167 were not significant, and only seven were inconsistent with it." Although this sounds supportive, all of his measures were indirect in nature, so findings were subject to widely diverging interpretations.

Containment Theory

Walter Reckless's (1961) *containment theory* is another control theory that examined both what motivates people to commit crime and what stops them:

> He argued that motivation to commit deviant acts could be provided by different "pushes" or "pulls." One could be pushed toward delinquent conduct by psychological factors such as restlessness, rebelliousness,

inner tension, impulsivity, or aggressiveness. Pushes toward delinquency can also come from one's social environment and include poverty or a lack of legitimate opportunities. One can be pulled by such factors as media portrayals of crime, the level of crime in one's neighborhood, and the presence of delinquent opportunities (Paternoster & Bachman, 2001, p. 77).

Given such pushes and pulls toward crime, restraints are needed to contain one's propensity for deviance. Thus, *inner containments* include one's self-concept and degree of self-control, and *outer containments* include social institutions such as families, schools, and so forth.

Social Bonding Theory

Travis Hirschi's book, *Causes of Delinquency* (1969), is the most cited version of social control theory. Known as *social bonding theory*, this theory asserts an inverse relationship between one's bond to society and the likelihood of engaging in delinquency—that is, the stronger one's bond to society, the less likely one is to commit acts of delinquency; and the weaker one's bond to society, the more likely one is to commit acts of delinquency. The social bond is the result of proper socialization, presumably of children by parents. The bond consists of four main elements, including attachment, commitment, involvement, and belief, as we showed in chapter 2. *Attachment* refers to how close one is to others, especially parents. *Commitment* means devotion to succeeding through conventional means, such as work and school. *Involvement* refers to the amount of time one spends engaged in legitimate activities such as recreation. Finally, *belief* means holding an allegiance to the law and widely accepted morals. As defined by Hirschi and Gottfredson (2001, p. 83), attachment is "the bond of respect, love, or affection," commitment is "the bond of aspiration, investment, or ambition," involvement is "the restriction of opportunity to commit delinquent acts by engaging in conventional activities," and belief is "the bond to conformity created by the view that criminal and delinquent acts are morally wrong."

As noted by Bohm (2001, pp. 90–91), delinquency is likely when there is "(1) inadequate attachment, particularly to parents and school, (2) inadequate commitment, particularly to educational and occupational success, (3) inadequate involvement in such conventional activities as scouting and sports leagues, and (4) inadequate belief, particularly in the legitimacy and morality of the law."

Hirschi tested his theory originally through a survey of roughly 4,000 junior and senior high school youths, and also used school records and police data. The main finding, consistent with the theory, was that boys who felt closer to their parents were less likely to report committing delinquent acts, as were boys who were less attached to their peers. Delinquents were also more likely to be having difficulties in school, including receiving poor grades and disrespecting school authorities (and thus presumably were less committed to legitimate success). Additionally, delinquents in Hirschi's study were found to have low educational and occupational aspirations. Finally, only some measures of involvement in conventional activities were related to delinquency in the predicted direction.

Hirschi hinted at the role that learning may play in delinquency by noting that associations with delinquent peers could increase delinquency in conditions where social controls were weak. Juveniles with a low stake in conformity were more likely to admit to greater involvement in delinquency when they were more exposed to delinquent peers, suggesting an interactive effect between social controls and social learning.

All of the elements of the bond to society are interrelated. Yet, the most important is supposedly attachment to others such as parents. As explained by Vold et al. (1998, p. 208): "Attachment is said to be the basic element necessary for the internalization of values and norms, and thus is related to Reiss' conception of personal controls and Nye's conception of internal and indirect controls." Originally, Hirschi maintained that attachment to even criminal parents would reduce the likelihood that a child would engage in delinquency, a prediction that runs opposite to social learning theory. The belief of inborn motivation to deviance was stated best by Hirschi (1969, p. 31) when he wrote "we are all animals and thus all naturally capable of committing criminal acts."

Low Self-Control Theory

Later Hirschi teamed with Michael Gottfredson (Gottfredson & Hirschi, 1990) to write *A General Theory of Crime*, where they offered the theory of *low self-control*. This theory explains antisocial behavior and criminality as a function of the interaction of low self-control and criminal opportunities. That is, when people with low self-control come across opportunities to engage in antisocial behavior and to commit crime, we should expect antisocial behavior and crime to result. Low self-control in childhood is "for all intents and purposes, *the* individual-level cause of crime" (Gottfredson & Hirschi, 1990, p. 232).

According to Grasmick et al. (1993, p. 6), low self-control is a personality trait that consists of six main elements including "impulsivity, a preference for simple rather than complex tasks, risk seeking, a preference for physical rather than cerebral activities, a self-centered orientation, and a volatile temper." Low self-control subsumes several personality traits. Some have asserted that each trait has its own effects on behavior; thus low self-control hides the independent effects of risk seeking and impulsivity (Polakowski, 1994; Rosay, 2000; Wood, Pfefferbaum, & Arneklev, 1993).

Low self-control depicts criminals as simpletons who commit crime because it "offers easy, short-term gratifications, such as excitement, small amounts of money, and relief from situational aggravations" (Evans et al., 1997, p. 476). Criminals are people who have "an enduring propensity to ignore the long-term consequences of behavior" (Longshore, Turner, & Stein, 1996, p. 212), people who generally have "moderately stable" levels of self-control (Polakowski, 1994).

This theory blames all antisocial behavior and criminality on low self-control, a trait that arises because of poor parenting. Low self-control is defined as "the tendency to avoid acts whose long-term costs exceed their immediate short-term benefits" (Hirschi & Gottfredson, 2001, p. 82).

> Everyone enjoys money, sex, power, excitement, ease, euphoria, and revenge. Everyone can see that crime provides a direct and easy way of obtaining them. So … the difference between offenders and nonoffenders is in their awareness of and concern for the long-term costs of crime—things such as arrest, prison, disgrace, and even eternal damnation … What distinguishes offenders from others is not the strength of their appetites but their freedom to enjoy the quick and easy and ordinary pleasures of crime without undue concern for the pains that may follow them. (Hirschi & Gottfredson, 2001, p. 90)

Low self-control is supposed to come about early in childhood within families where the parents do not closely supervise the children's behavior, do not recognize incorrect behavior by the children, and/or do not consistently punish the children for misbehaving. It is thought to be relatively stable across a person's life course so that children with low self-control will become adults with low self-control.

Low self-control, then, is natural and high self-control must be learned from the family. In the absence of good parents, children do not develop self-control and thus remain child-like in terms of their behavior even as adolescents and adults. According to Hirschi and Gottfredson (2001, p. 90):

> All of us, it appears, are born with the ability to use force and fraud in pursuit of our private goals. Small children can and do lie, bite, whine, hit, and steal. They also sometimes consider horrendous crimes they are too small to carry off. By the age of 8 or 10, most of us learn to control such tendencies to the degree necessary to get along at home and school. Others, however, continue to employ the devices of chil-

Figure 7.1 Low Self-Control

Family Environment ±	Individual Characteristics ±	Behavior
Inadequate supervision	1) Impulsivity	Delinquency
Failure to recognize deviant behavior	2) Preference for simple tasks	Criminality
Inconsistent punishment	3) Risk seeking behaviors	Analogous behavior
	4) Preference for physical activities	Academic difficulties
	5) Self-centered orientation	Employment problems
	6) Volatile temper	Difficulty in inter-personal relationships

Source: Adapted from Gottfredson and Hirschi (1990).

dren, to engage in behavior inappropriate to their age. The differences observed at ages 8 to 10 tend to persist from then on. Good children remain good. Not so good children remain a source of concern to their parents, teachers, and eventually to the criminal justice system.

As noted in figure 7.1, the source of low self-control is posited as external to the individual; specifically it comes from the family. It becomes internalized by the individual through socialization (or learning) and becomes a stable set of personality traits. As noted by Vold et al. (1998, p. 214): "Since these traits can be identified prior to the age of responsibility for crime, since there is considerable tendency for these traits to come together in the same people, and since the traits tend to persist through life, it seems reasonable to consider them as comprising a stable construct useful in the explanations of crime." To these scholars, low self-control is the important criminogenic factor.

This means no other factors other than opportunity explain criminality. In fact, Hirschi and Gottfredson (2001) assert that since crime is related to social and economic conditions, this is proof of low self-control. That is, being characterized by low self-control partially explains why people are poor and disadvantaged. Being poor and disadvantaged does not explain why one commits crime; instead, low self-control explains both criminal behavior and being poor and disadvantaged. This suggests that the relationship between social class and criminality is spurious, or false.

This theory not only explains crime, but also supposedly explains what Hirschi and Gottfredson call *analogous behaviors* (other antisocial and potentially harmful behaviors that are not illegal). "People who smoke and drink are more likely than people who do not smoke or drink to use illegal drugs, to cut classes, to cheat on tests, to break into houses, to rob and steal. People who rob and steal are more likely than people who do not rob and steal to smoke and drink, use illegal drugs, break into houses, and cheat on tests" (Hirschi & Gottfredson, 2001, p. 82). This theory suggests that all of these quick and easy ways of getting what one wants—all these crimes and analogous behaviors—are explained by the same underlying tendency of individuals.

As shown in figure 7.1, low self-control will also negatively affect a person's school and work performance, as well as relationships with other people. Individuals with low self-control will have difficulty in school, at work, and in marriages. They will gravitate to other people with low self-control on the streets. If the theory of low self-control is true, then relationships between these factors and criminality are also spurious, or false.

Age-Graded Informal Social Control Theory

In contrast to the theory of low self-control, the theory of *age-graded informal social control* (Sampson & Laub, 1993) assumes that there are not stable personality characteristics such as self-control that across for criminality across the life course. It is aimed at explaining the initiation, continuation, and cessation of delinquency and crime over one's life. This theory is based on data collected by Glueck and Glueck (1950) and is aimed at answering questions such as: "How is it that some juvenile delinquents … are able to turn their lives around and change their criminal behavior … while others … display a pattern of continuous antisocial behavior from childhood through adulthood? Can pathways to delinquency be explained? Once formed, can delinquent pathways be altered? In other words, are there 'turning points' in life?" The theory takes into account *trajectories,* or how people start out life either toward or away from crime; *transitions,* or major events in people's lives such as marriage; and *turning points,* or events that change people's life courses.

As noted by Laub et al. (2001, pp. 100–101), there is "a connection between childhood events and experiences in adulthood (continuity)" but "transitions or turning points can modify (change) the courses of life trajectories, redirecting pathways." This is different than what is assumed by those who claim that once trajectories or behavioral propensities are set in place, they are very difficult to change (e.g., see Vila, 1997). According to Laub et al. (2001, p. 103): "salient life events and social bonds in adulthood, especially attachment to work and to a spouse, can counteract, at least to some extent, the trajectories of early child development ... pathways to both crime and conformity are modified by key institutions to adulthood independent of prior differences in criminal propensity." However, it is not just getting married nor just getting a job that changes one's trajectory; instead, it is being involved in quality, fulfilling marriages and careers that supposedly accounts for why people desist from criminality (Farrington & West, 1995; Horney, Osgood, & Marshall, 1995).

It should be pointed out that testosterone levels fall during marriage as well, suggesting a possible interrelationship between bonds and biology (Mazur & Michalek, 1998). Marriage also reduces exposure to delinquent peers (Warr, 1998). Only integrated thought allows these types of relationships to be taken into account.

The theory of age-graded informal social control is organized around the notion of social control, "the idea that delinquency is more likely when an individual's bond to society is weak or broken" (Laub et al., 2001, p. 101). Since one's bonds to society's controlling institutions such as school, work, and family are not stable, whether or not a person commits delinquency and crime (and the extent of it) will also vary over time. The point of this theory is that when bonds to society are weak or broken, criminality is likely; however, bonds to society can be repaired and this helps explain *desistance from crime*, which is a term used to describe when people finally stop committing it.

Control Balance Theory

Most recently, Charles Tittle developed *control balance* theory, a general theory organized around the concept of control balance. "The greater the value of [an] act for extending [one's] sense of control ... relative to the potential consequences of [one's] actions (magnitude and potentiality of counter-controlling responses), the greater the chances that [one] will do it. This balancing of the control [one] might gain from deviant behavior against the control that will likely be directed back at [one] is called 'control balancing'" (Tittle, 2001, p. 316). The theory suggests that criminality begins when a person is provoked by another. When the provoked person can gain control relative to the control being exerted upon him or her, depending on various other factors that Tittle calls *contingencies*, he or she is likely to commit deviance. Contingencies include moral beliefs, level of self-control, affiliations with potential witnesses to deviant acts, subcultural associations, and so forth.

Other important elements of control balance include: "(1) a predisposition toward being motivated for deviance, (2) situational provocation that reminds a person of a control imbalance, (3) the transformation of predisposition into actual motivation for deviance, (4) opportunity for deviant response, and (5) the absence or relative weakness of constraint, so that the mental process of 'control balancing' will result in a perceived gain in control" (Tittle, 2001, p. 317). Predispositions come from desiring autonomy (the ability to govern oneself), an unbalanced control ratio (having less control over others than they have over you or having more control over others than they have over you), and blockage of goals (strain). The desire for autonomy is a constant, according to Tittle, something that all people learn early in their lives, whereas perceptions of strain and control balance vary by person.

When people become aware of their control imbalances, they are more likely to become motivated to deviance. Deviant behavior is not likely to occur, however, unless negative emotions arise from the perception of control imbalances or from goal blockage. Opportunity for deviance must obviously exist in order for any deviant act to occur, and individuals will typically commit the most serious acts of deviance that are reasonable for them and those that will achieve control balance and meet their goals. The theory views human beings as rational because it asserts that people will avoid acts of deviance that may be too costly or are likely to be unsuccessful.

Control balance is specifically aimed at explaining both deviance and conformity. The theory explains forms of deviance such as predation, defiance, submission, exploitation, and plunder (Tittle, 2001). The type of deviance one will commit depends mostly on the degree of control imbalance the person is experiencing. According to Tittle, the probability of deviance is greatest when one experiences a control surplus or a control deficit. The V-shaped diagram in figure 7.2 describes the probability of deviance relative to control balancing.

Figure 7.2 Control Balancing

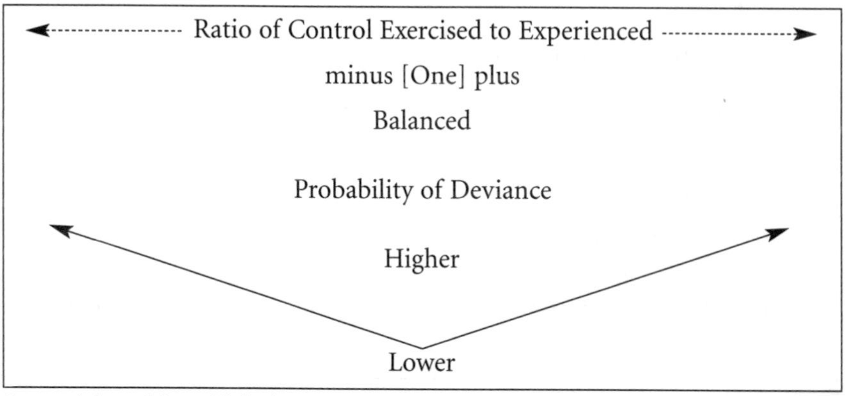

Source: Adapted from Tittle (1995, p. 183)

In terms of seriousness of deviance, the most serious forms of repressive deviance are most likely to be committed by those with the smallest control deficits. Those with the greatest deficits are likely to do the least serious deviance because that is the only kind of deviance they can realistically contemplate doing. Individuals with small control deficits ... can imagine getting away with more serious deviant acts; they will probably not face overwhelming possibilities of counter control ... [and] the most serious deviance is likely to be committed by those with the greatest control surplus—again because they can anticipate extending their control with the least chance of counter control. And those with relatively small control surpluses can imagine getting away with only the least serious forms of ... deviance. (Tittle, 2001, p. 325)

Summary of Social Control Theories

Although there are numerous social control theories, they all make essentially the same assertion, that in the absence of controls, antisocial and criminal behaviors are more likely. These controls are both within and outside of individuals. Figure 7.3 illustrates that controls of behavior can be inside or outside of people and does so utilizing the terms of social control theorists introduced in this chapter. In spite of the fact that the major social control theories were developed by different theorists over decades and that each used different terminology and concepts in the theories, they all essentially make the same assertion that factors inside and outside of us stop us from committing antisocial behavior and criminality; in the absence of such controls, antisocial and criminal behaviors should be expected.

Figure 7.3 Social Control Theories

Internal	External
Internal controls	External controls
Moral conscience	Stake in conformity
Inner containments	Outer containments
Bonds (attachment, commitment, involvement, belief)	Bonds (attachment, commitment, involvement, belief)
Self-control	Turning points

Source: Figure created by author.

Main Propositions of Social Control Theories

Given the predictions made by social control theories, the following propositions have been tested:

- Antisocial behavior is inversely related to the strength of one's bond to peers and families, including attachment, commitment, and involvement.
- Poor parenting increases low self-control and the risk of delinquent and antisocial behavior.
- Marriage and employment reduce the risk of criminality in adulthood.

Key Concepts of Family and Peer Studies

From the preceding propositions, the following concepts can be isolated and defined:

- Attachment
- Commitment
- Involvement
- Peers
- Families
- Poor parenting
- Low self-control
- Marriage
- Employment
- Delinquent behavior
- Antisocial behavior
- Criminality

Box 7.3 defines the key concepts of family and peer studies. Scholars have used these definitions to test the main propositions of family and peer studies. The findings of these tests are discussed in the following section.

Box 7.3 Definitions of Key Concepts of Family and Peer Studies

- *Attachment. Nominal*—the bond of respect, love, or affection shared within a family. *Operational*—evidence of the relative strength of respect, love, or affection shared within a family, as measured by self-report surveys and/or observations with families.
- *Commitment. Nominal*—the bond of aspiration, investment, or ambition one expresses to legitimate activities. *Operational*—evidence of aspiration,

investment, or ambition one expresses to legitimate activities as measured by self-report surveys and/or observations with families.

- *Involvement. Nominal*—the restriction of opportunity to commit delinquent acts by engaging in conventional activities. *Operational*—the amount of time one spends in legitimate conventional activities such as recreation, as measured by self-report surveys and/or observations with families.
- *Belief. Nominal*—the bond to conformity created by the view that criminal and delinquent acts are morally wrong. *Operational*—evidence of commitment or belief in the law, as measured by self-report surveys.
- *Peers. Nominal*—people who are close to a person; friends. *Operational*—friends identified by individuals in self-report surveys or surveys of parents and teachers.
- *Family. Nominal*—a group of people sharing a common bloodline who live in close conjunction to one another. *Operational*—a group of people sharing the same last name and same genealogy, who claim to be related to one another.
- *Poor parenting. Nominal*—a low degree of parental involvement, a low level of monitoring of children's behavior, poor supervision by parents, inconsistent or erratic discipline by parents, parental rejection of children. *Operational*—self-reported degree of involvement of parents in children's lives, amount of time spent by parents with children, evidence of consistent discipline practices; measured through surveys of parents or children, and less often through direct observations with parents and children.
- *Low self-control. Nominal*—a personality trait that consists of six main elements including impulsivity, a preference for simple rather than complex tasks, risk seeking, a preference for physical rather than cerebral activities, a self-centered orientation, and a volatile temper. *Operational*—the degree of impulsivity, preference for simple tasks, risk-seeking behavior, preference for physical tasks, self-centeredness, and volatile temper, according to self-reported attitudinal or behavioral measures or observations by parents or teachers.
- *Marriage. Nominal*—taking a legal oath to be married and committed to a partner for life. *Operational*—the degree of quality in a marriage, as measured by self-reported satisfaction of two adult partners in a legal marriage.
- *Employment. Nominal*—being involved in labor, typically on a full-time basis for pay. *Operational*—the degree of satisfaction and fulfillment of employment experiences, as measured by self-report surveys.

- *Delinquency. Nominal*—acts committed by juveniles that, if committed by adults, would be considered crimes by the criminal justice system. *Operational*—usually measured by official indicators such as arrests and adjudication of guilt in a court, also measured by self-report data and reports of observations of behaviors by parents and teachers.
- *Antisocial behavior. Nominal*—any behaviors that conflict with the prevailing norms of society and/or that are viewed as abnormal. *Operational*—any form of behavior defined as antisocial, measured by official crime reports, self-reported behaviors, or evaluations from others.
- *Criminality. Nominal*—committing any act that violates the criminal law. *Operational*—the number of times a person is arrested, is convicted in court for a violation of the criminal law, and/or self-reports violating the law.

Evaluation of Social Control Theories

In the following sections, we address social control theories. We assess the empirical validity of the theories, discuss the scope of the research, as well as address the conceptual clarity and the logical adequacy of the propositions.

Empirical Validity of Social Control Theories

When considering the possible validity of social control theories, it is important to describe how individual human beings develop from birth. It is obvious that children are born not knowing much, if anything; what they may know is represented by their reflexive and instinctive behaviors. They are not necessarily born good or bad, but really have the potential to end up either way. This is not to say that all people are born equal; recall from chapter 3 the *equality fallacy*, the belief that all people are equal in terms of abilities and advantages. The integrated systems perspective, used to organize the findings in this book, suggests that individuals experience variations in exposure to protective factors (things that decrease the likelihood of behaving in an antisocial way) and exposure to risk factors (things that increase the likelihood of behaving in an antisocial way). This means individuals are not equal in terms of the advantages and disadvantages they face, and they are not equal in terms of inborn abilities. Neither are they simply criminal or noncriminal since everyone violates the law. Antisocial behavior is made more or less likely based on exposure to protective and risk factors.

The natural development of children outlined by child development experts says a lot about social control theories. Box 7.3 outlines some key findings related to child development and human behavior.

Box 7.3 Child Development and Human Behavior

A clear picture of normal child and adolescent development emerges from the experts who study it such as the American Academy of Pediatrics (AAP) and the American Academy of Child & Adolescent Psychiatry (AACAP). These organizations have chronicled in great detail how parents can expect their children to grow over the life course. According to these organizations and other child development experts, behavioral problems begin early in life and steadily get worse until adolescence, where they peak.

The following is a brief summary of the normal state of human development according to the AAP, AACAP, and other experts. Young children do seem to know how to engage in some acts of very minor (but normal) deviance. For example, as adults, we seem to know it is inappropriate to stare at strangers. It would be considered deviant if an adult were to lean over the back of a booth in a restaurant occupied by other people and intentionally make eye contact with another without saying a word. We know that when two people are engaged in a conversation, it is not normal to interrupt while one is in the middle of a sentence. Adults usually do not run into the street without first looking both ways for traffic. More obvious, it is deviant for adults to urinate or defecate in their pants rather than in bathrooms. Young children normally do these things and have to learn *not* to do them. They learn, usually from their parent(s), that these behaviors are abnormal or deviant in all cases and potentially dangerous in some cases.

Children have to learn how *not* to engage in these behaviors and why these behaviors are abnormal in our culture. They learn this formally and informally, through discussion and subtle environmental cues in daily interactions. We teach our children, for example, not to take candy from a stranger, not to answer the door when it is someone they do not know, not to run out in front of cars, and so on. Thus, the research on human development appears to be supportive of the assumption of social control theories that deviant behavior is normal and has to be stopped though learning pro-social behavior. Yet, as you will see, learning plays a role not only in terms of conformity, but also in terms of criminality and antisocial behaviors.

As explained by Walsh (2002, p. 153): "The family is literally the 'nursery' of human nature ... The infant arrives in this world with all the biological equipment it needs to be human, but it is the family that takes hold of the protohuman and helps to mold it into a social being." In other words, humans are naturally inclined to be aimed at satisfying themselves; they must learn not to do this. "In the absence of interaction designed to promote empathy, identification, delayed gratification, a long time horizon, and prosocial values, the infant appears to exhibit older evolutionary scripts of adaptation which favor immediate gratification and egoism" (Brannigan, 1997, p. 425).

In fact, antisocial behavior is normal in children as young as one year, and particularly will be seen in the second and third years of life (known as the "terrible twos"). Children engage in deviance and learn not to when their parents respond with disapproval. Yet, *self-control*—being able to regulate or control one's impulses, emotions, and desires—starts to emerge early in life, in early and later childhood. In tracing the development of the typical child, AAP and AACAP lay out how and when babies, toddlers, and young children develop certain skills and abilities (American Academy of Pediatrics, 1999; Pruitt, 1998). At around the age of four months, babies begin to discover themselves primitively, being able to understand things that are associated with "me" and others that are associated with "not me." At about six months, babies start to recognize that they are independent, separate beings. And about the age of eight months, babies tend to understand "no" and can even obey the command.

Between the ages of eight and 12 months, babies learn *not* to do certain things based on reactions from others such as parents, which is described by AAP as "a major first step toward self-control" (p. 252). At around 12 months, babies begin to see the relationship between cause and effect. Between the ages of two and three years, children can use the word "no" to assert their own autonomy and control over situations. Each of these is an important precedent to the development of self-control. Yet, it takes "years of firm but gentle guidance" before babies/toddlers/children have the self-control to meet parental expectations (p. 283).

During these years, "the brain grows and develops significantly and patterns of thinking and responding are established ... The first years last forever" (American Academy of Pediatrics, 1998, p. 142). This is why the American Academy of Pediatrics suggests specific techniques to responsibly and positively impact brain development at different age periods.

AAP asserts that "your child will develop the ability to control his impulses very gradually. At two and three he'll still be very physical, using temper tantrums, pushing, shoving, and quarreling to get his own way. Most of these reactions are very impulsive; although he doesn't understand it, the whole point of his misbehavior is to find not only his limits but yours" (p. 321). At the age of four years, according to AAP, children still have a very simplified version of morality.

According to AACAP the moral development of children continues to evolve; "during elementary school, the child depends less upon the parent to define right

and wrong. Instead, behavior is influenced by internalized rules and by relationships with peers" (Pruitt, 1998, p. 126). This suggests the influence of peers
begin to be significant at around the age of five years.

AACAP asserts that by age six, children can understand how their own lives
and plans are limited by factors beyond their control including a consideration
for others: "Others have rights, motives, sensibilities, and feelings which must
be understood and taken into account." They are also much more likely than
during earlier periods of their lives to live up to their own developing sense of
right and wrong (Pruitt, 1998, p. 88). The American Academy of Pediatrics
(1998) suggests that most kids do not develop true empathy until around age seven.

So, it appears that we should not expect babies, toddlers, or young children
to effectively demonstrate self-control. It is something that takes much more
time to develop.

By adolescence, most children have developed to the point of holding the
dominant views of society including that the law is valid and necessary (Pruitt,
1999, p. 8). This is an important part of self-control. Yet, AACAP (1999)
claims: "Oppositional behavior is often a normal part of development for two
to three year olds and early adolescents." This means that self-control is not
learned until at least late adolescence, if not later. AACAP (2001) suggests that
early adolescents start to show more consistent evidence of conscience, but simultaneously experiment with potentially destructive behaviors such as unprotected sex and drug use, which signify low self-control.

In late adolescence as young people move toward greater independence, they
are better able to delay gratification, are increasingly stable emotionally, develop
a greater concern for others and concern for the future, and also have a greater
capacity for setting goals and insight, a greater interest in moral reasoning, as
well as more emphasis on personal dignity and self-esteem (AACAP, 2001).

In late adolescence, individuals tend to hold standards of behavior based
on broad, ethical principles. Further, since "older teenagers can grasp the full
implications of specific actions and circumstances, they are truly able to assume full responsibility for their own care. They can appreciate the cause and
effect relationship between destructive behaviors and low achievement, between good habits and good health … most can understand the nature of personal responsibility and anticipate the consequences of behavior. They have
begun to comprehend that what they do, the activities they engage in, and the
people they associate with can have repercussions in other areas of their lives
and in their future … the need for frequent and immediate gratification, which
characterizes early adolescence, begins to fade … as the teen approaches and
enters his twenties, he is more likely to abstain from such risky behaviors as drink-

ing, drug use, irresponsible sexual behavior, and reckless driving" (Pruitt, 1999, p. 57). This is suggestive of self-control.

Ultimately, "Children give up destructive behavior, not because they simply pass through the phase, but because parents set limits and censure certain aggressive behavior." Thus, the "process of repressing and controlling aggressive feelings is not innate, but rather a product of family education" (Pruitt, 1998, p. 104) which includes learning to control impulses (p. 136). Consistent, supportive, loving, and flexible parenting allows children to "learn to control their impulses and behavior, delay personal gratification, and respect other people and their rights" (p. 263). In other words, such parenting is associated with self-control. The American Academy of Pediatrics concurs: "Sometimes a child is aggressive because he has failed to learn self-control. Children develop self-control by learning from their parents what are acceptable limits to their aggressive impulses" (Schor, 1999, p. 227).

From the discussion in box 7.3, it is clear that child experts believe that deviant behavior is normal in children and adolescents. Breaking the rules, whether they are household rules, school rules, or societal rules (laws), should be expected of children and to a lesser degree, adolescents; they violate them in order to learn them. The way that families and peers respond to rule breaking then affects whether or not children and adolescents continue to engage in deviant behaviors. *Inconsistent discipline*, for example, is one of the most important risk factors for juvenile delinquency (McCord, 1991) because in conditions where children are not consistently rewarded and punished, it is difficult for them to learn the difference between right and wrong, to come to know which behaviors are tolerated and which are not.

According to the American Academy of Child & Adolescent Psychiatry (AACAP), "discipline is the set of methods by which parents guide and teach their children. You use discipline to teach right and wrong, to help a child incorporate a sense of limits and appropriate behavior, and to tolerate delayed gratification" (Pruitt, 1998, p. 69). The pay off of *consistent discipline*, according to AACAP, is the development in children of self-control. The American Academy of Pediatrics (1999) agrees, writing: "The main goal of discipline is to teach a child limits" (p. 217).

It is also important to understand that the importance of families and friends varies based on the stage of life one is in. That is, parents tend to be more important to individuals and have a greater impact on the behaviors of children at different periods over the course of one's life. Similarly, peer groups tend to be more important to individuals and have a greater impact on the behaviors of children at different periods over the course of one's life. Figure 7.4 il-

Figure 7.4 Parents and Peers: Which Matter When?

	Pre-Birth	Infant <1 yr	Toddler 1–2 yrs	Early Child 3–6 yrs	Later Child 7–12 yrs	Adolescence 13–17 yrs	Early Adult 18–24 yrs	Adult 25 yrs +
Family				→				→
Friends				Make Friends →				
			Antisocial Behavior Starts!!!	Delinquency Starts!!!			Crime Starts!!!	

Early Starters   Late Starters
Life course persistent   Adolescence limited

Source: Figure created by author.

lustrates that parents tend to be more important and have a greater impact through childhood, whereas friendships tend to be more important and have a greater impact during adolescence and early adulthood.

The arrows in the figure indicate the periods in which either parents or peers play a more important role in our behavior based on the relative impact they have on our lives during this period of our lives. The dashed lines suggest that the other group also has an effect but typically not as large an effect during that time period. The figure also illustrates at what time period antisocial, delinquent, and criminal behaviors tend to start, earlier for early starters and life course persistent offenders than for late starters and adolescent limited offenders. As examination of the figure shows that antisocial behavior and delinquency tend to precede peer associations in early starters. This supports the assertion of those scholars who suggest that peer influences tend to reinforce behavior that is already occurring rather than causing it.

According to the American Academy of Child & Adolescent Psychiatry (AACAP), children spend most of their time before school with parents, but by the first grade, "half of the child's waking hours will be spent in the company of peers" (Pruitt, 1998, p. 123). This is when peers start to become real important for understanding behavior of children. Like the AACAP, the American Academy of Pediatrics (1998) asserts that by the age of four or five years, peers begin to influence children's thinking and behavior. Prior to this time, parents have a much greater impact on behavior than peers, and likely continue to do so until adolescence.

The American Academy of Child & Adolescent Psychiatry (AACAP) asserts that adolescents pull away from their parents, and that conformity to friends tends to be viewed as more important (Pruitt, 1999). Yet, even when children are teenagers in high school who are developing rapidly and becoming adults and who may reject authority, they still need clearly defined rules of behavior, meaning their parents still impact their thinking and behavior. The rules, however, ought to be limited, important, and negotiable with respect (Pruitt, 1999, p. 8). Interestingly, teenagers tend to respond to peer pressure when it urges positively valued outcomes rather than negative ones (Pruitt, 1999).

Now that you understand some of the most important information regarding human development, we now turn to reviewing studies that test social control theories. Our particular focus is not only on tests of social control theories but also on studies of parenting more generally; our aim is to discover those risk factors that promote antisocial behavior in children and adolescents.

The earliest control theories are rarely if ever still tested. Even Hirschi's social bonding theory is rarely tested now. Studies have reported support for Hirschi's social bonding theory (e.g., see Kempf, 1993), but most of these studies are cross-sectional in nature (conducted at one time rather than over time). Longitudinal studies conducted over time have found less support for social bonding theory (Agnew, 1985, 1991). Studies show that problems in school (e.g., school discipline problems) are associated with problem behaviors such as drug use (Drapela, 2005). Further, students with lower grades tend to be more prone to delinquent behavior (Siennick & Staff; 2008), although such factors may vary by gender (Booth, Farrell, & Varano, 2008). Other research calls into serious question the validity of the "commitment" variable in social bonding theory. For example, a longitudinal study of more than 14,000 middle school students at various times by Felson & Staff (2006) found that the effects of academic performance on delinquency were spurious (false), owing themselves to other factors such as attachment to parents and low self-control.

Social Bonding

Empirical findings tend to be supportive of social control theories, but not as supportive as those for learning theories. For example, a review of scores of studies by Kempf (1993) found that some tests do not support the inverse relationship between social control and delinquency. Most telling about social control theory is a review of Hirschi's original data on self-reported delinquency, conducted three decades after Hirschi's original analysis (Greenberg, 1999). This study found that measures of social control such as attachment to parents, concern for teachers' opinions, involvement in school activities, and commitment to education have weak explanatory power for delinquency. Interestingly, this study also reported modest support for strain theory (discussed in chapter 9) and differential association theory. As noted by Greenberg (1999), it is at least plausible that larger level factors contribute to weak bonds in the family, suggesting theoretical integration is necessary to fully account for criminal behavior. We return to this issue later in the evaluation of social control theories.

One study of note found more support for social control theory than social learning theory (Costello & Vowell, 1999). This study, which assessed the effects of commitment to legal activities, attachment to school, and involvement in legitimate activities, found that social control measures were inversely related to self-reported delinquency in a sample of 4,075 white male high school students (using 1965 data). The authors concluded that the influence of peers was limited to providing opportunities for youth to engage in delinquency. This is consistent with the findings that unstructured socializing with peers is related to increased delinquency (Osgood et al., 1996).

Generally, studies that examine social control and social learning theories together tend to find support for both (Pardini, Loeber & Stouthamer-Loeber, 2005; Payne & Salotti, 2007). One study of 153 newly incarcerated felons (Alarid, Burton, & Cullen, 2000), found some support for their measures of differential association (individual definitions toward crime, others' definitions toward crime, and criminal friends) and social control (attachment to parents, attachment to friends, involvement, belief, and marital attachment). The findings varied slightly by gender and crime type, suggesting more complexity in the relationships than proposed by the original founders of the theories. The authors noted that their study was unique in that most samples on which these theories were tested consisted of juveniles and that their study did not rely only on self-reported delinquency data.

Both family and peer context variables are also found to be important for risk of violent victimization among adolescents. For example, teenagers living in households where the family context can be described as close with high levels of understanding between parent and child have less violent victimization, while children who are emotionally alienated from their parents have higher risks of victimization (Schreck & Fisher, 2004).

Low Self-Control

As for low self-control theory, Evans et al. (1997, p. 477) write that studies provide evidence that levels of self-control "are related to self-reported crime and intentions to break the law among juveniles, college students, and adults" ... it also "predicts future criminal convictions and self-reported delinquency" ... and has been "related not only to illegal conduct but also to analogous or imprudent behaviors" such as smoking and drinking. Longshore et al. (1996, p. 213) concurred that "crime and analogous acts are higher among people with low self-control."

A meta-analysis of studies testing low self-control theory showed that self-control, whether measured using a behavioral scale or an attitudinal scale, is a valid correlate of criminality (Pratt & Cullen, 2000). The meta-analysis examined 21 published studies of 17 different data sets that tested low self-control theory. According to Pratt and Cullen (2000), the results suggest not only that low self-control is an important predictor of criminality, but that it has general effects (explaining many types of crime). The same analysis demonstrated that studies that included social learning variables along with self-control variables found that social learning variables were equally strong predictors of criminality. Studies that included social learning variables explained roughly 15% more criminality than those that did not; still, the total variance explained by these studies was only about 35%, meaning that 65% of criminality was not explained by low self-control and social learning influences.

A major criticism of low self-control, according to the meta-analysis of Pratt and Cullen (2000), is that longitudinal studies are less supportive than cross-sectional studies. This runs counter to the assertions of Gottfredson and Hirschi that low self-control is a stable propensity across the life course. Still, according to Hirschi and Gottfredson (2001, p. 92), their explanation of antisocial and criminal behavior is consistent with the fact that differences between offenders persist over the life course (Gendreau, Little, & Goggin, 1996; Nagin & Paternoster, 1991). It also supposedly explains why rehabilitation efforts mostly do not work (Sherman et al., 1997), why intervention efforts are best aimed at children (Tremblay et al., 1992), why the criminal justice system does not reduce crime (Andrews et al., 1990), why crime can be prevented simply by increasing the efforts required to commit them (Murray, 1995; Clarke, 1983), why street criminality declines with age (Cohen & Land, 1987), why criminal specialization is rare (Britt, 1994), why criminal offenders also are involved in more accidents, suffer from more illnesses, and die earlier (Farrington & Junger, 1995), why offenders use more drugs (Boyum & Kleiman, 1995), why offenders commit more acts of deviance (Evans et al., 1997), why street criminals are less involved in legitimate, long-term careers, and why offenders are cognitively and intellectually lacking (Wilson & Herrnstein, 1985), and why family structure and practices are related to deviance (Loeber & Stouthamer-Loeber, 1986).

In their research of 642 undergraduate students at a major East Coast university, Piquero and Tibbetts (1996) found that low self-control had direct positive effects on intentions to shoplift and drive drunk, and on perceived pleasure to be gained from committing these acts. They also found that individuals with lower levels of self-control were less likely to experience shame due to shoplifting and driving drunk. Assuming these findings are generalizable to other portions of the population and to other forms of criminality, this means that individuals with lower levels of self-control are more likely to violate the law, in part because they perceive more pleasure from doing so and because they do not perceive their illegal acts to be shameful. From the studies conducted to date, there is a clear link between the theory of low self-control and rational choice. Other studies also support the theory (Love, 2006; Tittle, Ward & Grasmick, 2003; Vazsonyi & Crosswhite, 2004), although some studies call its ability to predict delinquency weak (Stylianou, 2002).

A study of 1,500 students from six cities found that self-control measured at an early age was associated with later victimization from crime, even after the researchers controlled for past victimization, delinquency, social bonds, and delinquent peer contact. Further, low self-control was related to association with deviant peers (Schreck, Stewart, & Fisher, 2006).

A study of more than 3,000 6th, 7th, and 8th graders in six Virginia middle schools found that not only was low self-control a strong predictor of self-reported delinquency and self-reported arrests, but also that the effects of ADHD on delinquency were largely through low self-control. Finally, parental monitoring and consistent discipline increased self-control as well as decreased delinquency (Unnever, Cullen & Pratt, 2003).

A study of more than 460 drug using female offenders found evidence that low self-control was associated with an increase risk of criminal victimization even after controlling for lifestyle factors (Stewart, Elifson, & Sterk, 2004). A study of about 800 12–13 year olds in secondary schools found that low self-control was associated with different forms of misbehavior and delinquency, as was being in or between the impulsive and self-protective developmental levels of development (Ezinga et al., 2008).

How Parents Impact Behavior

There is wide agreement about the effects of parenting on childhood behavior. Families contribute to criminality in at least three ways: (1) by genetic transmission; (2) by exposing children to risk factors in the physical and social environment; and (3) through child-rearing practices (McCord, 2001). The impact of genes on behavior was discussed in chapter 4. Below we discuss the impact of different risk factors of parenting including child-rearing practices.

Types of Parenting

Two dimensions around which to categorize parenting types include responsiveness and demandingness (Baumrind, 1996). Responsiveness refers to "the extent to which parents are approachable, warm, supportive and attuned to the needs of the child." Demandingness refers to "the extent to which parents exercise control over the child through supervision, disciplinary efforts, and willingness to confront the child when he or she disobeys" (Simons, Simons, & Wallce, 2004, p. 25).

Using these two dimensions results in at least four parenting styles—authoritative, authoritarian, permissive, and neglectful/rejecting parents. *Authoritative* parents are high in responsiveness and high in control. Authoritative parents are reasonable and flexible in nature.

Authoritarian parents are high in control and low in responsiveness. Authoritarian parenting consists of a parenting style where parents insist on a blind submission to authority by their children. Authoritarian parents attempt "to control a child's behavior and attitudes, stressing the importance of obedience to authority and discouraging discussion. Parents who use this method tend to rely upon punishment, which is often spanking or other physical measures" (Pruitt, 1998, p. 133).

Permissive parents are high in responsiveness and low in control. Overly permissive parents "tend to be warm and supportive, often to the point of indulging their child's every want, yet "they rarely set rules, explain moral principles, engage in monitoring, or confront disobedience" (Simons, Simons, & Wallce, 2004, p. 172). Permissive parents exercise "minimal control. Children of permissive parents are allowed to set their own schedules and activities. Permissive parents generally do not demand the same high levels of behavior as authoritarian and authoritative parents" (Pruitt, 1998, p. 133).

According to the American Academy of Child & Adolescent Psychiatry (AACAP): "Typically, when children have little self-control, their parents are permissive, have set no limits, and have let their children do whatever they wish. Sometimes parents use inappropriate means—physical punishment, for example—when responding to their children's negative behavior. These parents may erroneously believe that a spanking, or a similarly aggressive and abusive response, is a proper reaction when a child … misbehaves. However, physical punishment will not help a child learn to control his negative emotions or hostile behavior; rather, it teaches him to be aggressive when he is angry … When a child's aggressive behavior is met with more aggressive behavior from a parent, things usually get worse, not better" (Schor, 1999, p. 227). Further, "Hitting and spanking a child when you are angry teaches the child to use physical force to control others ... [and] may also undermine your efforts to teach your children to control their own anger" (Pruitt, 1998, p. 69).

The American Academy of Pediatrics (1998, p. 285) agrees writing that spanking does far more harm than good, and asserting that positive discipline is far more effective. The use of physical punishment (Carey, 1994), especially when applied in an impulsive fashion (Straus & Mouradian, 1998), is often found to be related to aggressive behavior in children.

Neglectful/rejecting parents are low in responsiveness and low in control. These are parents that either do not provide basic needs for their kids or reject them by not spending quality time with them and showing an interest in them.

Authoritarian, overly permissive, and neglectful parenting styles have all been linked to delinquency (Avenevoli, Sessa, & Steinberg, 1999; Haapasalo & Pokela, 1999; Mak, 1994; McCord, 1990, 2001). The American Academy of Child & Adolescent Psychiatry (AACAP) suggests that authoritative parenting "works best for teaching a range of values. Authoritative parenting combines emotional warmth with firmness while maintaining an open dialogue with the child" (Pruitt, 1998, p. 118). These parents operate "on the belief that both the children and the parent have certain rights and that the needs of both are important" (p. 133). Authoritative parents do not resort to force but rather use reason to explain why rules for behavior are important to understand and follow.

Since "children need support and nurturance combined with structure and control" authoritative parenting is seen as the most effective, and is associated with outcomes such as school achievement, psychological well-being, and social adjustment. Further, children raised by authoritative parents are less likely to suffer conduct problems and engage in delinquency (Simons, Simons, & Wallce, 2004, p. 26).

Figure 7.5 illustrates some of the factors that are present in "good parents" as well as "bad parents." The conditions on the left of the figure can be considered protective factors, things that "good parents" try to do for their kids, whereas the conditions of the right of the figure can be considered risk factors, things that "bad parents" do to their kids.

It is clear that "good parents"—those parents that provide numerous protective factors for their children—set standards for their children, monitor their children's behavior, provide consistent discipline, and avoid harsh punishments. The American Academy of Child & Adolescent Psychiatry (2001, 2004) writes that good parents also help develop responsibility in their kids, teach their children about respecting limits and to think before acting, model responsibility, and apply consequences in a fair and appropriate way.

Figure 7.5 Good and Bad Parents

Good	Bad
High attachment	Low attachment (neglect or rejection)
High supervision	Low supervision
Notice and correct antisocial behavior	Do not notice and correct antisocial behavior
Set standards of behavior and clearly communicate them	No standards of behavior or not clearly communicated (overly permissive)
Consistent discipline	Inconsistent discipline
Non-violent discipline	Violent discipline and abuse
No physical violence in presence	Physical violence in presence
Authoritative in nature	Authoritarian in nature
Law abiding and disapproving of deviance	Law breaking and approving of deviance

Source: Figure created by author.

According to Kumpfer and Alvarado (1998), good parenting involves supportive parent-child relationships, positive methods of discipline, good levels of monitoring and supervision of children, families who are advocates for their children, and parents who seek information and support for their children. The likelihood that parents will provide these conditions is affected by larger level factors, including but not limited to economic hardship, learning ineffective discipline practices from others, and authoritarian parenting styles (Simons et al., 1998). Other studies attribute risky behaviors to poor social background factors such as a lack of challenge from parents and schools (Hansen & Breivik, 2001).

Studies by sociologists and psychologists have found that affectionate treatment of children by parents tends to decrease antisocial behavior while abuse tends to increase it. Quality of parent-child relationships is negatively related to delinquency; i.e., the better the relationship, the lower the likelihood of offending behaviors (Ganem & Agnew, 2007).

The quality of parenting also likely impacts the effectiveness of disciplinary strategies used by parents to control the behavior of their children. For example, children with a positive relationship with their parents might respond better to physical discipline (i.e., punishment such as spanking) because they may see it "as a legitimate expression of parental concern for their welfare." Children with bad relationships with their parents may instead see it "as an expression of parental hostility and rejection." For this reason, spanking "may foster defiance and aggression when it is administered by cold, harsh, or uninvolved parents" (Simons, Simons, & Wallce, 2004, p. 70). However, spanking may be effective when it is "administered by a caring, supportive parents," so long as it is mild (rather than severe) and when the child is between the ages of 2 and 6 years old (rather than to older kids and pre-adolescents) (p. 75).

Also, parents who manage their lives well and who get along with others tend to have children who do the same. Given that parents and their children share not only environments but also genes, it is difficult to say which is more responsible for why these things run in families (Walsh, 2002). Logic suggests that both nature and nurture are important (Collins et al., 2000).

"Bad parents"—those parents that expose their kids to numerous risk factors—generally do the opposite as good parents. Risk factors for delinquency identified by the American Academy of Child & Adolescent Psychiatry (AACAP) include inadequate supervision, care and involvement by parents; neglectful, intolerant, and unloving parenting; excessive conflict among family members and intense marital discord; harsh and violent discipline and punishment; and inconsistent discipline (Pruitt, 1998, p. 265). Recall that risk factors are things that, when exposed to them, are likely to lead to antisocial and criminal behaviors.

Some of the above factors were identified by Gottfredson and Hirschi (1990) in their theory of low self-control. Most importantly for this theory, low maternal and paternal involvement are commonly found to be linked with delinquency, both serious and minor (Klein et al., 1997). Less monitoring by families is associated with higher levels of delinquency (Weintraub & Gold, 1991).

Important family factors for delinquency include degree of parental involvement, monitoring of children's behavior, discipline, and parental rejection (Loeber & Stouthamer-Loeber, 1986). Other important factors include deviant parental modeling, ineffective and erratic parental supervision, and parental endorsement of deviance (Akers, 2001). For example, a study of more than 500 adolescents showed that parental modeling predicted adolescents' alcohol misuse, drug use, as well as engagement in delinquency. The study also found effects of peer deviance on the same behaviors (Barnes et al., 2006).

It is also clear that abuse and child maltreatment are sources of delinquency (Goetting, 1994; Ryan, 2006; Schwartz, Rendon, & Hsieh, 1994; Smith & Thornberry, 1995). According to Jaffee et al. (2007: 231): "Children who are physically maltreated are at risk of a range of adverse outcomes in childhood and adulthood, but some children who are maltreated manage to function well despite their history of adversity." Their study of 1,116 twin pairs and their families found that boys who with above-average intelligence and whose parents had relatively few symptoms of antisocial personality were better able to resist the effects of maltreatment by parents. At the same time: "Children whose parents had substance use problems and who lived in relatively high crime neighborhoods that were low on social cohesion and informal social control were less likely to be resilient versus non-resilient to maltreatment." The authors suggest that children residing in multi-problem families are less able to rely on personal resources to function well and resist antisocial behavior. Children of abuse are 10 to 15 times more likely to be abusive themselves later in life (Simons, Simons, & Wallce, 2004, pp. 168–169).

According to Burgess and Drais (1999), child maltreatment results from interactions between ecological factors and child and parent traits. Each alters perceptions of parents about the potential benefits and costs associated with providing good child care for their children. Risk factors in the neighborhood and in the parents and children themselves interact to increase the likelihood that parents will assign a low priority to good parenting.

According to Walsh & Beaver (2009, p. 22), "early bonding and attachment are so vital to human beings, and ... abuse and neglect of children is ... injurious; experience is *physically* captured in the brain ... Chronic stress resulting from abuse/neglect can produce neuron death via the production of stress hormones, high levels of which lead to cognitive, motor, and social developmental delays."

Similarly, when children grow up in violent environments, "they expect hostility from others and behave accordingly. By doing so, they invite the very hostility they are on guard for, thus confirming their beliefs that the world is a dangerous and violent place, thus setting in motion a vicious circle of negative expectations and confirmations ... Children in our inner cities witness violence on an almost daily basis ... Witnessing and experiencing violence on a consistent basis gouges the lesson on the neural circuitry that the world is a hostile place in which one must be prepared to protect one's interests by violent means in necessary" (Walsh & Beaver, 2009, p. 22). Still, Wright et al. (2009, p. 84) point out that "humans are highly resistant to even the most pronounced environmental stresses." This is why it is important to take into account individual differences, because "the heat that melts the butter hardens the egg" (Walsh & Beaver, 2009, p. 9). That is, only some people in disadvantaged environments will react aggressively and violently.

Inadequate parenting directly promotes delinquent behavior, and also does so indirectly through promoting association with deviant peers. Simons et al. (1994, 1998, 2001), citing developmental research by Patterson, Reid, and Dishion (1991) and Patterson, Crosby, and Vuchinich (1992), suggested that both perspectives are correct. For early starters to delinquency, family influences are probably more important, whereas for late starters, peer influences are probably more important. This third hypothesis is most consistent with integrated theories of antisocial behavior and criminality.

According to Simons et al. (1994, p. 248): "Probably the most widely accepted interpretation [of the relationships between parenting, affiliations with deviant peers, and delinquency] is that inept parenting allows (or encourages) an adolescent to affiliate with deviant peers." Clearly, parents have an effect on children's peers. For example, a longitudinal study of more than 850 youth found that youths left structured activities (i.e., activities with adult leaders, regular meetings, and skill-building activities) spent time with peers not in those activities. Less participation in structured activities was associated with increased delinquency as well as hanging out on the streets. Further, those youth who did not feel valued and respected at home avoided structured activities when they were old enough to choose their own leisure activities. The authors concluded that "parents seem to play an indirect role in youths' leisure choices by contributing to youths' feelings associated with the home, but they might also play an indirect role in what happens once choices are made" (Persson, Kerr & Stattin, 2007: 203).

In a study of more than 4,000 eighth-grade students from thirty-six schools in ten cities, Osgood & Anderson (2004) found that time spent in unstructured settings socializing with friends had individual and contextual effects that explained much delinquency of adolescents attending different schools. Further, parental monitoring was found to have a strong contextual effect on unstructured socializing with friends.

How Antisocial Behavior Affects Parenting

There is a reciprocal relationship between antisocial behavior in childhood and parenting (Avenevoli et al., 1999; Simons et al., 2001). Early oppositional/defiant behavior undermines effective parenting, which then encourages associations with deviant peers. A study of more than 450 adolescents and their families found that parental conflicts over child rearing produced depressive symptoms and delinquency, and these occurrences worsened parental conflicts over child rearing (Cui, Donnellan & Conger, 2007).

Of course, the impact of parents on deviance depends on the nature of deviance. For example, Simons et al. (1994) found that for late starters of delinquency, quality of parenting was related to affiliation with delinquent peers and later criminal justice system involvement. For early starters to delinquency, quality of parenting influenced the development of oppositional/defiant behavior, which in turn increased deviant peers and subsequent criminal justice system involvement. Oppositional/defiant behavior in late childhood can actually erode quality of parenting and school commitment and result in greater associations with deviant peers (Conger & Simons, 1997; Simons et al., 1998). According to Simons et al. (1998), involvement in early delinquency leads to poor parenting practices, low school commitment, and associations with deviant peers, all of which increase the likelihood of committing more delinquency.

Age Graded Theory

Using the original data collected by the Gluecks, Sampson and Laub (1993) tested their age-graded social control theory and found that bonds to family and to school are inversely related to delinquency. Other family factors inversely related to delinquency noted by Laub et al. (2001, 102) include consistent parental discipline, parental monitoring of children, and attachment to the family, as noted earlier. Each of these facilitates linking the child to the family and ultimately to society through emotional bonds of attachment and direct forms of control, monitoring, and punishment. These same factors are important in schools.

Once a child is on a trajectory that includes serious delinquency and criminality, it is still possible to stop such behavior. As noted by Laub et al (2001, pp. 105–106): "The stability of criminal behavior patterns, especially aggression, throughout the life course is one of the most consistently documented patterns found in longitudinal research." At the same time, "most antisocial children do not become antisocial adults" meaning that behavior can be changed. It is bonds to controlling institutions in adulthood that can reduce the likelihood of antisocial behavior in adulthood.

Marriage seems to offer at least two protections from crime. First, marriage itself is a meaningful social bond, or stake in conformity. Second, marriage decreases associations with deviant peers (Maume, Ousey, & Beaver, 2005). The stability of relationships also matters as more stable relationships are associated with a decreased likelihood of offending persistence (Capaldi, Kim, & Owen, 2008).

Of course, involvement with romantic partners can also be criminogenic. For example, a study of more than 230 young adults found that adolescent delinquency and affiliation with deviant peers were associated with a higher likelihood of having an antisocial romantic partner as a young adult (Simons et al., 2002). Involvement with an antisocial romantic partner, in turn, had both a direct effect on crime as well as indirect influence through adult peer affiliations. For females, quality of the romantic relationship also predicted crime. The analyses revealed several moderating influences in addition to these mediating effects. For females, a conventional romantic partner, strong job attachment, and conventional adult friends all served to moderate the chances that a woman with a delinquent history would graduate to adult crime. In contrast, only conventional adult friends served this function for males.

Laub and Sampson (1993) followed a group of boys until age 70 years to determine which share of them persisted in crime and which of them desisted from crime. Their analysis demonstrated that three major events seemed to account for desistance from crime—marriage, work, and military service. Yet, it was not these institutions themselves that stopped offenders from persisting in crime, it was the caliber of them. That is, those youthful offenders who entered into quality and fulfilling marriages and careers, and those who successfully served in the military, tended to be more able to stop committing crimes. These social institutions gave offenders a stake in conformity, led to changes in routine activities (such as new friends), new responsibilities (such as children and bills), and direct supervision (by spouses, bosses, and superior officers).

The desistance of AL offenders can be understood by what Sampson and Laub (1999) called *turning points*. Turning points may only occur for some because "AL offenders have accumulated a store of positive attachments (they elicit positive responses from others) and academic skills (they are intelligent) that provide them with prosocial opportunities such as a good marriage and a good job" (Walsh, 2002, p. 137). AL offenders have been characterized as "psychologically healthy" (Moffitt, 1993, p. 690). Because of this psychological health, AL offenders are able to invest in the future through their social bonds; these investments lead to marriage, meaningful employment, and so forth, institutions that are not conducive for criminality at the street level.

In the absence of turning points, we'd expect that childhood antisocial behavior will lead to problems with adult social bonds, including economic dependency, educational attainment, attachment to the labor force, and quality of marital experiences. Those offenders who persisted in the Laub and Sampson study tended not to have military experience, and also tended either not to be married or to have never had a successful marriage; they also tended to have difficulties in work. Furthermore, incarceration was generally related to job instability in adulthood. Being unstable in terms of employment is a risk factor for adult criminality (unemployment is discussed in chapter 9). While this relationship is supportive of the theory, it also could be interpreted as evidence of labeling theory (discussed in chapter 8). The stability of antisocial behavior has been verified in other nations and using different kinds of data sources (Caspi & Silva, 1995).

Family Structure Variables

According to DeMuth & Brown (2004), approximately one-third of all children are born to unmarried mothers; more than one half of children will spend some of their lives in a single-parent family; finally, single-father families are the fastest growing family form. Evidence suggests it is family processes such as parent involvement, supervision, monitoring, and closeness that explain higher rates of delinquency among children living with single parents than with two parents.

Thus, family structure variables may influence behavior of children through social process variables. For example, a study of nearly 1,900 Canadian school children found that family structure was a significant predictor self-reported delinquent behaviors, and that the factor that accounted for this was low parental attachment (Kierkus & Baer, 2002). According to Simons, Simons, & Wallce (2004, p. 89), children raised by single parents are two to three times more likely to have conduct problems and engage in delinquency than those raised by two parents, probably due to less supervision and control within such families.

Blumstein (1995, p. 12) suggested that "teenage mothers, single-parent households, divorced households, [and] unwed mothers" all put children at a higher risk of antisocial behavior. Virtually every study of family disruption has found a positive relationship between divorce and separation and crime (Ellis, 1988; Loeber & Stouthamer-Loeber, 1986). Additionally, a review of more than 90 studies found that children from broken homes (e.g., divorced families) were less well psychologically adjusted, had lower self-esteem, and did worse in school than children from intact families (Amato & Keith, 1991). The effects of family disruption seem to be worse when family discord or breakup occurs early in a child's life.

Here we see a contradiction between what is good for children and what is good for the survival of the status quo American economy. As explained by Walsh (2002, p. 154), "the optimal family rearing environment is always one in which children are surrounded by many consanguineous individuals ... Unfortunately, such an arrangement does not fit the economic and social requirements of modern postindustrial societies" (also see Popenoe, 1993). In evolutionary terms, two parents are necessary for survival of children, but economic needs often require both parents to work.

Consistent with social control theories, studies show that associations between rates of out-of-wedlock birth and crime rates tend to be positive and very high (Mackey, 1997), in part because single parenthood encourages less well-being in children and a greater likelihood of associating with deviant peers in an unsupervised environment. According to Cleveland et al. (2000), mothers who are not married tend to be more impulsive and risky, tend to be sexually promiscuous, and are more likely to have low IQs. When a large number of unmarried women live in the same community, the results can include "weaker commitments of men toward women, more illegitimate births, increased sexual promiscuity, increased sexually transmitted diseases, greater misogyny, greater female depression, and an increase in women's liberationist sentiments as women become more conscious of the negative aspects of a low sex ratio" (Walsh, 2002, p. 186). Children raised in these environments logically may learn that these types of behaviors are normal, and their developing attitudes may be reinforced by single mothers who view their potential mates as unreliable (Anderson, 1999).

Other family structure factors believed to be important to understanding delinquency in children include economic well-being, family criminality, family size, single parenthood, and working mothers. Children raised in poverty "are at an increased risk for a variety of negative developmental outcomes, including conduct problems and delinquency," in part due to strains on good parenting and also due to the negative effects of economic strain on parental affect (Simons, Simons, & Wallce, 2004, p. 96–97).

Control Balance

Not many tests of control balance have been offered. One study of control balance theory by Baron & Forde (2006) found that control deficits and control surpluses were related to some crimes (i.e., assault and serious theft) but not others (i.e., minor theft). According to the authors: "Perceptions of thrill, deviant peers, deviant histories, and deviant values predicted violent and property crime, and perceptions of risk were related to the property offenses. Criminal peers also conditioned the impact of control surpluses and deficits on property offenses" (p. 335).

Scope of Social Control Theories

In tests of the theory, the scope of control theories appears narrow, as typically tests of these theories are limited to relatively minor acts of delinquency and criminality, those acts that can be considered normal. For example, one study of 440 high school youth in Israel assessed the effects of social controls on driving without a license and stealing from a mini-market (Cohen & Zeira, 1999). This study found little support for the theory. Another study of social control theory found little support even for minor acts of delinquency committed by fifth graders (Leonard & Decker, 1994). Other studies have tested the effects of social control on samples such as high school dropouts (Samuelson & Hartnagel, 1995). Yet, what social control theories seem well-equipped to explain is why aggressive and antisocial behaviors can be seen as normal in children who have not yet learned how to conform to the norms and laws of society.

Social control theories cannot account for why children who have strong attachments to parents and involvement in after-school activities still commit acts of delinquency. In a study of 213 boys in Washington, D.C., Chaiken (2000) found that nearly 80% were involved in some form of delinquency. Yet, in the entire sample, 92% reported having a caring adult in their lives. Additionally, 52% of the boys reported participating in sports during after-school hours. Social control theorists would suggest that these boys would be less likely overall to be involved in delinquency. This was not the case, but the study did show that nearly half of the boys (48%) reported never receiving adult supervision during the after-school hours; the 23% of the sample who reported receiving supervision every day after school were less delinquent than the group who received less supervision.

While we suggested in this chapter that much deviance may very well be normal, it is hard to view serious, violent acts of street criminality as normal. Clearly, factors other than a lack of social controls are required to explain these acts. It is more logical to place violent acts of elite deviance (e.g., corporate violence) in the context of normal behavior, because virtually anything is acceptable in the business realm, as long as it does not threaten the bottom line (i.e., as long as it turns a profit). Recent allegations against major corporations for defective products verify this, such as those claims made against Ford and Firestone for the rollover accidents that have cost hundreds of lives (Robinson and Murphy, 2008).

In terms of low self-control, it seems implausible to suggest that those who commit white-collar and corporate crimes come from dysfunctional families who provide poor supervision and guidance. According to Gottfredson and Hirschi, most white-collar offenders are characterized by low levels of self-control, but this claim has not been subjected to wide empirical testing. One study did examine the effects of social controls on sexual assaults by physicians and lawyers (Jacobs, 1994), and another on drunk drivers (Watkins, 1999), but these studies assessed the effects of criminal and disciplinary sanctions on such behaviors, making the findings more relevant for the areas of deterrence and labeling (discussed in chapter 8).

The theory of low self-control is aimed at explaining differences in the tendency to offend by persistent offenders. A study of nearly 1,000 individuals found that low self-control also predicts participation in, frequency of, and persistence in antisocial behaviors (Piquero, Moffitt, & Wright, 2007). Yet, if virtually all people commit acts of delinquency as juveniles (which they do), and virtually everyone occasionally commits acts of crime as adults (which they do), the most important fact about crime that needs to be explained is desistance—why some people stop and others do not. Low self-control theory does not seem able to do this, although some authors claim it can.

Morizot & Blanc (2007) claim desistance from criminality is a function of level of self-control and social integration. Yet, social bonds predict desistance from offending independent of a person's level of self-control (Doherty, 2006: 828). Further, biosocial research also shows that desistance from crime has a genetic component. For example, research into polymorphisms of the DAT1, DRD2, DRD4, 5HTT, and MAOA genes showed that genetic make-up plays a role, both independently and in conjunction with social factors, in desistance from crime (Beaver et al., 2008b).

Hirschi and Gottfredson are not entirely correct about criminal behavior being highest in adolescence and early adulthood: "This appears to be true for all, or almost all, crimes. It appears to be true as well for behavior similar to crime: accidents, legal drug use, promiscuous sexual activity. It appears to be true for all groups and societies, at all times and places, even in prisons. It is true whether crime is measured by police records or by asking people to report their own delinquent acts" (2001, p. 85). It goes without saying that Hirschi and Gottfredson's references to crime only apply to street crime. We don't think anyone would argue that acts such as white-collar crimes, corporate crimes, political crimes, and so forth are more likely in adolescence and early adulthood. So, low self-control theory cannot explain acts of elite deviance (discussed in chapter 1).

Perhaps white-collar criminals are characterized by low self-control but do not have to resort to street crimes for the simple fact that they have greater opportunities at work. If this is the case, many of Gottfredson and Hirschi's statements about the stability of low self-control would make sense. For example: "Children in trouble with teachers in the 2nd and 3rd grades are more likely to be in trouble with juvenile authorities at 15 and 16; they are more likely to serve prison terms in their 20s; they are more likely to have trouble with their families and jobs at all ages" (Hirschi & Gottfredson, 2001, p. 87). Of course, white-collar criminals rarely serve prison terms or even come to the attention of the criminal justice system (Robinson, 2002).

One limit of low self-control as an explanation is the assumption that all harmful behaviors, even those supposedly explained by the theory, are characterized by impulsivity. Even though much crime is relatively easy and requires little thought, much crime, especially property crime, requires diligence and patience (hardly something a person with low self-control can claim to possess).

As with all theories, it is not clear whether social control theories equally explain male and female behaviors. One study of delinquency suggests that both boys and girls are attached to controlling institutions, but that the effects of attachments to parents and having two parents in the household are more controlling for boys, while attachment to peers and to school reduce the severity of female delinquency (Anderson, Holmes, & Ostresh, 1999). This finding is consistent with studies showing that egalitarian and matriarchal family structures allow women to better control their sons' potential delinquent behaviors and that in patriarchal families, men are more likely to control their daughters than their sons (Avakame, 1997; McCarthy, Hagan, & Woodward, 1999). These studies tend to show not only that family structure plays a role in children's delinquency but also that peer influences matter, as well.

Higgins & Tewksbury (2006) suggest the self-control is associated with delinquency in both males and females, although the effects of self-control may vary by gender. Further, their study of 1,500 youth found that other factors were important for understanding delinquent behavior, including opportunity and peer associations. Other studies also suggest the importance of opportunity and peer influences (Tittle & Botchkovar, 2005).

Some do suggest that social control theories can adequately account for acts of deviance in various groups. One study of four different ethnic groups living in the Netherlands, for example, suggested that social control variables explained delinquency in all four groups (Junger & Marshall, 1997). The same study also found that associations with delinquent peers played a modest role in delinquency in the boys studied.

Conceptual Clarity of Social Control Theories

The main problem with the concepts in many social control theories are that many are not directly measurable. How does one measure factors such as inner containments, internal controls, conscience, and so forth? Hirschi's social bonding theory is measurable, but often the concepts attachment, commitment, and involvement are used interchangeably in studies, likely because each is so intimately related to the others.

Because of problems with the main concepts of self-control theory, some argue that it is really not a theory at all (according to the definition put forth in chapter 2). The only way to accurately assess whether individuals have low self-control is to observe how they behave in given contexts, or how they say they will behave. Of course, labeling a person as having low self-control and then using that label to explain the person's behavior constitutes the logical error of circular reasoning.

According to Wright et al. (1999, p. 488), "self-control itself is not difficult to measure ... it simply has not been measured often in the data sets most often used by criminologists." The presence of low self-control is verified by assessing two different types of measures; one is attitudinal and the other is behavioral. Criminologists assert that low self-control can be verified by asking people about their own attitudes and behaviors, or the attitudes and behaviors of others. Some assert that the best way to verify whether someone has low or high levels of self-control is to ask others—for example, asking teachers or parents whether a child is impulsive or lacks persistence in tasks (Wright et al., 1999, p. 490). According to Gottfredson and Hirschi (1993, p. 48): "Although we would agree that multiple measures are desirable, behavioral measures of self-control seem preferable to self-reports" since the latter "appear to be less valid the greater the delinquency of those to whom they are applied." Behavioral measures assess how people say they behave, whereas attitudinal measures assess how people say they prefer to behave. Each of these measures makes the theory tautological. Examine box 7.4, which contains an index of questions intended to establish one's level of self-control.

Box 7.4 Low Self-Control Scale

Impulsivity. I devote time and effort to preparing for the future.
I act on the spur of the moment without stopping to think.
I do things that bring me pleasure here and now, even at the cost of some future goal.
I base my decisions on what will benefit me in the short run, rather than in the long run.
Physical Activity. If I have a choice, I will do something physical, rather than something mental.
I feel better when I am on the move than when I am sitting and thinking.
I would rather get out and do things than read or contemplate ideas.
Compared to other people my age, I have a greater need for physical activity.
Risk Seeking. I test myself by doing things that are a little risky.
I take risks just for the fun of it.
I find it exciting to do things for which I might get in trouble.
Excitement and adventure are more important to me than security.
Self-Centered. I look out for myself first, even if it means making things difficult for other people.
I am not very concerned about other people when they are having problems.
I don't care if the things I do upset other people.
I try to get things I want, even when I know it's causing problems for other people.

Simple Tasks. I try to avoid projects that I know will be difficult.
When things get complicated, I quit or withdraw.
I do the things in life that are the easiest and bring me the most pleasure.
I avoid difficult tasks that stretch my abilities to the limit.
Temper. I lose my temper easily.
When I am angry at people, I feel more like hurting them than talking to them about why I am angry.
When I am really angry, other people better stay away from me.
When I have a serious disagreement with someone, it's usually hard for me to talk calmly about it without getting upset.

Source: Piquero, A., MacIntosh, R., & Hickman, M. (2000). Does self-control affect survey response? Applying exploratory, confirmatory, and item response theory analysis to Grasmick et al.'s self-control scale. *Criminology, 38* (3), 908.

As you can see, each of the items in box 7.4 assesses how a survey respondent says he or she would behave in a given situation, how he or she prefers to behave, and so on. Thus, each is an indicator of how someone behaves. People who say they would behave in a way consistent with low self-control theory (because they say they are more impulsive, physical, risk seeking, self-centered, simple, and bad tempered) are supposedly more likely to also say they commit crimes. Because low self-control is measured through self-reported behaviors and attitudes, the theory is tautological.

Given its underlying assumptions regarding human nature (e.g., individuals can rationally choose to behave or not), perhaps low self-control does not meet the definition of a theory put forth in chapter 2. You might think that we could tell if a person has low self-control based on whether he or she committed crimes, performed poorly at school and/or work, or had troubles with interpersonal relationships. Indeed, Gottfredson and Hirschi (1990) suggested just this. Yet, when criminologists cannot independently demonstrate the existence of a concept independent of the behavior they wish to explain, then the theory is tautological.

Let's say, for example, that the only way to know whether a man named Bob had low self-control is whether he committed crimes. A criminologist might then say, "Bob has low self-control." You, as an astute student, would ask, "How do you know Bob has low self-control?" The criminologist would then say, "Because Bob committed a crime." Tautological theories amount to saying "Bob is a criminal because he has low self-control, and we know Bob has low control because he commits crime." This is circular reasoning.

In the example, the criminologist labeled Bob with the personality trait of "low self-control" and then used that label to explain why Bob committed crime. Even though Bob's personality may be characterized by low self-control, the criminologist has no real evidence that Bob has low self-control other than the fact that Bob commits crime. This makes the theory tautological and the criminologist is engaging in circular reasoning.

In order to avoid these problems, criminologists must be able to independently verify the existence of the key concepts that are supposed to explain crime, aside from the crime they are attempting to explain. In the example of low self-control theory, this means criminologists must be able to prove the existence of low self-control without using crime or analogous behaviors as indicators of it (for a detailed discussion of measurement problems related to self-control, see Marcus, 2004).

According to Hirschi and Gottfredson (1990):

> In our view, the charge of tautology is in fact a compliment; an assertion that we followed the path of logic in producing an internally consistent result ... We started with a conception of crime, and from it attempted to *derive* a conception of the offender ... What makes our theory *peculiarly* vulnerable to complaints about tautology is that we explicitly show the logical connections between our conception of the actor and the act, whereas many theorists leave this task to those interpreting or testing their theory ... In a comparative framework, the charge of tautology suggests that a theory that is nontautological is preferable. But what would such a theory look like? It would advance definitions of crime and of criminals that are independent of one another ...

In fact, Gottfredson and Hirschi did a good job describing criminality, but not explaining it. Much criminality, indeed, is impulsive, risky, shortsighted, and stupid. But, this does not mean that impulsivity or risk seeking explains it. To assert this, without providing evidence independent of the behaviors being explained, leads to the problem of circular reasoning.

Hirschi offered a new operationalization of self-control (Hirschi, 2004, p. 543, emphasis in original) as "the tendency to consider the full range of potential costs of a particular act [which] moves the focus from the *long-term* implications of the act to its *broader* and often contemporaneous implications" Piquero & Bouffard (2007) tested this measure of self-control against traditional attitudinal measures on a sample of more than 200 university students and found it to be related to drunk driving and sexual coercion. They conclude "Hirschi's redefined self-control measure that considers all costs provided better predictive utility than Gottfredson and Hirschi's previous conceptualization of self-control as considering primarily long-term costs" (p. 19).

Wiebe (2006) adds two new components to low self-control—diligence and the tendency to neutralize one's guilt for wrongdoing—and shows in a study of more than 1,000 university students that they help better explain offending behaviors when added to Gottfredson & Hirschi's (1990) six elements of impulsivity, risk-seeking, shortsightedness, low frustration tolerance, self-centeredness, and a preference for physical activities. He defines *diligence* this way: "The essence of diligence lies in persisting in tasks, both simple and complex, in the absence of immediate tangible rewards. Persons with [low self-control], motivated by immediate gratification, seldom pursue their goals through diligence" (p. 521). *Neutralization* refers to ways in which individuals justify their deviant acts, as in techniques of neutralization (Sykes & Matza, 1957).

Marcus (2006, p. 38) takes great issue with the notion of self-control. He asserts that the belief that such a construct is stable across the life course "is at odds with decades of research on the structure of personality." He discusses the Five Factor Model (FFM) put forth by personality theorists and asserts that each element (i.e., agreeableness, intelligence, conscientiousness, extraversion, and neuroticism) is independent of the others and varies of the course of a person's life. Marcus asserts that "we have a relatively precise understanding of the logical links between these traits and deviant behavior. These links are in some cases completely incompatible with the logic of the [general theory of crime.] ..." (p. 39).

Logical Adequacy of Social Control Theories

Control theories, since they assume that people are born bad and are naturally likely to engage in delinquent acts as children, wrongly assume that all people have the same propensities to engage in antisocial behaviors. In chapters 4 and 5, you saw the evidence that people may have different propensities for antisocial behavior based on their biological makeup. Furthermore, they wrongly assume that all people have the same abilities to commit crimes and the same degree of motivation to commit crimes (Bohm, 2001, p. 92). According to Brannigan (1997, p. 425), when "interaction designed to promote empathy, identification, delayed gratification, a long time horizon, and prosocial values" is absent, "the infant appears to exhibit older evolutionary scripts of adaptation which favor immediate gratification and egoism." This would lend credibility to social control theories in general.

One strength of social control theories is that the view of human nature on which they are based is shared across at least three academic disciplines. Biologists such as Eysenck, psychologists such as Aichorn, and sociologists such as Durkheim all assume a natural drive to deviance that is either inborn or results from inadequate internal control mechanisms (Vold et al., 1998, p. 201, note 1). Further, you saw that major organization such as the American Academy of Pediatrics and the Academy of Child & Adolescent Psychiatry agree one problem with the notion of social control is its assumption that criminality will cause a person to lose something of value, his or her stake in conformity. What if deviance is expected, or if one is rewarded for committing it? Social control theories cannot account for crime in subcultures that value and reward criminal behavior (subcultures are discussed in chapter 9).

What is clear about social control theory is that it, alone, cannot explain why people commit crime or conform to social norms. For example, larger level factors such as economic status (i.e., poverty) may increase family stresses and result in supervision and discipline practices of parents and also may increase the likelihood of associating with criminal peers. As noted by Brannigan (1997, p. 413): "Background factors contribute to the demise of parental control structures and positive school attachment. These in turn make the boys vulnerable to becoming delinquent. Once delinquent, even allowing for all the previous variability, the boys are prone to a host of other social failures and further brushes with the law, right through until middle age."

Recent biosocial research shows it is also important to consider biological factors in conjunction with social factors like social control. For example, the effects of social control variables (e.g., school performance, meals with parents, friendships with deviants) are more pronounced in the presence of certain genetic polymorphisms (i.e., DAT1, DRD2, and MAOA genes). Guo, Roettger, & Cai (2008: 561) conclude that "a stronger social-control influence of family, school, or social networks reduces the delinquency increasing effect of a genetic variant, whereas a weaker social-control influence of family, school, and social networks amplifies the delinquency-increasing effect of a genetic variant."

As noted earlier, Gottfredson and Hirschi (1990) suggested that all crime and a whole host of analogous behaviors (e.g., smoking, drinking, engaging in unprotected sex) can be explained by one single factor. This ignores the rich evidence that numerous other personality factors are related to behavior. Low self-control theory also underestimates the influences of peers, blaming poor socialization by parents for delinquency (Andrews & Bonta, 1994). More problematic, it also may misspecify the meaning of low self-control as it combines the widely posited criminogenic personality factor of impulsivity (discussed in chapter 6) with other elements that may not even be needed to understand why people commit antisocial behaviors. This may be the most troubling criticism of the theory of low self-control—that it does not really add anything new to the criminological literature (Andrews & Bonta, 1998, p. 114). It merely combines many personality factors into one theory.

Even though parenting is important for self-control levels, studies suggest other measures of parenting efficacy are important for understanding delinquency by adolescents. For example, a study of more than 13,000 youths, including a high proportion of minority youths from middle-class and upper-middle-class backgrounds, found that not only did parenting matter but so too did family structure (i.e., family disruption) (Perrone et al. 2004). Further, parenting aside from its impact on self-control was found to be important for delinquency, as were deviant peers. The authors conclude that "it appears as though elements of social bond/social control (parental efficacy) and differential association/social learning (deviant peers) theories specify variables that are theoretically plausible and empirically defensible correlates of deviant behavior" (p. 308).

Gottfredson and Hirschi used legal but harmful behaviors (such as smoking and drinking) to explain criminal behaviors, providing no evidence of low self-control other than the fact that people behave in impulsive ways. In fairness to Hirschi and Gottfredson (2001, pp. 90–91), they noted that other family factors play some role in criminality; they specifically mentioned neglect, abuse, single-parent families, having a large number of children, and parental criminality. Each of these factors supposedly is an indicator of parental concern for children or is a condition that affects the abilities of parents to monitor and correct their children's behaviors.

A study of 750 African American children and their caregivers found that low self-control was positively associated with involvement in delinquency. Other effects of parental efficacy on delinquency were also identified. In the study, levels of self-control varied over time as a result of improvements in parenting, attachment to teachers, and association with pro-social peers (Burt, Simons, & Simons, 2006). Another longitudinal study of nearly 600 individuals found that self-control was related to peer rejection, association with deviant peers, and delinquency (Chapple, 2005). This calls into question the assertion of low self-control theorists that low self-control is a stable trait.

Winfree et al. (2006) studied nearly 1,000 students from 22 middle schools in six cities across the continental United States over several years. Their study showed that "levels of impulsivity declined during the entire 5 year period of the study; and, for its part, risk seeking showed no clear pattern of change, actually increasing slightly between 1995 and 1997 and then declining to levels below those observed in the study's 1st year." The authors thus conclude: "Our findings do not support self-control as an immutable and stable propensity" (p. 278).

Other studies who that factors other than self-control are important for understanding antisocial behavior. For example, level of psychopathy also matters when considering self-control (Wiebe, 2004), as does IQ (McGloin, Pratt & Maahs, 2004). Peter, LaGrange & Silverman (2003) found, in a study of 2,000 adolescents attending junior and senior high schools in a western Canadian city, that self-control and strain contributed to delinquency in an additive way.

A study of juvenile delinquency found that the effects of low self-control on delinquency partially depend on the availability of criminal opportunities, as measured in the study by the time juveniles spent with their friends and/or away from the supervision of their parents (Hay & Forrest, 2008). Further, the effects of low self-control may also depend on moral beliefs, meaning that people with high moral beliefs may be less likely to commit criminal behaviors (Schoepfer & Piquero, 2006; also see Antonaccio & Tittle, 2008).

Turner, Piquero & Pratt (2005) conducted a longitudinal study of more than 450 individuals and offered four major findings about their study of low self-control. First, parental socialization played a meaningful role in children's self-control. Second, school and neighborhood level socialization were also significant in the development of self-control. Third, school socialization efforts were only effective in increasing self-control in neighborhoods characterized with few problems (i.e., in disadvantaged neighborhoods), while parental socialization was important regardless of neighborhood environment. Fourth, school socialization mattered only when the family failed in its task of socializing children. To the degree that these other factors which contribute to delinquency in children are not considered by low self-control theory, it is logically incomplete.

It is possible, too, that low self-control theory is wrong about the major source of low self-control. Sources other than parenting are important for self-control, including but not limited to morality and social reactions from other spheres such as school and work (Latimore, Tittle & Grasmick, 2006). Further, parenting that instills responsibility for actions and good decision making is probably more important for the development of self-control than punitive parenting practices.

Low-self control is also largely heritable, challenging the concept that it arises from social sources (e.g., see Wright & Beaver, 2005). Wright et al. (2009, p. 83) assert that low self-control emanates from genetic impacts on the brain: "Neuroscience long ago classified [the inability to plan, to control emotional impulses, and the tendency to act on the spur of the moment] as executive functions — or higher order thought processes that vary across humans." Further, they claim: "*All* scientific data indicate that self-control is housed in the frontal and prefrontal cortex" of the brain.

AACAP (2008) concurs, writing: "Adolescents differ from adults in the way they behave, solve problems, and make decisions. There is a biological explanation for this difference. Studies have shown that brains continue to mature and develop throughout childhood and adolescence and well into early adulthood. Scientists have identified a specific region of the brain called the *amygdala* which is responsible for instinctual reactions including fear and aggressive behavior. This region develops early. However, *the frontal cortex*, the area of the brain that controls reasoning and helps us think before we act, develops later. This part of the brain is still changing and maturing well into adulthood."

AACAP also asserts: "Pictures of the brain in action show that adolescents' brains function differently than adults when decision-making and problem solving. Their actions are guided more by the amygdala and less by the frontal cortex." As a result, adolescents are more likely to act on impulse; misread or misinterpret social cues and emotions; get into accidents of all kinds; get involved in fights; and engage in dangerous or risky behavior, and are less likely to think before they act; pause to consider the potential consequences of their actions; and modify their dangerous or inappropriate behaviors.

A study by Beaver et al. (2008a) shows that more than half of low self-control is due to genetic variability. Low self-control often emanates from neurological impairments (Moffitt, 1993) that produce low IQ, hyperactivity, negative emotionality, impulsivity, and inattentiveness. These impairments can be produced by environmental factors such as maternal drug use during pregnancy, poor nutrition, and child abuse. They are also likely to result from low levels of serotonin and serotonin metabolites. Thus, "given an equal level of parenting, some children will develop self-control and others will not" (Walsh, 2002, p. 226).

One thing most sociological theories at the group level tend to ignore is that socialization is a two-way street. For example, the behavior of a child will directly affect parenting practices within a family: "Children bring with them traits that increase or decrease the probability of evoking certain kinds of responses when they interact with others. A well-behaved, pleasant, and compliant child generates different reactions from others than does a bad-tempered, moody, and mischievous child" (Walsh, 2002, p. 39). From a developmental perspective, children are born with certain propensities that are either reinforced by parental reactions to early behaviors or reduced by parental reactions to it. When children behave improperly, some parents may react with severe punishment, while others may simply give up and let their children have their way. These two approaches are likely to reinforce deviant behavior.

Walsh (2009) lays out an example of how problem behaviors in children might stress good parenting. Parents of difficult children may adopt coercive techniques in raising and disciplining their children, raising the odds of antisocial behavior, especially when coupled with problems in school as well as peer rejection or association with deviant peers. O'Connor et al. (1998) showed that children classified as at risk for antisocial behavior because of their genetic makeup tended to receive more negative parenting from their adoptive parents. Another adoption study found that children at risk for antisocial behavior who experienced negative parenting from their adoptive parents tended to commit more antisocial behavior than adopted children not considered at risk for antisocial behavior (Cadoret et al., 1995). The study also showed that, children at risk for antisocial behavior raised in loving adoptive families were no more likely to commit antisocial behavior.

Poor parenting tends to be correlated with low levels of serotonin in children (Pine et al., 1997). This likely means that children with low serotonin behave impulsively which produces less than adequate parenting, and inept parenting reinforces serotonin levels and children's behavior. None of this is recognized by social control theorists, because they do not utilize an interdisciplinary perspective in their approach to behavior.

Quality of good parenting can be viewed as having a significant genetic component if one looks at it in evolutionary terms. "Parents nurture and love their children because, well, they love them. They do so because ancestral parents who loved and nurtured their children saw more of them grow to reproductive age and pass on the genes underlying the traits we now define as love and nurturance" (Walsh, 2002, pp. 55–56). There is also significant chemistry involved in good parenting. For example, the presence of the neurotransmitter oxytocin, synthesized in the hypothalamus and stimulated by environmental events (including pregnancy and birth), is related to good maternal behavior, while the absence of it is associated with negative parenting including neglect and abandonment.

The importance of bonds between parent and child cannot be overstated. According to Rowe (1992, p. 402): "the affection dimension of child rearing appears to pull in more correlates with child behavior than any other dimension." There is actually a biological need for bonds between parents and children (Walsh, 2002). Basically, our brains require affection and if we do not get it early in life, the effects can be dramatic and far-reaching. Research shows that a failure to establish affectional bonds in childhood results in a diminished ability to form lasting and meaningful bonds in adulthood (Perry & Pollard, 1998; Shore, 1996; Zeifman & Hazan, 1997). The reason that affection is so important is because about 75% of our brain growth occurs outside the womb, after we are born. As explained by Walsh (2002, pp. 85–86): "Such a high degree of developmental incompleteness of the human brain assures a greater role for the [external] environment in its development than is true of any other species."

It should be no surprise that parental neglect, then, is strongly associated with criminality (Glaser, 2000; Heck & Walsh, 2000). For example, a study of 360 high-risk adolescents found that parenting was associated with school engagement and child well-being as well as the likelihood kids ran away. Childhood neglect by parents was related to victimization while sexual abuse and living in a more disadvantaged neighborhood were associated with poorer well-being. The more adolescents were engaged in school was associated with higher levels of well-being and a lower likelihood of delinquency (Tyler, Johnson, & Brownridge, 2008).

Childhood stress can lead to higher levels of stress hormones that lead to death of brain cells (Teicher et al., 1997) and is likely to produce delays in development in cognition, movement, and social behaviors (Gunnar, 1996). Low levels of attachment make it more difficult for an individual to adapt to the environment (Walsh, 2002). For a developmental perspective, the importance of quality parenting becomes clear: "Experience in adults alters the organized brain, but in infants and children it organizes the developing brain" (Perry & Pollard, 1998, p. 36). In other words, a child's brain can be wired for low attachment and affection very early in life.

Other Group Level Factors

Without doubt, there are other group level factors involved in criminality. As of yet, not many other factors have not been subjected to widespread empirical testing. Nevertheless, given the importance of peers and family members in the lives of most people, it is unlikely that other groups will reach the importance of these in terms of the effects they will have on an individual's behavior. Some have examined the effects of school level factors independent of the ones discussed in this chapter, but the weight of the evidence suggests that the most important aspect of school concerns peer influences as well as the potential protective value of an education. Recall that protective factors are specifically not examined in great depth in this book. Also not given great attention in the book is the influence of religion, thought to be a protective factor against antisocial behavior (see chapter 3).

Summary

In this chapter, you learned about group level factors as they impact antisocial and criminal behavior. A group was defined as a collective of individuals that are assembled together and have some unifying relationship. The most important groups for understanding behavior include parents and peers, or families and friends, although other groups also impact an individual's behavior.

The most important theories at this level of analysis include social learning and social control theories. Each asserts that groups are very important for understanding behavior, including families and friends, and that behavior is learned from these groups. Yet, the theories are based on opposite assumptions; social learning theories assume that an individual learns to commit crimes from these groups whereas social control theories assume that conformity must be learned from these groups.

Social learning theories include imitation, differential association, differential identification, differential reinforcement, observational learning, and social structural learning theories. Each of these theories asserts that criminality is learned through observations and/or interactions with other people as well as the media.

Social control theories include anomie, failure of personal and social controls, stake in conformity, containment, social bonding, low self-control, age-graded informal social control, and control balance theories. Each of these theories asserts that criminality should be expected in the absence of controls, some internal to individuals and others external to individuals.

A review of normal child/human development suggests that the assumption of social control theories is more accurate; that is, young people normally will engage in antisocial and deviant behavior and must learn to stop committing it. However, learning is also important for understanding antisocial behavior, delinquency, and criminality, especially in how it accounts for the continuation of antisocial behavior across the life course.

Since most people commit antisocial behavior and delinquency prior to developing meaningful peer interactions, peer influences cannot cause most antisocial behavior and delinquency, particularly for early starters and life course persistent offenders who engage in serious delinquency prior to making close friends. These offenders tend to seek out like-minded individuals after initiation into deviant behavior; such friendships then reinforce the likelihood of future deviance. For late starters and adolescent limited offenders, peer influences may very well help explain the initiation of delinquent and criminal behaviors.

The importance of families/parenting and friends/peers varies over the course of one's life. Generally speaking, family/parenting influences are much more important early in life, whereas friend/peer influences become more important during early to late adolescence.

Tests of social learning and social control theories have been supportive, although the latest control theories have not been subjected to widespread testing. Generally, the more time people spend with deviant peers, especially in unsupervised settings, the greater their odds of engaging in deviance. Additionally, studies of media portrayals of violence show clear and consistent evidence that exposure to media violence contributes to future violent behavior.

Tests of social bonding theory show that attachment to parents is inversely related to the likelihood of deviant behavior. Further, parents who supervise their kids, notice and correct their antisocial behavior, set standards of behavior and clearly communicate them, use consistent and non-violent discipline, and who abide by the law and disapprove of deviance have children that have a lower likelihood of engaging in delinquent behavior. Conversely, children who are not attached to their children, who neglect or reject them, who fail to adequately supervise them and notice and correct their antisocial behavior, who set no standards of behavior or do not clearly communicate them, who use inconsistent and violent discipline, who abuse their kids, who break the law and approve of deviance, and who are authoritarian or overly permissive in nature have children that have a higher likelihood of engaging in delinquent behavior.

In terms of prevention, evidence suggests that meaningful bonds to significant others (such as marriage) and institutions (such as work) are important for understanding desistance from crime. That is, even serious repeat criminals often stop committing crimes after entering into fulfilling marriages and careers.

There is a reciprocal relationship between parenting and antisocial behavior. Bad parenting tends to promote antisocial behavior in children and antisocial behavior in children strains good parenting. Further, good parenting can lessen the likelihood that children will associate with deviant peers. Several family structure variables are also associated with an increased risk of criminality, yet these variables rely on social process variables to account for the increased odds of antisocial behavior by children.

The scope of social bonding and social learning theories is probably larger than that established through research. Most tests of these theories have been conducted on relatively minor acts of deviance. Yet, recent studies show that control and learning factors play an important role in various forms of elite deviance, including some white-collar and corporate crimes.

Some theories at the group level of analysis such as differential association and the earlier social control theories are problematic in that they posit concepts that cannot be directly measured. Further, the theory of low-self control is tautological. Low self-control also clearly emanates from sources other than parenting, including biological sources such as genetics and brain dysfunction.

Discussion Questions

1. What is a group?
2. What groups likely have the most important influence on individual behavior?
3. What are the most important theories at the group level of analysis?
4. Do social learning theories and social control theories really make opposite predictions about human behavior? Explain.
5. What is imitation?
6. Outline the theory of differential association. Briefly discuss how the theory has been modified over time with the concepts of differential identification and differential reinforcement.
7. Briefly summarize Akers's social learning theory.
8. What is anomie?
9. Outline social control theories, including failure of personal and social controls, multiple control factors, containment theory, and social bonding theory.
10. What is meant by the term *stake in conformity?* How is it relevant for antisocial behavior?
11. Briefly summarize the theory of low self-control, the age-graded informal social control theory, and the control balance theory.
12. What does the evidence concerning normal human development suggest about the validity of social learning and social control theories?
13. List and discuss the main propositions related to peer and family studies.
14. Are social learning theories supported by empirical evidence? Explain.
15. Identify the possible interpretations of findings showing that people who commit antisocial behavior are more likely to have antisocial friends and spend more time with antisocial people.
16. According to the evidence, which tends to come first: antisocial behavior or associations with antisocial peers? Explain.
17. Are social control theories supported by empirical evidence? Explain.
18. What family conditions appear to be related to antisocial behavior?
19. Are the concepts of group level explanations of crime clearly defined? Explain.
20. What is the logical adequacy of group level explanations of crime?
21. What is the scope of group level explanations of crime?

8

Community and Organization Level Explanations of Crime

Introduction

Recall from chapter 3 that communities are synonymous with neighborhoods. Organizations are large groups. *Merriam-Webster's Collegiate Dictionary* (2008) defines an organization as the "administrative and functional structure" of an association; an association is "an organization of persons having a common interest." Communities and organizations are made up of groups (chapter 7) and comprise societies (chapter 9). Factors at this level of analysis include conditions of social disorganization (also known as differential social organization), the effects of routine activities and victim lifestyles, and the effects of punishment, including deterrence and labeling. These factors have been put forth by seemingly unrelated schools of thought. Each is included here because each represents the community or organization level of analysis.

Behavior in the Context of Communities and Organizations

Individuals come together to form meaningful groups in order to better their lives through symbiotic relationships. Communities and organizations are in essence large groups or congregations and collective of groups. The primary difference between a group and an organization is that a group tends to be smaller. Groups are also characterized by more frequent interactions between individual members. Members of a family or a peer group, for example, will spend much more time together than members of most organizations. For the purposes of this chapter, a community is treated as synonymous with a neighborhood. Criminologists have a long history of examining relationships with community level factors and crime rates. In fact, this may be the most popular level of analysis for the study of the etiology of crime (e.g., see Reiss & Tonry, 1986).

Organizations can best be understood through examples. Criminal justice organizations include police, courts, and corrections agencies. In 2006, U.S. civil and criminal justice systems employed more than two million persons. Further, federal, state, and local governments spent about $214 billion for police protection, corrections, and judicial and legal activities in that year—that is, to achieve justice and reduce crime (Robinson, 2009). This gives you a sense of how large criminal justice organizations are in the United States.

In addition to these public criminal justice organizations, there are also many private organizations affiliated with criminal justice. For example, there are national organizations such as the American Society of Criminology (*www.asc41.com*) and the Academy of Criminal Justice Sciences (*www.acjs.org*), and numerous regional organizations such as the Southern Criminal Justice Association (*www.scja.net*). Since this book is about why crime happens, we do not assert that these agencies actually play a role in the etiology of crime (or in its prevention for that matter). We simply use them as examples of organizations; each is essentially a large group with many individual and institutional members. There are also many private organizations, often called *interest groups,* that concern themselves with matters of criminal justice policy. One of the most successful is the National Rifle Association, which not only lobbies for gun ownership rights, but also for many other criminal justice policies (Walker, 1998).

For the purposes of this chapter, we examine the effects on crime of the main components of the criminal justice system. Using labeling theory and the research on deterrence, we examine the effects of police, courts, and corrections activities on crime in the United States. We begin with an examination of the most well-known community level factor, social disorganization, which arose out of the most influential theoretical "school of thought" in American criminology, commonly referred to as the Chicago School of Criminology.

Social Disorganization and Differential Social Organization

Chicago School

The so-called *Chicago School of Criminology* emerged largely as a result of environmental and social conditions that materialized at the turn of the 20th century in Chicago, including extensive foreign immigration. "Chicago at that time had a population of over 2 million; between 1860 and 1910 its population had doubled every ten years, with wave after wave of immigrants" (Vold, Bernard, & Snipes, 1998, p. 141). According to Figlio, Hakim, and Rengert (1986, p. xi), early sociological theorists in the Chicago School argued that urban areas were more crime-prone than rural areas: "Perhaps the most influential of these theorists was Louis Wirth, who observed that life in cities creates anomie at the societal level and alienation at the individual level. Similarly, Tonnies, Simmel, and Maine viewed urban living as essentially amoral and normless."

Virtually all criminological theories in the 20th century can be traced back to the writings of Emile Durkheim (discussed in chapter 9) and the Chicago School of Criminology. The Chicago School started in the early 1900s, as Robert Park investigated various social conditions of the city. In 1914, he was appointed to the Sociology Department at the University of Chicago. Park eventually became interested in the similarities between the natural distribution of plant life and the societal organization of human life. From the field of plant ecology, he borrowed two concepts that helped him form what he called the *theory of human ecology*. Felson (1983, p. 665) noted that this field of human ecology encompasses the field of the ecology of crime, but in turn it is encompassed by the more general field of ecology.

The first concept borrowed by Robert Park (1915, pp. 577–612) was from Eugenius Warming. Warming posited that plant communities were made up of individual organisms, each of which had its own characteristics. These characteristics, in combination, resembled the original organism. Thus, each plant community was analogous to a distinct organism. Park (1952, p. 118) saw the city in a similar way, as a *superorganism*. He noted that many areas existed where different types of people lived. Like the natural areas of plants, each area of the city had an organic unity of its own. Divisions in the city existed, including racial and ethnic divisions, income and occupational divisions, industrial and business divisions, and physical divisions created by architectural and natural structures.

The second concept Park borrowed from plant ecology revolved around how the balance of nature in an area changed. The primary mechanisms identified by Park were invasion, domination, and succession. As noted by Figlio et al. (1986, p. xi), "Park viewed communities as functionally specialized areas within an industrial economy. The patterning of communities was determined by competition, and changes were determined by invasion and social succession." These mechanisms can be seen in nature (e.g., the natural evolution of a pasture into a deciduous forest, where plant species invade, dominate, and eventually take over original species). They can also be seen in human societies (e.g., the shift from small, closely knit communities to large, unfamiliar cities through the process of immigration).

Later studies focused on ecological spatial patterns of cities, such as Burgess's (1928) concentric circles, Hoyt's (1943) sectors, and Shaw and McKay's (1929, 1942) work on delinquency areas. For example, Ernest Burgess, Park's associate, explored the processes of *invasion*, *dominance*, and *succession*. He used them to explain the growth of cities. According to Burgess, cities expand outward from the center of the city in patterns of concentric circles.

Concentric Zones

Burgess portrayed the city of Chicago in five zones. Figure 8.1 shows these zones. They include the loop, the zone in transition, the zone of workingmen's homes, the residential zone, and the commuters' zone. The loop was the central business district. The zone in transition was the oldest section of the city and was being invaded by business and industry. Residential housing there was deteriorated, and residents were generally poor immigrants. The zone of workers' homes was occupied by those who had managed to escape the zone in transition. The residential zone consisted of single-family houses and expensive apartments. Finally, the commuters' zone was a growing zone that was in the process of expanding outward through a process of invasion, dominance, and succession (Robinson, 1997).

Of course, the portrayal created by Burgess does not represent a perfect account of any given city. After all, any city contains natural areas such as lakes and rivers, and architectural features such as railroad tracks and highways. Nevertheless, within this framework, Burgess and Park studied Chicago and its social problems. The most crime reportedly occurred in the least desirable residential section of the city, which was the zone in transition.

Figure 8.1 Chicago's Concentric Zones

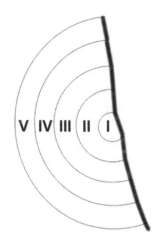

I --
(C

II

II

IV -- Residential Zone

V -- Commuters' Zone

Source: Figure created by author.

Clifford Shaw used Park's theories as a foundation for studying juvenile delinquency in Chicago. Shaw believed that juvenile delinquency resulted from the juvenile's detachment from conventional groups (recall the discussion of social control theory in chapter 7). He wanted to determine how this detachment occurred. Shaw felt that delinquent activities somehow came out of individuals' environments. Therefore, he analyzed characteristics of the neighborhoods out of which delinquents arose, and compiled case histories for individual delinquents, in order to find out how they had related to their environments. This means his analyses were limited to delinquents known to the criminal justice system through court records (Robinson, 1997).

Later, Henry McKay coauthored studies with Shaw. They produced maps that pinpointed the residences of juveniles involved in the justice system. Other maps showed percentages of the juvenile population who were involved in the criminal justice system. Through zone maps, a general tendency for concentration of delinquency emerged toward the city's center. Specific findings related to delinquency showed that it had roots in the physical and economic status of the neighborhood and in the population composition of the neighborhood. Specifically, the scholars found that areas with the highest official rates of juvenile delinquency were characterized by high industry and commerce, high levels of foreign-born families, and a low level of economic status (Robinson, 1997).

rganization and Collective Efficacy

types of findings, along with summary case studies of individual ents, led to the theory of *social disorganization.* Thomas and Znaniecki 8, p. 1128) defined social disorganization as a "decrease of the influence existing social rules of behavior upon individual members of the group." As summarized by Vold et al. (1998, p. 147): "The formal social organizations that existed in the neighborhood tend to disintegrate as the original population retreats. Because the neighborhood is in transition, the residents no longer identify with it, and thus they do not care as much about its appearance or reputation. There is a marked decrease in 'neighborliness' and in the ability of the people of the neighborhood to control their youth." This trend is worsened by high mobility of residents, high population turnover, culture conflict, high levels of immigration, and so on. Social disorganization is essentially anomie at the community or neighborhood level (Walsh, 2002, pp. 171–172). Anomie means a state of normlessness or confusion over right and wrong (more on this in chapter 9).

As explained by Walsh, social disorganization affects neighborhood crime rates in two ways: first, it erodes informal social control networks between neighbors; and second, it provides positive incentives to commit antisocial behaviors. According to Wilsktroem (1998), crime rate variations are affected by changes in community rules, resources, and routines. This means when conditions of social disorganization arise, families find it harder to assert authority over children; children find it more difficult to resist deviant temptations and are more likely to engage in behaviors that take them into dangerous and risky places where delinquency is likely to occur (which may very well be their own neighborhoods).

According to Veysey and Messner (1999, p. 159), social disorganization operates "through the processes of value and norm conflicts, cultural change and cultural vacuums, and the weakening of primary relationships. This, in turn, is believed to reduce internal and external social control, which then frees individuals to engage in deviant behavior." Characteristics of the community, including urbanization, residential mobility, racial or ethnic heterogeneity, socioeconomic status (SES), family disruption or single-parent households, and others, inhibit a community's ability to impose social controls over people in the community. This operates through processes such as reduced friendship networks, less involvement in community organizations, and less supervision of young people (Sampson & Groves, 1989). Social disorganization is also thought to increase associations between an individual and deviant peers (Cattarello, 2000), meaning social learning theory underlies the process of social disorganization.

The opposite of social disorganization is referred to as *collective efficacy*. Taylor (2001, p. 128) explained the differences between a socially disorganized neighborhood and one that is high in collective efficacy: "A locale is socially disorganized if several things are true: residents do not get along with one another; residents do not belong to local organizations geared to bettering the communities and thus cannot work together effectively to address common problems; residents hold different values about what is and what is not acceptable behavior on the street; and residents are unlikely to interfere when they see other youths or adults engaged in wrongdoing." An area has collective efficacy if conditions such as these prevail: "residents will work together on common, neighborhood-wide issues, will get along somewhat with one another, and will take steps to supervise activities of youth or teens taking place in the immediate locale." It consists of "several features of community social life including organizational participation ... informal social control ... and local social ties based on physical proximity." A neighborhood is high in collective efficacy if it is organized to fight crime. Taylor has taken the works of Shaw and McKay and turned them on their head; he has studied opposite conditions and labeled them collective efficacy.

Through the writings of Shaw and McKay, the ecological approach was committed to "the stability of the ecological substructure of the city" (Figlio et al., 1986). For example, Shaw and McKay saw the city's stable delinquency areas as "specialized habitation niches for low income migrants into the city" which "would be used by a succession of immigrant groups from different ethnic backgrounds at different time periods." Thus, even when the ethnic composition of the inner city changed from German and Irish to Italian and Polish, high crime rates were consistently found closest to the center of the city, because "as the social and economic situation of groups improved, they would move into the mainstream of American life, leaving space for the new immigrant groups" in the "breeding ground for the city's criminal population." Those who were left behind can be thought of as socially isolated from the middle class and truly disadvantaged (Wilson, 1987). The recognition of *hot spots* of crime (areas with a lot of crime) undoubtedly started here (Sherman, Gartin, & Buerger, 1989; Spring & Block, 1988).

Park and Burgess of the Chicago School originated their search into the etiology of deviance by describing environmental factors. Shaw and McKay essentially began attempts to explain why these environmental factors were important. In other words, "the work of Park and Burgess was used by Shaw and McKay to study the ecology of crime" (Jeffery, 1990, p. 260). For example, certain areas of Chicago characterized by high rates of delinquency were differentiated from areas with lower rates of delinquency, in terms of "physical, economic, and population characteristics" (Voss & Petersen, 1971, p. 87). Shaw and McKay then turned to "more subtle differences in values, standards, attitudes, traditions, and institutions" in order to explain such differences.

Examples of explanations of crime provided by "the Chicago sociologists" included urbanization, culture conflict, immigration, poverty, ecology, and socialization (Jeffery, 1990, p. 256). From this, American criminology turned largely to sociological variables in attempts to explain criminal and deviant behavior, leaving the physical environment behind (Jeffery & Zahm, 1993, p. 326). Thus, it was out of the early works of the ecological theorists that the sociological theories, which have been greatly emphasized in American criminology, arose. In support of this, Vold et al. (1998, p. 156) wrote that the "Chicago School of Human Ecology can be described as a gold mine that continues to enrich criminology today ... the social disorganization theory forms the basis for several other theories in contemporary criminology."

Despite the important position that social disorganization theory has played in American criminology, the theory and its key concept have been severely criticized. Later in the chapter we outline the main problems with the theory, but for now, let us differentiate social disorganization from differential social organization. *Differential social organization* is a term coined by Sutherland (1947) which simply suggests that no neighborhood is truly disorganized. Instead, neighborhoods may be organized differently, according to different rules of conduct, and thus differentially socially organized. Social disorganization implies a form of chaos in a neighborhood, which is inaccurate. Differential social organization implies a different set of values, attitudes, and way of life than traditional middle-class neighborhoods.

Main Propositions of Social Disorganization and Differential Social Organization

Given the predictions made by social disorganization theorists, the following propositions have been tested:

- Conditions of social disorganization, including poverty or low socioeconomic status (SES), residential mobility, instability or transiency, immigration, racial or ethnic heterogeneity, population density, physical disorder or incivilities, and family disruption or single-parent families, are related to high rates of street crime.
- Conditions of collective efficacy, including friendship networks, supervised teenage peer groups, and organizational participation, are related to low rates of street crime.

Key Concepts of Social Disorganization and Differential Social Organization

From the preceding propositions, the following concepts can be isolated and defined:

- Social disorganization
- Poverty or low socioeconomic status (SES)
- Residential mobility, instability, or transiency
- Immigration
- Racial or ethnic heterogeneity
- Population density
- Physical disorder or incivilities
- Family disruption or single-parent families
- Collective efficacy
- Crime rates

Box 8.1 defines the key concepts of social disorganization and differential social organization. Scholars use these concepts to test relationships between community conditions and crime rates.

Box 8.1 Definitions of Key Concepts of Social Disorganization and Differential Social Organization Studies

- *Social disorganization. Nominal*—an inability of inhabitants to control the behavior of residents and users of neighborhood space because of deleterious social conditions. *Operational*—any evidence of deleterious social conditions, including the presence of poverty, residential mobility, immigration, heterogeneity, population density, incivilities, and family disruption, typically measured using official sources of data such as government census data, and/or surveys of residents of a neighborhood and on-site observations of neighborhood conditions.
- *Poverty or low socioeconomic status (SES). Nominal*—the presence of lower-class people in a community. *Operational*—the proportion of lower-class people in a neighborhood, city, or other area, as measured by official government statistics such as census data.
- *Residential mobility, instability, or transiency. Nominal*—the degree of population turnover in a neighborhood. *Operational*—the degree of turnover among residents in a neighborhood, as measured by official

government data or surveys of residents that assess the relative stability of residential status.

- *Immigration. Nominal*—the amount of people moving into a neighborhood. *Operational*—evidence of large-scale moving by people from outside a neighborhood, as measured by government statistics such as census data.
- *Racial or ethnic heterogeneity. Nominal*—diversity of a neighborhood among races and ethnic groups. *Operational*—the degree of diversity in a neighborhood, as measured by government statistics such as census data.
- *Population density. Nominal*—a heavy concentration of people residing in an area. *Operational*—the number of people living in a neighborhood, as measured by government statistics such as census data.
- *Physical disorder or incivilities. Nominal*—the presence of untended property and untended people and behavior in an area. *Operational*—the degree of presence of conditions such as abandoned buildings with boarded or broken windows; abandoned lots with an accumulation of trash; litter in streets, walkways, and parking areas; graffiti on buildings and walls; groups of people loitering, arguing, or fighting on streets; derelicts and winos reclining in doorways and alleyways; poorly lighted streets and dark entries to buildings and alleys; and illegal drug activity, usually measured through surveys of residents and/or on-site observations.
- *Family disruption or single-parent families. Nominal*—the presence of single-parent families in a neighborhood. *Operational*—the degree of family breakup, single parents, or divorce, as measured by government statistics such as census data.
- *Collective efficacy. Nominal*—the degree of cohesion in a neighborhood. *Operational*—evidence that a neighborhood is well suited to protect itself from deviant influences, as measured by friendship networks, involvement in community organizations and activities, and supervision of children, usually measured in surveys of neighborhood residents.
- *Crime rates. Nominal*—an aggregate measure of crime in an area. *Operational*—an official measure of total crime divided by the population (crimes per capita), typically crimes known to the police.

Evaluation of Social Disorganization Theory

In the following sections, we address social disorganization theory. We assess the empirical validity of this theory, discuss the scope of the research, as well as address the conceptual clarity and the logical adequacy of its propositions.

Empirical Validity of Social Disorganization

Neighborhood Crime

There have literally been hundreds of studies testing relationships between various aspects of social disorganization and crime (Bursik, 1988; Bursik & Grasmick, 1993; Kubrin & Weitzer, 2003; Sampson, 1985; Sampson & Groves, 1989; Sampson, Raudenbush, & Earls, 1997; Sampson & Wilson, 1994; Sampson & Wooldredge 1987; Smith & Jarjoura, 1988; Stark, 1987; Taylor, 1997; Warner & Pierce, 1993; Warner & Rountree, 1997). Most of these studies have focused on community level factors and their relationship to neighborhood crime rates (Sampson, 2000). Stark (1987), for example, suggested that structural characteristics such as high population density, high levels of transiency, high poverty, mixed land uses, and dilapidation of buildings all lead to higher crime rates. A review by Sampson (1995) of numerous studies testing the effects of poverty on official crime rates found that poverty combined with residential mobility is associated with higher levels of violent street crime. Other factors at the community level associated with higher crime rates include high numbers of apartments and various forms of family disruption.

Sampson and Groves (1989) tested their model of social disorganization using data from 238 British neighborhoods. They found that urbanization, family disruption, SES, residential stability, and ethnic heterogeneity are all related to unsupervised peer groups, that SES is related to participation in community organizations, and that residential stability and urbanization are related to local friendship networks. They also found that family disruption and urbanization have direct effects on victimization, as do reduced friendship networks, less involvement in community organizations, and less supervision of young people. Specifically, friendship ties decrease robbery and burglary but not assault, rape, auto theft, or vandalism. These findings were supported in a replication (Lowenkamp, Cullen & Pratt, 2003).

As summarized by Veysey and Messner (1999, p. 169):

> SES affects both organizational participation and supervision of peer groups. Poor communities lack money and resources, and therefore, have fewer organizational opportunities for youth and adults. In ad-

dition, poverty is believed to undermine formal and informal social controls, thus affecting the community's ability to monitor youth. Urbanization is negatively related to friendship networks and reduced organizational participation. Ethnic heterogeneity reduces community consensus and increases distrust among community members. Communities then become fragmented along ethnic lines, which impedes communication and, therefore, effective supervision of youths. Family disruption directly affects community members' ability to supervise teenage peer groups. Finally, residential mobility is predicted to disrupt friendship networks.

At the same time, conditions of social disorganization are related to an increased likelihood of associating with deviant peers (Cattarello, 2000), suggesting the importance of associations in deviant behavior (discussed in chapter 7).

A study of juvenile violence in rural areas (Osgood & Chambers, 2000) found that residential instability, ethnic heterogeneity, and family disruption are associated with higher arrest rates for rape, assault, and weapons offenses. Yet, the study found no relationships between these crimes and poverty or unemployment, which is not surprising given the research in this area (poverty and unemployment are discussed in chapter 9).

Social and economic disadvantage are associated with higher murder rates (Strom & MacDonald, 2007), as are other neighborhood characteristics (Kubrin & Herting, 2003; Titterington, Vollum & Diamond, 2003). A study of more than 1,100 people living in thirty-one residential units found that people living in economically disadvantaged areas were more likely to perceive their immediate surroundings in negative terms while people living in residential units characterized by higher levels of collective efficacy reported fewer problems with neighborhood incivilities (Reisig & Cancino, 2003).

A study by Kubrin (2003) found that residential instability was related to felony killings, while economic disadvantage was associated with all of the homicide categories he studied. Kubrin & Wadsworth (2003) found that concentrated disadvantage was associated with some forms of murders while residential instability was related to gang homicide. Another study of homicide found evidence that changes in economic conditions predicted levels of acquaintance homicides and especially instrumental homicides (felony murders) (Pratt & Lowencamp, 2002). Further, studies show that income inequality is related to higher murder rates (Wang & Arnold, 2008). Income inequality is discussed further in chapter 9.

A study of 153 central cities found that a decline in manufacturing employment relative to service employment increased aggravated assault, larceny, and burglary rates, while an increase in poverty raised rape and larceny (Oh,

2005). A study of more than 1,700 people across 95 census tracts in a Northern California city compared with neighborhood characteristics derived from Census 2000 measures showed that neighborhood poverty was related to higher rates of drug activity (Freisthler et al., 2005).

As for why poverty tends to be found to be related to higher rates of offending, Fergusson, Swain-Campbell, & Horwood (2004) provide a good account. In their longitudinal study of more than 1,200 children through age 21 years, socio-economic disadvantage during childhood was associated with increases in self-reported crime and officially recorded convictions. Parental, individual, school, and peer factors intervened between socio-economic disadvantage and crime, meaning social structural factors impact social process factors prior to impacting crime.

The authors note that "family, individual, school and peer factors combined accumulatively to place young people from socio-economically disadvantaged backgrounds at increased risk of later crime. Specifically, the analysis suggested that increased socio-economic disadvantage was related to increased:

1.   Family adversity, including: higher rates of physical punishment and child abuse; reduced levels of maternal care; changes in parental figures; low attachment to parents; and parental criminality.
2.   Childhood adjustment problems, including conduct and attentional problems.
3.   School problems, including: truancy; educational underachievement; suspension from school; and low scholastic ability.
4.   Affiliations with delinquent and substance using peers (p. 963)

A study of sixty-six neighborhoods in a southern state found that neighborhood disadvantage and stability affect neighborhood levels of strain which are associated with levels of violence (Warner & Fowler, 2003). Strain can be understood as frustration and stress, and is discussed in greater depth in chapter 9.

According to many studies, different elements of social disorganization are interrelated because they affect one another. For example, Rountree and Warner (1999) found that community stability increases the proportion of women in the community with close ties, and that ethnic heterogeneity lessens ties between women in the community. Furthermore, not all aspects of social disorganization have equal effects on crime; some elements of social disorganization are mediated by others while some act directly on crime (Taylor, 2001). For example, Veysey and Messner (1999) measured the effects of SES, residential mobility, ethnic heterogeneity, family disruption, urbanization, friendship networks, unsupervised teenage peer groups, and organizational participation on total victimization rates from street crimes. They found that their measure of unsupervised peer groups was the strongest predictor of victimization, followed by urbanization and family disruption. They also found that SES and urbanization are related to organizational participation, and that urbanization and residential stability are related to friendship networks. SES is largely mediated by organization participation and peer groups, meaning that poverty interferes with a community's ability to participate in organizations and to supervise children.

The effects of social disorganization depend in part on neighborhood characteristics not usually measured by social disorganization theorists. For example, Rountree and Warner (1999), in a study of crime in Seattle, found that female social ties are more closely related to lower violent crime rates and that these ties are most effective when communities are characterized by fewer female-headed households. The suspected reason that female-headed households have a greater difficulty controlling crime is that men provide monetary support for families, which allows a greater assurance of supervision of children and the potential for a strong authority figure in the household. Ties to the community imply that neighbors know each other and share things, watch out for each other, and so on. Additionally, the effects of social ties on assault are dependent in part on race (Warner & Rountree, 1997).

Social and Human Capital

From these studies, it can be argued that areas characterized by what scholars call social disorganization lack social capital and human capital, both of which are needed to prevent social problems in the community. Scholars contend that low levels of social capital, also referred to as collective efficacy (Taylor, 2001, p. 128), combine with larger level factors in society such as income inequality (discussed in chapter 9) to increase crime rates. One study illustrated this link, showing that burglary and violent crimes are associated with higher levels of income inequality when social capital is low (Kawachi, Kennedy, & Wilkinson, 1999). High crime areas also tend to be characterized by other negative social conditions, including overall mortality rates.

Collective efficacy is associated with lower rates of homicide among partners (Browning, 2002), especially in the presence of certain partner- and individual-level factors such as race, relationship status, and social support (Van Wyk et al., 2003). A study of more than 1,100 citizens in Michigan found that measures of collective efficacy (i.e., mutual trust and solidarity) are major sources of residents' lower perceived levels of incivility and burglary (Cancino, 2005).

When discussing the role of mass incarceration in the United States in the development of social disorganization, Rose and Clear (1998, p. 456) differentiated between the effects of an incarceration in a socially organized and a socially disorganized neighborhood: "Socially organized areas have sufficient assets and resources to overcome the loss of an offender's asset in order to remove the offender's liability from the neighborhood. In socially disorganized areas, however, assets are already sufficiently depleted that the neighborhood feels the loss of the asset just as it rejoices in the loss of the liability." This is related to the notions of social capital and human capital. *Social capital* is "the social skills and resources needed to effect positive change in neighborhood life. It is the aspect of structured groups that increases the capacity for action oriented toward the achievement of group goals (Hagan, 1994) ... Social capital is the essence of social control for it is the very force collectives draw upon to enforce order. It is what enables groups to enforce norms, and, as a result, to increase their level of informal control." *Human capital* is "the human skill and resources individuals need to function effectively, such as reading, writing, and reasoning ability. It is the capital individuals acquire through education and training for productive purposes (Hagan, 1994) ... neighborhoods rich in social capital exert more control over individual residents, thus helping to produce more highly educated, employable, and productive members of the community."

Factors of social disorganization make it more difficult for community members to regulate the behavior of their residents: "Poverty, family disruption, and residential instability ... result in anonymity and the lack of relationships among neighborhood residents and low participation in community organizations and in local activities" (Vold et al., 1998, p. 152). Studies tend to consistently find relationships between high levels of poverty, residential mobility, racial heterogeneity, population density, single-parent households, and rates of both property and violent crime (Petee & Kowalski, 1993; Petee, Kowalski, & Duffield, 1994; Warner & Pierce, 1993). Regardless of who lives in a community, these conditions will breed street crime and other social problems.

Consider adolescent delinquency, for example. Sampson (2000) used data from 80 Chicago neighborhoods to explore how changes in residential stability and neighborhood advantages are related to measures of informal social control. He reported that concentrated poverty and low levels of residential stability are associated with higher rates of juvenile delinquency. The main causal factor in the relationship is level of informal social control; high levels of informal social control inhibit delinquency (discussed in chapter 7). Similarly, Taylor (1996) found that high levels of neighborhood stability are related to higher levels of local attachment and social involvement.

Similarly, studies show that, even after controlling for known risk factors of violence (e.g., family supervision and structure, school attachment, and peer delinquency), young people who witness violence in their neighborhoods are more likely to commit assaultive behaviors and carry weapons (Patchin et al., 2006). A study of more than 160 students attending two elementary schools in economically disadvantaged, high risk neighborhood in Detroit, Michigan found that exposure to community violence was associated with more symptoms of depression and feelings of hopelessness. However, parental monitoring lessened this effect somewhat (Ceballo et al., 2007).

This suggests the importance of the family in informal community social controls. You saw in chapter 7 how the family can both produce and reduce criminality. Social disorganization rests on the assumption that families are less able to monitor and correct the behavior of their children when conditions of social disorganization prevail. Yet, the effects of social disorganization variables on crime depend on other factors. This means that traditional social disorganization theory is not logically complete. Other factors also appear to be important for helping understand some of the relationships between crime and community factors in urban areas. For example, people living in conditions of social disorganization may over time begin to see deviance as normal or not so bad and/or as a legitimate response to economic deprivation (Anderson, 1999). If true, this implicates learning (discussed in chapter 7) and strain (discussed in chapter 9) approaches as important. Social disorganization also affects quality of parenting. According to Simons et al. (1998, 2001), living in poor neighborhoods produces present-orientation in parents, as well as poor organizational and planning skills. It also increases the chance of experiencing strain and reduces social support. This means social control mechanisms may also be important.

Hoffman (2003) demonstrates that factors such as the percentage of unemployed or out-of-workforce males, the proportion of female-headed households, and the percent living below the poverty line are associated with higher rates of delinquency in neighborhoods. He also specifies several protective factors that can lessen the negative impacts of such social disorganization factors, including "definitions that oppose delinquent behavior, peer reinforcement of prosocial activities, absence of stress, solid attachment to parents, sufficient parental supervision, and involvement in conventional activities" (p. 776). Each of these is a form of informal social control, which are found in higher levels in lower crime neighborhoods (Silver & Miller, 2004).

Neighborhood stability (i.e., low residential mobility and high parental support and monitoring) is associated with lower rates of delinquency (Cantillon, 2007). According to Saegert & Winkel (2004: 219): "When neighbors exercise informal social control, they limit the likelihood of crime by creating the network conditions associated with social capital: communication, closure, and the ability to apply sanctions to enforce norms."

However, racially motivated crimes against Blacks are more common in socially organized areas with high levels of informal social controls whereas racially motivated crimes against whites tend to be more common in socially disorganized areas (Lyons, 2007).

Race and Social Class

Findings from tests of theories at the community level also inform the debate about race and crime (discussed in chapter 9). For example, Walsh (2002, p. 170) interpreted the findings of the Chicago School by claiming "there may be certain areas possessing characteristics that persist over the decades that infect individuals exposed to them in ways that increase the likelihood of antisocial behavior regardless of their race or ethnicity." He further noted:

> Group differences in behavior are probably almost entirely structural and cultural in origin ... [and] it is hardly valid when applied to individuals . .. the majority of inhabitants of even the worst neighborhoods [do] not acquire criminal records ... Thus, there must be something about individuals also that either promotes or resists crime. Individuals within racial and ethnic groups may vary widely on the traits and characteristics that place them differentially at risk for antisocial behavior.

Walsh made the mistake of concluding that there are true crime differences between races, saying that Blacks in a wide range of countries exhibit more criminality than Whites and Asians. He cited studies showing how well the percent of Black inhabitants predicts murder and other street crimes (Chilton, 1986; Laub, 1983; Sampson, 1985). As we point out in chapter 9, however, such studies rely almost exclusively on official crime statistics, which is problematic because official agencies of social control are focused on the behaviors of some people more than others (Robinson, 2009). Even if studies show actual differences in criminality among races, however, they cannot be used to conclude that people of color are more dangerous, because they focus only on street crimes, which actually cause far less damage than many other harmful acts such as elite deviance (discussed in chapter 1).

Furthermore, disadvantages of social class seem to account much better for street criminality than does race (Robinson, 2009). Social disorganization is essentially a composite measure of neighborhood disadvantage. When Blacks experience conditions of social disorganization, such as poverty, they tend to do so in a much more perverse way than Whites. Black poverty is more concentrated than White poverty; White poverty is more dispersed across residential areas (Sampson, 1995; Sampson & Wilson, 2000). In fact, one study found that the most disadvantaged neighborhoods in a major city were almost entirely comprised of Black residents (Wilkstrom & Loeber, 2000). According to Wilkstrom and Loeber (2000), protective factors are highest in the best neighborhoods, whereas risk factors are more concentrated in the worst neighborhoods. Not surprisingly, self-reported delinquency is highest in the most disadvantaged neighborhoods where the highest levels of risk factors and lowest levels of protective factors are found. Young boys at the highest risk for antisocial behavior, based on the presence of individual risk factors, commit antisocial behaviors at about the same level regardless of level of disadvantage. Finally, neighborhood factors appear to have the greatest influence on children already at risk for antisocial behavior, but disadvantaged neighborhoods do appear to propel low-risk children into antisocial behavior.

Incivilities

The study of *incivilities* informs the findings from tests of social disorganization theory. Incivilities have been generally described as "untended property" and "untended people and behavior" (Wilson & Kelling, 1982). More specifically, these include abandoned buildings with boarded or broken windows; abandoned lots with an accumulation of trash; litter in streets, walkways, and parking areas; graffiti on buildings and walls; groups of people loitering, arguing, or fighting on streets; derelicts and winos reclining in doorways and alleyways; poorly lighted streets and dark entries to buildings and alleys; and the presence of illegal drug activity (Covington & Taylor, 1991; Hunter, 1978; Lewis & Salem, 1981; Rohe & Burby, 1988).

These conditions have been variously referred to as "signs of crime" (Skogan & Maxfield, 1981), "early signs of danger" (Stinchcombe et al., 1980), "urban unease" (Wilson, 1968), "perceived neighborhood problems" (Gates & Rohe, 1987), "non-normal appearances" (Goffman, 1971), "disorder" (Skogan, 1981), "soft crimes" (Reiss, 1985), "prelude to trouble" (Skolnick, 1966), and "cues to danger" (Warr, 1990). It is not surprising that environmental conditions are also associated with high rates of actual victimization, especially for offenses such as robbery (Camp, 1968; Tiffany & Ketchel, 1979), rape (Stoks, 1983), and burglary (Robinson, 1997, 1999; Taylor & Nee, 1988).

According to Robinson (1998b), the presence of incivilities can be understood as an indication that an area is low in aesthetics. Aesthetics refers to beauty-qualities that are pleasing to the senses. Insofar as environmental characteristics of urban areas are concerned, the term may be generally taken to include well-maintained buildings, neat vacant properties as well as grounds immediately surrounding buildings, clean streets/parking areas/walkways, attractive natural foliage and plantings, bright night-lighting of all public use areas, and orderly, unobtrusive behavior of people. In essence, a high level of aesthetics is equivalent to a low level of incivilities.

A number of research studies have reported a significant relationship between conditions of incivility (or aesthetics) and fear of crime and/or perception of risk for victimization (Appleton, 1975; Biderman et al., 1967; Box, Hole, & Andrews, 1988; Covington & Taylor, 1991; Gates & Rohe, 1987; Greene & Taylor, 1988; Hunter, 1978; Lewis & Maxfield, 1980; Lewis & Salem, 1986; Maxfield, 1984, 1987; Pate et al., 1986; Skogan, 1986; Taylor, Shumaker, & Gottfredson, 1985; Wilson, 1968). Areas with incivilities increase fear of crime and perceptions of crime risk.

Sampson and Raudenbush (2001) studied key relationships between disorder and crime in 196 urban Chicago neighborhoods. The results of the study suggest that crime stems from the same conditions as disorder-neighborhood conditions such as concentrated poverty. As explained by the researchers:

> disorder may operate in a cascading fashion by motivating residents to move out of their neighborhoods, thereby increasing residential instability. And because people move only if they have the financial means to do so, outmigration would increase the concentration of poverty among those left behind. Since residential instability and concentrated poverty are associated with lower collective efficacy and higher crime and disorder, over the course of time this process would lead to more crime and disorder.

This study found a link between disorder and robbery but suggested that the relationship is spurious, or caused by other factors such as poverty, high levels of immigrant populations, and mixed land uses. These factors decrease collective efficacy, or the ability of residents to reduce crime in their own neighborhoods.

A longitudinal study of crime data from the British Crime Survey (1984–1992) found that low SES, ethnic heterogeneity, family disruption, and residential instability increase neighborhood disorder (incivilities) and that community cohesion reduces disorder (Markowitz et al., 2001). This study also suggested that incivilities interfere with the ability of a community to defend itself against crime.

Scope of Social Disorganization Theory

The scope of social disorganization theory is broad in the sense that it seems to be related to a wide range of street crimes but narrow in the sense that it is not related to acts of elite deviance. For example, tests of social disorganization have been used to explain homicide (Bachman, 1991; Frye & Wilt, 2001), gang membership and related criminality (Toy, 1992), assault and theft (Rollin, 1997), convenience store robbery (D'Alessio & Stolzenberg, 1990), drug use (Bell, Carlson, & Richard, 1998), school disorder (Welsh, Stokes, & Greene, 2000), violence among discharged mentally ill patients (Silver, 1999), suicide (Nomiya, Miller, & Hoffman, 2000), and even cyberspace deviance (Evans, 2001). Furthermore, it is related to higher levels of fear of crime and perceptions of crime risk (Taylor, 1997).

The scope of social disorganization seems limited to street crimes, particularly street crimes committed within urban areas. At least one study found that conditions of residential instability, family disruption, and ethnic heterogeneity explained rural violence committed by juveniles in 264 counties (Osgood & Chambers, 2000), but this study used arrests for homicide, rape, assault, robbery, and weapons offenses as a measure of crime. Other studies have also related social disorganization to measures of citizens' calls for police assistance (Warner & Pierce, 1993), self-reports of victims (Sampson, 1985; Sampson & Groves, 1989), and self-reports of offenders (Elliott et al., 1996; Gottfredson, McNeil, & Gottfredson, 1991).

Of course, tests of social disorganization cannot explain individual behavior. Instead, they are aimed at explaining variations in crime rates. This is not the same thing as individual behavior. An example clarifies the point. Studies of neighborhoods show that crime rates are highest in neighborhoods with higher levels of social disorganization. These neighborhoods tend to have higher levels of minority residents (indeed, minority residents or racial or ethnic heterogeneity is one commonly used measure of social disorganization). To conclude, however, that higher crime rates in socially disorganized areas are attributable to the fact that they house more Blacks and Hispanics is incorrect. Given that police enforcement behaviors are more aimed at neighborhoods containing higher levels of African Americans (Rollin, 1997), it is possible that higher crime rates are actually a better indication of police behavior than of residents' behavior (Robinson, 2009). For example, many studies show that mere presence of racial minorities in a community is associated with higher arrest rates for offenses such as drug crimes, not necessarily because there is actually more drug use in the area (e.g., see Mosher, 2001).

Conceptual Clarity of Social Disorganization Theory

Some point out that key concepts of social disorganization are difficult to measure because they are not defined clearly. For example, the concept of economic deprivation, often measured through poverty rates and unemployment rates, ignores other economic factors that may also be related to crime. According to Bausman (2000), this has led to some inconsistent results in tests of unemployment, poverty, and crime (discussed in chapter 9).

Most problematic, some measures of social disorganization itself often include measures of crime, raising the problem of tautology. As explained by Veysey and Messner (1999, p. 159): "Variation in official crime rates across communities is likely to reflect not only variation in crime but also variation in social control, which might itself systematically be related to the hypothesized determinants of social disorganization."

Part of the tautology problem arises because social disorganization cannot be directly measured. "Perhaps the most important limitation of virtually all of the research on social disorganization theory ... is the lack of any direct measure of social disorganization itself. Indicators for many of the structural elements thought to cause social disorganization, such as poverty and residential mobility, are routinely collected, but direct indicators of social disorganization are lacking in standard data sources. To compensate, researchers have been forced to infer social disorganization processes that they cannot, in fact, observe in their data to interpret observed associations" (Veysey & Messner, 1999, p. 159). The research by Sampson and Raudenbush that measures the degree of collective efficacy in a neighborhood is promising because it is the closest we can come to measuring social disorganization.

The concept of incivilities is also tautological. Sampson and Raudenbush (1999) pointed out that many forms of disorder, such as graffiti, public drug use, and loitering, are actually crimes. Thus, a relationship between incivilities and crime should be expected. As noted by Markowitz et al. (2001, p. 295): "Moreover, even if disorder and other crimes are considered conceptually distinct, it may be that any association between them is due to common causes, such as collective efficacy and neighborhood demographic structure." This means the relationship may be spurious, as noted earlier.

Logical Adequacy of Social Disorganization Theory

The main propositions of tests of social disorganization theory seem valid on their face. They appeal to our common sense about the role of community level factors in crime. Yet, there are problems with this approach in isolation from others.

For example, findings suggesting relationships between measures of social disorganization, lack of social cohesion among community members, and delinquency may very well be spurious (Bohm, 2001). There may be some larger level factors at the society level that account for all of these phenomena.

Social disorganization theorists ignore the role of discrimination and of intentional planning of powerful elites; thus they address the symptoms of the problem rather than the problem (Bohm, 2001).

Tests of social disorganization can lead to circular reasoning because they use the concept of social disorganization to explain delinquency and criminality, but often use delinquency and criminality as indicators of social disorganization (Bohm, 2001, p. 71). This is a problem with logic caused by tautological concepts, discussed earlier.

Findings suggest that *overprediction* is a problem, as well meaning that we should expect a lot more delinquency and crime among people who live in environmental conditions described by social disorganization theorists (Bohm, 2001). In fact, only a very small portion of people residing in conditions described as social disorganization actually become persistent delinquents and criminals (and even a smaller portion come to the attention of criminal justice officials). This is a problem that characterizes virtually all criminological theories as you have seen throughout this book. Even during the time of the original studies by Chicago School theorists, some ethnic groups in the city of Chicago seemed to be more resistant to the effects of social disorganization than others, something that cannot be explained by the theory (Einstatder & Henry, 1995).

The use of official crime rate data raises the troublesome issue of class bias. If police are in socially disorganized communities, shouldn't we expect there to be more crime known to the police in those areas? This is a major weakness of theories such as social disorganization.

Another problem with tests of social disorganization theories is that they cannot resolve the debate about causal order: which comes first, crime or social disorganization? Much research shows that crime often precedes social disorganization and is a source of it. It appears that the relationship is reciprocal (Bellair, 1996; Skogan, 1991). According to Markowitz et al. (2001, p. 297):

> Clearly, there is some evidence, although mixed, that crime is not only an important personal event, having consequences for both offenders and victims, but also that crime rates and the presence of disorder are important social facts, having consequences for social areas. It seems reasonable to expect that people avoid living, working, and playing in high crime areas. If they can afford to live elsewhere, they do; if they live there, they move out; and if they live there and cannot afford to move, they withdraw from social life or sharply alter their social interaction to avoid being victimized.

The original propositions associated with social disorganization theory are also very simplistic in their characterization of how informal social control operates. In fact, there are at least three levels of informal social controls that have now been identified by scholars. For example, Bursik and Grasmick (1993) identified the following levels:

- *Private.* Social control exercised by important people such as family members and close friends.
- *Parochial.* Social control exercised by relatively less important people such as acquaintances and neighbors.
- *Public.* Social control exercised in conjunction with outside assistance (e.g., with government agencies).

According to Taylor (1997, p. 114):

> The control processes operating at each level are qualitatively different. The primary level of control "is grounded in the intimate informal primary groups that exist in the area ... Social control is usually achieved through the allocation or threatened withdrawal of sentiment, social support, and mutual esteem" (Bursik & Grasmick, 1993, p. 16). At the parochial level, control is achieved through "the effects of the broader local interpersonal networks and the interlocking of local institutions such as stores, schools, churches, and voluntary organizations" (p. 17). Parochial control relies on "weak" ties and secondary groups, both perhaps emerging partly from participation in local institutions. Public control is achieved by local organizations as they "secure public goods and services that are allocated by agencies located outside the neighborhood" (p. 17).

Recent research is more logical in its conception of informal social control networks. For example, Taylor (1997) asserted that the street block, commonly referred to as a *face block* in research, is in essence a closely knit neighborhood or community. Residents on a block share a common "psychogeography" according to Taylor, or a common sense of community based on their proximity to one another. Strongly bonded blocks would deter criminality, according to social disorganization theorists, for the following reasons: (1) because people get to know each other through their interactions; (2) because as people get to know each other, they are more likely to be neighborly and look out for each other; (3) because the neighborhood will develop norms for acceptable behavior; and (4) because community activities will not only specify opportunities for criminality but also inhibit them. Such a neighborhood would be characterized by a greater ability to recognize outsiders and to cooperate in protecting common space. If such street blocks are characterized by higher levels of nonresidential land uses (e.g., fewer homes but more vacant lots or businesses), they will likely be characterized by more physical deterioration (Taylor et al., 1985), including conditions of incivilities.

Finally, tests of social disorganization rarely consider individual level factors. It may be true that social disorganization persists in given neighborhoods because of the people who live there. Some people most prone to deviance may also be more prone to living in poverty and remaining in slum areas because of low ambition and other negative personality traits (discussed in chapter 6).

As explained by Cattarello (2002, p. 34), Shaw and McKay originally referred to individual level factors in their research. "Shaw and McKay did not believe that macro-level community characteristics influenced delinquency directly; rather, they considered their influence on delinquency to be indirect. Shaw and McKay believed that neighborhood-level ecological conditions and informal social control networks influenced delinquency by affecting individuals' social bonds, such as the family and the school ... as well as peer associations." This point is well taken, but clearly Shaw and McKay did not suggest individual level factors like those discussed in chapters 4, 5, and 6 of this book, nor have any other social disorganization theorists since.

Routine Activities and Victim Lifestyles

Routine Activity Theory

According to *routine activity theory,* crime results from the convergence of three elements in time and space: a presence of likely or motivated offenders, a presence of suitable targets, and an absence of capable guardians to prevent the criminal act (Cohen & Felson, 1979; Cohen, Felson, & Land, 1980; Felson, 1983, 1987, 1994, 1995; Kennedy & Baron, 1993; Kennedy & Forde, 1990a,b; Massey, Krohn, & Bonati, 1989; Maxfield, 1987; Miethe, Stafford, & Long, 1987; Roncek & Maier, 1991; Sherman, 1995; Sherman et al., 1989).

A *likely offender* includes anyone with an inclination to commit a crime (Felson, 1983). A *suitable target* includes any person or thing that may evoke criminal inclinations, which would include the actual value of the target and the monetary and symbolic desirability of it for offenders, the visibility to offenders or their informants, the access to it, the ease of escape from the site, as well as the portability or mobility of objects sought by offenders (Felson, 1983). *Guardians* are people who can protect a target (Eck & Weisburd, 1995), including friends and formal authorities such as police and security personnel; *intimate handlers* such as parents, teachers, coaches, friends, and employers; and *place managers* such as janitors and apartment managers (e.g., see Eck, 1994; Eck & Weisburd, 1995; Felson, 1986, 1995). According to Eck (1994), potential targets are supervised by guardians, potential offenders by handlers, and potential places of crime by place managers. The guardian, handler, and manager must be absent or ineffective from the potential target, the potential offender, and the place, respectively, for crime to occur (Eck & Weisburd, 1995).

An *absence of capable guardians* can be produced by average citizens going about their daily life (Felson, 1983). In fact, the most important guardians are ordinary citizens going about their daily routines (Felson, 1994). The typical guardian is not a police officer or security guard in most cases, but is a neighbor, friend, relative, bystander, or owner of property (Clarke & Felson, 1993). This means that routine activities of potential victims can not only facilitate criminal victimization, but also prevent it.

Routine activities include "any recurrent and prevalent activities which provide for basic population and individual needs, whatever their biological or cultural origins ... including formalized work, leisure, social interaction, learning ... which occur at home, in jobs away from home, and in other activities away from home" (Cohen & Felson, 1979). Routine activities are the means people use to satisfy their needs, which are specific to their lifestyles. When these routine activities are performed within or near the home, lower risks of property crime are expected because they enhance guardianship capabilities (Cohen & Felson, 1979; Felson, 1983; Felson, 1987). That is, since higher levels of guardianship increase the likelihood that offenders will be seen, the risk for criminal victimization is reduced.

Routine activity theory was used by Cohen and Felson (1979) to explain rising crime rates in the United States. Other theories, according to the authors, could not account for the rise. The theory points to factors unique to lifestyles of potential offenders and victims as they are affected by larger social processes. The importance of victim lifestyles is also indicated by the *lifestyle/exposure theory*, which was developed by Hindelang, Gottfredson, and Garofalo (1978; also see Goldstein, 1994; Maxfield, 1987; Miethe et al., 1987). This model of criminal events links victimization risks to the daily activities of specific individuals, especially potential victims (Goldstein, 1994; Kennedy & Forde, 1990a).

Lifestyle/Exposure Theory

Lifestyles are patterned, regular, recurrent, prevalent, or "routine activities" (Robinson, 1997; also see Cohen & Felson, 1979; Felson, 1994; Garofalo, 1987; Hindelang et al., 1978). Lifestyles consist of the activities that people engage in on a daily basis, including both obligatory activities and discretionary activities. LeBeau and Coulson (1996; also see LeBeau & Corcoran, 1990) asserted that: "The former are activities that *must* be undertaken while the latter because they are pursued by choice are called discretionary. An activity is discretionary if there is a greater chance of *choice* than constraint, and obligatory if there is a greater degree of constraint than choice."

The lifestyle/exposure model suggests that lifestyles, which encompass differences in various demographic factors (e.g., age, sex, marital status, family income, and race), affect daily routines of people and thus vulnerability to criminal victimization (Kennedy & Forde, 1990). Because lifestyles vary, victimization is not evenly distributed across space and time (Garofalo, 1987, p. 26). Specifically, lifestyles influence a person's exposure to places and times with differing risks of victimization and frequency of associations with potential offenders. A similar theoretical model developed by Kennedy and Forde (1990) suggested that background characteristics affect time spent in risky activities that lead to dangerous results (i.e., criminal victimization).

Main Propositions of Studies of Routine Activities and Victim Lifestyles

Given the predictions made by routine activities and victim lifestyle theorists, the following propositions have been tested:

- For a crime to occur, it requires the convergence of three elements in time and space: a presence of likely or motivated offenders, a presence of suitable targets, and an absence of capable guardians to prevent the criminal act.
- Routine activities in a community or neighborhood affect crime rates in the area.
- Lifestyles of potential victims, including obligatory and recreational activities, affect the risk of criminal victimization.

Key Concepts of Studies of Routine Activities and Victim Lifestyles

From the preceding propositions, the following concepts can be isolated and defined:

- Likely or motivated offenders
- Presence of suitable targets
- Absence of capable guardians
- Routine activities
- Lifestyles

- Obligatory activities
- Recreational activities
- Crime rates
- Criminal victimization

Box 8.3 defines the key concepts of routine activities and victim lifestyles. Scholars also use these concepts to test relationships between community conditions and crime rates.

Box 8.3 Definitions of Key Concepts of Routine Activities and Victim Lifestyles

- *Likely or motivated offenders. Nominal*—the presence of a person who is inclined to commit crime. *Operational*—the number of criminals in a given area, usually measured as the total number of persons in a neighborhood, street block, census tract, or city that are young, male, and have other statuses held to be more likely to commit crime.
- *Presence of suitable targets. Nominal*—the presence of anything of value. *Operational*—evidence of valuable property suitable for offending as measured by government statistics such as census data or surveys of residents.
- *Absence of capable guardians. Nominal*—the lack of presence of a person or persons who will defend a property against crime. *Operational*—evidence that property is left unguarded, typically measured by surveys of residents and occupants of places that assess how often property is left unguarded and/or on-site observations.
- *Routine activities. Nominal*—the behaviors a person engages in on a daily and nightly basis. *Operational*—the volume and regularity of behaviors engaged in on a daily and nightly basis, usually measured from surveys of people and/or on-site observations.
- *Lifestyles. Nominal*—the behaviors a person engages in on a daily and nightly basis, including obligatory and recreational activities. *Operational*—the volume and regularity of behaviors engaged in on a daily and nightly basis, usually measured from surveys of people and/or on-site observations.
- *Obligatory activities. Nominal*—behaviors that people engage in that are required of them such as work and school. *Operational*—the number of hours a person spends engaged away from home and/or property for the purposes of work and school, assessed through surveys.

- *Recreational activities. Nominal*—behaviors that people engage in that are optional such as recreation. *Operational*—the number of hours a person spends engaged away from home and/or property for the purposes of recreation, assessed through surveys.
- *Crime rates. Nominal*—an aggregate measure of crime in an area. *Operational*—an official measure of total crime divided by the population (crimes per capita), typically crimes known to the police.
- *Criminal victimization. Nominal*—being harmed by crime. *Operational*—whether or not a person is physically injured or loses property by crime, typically measured by surveys of potential victims of crime.

Evaluation of Routine Activity and Lifestyle/Exposure Theory

In the following sections, we address routine activity and lifestyle/exposure. We assess the empirical validity of this theory, discuss the scope of the research, as well as address the conceptual clarity and the logical adequacy of its propositions.

Empirical Validity of Studies of Routine Activities and Victim Lifestyles

A large body of research illustrates relationships between routine activities, victim lifestyles, and criminal victimization. In the original study of routine activity theory, Cohen and Felson (1979) found that daytime burglaries increased over time along with time spent outside of the home during the day. Additionally, Miethe et al. (1987) found that persons with low daytime and nighttime activity outside of the home have the lowest risk of property victimization, and people who find themselves away from the home due to daytime and nighttime activity have the highest risks for crime victimization. Similarly, in a study of violent rural crime in Alabama, Spano and Nagy (2005) found that social guardianship reduced the risk of assault and robbery victimization and that social isolation at the individual level was a strong risk factor for robbery and assault victimization.

Overall, the findings from routine activity research indicate that the risk for criminal victimization varies "among the circumstances and locations in which people place themselves and their property" (Cohen & Felson, 1979, p. 595). Specifically, victimization rates vary inversely with age and are lower for people with "less active" statuses such as keeping house, being unable to work, being retired, and so forth (p. 596). However, Cohen and Felson did not actually measure activity levels associated with each status. In fact, lifestyles or routine activities of potential victims are typically inferred from demographic variables; they are rarely directly measured (Akers, 1994; Kennedy & Forde, 1990a,b; Maxfield, 1987; Miethe et al., 1987; Moriarty & Williams, 1996; Sampson & Wooldredge, 1987). One study of note that actually measured routine activities directly through on-site observations found support for the proposition that increased activity around residences is associated with a lower risk for burglary victimization (Robinson, 1999).

Numerous studies have shown relationships between daily activities of individuals and their likelihood of criminal victimization (Riley, 1987). In other words, what people do and how they behave places them at either more or less risk of criminal victimization (Maxfield, 1987; Miethe et al., 1987; Sampson & Wooldredge, 1987). For example, offender and victim activities influence the selection of victims by serial sex offenders (Beauregard, Rossmo, & Proulx, 2007). Further, lifestyle variables such as drug use, belonging to a gang, carrying a gun, and employment status have been linked with one's likelihood of becoming a victim of violent crime (Armstrong & Griffin, 2007; Spano, Freilich, & Bolland, 2008; Taylor et al, 2008). Engaging in activities away from the home is associated with a higher likelihood of violent victimization, as is having friends with delinquents (Schreck & Fisher, 2004). A study by Nofziger & Kurtz (2005) of a nationally representative sample of juveniles ages 12 through 17 found having a violent lifestyle (i.e., being exposed to violence through witnessing violence, having associations with violent peers, and experiencing violent victimization) was associated with violent behavior.

These studies raise some interesting questions. For example, does an active lifestyle promote or inhibit criminal victimization? According to Sampson and Wooldredge (1987), an active lifestyle increases victimization risk by increasing the likelihood that potential offenders will find suitable targets with low levels of guardianship. An active lifestyle may not necessarily increase one's risk of criminal victimization. For example, if there is a great deal of activity by residents, neighbors, or passersby around a residence, then this activity may serve to decrease the likelihood that a property offender will victimize a residence. In fact, many property offenders are nonconfrontational and want to avoid being seen by residents, neighbors, or passersby (Cromwell, Olson, & Avary, 1991; Tunnell, 1994; Wright & Decker, 1994).

The Impact of Social Disorganization

Routine activities and victim lifestyles depend in part on social disorganization (Moriarty & Williams, 1996; Robinson, 1997), because conditions of social disorganization affect routine activities in communities (Andresen, 2006; Davison, 1996; Hipp, 2007; Rice & Smith, 2002). If true, studies should show interrelationships between measures of social disorganization and routine activities.

One of the first studies to demonstrate a contextual relationship between social disorganization and routine activities was conducted by Miethe and McDowall (1993), who reported that measures of target attractiveness and guardianship alter burglary risks for people living in more affluent neighborhoods when there is little population mobility. In conditions of social disorganization, this relationship is not seen. Other research also demonstrates that the effects of routine activity variables depend, in part, on the degree of social disorganization present. For example, Rountree, Land, and Miethe (1994) surveyed more than 5,000 adults living on 600 city blocks in Seattle to assess the effects of exposure to motivated offenders, target attractiveness, and guardianship, as well as neighborhood incivilities, ethnic heterogeneity, and population density on risks for burglary and violent crime victimization. They found that risk for violent victimization is increased by high levels of exposure to outside activity, and that burglary victimization is increased by target attractiveness and neighborhood incivilities. Burglary risk is also affected by ethnic heterogeneity, but this effect is reduced by high levels of incivilities. Neighborhood incivilities and high population density are also related to a greater risk for violent crime.

Smith, Frazee, and Davison (2000) also found that the effect of some social disorganization and routine activity factors on robbery depends on other factors. Their research showed that robbery was affected by the number of African Americans in the community, by single-parent households, by the proportion of households of low assessed value, by distance from the center of the city, and by the number of owner-occupied households. It was also affected by the number of vacant parking lots. Yet, the effects of vacant parking lots and owner-occupied households were greater in the downtown area of the city of study.

A study of social disorganization and routine activities found that high unemployment (social disorganization theory) and the presence of young populations (routine activity theory) were the strongest predictors of automotive theft, breaking and entering, and violent crime in Vancouver, British Columbia (Andresen, 2006). Further, population turnover and routine activities associated with households affect the risks of victimization (Xie & McDowall, 2008).

The effects of many neighborhood specific factors (e.g., schools, businesses, playgrounds) and crime often depends on other factors such as physical disorder and residential instability. In contrast, the effect of playgrounds on violence is moderated by residential instability (Wilcox et al, 2004).

Similar variables (residential turnover and activity patterns of household members) impact rates of household victimization (Xie & McDowall, 2008). Such factors (young males and poverty) also are related to drug dealing in neighborhoods (Freisthler et al., 2005). Another study finds social disorganization (number of single-parent families and African Americans) and routine activity variables (the flow of traffic of motivated offenders, the level of guardianship) important for understanding auto theft (Rice & Smith, 2002). Studies of burglary in numerous countries also find evidence in support of these theories (e.g., see Coupe & Blake, 2006; Tseloni et al., 2004).

Scope of Routine Activity and Lifestyle/Exposure Theory

Cohen and Felson (1979) used the routine activity approach to explain increasing crime trends from 1947 to 1974, which other theories supposedly have failed to account for (Cohen & Felson, 1979). Cohen and Felson (1979, p. 598) found that increasing crime rates corresponded to time spent outside of the home and rates of out-of-town travel by residents. Daytime burglaries increased over time along with time spent outside of the home during the day (p. 600). Cohen and Felson also found positive and statistically significant relationships between their "household activity ratio" and each official crime rate change (p. 602).

The routine activity theory is said to apply to direct contact predatory violations (Glaser, 1971, p. 4) where "someone definitely and intentionally takes or damages the person or property of another" (Cohen & Felson, 1979, p. 589; also see Clarke & Felson, 1993). It is "concerned primarily with predatory crimes involving individuals and their personal property, and they are geared more to instrumental than expressive crimes" (Hough, 1987; also see Felson, 1987). As such, this theory is supposedly more applicable to property crime (Bennett, 1991). Violent crimes are often expressive (i.e., spontaneous, impulsive) rather than instrumental acts (e.g., directed toward an economic end) (Miethe et al., 1987). Hence, if motivated offenders engage in a conscious selection of suitable targets who lack guardianship, the spontaneous nature of most violent crimes is incongruent with the strictly rational characterization of human behavior underlying routine activity theory.

Some studies have shown that their measures of routine activities are associated with violent victimizations (Kennedy & Forde, 1990a,b; Messner &

Tardiff, 1985). Using data from the Canadian Urban Victimization Survey, Kennedy and Forde (1990) showed that personal crime is dependent on exposure which comes from following certain lifestyles, especially for young males who are more likely to be exposed to conflict situations and react in a deviant manner. The likelihood for victimization by the crime of breaking and entering also was found to vary by the types of activities that take people away from their homes for extended periods of time. Stahura and Sloan (1988) found that some of their measures of motivation, opportunity, and guardianship have direct and indirect effects on both violent and property crime rates.

In 1987, Felson argued that routine activities can be used to account for all four types of crime: exploitative, mutualistic, competitive, and individualistic. *Exploitative crime* "involves persons acting in different roles, in which one illegally seizes or tries to seize control over the person or property of another"; *mutualistic crime* "includes so-called victimless offenses, in which two or more persons cooperate to violate the law, playing different roles in the process"; *competitive crime* means when "different offenders act illegally so that gain by one means loss by another"; and *individualistic crime* includes "suicide, solo drug abuse, or any other violation by lone individuals that is contingent upon the absence of interference by others" (Felson, 1983, pp. 665–666).

Bennett (1991) tested the macrostructural tenets of the routine activities approach on a sample of 52 nations over a 25-year period (1960–1984). He found that:

> the routine activities approach ... is most appropriate when the social structure is defined by the following characteristics: (1) an income per capita (target attractiveness) between the low and the high range, (2) a level of hard-goods manufacturing (target accessibility) between the low and moderately high range, (3) a level of inequality (motivation) that is high or when relative inequality is prevalent, (4) a low level of urbanization (proximity), and (5) a low to moderately high proportion of women in the work force (guardianship) (p. 147).

The lifestyle exposure approach best explains intergroup differences in criminal victimization. According to Maxfield (1987b, p. 277), "crimes against persons formed the basis for the initial development of lifestyle theory" by Hindelang et al. (1978), or direct contact predatory violations (Garofalo, 1987). Maxfield suggested that this is due to the fact that "lifestyle" relates more to individuals than to households. Garofalo (1987) claimed that the lifestyle model is applicable to many types of property crimes, "particularly household burglary, non-commercial larceny, and vehicle theft." Miethe et al. (1987) found that the odds of violent victimization increased with frequency of nighttime activity, and the odds of property victimization increased with frequency of nighttime activity and activity outside the home.

Concerning burglary, Sampson and Wooldredge (1987) found the highest victimization risks for single-headed households, younger households, and households left unguarded and empty. Similarly, Stack (1995, p. 204) found that the higher the percentage of "temporary residences" (i.e., "suitable targets marked by low guardianship") in an area, the higher its burglary rate.

Although most research on lifestyle/exposure theory has been conducted with regard to street crime, a study of nearly 1,000 adults from a statewide survey in Florida found that "remote-purchasing activities increase consumers' risk of being targeted for fraud" whereas low self-control was found to associated with an increased risk for fraud victimization (Holtfreter, Reisig, & Pratt, 2008).

Conceptual Clarity of Routine Activity and Lifestyle/Exposure Theory

The main concepts of routine activity and lifestyle exposure theories are clearly defined and easy to understand. However, some confuse the two theories since they are so similar. In fact, the definition of routine activities includes references to people's lifestyles. Unfortunately, lifestyles and routine activities are rarely measured directly by on-site observations of activities of offenders and potential victims.

Logical Adequacy of Routine Activity and Lifestyle/Exposure Theory

The main propositions of tests of routine activity and lifestyle/exposure theory seem valid on their face. They appeal to our common sense about the role of community level factors in crime. Yet, routine activities generated by lifestyles of offenders and victims do not explain why crime happens or why a person is victimized; instead, these theories fill in the gap of traditional criminological theories by helping account for the role of opportunity in crime and victimization. These theories do not explain criminality well, for they rarely even deal with the behavior of offenders. No theory is complete without assessing the role of opportunity in crime. Routine activity and lifestyle exposure theories explain how opportunities created by potential victims affect overall crime.

One significant problem concerning these theories should be pointed out. When relationships between lifestyles and crime are studied, dependent variables typically consist of some composite measure of crime (see Thompson & Fisher, 1996). Composite measures of crime are most used by researchers rather than distinct measures of individual crime types (Bennett, 1991; Maxfield, 1987; Thompson & Fisher, 1996), making it nearly impossible to differentiate the effects of lifestyles on different types of criminal victimization. It is problematic because lifestyle/exposure theory is "crime specific" (Bennett, 1991, p. 158; Thompson & Fisher, 1996). For example, crimes such as burglary and theft may create different opportunities for offenders:

> For a burglary to occur, an offender has to break and enter a home to get the desired goods. An offender who commits a larceny, on the other hand, may ride off with a bicycle left out on the lawn or steal something from the porch of a home. These examples demonstrate that the opportunity structures for burglary and larceny are different and therefore the two crimes must be examined separately in research. (Thompson & Fisher, 1996, p. 52; also see Gottfredson, 1984; Maxfield, 1987; Sampson & Wooldredge, 1987)

Deterrence and Labeling

When the criminal justice system catches, convicts, and punishes criminals, does this reduce crime or does it produce more crime? The answer is a matter of debate between *deterrence* theorists and *labeling* theorists. Deterrence theorists suggest that punishment reduces crime; labeling theorists suggest that it may actually increase crime. Each of these schools of thought is discussed here.

Types of Deterrence

Deterrence is based on the logical notion that being punished for criminal activity will create fear in offenders so that they will not want to commit crime. Scholars suggest there are at least two types of deterrence, *special or specific deterrence* and *general deterrence*. The former can be understood as punishing an offender with the specific intent of instilling fear in that offender so that he or she will not commit crimes in the future. The latter involves punishing offenders in order to instill fear in society generally so that the rest of us will not want to commit crime. So, special or specific deterrence is aimed at stopping a known criminal offender from committing future crimes, while general deterrence is aimed at teaching the rest of us a lesson about what might happen to us if we were to commit crimes. The belief in deterrence is evident in all that we do in the United States to fight crime, including:

- **Probation**—Offenders on probation are "hassled" by their probation officer and must follow many rules that they would not have to follow even in prison. Thus, they should be deterred from committing future crimes for fear that they might be put on probation again.
- **Incarceration**—Prisons and jails are horribly violent and repressive places. Any criminal who goes to prison ought to be afraid to come back. Additionally, all of society should fear suffering the pains of imprisonment. Thus, crime will be specially and generally deterred.
- **Boot camps**—Juvenile offenders are forced to go to classes, work, and train through various physical fitness activities. It is hoped that juveniles will fear being forced to undergo such strenuous conditions again in the future, thereby deterring juvenile delinquency.
- **Chain gangs**—Forcing inmates to work on the side of the road doing hard labor not only instills fear in those inmates, but also shows others what can happen if they commit crimes. Thus, crime is specially and generally deterred.
- **Death penalty**—Not only does the death penalty incapacitate the offender, it sends a message to all of society that anyone who commits murder can be executed for his or her offense.

Assumptions of Deterrence

Deterrence as a justification for punishment assumes that offenders are hedonistic or pleasure seeking (e.g., crime provides various pleasures), offenders seek to minimize costs or pains associated with crimes (i.e., they do not want to get caught and be punished), and offenders are rational (i.e., they choose to commit crime after weighing the potential costs or punishments and benefits or rewards). Such assumptions are beyond direct empirical observation, but most criminologists assume that offenders are rational. There are many criminologists—for example, rational choice theorists—who believe that we do (Clarke, 2001).

Elements of Punishment

In order for punishment to effectively deter would-be offenders, punishment must be certain (or at least likely), swift (or at least not delayed by months or years), and severe enough to outweigh the pleasures associated with crimes. Of these requirements, the one that is most important is *certainty* (Robinson, 2009). The more likely that punishment is to follow a criminal act, the less likely the criminal act will occur. Think of this example: if a lightning bolt was guaranteed to strike from the sky upon an offender when he or she committed theft of property, how many thefts do you think we would have each year in America? Probably not many, for if it was absolutely certain that some higher being in the sky would strike you dead upon stealing someone else's property, then everyone would refrain from committing theft so as to remain alive.

Such punishment would be certain, swift, and severe. But, do not be misled by this example. For deterrence to be effective, it must be certain and somewhat swift, but it only has to be severe enough to outweigh the pleasure gained by the offense. This means death by lightning strike is not required for most crimes, which are relatively mundane in nature. Noted Italian criminologist Cesare Beccaria wrote in his 1776 book, *An Essay on Crime and Punishments,* that:

> The certainty of punishment, even though it be moderate, will always make a stronger impression than the fear of one more severe if it is accompanied by the hope that one may escape that punishment, because men are more frightened by an evil which is inevitable even though minor in nature. Further, if the punishment be too severe for a crime, men will be led to commit further crimes in order to escape punishment for the crime ... It is essential that it be public, prompt, necessary, minimal in severity as possible under given circumstances, proportional to the crime, and prescribed by the laws. (pp. 58–59)

As you will see later in the chapter, empirical studies of deterrence support this original statement about punishment.

Symbolic Interactionism

Labeling theories are interesting particularly because they not only deny that the criminal justice system deters crime, they also blame serious, repeated, or career criminality on the criminal justice system. They are based on the logic of *symbolic interactionism,* the notion that people define themselves based on how they perceive others view them. Symbolic interactionism arose out of the work of George Herbert Mead, John Dewey, W.I. Thomas, and Charles Horton Cooley (Matsueda, 2001). According to these scholars, individuals construct meanings for their own lives based on interactions with others. People form their identities or self-images through assuming the role of other people in their key reference groups. Vold et al. (1998, p. 219) noted that "human actions are best understood in terms of the *meaning* that those actions have for the actors, rather than in terms of preexisting biological, psychological, or social conditions."

Dramatization of Evil

Frank Tannenbaum (1938, pp. 19–20) coined the term *dramatization of evil* to describe how society through its shaming institutions creates delinquency:

The process of making the criminal ... is a process of tagging, defining, identifying ... it becomes a way of stimulating, suggesting, and evoking the very traits that are complained of. If the theory of relation of response to stimulus has any meaning, the entire process of dealing with the young delinquent is mischievous insofar as it identifies him to himself or to the environment as a delinquent person. The person becomes the thing he is described as being.

Self-Fulfilling Prophecy

Labeling theorists assert that through the "process of signification" (Matza, 1969), society creates a *self-fulfilling prophecy* (Matsueda, 2001)—it produces the very thing it is trying to prevent through its efforts at shaming. This has also been called *role engulfment* (Schur, 1971), whereby "when deviant labels are applied, persons being labeled tend to get 'caught up in' the deviant role, organizing their identities and activities around that identity. That is, one who is role-engulfed both thinks of oneself and is thought of by others in terms of the deviant identity" (Paternoster & Bachman, 2001, p. 220).

If the label is accepted, it becomes believed by the labeled person. Ultimately, if it affects the person's self-image—the way a person views himself or herself—"deviant" or "delinquent" or "criminal" becomes the person's *master status* (Becker, 1963), which is the most important status a person has to which all other statuses are secondary (Paternoster & Bachman, 2001).

One result of being labeled is exclusion (Becker, 1963), which includes being denied opportunities in work, school, and so forth. Criminologists assert that frustration arising out of being denied opportunities is a significant source of strain or stress and ultimately criminality (strain theory is discussed in chapter 9).

Primary and Secondary Deviance

Edwin Lemert's (1951) labeling theory is probably the most discussed of all. It, like all other labeling theories, views childhood and adolescent deviance as normal behavior. Most people commit acts of delinquency as juveniles but usually outgrow their youthful indiscretions. Labeling theory asserts that when people are formally recognized as deviants, they are less likely to outgrow their normal deviant behavior because their self-image has been changed. As explained by Matsueda (2001, p. 225): "At least in some cases, had the child's early acts of misbehavior been essentially ignored—attributed to normal childhood immaturity—the child would have aged out of the misbehavior, rather than continued on a path of crime."

The term Lemert used to describe this normal deviance that is committed prior to being labeled is *primary deviance,* which he saw as caused by numerous biological, psychological, and/or sociological factors. These acts, if not formally recognized by people in positions of power (whether they be police, parents, teachers, or others), do not lead to significant losses of status or opportunity for juveniles: "Primary deviance tends to be situational, transient, and idiosyncratic" (Matsueda, 2001, p. 225).

If a primary deviant is caught, recognized as a deviant, and ultimately accepts the label as accurately descriptive of his or her behavior and basic personality, the primary deviant will likely go on to commit *secondary deviance.* Secondary deviance is that behavior which occurs after the labeling process and is attributable to being labeled. It "has major consequences for a person's status, relationships and future behavior" (Matsueda, 2001, p. 225). While primary deviance is caused by criminological factors identified by numerous theories, these factors do not explain secondary deviance. Instead, the label takes over and is reinforced when other people respond to the person in ways consistent with his or her new identity.

Whether or not a label sticks depends

> *in part* on what one has done and *in part* on who one is. The implication of this is that one can expect a more potent social reaction (a more serious label) from authorities when the alleged infraction is of a more serious rule, and when one either lacks the resources to resist the reaction or, because of one's personal attributes one more closely resembles commonly held stereotypes about the "kind of person" likely to break such a rule. (Paternoster & Bachman, 2001, p. 217)

Numerous scholars have illustrated what the "stereotypical criminal" looks like (Reiman, 2006). Mostly because of mainstream media accounts that characterize atypical crimes (i.e., random and bizarre acts of violence committed by strangers), the everyday American citizen carries around the image in his or her head of the street criminal, a young, urban, minority male (Robinson, 2009).

This does not mean, however, that the validity of labeling theories depends on findings showing that relatively powerless groups are more harshly punished or more likely to be labeled as deviants or troublemakers. As noted by Matsueda (2001, p. 232), labeling theorists "never argued that extralegal factors should have greater effects on labeling than actual rule-breaking."

According to Sherman (1993), whether or not a label leads to criminality depends on other factors, as well. Sometimes labels can produce further criminality, sometimes they actually prevent crime, and sometimes they have no effects. One factor that is important is how well one is bonded to society (i.e., how well one is committed to and involved in conventional life). When a person is not bonded to conventional society, the effects of a label will likely be less significant. It also depends on how the sanction is imposed. When it is imposed with respect, it is less likely to produce future criminality. When it is imposed with condemnation, it is more likely to produce future criminality.

Reintegrative Shaming

Braithwaite (1989), in his theory of *reintegrative shaming*, concurs. Any society's crime rate is related to how it communicates shame toward deviance (Braithwaite, 2001). When societies shame offenders in a demeaning way not aimed at restoring offenders as well as victims and their communities, it is likely to produce more deviance. Braithwaite calls this type of shaming *stigmatization*. Reintegrative shaming, in contrast, involves shaming that is aimed at restoration of the offender. This type of shaming, according to Braithwaite, is more likely to reduce the likelihood of offending, and so it is a form of deterrence. This type of shaming is followed by a ceremony of forgiveness after the wrong is disapproved of and punished.

An interesting parallel with reintegrative shaming as an official means of punishing offenders occurs within families. To parents, punishment is a natural way to correct the behavior of their children. In fact, organizations such as the American Academy of Pediatrics (AAP) suggest specific ways to discipline and not to discipline children. These were discussed in chapter 7. Braithwaite (2001, p. 244) summarized the type of research that led to recommendations by the AAP and other experts in child rearing: "The evidence is strong that American families that confront wrongdoing while sustaining relationships of love and respect for their children are the families most likely to raise law-abiding citizens." Parents who take a hands-off or disinterested approach to child discipline and parents who are overbearing and harsh disciplinarians tend to have children who end up misbehaving much more often than parents who discipline with a calm sense of respect and dignity: "What seems particularly criminogenic is harsh, unreasoning, and punitive discipline combined with rejection of the child." This is consistent with Laub and Sampson's theory of *age-graded social control* and the other evidence discussed in chapter 7 with regard to parenting.

Differential Social Control

One of the most recent labeling theories is *differential social control*, by Matsueda and his colleagues (Bartusch & Matsueda, 1996; Heimer, 1996; Heimer & Matsueda, 1994; Matsueda, 1992). This theory is aimed at explaining both primary and secondary deviance; secondary deviance is attributable to label-

ing by people important in the lives of juveniles while primary deviance is attributable to a process of role taking where people confronted with problems
adjust their behaviors in line with their revised view of themselves. The theory includes not only labeling but also learning from peers and the family.

An interesting fact generated by labeling theorists is that deviance is, in essence,
invented because it is socially created (Becker, 1963). Matsueda (2001, p. 226)
explained that since "society creates deviance by making rules and then labeling
people for violating those rules," we basically get as much deviance as we want.
Erikson (1962, p. 11) went even further when he suggested: "Deviance is not a
property inherent in certain forms of behavior; it is a property conferred upon
these forms by the audiences which directly or indirectly witness them."

This is not to say that all we have to do to prevent deviant behavior is simply not label it deviant; this would only eliminate *deviance*. The behaviors
themselves would still exist. It is the behaviors that must be explained by labeling theory in order for it to enjoy empirical support.

Main Propositions of Deterrence and Labeling

Given the predictions made by deterrence and labeling theorists, the following propositions have been tested:

- Punishment administered by the criminal justice system will deter crime
  if it is certain, swift, and severe enough to outweigh the pleasures associated with committing crime.
- Labeling of criminal offenders changes the self-image of offenders so that
  they accept the label and commit acts of secondary deviance.
- Reintegrative shaming lowers the risk of recidivism.

Key Concepts of Deterrence and Labeling

From the preceding propositions, the following concepts can be isolated
and defined:

- Punishment by the criminal justice system
- Deterrence
- Certain punishment
- Swift punishment
- Severe punishment
- Labeling
- Self-image of offenders

- Secondary deviance
- Reintegrative shaming
- Recidivism

Box 8.4 defines the key concepts of deterrence and labeling. Scholars also use these concepts to test relationships between community conditions and crime rates.

Box 8.4 Definitions of Key Concepts of Deterrence and Labeling

- *Punishment by the criminal justice system. Nominal*—the administration of a painful consequence for behavior by the police, courts, and corrections. *Operational*—the presence of arrest, conviction, and/or sentence for a criminal act, as measured by official statistics from the police, courts, and correctional facilities.
- *Deterrence. Nominal*—the absence of future criminal behavior after punishment. *Operational*—the absence of future criminal behavior after punishment, typically inferred from reduced crime rates known to the police or recidivism rates reflected in court statistics.
- *Certain punishment. Nominal*—a high likelihood of receiving punishment after the commission of a criminal act. *Operational*—the proportion of criminal acts committed, as reflected in self-report studies or official crime statistics, relative to the number of criminal acts that receive punishment, as reflected in court statistics.
- *Swift punishment. Nominal*—the amount of time that passes between the commission of a criminal act and punishment. *Operational*—a short amount of time between the commission of a criminal act and punishment (typically hours, days, weeks, or months), as measured in police and court statistics.
- *Severe punishment. Nominal*—when the pleasure associated with criminality is outweighed by the pain derived from punishment. *Operational*—any indication that pleasure associated with criminality is outweighed by the pain of punishment, as measured in a survey of offenders.
- *Labeling. Nominal*—when an offender formally is identified by the justice system as a delinquent, deviant, criminal, or a similar term. *Operational*—when an offender formally is identified by the justice system as a delinquent, deviant, criminal, or a similar term, as measured through a survey of offenders, their family members, and/or official court records.
- *Self-image of offenders. Nominal*—the way in which a person views himself or herself. *Operational*—the way in which a person views

himself or herself, as measured in a survey before and after being labeled by the criminal justice system.

- *Secondary deviance. Nominal*—any criminal act committed after the labeling process. *Operational*—any criminal act committed after the labeling process, as shown by a self-report survey and/or court records.

- *Reintegrative shaming. Nominal*—the productive and/or positive labeling of an offender with the intent of restoring him or her to respected status in the community. *Operational*—the productive and/or positive labeling of an offender with the intent of restoring him or her to respected status in the community, as measured by participation in a program of reintegrative shaming and by assessing the effects of the program on the offender in a survey.

- *Recidivism. Nominal*—criminal activity after a sentence has been served. *Operational*—any evidence of criminal activity after a sentence has been served, usually verified by official records such as an arrest or conviction for another criminal act and/or by self-report data.

Evaluation of Deterrence and Labeling Theory

In the following sections, we address deterrence and labeling theory. We assess the empirical validity of this theory, discuss the scope of the research, as well as address the conceptual clarity and the logical adequacy of its propositions.

Empirical Validity of Deterrence and Labeling

Deterrence

Contemporary research into deterrence supports original speculation by classical theorists. For example, Blumstein (1995, pp. 408–409) wrote:

> Research on deterrence has consistently supported the position that sentence "severity" (that is, the time served) has less of a deterrent effect than sentence "certainty" (the probability of going to prison). Thus, from the deterrence consideration, there is clear preference for increasing certainty, even if it becomes necessary to do so at the expense of severity.

The problem with punishment in the United States is that punishment is anything but certain. For every 100 serious street crimes (as measured in the National Crime Victimization Survey), about 40 are known to the police (as measured in the Uniform Crime Reports). Of these 40, only about 10 will lead to an arrest. Of these, some will not be prosecuted; some will be prosecuted, but will not be convicted. Only about 3 of the original 100 will lead to an incarceration. Thus, roughly 10% of serious crime leads to an arrest; 3% leads to a serious consequence like prison or jail.

Formal punishment is anything but certain in America, and offenders know this. They tell criminologists that they know from personal experiences and from experiences of fellow criminals that their risks of getting apprehended by the police and convicted in court are very low (Cromwell, 1995). Since there are only 3 police officers in America for every 1,000 citizens (Robinson, 2009), is this surprising? Police must be present on the streets to detect criminality. With so few police and so few people willing to report criminal activity, criminal justice system activity cannot be considered a successful deterrent (Robinson, 2009).

What many offenders do tell us, and what is evident from their offending patterns, is that the great bulk of criminal behavior seems to be motivated by the desire to obtain short-term, immediate pleasures and gains. Long-term concerns about potential punishments seem not to enter the minds of most offenders (see the discussion of impulsivity in chapter 6). If they thought there was a good chance of getting caught, after all, offenders would not likely engage in their criminal behaviors, especially if offenders are rational as criminologists tell us.

The main problem with deterrence as a justification for punishment is that it is impossible to demonstrate empirically that deterrence works. How can one prove *the absence* of criminal activity as a result of some criminal justice policy or program? This is why many criminal justice scholars argue that there is no empirical evidence supporting deterrence (Bohm, 2001). At the same time, others claim that deterrence clearly exists. According to Paternoster and Bachman (2001, p. 16),

> numerous studies tested the prediction that crime rates are lower when the objective properties of punishment are higher, and much of this research provided some support for deterrence theory (Gibbs, 1975; Nagin, 1978) ... most data seemed to show some deterrent effect for certain punishment. The evidence with respect to the severity of punishment was much less supportive.

The problem with this type of research into actual punishment levels and subsequent crime reductions is that the intervening variable of deterring the offender is not measured. Furthermore, deterrence researchers often make the ecological fallacy of assuming that reductions in crime rates are attributable to changes in the thought processes of individuals.

It is clear that punishment can only deter when it is credible and meaningful to the would-be offender. Many scholars have spent time with known offenders, both incarcerated and in the free world, in order to discover their motivations and mechanisms for committing crimes. Essentially, offenders learn from personal experience that their likelihood of getting punished is extremely low in the United States. That is, their perception of punishment (or perceived punishment) is low and so it cannot cause fear to prevent them from committing crimes. Many studies assessing the relationship between perceived punishment and likelihood of committing crime have found little empirical support (Bachman, Paternoster, & Ward, 1992; Klepper & Nagin, 1989; Paternoster, 1987).

Studies of aggregate crime data show evidence that is consistent with deterrence. For example, some studies show that an increased police presence leads to reductions in street crime (Levitt, 1997; Marvell & Moody, 1996; also see studies reviewed in Sherman et al., 1997) and that police interventions into hot spots of crime lead to reductions in those areas (Sherman, 1995; Sherman & Rogan, 1995; Sherman & Weisburd, 1995). Paternoster and Bachman (2001, p. 18) summarized the state of the knowledge: "While not all of the findings are supportive of a deterrent effect, the collective landscape of findings does seem to suggest that offenders are sensitive to the risks and costs of doing crime." That offenders sometimes weigh the potential benefits and costs of offending before they commit crimes is not necessarily evidence of the deterrent effect of criminal justice activity.

Sherman et al. (1998) summarized what works, what is promising, and what does not work in the justice system to prevent crime. They concluded that extra police patrols reduce crime in hot spots, that monitoring of high-risk repeat offenders by specialized police units is effective as is incarceration for these offenders, that on-scene arrests of domestic violence suspects can reduce recidivism, and that rehabilitation programs in and out of prison focused on risk factors can reduce drug use. They concluded that the following programs are promising: proactive drunk driving arrests with breath tests, police showing greater respect to offenders, polite field interrogations of suspects, mailing arrest warrants to suspects who leave the scene before arrests, higher numbers of police officers in cities, gang monitoring by police and probation officers, prison-based vocational training for adult offenders, sound crime analysis, proactive arrests for carrying concealed weapons, drug courts, drug treatment in jails followed by urine testing in the community, intensive supervision and aftercare for juveniles, and fines. The rest of criminal justice system activity does not work to prevent crime, or the effects are unknown, according to the authors.

Some studies find evidence in support of deterrence (Bushway & Reuter, 2008; Helland & Tabarrok, 2008; Levitt, 2004; Lochner, 2007; Matsueda et al., 2006; Sitren & Applegate, 2007). For example, a study of offenders under intensive supervision probation (ISP) in New Jersey suggests that perceptions of risks for violating ISP were associated with an increased likelihood of successfully completing ISP (Pogarsky, 2007). This does not mean, however, that such offenders would not offend again upon completion of ISP. Similarly, Weisburd, Enat, & Kowalski (2008) found that probationers in New Jersey who faced an increased risk of violation to prison for nonpayment of fines were more likely than the other probationers to pay their fines. Again, this does not mean that such offenders would not reoffend.

It is logical to assume that some offenders will be deterred by criminal punishment, but the effect of punishment on likely criminal behavior probably depends on several other factors (Pogarsky, 2008; Pratt et al., 2006; Tittle & Paternoster, 2000). As noted by Nagin (2008): "Just like medications for treatment of disease have no single effect across type of medication and disease, we cannot expect that all sanctions will be equally effective."

Some of these factors would include likelihood of offending based on the type of crime being studied (Pogarsky, Kim, & Paternoster, 2005), social factors such as number of deviant peers (Matthews & Agnew, 2008) as well as personality characteristics such as low self-control (Paternoster et al., 1997), although not all studies find this to be true (Wright et al., 2004). In fact, Wright et al (2004) suggest that studies of the deterrent effects of punishment may underestimate the actual deterrent effect given that they are often tested on law-abiding citizens with high moral beliefs. They conclude: "Many social processes bear upon criminal behavior, and whatever the nature of their effect, whether to increase or decrease criminal behavior, they have their greatest impact on individuals with personal characteristics, both psychological and biological in origin, that increase their proclivity to crime" (p. 207).

Studies of the effects of prison on crime rates tend to find larger incapacitative effects on future crimes than deterrence effects (Bhati and Piquero, 2007). This suggests that the main crime reduction effect of imprisonment is not deterrence but rather incapacitation. That is, if we can lock up the offenders most likely to reoffend, we ought to expect a reduction in crime since they are not able to offend in the free world (except in the cases where they run criminal enterprises from behind bars).

The research has great import for criminal justice policy. For example, should states get tougher and sentence offenders to longer periods of crime? In 1982, the state of California passed Proposition 8 which imposed a mandatory prison term for selected crimes by repeat offenders. Specifically, those convicted of murder, rape, robbery, burglary of a residence, and firearm assault were to receive a 5-year sentence enhancement for each prior conviction of a serious felony offense (Cook, 2006).

One study suggested this change led to declines in serious crimes in the state (Kessler & Levitt, 1999). Yet, a more sophisticated follow-up study found this not to be true (Webster, Doob & Zimring, 2006). One of the authors of the original article later wrote that "crimes were falling everywhere in the United States at the same time ... and ... crimes began falling before the passage of the law" (Kessler, 2007: 459). A subsequent analysis of the data also suggests no deterrent effect of the policy (Raphael, 2006). Studies of sentencing enhancements such as three strikes laws are just as likely to find evidence of increased criminality as they are to find evidence of decreased criminality (Kovandzic, Sloan & Vieraitis, 2004).

Based on the wide body of literature available, it is a safe conclusion that efforts other than punishment offer greater reductions in recidivism. For example, studies of drug treatment show much better results than incarceration (Hung-En, 2003). Further, restorative justice practice is better equipped to heal not only criminal offenders but their victims as well (Roche, 2006; Tyler, 2006). A study of *reintegrative shaming* on 652 tax offenders found that taxpayers who felt that their enforcement experience was reintegrative in nature were less likely to report having evaded their taxes two years later (Murphy & Harris, 2007).

Labeling

According to Paternoster and Bachman (2001, p. 220), "there is really no solid consensus in the field as to the validity of [labeling] theory." Matsueda (2001, p. 233) added that "research has not contradicted labeling theory, but neither has it yielded strong support." This owes itself partly to the fact that many do not consider it to actually be a theory but instead a perspective, and partly to the fact that parts of it are not directly testable.

It is clear that many criminals do not actually view themselves as criminals (Yochelson & Samenow, 1976). Instead, they use *techniques of neutralization* (Sykes & Matza, 1957) to justify their actions (e.g., "I am not responsible for my actions," "I had to do it for my family," "Everyone else does it so what's the big deal?"). Vold et al. (1998, p. 221) suggested that "criminal behaviors are frequently committed by persons who do not conceive of themselves as criminals. To maintain a noncriminal self-image, these persons 'define the situation' so that they can maintain their actions are not really crimes. They are free to continue committing criminal behaviors without changing their self-image."

Labeling theory also assumes that all people reject labels such as criminal or deviant. Some criminals, at least, welcome such labels and actually pursue them (Robinson, 2009). Subcultural theories may explain this phenomenon (discussed in chapter 9).

Based on the research, it is clear that labeling does occur (Robinson, 2009). Moreover, it is clear that some people are more likely to be labeled than others (Paternoster & Iovanni, 1989). In his book, *Controlling the Dangerous Classes,* Shelden (2007) illustrated how the American criminal justice system has always been aimed at controlling certain segments of the population even though these groups do not necessarily commit more than their share of criminality (also see Reiman, 2006; Robinson, 2009). Given the focus on juvenile delinquency by labeling theorists, the recent study released by the U.S. Department of Justice (which found that the juvenile justice system in America is biased at every stage of the process) speaks volumes to the proposition that labels are applied differentially to some segments of the population (Pope, Lovell, & Hsia, 2001).

The problem with labeling theories is they are unable to directly illustrate with empirical evidence that a person's self-image changes after being labeled. Figure 8.2 depicts the labeling process. Note the part of the model that is spiraled. This is the part that is difficult to measure.

Studies of the effects of criminal sanctions show that an arrest and/or conviction increases the likelihood of employment difficulties (e.g., Bushway, 1998; Freeman, 1991; Sampson & Laub, 1993). Consistent with the labeling approach, Bushway (1998) explored the issue of whether the stigma of arrest causes harm to individuals who apply for jobs after arrests. Their research was longitudinal in nature and conducted on 1,725 youth. It found that formal

Figure 8.2 The Labeling Process

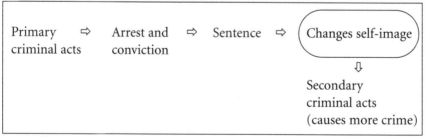

Source: Figure created by author.

contact with the criminal justice system directly damaged job prospects, even after controlling for level of offending. This study did not demonstrate that arrests and the resulting job instability actually increased later criminality, nor did it show that individual's self-concepts were changed as a result of the arrest. Therefore, even though the findings are consistent with labeling theories, they are not directly supportive of them.

Kurlychek, Brame, & Bushway (2007: 78) note that there is a "substantial body of evidence suggesting that those with criminal records are likely to face important disadvantages in many activities and endeavors. Limited access to jobs, public housing, student loans, and other types of activities have all become more commonplace in recent years." Yet, in their own study of 670 males through age 32 years, they found no evidence of increased criminality as a result of a criminal conviction. Further, the authors explain, "if a person with a criminal record remains crime free for a period of about 7 years, his or her risk of a new offense is similar to that of a person without any criminal record" (p. 80).

However, in a study of 1,000 people followed over a nine year period between the ages of 13 and 22 years, Bernburg & Krohn (2003) found evidence consistent with the labeling perspective. The authors found that court intervention during adolescence influences criminal involvement in early adulthood "when individuals become fully affected by blocked life chances shaped by education and employment ... [I]n addition to the indirect effects that both intervention by the police and the juvenile justice system have on adult crime, official intervention also directly influences subsequent criminality ... even after controlling for educational attainment, [and] employment" (p. 1310).

Using the same data, Berburg, Krohn & Rivera (2006: 67) also find that "juvenile justice intervention positively affects subsequent involvement in serious delinquency through the medium of involvement in deviant social groups, namely, street gangs and delinquent peers." The study found evidence that teenagers adjudicated delinquent by courts were "substantially more likely than their peers to become members of a gang in a successive period" and that "the peer networks of these youth ... tend to become increasingly nonconventional in the sense that they are more likely to be involved in peer networks that have high levels of delinquency" (pp. 81–82). Another study of more than 400 Midwestern adolescents found not only that labeling maintains deviant behavior but also that is strains good parenting practice (Stewart et al, 2002).

Of the studies that have been conducted, scholars suggest that stigmatization affects the development of deviant self-image but that deviant self-image does not produce delinquency necessarily. Typically, after labeling occurs, delinquency is not an immediate outcome but is preceded by other factors such as associations with deviant peers and school experiences. This tends to support the theory of *differential social control* (e.g., Adams, 1996; Adams & Evans, 1996; Hagan & McCarthy, 1997; Lotz & Lee, 1999; Rolison, 1993; Sampson & Laub, 1997). A study of arrests for domestic violence showed that arrested individuals are more likely to reoffend when they have a low stake in conformity (e.g., when they are unemployed and/or unmarried) (Sherman et al., 1992).

A study of the Las Vegas Drug Court using reintegrative shaming (Miethe, Lu, & Reese, 2000) found that the court actually ended up stigmatizing offenders despite being aimed at reintegration. The result was higher rates of recidivism (repeat offending) for drug court clients than for drug offenders handled outside of the court. The authors suggested this was evidence of labeling. However, their study did not actually assess how the process of the drug court affected the self-image of the offenders. Thus, their recidivism cannot be attributed to labeling necessarily.

Another problem with labeling is its overemphasis on the role of official agents of social control (Vold et al., 1998), although this applies only to the early labeling theories and not to the more recent ones that suggest that the most important labels are those applied by informal sources (Heimer & Matsueda, 1994). It is obvious that the reactions of the criminal justice system to our behavior is of less importance than the reactions of our families and close friends.

With regard to both labeling theory and deterrence, it seems clear from the available evidence that concerns about informal sanctions are more important than concerns about formal sanctions. This is "because they are more often experienced than formal reactions, are given by social others who are more important in the lives of those being labeled than formal authorities, and generally occur earlier in life when they can have their greatest impression" (Paternoster & Bachman, 2001, p. 218).

Much recent research illustrates that being labeled in a negative way by normal, everyday people (e.g., parents, friends, teachers) is more likely to increase future deviant behavior than being labeled by formal agencies of social control (e.g., police, courts, corrections) (Bartusch & Matsueda, 1996; Heimer, 1996; Heimer & Matsueda, 1994; Matsueda, 1992). Similarly, it seems that what deters people from committing crimes, particularly serious crimes such as murder, is that most people think such acts are wrong and they are afraid of consequences related to the loss of family contact, status, respect, and love. According to Braithwaite (2001, p. 244): "My theory is that it is exposure early in our lives to the idea of the shamefulness of murder that puts it off the deliberative agenda of responsible citizens. This is why it makes no difference to most people whether the punishment for murder is the electric chair or prison." If it is true that potential informal sanctions affiliated with deviance reduce the likelihood that a person will commit a crime, this means that deterrence would only work for individuals who have something to lose, or a *stake in conformity,* a factor implicated by social control theorists (discussed in chapter 7).

Given the evidence, it would seem that much criminal justice system activity actually encourages criminality rather than discouraging it. One example of this is that a policy of mass incarceration will encourage social disorganization in communities and erode the capacity of families to protect their children from bad influences (Bursik & Grasmick, 1993; Sampson, 1987; Sampson & Groves, 1989). Communities with high rates of incarceration tend to experience higher rates of family disruption, single-parent families, and births by young adults who are unmarried (Rose & Clear, 1998). These are risk factors associated with higher crime rates. "The more society builds prisons, the more it cultivates the crime problem for which building is proposed as a solution. A crime control strategy that looks only to coerce compliance from members of communities and that ignores the ways in which it can strengthen the neighborhood's internal mechanism of social control is worse than neutral. It is self-defeating" (Rose & Clear, 1998, p. 474).

Scope of Deterrence and Labeling Theory

It is difficult to specify the scope of deterrence and labeling theories. After all, deterrence is meant to explain *noncrime* (i.e., crime that does *not* happen). It is not aimed at explaining why people commit crimes, unless scholars reverse the propositions and assert that uncertain, slow, and weak punishment explains why people commit crimes. In this case, the theory would be limited to explaining crimes committed for profit.

As explained in this chapter, labeling theory seeks to account for secondary deviance, acts committed after a person has come to the attention of formal agents of social control and has been labeled a criminal; thus, obviously, it does not explain primary deviance, or acts committed before a person has come to the attention of formal agents of social control and been officially called a criminal. Proponents of labeling theories suggest that primary deviance is normal and caused by various factors. It is secondary deviance that should be of most importance, they suggest, because secondary deviance is indicative of abnormal behavior (i.e., it is persistent, repetitive criminality). The theory accounts for all crimes after a person is labeled.

Conceptual Clarity of Deterrence and Labeling Theory

The main concepts of labeling and deterrence theories are clearly defined. Yet, some cannot be directly measured with the empirical senses. For example, what is a self-concept and how can it be measured? The only option is to ask offenders how they feel about themselves. They are likely to offer excuses for their criminality, including that they were labeled by the system and so the system got what it deserved. Whether or not we can trust offenders to tell us the truth is a matter of heated debate.

Logical Adequacy of Deterrence and Labeling Theory

The main propositions of tests of deterrence and labeling theory seem valid on their face. They appeal to our common sense about the role of organization level factors in crime. Yet, studies of labeling and deterrence are characterized by the same basic weaknesses as other approaches at this level of analysis. Each states propositions that are not directly testable, mostly because they do not define their concepts in ways that can be subjected to empirical testing, as explained earlier. Even though each makes sense, labeling theories wrongly assume that all people are meaningfully affected by actions of official agents of the government, that people do not want to be seen as deviant or criminal, and that individual differences are not important for accounting for why some people continue on with their criminal acts while others don't. They also cannot empirically demonstrate how many acts of criminality never occur because potential offenders are deterred from committing crimes due to fear of punishment by the criminal justice system. The same can be said for deterrence theories, which also ignore these issues.

Other Community and Organization Level Factors

As with the other levels of analysis, there are undoubtedly other community and organization level factors that contribute to antisocial behavior. Some of these would include affiliations with organizations (as in the theory of social disorganization) as well as activity by organizations. Each of these would likely not only affect crime rates but also might help account for individual behavior. Such studies are beyond the scope of this book.

Summary

In this chapter, you learned about community and organization level factors as they impact antisocial and criminal behavior. Communities are usually treated synonymously with neighborhoods, although in social disorganization theory a community is viewed as a neighborhood that is capable of defending itself from criminality. Organizations are large groups whose members are not as close and who do not spend as much time together as those in smaller groups.

Social disorganization theory was originally aimed at accounting for why certain areas of large cities tend to house higher rates of delinquency and crime regardless of who lives there. An area is socially disorganized if residents are unable to prevent delinquency and criminality due to environmental conditions such as poverty, unemployment, population density, turnover, and heterogeneity, single parent families, and so forth. These factors diminish community participation, supervision of children, friendship networks, and therefore erode collective efficacy. Structural conditions most commonly found in larger, inner-city areas impede informal social control in families and neighborhoods, thereby increasing the odds of criminality. Social disorganization also increases the odds of family adversity, school problems, and perceptions of strain.

The scope of the theory is generally limited to street crime, particularly that committed by urban males. A major limitation of the theory is that it does not specify from where it is that social disorganization arises. Yet, studies demonstrate that economic and social conditions produced by elite decision-makers erode social and human capital, two factors necessary for collective efficacy.

Areas characterized by social disorganization also tend to have higher rates of incivilities, defined as untended people and places. Yet, incivilities do not produce criminality but instead seem to be an indicator of social disorganization.

Routine activity theory and lifestyle exposure theory focus mostly on explaining differential risks of criminal victimization based on activity patterns and lifestyles of potential victims and offenders, although routine activity theory was originally applied to crime rate trends. The scope of such theories seems limitless, although they have been applied almost exclusively to street crime victimization.

Finally, deterrence and labeling theories make opposite assertions about the impact of criminal punishment on future criminality. The former suggests criminality can be prevented using punishment, particularly if it is certain, as well as swift and severe enough to outweigh pleasures associated with criminality. The latter suggests future criminality is made more likely when punishment is applied, particularly when applied in a hateful, harmful way that limits future opportunities for legitimate success and when it damages the self-image of offenders. A review of the research shows that the likelihood of criminal punishment is very slim for even most serious offenders, calling into question the deterrent value of most criminal punishment. Although we know that labeling occurs and that labels such as "delinquent" and "criminal" are more likely to be applied to certain segments of the population, research has not been able to show conclusively that this increases the odds of future criminality. What is fairly clear is that informal sources of control such as families seem to hold much more promise for deterring future criminality, as well as sustaining it by applying destructive labels.

Discussion Questions

1. What is a community?
2. What is an organization?
3. What is meant by the term *social disorganization*? Briefly outline the development of this theory.
4. What characteristics of a community or neighborhood are present in conditions of social disorganization?
5. Is it really possible for a community or neighborhood to be socially disorganized? Explain.
6. List and discuss the main propositions at the community and organization levels of analysis.
7. Is the theory of social disorganization supported with empirical evidence? Can it explain antisocial behavior of an individual? Explain.
8. What is downsizing? How might it be related to antisocial behavior?
9. What are incivilities? How are they related to antisocial behavior?
10. What are routine activities and lifestyles? How are they related to criminal victimization?
11. What is the relationship between social disorganization and routine activities?
12. Contrast the main propositions of deterrence and labeling theories.
13. Does the criminal justice system deter crime or produce crime? Explain.
14. Contrast primary deviance with secondary deviance.
15. Is criminal justice activity in the United States consistent with reintegrative shaming? Explain.
16. Are the concepts of community and organization level explanations of crime clearly defined? Explain.
17. What is the logical adequacy of community and organization level explanations of crime?
18. What is the scope of community and organization level explanations of crime?

9

Society Level
Explanations of Crime

Introduction

Recall from chapter 3 that societies are the largest level of analysis considered in the integrated systems perspective. Societies are made up of communities and organizations (chapter 8), which are made up of groups (chapter 7), which are made up of individual organisms (chapter 6) that are comprised of organs (chapter 5) and cells (chapter 4). Thus, all the previous subsystems exist within societies. Because of this, it is wise to think of society as the appropriate level within which to attempt to integrate all factors related to antisocial behavior and criminality (theoretical integration). In this chapter, we present societal level factors that increase the probability of antisocial and criminal behaviors; in the final chapter, we attempt to summarize the integrated relationships between these society level factors and factors from other levels of analysis that have been discussed in previous chapters.

Behavior in the Context of Society

All behavior occurs in a *society* and thus has effects on that society. According to *Merriam-Webster's Collegiate Dictionary* (2009), a society is "an enduring and cooperating social group whose members have developed organized patterns of relationships through interaction with one another; a community, nation, or broad grouping of people having common traditions, institutions, and collective activities and interests." For the purposes of this chapter, society refers to a collective of people with common traditions, institutions, and activities and interests. The specific factors discussed in this chapter refer to those in American society but are relevant for other societies with similar structural elements, as well as similar traditions, institutions, and activities and interests.

Every society has a unique *social structure,* which symbolizes the main, permanent, interrelated features of the society that determine how the society as a whole functions. A society's social structure contains various institutions and includes the regular, persistent social relations shared by individual members and between groups and communities: *Institutions* are the significant practices and organizations in a society or culture, including economic institutions, political institutions, educational institutions, moral institutions, and so forth. As explained by Bohm (2001, pp. 104, 138), "human beings are the creators of the institutions and structures that ultimately dominate and constrain them ... Human beings not only shape the world, but also are shaped by it." The meaning of social structure is perhaps best explained by Hagan (1989, p. 1): "Social structure is formed out of relations between actors." This means social structure results from human behavior; in turn future human behaviors are shaped and constrained by social structural features so that the result is structured action (Messerschmidt, 1997).

Society also includes the general culture of the society as a whole and the various subcultures that exist within the society. A *culture* can be understood as "the integrated pattern of human knowledge, belief, and behavior that depends upon man's capacity for learning and transmitting knowledge to succeeding generations; the customary beliefs, social forms, and material traits of a racial, religious, or social group"*(Merriam-Webster's Collegiate Dictionary,* 2009). A *subculture* is a culture within a culture, or more specifically, "an ethnic, regional, economic, or social group exhibiting characteristic patterns of behavior sufficient to distinguish it from others within an embracing culture or society"*(Merriam-Webster's Collegiate Dictionary,* 2009). The various events that occur within society's institutions, its general culture, and various subcultures make up the *social processes* of the society, or the way in which the society itself generally operates.

Criminologists have historically differentiated between social structural theories and social process theories. *Social structural theories* concern the main institutions of society and the effects of class, race, ethnic, and gender stratification on behavior; *social process theories* concern social-psychological processes such as socialization in families, peer groups, and schools and their effects on behavior (Brown, Esbensen, & Geis, 2001; Paternoster & Bachman, 2001). Social structural theories include anomie and strain theories (discussed in this chapter), social disorganization and ecological theories (discussed in chapter 8), and cultural deviance or subcultural theories (discussed in this chapter). Social process theories include social learning theories and social control theories (discussed in chapter 7), and labeling theories (discussed in chapter 8). Box 9.1 summarizes the main propositions of each of these theories of crime.

Box 9.1 Leading Social Structural and Social Process Theories

Social Structural Theories
- *Anomie and strain theories.* Criminality is caused by sudden or dramatic changes in society and by economic or emotional frustration.
- *Social disorganization and ecological theories.* Criminality is caused by social disorder, physical deterioration, and other conditions in the physical environment (e.g., industrialization, urbanization, immigration, family breakdown) that interfere with informal social control networks (e.g., families).
- *Cultural deviance or subcultural theories.* Criminality is caused by conflicts between social groups; criminality is most found in some groups of people living in the larger society who have values, norms, and attitudes that are inconsistent with mainstream society.

Social Process Theories
- *Social learning theories.* Criminality is learned in a process of communication between individuals; people learn not only how to commit crime but also how to justify their illegal acts.
- *Social control theories.* Criminality is normal and expected in the absence of social control. To the degree that people do not have a stake in conformity, they are free to deviate; conformity is achieved when people are adequately bonded to society, attached to other people, committed to legal rules, and involved in legitimate activities.
- *Labeling theories.* Criminality is normal and caused by a variety of factors; repetitive acts of deviance and criminality and career criminality are explained by the labeling of individuals by agencies of formal social control (such as the criminal justice system) and by informal

sources (such as parents). After an individual is labeled as a criminal, his or her self-concept is damaged; the individual begins to see himself or herself as a criminal and thus commits more criminal acts. Further, legitimate opportunities for success are blocked, increasing the risk of criminality.

Social structure theories and social process theories are based on different assumptions and are aimed at explaining different things. Social structure theories see antisocial behavior and criminality emanating from the structural elements of society; thus *crime rates* are a function of the characteristics of society. They tend to "assume that crime is primarily a lower-class problem and point to flaws within the social structure that increase the odds of a person within that social structure resorting to illegal behavior"; these theories seem to have great relevance for the disproportionate involvement in the criminal justice system by minorities. Finally, social structure theories "are designed specifically to account for the higher rates of crime that ... characterize the lower class echelon of the American class structure" (Brown et al., 2001, p. 284). Alternatively, social process theories see antisocial behavior and criminality emanating from an individual's social interactions and experiences with adverse social processes. These theories "typically do not approach crime and delinquency as primarily a lower-class problem; one of their strengths is that their explanatory power cuts across social classes and economic strata ... [yet] they are consistent with a pattern of crime and delinquency weighted toward members of the lower class. Features of the social structure may unevenly expose members of the lower class to adverse social processes, which in turn could translate to higher rates of deviance" (Brown et al., 2001, p. 321). In these theories, daily interactions with peers, family members, and other groups are most important for understanding individual crimes.

Typically, social structure and social process theories are tested in isolation from one another and are only occasionally integrated. In chapter 10, you will learn how some scholars have attempted to integrate some of these theories. Because these theories typically are not interdisciplinary, the efforts have generally proved fruitless. Furthermore, social structure theories cannot directly explain individual behavior very well without turning to social processes. As explained by Agnew (1999, p. 123), macro level theories (social structure theories) are aimed at explaining crime rates rather than individual behavior. Thus, they

> explicitly or implicitly draw on micro theories [social process theories] when they explain how community-level variables lead individuals to engage in crime (and thereby produce crime rates). Social

disorganization theory draws on social control theory, with disorganization theorists pointing to those community characteristics that ultimately reduce the level of social control to which individuals are subject. Subcultural deviance theory draws on differential association / social learning theory, with subcultural theorists arguing that community values and norms lead some individuals to define crime as a desirable or justifiable response in certain situations. Relative deprivation theory draws on Merton's (1938) version of strain theory, with deprivation theorists arguing that high levels of income or socioeconomic inequality lead some individuals to experience strain or frustration.

Since we take a systems approach in this book, we posit that society is an integrated, living system made up of parts that are interdependent. Based on the arguments of scholars such as sociologist and philosopher Herbert Spencer, we hold that societies are alive, much like an individual organism; its subsystems include communities, organizations, groups, individual organisms, and organs and cells of individuals. Each of these components is part of society and each, through its normal operations, results in changes in society's social structures; this is similar to how changes in cells and organs produce changes in individuals. Changes to societal structures result in changes in social processes and thus individual behavior.

This systems perspective is rarely assumed by criminologists and other scholars who study behavior, a fact that is ironic considering the roots of American criminology. Early American sociologists/criminologists viewed communities as organisms and even used concepts from the natural or hard sciences to describe them. Recall the Chicago School of Criminology discussed in chapter 8, which specifically borrowed its key concepts from the natural sciences.

In the final chapter of this book, we return to the metaphor of society as an organism and offer an integrated systems theory of antisocial behavior. In this chapter, we discuss factors unique to the social structure of American society, including anomie and strain, culture conflict, criminal subcultures, and race, class and gender. Other social structural factors, such as social disorder, physical deterioration, and other conditions in the physical environment that interfere with social control networks (social disorganization) were discussed in chapter 8 because of their roots in the community level of analysis. The influence of labeling by criminal justice organizations was also discussed in chapter 8. Factors related to social processes were discussed in chapter 7 (social learning and social control), the chapter pertaining to the group level of analysis.

Anomie and Strain

Anomie Theory

Anomie is a term that roughly means a state of normlessness or a breakdown in basic norms of a society. It occurs when societal institutions can no longer regulate members of society, and when individual members of society no longer feel integrated into the whole; thus, anomie can also be understood as a lack of regulation and integration. The term "anomie" was put forth by French sociologist Emile Durkheim in two books, *The Division of Labor in Society* (1893) and *Suicide* (1897). The theoretical statements by Durkheim were later developed into a major strain theory by Robert Merton (1938), into subcultural theories by Albert Cohen (1955) and Richard Cloward and Lloyd Ohlin (1960), and into a social control theory by Travis Hirschi (1969). In other words, each of these theories traces its main ideas back to the works of Emile Durkheim (Vold, Bernard, & Snipes, 1998).

In *The Division of Labor in Society*, Durkheim described how as societies developed economically and socially, they shifted from *mechanical* societies to *organic* societies. The main features of each of these societies are described in figure 9.1. Durkheim claimed that as societies became larger and more advanced, institutions like the family would be less able to regulate (or control) members' behaviors. Furthermore, labor would be less specialized in larger societies and thus many more people would exist with no specialized skills to offer to the labor force. In smaller societies where labor was more specialized, each member of the group would have a specific role in the workplace and thus have a stake in conformity, or reason to conform.

Figure 9.1 Durkheim's Conception of Anomie

Mechanical Society	Organic Society
Simple	Complex
Small	Large
Homogenous	Heterogeneous
Specialized labor	Unspecialized labor
Strong consensus over moral values	Weak consensus over moral values
Behavior controlled by informal means (e.g., family)	Behavior controlled by formal means (e.g., police)

Source: Figure created by author.

As society became more heterogenous, the likelihood of conflict would increase because not all groups in the society would necessarily agree about what is right and wrong. Thus, the *collective conscience* of the society—the basic sense of morality of the times in the society—would be threatened, meaning that informal social controls instilled by families, peers, and so on would be less effective at controlling behaviors of individual members. This means formal social controls, like those imposed on us by the threat of punishment from the criminal justice system, would become more important in organic societies. Perhaps the explosion in imprisonment in the United States over the past 30 years serves as evidence that Durkheim was right, especially given that resulting crime rate reductions are small; the use of imprisonment is serving some function other than crime reduction (Robinson, 2002).

In *Suicide,* Durkheim argued that conditions of anomie make it less likely that individuals will be regulated by the morals of society and less integrated into the whole of society. For example, in periods of rapid economic decline, Durkheim suggested that suicides would increase as some individuals were unable to deal with the consequences. In conditions of rapid economic growth, other individuals would find themselves wanting more (egoism), and would be unable to deal with the increased freedom to deviate. These individuals may end up committing suicide. Another possible outcome of anomie is higher crime rates. Following this logic, the people most likely to commit crime would be those who were not regulated by society's morals and those not integrated into the mainstream of society.

The theory of anomie assumes that humans are in possession of desires and appetites that need to be controlled by outside forces. For example, Durkheim (1897, p. 257) wrote: "It is everlastingly repeated that it is man's nature to be eternally dissatisfied, constantly to advance, without relief or rest, toward an indefinite goal. The longing for infinity is daily represented as a mark of moral distinction." In smaller, mechanical societies, societal institutions are more effective at controlling members' behaviors. Children growing up in a small, closely knit community will learn that aggressiveness is only tolerated in certain circumstances by being corrected by their parents, town leaders, and so forth. Virtually everyone will assist in correcting wayward children. As adolescents, some individuals may continue to test the limits of proper behavior and will also be sanctioned by local leaders. In a larger and more complex organic society, such practices will be less effective, in part because members of the community will be less likely to know about misbehaviors, and also because there may be less agreement about whether children are misbehaving (anomie implies that no clear normative expectations exist). Thus, crime will increase and formal means of social control will be used to deal with behaviors perceived and/or declared to be wrong by societal leaders. Walsh (2002, p. 100) described conditions of anomie as *releasers* of criminality because they supposedly allow humans to behave as if there were no constraints on their behavior, more like they might if they were living in isolation from society.

Social Structural Stain Theory

A related line of reasoning has been referred to as strain theory. Anomie exists when a society is characterized by *strain* (Vold et al., 1998); when a neighborhood experiences strain, it is called *social disorganization* (discussed in chapter 8). *Social structural strain* is a term put forth by Robert Merton is his book, *Social Theory and Social Structure* (1938). Strain occurs when an individual wants something (goals) but cannot obtain it legally (because the means are not available). Consider, for example, a person who aspires to buy a house, raise a family, and buy nice things. If this individual adheres to legal means (formal education, hard and honest work, deferred gratification, savings) but does not achieve his or her goals, he or she will experience feelings of strain. As explained by Vold et al. (1998, p. 173), "people in situations of 'social structural strain' (i.e., people who cannot achieve culturally valued goals through legitimate means provided by the social structure) may feel 'strained' (i.e., may feel stressed, frustrated, anxious, depressed, and angry), and [these] feelings are the actual cause of the higher crime rates associated with these people."

Strain theory does not assume that people are naturally bad or likely to commit criminal and antisocial behaviors; rather, our desires and appetites come from the dominant culture in our country, which stresses the goal of acquiring as much wealth as possible. The problem, according to Merton, is that wealth should only be acquired through legitimate means, which are structured by social class—that is, equal opportunities for success are not equally available to all. Is it possible that America's economic system of capitalism actually encourages us to be greedy and self-indulgent, to pursue our own wants and desires without regard for others? William Bonger, in *Criminality and Economic Conditions* (1916), argued that this is the case. If this is true, then it is capitalism that makes people egoistic and selfish rather than human nature. While Durkheim viewed society as a preventive factor against deviance (if anomie was not prevalent), Merton and Bonger saw society as a criminogenic factor.

Merton put forth five modes of adaptation, or ways of adapting to strain. These include conformity, innovation, ritualism, retreatism, and rebellion. *Conformists* abide the law despite feelings of strain, whereas *innovators* create illegitimate means to achieve their goals. *Ritualists* simply go about abiding by the legitimate means of hard work despite that they are not really aimed at ac-

Figure 9.2 Merton's Modes of Adaptation to Strain

	Goals	Means
Conformity	+	+
Innovation	+	−
Ritualism	−	+
Retreatism	−	−
Rebellion	+ −	+ −

+ indicates goals or means are available and accepted
− indicates goals or means are not available and accepted
+ and − indicates goals or means were once available but have been replaced with new goals and means

Source: Adapted from Merton (1938).

quiring material wealth. *Retreatists* give up and withdraw into drug abuse and other deviant outlets. *Rebels* create not only their own means but also their own goals by substituting those of their own subculture with those of the larger society. Supposedly, criminality is most found among innovators who create illegitimate means to achieve their goals, followed by rebels who may create illegitimate means to achieve their goals, and finally, retreatists who may commit crimes under the influence of drugs. One problem is that it is not clear why most people conform despite experiencing strain and why some people react to strain by innovating while others react by retreating or rebelling. This issue is discussed later in the section on evaluating society level explanations.

Because legitimate opportunities are least prevalent in areas inhabited by lower-class people, Merton's strain theory expects higher crime rates among the nation's poor. It is anomie, one major contradiction or irony of our society, that explains higher criminality. People who experience strain may innovate by creating their own illegitimate means to achieve their goals. The modes of adaptation posited by Merton are depicted in figure 9.2.

Institutional Anomie Theory

Steven Messner and Richard Rosenfeld, in *Crime and the American Dream* (1994), attributed high crime rates in the United States to our allegiance to the "American Dream," which is the "broad cultural ethos that entails a commitment to the goal of material success, to be pursued by everyone in society, under conditions of open, individual competition" (p. 6). Messner and Rosenfeld suggested that other important societal institutions such as the family, schools, and even places of worship have become subservient to the needs of the economy—that is, the relative well-being of other institutions is of secondary importance to the health of the economy. Since the "primary task for noneconomic institutions such as the family and schools is to inculcate beliefs, values, and commitments other than those of the marketplace" (Vold et al., 1998, p. 176), when these institutions are weakened, we should not expect them to be as effective in controlling wayward behaviors. This *institutional anomie theory* is an extension of Merton's structural strain theory, which only examined the effects of the illegitimate economic opportunity structure on crime rates.

According to Messner and Rosenfeld, in order for society to function appropriately, societal institutions must be coordinated and cooperate. However, America's most cherished values are rooted in economic concerns. The welfare of the economy takes precedence in society in three ways:

1. *Devaluation of noneconomic institutional functions and roles*—for example, those who perform family-oriented tasks such as childcare are paid very little in the United States; educational pursuits are often reduced to the relevance they have for assisting one with earning money and with career advancement; people see the primary purpose of government as encouraging and assisting with economic growth;

2. *Accommodation to economic requirements by other social institutions*—for example, families often must make serious sacrifices in terms of time spent together so that both parents can work full-time; students in public schools are encouraged to raise money for their schools by selling products for corporations whereby a portion is donated to the school; politicians depend on donations by lobbyists for major corporations, wealthy individuals, and political action committees to raise enough money to compete in and win elections;

3. *Penetration of economic norms into other institutional domains*—for example, a bottom line, business-like mentality is utilized in families, schools, and law-making activities in much of what they do.

When other institutions in society such as the family are prioritized less than the economy, higher crime rates result.

Contextual Anomie/Strain Theory

Robinson and Murphy (2008) extended strain, anomie, and institutional anomie theories by creating *contextual anomie/strain theory*. This theory, aimed at explaining corporate crimes of the wealthy, posits that the main sources of criminality are:

- Prioritization of the goals associated with the American Dream over the legitimate means to achieve those goals (Merton's anomie theory);
- Frustration produced by goal blockage whereby individuals are unable to achieve the goals associated with the American Dream, regardless of how much they have (Merton's strain theory);
- Prioritization of the economy over other noneconomic institutions in America (Messner and Rosenfeld's institutional anomie theory); and
- Greater presence of opportunities for deviance in some situations than in others (Cloward and Ohlin's differential opportunity theory).

Although this new theory makes the same basic assertions as previous anomie and strain theories, one major difference is the supposed scope of the theory. The theory is aimed at explaining elite deviance rather than street crime. Robinson and Murphy thus focus on property crimes committed by corporations (e.g., fraud) as well as violent crimes committed by corporations (e.g., selling defective products).

The question these theorists try to answer is, why do corporations, who already have everything they could possibly need, still commit such crimes? The answer, according to Robinson and Murphy, is *greed*, greed that is first learned in the context of American society, but that is also more present in the corporate world. Thus, another major difference of this theory is its explicit focus on "additional pressures that occur in given contexts in American society, such as in the workplace." That is, the argument is that "there are contexts in American society whereby individuals, groups, and subcultures are not only living under the pressures to achieve the American Dream that the rest of us live, but also additional pressures to do so that are unique to the given contexts in which they find themselves—hence the name contextual anomie/strain theory" (Robinson and Murphy, 2008: p. 42).

Robinson and Murphy (2008: p. 42) predict that "people working in big business—the corporation—have additional pressures to achieve wealth that emanate from the subcultures of their workplace ... in big business, individuals are exposed to additional pressures to achieve wealth through any means, to 'maximize wealth' by whatever means necessary, including greed." Robinson and Murphy thus add a new mode of adaptation to strain called *Maximization* which they define as the "the concomitant utilization of legitimate and illegitimate means of opportunity in pursuit of wealth ... maximization occurs when elites use illegal means simultaneously with legal means to achieve their goals of wealth or profit." Robinson and Murphy thus proposed that it is possible to engage in *Conformity* and *Innovation* at the same time.

General Strain Theory

A disjunction between financial goals and means available to achieve them is not the only source of strain. Robert Agnew (1992) developed *general strain theory*, which suggests that "delinquency can occur in response to noxious circumstances and situations" (Mazerolle & Maahs, 2000, p. 754). These include negative interpersonal relationships which can create negative emotions or feelings of strain in individuals that increase their likelihood of criminality. General strain can be experienced when one is prevented from achieving his or her goals by other people, when one loses something of financial or sentimental value, or when one experiences some undesirable stimulus. According to this theory, delinquency is a normal reaction to strain, in fact it is a means to cope with it (Brezina, 1996). Delinquency is viewed as a rational, problem-solving behavior committed by an individual dealing with emotional strain. In essence, general strain suggests that antisocial behavior and criminality are a function of negative affective states such as anger, frustration, depression, and so on.

Agnew also pointed out that perceptions of strain can increase deviant behavior if they are anticipated in the future and if they are vicarious in nature (i.e., suffered by people close to you). Further, strains actually experienced— called *objective strains*—have more of an impact on behavior than those sources of stress that are subjectively interpreted—called *subjective strains* (Froggio & Agnew, 2007).

According to Agnew, general strain is more likely to lead to aggressive responses when they are high in magnitude, seen as highly unjust, and when people are unable to correct them through legitimate means. For example, if a person is prevented from achieving some goal, loses something of value, or experiences some undesirable stimulus that is very stressful and results from an unjust action of another, that person would be likely to respond with aggression if he or she could not resolve the problem through other means.

Main Propositions of Studies of Anomie and Strain

From the preceding discussion, it is clear that Durkheim, Merton, Messner, Rosenfeld, and Agnew made some specific predictions about criminality and other forms of antisocial behaviors. The main propositions pertaining to anomie and strain include:

- Conditions of anomie lead to high crime rates.

- Social structural strain increases the likelihood of crime and antisocial behavior.
- Institutional anomie increases crime rates.
- Contextual anomie/strain increases crime.
- General strain increases the likelihood of delinquency and antisocial behavior.

Key Concepts of Studies of Anomie and Strain

From the preceding propositions, the following concepts can be isolated and defined:

- Anomie
- Social structural strain
- General strain
- Institutional anomie
- Contextual Contextual anomie/strain
- Crime rates
- Antisocial behavior
- Delinquency

Box 9.2 defines the key concepts of studies of anomie and strain. Scholars have used these definitions to test the main propositions of studies of anomie and strain. The findings of these tests are discussed in the following section.

Box 9.2 Definitions of Key Concepts of Studies of Anomie and Strain

- *Anomie. Nominal*—a general state of normlessness or confusion over right and wrong produced by rapid growth of communities, increased heterogeneity, and economic change. *Operational*—any indication of confusion over (im)moral behaviors or an allegiance to clearly immoral and selfish behaviors reported by respondents in a survey; often anomie is assumed in the presence of such large-scale societal changes.
- *Social structural strain. Nominal*—frustration experienced by individuals unable to achieve their goals through legitimate institutional means. *Operational*—reported feelings of frustration associated with being unable to achieve financial goals, usually measured in self-report surveys.
- *General strain. Nominal*—negative emotions generated when one is prevented from achieving his or her goals by other people, by losing something of financial or sentimental value, or by experiencing some

undesirable stimulus. *Operational*—any indication of negative emotion, usually measured by self-report surveys where respondents are asked about problems in their lives, with their parents, with their peers, with their spouses, and so on.

- *Institutional anomie. Nominal*—feelings of pressure to succeed generated by a strong economy and weak controlling institutions such as the family, polity, and religion. *Operational*—feelings of pressure as measured by self-report surveys present in a strong economy in conjunction with conditions of family disruption, low political participation, and low religious affiliations; conditions of economic strength, family disruption, and political participation are typically obtained from government data sources.
- *Contextual anomie/strain. Nominal*—feelings of pressure to succeed and greed generated by additional pressures to achieve wealth in the context or work. *Operational*—feelings of pressure to succeed and greed generated by additional pressures to achieve wealth in the context or work as measured by self-report surveys.
- *Crime rates. Nominal*—an aggregate measure of crime indicating how much crime is present in a given area such as a neighborhood, state, or nation. *Operational*—usually measured by the number of crimes known to officials (e.g., police) divided by the population of the area (crimes per capita).
- *Antisocial behavior. Nominal*—any behaviors that conflict with the prevailing norms of society and/or that are viewed as abnormal. *Operational*—any form of behavior defined as antisocial, measured by official crime reports, self-reported behaviors, or evaluations from others.
- *Delinquency. Nominal*—acts committed by juveniles that, if committed by adults, would be considered crimes by the criminal justice system. *Operational*—usually measured by official indicators such as arrests and adjudication of guilt in a court, also measured by self-report data and reports of observations of behaviors by parents and teachers.

Evaluation of Anomie and Strain Theories

In the following sections, we address anomie and strain theories of crime. We assess the empirical validity of these theories, discuss the scope of the research, as well as address the conceptual clarity and the logical adequacy of their propositions.

Empirical Validity of Studies of Anomie and Strain

Anomie Theory

Studies examining the effects of anomie tend to be conducted at high levels of analysis such as the society level; thus they examine the effects of anomie on crime rates rather than on individual behaviors. Interestingly, when it comes to the effects of normlessness or anomie and crime rates, official measures of crime suggest that property crime rates between the 1830s and 1930s in France (where Durkheim developed his anomie theory) actually decreased despite the conditions of anomie generated by the French and Industrial Revolutions (Lodhi & Tilly, 1973). According to Vold et al. (1998, p. 135): "The statistics for violent crime remained approximately stable over the same period, with some tendency toward decline." McDonald (1982) asserted that crime rate data were available to Durkheim at the time of his studies; he simply did not examine them. Assuming the accuracy of these data, official crime rates did not increase during the time when anomie developed according to Durkheim.

Most contemporary studies have shown a positive relationship between conditions of anomie and official property crime rates, meaning that higher anomie is associated with higher crime rates (LaFree & Kick, 1986), and at least one study found a relationship between modernization and homicide rates (Ortega et al., 1992). An analysis of nearly 20 studies of urbanization and industrialization (factors relevant for anomie theory and social disorganization) reported consistent relationships between these conditions and property crime rates. However, these studies hold that changing values are not the significant causal mechanism underlying higher crime rates (Neuman & Berger, 1988). This runs counter to Durkheim's theory (Vold et al., 1998, p. 136).

One thing that economic change can bring, however, is income inequality, a condition consistently related to higher homicide rates. *Income inequality* is typically measured by comparing the incomes of the upper classes with those of the lower classes; a larger gap between the two suggests crime rates are likely to be higher. In this case, it is the inequality that is important for explaining higher crime rates rather than normlessness or anomie. We return to studies of income inequality later in this chapter when discussing the impact of social class on crime. Durkheim's basic hypothesis that economic development will increase violent crime rates has been directly refuted in other research as well (Bennett, 1991).

It is not anomie, per se, that increases crime rates, despite claims that the economic pressure exerted on families and other social institutions interferes with their ability to control behavior. For example, a study of young people from 11 rural counties in North Carolina found that parent risk factors such as substance abuse, mental illness, lack of education, and involvement with crimi-

nal justice had significant impacts on children's likelihood of experiencing economic strain and instability. These factors, in turn, can pressure individuals to
criminality (Phillips et al., 2006).

Institutional Anomie Theory

Both institutional anomie theory (Messner & Rosenfeld, 1994) and general
strain theory (Agnew, 1992) have received tremendous attention by scholars,
leading to a revival of classic anomie and strain theories (Adler & Laufer, 1999).
The former suggests that the effects of the economy and economic change depend on the relative strength of other, noneconomic societal institutions.
Specifically, when other institutions such as polity, religion, education, and
the family are unable to regulate human impulses generated by the economy,
criminality and deviance are more likely (Chamlin & Cochran, 1995). If this
theory is true, then the relationship between poverty and crime would be
strongest when other social institutions are weak (Jensen, 1996; Messner &
Rosenfeld, 2001). The effects of poverty on crime are discussed later in this
chapter.

Studies by Chamlin and Cochran (1995) and Messner and Rosenfeld (1997,
1998) found that when noneconomic institutions are strong, the effects of economic pressure on both property crimes and violent crimes are weaker. An international study of homicide rates reported that countries which protect their citizens
from intrusions of the economy (e.g., income inequality) through social welfare
policies are characterized by lower levels of homicide (Savolainen, 2000).

An examination of crime rate changes in Russia after the fall of commu-
nism suggested that global anomie may contribute to higher crime rates (Passas, 2000). Passas asserted that the process of globalization (the spread of
capital, labor, management, news, and data across country borders) is criminogenic. Globalization is pursued by transnational corporations, transnational media organizations, intergovernmental organizations, and
nongovernmental organizations. According to Passas, the spread of capitalism
to the former Soviet Union led to anomie and crime in Russia in the 1990s.
The key mechanisms he identified as relevant for understanding increased
crime rates in Russia included the resulting increased inequalities, greater
amounts of poverty, and the promotion of unsustainable growth. Results included increased street crime, increased corporate crime, increased corruption, increased ecosystem deterioration, as well as lower worker productivity,
higher unemployment, and a disappearance of traditional safety nets. Passas
asserted not only that globalization provides more motivation and opportunities
to commit deviance, but also that it leads to a less efficacious institutional con-

trol system. "Means-ends discrepancies are caused by a strong cultural emphasis on monetary or material success goals for all members of society, while a good number of them do not have a realistic chance to attain them" (p. 21). This is social structural strain. "Socially distant referents are constantly introduced and sustained through the school, family, politics, workplace, media, advertising, and even religion (Passas, 1994). Regardless of their social background and the social capital available to them, people are urged to desire more than they have" (p. 21). This can lead to anomie:

> Success stories of going from rags to riches make the American Dream even more believable. As this cultural theme is internalized, competitive forces and consumerism foster normative referents on what is "normal" and appropriate. The widely internalized egalitarian discourse clashes in practice with widespread inequality (power and economic asymmetries). Consequently, those members who fail to meet such comparative and normative standards are likely to experience relative deprivation and frustration ... A good part of the deviance is an individual search for a solution to these structural problems (p. 22).

To some degree, Passas may have been referring to general strain, as well:

> If the deviant adaptation is successful (i.e., perpetrators are not caught or adequately punished), this adaptation may become normative for others in a similar context. To the extent that this solution is available to them (demand for illicit goods or services, access to illegitimate opportunity structures), they may adopt this role model—and may be expected by their significant others to follow this path—even though the original source of strain has by now been eclipsed. Unless effective control measures are taken, this process continues in a vicious cycle toward higher rates of deviance and widespread anomie.... (p. 23)

In other words, at some point, cultural influences take over.

Although the examination of globalization and crime by Passas is informative, there are little empirical data to prove that anomie is the actual culprit for increased crime rates. As Passas pointed out, eventually financial strain does not actually need to be directly experienced by a person to lead to deviance; rather, as deviance becomes normalized over time, people may simply learn that criminality and deviance are acceptable means to achieve their goals. This is an important point to remember, for anomie and strain may be less proximate than other criminogenic factors in terms of causal ordering when explaining crime.

In terms of the effects of anomie and strain on individuals, it is not proper to draw conclusions about individual behavior from crime rate data. For example, it is not proper to conclude that any given individual living in conditions of anomie will commit crime even when findings suggest that anomie is related to higher crime rates. Making conclusions from a higher level of analysis to a lower level constitutes the ecological fallacy (Robinson, 1950).

Structural Strain Theory

Studies examining the relationship between strain and antisocial behavior and criminality tend to be conducted at lower levels of analysis, including the individual level; these studies can more appropriately be used to draw conclusions about individual behavior. Studies of strain also tend to find positive relationships. For example, strain has been associated with increased incidence of violence, property crimes, and drug use (Slocum, Simpson, & Smith, 2005). Perceptions of strain by individuals appear to be related to increased antisocial behavior and criminality, so that the greater one experiences strain, the more likely he or she is to commit an official act of criminality. Social structural strain has probably been the most studied factor in criminology, at least until the development of general strain theory in the 1990s.

Perceptions of deprivation relative to others are associated with increased negative emotions, which are correlated with a higher risk of antisocial behavior (Stiles, Liu, & Kaplan, 2000). In a study of more than 6,000 individuals, Stiles et al. (2000) showed that perceptions of economic deprivation relative to others (a type of strain called *relative deprivation*) lead to negative self-feelings, which then motivate deviant behaviors.

General Strain Theory

The most consistent findings with regard to strain theories are for general strain theory. These studies tend to find a positive relationship between experiencing general strain and delinquency of all sorts (Mazerolle & Maahs, 2000). Many studies report that general strain is related to minor and moderate acts of deviance by juveniles (Agnew & White, 1992; Agnew & Brezina, 1997; Brezina, 1996; Broidy & Agnew, 1997; Hoffman & Miller, 1998; Hoffman & Su, 1997; Mazerolle & Piquero, 1998; Mazerolle & Piquero, 1997; Paternoster & Mazerolle, 1994). One study also suggested a link between spiritual alienation, which is conceptualized as an element of general strain, and criminality among some groups of people such as the poor and minorities (Martin, 2000). Even stress during traveling in traffic may be a source of antisocial behavior among youth (Ellwanger, 2007).

In a study of more than 700 Korean youth, Moon, Burton & McCluskey (2008) found that some of their measures of strain (family conflict, parental punishment, teachers' punishment, financial strain, examination-related strain, being bullied, and criminal victimization) were associated with a higher risk of delinquency, whereas others were not. Similarly studies of middle school youth show evidence of strain-delinquency links in school and peer domains (De Coster & Kort-Butler, 2006). These findings, taken as a whole, suggest that harmful acts committed by juveniles (delinquency) are attributable to negative emotional states produced by a wide range of sources.

Another source of general strain is child abuse and neglect (discussed in chapter 7). Studies of abuse victimization find that physical and sexual abuse during childhood and adolescence may be important predictors of adult criminality (Cernkovich, Lanctôt, & Giordano, 2008; Rebellon & Van Gundy, 2005) as well as drug use by young people (Lo, Kim, & Church, 2008). Studies of trauma experienced by youth also show evidence that trauma is associated with adolescent offending as well as "health-risking sexual behavior" (Smith, Leve, & Chamberlain, 2006).

According to Widom (2000, p. 3): "Childhood physical abuse, sexual abuse, and neglect have both immediate and long-term effects. Different types of abuse have a range of consequences for a child's later physical and psychological well-being, cognitive development, and behavior." Yet, abuse and neglect usually co-occur with other conditions of "chronic adversity," such as "parental alcoholism, drug problems, and other inadequate social and family functioning." Thus, there are reciprocal relationships between multiple risk factors that result in abuse and neglect. According to Widom, physical consequences of abuse and neglect include brain damage (discussed in chapter 5 as a risk factor for antisocial behavior); psychological consequences include low self-esteem, anxiety, depression, and substance abuse (discussed in chapter 6 as risk factors for antisocial behavior); and cognitive effects include attention deficits, learning disorders, and poor school performance (discussed in chapters 6 and 7 as risk factors for antisocial behavior). Widom's study of more than 900 people victimized in childhood showed reduced IQ among the victimized group relative to a control group, reduced schooling in the victimized group relative to the control group, higher levels of employment problems in the victimized group relative to the control group, and higher levels of interpersonal relationships in the victimized group relative to the control group. The victimized group was also more likely to be arrested as juveniles and adults. A later follow-up of this study (Widom & Maxfield, 2001) showed that being abused or neglected as a child increased the likelihood of arrests as a juvenile by 58%, as an adult by 28%, and as an adult for a violent crime by 30%. Maltreatment at the hands of caregivers was found to encourage early starter offending, more frequent offending, and more serious offending.

General strain can be useful to criminologists and policy-makers concerned about real-world problems such as unemployment. For example, Baron (2008) showed, in a study of 400 homeless street youths, that the effect of unemployment on crime was conditioned by anger and impacted by other factors such as monetary dissatisfaction. Other factors related to increased antisocial behavior included negative subjective perceptions, the lack of state support, a decrease in social control, prolonged homelessness, associated with peers, deviant values, and a lack of fear of punishment.

Some studies find that the effects of strain on behavior vary by factors such as race and gender. For example, Baron (2007) showed, in a "high risk" sample of 400 homeless street youths that homelessness, monetary dissatisfaction, and relative deprivation were linked differentially to property and violent crime based on gender. In a study of general strain theory, Jang (2007) found that African American women were most likely to report strains concerning issues such as physical health, interpersonal relations, and gender roles in the family but were less likely to note work-related, racial, and job strain than African American men. Additionally, black women were less likely than black men to utilize deviant coping strategies as a result of strain, probably because they instead experienced depression and anxiety whereas black men were more likely to respond with anger.

Scope of Anomie and Strain Theories

It is widely believed that the scope of anomie and strain theories is limited to profit-motivated crimes (Chamlin & Cochran, 1995) since usually tests attempt to discover the effects of these factors on property crimes. Because the original statement of strain theory by Merton (1938) suggested that the inability to achieve financial goals led to strain, one would expect the theory to best account for street crimes committed by people who cannot achieve their legitimate goals through legitimate means. This leads to one significant criticism of anomie, strain, and subcultural theories—each assumes that members of the lower class want to be like the middle class and that they will do anything to achieve this status (Vold, 1979). Their frustration with being unable to achieve their goals explains their criminality. Because of this assertion, these theories have almost exclusively been used to explain lower-class crime, suggesting the scope of the theories is very small.

As you recall, Miller (1958) alone suggested that the lower class consisted of cultural groups with their own values and beliefs. We now know he was wrong given that studies consistently demonstrate that members of the lower class generally espouse the same goals and values as members of the middle class (Bohm, 2001). Given that most members of the lower class have the same goals and continue to abide by the law even when legitimate means to achieve their goals are blocked, how can strain explain their criminality? Furthermore, it seems that many delinquents do appear to have low aspirations (goals); yet they also tend to have very low expectations (Martin, Mutchnick, & Austin, 1990). If this is true, strain would not be experienced because these juveniles do not actually expect to achieve much. It may be low aspirations and expectations are associated with an increased likelihood of street crime.

However, it is now apparent that for many people, no matter how much they attain, they still want more (Friedrichs, 1996; Robinson & Murphy 2008). If this is true, then strain may explain even white-collar and corporate crime, especially to the degree that profit motives are stressed through literally any means necessary. Yet, at least one study calls into question the applicability of general strain theory to corporate and white-collar type offending (Langton & Piquero, 2007).

One study found evidence of a link between strain and occupational crime in nursing homes, including employee theft of patients' belongings and abuse of patients (Van Wyk, Benson, & Harris, 2000). If strain can be experienced by people in the middle and upper classes, and if no matter how much a person acquires he or she will always want more, we should expect strain to explain a great deal of criminality. Alternatively, if strain is experienced by all people, it is not a variable since, by definition, it does not vary. The recent scandals caused by large American corporate crimes serve as evidence that many very wealthy people seem to not be satisfied with being filthy rich and are willing to cause tens of billions of dollars of damages in order to acquire more.

Brezina's (1996, p. 55) study of general strain theory found that very minor acts of delinquency were committed in response to emotional strain. He wrote that:

> strain leads to a range of negative affective states, including feelings of anger, resentment, anxiety, and depression ... delinquency represents a partially successful adaptation to strain. Adolescents who respond to strain with delinquency appear to experience fewer of the negative emotional characteristics of strain. Although delinquent behaviors do not eliminate the emotional consequences of strain, they do seem to be associated with modest relief from strain's effects on anger, resentment, anxiety, and depression. Presumably, delinquent behaviors enable adolescents to escape or avoid strain, compensate for the adverse effects of strain, and/or satisfy desires for retaliation and revenge.

Again, the main elements of general strain include being prevented from achieving goals by other people, losing something of financial or sentimental value, or experiencing some undesirable stimulus. Hoffman and Su (1997) found that experiences of strain such as these are modestly related to self-reported delinquency and drug use, with no differences among male and female adolescents.

General strain theory apparently accounts for some acts of self-reported delinquency among known offenders (Leeper-Piquero & Sealock, 2000). It also accounts for some female delinquency and criminality. For example, Katz (2000) found that childhood victimization experiences were related to juvenile delinquency in girls, and that racial discrimination, sexual discrimination, and domestic violence victimization as an adult explained female criminality. If this holds true in other samples of women, it suggests that the conditions which typically produce victimization experiences will also produce more future criminality.

General strain may also help us understand the gender differences in adult criminality. Broidy and Agnew (1997) suggested that men and women experience different types of strain and react to them differently. Apparently, strain experienced by men tends to be more conducive to serious criminality, while strain experienced by women tends to be more conducive to family violence, escape behaviors, and self-harmful behaviors. Additionally, female strain is more likely than male strain to be accompanied by other emotional states, such as depression, guilt, and anxiety. Finally, men may respond to strain more violently because of other factors, including different coping mechanisms, less social support, and a greater disposition to engage in violence. According to Broidy and Agnew (1997), women may experience more gender-based discrimination, more strain from others' expectations, and strain associated with lower family and job role prestige, whereas men may suffer from more financial strain, interpersonal conflict, and criminal victimization.

Conceptual Clarity of Anomie and Strain Theories

Generally, the concepts of studies of anomie and strain are easy to understand because their nominal definitions are clear. Standing in society is measured in numerous ways, including absolute poverty, unemployment, and income inequality. Each of these measures is understandable, but accurate measures of these variables are hard to obtain. For example, official unemployment rates are available from the government, yet they do not include people unemployed who are not actively seeking work, nor do they include people in the nation's prisons and jails because they are not counted as part of unemployment figures (Robinson, 2009). The measures of both unemployment and delinquency affect the findings in studies (Vold et al., 1998, pp.

111–114). Income inequality can be measured in so many ways that it is not certain which measures are better. Logic suggests that people must be aware of income inequality (relative deprivation) before it will actually affect their behavior. Typically, the concept of income inequality is not developed with this in mind.

Logical Adequacy of Anomie and Strain Theories

Propositions stated by anomie, and strain theorists are logically stated. The predictions made by these theories are easy to understand and seem valid on their face (face validity). Yet, each is partial and incomplete.

In isolation, there are simply too many questions left unanswered by societal level theories such as strain. Here are some examples:

- Why do most people conform despite experiencing strain (Akers, 1999)?
- What explains the large amount of conformity even among the lower class (Costello, 1997)?
- Why do some people react to strain by innovating while others react by retreating or rebelling (Bohm, 2001)?
- Do humans choose how to adapt to strain? If so, are some people more able to choose to abide by the law than others (Vold et al., 1998)?
- Why do conformists, those that generally abide by the law even in the face of strain, still commit some crimes? Is it because criminality is normal in America (Robinson, 2009)?

It is only when other factors are taken into account that questions such as these can be answered.

Like all other single-factor theories, anomie and strain theories ignore the role of other important factors, such as social control, learned techniques for crime, and the presence or absence of illegitimate opportunities (Cullen & Wright, 1997; Tittle, 1995). This is problematic because when such factors are not considered, we cannot fully understand behavior. For example, general strain is more likely to produce delinquency in the presence of other deviant peers and when youth already hold deviant values (Mazerolle & Maahs, 2000). This is a good reminder for the importance of integrated theories, as one single factor simply cannot be used to explain antisocial behavior or criminality. Similarly, it has been demonstrated that the effects of strain depend on the person's developmental stage in life (Menard, 1995); thus theories focusing on strain should be developmental in nature (see chapter 10).

Anomie and strain theories also ignore individual propensities for criminality and tend to ignore the source of goals in our culture, especially corporate marketing and so forth (Bohm, 2001). Thus, it can confidently be concluded that the factors identified in this chapter are not sufficient for explaining why any given person commits antisocial or criminal behaviors.

There are several notable relationships between anomie, strain, and biology (Walsh, 2000), all of which are ignored by anomie and strain theorists. First, conformity itself may have a genetic basis. As suggested by Walsh (2002, p. 60), humans may "cooperate and act altruistically because we tend to feel good when we do, expect to be rewarded in kind, and because such behavior confers valued social status on us by identifying us as persons who are kind, reliable, and trustworthy." If this is the case, then the fact that all people spend most of their time conforming has its roots in genetics.

Second, the negative emotionality component of Agnew's general strain theory has a very strong genetic component. Based on the complicated mathematical formulas used by scientists, it is suggested that more than 50% of negative emotionality is heritable (McGue, Bacon, & Lykken, 1993). Many of the protective factors mentioned by Agnew are also heritable, including temperament, intelligence, creativity, problem solving, self-efficacy, and self-esteem.

Third, one's place in the status hierarchy is affected by brain chemistry (i.e., neurotransmitters). According to Walsh (2002, p. 119), "serotonin levels and self-esteem, status, impulsivity, and violence are consistently found among human males ... (Raine, 1993; Virkkunen, Goldman, & Linnoila, 1996; Virkkunen & Linnoila, 1990)."

Early conflict theorists such as Bonger were aware of individual differences, including altruism and egoism, and thought they were important. Institutional anomie theory assumes the presence of a personality trait not measured, called egoism (or selfishness) by psychologists (e.g., Weigel, Hessing, & Elffers, 1999). This trait is associated with antisocial behavior. The problem with capitalism is that it generates egoism and interferes with altruism (or charity). Because the United States has a capitalistic economy, we have a lot of crime. There is no way to know what would happen with a trend toward greater socialism, but studies of socialist countries also show numerous forms of crimes, including violent atrocities against citizens by powerful rulers.

Tests of the propositions stated in this chapter have been plagued with some other problems related to the logic of the propositions. For example, studies assessing the relationship between unemployment and crime rates tend to be conducted with cross-sectional research rather than longitudinal designs. This means that the effects of unemployment on crime over time are not actually determined; rather, scholars can only say that there is a relationship between the factors at a given time (Kapuscinski, Braithwaite, & Chapman, 1998). This can lead to inconsistent findings since the effects may vary over different historical time periods (Britt, 1997). Developmental theories (discussed in chapter 10) stress the importance of studying the etiology of criminality, delinquency, and deviance as it occurs over the life course. Furthermore, findings in studies of income inequality can be confused because of the problem of multicollinearity, which suggests that the effects of inequality on crime rates depend on other factors (Vold et al., 1998).

Culture Conflict and Criminal Subcultures

Culture Conflict

As explained in the previous section on anomie and strain, as a society becomes more heterogenous, one outcome is conflict between groups. The process of *culture conflict* was explained by Thorsten Sellin in *Culture Conflict and Crime* (1938). In societies made up of various subcultural groups, conflicts are likely because groups have different *conduct norms*—rules that specify how individuals are expected to behave in given situations. *Primary cultural conflict* occurs between two different cultures. *Secondary cultural conflict* occurs between subcultures of the same culture. In this case, one group tends to have its norms, attitudes, and beliefs enacted into the law while the other groups lose. The law then may conflict with the norms, attitudes, and beliefs of the losing groups, meaning that if members of the losing groups do not change their behaviors to be consistent with the law, they will more than likely have run-ins with agents of formal social control (such as law enforcement officers).

Similarly, sociologist George Vold (1958) posited that group conflict would ultimately result in some groups not having their will enacted into law. These groups, whom Vold called *minority power groups*, would have their behaviors defined as crimes while the harmful behaviors of the majority power group would not be called crimes or would not be considered serious. Robinson (2009) shows how the criminal law is made by wealthy, powerful Caucasian men; "crimes" consist of any behaviors viewed as threatening to the status quo (Reiman, 2006). To the degree that this is true, then power relations become important for understanding why some groups get into trouble with the law and are faced with greater involvement in the criminal justice system than others (Hagan, 1989). That is, groups that are most differentiated from the mainstream will be confronted with more conflict, especially in heterogenous societies.

Furthermore, groups that lose may be left geographically isolated from the mainstream living in conditions of social disorganization. Consistent with conflict criminology, Vold et al. (1998, p. 254) predicted: "Because of the processes of criminal law enactment and enforcement ... the official crime rates of individuals and groups will tend to be inversely proportional to their political and economic power, independent of any other factors that might also influence the distribution of official crime rates (e.g., social, psychological, or biological factors affecting the behavior of offenders or the behavior of criminal justice agents)."

Similarly, critical criminologists see *inequality of power* as the primary cause of street crime. To them, street crime is a form of rebellion against the powerful classes in the capitalistic economy (Bonger, 1916). Those people who have little to offer the economy, are left marginalized, demoralized, poor, and unemployed or underemployed (Taylor, Walton, & Young, 1974). Conflict and critical criminologists each assume that society is characterized by conflict between different segments of society. According to these criminologists, these are the primary factors that produce crime:

> All behavior, including criminal behavior ... is the result of people acting in ways consistent with their social positions. Whether white-collar crime or ordinary street crime, crime is a response to a person's social situation. The reason members of the subordinate groups appear in official criminal statistics more frequently than members of dominant groups is that the latter are better able than the former to ensure that the responses of subordinate group members to their social situations will be defined and reacted to as criminal ... the amount of crime in society is a function of the extent of conflict generated by *stratification, hierarchical relationships, power differentials,* or the ability of some groups to dominate other groups in that society. Crime, in short, is caused by *relative powerlessness.* (Bohm, 2001, p. 111)

Although culture conflict studies do not assess these factors directly, they assume, as do critical and radical criminologists, that the most important criminogenic factors are located in society's political and economic institutions, which are each part of the society's overall culture.

Subcultural Theories

Related to the theory of culture conflict are *subcultural theories*. There are several theories that focus on subcultures as important for explaining antisocial behavior and criminality. Recall that subcultures are cultures within the larger culture, or groups within society that have their own unique values, groups, beliefs, attitudes, and way of life.

There are many subcultures within American society that can be identified based on ethnicity, religious affiliation, profession, or even recreational preferences. The key point to remember is that for a group to be considered a subculture it must somehow be different from the larger society. Examples of subcultural studies by criminologists and criminal justice scholars include criminality among street gangs, delinquency among male youth, and deviance and corruption among police officers.

Subcultures can develop naturally, for example, when a group of families from another country moves to the United States. They also can develop in response to shared perceptions of strain. Subcultural theories tend to focus on lower-class criminality, especially that committed by young males in gang situations. They include Albert Cohen's (1955) *theory of the middle-class measuring rod*, which posits that a form of strain called status frustration produces delinquency. Another subcultural theory is Richard Cloward and Lloyd Ohlin's (1960) *theory of differential opportunity*, which posits not only that legitimate means are structured by society, but so too are illegitimate opportunities. Walter Miller's (1958) theory of *focal concerns* is also a subcultural theory, which holds that lower-class values are distinct from the middle class and are more likely to lead to criminality. Each of these theories is briefly summarized as follows.

Middle-Class Measuring Rod

Cohen's (1955) theory aimed to explain the malicious acts of delinquent gangs. In studying working-class children, Cohen found that they were very loyal to their gangs and gave great import to short-run hedonism, feeling good here and now. Cohen explained delinquency among young males as a function of *status frustration*, being unable to achieve the goals of middle-class children. According to Cohen, teachers and others in positions of power to evaluate children evaluate them based on middle-class values, or a middle-class measuring rod. Juveniles from the lower class are not well equipped to live up to middle-class standards and thus are more likely to fail and become frustrated. These juveniles may then drop out of school and hang out with other peers in the same boat, making delinquency more likely.

Differential Opportunity

Cloward and Ohlin (1960) noted that not all youth respond to this frustration in the same manner. Some cannot respond by committing serious criminal acts because they do not have sustained, illegitimate opportunities available to them. It is only when illegitimate opportunities to make money are available that *criminal gangs* will develop. When neither legitimate nor illegitimate opportunities are available, juveniles may become frustrated and violent, and form what Cloward and Ohlin called *violent gangs*. Finally, when juveniles fail at legitimate activities and crime, they may simply withdraw into *retreatist gangs*.

Focal Concerns

Miller (1958) disagreed with the other subcultural theorists who saw lower-class values as developing in reaction to frustration with failure. Miller saw lower-class culture as distinctly different than middle-class culture, such that their allegiance to criminal values, or *focal concerns*, makes them more likely to engage in criminality. Miller posited that members of the lower class give greater value to getting into trouble, toughness, street smarts, excitement, fate, and autonomy. In essence, to lower-class youth, delinquency is relatively more normal because of their unique culture.

Main Propositions of Studies of Culture Conflict and Criminal Subcultures

- Culture conflict is associated with high crime rates.
- Status frustration produces aggression.
- An allegiance to subcultural values increases the likelihood that members of subcultures will commit acts of antisocial behavior.

Key Concepts of Studies of Culture Conflict and Criminal Subcultures

From the preceding propositions, the following concepts can be identified:
- Culture conflict
- Status frustration
- Subcultural values
- Crime rates
- Aggression
- Antisocial behavior

Box 9.3 defines the key concepts of studies of culture conflict and criminal subcultures. Scholars have used these definitions to test the main propositions of studies of culture conflict and criminal subcultures. The findings of these tests are discussed in the following section.

Box 9.3 Definitions of Key Concepts of Studies of Culture Conflict

- *Culture conflict. Nominal*—disagreement over rules that specify how individuals are expected to behave in given situations, including conflicts between two different cultural groups and between subcultures of the same culture. *Operational*—any signs of tension, disagreements, or fighting behaviors between two different cultural groups or between subcultures of the same culture, usually measured by surveys of residents and/or gang members and official crime reports.
- *Status frustration. Nominal*—feelings of strain associated with being unable to achieve goals rooted in cultural expectations. *Operational*—perceptions of strain associated with one's status as measured through self-report surveys or evaluations from others such as parents and teachers.
- *Subcultural values. Nominal*—the unique values, norms, beliefs, and attitudes of smaller groups within society. *Operational*—self-reported values, norms, beliefs, and attitudes of respondents affiliated with an identified subculture.
- *Crime rates. Nominal*—an aggregate measure of crime indicating how much crime is present in a given area such as a neighborhood, state, or nation. *Operational*—usually measured by the number of crimes known to officials such as police divided by the population of the area (crimes per capita).
- *Aggression. Nominal*—any act or behavior aimed at harming another committed with hostile intent. *Operational*—violent or property crimes, usually measured in official crime reports such as crimes known to the police and/or in self-report surveys.
- *Antisocial behavior. Nominal*—any behaviors that conflict with the prevailing norms of society and/or that are viewed as abnormal. *Operational*—any form of behavior defined as antisocial, measured by official crime reports, self-reported behaviors, or evaluations from others.

Evaluation of Culture Conflict and Subcultural Theories

In the following sections, we address culture conflict and subcultural theories of crime. We assess the empirical validity of these theories, discuss the scope of the research, as well as address the conceptual clarity and the logical adequacy of their propositions.

Empirical Validity of Studies of Culture Conflict and Subcultures

Culture Conflict

Most studies of culture conflict and behavior tend to show a positive relationship between culture conflict and official crime rates, so that conditions of culture conflict are related to higher official crime rates. This factor is rarely studied relative to other explanations of crime, in part because of its negative cultural assumptions and suspected low scope (Miller & Cohen, 1997). Culture conflict has been tested in settings where two groups reside in close proximity to one another, for example, for socially disruptive behaviors in native Alaskan villages (Lee, 1995). Scholars suggest that minor and moderate disagreements often lead to serious criminality and even sustained violence. Consider, for example, the ever escalating violence between Israelis and Palestinians in the Middle East. Significantly, while cultural differences may initiate acts of violence, it is certain that these differences are not necessary for violence to be sustained. Eventually, violence begets violence just for the sake of vengeance and retaliation.

Subcultural Theories

Subcultural studies focus almost exclusively on street crimes committed by male youths, usually in the context of gang activity. The theories on which these studies are based assume that there is something different about the norms, values, attitudes, and beliefs among subculture members that makes them more likely to violate the law.

Overall, subcultural theories enjoy little empirical support. Members of even deviant, delinquent, or criminal subcultures rarely report different values than those held by the mainstream (Kornhauser, 1978; Hagan et al., 1998). Studies of violent crimes on the street have found that they are better explained by other factors, including legitimate and illegitimate opportunities produced by normal activities of and encounters between everyday citizens (Kennedy & Baron, 1993; Kennedy & Forde, 1990a).

Despite the assertions that subcultures tell us little about antisocial behavior and criminality, studies have examined the effects of criminality produced by subcultures such as popular music subcultures (Rosenbaum & Prinsky, 1991), so-called supergangs (Baker, 1999), biker gangs (Valdez, 2001), and the hip hop underground (Ferrell, 1997, 1998). The latter studies explored the "hip hop graffiti underground—a deviant/criminal subculture organized by a marginalized population possessing few traditional economic and political resources — in successfully broadcasting itself" by painting their signs and symbols on freight trains (Ferrell, 1998, p. 15). According to Ferrell, such subcultures develop in reaction to shared perceptions of strain (in this case, being shut out of cultural spaces); their "crimes" (in this case, graffiti art) act as a means of sharing meanings and identities across spaces owned by others.

As you might guess, subcultural theories have tended to focus on subcultures perceived as deviant by mainstream thinkers, including criminologists, sociologists, anthropologists, and so forth. Not surprisingly, then, one recent study suggested that worry over subcultural diversity is predictive of both fear of crime and fear of gangs (Lane & Meeker, 2000). This finding makes sense in the context of other findings where fear is based partially on being forced to live near people who are different than you (Merry, 1981; Skogan, 1995).

Hagan et al. (1998, p. 309) summarized the debate about subcultural theories as follows:

> Criminologists frequently disagree about the meanings, origins, and influences of subcultures; about whether and in what form subcultures exist, and if so, about where subcultures come from, and the nature and extent of subcultural influences on individuals and groups. At the core of this debate are conflicting assumptions about whether subcultural crime and delinquency are wholesale rejections or subterranean reflections of core values of the dominant culture; and therefore, about whether the problems of crime and delinquency come primarily from outside, or whether they often are generated through subterranean values that come from inside the dominant culture itself.

These authors suggest that American culture is conducive to group delinquency because of its promotion of self-interest over all other values and institutions; this suggestion is more in line with the assertions of anomie and strain theories discussed earlier. Their point is significant for the influence of subcultures, however, because it shows that some subcultures are actually part of the dominant culture, including corporations who pursue profit at any cost, even through "respectable crimes" committed in the course of daily business operations (Sutherland, 1977a, 1977b). The evidence that American corporations encourage tremendous pressure (or strain) on their white-collar employees to violate ethical and even legal standards in order to succeed (Coleman, 1998; Robinson & Murphy, 2008) suggests that this is a significant criminal subculture that is often ignored by criminologists.

Scope of Culture Conflict and Subcultural Theories

Culture conflict and subcultural theorists clearly have very limited scope. Ideally, each is aimed at explaining why some groups of people supposedly commit more crimes than others; in reality, these theories tend to account for why some groups come to the attention of the criminal justice system more than others. There are obviously group dynamics that help us understand why group members have a greater allegiance to deviance than nongroup members. Gang violence, for example, only makes sense in the context of gang membership and a criminal value system. One could argue that virtually all criminality requires membership of some sort, since so little of it is committed solo. To the degree that this is true, subcultural factors seem to explain a lot of criminality. We suggest that subcultural theories as stated actually explain very little antisocial behavior, and it tends to be street crimes committed by young males in the context of gang membership.

Conceptual Clarity of Culture Conflict and Subcultural Theories

One significant problem exists with the concept of culture conflict. By definition, conflicts include numerous criminal acts. Thus, culture conflict tends to be verified by the presence of clashes between groups (e.g., gang fights). This makes the concepts tautological since culture conflict is true by definition. Culture conflict cannot be used to explain criminality when a significant part of culture conflict is crime.

Logical Adequacy of Culture Conflict and Subcultural Theories

Propositions stated by culture conflict and subcultural theorists are logically stated. The predictions made by these theories are easy to understand and seem valid on their face (face validity). Yet, because these theories were developed in isolation from one another, each is partial and incomplete. Factors from these theories can be isolated and incorporated into an integrated theory, like the one presented in chapter 10. In such an approach, the key questions become: (1) which concepts should be retained and which should be left out? and (2) which factors play a role and how much of a role do they play in antisocial behavior? These questions are addressed in chapter 10.

Some of the factors from this chapter are indeed left out, such as subcultural values. Criminal values are not necessary to commit crimes. In chapter 7, you saw that when crime is learned, it is usually through the processes of imitation and reinforcement; definitions or attitudes are less important. Of greater importance is how criminal values arise. Subcultural theories do not explain this very well, but instead merely describe how different subcultures hold different values.

Race, Class, and Gender

There is great disagreement among scholars about relationships between race, class, and criminality. Some have claimed that these extralegal factors dictate to a large degree whether a person will commit criminal acts. Others disagree and assert that people of all races and classes commit antisocial behaviors; it's just that our system of criminal justice disproportionately focuses on the acts of racial minorities and poor people, meaning that they will be most likely to be identified as criminals.

There is no question that the criminal justice system disproportionately arrests, convicts, and punishes poor people and racial and ethnic minorities (Robinson, 2009). This does not mean, however, that there is an association between race, class, and criminality; it may signify some form of discrimination against relatively powerless people. According to Walker, Spohn, and Delone (2007), discrimination against racial minorities and poor people has "a direct impact on crime and criminal justice" and accounts for many of the racial disparities in the criminal justice system. One study by Mosher (2001), for example, reported that racial composition of cities is a good predictor of drug arrests, regardless of the level of crime. Other research shows strong evidence of increased police brutality and civil rights complaints against minorities and people living in areas of inequality (Holmes, 2000; Lanza-Kaduce & Greenleaf, 2000). Disproportionate contact with the police (such as drug arrests) may actually promote further criminality by creating criminogenic conditions such as single-parent families, greater poverty, and so forth (Hagan & Coleman, 2001). And not to be forgotten, dozens of studies have now confirmed the existence of racial profiling—the use of race by police to pull over and search drivers and their cars (Barlow and Barlow, 2002; Batton and Kadleck, 2004; Bostaph, 2007; Buerger and Farrell, 2002; Engel and Calnon, 2004; Gross and Barnes, 2002; Harris, 1999; Lamberth, 1997; Langan et al., 2001; Lundman, 2004; Lundman & Kaufman, 2003; Meehan and Ponder, 2002; Peruche and Plant, 2006; Petrocelli, Piquero, and Smith, 2003; Romero, 2006; Schafer et al., 2006; Tomaskovic-Devey et al., 2006; Warren et al., 2006).

Race

According to Walker et al. (2007), race refers to the "major biological divisions of mankind," including Caucasian, Negroid, and Mongoloid. It has long been held in the social sciences that it is difficult to differentiate races of people based on biological characteristics related to behavior (Yinger, 1994). Sociologists say race is really a social construct determined by politically and culturally dominant groups in society (Walker et al., 2000, p. 5). However, according to Wright (2009), there are indeed meaningful biological differences between races, including genetic differences. Still, he does acknowledge that there is more genetic variation within races than between them.

Social Class

Social class is not an exact term, but refers more or less to resources owned or income earned per year. The US Census Bureau collects and presents data with regard to measures such as income and social class. After determining income level of Americans, people are placed into quintiles (fifths) based on how much money they earn. Then, based on household characteristics, people are considered poor if they do not make more than a designated amount of money each year. For 2007, the poverty threshold for a family of four was $21,203. Thus, to be considered poor, a family of four must make less than this amount. Research demonstrates that the federal poverty measure does not adequately capture the true amount of poor people in the United States, because the measure is based on an old formula that does not take into account current financial obligations of families (such as child care and health care). The true number of poor people based on those that do not earn a living wage is far more than the 12.5% poverty rate reported by the US Census Bureau (Robinson, 2009).

Gender

Finally, gender refers to differences between the sexes based on both biology and social factors. Although the US Census Bureau as well as most criminal justice agencies collect and present data with regard to sex (i.e., male or female), this hardly captures the meaning that sociologists and other social scientists attribute to gender, that it really refers to the socially constructed roles that people in society consider appropriate for men and women.

Relationships between Race, Social Class, and Gender

There is an intimate relationship between race and social class in the United States. Specifically, racial and ethnic minorities are disproportionately likely to be poor and be exposed to harmful environmental conditions. For example, nearly seven out of every eight people in America's poorest areas are minorities. In these areas, there is far greater despair and deterioration than in the suburbs and rural areas of the country (Beckett & Sasson, 2000, p. 37). Walker et al. (2000, pp. 62–65) explained the differences in social class standing between racial and ethnic groups on the basis of income, wealth, employment, and poverty rates. Income (a measure of how much money a family earns in a year) for African Americans is about 60% of that for Caucasians. Wealth (a measure of all things accumulated) is nearly 11 times lower for African Americans than for Caucasians. Meanwhile, the unemployment rate is more than twice as high for African Americans than for Caucasians. Poverty rates are also higher for African Americans than for Caucasians. Finally, child poverty rates are almost three times higher for African Americans than for Caucasians.

While Caucasians make up most people living in poverty, this is only because whites make up the majority of those living in the country. The rate of poverty is higher for minorities, particularly African Americans, who account for only 12% of the general population. In 2007, poverty rates were highest for blacks (24.5%) than Asians (10.2%) and whites (8.2%) (US Census, 2008). Further, black households have the lowest median income ($33,916), versus $66,103 for Asian households, $54,920 for white households, and $38,679 for Hispanic households (US Census, 2008).

Excluding biological arguments, there are essentially two competing explanations as to why African Americans are more likely to suffer from poverty than Caucasians. According to Smith (1995, p. 107), *cultural perspectives* "emphasize the values, beliefs, attitudes, and lifestyles" of the poor while *structural perspectives* "emphasize enduring features of the economic and social systems." That is, one view sees the problem as coming from within the people who are poor, whereas the other sees the problem as emanating from outside of poor people.

Even if there is a culture unique to people of color or the poor (meaning that they would make up subcultures in America), it may emerge from the U.S. capitalist economy (Lewis, 1966). Such is the claim by *Marxist criminologists*, who hold that crime is a reaction to oppression and domination at the bottom of the capitalist economy. Lynch and Stretesky (2001) outlined the significant criminogenic factors in Marxist terms. Unemployment is a key factor in accounting for this culture or way of life, which has always been higher for

African Americans and Hispanics than Caucasians. Unemployment rates are associated with rates of murder, suicide, mental illness, divorce, separation, child abuse, and drug abuse (Smith, 1995, pp. 131–132). Areas with higher rates of male joblessness are also found to have higher rates of delinquency (Hoffman, 2003). It is also related to female-headed household status (De-Fronzo, 1996), itself a correlate of higher crime rates.

Cultural explanations of poverty ignore structural correlates of poverty. As explained by Kushnick and Jennings (1999, p. 1), poverty is produced by larger structural factors such as the "increasing imbalance in the distribution of wealth, with the rich continually becoming richer; the unbridled mobility of capital, both in finance and in production; and the prevalence of low wages coupled with levels of relatively high unemployment of certain groups."

Anomie and strain theorists would claim that the poor have been forced either to retreat into unemployment and drug use or to innovate by selling black market goods (e.g., drugs). When the poor turn to illegal activity to tilt the scales in their favor, they are then more likely to have run-ins with the law. *Radical criminologists* assert that the greater the gap between the rich and the poor, the more crime we should expect.

> However, it is important to understand that ... the destructive effects of capitalism, such as crime, are not caused directly by income or property inequality or poverty per se. Rather, crime is a product of the political economy that, in capitalist societies, encourages an individualistic competition among wealthy people and among poor people and between rich and poor people ... and the practice of taking advantage of other people ... The class struggle and exploitation, in turn produce crime, income or property inequality, poverty, and many of the other problems that are characteristic of a capitalist society ... crime in capitalist societies is often a rational response to the circumstances in which people find themselves in the individualistic and competitive struggle to acquire material wealth. (Bohm, 2001, p. 115)

This means that institutions in U.S. society produce criminogenic processes. These processes help us understand crime rate differences between people of different races and classes.

Relationships between social class and gender have also been identified (McCall, 2001; Grusky, 2008). For example, it is widely acknowledged that women earn less per hour than men even for the same jobs, which is to say roughly $.75 for every dollar earned by men (Jacobsen, 2007). Women are more likely than men to be poor, and are also more likely to be raising children in poverty.

Main Propositions of Race, Class, and Gender Studies

The most telling propositions concerning race and class that have been subjected to empirical tests include:

- People of color are more likely than Caucasians to commit criminal acts.
- People of the lower class are more likely than people of the middle class and upper class to commit criminality.
- Unemployment is associated with high crime rates.
- Income inequality is associated with high crime rates.
- Men are more likely to be engaged in criminality than women.

Key Concepts of Race and Class Studies

From the preceding propositions, the following concepts are identified:

- People of color
- Caucasians
- Lower-class citizens
- Middle-class citizens
- Upper-class citizens
- Unemployment
- Income inequality
- Men
- Women
- Criminality
- Crime rates

Box 9.4 defines the key concepts of studies on race and class. Scholars have used these definitions to test the main propositions of race and class studies. The findings of these tests are discussed in the following section.

Box 9.4 Definitions of Key Concepts on Race and Class

- *People of color. Nominal*—racial and ethnic minorities, including but not limited to African Americans and Hispanics. *Operational*—self-reported affiliation with a particular racial or ethnic group, such as African American or Hispanic.
- *Caucasians. Nominal*—members of society who are not racial or ethnic minorities. *Operational*—self-reported affiliation with the Caucasian or White race.

- *Lower-class citizens. Nominal*—people who are unemployed, under-employed, or employed but who earn little money annually. *Operational*—making less income per year than a specific amount, usually set by the federal government for a family of four.
- *Middle-class citizens. Nominal*—people who are usually employed and who earn an adequate amount of income. *Operational*—making a specified amount of money each year so that annual income is relatively close to the median American income, usually specified by the federal government.
- *Upper-class citizens. Nominal*—people who are usually employed and who earn more money than they generally need. *Operational*—making a specified amount of money each year so that annual income is much more than the median American income, usually specified by the federal government.
- *Unemployment. Nominal*—not being employed in a legal job full-time or part-time. *Operational*—the number of people per capita who are not employed but who are seeking employment, as measured by government statistics.
- *Income inequality. Nominal*—the gap in job pay between the poor and wealthy classes. *Operational*—the dollar figure that separates the average income of the wealthy from the average income of the poor, usually measured by a composite index of wealth owned, mostly attributable to annual household income.
- *Men. Nominal*—male human beings. *Operational*—human beings who identify themselves as men.
- *Women. Nominal*—female human beings. *Operational*—human beings who identify themselves as women.
- *Criminality. Nominal*—committing any act that violates the criminal law. *Operational*—the number of times a person is arrested, is convicted in court for a violation of the criminal law, and/or self-reports violating the law.
- *Crime rates. Nominal*—an aggregate measure of crime indicating how much crime is present in a given area such as a neighborhood, state, or nation. *Operational*—usually measured by the number of crimes known to officials such as police divided by the population of the area (crimes per capita).

Evaluation of Race, Class, and Gender Studies

In the following sections, we address studies of race, class, gender and crime. We assess the empirical validity of these approaches, discuss the scope of the research, as well as address the conceptual clarity and the logical adequacy of their propositions.

Empirical Validity of Race, Class, and Gender Studies

Hundreds of studies have assessed relationships between criminality and race, social class, and gender. These studies do tend to show that people of color, poor people, and men commit more street crime than you would expect given their percentage of the general population (Robinson, 2009). Remember from chapter 1, however, that other forms of antisocial behavior (such as elite deviance) are much more harmful to Americans than street crime. These acts tend to be committed primarily by wealthy Caucasian men, if for no other reason than these are the types of acts they have more opportunity to commit (recall the theory of differential opportunity discussed earlier). Another way to think of it is that wealthy people don't have to resort to acts of street crime in order to achieve their goals; they have other opportunities to achieve their goals, both legitimate and illegitimate. And for various reasons, white men are more likely to be wealthy.

Official Data Sources

One way to assess whether people of color and members of the lower classes commit more criminality is to examine the various sources of data available to criminologists. Major sources of crime data include the Uniform Crime Reports (UCR), the National Criminal Victimization Survey (NCVS), and self-report studies. The UCR is a measure of crimes known to the police, crimes cleared by arrests, and arrests. Official rates of offending from the UCR are in fact higher in poor, minority communities and for African Americans generally (Kennedy, 1997; Tonry, 1995). Yet, relying on the UCR and other such official statistics for discovering offender characteristics is flawed and can create misconceptions about who is dangerous and who should be feared. There is evidence, for example, that victims of violent crime are more likely to report their victimizations to the police when the offenders were African Americans (Hindelang, 1978).

According to Miller (1997, p. 29): "Relying on 'experience' emanating from the justice system is dicey even in the best of circumstances. Its rituals and procedures distort social realities and feed stereotypes at virtually every step."

Figure 9.3 Arrests by Race

Crime	White	Black
Violent crime	59%	39%
Murder	41%	57%
Rape	65%	33%
Robbery	42%	56%
Assault	63%	35%
Property crime	68%	29%
Burglary	69%	29%
Theft	69%	29%
Car theft	63%	35%
Arson	76%	22%
Drug abuse violation	64%	35%

Source: Sourcebook of Criminal Justice Statistics [On-line]. Available: *http://www.albany.edu/sourcebook/pdf/t4102006.pdf*

The UCR is a more valid measure of police experience than crime, because it measures the behavior of police rather than criminal offenders; therefore, it is not surprising that over 40% of individuals who are arrested for felonies are not prosecuted or have their cases dismissed at first appearance (Miller, 1997).

UCR arrest statistics show that African Americans are overrepresented among arrestees for virtually every type of street crime. Figure 9.3 shows arrest statistics for various crimes by race. These statistics tend to create myths about who is dangerous and guilty. If we relied on arrest statistics to develop composites of "dangerous classes," we would not get an accurate picture of those that most threaten us. As noted by Walker et al. (2000, p. 37), "the picture of the typical offender that emerges from official arrest statistics may be racially distorted. If police target enforcement efforts in minority communities or concentrate on crime committed by racial minorities, then obviously racial minorities will be overrepresented in arrest statistics."

Take the crimes of murder and robbery, for example. Murder is but one way of killing people. Robbery is but one form of taking property. If you examine these statistics only, you see that African Americans, who make up only 12% of the US population, commit about half of the murders and robberies in any given year. From this you could rightly conclude that blacks are overrepresented among murderers and robbers. However, it would be wrong to conclude from this that blacks are more dangerous than whites. Why? Because there are other forms of killing and property-taking beside murder and robbery, and these forms are overwhelmingly committed by whites. Such acts would include deaths due to defective products and workplace safety violations. We showed in chapter 1 that these acts are more dangerous and costly than street crimes such as murder and robbery. They also tend to be committed by whites.

The NCVS is a measure of self-reported victimizations, including crimes reported to the police and crimes not reported to the police. The NCVS is generally thought to be a more valid measure of criminal behavior than the UCR. The NCVS shows that households headed by African Americans have higher victimizations than Caucasian households. Also, African Americans are more likely than Caucasians to suffer from personal criminal victimizations. Finally, one's lifetime risk of being victimized by some violent street crimes is highly correlated with one's race. When it comes to being victimized by the crime of robbery, the African American risk is about 50% while the Caucasian risk is about 25%. Approximately 50% of American homicides in 2006 were African Americans, even though they only make up 12% of the U.S. population. For African American males, the risk of homicide is eight times the rate of Caucasian males. And for young males, the risk is ten times higher for African Americans than for Caucasians. African American males, who make up only 6% of the population, consist of about 20% of the nation's homicides (Walker et al., 2007).

Similarly, according to the Bureau of Justice Statistics (2009), property crime victimization rates were higher for blacks (186 of 1,000 black households) than whites (157 of 1,000 white households). Specifically, burglaries were experienced by 42 of 1,000 black households and 29 of 1,000 white households, the rates of motor vehicle theft were 15 per 1,000 black households and 7 per 1,000 white households, and the theft rate was 128 per 1,000 black households and 121 per 1,000 white households.

Figure 9.4 illustrates trends in violent crimes according to the NCVS. While trends for whites and blacks have declined significantly in recent years, the figure shows clearly that the rate of victimization has always been higher from African Americans than for Caucasians. Since most street crimes are intraracial in nature, logic would dictate that African American people are disproportionately committing street crimes against their own households and persons. Yet, higher victimization rates are partially a function of social class because household victimization rates are highest in inner cities. Additionally, these numbers only refer to street crimes.

These government statistics show that people of color commit more street crime than one would logically expect given their proportion of the population. For example, the NCVS also shows that victims report a higher percentage of victimizations at the hands of African Americans than one would expect

Figure 9.4 Trends in Violence by Race

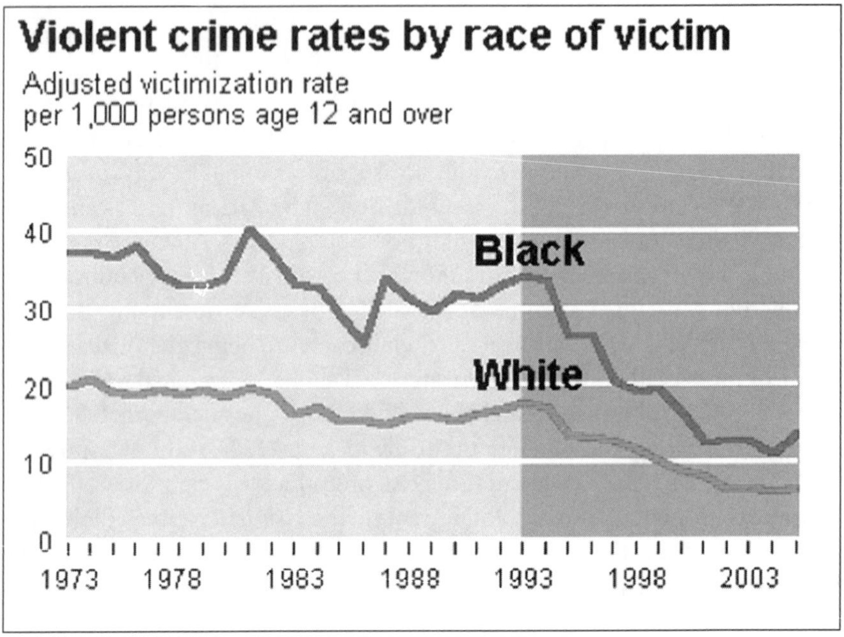

Violent crime rates by race of victim

Adjusted victimization rate
per 1,000 persons age 12 and over

Source: Bureau of Justice Statistics [On-line]. Available: *http://ojp.usdoj.gov/bjs/glance/race.htm*

given their percentage of the population (Kennedy, 1997, p. 23): "African Americans are overrepresented as offenders for all of the offenses" of the NCVS (Walker et al., 2000, p. 42). The validity of NCVS data in this regard is questionable, since the NCVS researchers must rely on victims' perceptions of their offenders (Robinson, 2009).

As for gender, women are less likely to be victimized by crime, less likely to commit it, less likely to be arrested, less likely to be convicted, less likely to be sentenced to prison or jail, and generally are sentenced to less time than men (Robinson, 2009). Starting with victimization, the Bureau of Justice Statistics (2009) states that rates of violent victimization are higher for men in every category except sexual assault. Figure 9.5 illustrates trends in violent crimes according to the NCVS. While trends for men and women have declined significantly in recent years, the figure shows clearly that the rate of victimization has always been higher from men than for women.

Arrest data show that men are disproportionately arrested for every crime, including corporate and white-collar offenses. There are likely social and bio-

Figure 9.5 Trends in Violence by Gender

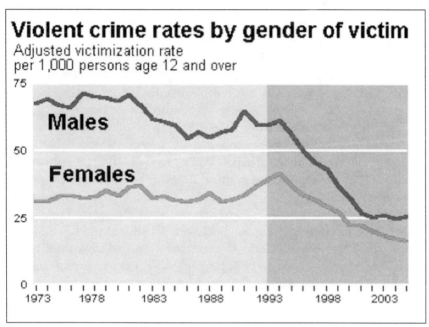

Source: Bureau of Justice Statistics [On-line]. Available: *http://ojp.usdoj.gov/bjs/glance/vsx2. htm*

logical reasons for the fact that men commit more violent and property crimes than women. Social reasons pertain to the impact of early and later socialization, as suggested by *social learning theories.* Biological reasons pertain to hormonal and body differences (e.g., see Walsh & Beaver, 2009).

In terms of criminal justice processing, police, courts, and corrections are generally less punitive toward women. This may be due to what Belknap (1996: 69–70) calls the *chivalry or paternalism hypothesis.* For example, even though women commit more than 10% of all murders in any given year, they make up less than 2% of all people on death row and 1% of all executions (Robinson, 2008).

There is also some evidence of what Belknap calls the *evil woman hypothesis,* which posits that women will be treated more harshly for similar crimes than men. Morgan-Sharp (1999: 384) suggests that the criminal justice network is tougher on women when they "do not adhere to prescribed gender roles." This suggests that women may be reacted to more harshly by courts when they do things that are not generally expected of them (Chesney-Lind and Pasko, 2004).

Self-Report Studies

Self-report studies provide some unique insight into criminal behavior by assessing the degree to which respondents admit to engaging in criminal behaviors. Self-report studies question the disparities found in official criminal justice statistics such as the UCR (e.g., see Pope, 1979). Although the UCR may suggest that African Americans commit a disproportionate amount of crime because they are more likely to get arrested by the police, self-report studies do not show such patterns. Instead, self-report studies show rates of offending in middle-class minority communities are equivalent to those in the general population. Earlier self-report studies showed little or no differences in self-reported delinquent and criminal behavior between different groups (Robinson, 2009).

Since early studies typically assessed minor acts of delinquency, more recent studies assess more serious criminal behaviors. According to Tittle and Meier (1990), studies assessing relationships between social class and crime show "mixed results" and according to Akers (1996, p. 127): "Self-report studies find class and race variations in criminal and delinquent behavior, but they are not as great as class and race differences in officially arrested, convicted, and/or imprisoned populations." So, when unemployed citizens are disproportionately found in incarcerated populations (Chiricos & Bales, 1991), it is not likely due to their increased involvement with criminal behavior. Nor can the overrepresentation of African Americans in the criminal justice system be explained solely by their higher involvement in criminal behavior. There is some evidence that African Americans tend to underreport their involvement in criminality (e.g., see Hindelang, Hirschi, & Weis, 1981; Robinson, 2009), but no one knows for sure whether this is true.

One notable study related to institutional anomie theory (Cernokovich, Giordano, & Rudolph, 2000) reported that of a sample of Americans, African Americans were more committed to the American Dream than Caucasians:

> Our data indicate that African Americans maintain a very strong commitment to the American Dream. Blacks report higher levels of commitment to economic success than do their White counterparts and indicate that they are prepared to work harder and sacrifice more to realize them. Even though the young Black adults in our study report low incomes and are more likely to be unemployed than are Whites, they continue to maintain a very strong commitment to the American Dream. Such a commitment in the face of economic adversity may be due to the role of economic and material success as symbols of success—they function as tangible indicators for many African Americans

that, despite the many disadvantages to which they are subjected, they have in fact "made it." (p. 272)

In this particular study of race, crime, and strain, the authors found that strain did not account for criminality of the subjects. In fact, respondents with a lower desire for success were found to commit more deviance, whereas a high desire for success was more likely to ensure conformity. This calls into question not only strain theory but also social control theory (discussed in chapter 7), as well as our commonly held belief that blacks are more criminal than whites.

Strains Associated with Poverty

In terms of social class, it is certainly logical to assert that living in conditions of poverty ought to be associated with an increased risk for criminality. There are three main areas of research that address this logical assertion: (1) research that assesses the relationship between social class and crime directly, (2) research that assesses unemployment and crime, and (3) research that examines economic inequality and crime.

First, living in poverty has been associated with increased rates of depression and other forms of mental illnesses, as well as joblessness, family disruption, and community instability (Pearson, 2000). In addition, the effects of poverty on children can be dramatic because "children born into poverty have an increased risk of neurological developmental delays because of malnutrition, less access to medical attention, low levels of physical and mental stimulation, a greater probability of abuse and neglect, and a generally unsafe environment" (Walsh, 2002, p. 96; also see Shore, 1996; Vila, 1997). Criminologists have also claimed that the poor have less contact with proper role models and less ability to participate in controlling institutions such as community groups (Skogan, 1990; Wilson, 1987). Furthermore, poor children are more likely to come from single-parent families who have less ability to supervise their children, and the children may suffer from worse nutrition and have less access to educational, vocational, and recreational opportunities. Criminological theories such as social disorganization (discussed in chapter 8), anomie and strain, and social bonding (discussed in chapter 7) have historically attributed such environmental conditions to increased risks for criminality and to higher crime rates (Bohm, 2001; Vold et al., 1998).

For all these reasons, we might expect poor people to commit more crime than people in the middle and upper classes. Yet, according to Tittle and Meier (1990, p. 292): "Research published since 1978, using both official and self-reported data suggests ... that there is no pervasive relationship between [social class] and delinquency." Jensen and Thompson (1990, p. 1021) similarly concluded that "class, no matter how defined, contributes little to explaining variation in self-reports of common delinquency." If true, this means acts committed by juveniles are not attributable to social class.

In terms of adult crime, Vold et al. (1998, p. 108) wrote that:

> If crime is caused by poverty ... there should be more crime in places and at times where there are more poor people. Thus ... studies have compared times of economic depression with times of economic prosperity, and wealthy areas of a country with poor areas, to see if there are any systematic differences in their crime rates. Later studies looked at whether there is any systematic relationship between crime rates and unemployment rates, and whether crime is associated with economic inequality, that is with poverty that exists next to wealth.

According to these authors, there is still disagreement about findings and their meaning.

Poverty, Wealth, and Crime

A great number of these studies have assessed the relationship between poverty and violent crimes such as homicide. These studies should find a clear relationship between poverty and homicide since killings on the street are about the only kind of killings called murder. However, studies do not report consistent findings. Studies addressing other types of crimes have also found inconsistent results, thus Vold et al. (1998, p. 122) concluded that "the direct effect of poverty on crime is weak and probably is conditional on other community factors." One study by Patterson (1991) reported a positive relationship between levels of absolute poverty and neighborhood rates of violent and property crimes.

One very interesting study examined the relationship between financial resources and delinquency (Wright et al., 2001). Specifically, the study tested the hypothesis that resources of adolescents acquired through work and parental allowance would lead to increases in self-reported delinquency and drug use. Wright et al. found a modest relationship between having money in adolescence and some acts of delinquency and drug use. Interestingly, the relationship holds true, even after controlling for many other criminogenic factors. The authors suggested that having money is associated with greater dating behaviors and having more friends. This increases the likelihood of being influenced by deviant peers. This finding, supported by similar research, raises serious questions about the suspected relationship between low social class and crime. Furthermore, the authors found that desire to have money was not associated with increased delinquency or drug use, raising some question about the validity of strain theory for explaining delinquency.

This particular study is important for at least three other reasons. First, Wright et al. also found that low self-control (discussed in chapter 7) was a significant predictor of delinquency and drug use, as suggested by Gottfredson and Hirschi (1990). According to the authors, a better economy, spurred in part by corporate efforts to target and spur adolescent spending, will logically lead to more delinquency in society; thus corporate exploitation of adolescent low self-control may be an important factor for explaining why kids get into trouble with the law. This study suggested that money gives teenagers access to the more disreputable side of adolescence. Second, the study suggested that behaviors begun in adolescence may follow kids into adulthood, as behavior is self-reinforcing and likely to be repeated once it is started and rewarded. Finally, despite the findings that adolescents place great value on having money, the study also cited evidence that adults value more than just money, including the importance of family life.

Robinson and Murphy (2008) show clearly that wealthy people also commit an enormous amount of crime. Further, the crimes they tend to commit are much more harmful to society than street crimes committed by the poor. For example, fraud causes losses in the hundreds of billions of dollars every year, compared to less than $20 billion for all thefts. Further, deaths produced by defective products and hazardous working conditions dwarf all deaths caused by murder every year (see chapter 1).

Unemployment and Crime

In terms of unemployment, people who are unemployed and cannot find work may commit property and drug crimes for income. Singh (1991, p. 509) claimed that: "Unemployment and growing isolation from the mainstream economy have led to unwed parenting, dependency, lawlessness, joblessness, and school failure." The research into unemployment, however, is less clear. Some suggest that there is a weak relationship between crime and unemployment, including for homicide (Land, McCall, & Cohen, 1990). Chiricos (1987) reviewed nearly 70 studies of unemployment and crime and found generally consistent positive relationships; this effect was seen when community rates of unemployment and crime were studied rather than national rates. Land et al. (1990) noted that at lower levels of analysis such as the community level, the relationship was generally positive. More recent research has also found similar results; for example, Witt, Clarke, and Fielding (1999) reported positive relationships between male unemployment and four property crime rates.

The most significant problem about unemployment is that it has disproportionate consequences for people in the nation's inner cities (Wilson, 1984), where we also see the highest street crime rates. This does not suggest that the people there are somehow different, as subcultural theories would suggest; instead, structural disadvantages accumulate there, including poverty, family disruption, poor health care, and so forth. The criminal behaviors are not unique to ghettos and thus they cannot be unique to the people who live there. Interestingly, getting arrested also increases the likelihood of later unemployment (Hagan, 1993). Bushway (1998) suggested that an arrest can lead to diminished employment possibilities, consistent with the labeling perspective discussed in chapter 8.

Income Inequality and Crime

Some research shows a positive relationship between income inequality and crime, although findings for different types of crime are inconsistent (Witt et al., 1999). According to Hsieh and Pugh (1993), who reviewed more than 30 studies assessing relationships between poverty, income inequality, and violent crimes, almost all of the studies found positive relationships between income inequality and homicide, assault, robbery, and rape. Other research into income inequality has produced similar findings (Fowles & Merva, 1996; Hagan & Peterson, 1994). A review of 45 studies by Vieraitis (2000) described relationships between income inequality, poverty, and violent crimes: (1) inequality and homicide is typically positive, (2) poverty and homicide is typically positive, and (3) inequality and assault is typically positive. Other studies have shown positive results as well, but they are not *statistically significant*, meaning the authors could not assure that their findings were not due to random chance.

Despite these apparently consistent findings, neither homicide rates (as reflected in the UCR) nor violent crime rates (from the NCVS) have increased as the gap between the upper and lower classes has widened. This suggests that the relationship between poverty, income inequality, and criminality is not as straightforward as posited by scholars. For example, the past 20 years have produced higher incomes for the top 40% of wage earners in the United States, whereas the bottom 60% actually earn a smaller share of the total national income today (Harrigan, 2000). Since 1974, the wealthy have captured more of the national income, while the rest of us have received less. In fact, the top 1% of the wealthy now own an astounding 40% of the nation's wealth. In 1974, the average CEO of America's 200 largest companies earned 35 times as much as its average worker, but in 1990, the average CEO earned 150 times as much (Frank, 1994).

According to Robinson and Murphy (2008), CEO salaries are outlandishly high relative to the average employee. In 2006, the average CEO of a major company (earning at least $1 billion in annual revenue) was paid an average of

$42,400 every day, or $10.98 million per year. This is approximately 262 times what the average worker at these companies made, which was $41,861 in 2005. Stated differently, the average worker made about $400 less for an entire year's salary than the average CEO made every single day of the year! Further, the salaries of these CEOs were more than 364 times that of the average American worker.

From 2000 through 2005, CEO salaries grew 84 percent. During this same time, workers' salaries fell approximately 0.3 percent. In other words, the gap between the rich and the poor—called *income inequality*—is growing. And the gap in salary does not fully capture the true disparities between the highest paid and the lowest paid employees because it does not include the numerous perks received by CEOs. In 2006, the CEOs of America's top twenty companies were paid an average of $438,342 in perks annually, not including pension benefits.

In 2006, CEOs at major US corporations earned an average of $1.3 million in pension gains. Amazingly, only about 59 percent of American households led by a forty-five- to a fifty-four-year-old and 36 percent of households headed by individuals sixty-five years and older report having any retirement account; the annual growth and total amount of such accounts is quite small by comparison to CEOs.

The top twenty highest paid CEOs earned an average of $36.4 million in 2006, which is "38 times more than the 20 highest-paid leaders in the non-profit sector and 204 times more than the 20 highest-paid generals in the U.S. military." Yet, this pales in comparison to the top twenty private equity and hedge fund managers, who made an average of $657.5 million per year in 2006—22,255 times the average salary of American workers!

Because of an aging population, a better economy, the waning of turf wars over illicit drug markets, and increases in probation and incarceration, street crime has not increased despite these conditions. Over the long term, we'd expect this growth in income inequality to produce higher rates of violent crime.

Because of changes in the tax codes and due to business practices such as downsizing, or mass layoffs (Robinson & del Carmen, 1999), America is becoming more and more unequal in terms of income. Downsizing also obviously affects unemployment. One study reported that a decline in manufacturing jobs in the nation's 100 largest cities between 1970 and 1990 not only resulted in greater unemployment, but also was related to increases in official crime rates (White, 1999). White (1999, p. 89) hypothesized about what he might find:

> When manufacturing companies reduce the number of their employees or depart from a city, fewer stable, higher-paying jobs are available to workers without high school diplomas or college degrees.

These residents then must accept lower-paying jobs that are less likely to provide benefits such as health insurance. Alternatively they may turn to an adaptive lifestyle that involves a combination of part-time work, part-time welfare, and part-time crime. The massive reduction in high-paying blue-collar jobs thus reduces the overall living standards in the city. Fewer jobs are available for these residents; if the skilled manufacturing jobs are replaced, they are replaced by lower-paying jobs, often part-time jobs without benefits.

The result of these processes should be higher unemployment, higher poverty, and higher economic crimes. In this study, absolute poverty turned out not to be related to official crime rates, but a decline in manufacturing jobs and increases in unemployment were related to increased rates of burglary, drug offenses, and robberies; declines in manufacturing jobs were also related to higher rates of aggravated assault.

Some research has shown that countries with higher levels of inequality also have higher rates of murder (Land, McCall, & Cohen, 1990; Messner & Tardiff, 1986; Sampson, 1995). Additionally, about one half of all murders in the United States occur in large cities, which are inhabited by less than one fifth of the population. Within these cities, rates of homicide are 20 times the national average in areas where poverty is highly concentrated (Sheman et al., 1997). This suggests that the relationship between poverty and violent crime is strongest in the nation's inner cities where poverty is most concentrated (Hagan, 1994).

A recent study of homicide trends in 83 US cities with populations of more than 100,000 people found that resource deprivation was associated with homicide. Thus, cities with more families living in poverty, greater income inequality, reductions in family income, as well as other factors such as single parents and population turnover, had higher rates of homicide (McCall, Parker, & MacDonald, 2007).

Scope of Race, Class, and Gender Studies

Studies examining the relationship between race, class, gender and crime also have a very limited scope. People of one skin color are no more likely to commit acts of antisocial behavior than people of another skin color. Poor people are no more likely to commit acts of antisocial behavior than middle-class or wealthy people. What seems to be best accounted for by race and class features is the type of crimes that are committed by each; economic conditions largely determine the type of crime one commits based on the legitimate and illegitimate opportunities one is afforded (Vold et al., 1998, p. 168). Poor people, who are disproportionately likely to be members of racial minorities, are more likely to commit street crimes than the nonpoor. Concomitantly, wealthy people, who are disproportionately likely to be Caucasians, are more likely to commit white-collar deviance than the nonwealthy. Finally, middle-class people are most likely to commit the types of crimes where opportunities are greatest for them, typically in their occupations. Factors related to social class, including unemployment and income inequality, tend to best explain community differences in official crime rates, most notably violent crime such as homicide (Vieraitis, 2000), suggesting that police may become alerted to potential problem populations by policy makers.

There is little doubt that there is a relationship between a society's economic institutions and its crime rates, even violent crime rates. As explained by Agnew (1999, p. 124), areas with higher crime rates

> tend to be low in economic status, with economic status being measured in terms of such variables as income, poverty, unemployment, welfare, occupation, education, inequality, owner-occupied dwellings, and substandard housing. Economic deprivation, in fact, is perhaps the most distinguishing characteristic of high-crime communities (see, especially, Land, McCall, & Cohen, 1990; Sampson, Raudenbush, & Earls, 1997). High-crime communities also tend to be large in size and high in population density, overcrowding, residential mobility (particularly poor communities), and percentage non-White. Although these variables usually have significant zero-order correlations with community crime rates, their effect on crime is sometimes reduced to insignificance in multivariate analyses. A key variable that partly mediates the relationship between at least certain of these variables and community crime rates is family disruption, usually measured by divorce/separation rates and/or female-headed households (see Sampson, 1995).

In terms of violent crime rates, Currie (1997) identified several factors within market societies that produce higher rates: "the progressive destruction of livelihood"; "the growth of extremes of economic inequality and material deprivation"; "the withdrawal of public services and supports, especially for families and children"; "the erosion of informal and communal networks of mutual support, supervision, and care"; "the spread of materialistic, neglectful, and 'hard' culture" which includes "brutal individual competition and consumption over the values of community, contribution, and productive work"; "the unregulated marketing of the technology of violence"; and "the weakening of social and political alternatives." How these factors contribute to the behavior of specific individuals is not clear unless social process factors are also taken into account.

Conceptual Clarity of Race, Class, and Gender Approaches

People generally understand what race, class, and gender mean, yet measuring them in studies has proven more difficult. Although absolute measures of poverty, such as annual household income, are available, scholars must rely on self-reported measures of race to study the effects of race on crime. Further, although numerous sources of statistical information with regard to criminal involvement and criminal justice involvement of men and women are available, many social scientists take issue with the notion that sex (i.e., male or female) is equivalent to gender. To the degree that gender refers to roles played in society and/or the way people view themselves, variables related to gender are much harder to measures.

As for race, *racial formation theory* shows that race is not a static and fixed concept (Omi & Winant, 1994). The emergence of a modern conception of race did not occur until the rise of Europe and the arrival of Europeans in the Americas. Early European settlers found individuals in the Americas who looked and acted differently. The people native to the Americas challenged the "pre-existing conceptions of the origins and possibilities of the human species" (Omi & Winant, 1994, p. 61). The discovery of these new people led "white" settlers to justify exploiting and enslaving "natives" and eventually African slaves through the religious justification that Europeans were children of God, and chosen to bring Christianity to "others."

Over time religious justifications for racial differences gave way to scientific ones (Omi & Winant, 1994). These scientific explanations focused upon supposedly biological differences, ranging from cranial capacity to social Darwinism, which posited whites as more intellectually developed and having a superior culture. Today scientific explanations for racial difference are giving way to social and political explanations. As a result of prior efforts and struggles, a current consensus has been reached that race is not biologically given but a socially constructed way of differentiating humans beings from one another (Omi & Winant, 1994).

Races do not correspond to a distinct biological or genetic trait, they are instead a product of societies need to create categories of people for reasons, that are often disingenuous. People with common origins do share certain physical traits, but these traits constitute an extremely small amount of humans' genetic makeup, and we are all quite common despite the physical difference of skin color.

Logical Adequacy of Race, Class, and Gender Approaches

Propositions related to social class, race, and gender are logically stated. The predictions made by these theories are easy to understand and seem valid on their face (face validity). Yet, because these theories were developed in isolation from one another, each is partial and incomplete.

More recent theoretical approaches recognize the interplay between demographic factors such as race, class, and gender. For example, *intersectionality theory* holds that discrimination and privilege result from the intersecting effects of societal signifiers (Collins, 2000). A *social signifier* is any characteristic or trait that identifies an individual within a society. Examples of social signifiers include skin color, gender, physical appearance, age, and sexual preference. Individuals can experience different forms and combinations of oppression or privilege based on any of these signifiers. Further, factors such as race, gender, class, and ethnicity all intersect and lead to additional oppression and privilege. For example, being black, poor, and male means a higher risk of incarceration. The individual's race is a factor as is his social class and sex; yet when combined the risk of incarceration is much higher than when in isolation. No single factor is more important than the other in the overall system of privilege and oppression.

The place where socio-cultural factors of oppression meet is referred to as the *matrix of domination*. In capitalist societies, like the United States, the matrix of domination also functions as a matrix of privilege (Johnson, 2006). That is to say that there is more than one factor that is relevant to an individual being considered privileged, and the resulting privilege that individual receives leads to domination over others who are considered inferior. This explains how individuals can be considered privileged in one sense while being unprivileged in another. An example is a white homosexual male. This individual would typically be considered privileged because he is male and white. However he might also be considered underprivileged because of his sexual orientation. Therefore, he might not be afforded the same opportunities and advantages as heterosexual white males.

The dynamics of capitalism lead to a system of privilege and a conception of life that is also not easy to delineate. As noted by Johnson (2006, p. 51), "the dynamics of gender and race are so bound up with each other that its hard, if not impossible, to tell where one ends and the other begins." This is not to say that one cannot tell the difference between race and gender when it comes to discrimination. What it means is that privilege and lack of privilege take different forms that are connected in ways that sometimes are not obvious. Johnson gives the example of white men justifying their domination over black men by painting them as sexual predators that pose a significant threat to white women. At the same time white men tend to portray white women as pure and in need of protection from white men, therefore placing them in a position of subordination.

The matrix of domination is relevant to criminality as well as criminal justice processing. First, being oppressed can lead to perceptions of financial strain as well as feelings of general strain which may lead to an increased likelihood of criminality. Second, criminal justice discrimination can be based on white privilege and/or male domination. For example, there is evidence that those who kill whites and especially those who kill white females will be treated more severely when it comes to application of the death penalty (Robinson, 2008).

Critical race theory posits that racism is normal in American society (Delgado & Stefancic, 2005). Further, it has become so engrained within American culture and institutions that it is hard to recognize. Discrimination plays to the advantage of the dominant racial group within society, which in America is whites. Similarly, Omi and Winant's (1994) racial formation theory, suggests that ever changing socially constructed formations of racism combine with extra legal factors to create hegemony in society. *Hegemony* is societal domination of one racial group by consent of other racial groups, and it is achieved by a combination of coercion and consent.

Racial formation theory posits that race is a product of socially constructed thought used to the advantage of a dominant social class. According to Omi Winant (1994, p. 55), posit that race in the United States is an "unstable and "de-centered" complex of social meanings constantly being transformed by political struggle." Social and historical processes have, in essence always defined the particular features that supposedly make individuals members of a certain race. In fact humans of all skin colors are almost genetically identical. This means that humans of all skin colors are far more similar biologically than different. Omi and Winant (1994, p. 55) expound upon the thought that race is a socially constructed device and a cultural representation, through racial formation theory, "racial formation is the socio-historical process by which racial categories are created, inhabited, transformed, and destroyed."

Racial formation theory holds that social value and worth based upon race permeate American society, through both micro and macro-level social processes. Micro-level social processes are encounters and individual interactions with other people throughout everyday life (Omi & Winant, 1994). This often involves encounters with members of different races and pre-judging these individuals with preconceived notions of a racialized social structure. The *racialized social structure* is established through macro-level social processes. Macro-level social processes relate to the social structures and common ideologies that define what it means to be a member of certain races within America. Through both micro and macro-level processes individuals in American society become aware of their own racial identity and racial classifications of others subconsciously and without any formalized training as to what classifies race. Social processes are carried out through what Omi and Winant (1994, p. 56) define as racial projects. A *racial project* is "simultaneously an interpretation, representation, or explanation of racial dynamics, and an effort to reorganize and redistribute resources along particular racial lines."

Other Society Level Factors

Vold et al. (1998, p. 330), after offering a series of propositions summarizing relationships between criminogenic factors, wrote: "It may be true, and it is even quite likely, that some of [the stated relationships] are false." This means that even in the face of a good bit of supportive empirical evidence, some factors discussed in this chapter may prove ultimately *not* very useful for explaining criminality and antisocial behavior. Similarly, there may very well be other societal level factors not discussed here that are conducive to criminality and other forms of antisocial behaviors. Future research will have to uncover these factors.

There are also undoubtedly criminogenic factors at a higher level of analysis than society that may help understand why individuals commit criminal acts and antisocial behaviors. Miller's integrated systems perspective (discussed in chapter 3) is the basis for this book and the integrated systems theory of antisocial behavior we offer in the next chapter. In this perspective, Miller discusses the *super society* level of analysis, which is actually the highest level of analysis. The super society would include criminogenic factors found outside of society (in this case, like those found in other societies outside of the United States). Scholars certainly study how developments in the world affect the United States and its crime rates; yet, this book seeks to posit criminogenic factors that help explain why individuals commit crimes and antisocial behaviors. Scholars considering how events occurring outside the United States affect the behavior of particular individuals within the United States have difficulty doing more than merely speculating. Thus, super society level factors are not included in this analysis. This is not to say that they are irrelevant; since the focus of this book is on the antisocial behaviors of individuals, these factors are of less importance than factors found from the cell level of analysis through the society level of analysis.

Summary

In this chapter, you learned about society level factors as they impact anti-social and criminal behavior. A society was defined as a collective of people with common traditions, institutions, activities and interests. Societies are made up of social structures—the main institutions of the society including economic, political, education, and moral institutions, as well as a dominant culture and various subcultures. The social processes of a society refer to the way in which the society tends to operate. Social structural theories tend to focus on the main institutions in society and how they impact criminality whereas social process theories focus on the social-psychological processes such as socialization in families and among peers.

The main social structure theories include anomie and strain theories, so-cial disorganization and ecological theories, and cultural deviance and sub-cultural theories. The main social process theories include social learning theories, social control theories, and labeling theories. Social structure theo-ries tend to be used to explain crime rate variations within a society whereas social process theories tend to be used to explain individual criminality. Social structure theories generally rely on social processes to explain individual be-havior.

Anomie theory posits that a breakdown in social norms caused by wide-spread changes in society can lead to increased risks of suicide and antisocial behavior. As people are less integrated into society they are less regulated by its rules and thus freer to deviate. Institutional anomie theory points out that one source of anomie is an allegiance to the American Dream, a broad cultural ethos that entails a commitment to the goal of material success. Institutional anomie theory suggests that the social institutions in society responsible for instilling important noneconomic values in citizens—families, schools, and places of worship—are weakened are less prioritized relative to the economy, crim-inality is more likely to result.

Institutional anomie theory suggests that the welfare of the economy takes precedence in society in three ways: devaluation of noneconomic institutional functions and roles, accommodation to economic requirements by other so-cial institutions, and penetration of economic norms into other institutional domains.

Strain theory posits that criminality is more likely when an individual can-not achieve his or her goals through legal means such as school and work. Since legitimate means for success tend to be structured by social class, op-portunities for success are not equally available to all. People who do not have legitimate means to achieve their goals may create new means to achieve wealth through a process called innovation. Innovation is one of five modes of adaptation to strain and is most likely to lead to criminality.

Contextual anomie/strain theory combines previous iterations of anomie and strain theories and suggests that criminality results due to the goals of the American Dream being prioritized over the means to achieve them, frustration due to goal blockage, and a prioritization of the economy above other institutions in society. The theory is aimed at explaining elite deviance and holds that one major source of it is greed promoted both inside and outside of corporations. A new mode of adaptation to strain is offered — Maximization — which entails conforming to the law and breaking it at the same time.

General strain theory adds that other sources of strain besides financial strain can lead to aggressive acts. General strain can occur when one is prevented from achieving any goals, when one loses something of value, or when negative emotions arise due to other negative experiences. Negative emotions produce aggression even in cases where strain is anticipated in the future or are suffered by others close to you, especially when they are high in magnitude, seen as unjust, and when people are unable to correct them through legitimate means.

Generally, relationships have been found between conditions of anomie and property crime rates. Further, institutional anomie appears to be associated with higher murder rates as well as various forms of corporate crime. Strain is also associated with higher crime rates, including property crimes, violence, and drug use. General strain can be produced by child abuse and neglect, sexual abuse, and discrimination, and is associated with various forms of deviance, delinquency, and criminality. It also is correlated with various negative psychological outcomes such as low self-esteem, anxiety, and depression, as well as cognitive outcomes such as attention deficits, learning disorders and poor school performance.

Culture conflict theory highlights the importance of conflicts between and within groups for criminality. Primary and secondary culture conflicts occur and minority power groups tend to be most harmed. Relative powerlessness is a source of criminality. Various subcultural theories have been put forth over the years, which suggest that values unique to groups within society can lead to antisocial behavior when they conflict with dominant norms. However, these theories are not well-supported in empirical tests. Differential opportunity theory offers the important insight that not only are legitimate opportunities in society limited, so too are illegitimate opportunities. This means that the likelihood of criminality among different groups will vary based on opportunities to commit crimes.

Studies of race, class and gender tend to find that the poor, people of color, and men are more involved in street criminality. However, the wealthy and whites are more involved in elite deviance, suggesting that factors like social class and race are most important for understanding the type of crimes people commit. People of color are more likely to earn lower incomes, have less wealth, be poor, and unemployed, suggesting a higher incidence of strain and criminality. This supports the structural perspective more than the cultural perspective. Finally, unemployment is consistently found to be related to higher property crime rates, and income inequality is most consistently found to be related to higher violent crime rates.

Discussion Questions

1. What is meant by the term *society*?
2. Contrast social structure with social process.
3. What is anomie? What is strain?
4. List and define Merton's five modes of adapting to strain. Which is most relevant for understanding antisocial behavior? Explain.
5. List and discuss the main propositions related to anomie, strain, and antisocial behavior.
6. Does empirical evidence support anomie and strain theories? Explain.
7. What is meant by the term *general strain*?
8. What is culture conflict?
9. What is a subculture? Provide some examples.
10. List and discuss the main propositions related to culture conflict, subcultures, and antisocial behavior.
11. Does empirical evidence support culture conflict and subcultural theories? Explain.
12. What do scholars mean by the terms *race* and *social class*?
13. Why are most racial and ethnic minorities poorer than Caucasians? Explain.
14. List and discuss the main propositions related to race, social class, and antisocial behavior.
15. Does empirical evidence support the claim that racial and ethnic minorities and the lower class commit more crime? Explain.
16. Identify and briefly discuss the relationships between unemployment, income inequality, and crime.
17. Are the concepts of society level explanations of crime clearly defined? Explain.
18. What is the logical adequacy of society level explanations of crime?
19. What is the scope of society level explanations of crime?

10

An Integrated Systems
Theory of Antisocial Behavior

- Introduction
- The logic of integration
- Some examples of integration
- Summary of criminogenic factors
- Putting it all together: An integrated systems theory of antisocial behavior
- Summary of the integrated systems theory of antisocial behavior
- Policy implications: Logical strategies deduced from the integrated systems theory of antisocial behavior
- Summary

Introduction

In this final chapter, we briefly outline relationships between the important criminogenic factors discussed in previous chapters and then put forth a "new" integrated systems theory of antisocial behavior. Since there have been so many other efforts to produce integrated theories, in this chapter we also provide a general summary of some of these theories. Despite these efforts, virtually no previous attempts have outlined and discussed relationships between and among the criminogenic factors discussed in this book. The integrated theory of antisocial behavior put forth in this chapter goes at least two steps further than most other integrated theories: first, we explicitly state propositions that can be tested with empirical evidence; and second, we visually diagram the relationships between criminogenic factors. The integrated systems theory of antisocial behavior offered in this chapter is also different because it is organized around the levels of analysis in the integrated systems perspective introduced in chapter 3 and discussed in chapters 4 through 9.

The theory is interdisciplinary, meaning that it attempts to integrate contributions of all useful academic disciplines. An interdisciplinary approach to explaining antisocial behavior and criminality, where available knowledge from all useful disciplines is applied to the problem of culpable harmful behaviors, would make criminological theory much more effective at explaining antisocial behavior and criminality. Barak (1998, p. 15, citing Arrigo, 1994) provided a similar rationale for integrating theories of criminality from numerous academic disciplines, claiming that integrated approaches to explaining crime "offer a more cogent explanation for promoting objective science than other strategies."

There are three important points to remember: first, the effects of exposure to any of the factors discussed in this chapter are partially determined by the frequency, regularity, intensity, and priority of the exposure (see chapter 3); second, some factors certainly have greater effects at different time periods over the life course, based on the assertions of *developmental criminology* (discussed briefly in this chapter); and third, different types of antisocial behaviors are likely explained by slightly different groups or patterns of factors specific to each type of antisocial behavior. The theory offered here is meant to explain why an individual would be more likely to commit antisocial behaviors generally. It is not meant to explain any particular type of criminality. Recall from chapter 1 that the behaviors of most interest are maladaptive behaviors that are violent or aggressive in nature.

The Logic of Integration

Theoretical integration was introduced in chapter 3 in the discussion of *perspectives.* You saw some of the advantages and disadvantages to approaches that attempt to combine distinct explanations of behavior into one theoretical model. We believe that theoretical integration is neither new nor particularly innovative, but more specific integrative theories are currently being developed and their value has very recently been specified much more clearly (e.g., see Bernard & Snipes, 1996; Messner, Krohn, & Liska, 1989; Marenin, 1994; Miethe & Meier, 1994; Roundtree, Land, & Miethe, 1994; Tittle, 1995; Vila, 1994).

As is obvious by the evidence presented throughout the book, criminological theory is still fragmented among various schools of thought. For example, Barak (1998) mentioned the existence of positivist criminology, classical criminology, neoclassical criminology, functionalist criminology, conflict criminology, critical criminology, radical criminology, realist criminology, cultural criminology, feminist criminology, peacemaking criminology, biosocial criminology, anarchistic criminology, deconstructionist criminology, and postmodernist criminology. Much of the research discussed in this book comes from scholars affiliated with some of these camps. Some of the schools of thought are not included because they are not consistent with empirical science.

As we attempted to show in this book, knowledge about delinquency, criminality, antisocial behaviors, and aggression is partial and incomplete because of the discipline's fragmentation and also because of its historical allegiance to nonintegrated theories of crime. Barak (1998, p. 4) claimed that "such a proliferation of criminologies is not warranted and that it diminishes the field's ability to consolidate the various bodies of knowledge and to impact public policy"; therefore, various bodies of knowledge within criminological theory need to be integrated. Vila (1994) concurred, suggesting that criminological theory is not being used to formulate crime control policy because of its fragmented nature.

Scholars are increasingly coming to realize that *theory competition,* where one theory is compared to another in its ability to explain more or less criminality (Paternoster & Bachman, 2001), is a waste of time. We simply are not learning much about why behavior happens by studying small aspects of it (e.g., social factors) in isolation from so many other aspects of it (e.g., biological factors).

Part of this stems from the problem of *disciplinary myopia* discussed in chapter 3; criminologists tend to have limited vision with respect to knowledge being generated outside of the discipline (e.g., see Robinson, 1998). According to Vila (1994, p. 316), scholarship tends to be "largely congruent with its authors' academic disciplines—disciplines whose boundaries exist in our minds and institutions, but not in reality." Thus, "in order to understand criminal behavior we sometimes must eschew the intellectual comfort and safety of balkanized academia and venture across interdisciplinary frontiers" (p. 332). The result of disciplinary myopia in criminological theory is *reductionism,* or reducing the explanations of antisocial and criminal behavior to only factors within one discipline. According to Bohm (2001, p. 134): "analyses of the causes of crime generally have not been interdisciplinary. The questions that have been asked and the answers that have been given, for the most part, have remained within the province of a particular academic discipline. The result has been biological reductionism, psychological reductionism, sociological reductionism, and so forth."

As we showed in the book, the most neglected of all the disciplines in criminological theory is probably biology. For example, there have been over 150 studies on electrodermal and cardiovascular activity and crime, and hundreds more on electroencephalograms (EEGs) and delinquency, but such research has received little attention within criminology and is rarely included in basic theory texts (Raine, 1993, p. 157). As noted by Vila (1994, p. 324):

> Theories that acknowledge a role for biological factors in influencing human behavior — or even use [biological terms] — often are discounted out of hand by social scientists as deterministic or irrelevant ... Biological factors, so the argument goes, are philosophically incompatible with human free agency. Moreover, even if biology plays a role, it does not provide information about how to deal with social problems because biological characteristics are immutable. Worse still, any acceptance of a role for biological factors opens the door to the horrors of eugenics and racism.

We discussed the validity of these concerns in chapters 4 and 5. The bottom line is that biological factors such as genetics and brain structure and function play a major role in human behavior generally, and some role in maladaptive behaviors in particular. They also account for conditions such as low self-control, the very criminogenic factor identified by Gottfredson and Hirschi (1990) in their theory of low self-control (discussed in chapter 7). This is why biological factors are included in the integrated systems theory of antisocial behavior presented in this chapter.

As discussed in chapter 3, theoretical endeavors within criminology are undertaken by sociological traditionalists, multidisciplinary specialists, and interdisciplinary generalists, who differ with regard to their approaches to studying criminal behavior (Barak, 1998). Recall that *sociological traditionalists* claim that sociological explanations of crime are the most or even the only valid explanations; these theorists focus entirely on social factors; this is sociological reductionism. *Multidisciplinary specialists* highlight the importance of their own disciplines (such as sociology) but at least acknowledge that other disciplines are also important to studying behavior; these theorists make limited efforts to include not only social factors but also psychological and perhaps biological factors. *Interdisciplinary generalists* are open to knowledge about behavior that can be gleaned from studying other disciplines. This book has taken the latter approach, in an effort to integrate the most important criminogenic factors from all academic disciplines. The importance of an interdisciplinary theory cannot be overstated. Human behavior is affected by all kinds of factors. Since these factors are studied by so many different disciplines, theories of behavior must be interdisciplinary.

Some Examples of Integration

There are many integrated theories in criminological theory. Box 10.1 provides a few of the most well-known examples of integrated theories of crime. Most attempts to develop integrated theories integrate criminogenic factors generated within only one academic discipline, tending to reinforce the disciplinary boundaries of academic knowledge related to crime rather than breaking the boundaries down. Barriers between disciplines need to come down to truly achieve theoretical integration. There are, after all, no real dividing lines in knowledge (Jeffery, 1990; Barak, 1998). According to Vila (1994), there really is not a true integrated theory of criminality, for no theory has yet to identify and outline relationships between factors across all levels of analysis.

Box 10.1 Some Examples of Integrated Theories of Crime

- *Elliot's integrated theory*—(Elliott et al., 1985, 1994). Living in conditions of social disorganization is related to low levels of socialization at home, which produces high levels of perceived strain, a weakened bond to community institutions, rejection of conventional values, and an increased likelihood of associating with deviant peers, who provide reinforcement for deviant behavior.
- *Farrington's integrated theory*—(Farrington, 1989, 1993, 1994, 1995). Conditions such as poverty and large families with criminal parents and siblings produce children who receive low levels of supervision and harsh or inconsistent discipline, which increases associations with deviant peers and antisocial behavior.
- *Thornberry's integrated theory*—(Thornberry, 1987, 1997; Thornberry et al., 1998). Living in conditions of social disorganization decreases attachment to parents, decreases commitment to school, and erodes belief in conventional values, thereby increasing the risk of antisocial behavior, which when committed, encourages associations with deviant peers and further antisocial behavior.
- *Shoemaker's integrated theory*—(Shoemaker, 1996). Structural conditions such as anomie, social disorganization, and economic and political conditions interact with individual characteristics such as biological and personality traits to lead to reduced controls by conformist adults and to lowered self-esteem; these conditions in turn increase the influence of peers on deviant behavior and produce delinquency.

- *Colvin's integrated theory*—(Colvin, 2000). Interpersonal coercion (use or threat of force to achieve cooperation through fear) and impersonal coercion (economic and social pressures caused by unemployment, poverty, and competition) generated in families, peer groups, work environments, and society generally creates coercive ideation and ultimately coercive crime in people who experience it.
- *Agnew's general theory*—(Agnew, 2002). Individuals are more likely to commit criminal acts when they are in environments where the risk of condemnation or sanction is low (such as when living with poor parents), they possess personality traits that reduce their concern with condemnation or sanction (such as low self-control and irritability), and they face strong pressures and incentives to engage in these behaviors (due to factors such as negative school experiences and deviant peers).

The theories in box 10.1 represent a major improvement over traditional criminological theories, or what Tittle (1995, p. 1) called "simple theories." Most theories of criminality are simple because they are made up of "one or two explanatory principles involving only a few variables that are assumed to apply to all instances of the particular form of deviance being explained." As explained by Bohm (2001, p. 134): "The problem with simple theories … is that they may seem reasonable, have some (but never compelling) empirical support, and have attracted followers, but none of them has much explanatory power." It appears then that a better theory would be more complex, one that includes factors from all levels of analysis and all academic disciplines. Such a theory should be driven by empirical evidence, should specify the temporal ordering between variables, and should consider reciprocal influences between variables (as discussed in chapter 3). In the integrated systems theory of antisocial behavior we offer later in this chapter, we attempt to do just this.

One type of integration is *propositional integration* (e.g., see Liska, Krohn, & Messner, 1989). Propositional integration includes *end-to-end integration* (where one proposition is used to predict another), *side-by-side integration* (where one proposition explains one type of crime and another proposition explains another type of crime), and *up-and-down integration* (where one proposition subsumes other related propositions). None of these approaches actually synthesizes knowledge from multiple theories; instead they tend to represent new specifications of older theories where factors from single- or multifactor theories have either been added or subtracted. True integration requires specification of interactive effects between key concepts and behavior.

Another type of integration is *conceptual integration* (e.g., see Liska et al., 1989). Conceptual integration takes concepts from different academic theories and puts them together into a single theory. These theories tend to add concepts only from theories within the same academic discipline, which is myopic and incomplete. The risk factor approach discussed in chapter 3 is consistent with conceptual integration, but it requires acknowledging criminogenic factors identified by all academic disciplines.

Perhaps the most convincing argument regarding theoretical integration to date is Bryan Vila's (1994) *general evolutionary ecological paradigm*. According to Vila, ecological level factors, macro level factors, and micro level factors interact to produce an individual's strategic style which then increases or decreases a person's likelihood of criminality. Ecological level factors are "interactions between individuals, their activities in a physical environment, and their interactions with the physical environment," macro level factors are "systematic interactions between social groups," and micro level factors are "how an individual becomes motivated to commit a crime" (Vila, 1994, p. 326). A person's strategic style can be best understood as how the person regularly behaves, which would include his or her preferred way of dealing with problems, adapting to stress, and pursuing goals.

Vila posited the following view of human nature and behavior: "Humans are complex, dynamic, and self-reinforcing systems. Very small differences between individuals, combined with early random events and systematic processes, tend to 'push' development toward different styles of behavior. Eventually, we 'lock into' a particular style. Once a strategic style dominated by antisocial and criminal behavior is locked in, it is very difficult to change" (p. 338). According to Vila, various criminogenic factors come together and interact to affect the probability of criminality in any given person. This paradigm is not deterministic, but rather "treats human behavior as the outcome of systematic processes that are dynamic, complex, and self-reinforcing; that is, they involve ongoing interactions between many interconnected components, and the action of one component in the system affects subsequent actions of other components" (p. 312). Whether or not a person becomes motivated to commit criminal acts, then, results from "interactions over the life course between biological, sociocultural, and developmental factors" (p. 315).

Vila provided an excellent example of how criminal behavior might emerge according to this paradigm. For some individuals, their

> parents may transmit genes that—in conjunction with pre-, peri-, and post-natal experiences—cause offspring to develop nervous and organ systems which make them more difficult and irritable. This affects the probability that they will bond properly with a parent, especially if that parent is under extreme stress from economic, social, or

personal factors ... The parent/child bond affects how strongly a child values parental approval: weakly bonded children tend to be much more impulsive and difficult to control. This situation can initiate a vicious cycle in which a child receives less affection and nurturance because of misbehavior and therefore seeks less and less to please. Over time, the child develops his or her strategic style in a setting where rewards often are unpredictable as parents struggle with alternating resentment and desire to nurture. Because the child perceives rewards as undependable, he or she learns to grasp immediately opportunities for short-term gratification rather than to defer them for future rewards. In this setting, a child is also less likely to acquire conventional moral beliefs. In addition, the risk of physical and emotional child abuse—which further tend to fuel this vicious spiral toward criminality—may be greater. (p. 323)

Children who develop such impulsive behaviors will be less likely to succeed in school and thus the children will be further disadvantaged and more likely to engage in delinquent acts. Engaging in delinquency can further erode opportunities to succeed legitimately, leading to a child that could be viewed as truly disadvantaged and likely to continue into adult criminality. Note how this hypothetical scenario is consistent with the evidence discussed throughout this book.

Early experiences in childhood are very critical according to Vila's paradigm for it is in childhood that one's *strategic style* (way of behaving under normal circumstances) emerges. One's strategic style is virtually set before reaching adulthood because the brain is less susceptible to change due to outside influence (discussed in chapter 5). As explained by Vila: "People generally exhibit a preferred style for dealing with problems by middle childhood ... The evidence for this consistency is particularly strong for aggressive and antisocial behaviors" (p. 315). This is not to say that a person and his or her behaviors cannot be changed, it is just far less likely in adulthood to modify the way a person behaves than in childhood: "Although development is a lifelong process, early circumstances, events, and characteristics such as strategic style tend to be self-reinforcing" (p. 316). In other words, one's trajectory to delinquency and criminality begin early in life (Sampson & Laub, 1993).

Note that strategic style is very similar to the notion of personality (discussed in chapter 6), which summarizes the way in which an individual normally behaves. To the degree that one's strategic style or personality becomes set early in life and is difficult to change, it is certain that it emerges from early experiences and the effects of those experiences on the brain—that is, the pathways between neurons in the brain become hard wired. Because of this, it may then be possible to explain all major forms of antisocial behavior with the same or similar set of integrated factors; whatever factors account for the development of the strategic style or personality would be the key factors for accounting for the likelihood of antisocial and criminal behavior. We call this set of risk factors a *constellation of risk factors*.

Vila (1994, p. 315) wrote that "most contemporary criminological research is flawed because it fails to distinguish between criminality and illegal criminal acts [crime], allowing the state rather than the scientist to define the dependent variable ... Research that confuses these concepts is confounded because it treats different types of crimes as unique behaviors." In contrast, Vila's paradigm views crimes as "highly situation specific manifestations of an underlying strategic style favoring behaviors that are impulsive, self-centered, or harmful to others—many of which may not be considered criminal" ... thus Vila's paradigm says we should focus "attention on fundamental attributes of criminal behaviors rather than on political legal definitions of acts as crimes."

Vila's paradigm (what he defined as "a pre-theory whose role is to help us see a previously obscure puzzle in a new way", p. 338) is very important, but does not give us a theory with specific testable propositions per se. Specific theories, however, can be derived from this paradigm (or at the very least they can be consistent with it). Next in this chapter, we develop the integrated systems theory of antisocial behavior, which we hold to be consistent with the Vila paradigm. We begin by providing a summary of criminogenic factors discussed in the previous chapters of the book. As you will see, these are very similar, and in some cases identical, to those posited by Vila. According to Vila, some of these criminogenic factors are heritable through genes, and others are heritable through cultural transmission (or what most sociologists call learning, discussed in chapter 7). The integrated systems theory of antisocial behavior is based on these same assertions, as you saw in previous chapters.

Summary of Criminogenic Factors

In this book, we evaluated the research into criminogenic factors studied by various academic disciplines and organized them in appropriate levels of analysis, from cell to society. From this examination, we make the following conclusions:

1. All behaviors are the result of gene-environment interaction. Genes do not cause behavior; they predispose individuals to react to environmental stimuli in certain ways, meaning some will be more likely to behave in

an antisocial manner. Genes are linked to numerous factors relevant for antisocial behavior, including but not limited to personality, drug use and abuse, IQ, violence, and mental illness (chapter 4).

2. The majority of our genes determine brain chemistry and influence neurotransmitter levels in the brain. Levels of neurotransmitters in the brain affect behavior (e.g., low levels of serotonin increase the risk of antisocial behavior). Levels of enzymes in the brain also affect behavior (e.g., low levels of monoamine oxidase [MAO] increase the risk of antisocial behavior). Levels of hormones in the body affect behavior (e.g., high levels of testosterone and low levels of cortisol increase the risk of antisocial behavior). Neurotransmitter levels in the brain and hormones are affected by numerous environmental conditions, including but not limited to stress, diet/nutrition, drug use and abuse, and environmental toxins (chapter 5).

3. Brain dysfunctions caused by external sources such as maternal drug use during pregnancy, poor diet/nutrition, and stress during pregnancy, as well as use and abuse of drugs by individuals, poor diet/nutrition, exposure to environmental toxins, and head injury, are associated with an increased risk of antisocial behavior. Maternal drug use during pregnancy is associated with an increased likelihood of brain damage to the fetus, as well as birth complications such as low birth weight, low IQ, and learning disabilities. Exposure to toxins such as lead is associated with attention deficits, lower IQs, learning disabilities, and personality changes. Brain dysfunction generally leads to changes in neurotransmitter levels in the brain, cognitive deficits, learning disabilities, school failure, experiences of general strain, and ultimately an increased likelihood to live in conditions of poverty. All of these conditions are associated with an increased risk of antisocial behavior (chapter 5).

4. Personality is a product of gene-environment interaction (e.g., temperament is influenced by genetics and character is influenced by learning). Certain personality characteristics such as impulsivity, low-self control, negative emotionality, and low social perspective taking are associated with an increased risk of antisocial behavior. There is a reciprocal relationship between personality of a child and general parenting style and use of discipline, meaning that children partially determine the way their parents raise them. Nevertheless, personality characteristics are more accurately descriptive of antisocial behaviors rather than explanatory because personality is behavior (chapter 6).

5. Systems in the body such as the autonomic nervous system (ANS) affect behavior. ANS processes are affected by brain dysfunction and by larger level factors such as stress. ANS hypoarousal is suggestive of difficult condi-

tionality and is associated with an increased risk
(chapter 6).

6. Levels of intelligence have not been definitively lin
verbal IQ is related to an increased risk of antisoc
predicts later occupational problems and socioe
level is affected by genetics and environmental _
dysfunction. High IQ is also linked to antisocial behavior, but it is ·/ r
cally in the form of elite deviance rather than street crime (chapter 6).

7. The presence of a major mental illness affects behavior. Serious mental
illnesses are brain disorders (chemical imbalances of the brain) and are
associated with an increased risk of antisocial behavior only under certain
conditions (e.g., when a person is suffering from delusions, is using and/or
abusing drugs, and is not receiving treatment). Neurotransmitter levels
in the brain, influenced by genes and by use/abuse of drugs by an individual, are associated with mental illness. The relationship between mental illness and drug use/abuse is reciprocal in nature (chapter 6).

8. The foods, drinks, and drugs consumed by individuals affect neurotransmitters in the brain and ultimately behavior. Conditions such as hypoglycemia are associated with an increased risk of antisocial behavior. Poor
diet is associated with an increased risk for poor mood, hyperactivity, conduct disorder, attention deficit hyperactivity disorder, drugs abuse, aggression, and antisocial behavior. Most criminality arising from drugs is
attributable to illicit drug markets rather than drug use per se. The drug
that contributes most to antisocial behavior through pharmacological effects on the brain is a legal drug—alcohol (chapter 6).

9. Numerous family influences affect behavior. Inconsistent discipline, violent discipline, and unaffectionate parenting are associated with an increased risk of early antisocial behavior, and with associations with deviant
peers and poor school performance. Authoritative parenting is much more
effective than authoritarian and overly permissive parenting. Ineffective
parenting affects neurotransmitters in the brain of children. Low self-con
trol is not only produced by ineffective parenting but is also associ·
with genetics and brain dysfunction (chapter 7).

10. Larger level factors, such as poverty, unemployment, and eco·
rivation, produce family disruption, which is associated wi·´
likelihood of associations with deviant peers in unsupe·
an increased risk of antisocial behavior (chapter 7ꞌ

11. Numerous peer influences affect behavior. The·
ship between associations with deviant peers
tisocial behavior tends to precede deviant ass\

with deviant peers reinforce the likelihood of future antisocial behavior by affecting neurotransmitter levels in the brain (chapter 7).

12. Studies of media portrayals of violence demonstrate that exposure to violence in the media is associated with an increased risk of further violence (chapter 7).

13. Early antisocial behavior is associated with an increased likelihood of economic dependency, low educational attainment, occupational problems, and relationship problems, all of which are associated with an increased risk of continued antisocial behavior (chapter 7).

14. Larger level factors such as poverty, income inequality, and residential mobility in a community increase exposure to general strain, which stresses the ability of families to protect children from antisocial influences (chapter 7).

15. Experiences of general strain influence levels of stress hormones in the body, which can increase the likelihood of brain dysfunction, cognitive deficits, and antisocial behavior (chapter 7).

16. Living in conditions of social disorganization is associated with an increased likelihood of being identified as a criminal, most notably those that are most subjected to police focus. Living in conditions of poverty and urbanization is associated with reduced participation in community organizations. Living in conditions of high residential mobility, population heterogeneity, and family disruption is associated with less supervision of peer groups in the neighborhood and less interactions with neighbors. Such conditions stress effective parenting and are associated with an increased likelihood of exposure to general strain and risk of victimization from street crime (chapter 8).

17. Routine activities in an area and individual lifestyles of residents are associated with risk of criminal victimization. The routine activities of a neighborhood are associated with conditions of social disorganization (chapter 8).

18. Being identified as a delinquent, criminal, or deviant is associated with an increased risk of antisocial behavior when the labeling process is destructive, harmful, and/or demeaning rather than restorative, particularly when the labeling process is informal in nature (e.g., occurring in family settings) (chapter 8).

19. Exposure to general strain increases the likelihood of antisocial behavior. There are numerous sources of general strain, including structural or economic strain, criminal victimization, and perceptions of discrimination. Another source of strain comes from families—child maltreatment such as neglect and abuse. Physical consequences of abuse and neglect include brain damage; psychological consequences include low self-esteem, anxiety, depression, and substance abuse; and cognitive effects include re-

duced IQ, attention deficits, learning disorders, poor school performance, and an increased risk of employment and interpersonal relationship problems (chapter 9).

20. Egoism or selfishness created by an allegiance to materialistic goals is associated with an increased risk of antisocial behavior. At the same time, low aspirations for materialistic success are associated with an increased risk of antisocial behavior (chapter 9).

21. The dominance of the economy over other noneconomic institutions in society (e.g., greed promoted within the corporate world) result in higher crime rates within a society (chapter 9).

22. Minority race and ethnicity status and low social class positions are associated with an increased likelihood of being identified as a criminal, but are not associated with increased risk of antisocial behavior per se. These factors may help us understand why certain individuals commit the types of antisocial acts they commit. Whether any individual commits an antisocial act depends on the presence of illegitimate opportunities (chapter 9).

23. Unemployment rates are associated with increased crime rates, notably property crime rates (chapter 9).

24. Conditions of income inequality are associated with increased crime rates, especially violent crimes such as homicide (chapter 9).

Note that these conclusions are stated in isolation from one another. In some of the statements, we illustrate how various factors affect one another and result in antisocial behavior. Yet, in order to conclude the development of the integrated systems theory of antisocial behavior, we must now illustrate how these conditions interact to increase the risk of antisocial behavior within a given individual.

As explained by Vila (1994), the most important question for theorists to answer is, which variables or factors at what level of analysis interact in what ways to produce criminality? Specifically: "What relationships and processes tend to be fundamentally important for understanding changes over time in the ... behaviors of any social organism?" (p. 313). We hope the integrated systems theory of antisocial behavior offers an answer for these questions.

Putting It All Together: An Integrated Systems Theory of Antisocial Behavior

In this book, we have assessed multiple relationships to identify the risk factors that increase the likelihood of an individual engaging in antisocial be-

Figure 10.1 The Integrated Systems Theory of Antisocial Behavior, Part 1: Early Risk Factors

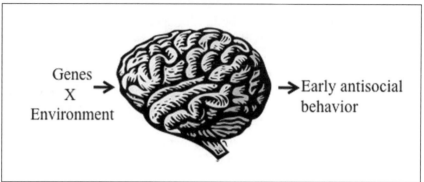

Genes X Environment → → Early antisocial behavior

Source: Figure created by author.

haviors. This does not represent a theory, per se. A complete theory needs to specify interactions between key variables. Next, we identify likely relationships between the various criminogenic factors and discuss how these interactions increase the likelihood of antisocial behaviors. With this theory, we do not assert a single cause or even multiple causes of criminality; rather we posit that antisocial behavior is made more likely when various factors are present and interact. As noted at the outset of this chapter, different forms of antisocial behaviors are likely explained by different groups of factors. The *constellation of risk factors* offered here is thought to increase the likelihood of antisocial behavior generally, because it increases the likelihood that an individual will develop a strategic style or personality that is conducive to antisocial behavior.

Some factors are left out of this theory because they are not testable, not falsifiable, and thus not useful for the advancement of our scientific understanding of criminality (see chapter 3). Other factors have been left out because the weight of the evidence suggests they are not valid, they are of little importance, or they have been falsified. Finally, other factors are not explicitly included because they are subsumed under other factors, as we will explain in this chapter.

Figure 10.1 begins the introduction of our theory of antisocial behavior, which we refer to as the Integrated Systems Theory (IST) of antisocial behavior. As shown in the figure, propensities for antisocial behavior begin at the moment of conception, when genes are passed down from parent to child. The brain is a product of genetic-environmental interaction. Factors here are enough to put one on a trajectory for antisocial behavior (e.g., abnormal neurotransmitter, enzyme, and hormone levels).

Figure 10.2 The Integrated Systems Theory of Antisocial Behavior, Part 2: The Role of Parenting

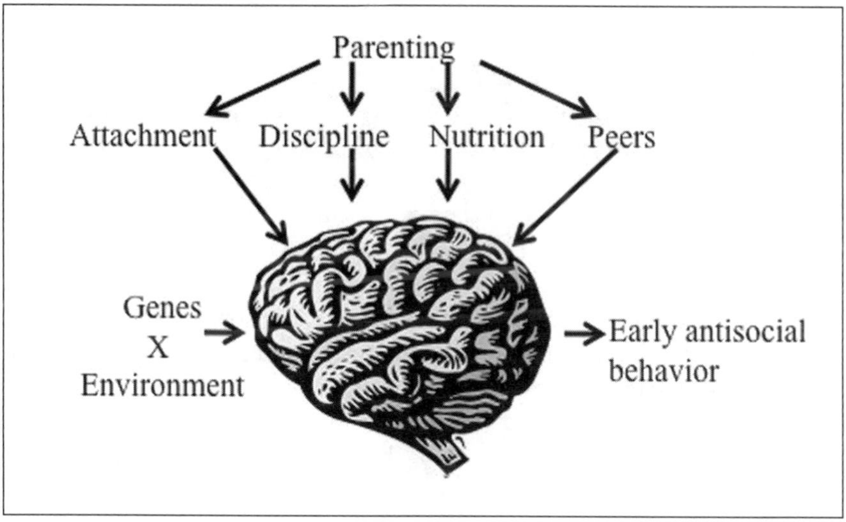

Source: Figure created by author.

Specifically, genes influence levels of brain chemistry (neurotransmitters and enzymes) and influence levels of hormones in the body. Low levels of serotonin increase the risk of antisocial behavior. Furthermore, low levels of the enzyme MAO increase the risk of antisocial behavior, as do high levels of the hormone testosterone and low levels of the stress hormone cortisol. Keep in mind that levels of these neurotransmitters, enzymes, and hormones are also affected by prenatal conditions, including drug use/abuse during pregnancy, unhealthy diet/nutrition during pregnancy, and stress during pregnancy. This means the impact of family conditions on behavior starts before birth.

Figure 10.2 adds the impact of parenting as shown in the book. Parenting impacts the brain of the child through four primary ways—attachment, discipline, nutrition, and peers. Thus, the less attached kids are to their parents, the more at risk to antisocial behavior, the less consistent and the more violent the discipline, the more at risk to antisocial behavior, the worse the diet of the child, the more at risk to antisocial behavior, and the worse the parent, the more likely the child is to associate with bad peers (which would reinforce deviant behavior).

Family conditions obviously affect diet/nutrition of children since parents largely determine what children eat. Family conditions also affect IQ level/cognition of children, the likelihood of drug use/abuse in adolescents, and experiences of general strain. Each of these relationships is thought to be reciprocal given that what affects a child will affect all the groups he or she is part of, including the family. Finally, family conditions also affect peer associations, and peer associations affect family conditions; thus the relationship is reciprocal. Specifically, parental failure to love, supervise, and consistently and non-violently discipline children increases the likelihood that children will associate with deviant peers, and associations with deviant peers interfere with the ability of families to correct the behavior of their children.

Other factors not depicted in the figures impact brain functions, as well, including consumption of drugs, nutritional intake, and exposure to environmental toxins. Relationships between brain chemistry and drugs and nutrition are likely reciprocal, since once brain chemistry is changed, it will increase cravings for certain drugs and foods. Abnormal levels of neurotransmitters can also trigger severe mental illnesses.

Destructive labeling can also affect these substances. Recall that the type of labeling most likely to impact behavior is that which occurs in informal settings such as families. We do not visually depict the impact of these factors on behavior because we suspect they are subsumed under factors such as parental attachment and discipline, peer influences, and so forth. For example, parents who see their kids as trouble-makers will spend less time with their kids, be less attached to them, and will resort to inconsistent and violent discipline.

Since brain dysfunction suggests abnormal brain activity, logic suggests that forms of it such as head injury will affect levels of neurotransmitters, enzymes, and hormones. In the book, we identified six sources of brain dysfunction, including harmful prenatal conditions, harmful family conditions, abnormal diet/nutrition, perceptions of strain, drug abuse, and exposure to environmental toxins. Relationships between brain dysfunction and the following factors are reciprocal: harmful family conditions, abnormal diet/nutrition, and drug abuse. This means once brain dysfunction is experienced, it is likely that family conditions will worsen as parents struggle to deal with the outcomes, and individuals with brain dysfunctions will be more susceptible to abnormal diets and drug abuse because people experiencing brain dysfunction will be more likely to consume things that make them feel better (as a form of self-medication).

Recall that outcomes of brain dysfunction include many individual level outcomes, including increased risks for family disruption, abnormal diet, and drug abuse, as well as lower verbal IQ and cognitive deficits and mental illness. Another result of brain dysfunction that we identified in the book is ANS hypoarousal, which is also produced by stress or perceptions of strain. Several of these organism level risk factors increase the likelihood of early antisocial behavior, including abnormal diet/nutrition, low verbal IQ/cognitive dysfunction, drug use/abuse, mental illness under the circumstances we discussed in the book, and ANS hypoarousal. It is likely that the relationships between antisocial behavior and verbal IQ/cognitive dysfunction, drug use/abuse, and mental illness are reciprocal, because once antisocial behavior begins, individuals are at greater risk for experiences that impair cognition and for situations where drug use and abuse are prevalent. It is also more likely that they will be diagnosed with minor if not serious mental illnesses. Low verbal IQ/cognitive problems also lead to perceptions of strain and likely increase the risk of associating with others with similar problems. We do not depict these relationships in the figure so that the theory remains more parsimonious.

Both drug use/abuse and mental illness can result from experiences of general strain; each can be considered a means of coping with negative or noxious stimuli. Strain is not depicted in the figure because it is perceived in the brain. Since general strain is caused by so many different factors, we cannot possibly include it in our figure but we do acknowledge that factors such as low attachment to parents and inconsistent and/or violent discipline by parents strains children and increases the risk of antisocial behavior. There is also a reciprocal relationship between drug use/abuse and mental illness. Drug use often serves as a trigger for major brain disorders such as manic depression, and people with major mental illnesses often use/abuse drugs as a form of self-medication.

Figure 10.3 adds the impact of social disorganization. We call it "community characteristics" because we are referring to factors like SES of the neighborhood, population turnover, heterogeneity, etc. Note that we specify that social disorganization is produced by political decision-making of elites. Factors such as tax policy, corporate policy (e.g., outsourcing of jobs, downsizing of workforces and so forth) directly lead to conditions of economic deprivation, unemployment and income inequality that lead to less effective social controls in communities.

We suggest that such factors strain good parenting (e.g., the ability of parents to spend time with and supervise their kids). Conditions of social disorganization such as poverty, population heterogeneity, and residential mobility make it harder for families to regulate the behavior of their children and peers. These conditions also make it more difficult for residents to participate in community organizations. Low levels of community participation increase the ability of deviant peers to congregate without adequate supervision. We do not include community participation and peer networks here because these factors are subsumed under the impact of community characteristics on parenting. Conditions of social disorganization, such as poverty and urbanization, increase the likelihood of exposure to environmental toxins, as it is in the poor, inner-city neighborhoods of our nation where these toxins are at their highest levels. Poverty also is detrimental to healthy pregnancies as is exposure to

Figure 10.3 The Integrated Systems Theory of Antisocial Behavior, Part 3: The Role of Community Characteristics

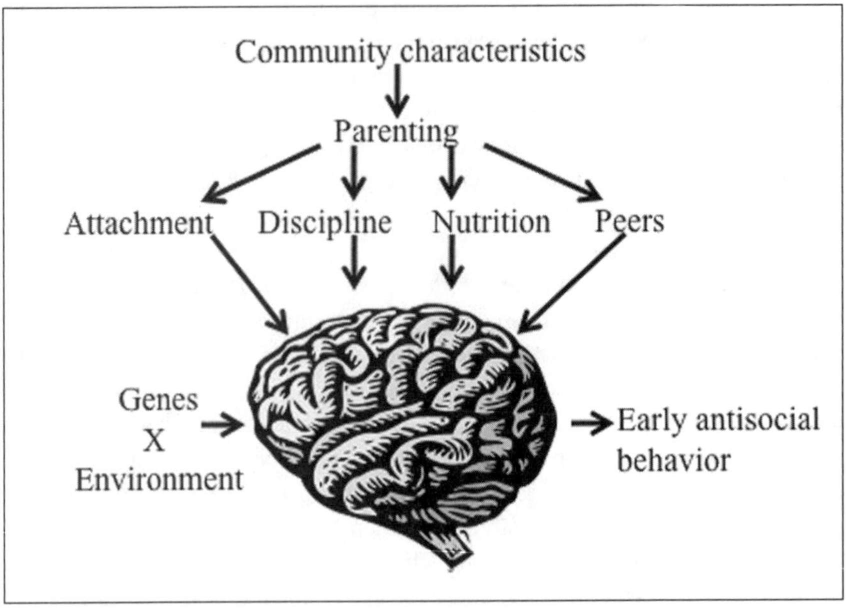

Source: Figure created by author.

environmental toxins. Living in poverty (especially in a society as rich as America) increases perceptions of strain.

Living in conditions of social disorganization also increases the risk that an individual will be labeled in a destructive manner by agencies of social control, largely because socially disorganized areas are the most heavily patrolled areas by the police. Being a member of a racial or ethnic minority (i.e., African American or Hispanic) and/or being a member of the lower class increases the risk of destructive labeling, as well. Being labeled as a delinquent, criminal, or deviant (especially when by informal sources such as parents and teachers) increases the likelihood of employment problems, relationship problems, and associations with deviant peers. Such problems with employment, relationships, and associating with other antisocial people will increase the risk of continued antisocial behavior, as noted earlier.

Social disorganization also is related to patterns of routine activities in a community as a result of lifestyles of residents and space users, which thus affect peer associations and the likelihood that one will engage in antisocial behavior. The effect of lifestyle patterns on antisocial behavior is through the creation of suitable opportunities for antisocial behavior.

Figure 10.4 The Integrated Systems Theory of Antisocial Behavior, Part 4: The Full Model

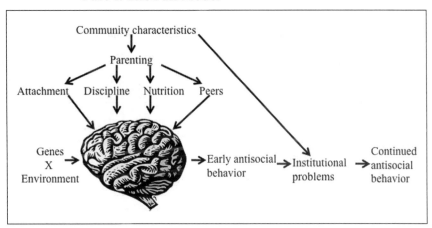

Source: Figure created by author.

Figure 10.4 adds the factors that tend to sustain antisocial behavior (associations with deviant peers, as well as relationship and employment problems). We call these "institutional problems" which refer to problems with the institutions of peers, romantic relationships, and work. These can also be "turning points" that lead to desistance from crime when people connect to good peers and enter into positive and fulfilling marriages and careers. Community characteristics also effect these institutions, suggesting that people living in poverty will have more opportunities for associating with deviant peers in certain neighborhoods as well as more strain that will likely lead to relationship and employment problems. Note that figure 10.4 is a much more parsimonious or simple version of the theory originally presented in the first edition.

As illustrated in this book, peer associations are often preceded by early antisocial behavior, so that people with like outlooks on life and certain characteristics flock together. Yet, peer associations are also reinforced by antisocial behavior so that the relationship is reciprocal. Associations with deviant peers often interfere with employment opportunities and experiences and with other relationships. Each of these relationships is reciprocal because problems in employment and other interpersonal relationships can increase the importance of peer associations. As associations with deviant peers typically follow early antisocial behavior, reinforcement of antisocial behavior occurs in the group context, making continued antisocial behavior more likely, a relationship that is reciprocal, as well. Both employment problems and relationship prob-

Figure 10.5 Development of Antisocial Behavior in the Integrated Systems Theory

Pre-Birth/ Birth	Early Childhood	Adolescence	Early Adulthood
Genetics			
Maternal drug use/abuse ——————————————————➤			
Maternal diet/nutrition ——————————————————➤			
Stress during pregnancy ——————————————————➤			
Exposure to environmental ——————————————————➤ toxins			
	Diet/nutrition ———————————————➤		
	Family influences ———————————————➤		
	Neurotransmitters/ ———————————————➤ enzymes		
	Brain dysfunction ———————————————➤		
	Environmental toxins ———————————————➤		
	Verbal IQ/cognition ———————————————➤		
		Hormones ———————➤	
		Drug use/abuse ———————➤	
		Mental illness ———————➤	
		Peer influences ———————➤	
		Strain ———————➤	
		Destructive labeling ———————➤	
			Employment problems ➤
			Relationship problems ➤

Source: Figure created by author.

lems increase the risk of continued antisocial behavior, and antisocial behavior likely will increase these problems. Employment problems and relationship problems also feed off each other meaning there is a reciprocal relationship between these factors.

Figure 10.5 incorporates these factors into a developmental time line, suggesting greater or lesser import for some factors at different times over the life course. Although research shows there may be more than one path to antisocial behavior, figure 10.5 simply illustrates when risk factors from the integrated systems theory of antisocial behavior are likely to first influence a person's behavior. This is based on the growing literature of developmental criminology (e.g., see Benson, 2002; Piquero & Mazerolle, 2001). Kumpfer and Alvarado (1998) are among those who posit more than one developmental pathway to antisocial behavior in children. They include (1) the early authority conflict pathway which begins with stubborn behaviors and evolves into defiant behavior and ultimately into avoidance of authority figures, (2) the covert pathway which begins with minor antisocial behaviors and develops into more serious delinquent acts, and (3) the overt pathway which begins with minor aggression and leads to more serious physical violence. The research suggests that these pathways are encouraged by inept parenting and by low attachment with parents (as discussed in chapter 7). Children on more than one pathway are at greatest risk for sustained antisocial behavior in adulthood (Huizinga, et al. 1998; Kelley et al., 1997). Regardless of how many developmental trajectories lead to antisocial behavior, they all begin at the moment of conception and are reinforced in early childhood and adolescence. Each also begins with early but minor forms of antisocial behavior.

As you see in figure 10.5, several of these risk factors begin before birth, such as inheriting genetic propensities, maternal drug use/abuse during pregnancy, maternal diet/nutrition during pregnancy, stress during pregnancy, and exposure to environmental toxins during pregnancy. The effects of diet/nutrition, family influences, chemical imbalances in neurotransmitter and enzyme levels, brain dysfunction, environmental toxins, hypoarousal of the ANS, and low verbal IQ/cognitive problems are likely to begin in early childhood. The risk factors of hormones, drug use/abuse, mental illness, peer influences, general strain, and destructive labeling are most likely to occur during adolescence. Finally, employment problems and relationship problems are most likely to occur in early adulthood.

This developmental time line is not meant as an absolute; it is simply a way of visualizing when certain risk factors are most likely to begin to have deleterious effects on individuals. Recall from chapter 3 that the earlier that risk factors begin to influence people (priority), the greater the likelihood that individuals will commit acts of antisocial behavior.

Summary of the Integrated Systems Theory of Antisocial Behavior

The integrated systems theory of antisocial behavior attempts to advance the state of theories of criminal and antisocial behavior past its myopic state by illustrating how risk factors at different levels of analysis from different academic disciplines interact to increase the probability that a person will commit antisocial behavior. Of particular interest is repeated, maladaptive or harmful forms of antisocial behaviors. Even though we think the theory is new, we do not pretend that we have invented the wheel. Certainly, the main premise of this theory is nothing new.

This theory is consistent with many other schools of thought, developed in other disciplines, some of which we have not even discussed in the book. An example from sociology is the idea of *developmental sociology* (Tsamis, 1998). This school of thought is an attempt to document the factors that create early onset of aggressive behavior and that persist over the years. The relevant factors according to this approach include underlying attention problems associated with impoverished environments before and after birth. Developmental sociologists assert that a trajectory is set in place toward academic and social difficulties, delinquency, and so forth; the process of criminality becomes entrenched when a person is labeled by formal authorities. As you can probably see in the figures in this chapter, the factors discussed by Tsamis are included in the integrated systems theory of antisocial behavior.

Now it is time to test this theory so that it can be evaluated using the criteria from chapter 2. Is there evidence that the theory is valid? Are the propositions logically stated? Are the concepts clearly defined? We do believe the theory will be supported if appropriate data are collected. Because the propositions have been laid out, and because the key concepts have been defined in a testable format, it is possible with the right data set to test all or parts of the theory. Since the theory is consistent with empirical evidence—built around previous tests of the risk factors presented—the main premises should be supported in future tests.

Tests of the integrated systems theory of antisocial behavior should be conducted using longitudinal data that are sensitive to the trajectory we have laid out in this book (see figure 10.5). Scholars must test for reciprocal relationships or two-way causality and the interactive effects that we have discussed in this book. The theory does not require that all the risk factors in the model be present for antisocial behavior to occur; rather, we assert that the more factors are present, the greater the likelihood that antisocial behavior will occur. Recall from chapter 3 that theory is probabilistic, meaning that the presence of these risk factors increases the likelihood of antisocial behavior.

Because all individuals are different in their biological makeup and social experiences, factors will affect people differently. As discussed in chapter 3 and earlier in this chapter, the effects of the risk factors on behavior will depend on the frequency, regularity, intensity, and priority of a person's exposure, so that the more times a person is exposed (frequency), the more consistently one is exposed (regularity), the earlier a person is exposed (priority), and the stronger the factor (intensity), the more likely antisocial behavior will occur. Finally, the presence of protective factors will counteract the effects of risk factors, especially if exposure to them is frequent, is regular, and begins early in life, and if the protective factors are many. We did not discuss protective factors at great length in this book because they tend to be the opposite of risk factors, as discussed in chapter 3.

Policy Implications: Logical Strategies Deduced from the Integrated Systems Theory of Antisocial Behavior

Recall from chapter 2 that all explanations of criminality can be used to derive policy implications for reducing crime; theories of crime suggest what should be done to reduce crime. When theories put forth causes of criminality, logical policies would call for the elimination of those causes. From a probabilistic argument, such as that of the integrated systems theory of antisocial behavior, logical policies would entail reducing one's exposure to the risk factors that increase the probability that one will behave in an antisocial fashion, and/or increasing one's exposure to protective factors that reduce the probability that one will behave in an antisocial fashion (see chapter 3).

This book is not specifically about preventing antisocial behavior, but ultimately the findings of studies mentioned in the book will lead to the development of policies aimed at preventing criminality and other antisocial behaviors. In the following paragraphs, we briefly summarize logical crime prevention implications based on the findings of the book.

Based on the findings we discussed throughout the book and the logic of how antisocial behavior arises according to the integrated systems theory of antisocial behavior, the prevention of antisocial behavior should entail what Vila (1994, p. 330) called *nurturant strategies* or "attempt[s] to forestall the development of criminality by improving early life experiences and channeling child and adolescent development." Nurturant strategies include efforts to allow and encourage individuals to develop their fullest potential, to increase adaptive behaviors, and to minimize the development of maladaptive, aggressive, and antisocial behaviors. They can thus be related to "restorative justice," aimed at restoring offender, victim, and community to previctimization status (to the degree possible) (Karp, 2001; Maxwell & Morris, 2001; Roach, 2000; Smith, 2001; Smith-Cunnien & Parilla, 2001); the primary difference with nurturant strategies is that they are proactive rather than reactive and thus aimed at crime prevention rather than crime control.

Crime nurturant strategies are a long-term investment in the future of the nation, its communities, and its citizens. It is opposite to most criminal justice policies in the United States, which are relatively unplanned and often based on illogical or incomplete ideas about criminality; most criminal justice policies are aimed at short-term gains in crime control without regard for future long-term consequences (Robinson, 2002). For example, mass incarceration (see chapter 8) as a means of crime reduction leads to social disorganization in the nation's inner cities, reduces the number of men and father figures in a community, and creates criminogenic factors (such as lower levels of community participation and lower levels of supervision of peer groups in the community) that may do more harm than good in the long run. Vila et al. (1997) argued that America's hateful and sensationalistic approach to crime reduction defers attention away from strategies that would be more effective, such as addressing child developmental health problems, education problems, and other developmental problems.

According to Vila (1994), benefits of nurturant strategies implemented in year one will not be seen for approximately 15 years; it takes this long for children born in year one to reach the age of the "delinquency peak." In actuality, results of nurturant strategies will be witnessed in less than 15 years, because antisocial behavior begins long before the age of 15 for many children, as do many other negative consequences of the risk factors discussed in this book. Not much has been written about these strategies, although Vila and colleagues have expanded on the original ideas (e.g., Cohen, 1997; Farrington, 1997; Howell, 1997; Land, 1997; Levitt, 1997; Machelek, 1997; Mealey, 1997; Richerson, 1997; Savage & Vila, 1997; Savage & Vila, in press; Vila, 1997; Walsh & Ellis, 1997; Wolf, 1997; Zimring, 1997).

The nurturant crime prevention strategies justified by the integrated systems theory of antisocial behavior can basically be boiled down to these two:

1. Reduce one's exposure to the risk factors identified in this book.
2. Increase one's exposure to the opposite of the risk factors in this book—the protective factors (e.g., the opposite of ineffective parenting is effective parenting, the opposite of inconsistent discipline is consistent discipline, the opposite of poor diet/nutrition is a healthy diet).

In making efforts to achieve these goals, the goal specifically is to reduce the frequency, regularity, intensity, and priority of the exposures to the risk factors identified in the book and to increase the frequency, regularity, intensity, and priority of the exposures to their opposites, or protective factors. Of most importance is reducing the clustering of disadvantages, for the cumulative effect of exposure to numerous risk factors is far worse than the periodic exposure to one or two risk factors. As shown in this book, risk factors tend to co-occur (called comorbidity). The constellation of risk factors shown in figure 10.1 illustrates how cumulative disadvantage puts some at far greater risk for antisocial behavior than others.

Given that the sources of antisocial behavior are so diverse, we believe it is warranted to consider crime prevention implications before making any and all government policies, business decisions, and so forth. In the following pages, we provide some examples from the research presented in this book, beginning with possible cell level implications all the way up to society level implications.

There is much speculation that in the very near future it will be possible to alter genetic makeup to reduce the likelihood that an individual will become antisocial, and/or to replace particular genes in people generally to reduce overall rates of antisocial behavior. Such possibilities bring forth thoughts of past efforts to use biological research to control certain segments of the population, including the eugenics movement (Robinson, in press).

The findings of genetic studies may ultimately be used to prevent criminality in people who have already offended (crime control) or to prevent it in people who have yet to commit serious, sustained criminality (crime prevention). Exactly how genetics research is used in a society is not a question to be answered by those conducting genetic studies, but instead is a social policy issue to be decided by members of the society.

Several main points need to be made up front with regard to developing policy implications from studies of genetics and behavior. Consider cautions we discuss in box 10.2.

Box 10.2 Cautions about Crime Prevention at the Cell Level

It really is partial and incomplete to outline policy implications that address only one level of analysis, such as the cellular level of analysis. Human behavior results from the interactions of numerous factors at several levels of analyses (discussed in chapter 3). Recall that genes do not express themselves in the absence of environmental factors; this means that many of the most important crime control and prevention policies will involve alterations to environmental conditions rather than one's genes. In fact, in a cost-benefit analysis, it may make more sense to change the environmental conditions that trigger genes to express themselves in the form of antisocial behavior, given that so many people are exposed to them at one time.

Additionally, even when particular genes are identified by scientists as relevant for increasing the probability of antisocial behavior, individuals with these genes may not ever commit repetitive antisocial behaviors. It is not appropriate to assume that just because an individual has a trait found in antisocial populations that the individual will also behave in an antisocial fashion.

Policy implications derived from genetics (indeed, from any theory) are potentially troubling because they question our assumptions about free will and moral responsibility: "Ethical, legal, and social issues arise about behavioral genetics largely because the explanations and predictions about human behavior generated by this science compete in the wider culture with other explanations of human behavior ... [for example] that human behavior is more often than not the exercise of free will" (Bloom et al., 2000, p. 36). If our genes play a role in determining our personalities and behavioral propensities, then free will is a myth. If free will is a myth, then the legitimacy of state power is called into serious question, for state power is only legitimate if citizens freely submit to it. State power includes the criminal justice activities of police, courts, and corrections ... "in the law you cannot be found guilty and punished (legal responsibility) for an action if you were not free to have done otherwise ... you do not face a burden of proof to show you are free. You are presumed to be free and, therefore, others face a burden of proof to show that you lack freedom" (Bloom et al., 2000, p. 36).

Given these important notes, there are essentially three possible crime control and crime prevention policy implications of genetics research: alteration of genetics, alteration of environmental triggers and insulators, and the medicalization of behavior. First, it is not likely that members of society will ever completely support alterations of genetics for the purposes of preventing crime. Furthermore, it is not called for. The policy implications of genetics studies are typically the same as those made by studies of environmental factors. As explained by Walsh (2002, p. 231): "Whatever biological therapies we eventually come up with, they almost certainly will not be genetic. As has been constantly emphasized, there are genes that bias traits in certain directions, but there are no genes that lead directly to any kind of nontrivial behavior. Genes act in concert with other genes, and collectively, they act in concert with the environment." This means that the policy implications of genetic studies point to alterations of the environment. This is especially true given that the same traits that produce many antisocial behaviors also produce many prosocial behaviors. Doing away with one gene that codes for proteins that encourage one trait related to antisocial behavior will wipe out the trait rather than its behavioral manifestations—for example, aggression will be wiped out in all its forms, including prosocial behaviors.

The medicalization of behavior involves regulating brain chemistry through the admission of legally prescribed drugs. Since genes partially determine neurotransmitter levels in the brain, genetic abnormalities can lead to unusually high or low levels of brain chemicals that affect behavior. One way to return brain chemistry to more normal levels is with the administration of drugs under the care of psychiatrists. This should never be done in isolation from other therapies, such as counseling.

Strategies at the organ level of analysis are aimed at regulating levels of neu-rotransmitters, enzymes, and hormones, primarily through eliminating the environmental conditions that produce abnormal levels. In addition, these substances can be regulated with medicine, suggesting the medicalization of be-havior. Drugs can be administered to counteract the effects of abnormal brain chemistry and abnormal levels of hormones. These efforts are reactive and thus are less likely to be effective at preventing criminality.

A more promising line of approach entails reducing the conditions that pro-duce organ level risk factors. For example, stress during pregnancy, drug use or abuse during pregnancy, and unhealthy diet/nutrition are all sources of brain dysfunction. Other sources include exposure to environmental toxins, head injury, drug use/abuse, child abuse/neglect, and unhealthy diet/nutrition. Successful crime prevention will address these factors. Finally, treatment is available for people suffering from traumatic brain injuries because of acci-dents and similar experiences. Never should we rely exclusively on medical treatments, for by themselves they are not as effective at changing behavior as when used in conjunction with other treatments (NAMI, 2002).

Logical policies stemming from organism level explanations suggest that changes ought to be made to the organism level factors that increase the like-lihood of committing antisocial behavior. Some go as far as to suggest that or-ganism level factors must be specifically considered. For example, Moffitt suggested that any crime prevention policy "that ignores either low IQ or im-pulsivity as risk factors for delinquency will be ill-informed by social science research" (quoted in Crime-Times, 1995, Volume 1, 3: 2). According to Tardiff "A wide range of medical illnesses have been found to be associated with vio-lent behavior. Many of these are treatable and reversible" (quoted in Crime-Times, 1995, Volume 1, 3: 2).

Thus, our two options are either to prevent exposure to organism level risk factors or to treat people who have been exposed. As suggested in chapter 6, treatment for mental illnesses and poor diet is relatively successful, which is good news for crime control. The most successful approaches to treat mental illness are a combination of medicine and counseling therapies (NAMI, 2002). IQs can be slightly raised through educational programs, but it is not clear that it is possible to change someone's personality once it becomes established early in life. Remember that personality is the same thing as behavior, so once a be-havioral pattern (or trajectory) becomes established early in life, it is very dif-ficult to change. This means efforts ought to be aimed at preventing the development of antisocial behavior beginning at birth and before. Similarly, once drug use becomes drug abuse, brain damage can occur and make reversing one's behavioral propensities more difficult. If this theory is correct, we must focus our efforts at preventing harmful drug abuse; this can be done by attempting to stop drug use entirely (which will fail) or more realistically to stop people from abusing drugs. Efforts should be focused at the very small percentage of users, based on family history, who are at greatest risk for abuse.

The most successful crime prevention strategies will likely be directed at the larger levels of analysis, including the group level, the community and organization level, and the society level. Efforts to prevent exposure to risk factors at these levels of analysis can be considered *primary crime prevention* (Robinson, 1999) because they are aimed at everyone in society, at all places and times. Primary crime prevention strategies can be differentiated from secondary crime prevention and crime control (also known as tertiary crime prevention). *Secondary crime prevention* is only aimed at particular people at particular times. As mentioned earlier, *crime control* or *tertiary crime prevention* is aimed at people who have already engaged in antisocial behavior. It makes more sense to direct crime prevention strategies at as many people as possible; this entails strategies at the group level, community and organization level, and society level.

Efforts should be made to reduce all individuals' exposure to deviant peers, especially in unsupervised settings, as well as family conflict and disruption, abuse, neglect, and harsh, authoritarian style discipline. These factors increase one's risk of early antisocial behavior, which then increases the risk that individuals will associate with deviant peers, have trouble at school and work, be labeled a troublemaker, and continue on to more serious and sustained antisocial behavior. Efforts should be made to educate parents about the harmful effects of these factors and to encourage good, supportive, loving, egalitarian families who are authoritative (but not physical) and consistent in their use of discipline.

Efforts also need to be directed at reducing the conditions of social disorganization discussed in the book, especially poverty, an unfettered expansion of urbanization, and residential mobility. A complete antisocial prevention policy will make it possible for people to make a decent living while still being heavily and meaningfully involved in raising their children, monitoring their children's behavior, interacting with neighbors, and participating in meaningful community organizations. This means businesses must allow and even encourage people to work more flexible schedules; provide affordable, on-site day care and supervision for children of employees; and permit employees to pattern their lifestyles in ways that reduce their exposure to criminal victimization. Since meaningful and fulfilling employment can be turning points away from deviance, we must do whatever it takes to ensure that people find such employment.

In neighborhoods, residential heterogeneity can encourage antisocial behavior, but only if people refuse to get to know each other based on their cultural, racial, and ethnic differences. Thus, appreciation of diversity and multicultural tolerance must be promoted and celebrated in the nation's cities. Crime prevention policies must be taken out of the context of politics so that we can invest our money in the programs that work. We must also strive toward restorative justice rather than applying negative labels to offenders. Destructive labeling produces more antisocial behavior, not less.

Major emphasis must be placed on addressing employment and relationship problems of all individuals. Healthy and fulfilling marriages are helpful for preventing antisocial behavior in adulthood (but they do not guarantee it). Additionally, two parents are more able than one parent to supervise, monitor, and correct their children's behavior in a consistent and healthy way. Thus, policies that ensure people are ready for marriage will prevent antisocial behavior, just as birth control education programs will prevent unwanted pregnancies. All sources of general strain must also be addressed, including discrimination and victimization. People will always experience negative emotions, but in the absence of legitimate means of directing frustration and anger, they will resort to antisocial behavior as a means for coping with strain. Thus, we must give people opportunities to vent when they perceive injustice and experience noxious stimuli. Counseling programs at places of employment and in schools are good examples. Additionally, government and major corporations must stop encouraging antisocial behavior through their policies of crime reduction and business, respectively. Two examples discussed in this book come to mind. A policy of mass incarceration will not only fail to reduce crime in the long run, but is likely to increase it. And mass layoffs by corporations (downsizing) encourage crime in several ways. As we mentioned earlier, all government and business executives should be required by law to consider the implications for crime and antisocial behavior before they implement policies. Finally, to the degree that big business harms Americans through fraud, illegal dumping of chemicals, and so forth, they must be held accountable, not only for the sake of justice, but also for the purposes of preventing criminality that results from their harmful behaviors.

Summary

In this chapter, we revisited the logic of theoretical integration first discussed in chapter 3. After discussing two brief examples of integration, we summarized relationships between the risk factors discussed in the whole book and antisocial behavior. Then, we illustrated how these risk factors come together and interact to increase the risk of antisocial behavior by presenting the integrated systems theory of antisocial behavior. After briefly discussing how these risk factors are likely to affect individuals over the life course, we turned to a discussion of the logical policy implications deduced from the integrated systems theory of antisocial behavior. We suggested nurturant crime prevention strategies as the most logical approach to reduce antisocial behavior.

Discussion Questions

1. In what ways is theoretical integration superior to theory competition?
2. Briefly summarize the integrated theories of crime introduced in this chapter. What are the weaknesses of these theories?
3. List and define the different types of integration available to scholars.
4. Briefly summarize Vila's general evolutionary ecological paradigm.
5. What is meant by the term *strategic style*? How is this term similar to personality?
6. Create an outline that summarizes the main findings of the book.
7. Summarize the integrated theory of antisocial behavior. What are the main propositions of this theory?
8. Locate a real-life case of a sensationalized crime and apply the integrated theory of antisocial behavior to explain it.
9. Which risk factors in this theory are most likely to emerge before birth and at birth?
10. Which risk factors in this theory are most likely to emerge in early childhood?
11. Which risk factors in this theory are most likely to emerge in adolescence?
12. Which risk factors in this theory are most likely to emerge in early adulthood?
13. What are nurturant strategies?
14. What is restorative justice?
15. Outline the main policy implications for prevention of antisocial behavior that can be deduced from the integrated systems theory of antisocial behavior.
16. Which policy implications would be most successful and which would not? Explain.

References

Abbar, M., Courtet, P., Bellivier, F., Leboyer, M., Boulenger, J., Castelhau, D., et al. (2001). Suicide attempts and the tryptophan hydroxylase gene. *Molecular Psychiatry, 6*(3), 268–273.

Adams, M. (1996). Labeling and differential association: Towards a general social learning theory of crime and deviance. *American Journal of Criminal Justice, 20*(2), 147–164.

Adams, M., & Evans, T. (1996). Teacher disapproval, delinquent peers, and self-reported delinquency: A longitudinal test of labeling theory. *Urban Review, 28*(3), 199–211.

Adler, F., & Laufer, W. (1999). The legacy of anomie theory. *Advances in Criminological Theory, 6.* Somerset, NJ: Transaction.

Agazarian, Y., & Gantt, S. (2000). *Autobiography of a theory: Developing the theory of living human systems and its systems-centered practice.* Philadelphia: Jessica Kingsley.

Agnew, R. (1989). A longitudinal test of the revised strain theory. *Journal of Quantitative Criminology, 5,* 373–387.

Agnew, R. (1992). Foundation for a general strain theory of crime and delinquency. *Criminology, 30*(1), 47–87.

Agnew, R. (1997). Stability and change in crime over the life course: A strain theory explanation. In T. Thornberry (Ed.), *Developmental theories of crime and delinquency.* New Brunswick, NJ: Transaction.

Agnew, R. (1999). A general strain theory of community differences in crime rates. *Journal of Research in Crime and Delinquency, 36*(2), 123–155.

Agnew, R., & Brezina, T. (1997). Relational problems with peers, gender, and delinquency. *Youth and Society, 29,* 84–111.

Agnew, R., & White, H. (1992). An empirical test of general strain theory. *Criminology, 30*(4), 475–499.

Agnew, R., Brezina, T., Wright, J., & Cullen, F. (2002). Strain, personality traits, and delinquency: Extending general strain theory. *Criminology, 40*(1), 43–72.

Akers, R. (1985). *Deviant behavior: A social learning approach* (3rd ed.). Belmont, CA: Wadsworth.

Akers, R. (1991). Self-control as a general theory of crime. *Journal of Quantitative Criminology, 7*(2), 201–211.

Akers, R. (1992). *Drugs, alcohol, and society: Social structure, process, and policy.* Belmont, CA: Wadsworth.

Akers, R. (1994). *Criminological theory: Introduction and evaluation.* Los Angeles: Roxbury.

Akers, R. (1996). Is differential association/social learning cultural deviance theory? *Criminology, 34*(2): 229–247.

Akers, R. (1997). *Criminological theory: Introduction and evaluation* (2nd ed.). Los Angeles: Roxbury.

Akers, R. (1998). *Social learning and social structure: A general theory of crime and deviance.* Boston: Northeastern University Press.

Akers, R. (1999). Social learning and social structure: Reply to Sampson, Morash, and Krohn. *Theoretical Criminology, 3,* 477–493.

Akers, R. (2001). *Criminological theory: Introduction and evaluation* (3rd ed.). Los Angeles: Roxbury.

Akers, R., & Cochran, J. (1985). Adolescent marijuana use: A test of three theories of deviant behavior. *Deviant Behavior, 6,* 323–346.

Akers, R., & Lee, G. (1996). A longitudinal test of social learning theory: Adolescent smoking. *Journal of Drug Issues, 26,* 317–343.

Akers, R., Krohn, M., Lana-Kaduce, L., & Radosevich, M. (1979). Social learning and deviant behavior: A specific test of a general theory. *American Sociological Review, 44,* 635–655.

Alarid, L., Burton, V., Jr., & Cullen, F. (2000). Gender and crime among felony offenders: Assessing the generality of social control and differential association theories. *The Journal of Research in Crime and Delinquency, 37*(2), 171–199.

Alessio, V., Kiesner, J., Massimiliano, P., and Massimo Santinello (2008). Antisocial behavior and depressive symptoms: Longitudinal and concurrent relations. *Adolescence, 43* (171), 649–660.

Alm, B., Humble, K., Leppert, J., Sorensen, S., Tegelman, R., Thorell, L., & Lidberg, L. (1996). Criminality and psychopathy as related to thyroid activity in former juvenile delinquents. *Acta Psychiatry Scandinavia, 94*(2), 112–117.

Alpert, J., & Fava, M. (1997). Nutrition and depression: The role of folate. *Nutrition Review, 55*(5), 145–149.

Amato, P., & Keith, B. (1991). Parental divorce and adult well-being: A meta-analysis. *Journal of Marriage and the Family, 53,* 43–58.

American Academy of Child & Adolescent Psychiatry (1999). Children with oppositional defiant disorder. Retrieved December 16, 2008 from: *http://www.aacap.org/cs/root/facts_for_families/children_with_oppositional_defiant_disorder.*

American Academy of Child & Adolescent Psychiatry (2001). Normal adolescent development, part one. Retrieved December 16, 2008 from: *http://www.aacap.org/cs/root/facts_for_families/normal_adolescent_development_part_i.*

American Academy of Child & Adolescent Psychiatry (2001). Normal adolescent development, part two. Retrieved December 16, 2008 from: *http://www.aacap.org/cs/root/facts_for_families/normal_adolescent_development_part_ii.*

American Academy of Child & Adolescent Psychiatry (2001). Parenting: Preparing for adolescence. Retrieved December 16, 2008 from: *http://www.aacap.org/cs/root/facts_for_families/parenting_preparing_for_adolescence.*

American Academy of Child & Adolescent Psychiatry (2004). Discipline. Retrieved December 16, 2008 from: *http://www.aacap.org/cs/root/facts_for_families/discipline.*

American Academy of Child & Adolescent Psychiatry (2008). Fighting and biting. Retrieved December 16, 2008 from: *http://www.aacap.org/cs/root/facts_for_families/fighting_and_biting.*

American Academy of Child & Adolescent Psychiatry (2008). The teen brain. Retrieved December 16, 2008 from: *http://www.aacap.org/cs/root/facts_for_families/the_teen_brain_behavior_problem_solving_and_decision_making.*

American Academy of Child & Adolescent Psychiatry. (2002). Facts for families. Retrieved from *www.aacap.org/publications/factsfam.*

American Academy of Pediatrics (1998). *Caring for your baby and young child: Birth to age 5.* New York: Bantam Books.

American Medical Association. (1999). Rehabilitation of persons with traumatic brain injury. *Journal of the American Medical Association, 282*(10), 974–983.

Anderson, B., Holmes, M., & Ostresh, E. (1999). Male and female delinquents' attachments and effects of attachments on severity of self-reported delinquency. *Criminal Justice and Behavior, 26*(4), 435–452.

Anderson, E. (1999). *Code of the street: Decency, violence, and the moral life of the inner city.* New York: W. W. Norton.

Anderson, S., Bechara, A., Damasio, H., Tranel, D., & Damasio, A. (1999). Impairment of social and moral behavior related to early damage in human prefrontal cortex. *Nature Neuroscience, 2*(11), 1032–1037.

Andresen, M. (2006). A spatial analysis of crime in Vancouver, British Columbia: A synthesis of social disorganization and routine activity theory. *Canadian Geographer, 50*(4), 487–502.

Andrews, D., & Bonta, J. (1994). *The psychology of criminal conduct.* Cincinnati, OH: Anderson.

Andrews, D., & Bonta, J. (2006). *The psychology of criminal conduct* (4th edition). Cincinnati, OH: Anderson Publishing Company.

Andrews, D., Zinger, I., Hoge, R., Bonta, J., Gendreau, P., & Cullen, F. (1990). Does correctional treatment work? A clinically relevant and psychologically informed meta-analysis. *Criminology, 28*, 369–404.

Andrews, T., Rose, F., & Johnson, D. (1998). Social and behavioral effects of traumatic brain injury in children. *Brain Injury, 12*(2), 133–138.

Antonaccio, O., & Tittle, C. (2008). Morality, self-control, and crime. *Criminology, 46*(2), 479–510.

Appleton, J. (1975). *The experience of place.* London: Wiley.

Armstrong, G., & Griffin, M. (2007). The effect of local life circumstances on victimization of drug-involved women. *Justice Quarterly, 24*(1), 80–105.

Arneklev, B., Grasmick, H., Tittle, C., & Bursik, R., Jr. (1993). Low self-control and imprudent behavior. *Journal of Quantitative Criminology, 9*(3), 225–247.

Arrigo, B. (1994). *The peripheral core of law and criminology: On postmodern social theory and conceptual integration.* Paper presented at the annual meeting of the American Society of Criminology, Miami, FL.

Asberg, M., Traskman, L., & Thoren, P. (1976). 5-HIAA in the cerebrospinal fluid: A biochemical suicide predictor? *Archives of General Psychiatry, 33*(X), 1193–1197.

Asnis, S., & Smith, R. (1978). Amphetamine abuse and violence. *Journal of Psychedelic Drugs, 10*, 317–377.

Avakame, E. (1997). Modeling the patriarchal factor in juvenile delinquency: Is there room for peers, church, and television? *Criminal Justice and Behavior, 24*(4), 477–494.

Avenevoli, S., Sessa, F., & Steinberg, L. (1999). Family structure, parenting practices, and adolescent adjustment: An ecological examination. In E. Hetherington (Ed.), *Coping with divorce, single parenting, and remarriage: A risk and resiliency perspective.* Mahwah, NJ: Lawrence Erlbaum Associates.

Babiak, P., & Hare, R. (2006). *Snakes in suits: When psychopaths go to work.* New York: Harper Collins.

Babinski, L., Hartsough, C., & Lambert, N. (1999). Childhood conduct problems, hyperactivity-impulsivity, and inattention as predictors of adult criminal activity. *Journal of Child Psychology and Psychiatry, 40*(3), 347–355.

Bachman, R. (1991). An analysis of American Indian homicide: A test of social disorganization and economic deprivation at the reservation county level. *Journal of Research in Crime and Delinquency, 28*(4), 456–471.

Bachman, R., Paternoster, R., & Ward, S. (1992). The rationality of sexual offending: Testing a deterrence/rational choice conception of sexual assault. *Law and Society Review, 26*, 434–472.

Backlar, P. (1998). Criminal behavior and mental disorder: Impediments to assigning moral responsibility. *Community Mental Health, 34*(1), 3–12.

Badcock, C. (2000). *Evolutionary psychology: A critical introduction.* Cambridge, England: Polity Press.

Baer, J., Barr, H., Bookstein, F., Sampson, P., & Streissguth, A. (1998). Prenatal alcohol exposure and family history of alcoholism in the etiology of adolescent alcohol problems. *Journal of Studies on Alcohol, 59,* 533–543.

Bagozzi, R., & Warshaw, P. (1992). An examination of the etiology of the attitude-behavior relation for goal-directed behavior. *Multivariate Behavioral Research, 27,* 601–634.

Baier, C. (2001). If you love me, keep my commandments: A meta-analysis of the effect of religion on crime. *The Journal of Research in Crime and Delinquency, 38*(1), 3–22.

Baker, T. (1999). Supergangs—Or organized crime? *Law & Order, 47*(10), 192–197.

Balaban, E., Alper, J., & Kasamon, Y. (1996). Mean genes and the biology of aggression: A critical review of recent animal and human research. *Journal of Neurogenetics, 11,* 1–43.

Baldry, A., & Farrington, D. (2000). Bullies and delinquents: Personal characteristics and parental styles. *Journal of Community and Applied Social Psychology, 10*(1), 17–31.

Baldwin, J. (1990). The role of sensory stimulation in criminal behavior, with special attention to the age peak in crime. In L. Ellis & H. Hoffman (Eds.), *Crime in biological, social, and moral contexts.* New York: Praeger.

Bandura, A. (1969). *Principles of behavior modification.* New York: Holt, Rinehart, & Winston.

Bandura, A. (1973). *Aggression: A social learning analysis.* Englewood Cliffs, NJ: Prentice-Hall.

Bandura, A. (1977). *Social learning theory.* New York: General Learning Press.

Banks, T., & Dabbs, J. (1996). Salivary testosterone and cortisol in a delinquent and violent urban subculture. *Journal of Social Psychology, 136*(1), 49–56.

Barak, G. (1998). *Integrating criminologies.* Needham Heights, MA: Allyn & Bacon.

Barkley, R. (1997). *ADHD and the nature of self-control.* New York: The Guilford Press.

Barlow, D., & Barlow, M. (2002). Racial profiling: A survey of African American police officers. *Police Quarterly, 5*(3), 334–358.

Barnes, G., Hoffman, J., Welte, J., Farrell, M., & Dintcheff, B. (2006). Effects of parental monitoring and peer deviance on substance use and delinquency. *Journal of Marriage & Family, 68*(4), 1084–1104.

Baron, S. (2007). Street youth, gender, financial strain, and Crime: Exploring Broidy and Agnew's extension to general strain theory. *Deviant Behavior, 28*(3), 273–302.

Baron, S. (2008). Street youth, unemployment, and crime: Is it that simple? Using general strain theory to untangle the relationship. *Canadian Journal of Criminology & Criminal Justice, 50*(4), 399–434.

Baron, S., & Forde, D. (2007). Street youth crime: A test of control balance theory. *Justice Quarterly, 24*(2), 335–355.

Bartusch, D., & Matsueda, R. (1996). Gender, reflected appraisals, and labeling: A cross-group test of an interactionist theory of delinquency. *Social Forces, 75*, 145–177.

Bartusch, D., Lynam, D., Moffitt, T., & Silva, P. (1997). Is age important? Testing a general versus a developmental theory of antisocial behavior. *Criminology, 35*(1), 13–48.

Bateman, D., & Chiriboga, C. (2000). Dose-response effect of cocaine on newborn head circumference. *Pediatrics, 106*(3), e33.

Batton, C. & Kadleck, C. (2004). Theoretical and methodological issues in racial profiling research. *Justice Quarterly, 7*, 30–64.

Baumrind, D. (1996). Parenting: The discipline controversy revisited. *Family Relations, 45*, 405–414.

Bausman, K. (2000). Reconceptualizing the link between economic deprivation and crime: A metropolitan/nonmetropolitan comparison of social disorganization theory. *Dissertation Abstracts International, A: The Humanities and Social Sciences, 60*(8), 3143-A.

Beauregard, E., Rossmo, D., & Proulx, J. (2007). A descriptive model of the hunting process of serial sex offenders: A rational choice perspective. *Journal of Family Violence, 22*(6), 449–463.

Beaver, K. (2008). *The nature and nurture of antisocial outcomes.* New York: LFB Scholarly Press.

Beaver, K., & Holtfreter, K. (2009). Biosocial influences on fraudulent behaviors. *The Journal of Genetic Psychology.* Forthcoming.

Beaver, K., Wright, J., & Delisi, M. (2008). Delinquent peer group formation: Evidence of a gene X environment correlation. *Journal of Genetic Psychology, 169* (3), 227–244.

Beaver, K., Wright, J., & Walsh, A. (2008). A gene-based evolutionary explanation for the association between criminal involvement and number of sex partners. *Social Biology, 54*(Spring), 47–55.

Beaver, K., Wright, J., Delisi, M., & Vaughn, M. (2008a). Desistance from delinquency: The marriage effect revisited and extended. *Social Science Research, 37*(3), 736–752.

Beaver, K., Wright, J., Delisi, M., & Vaughn, M. (2008b). Genetic influences on the stability of low self-control: Results from a longitudinal sample of twins. *Journal of Criminal Justice, 36*(6), 478–485.

Beaver, K., Wright, J., Delisi, M., Daigle, L., Swatt, M., & Gibson, C. (2007a). Evidence of a gene x environment interaction in the creation of victimization: Results from a longitudinal sample of adolescents. *International Journal of Offender Therapy and Comparative Criminology, 51*(X), 620–645.

Beaver, K., Wright, J., Delisi, M., Walsh, A., Vaughn, M., Boisvert, D., & Vaske, J. (2007b). A gene x gene interaction between DRD2 and DRD4 is associated with conduct disorder and antisocial behaviors in males. *Behavioral and Brain Functions, 3.*

Beccaria, C. (1776). *An essay on crime and punishment.* London: C. Mitchum.

Bechara, A., Damasio, A., Damasio, H., & Anderson, S. (1999). Insensitivity to future consequences following damage to human prefrontal cortex. *Cognition, 50, 7.*

Becker, H. (1963). *Outsiders: Studies in the sociology of deviance.* New York: Free Press of Glencoe.

Beckett, K., & Sasson, T. (2000). *The politics of injustice: Crime and punishment in America.* Thousand Oaks, CA: Pine Forge Press.

Beirne, P., & Messerschmidt, J. (2000). *Criminology* (3rd ed.). Boulder, CO: Westview Press.

Beitchman, J., Baldassarra, L., Mik, H., Deluca, V., King, N., Bender, D., Ehtesham, S., & Kennedy, J. (2006). Serotonin transporter polymorphisms and persistent, pervasive childhood aggression. *American Journal of Psychiatry, 163*(X), 1103–1105.

Belfrage, H. (1998). A ten-year follow-up of criminality in Stockholm mental patients: New evidence for a relation between mental disorder and crime. *British Journal of Criminology, 38*(1), 145–155.

Belknap, J. (1996). *The invisible woman.* Belmont, CA: Wadsworth.

Bell, D., Carlson, J., & Richard, A. (1998). The social ecology of drug use: A factor analysis of an urban environment. *Substance Use and Misuse, 33*(11), 2201–2217.

Bellair, P. (1996). The consequences of crime for social disorganization theory: An examination of reciprocal effects between crime and social interaction. *Dissertation Abstracts International, A: The Humanities and Social Sciences, 56*(10), 4154-A.

Benda, B. (1990). Crime, drug abuse, and mental illness: A comparison of homeless men and women. *Journal of Social Service, 13*(3), 39–60.

Benda, B. (1995). The effect of religion on adolescent delinquency revisited. *The Journal of Research in Crime and Delinquency, 32*(4), 446–466.

Benda, B. (1997). An examination of reciprocal relationship between religiosity and different forms of delinquency within a theoretical model. *The Journal of Research in Crime and Delinquency, 34*(2), 163–186.

Benda, B., & Corwyn, R. (1997). Religion and delinquency: The relationship after considering family and peer influences. *Journal for the Scientific Study of Religion, 36*(1), 81–92.

Benda, B., Pope, S., & Kelleher, K. (2006). Church attendance or religiousness: Their relationship to adolescents' use of alcohol, other drugs, and delinquency. *Alcoholism Treatment Quarterly, 24*(1/2), 75–87.

Bennett, C., & Brostoff, J. (1997). The health of criminals related to behavior, food, allergy, and nutrition: A controlled study of 100 persistent young offenders. *Journal of Nutritional and Environmental Medicine, 7*, 359–366.

Bennett, C., McEwen, L., McEwen, H., & Rose, E. (1998). The Shipley Project: Treating food allergy to prevent criminal behavior in community settings. *Journal of Nutritional and Environmental Medicine, 8*, 77–83.

Bennett, R. (1991). Development and crime. *Sociological Quarterly, 32*(3), 343–363.

Bennett, R. (1991). Routine activities: A cross-national assessment of a criminological perspective. *Social Forces, 70*(1), 147–163.

Benson, M. (2002). *Crime and the life course: An introduction.* Los Angeles: Roxbury.

Benton, D., & Cook, R. (1991). The impact of selenium supplementation on mood. *Biological Psychiatry, 29*(11), 1092–1098.

Benton, D., & Roberts, G. (1991). Vitamin and mineral supplements improve the intelligence scores and concentration of six-year-old children. *Personality and Individual Differences, 12*(11), 1151–1158.

Berenbaum, S., & Resnick, S. (1997). Early androgen effects on aggression in children and adults with congenital adrenal hyperplasia. *Psychoneuroendocrinology, 22*, 505–515.

Bernard, T. (2001). Integrating theories in criminology. In R. Paternoster & R. Bachman (Eds.), *Explaining crime and criminals.* Los Angeles: Roxbury.

Bernard, T., & Snipes, J. (1996). Theoretical integration in criminology. In M. Tonry (Ed.), *Crime and justice: A review of research.* Chicago: University of Chicago Press.

Bernburg, J., & Krohn, M. (2003). Labeling, life chances, and adult crime: The direct and indirect effects of official intervention in adolescence on crime in early adulthood. *Criminology, 41*(4), 1287–1318.

Bernburg, J., Krohn, M., & Rivera, C. (2006). Official labeling, criminal embeddedness, and subsequent delinquency: A longitudinal test of labeling theory. *Journal of Research in Crime & Delinquency, 43*(1), 67–88.

Bernhardt, P. (1997). Influences of serotonin and testosterone in aggression and dominance: Convergence with social psychology. *Current Directions in Psychological Science, 6*(2), 44–48.

Bhati, A., & Piquero, A. (2007,). Estimating the impact of incarceration on subsequent offending trajectories: Deterrent, criminogenic, or null effect? *Journal of Criminal Law & Criminology, 98*(1), 207–253.

Biderman, A., Johnson, L., McIntyre, J., & Weir, A. (1967). *Report on a pilot study in the District of Columbia on victimization and attitudes toward law enforcement.* Washington, DC: U.S. Government Printing Office.

Biederman, J., Fardone, S., Mick, E., Spencer, T., Wilens, T., & Kiely, K., et al. (1995). High risk for attention deficit hyperactivity disorder among children of parents with childhood onset of the disorder: A pilot study. *American Journal of Psychiatry, 152*(3): 431–435.

Birch, E., Garfield, S., Hoffman, D., Uauy, R., & Birch, D. (2000). A randomized controlled trial of early dietary supply of long chain polyunsaturated fatty acids and mental development in term infants. *Developmental Medicine and Child Neurology, 42,* 174–181.

Bjork, J., Dougherty, D., Moeller, F., Cherek, D., & Swann, A. (1999). The effects of tryptophan depletion and loading on laboratory aggression in men: Time course and a food-restricted control. *Psychopharmacology, 142*(1), 24–30.

Blackburn, R. (1998). Criminality and the interpersonal circle in mentally disordered offenders. *Criminal Justice and Behavior, 25*(2), 155–176.

Blanco, C., Orensanz-Muñoz, L., Blanco-Jerez, C., & Saiz-Ruiz, J. (1996). Pathological gambling and platelet MAO activity: A psychobiological study. *American Journal of Psychiatry, 153*(1), 119–121.

Bloom, M., Cutter, M., Davidson, R., Dougherty, M., Drexler, E., Gelernter, J., et al. (2000). *Genes, environment, and human behavior.* A report of the Biological Sciences Curriculum Study (BSCS). Colorado Springs, CO: BSCS.

Blount, E. (2002). *Occupational crime: Deterrence, investigation, and reporting in compliance with federal guidelines.* New York: CRC.

Blum, K., & Payne, J. (1991). *Alcohol and the addictive brain: New hope for alcoholics from biogenetic research.* New York: Free Press.

Blumer, H. (1969). *Symbolic interactionism.* Englewood Cliffs, NJ: Prentice-Hall.

Blumstein, A. (1995). A LEN interview with Professor Alfred Blumstein of Carnegie Mellon University. *Law Enforcement News, 21,* 10–13.

Blumstein, A., Farrington, D., & Moitra, S. (1985). Delinquency careers. In M. Tonry & N. Morris (Eds.), *Crime and justice: An annual review of research.* Chicago: University of Chicago Press.

Bodel, M. (1994). Psychological pollution. *Social Work, 39*(6), 632–635.

Boeringer, S., Shehan, C., & Akers, R. (1991). Social contexts and social learning in sexual coercion and aggression: Assessing the contribution of fra-
ternity membership. *Family Relations, 40,* 558–564.

Bohm, R. (2001). *A primer in crime and delinquency* (2nd ed.). Belmont, CA:
Wadsworth.

Bohm, R. (2007). *Deathquest III. An introduction to the theory & practice of capital punishment in the United States* (3rd Ed.). Cincinnati, OH: Anderson.

Bonger, W. (1916). *Criminality and economic conditions.* Boston: Little, Brown.

Book, A., Starzyk, K., & Quinsey, V. (2001). The relationship between testosterone
and aggression: A meta-analysis. *Aggression and Violent Behavior, 6*(X), 579–599.

Booth, J., Farrell, A., & Varano, S. (2008). Social control, serious delinquency,
and risky behavior: A gendered analysis. *Crime & Delinquency, 54*(3), 423–456.

Bostaph, L. (2007). Race and repeats: The impact of officer performance on
racially biased policing. *Journal of Criminal Justice, 35*(4), 405–417.

Boston Physicians for Social Responsibility. (2000). *In harm's way — Toxic
threats to child development.* Retrieved from *www.igc.org/psr/ihw.htm.*

Bothamley, J. (1993). *Dictionary of theories.* London: Gale Research International.

Botting, N., Powls, A., Cooke, R., & Marlow, N. (1997). Attention deficit hyperactivity disorders and other psychiatric outcomes in very low birthweight
children at 12 years. *Journal of Child Psychology and Psychiatry, 38*(8), 931–941.

Boulding, K. (1978). *Ecodynamics: A new theory of social evolution.* Beverly
Hills, CA: Sage.

Boutwell, B., & Beaver, K. (2008). A *biosocial* explanation of delinquency ab-
stention. *Criminal Behaviour & Mental Health, 18*(1), 59–78.

Boutwell, B., Beaver, K., & Gibson, C. (2009). Prenatal exposure to cigarette
smoke and childhood externalizing behavioral problems: A propensity
score matching approach. Unpublished manuscript.

Box, S., Hale, C., & Andrews, G. (1988). Explaining fear of crime. *British Journal of Criminology, 28,* 340–356.

Boyum, D., & Kleiman, M. (1995). Alcohol and other drugs. In J. Wilson &
J. Petersilia (Eds.), *Crime.* San Francisco: ICS.

Braithwaite, J. (1989). *Crime, shame, and reintegration.* New York: Cambridge
University Press.

Braithwaite, J. (1995). *Crime, shame, and reintegration* (2nd ed.). New York: Cambridge University Press.

Braithwaite, J. (2001). Reintegrative shaming. In R. Paternoster & R. Bachman (Eds.),*Explaining crime and criminals.* Los Angeles: Roxbury.

Brannigan, A. (1997). Self-control, social control and evolutionary psychology:
Towards an integrated perspective on crime. *Canadian Journal of Criminology, 39*(4), 403–431.

Brantingham, P., & Brantingham, P. (1984). *Patterns in crime*. New York: MacMillan.

Breakey, J. (1997). The role of diet and behavior in childhood. *Journal of Pediatric Child Health, 33*, 190–194.

Brennan, P., & Mednick, S. (1990). *Childhood psychopathology as a predictor of violent criminal behavior*. Paper presented at the annual meeting of the American Psychological Association, Atlanta, GA.

Brennan, P., Grekin, E., & Mednick, S. (1999). Maternal smoking during pregnancy and adult male criminal outcomes. *Archives of General Psychiatry, 56*, 215–219.

Brennan, P., Raine, A., Schulsinger, F., Kirkegaard-Sorensen, L., Knop, J., Hutchings, B., et al. (1997). Psychophysiological protective factors for male subjects at high risk for criminal behavior. *American Journal of Psychiatry, 154*(6), 853–855.

Breslau, N., Kilbey, M., & Andreski, P. (1993). Nicotine dependence and major depression. New evidence from a prospective investigation. *Archives of General Psychiatry, 50*, 31–35.

Brezina, T. (1996). Adapting to strain: An examination of delinquent coping responses. *Criminology, 34*(1), 39–60.

Britt, C. (1994). Versatility. In T. Hirschi & M. Gottfredson (Eds.), *The generality of deviance*. New Brunswick, NJ: Transaction.

Britt, C. (1997). Reconsidering the unemployment and crime relationship: Variation by age group and historical period. *Journal of Quantitative Criminology, 13*(4), 405–428.

Brizer, D. (1988). Psychopharmacology and the management of violent patients. *Psychiatric Clinics of North America, 11*(X), 551–568.

Broidy, L., & Agnew, R. (1997). Gender and crime: A general strain theory perspective. *Journal of Research in Crime and Delinquency, 34*(3), 275–306.

Brown, G., Ebert, M., Goyer, P., Jimerson, D., Klein, W., Bunney, W., & Goodwin, F. (1982). Aggression, suicide, and serotonin: Relationships to CSF amine metabolites. *American Journal of Psychiatry, 139*(X), 741–746.

Brown, G., Goodwin, F., Ballenger, J., Goyer, P., & Major, L. (1979). Aggression in humans correlates with cerebrospinal fluid amine metabolites. *Psychiatry Research, 1*(X), 131–139.

Brown, S., Esbensen, F., & Geis, G. (2001). *Criminology: Explaining crime and its context* (4th ed.). Cincinnati, OH: Anderson.

Browning, C. (2002). The span of collective efficacy: extending social disorganization theory to partner violence. *Journal of Marriage & Family, 64*(4), 833–850.

Brunner, H., Nelen, M., Breakfield, X., Ropers, H., & Van Oost, B. (1993). Abnormal behavior associated with a point mutation in the structural gene for monoamine oxidase A. *Science, 262*(5133): 578–580.

Buckley, W. (1968). *Modern systems research for the behavioral scientist.* Chicago: Aldine.

Buerger, M., & Farrell, A. (2002). The evidence of racial profiling: Interpreting documented and unofficial sources. *Police Quarterly, 5*(3), 272.

Bureau Of Justice Statistics (2009). Victim characteristics. Retrieved January 13, 2009 from: *http://ojp.usdoj.gov/bjs/cvict_v.htm#prace.*

Bureau of Justice Statistics. (1996). Crime facts. Retrieved from *www.ojp.usdoj.gov/bjs.*

Bureau of Justice Statistics. (2001). Drugs and crime facts. Retrieved from *http://www.ojp.usdoj.gov/bjs/dcf/contents.htm.*

Bureau of Justice Statistics. (2001). Expenditures for justice. Retrieved from *www.ojp.usdoj.gov/bjs.*

Burgess, E. (1928). The growth of a city. In R. Park, E. Burgess, & D. McKenzie (Eds.), *The city.* Chicago: University of Chicago Press.

Burgess, R., & Akers, R. (1968). A differential association-reinforcement theory of criminal behavior. *Social Problems, 14,* 128–147.

Burgess, R., & Drais, A. (1999). Beyond the "Cinderella effect": Life history theory and child maltreatment. *Human Nature, 10*(4), 373–398.

Bursik, R. (1988). Social disorganization and theories of crime and delinquency. *Criminology, 26,* 519–551.

Bursik, R., & Grasmick, H. (1993). *Neighborhoods and crime: The dimensions of effective social control.* New York: Lexington.

Burt, A., Mcgue, M., Carter, L., & Iacono, W. (2007). The different origins of *stability* and change in *antisocial* personality disorder symptoms. *Psychological Medicine, 37*(1), 27–38.

Burt, C., Simons, R., & Simons, L. (2006). A longitudinal test of the effects of the parenting and the stability of self-control: Negative evidence for the general theory of crime. *Criminology, 44*(2), 353–396.

Bushway, S. (1998). The impact of an arrest on the job stability of young white American men. *The Journal of Research in Crime and Delinquency, 35*(4), 454–479.

Bushway, S., & Reuter, P. (2008). Economists' contribution to the study of crime and the criminal justice system. In M. Tonry (Ed.), *Crime and justice: A review of.*

Buss, D. (1995). Evolutionary psychology: A new paradigm for psychological science. *Psychological Inquiry, 6,* 1–30.

Byrne, J., & Sampson, R. (1986). *The social ecology of crime.* London: Springer-Verlag.

Cadoret, R., Langbehn, D., Caspers, K., Troughton, E., Yucuis, R., Sandhu, H., & Philibert, R. (2003). Associations of the serotonin transporter promoter polymorphism with aggressivity, attention deficit, and conduct disorder in an adoptee population. *Comprehensive Psychiatry, 44*(X), 88–101.

Cadoret, R., Yates, W., Troughtan, E., Woodworth, G., & Stewart, M. (1996). An adoption study of drug abuse/dependency in females. *Comprehensive Psychiatry, 37*(2), 88–94.

Cadoret, R., Yates, W., Troughton, E., Woodworth, G., & Stewart, M. (1995). Genetic-environmental interaction in the genesis of aggressivity and conduct disorders. *Archives of General Psychiatry, 52*(X), 916–924.

Camp, G. (1968). *Nothing to lose: A study of bank robbery in America.* Doctoral dissertation, Yale University, New Haven, CT.

Campbell, A. (1999). Staying alive: Evolution, culture, and women's intrasexual aggression. *Behavioral and Brain Sciences, 22,* 203–214.

Cancino, J. (2005). The utility of social capital and collective efficacy: Social control policy in nonmetropolitan settings. *Criminal Justice Policy Review, 16*(3), 287–318.

Cantillon, D. (2006). Community social organization, parents, and peers as mediators of perceived neighborhood block characteristics on delinquent and prosocial activities. *American Journal of Community Psychology, 37*(1/2), 111–127.

Capaldi, D., Kim, H., & Owen, L. (2008). Romantic Partners' influence on men's likelihood of arrest in early adulthood. *Criminology, 46*(2), 267–299.

Capra, F. (1996). *The web of life: A new scientific understanding of living systems.* New York: Anchor Books.

Carey, T. (1994). Spare the rod and spoil the child: Is this a sensible justification for the use of punishment in child rearing? *Child Abuse and Neglect, 18*(12), 1005–1010.

Carlson, N. (1994). *Physiology of behavior.* Boston: Allyn & Bacon.

Carlton, R., Ente, G., Blum, L., Heyman, N., Davis, W., & Ambrosino, S. (2000). Rational dosages of nutrients have a prolonged effect on learning disabilities. *Alternative Therapies, 6*(3), 85–91.

Carmelli, D., Swan, Ga., Robinette, D., & Fabsitz, R. (1992). Genetic influence on smoking: A study of male twins. *New England Journal of Medicine, 327*(12): 829–833.

Cases, O., Seif, I., Grimsby, J., Gaspar, P., Chen, K., Pournin, S., et al. (1995). Aggressive behavior and altered amounts of brain serotonin and norepinephrine in mice lacking MAOA. *Science, 268:* 1763–1766.

Caspi, A., & Silva, P. (1995). Temperamental qualities at age 3 predict personality traits in young adulthood: Longitudinal evidence from a birth cohort. *Child Development, 66,* 486–498.

Caspi, A., Begg, D., Dickson, N., Langley, J., Moffitt, T., McGee, R., & Silva, P. (1995). Identification of personality types at risk of poor health and injury in late adolescence. *Criminal Behaviour and Mental Health, 5*(4), 330–350.

Caspi, A., Henry, B., McGee, R., Moffitt, T., & Silva, P. (1995). Temperamental origins of child and adolescent behavior problems: From age three to age fifteen. *Child Development, 66*, 55–68.

Caspi, A., Mcclay, J., Moffitt, T., Mill, J., Martin, J., Craig, I., Taylor, A., & Poulton, R. (2002). Role of genotype in the cycle of violence in maltreated children. *Science 297*(X), 851–854.

Caspi, A., Moffitt, T., Silva, P., Stouthamer-Loeber, M., Krueger, R., & Schmutte, P. (1994). Are some people crime-prone? Replications of the personality-crime relationship across countries, genders, races, and methods. *Criminology, 32*(2), 163–195.

Cattarello, A. (2000). Community-level influences on individuals' social bonds, peer associations, and delinquency: A multilevel analysis. *Justice Quarterly, 17*(1), 33–60.

Cauffman, E., Steinberg, L., & Piquero, A. (2005). Psychological, neuropsychological, and physiological and physiological correlates of serious antisocial behavior in adolescence: The role of self-control. *Criminology, 43*(1), 133–175.

Ceballo, R., Ramirez, C., Hearn, K., & Maltese, K. (2003). Community violence and children's psychological well-being: Does parental monitoring matter? *Journal of Clinical Child & Adolescent Psychology, 32*(4), 586–592.

Cernkovich, S., Giordano, P., & Rudolph, J. (2000). Race, crime, and the American dream. *The Journal of Research in Crime and Delinquency, 37*(2), 131–170.

Cernkovich, S., Lanctôt, N., & Giordano, P. (2008). Predicting adolescent and adult antisocial behavior among adjudicated delinquent females. *Crime & Delinquency, 54*(1), 3–33.

Chaiken, M. (2000, March). Violent neighborhoods, violent kids. *Juvenile Justice Bulletin*, March.

Chamlin, M., & Cochran, J. (1995). Assessing Messner and Rosenfeld's institutional anomie theory: A partial test. *Criminology, 33*(3), 411.

Chan, A., Keane, R., & Robinson, J. (2001). The contribution of maternal smoking to preterm birth, small for gestational age and low birth weight among Aboriginal and non-Aboriginal births in South Australia. *Medical Journal, 174*(8), 389–393.

Chapple, C. (2005). Self-control, peer relations, and delinquency. *Justice Quarterly, 22*(1), 89–106.

Checkland, P. (1999). *Systems thinking, systems practice.* New York: J. Riley.

Chesney-Lind, M., & Pasko, L. (2004). *The female offender: Girls, women, and crime.* Thousand Oaks, CA: Sage.

Chilton, R. (1986). Urban crime rates: Effects of inequality, welfare dependency, region, and race. In J. Byrne & R. Sampson (Eds.), *The social ecology of crime.* New York: Springer-Verlag.

Chiricos, T. (1987). Rates of crime and unemployment: An analysis of aggregate research evidence. *Social Problems, 34*(2), 187–211.

Chiricos, T., & Bales, W. (1991). Unemployment and punishment: An empirical assessment. *Criminology, 29*(4): 701–724.

Chudler, E. (2001). *Neuroscience.* Retrieved from *http://faculty.washington.edu/ chudler/ neurok.html.*

Clark, W., & Grunstein, M. (2000). *Are we hardwired? The role of genes in human behavior.* New York: Oxford University Press.

Clarke, P. (1998). Tobacco smoke, smoking, genes, and dopamine. *Lancet, 352*(9122), 84–85.

Clarke, R. (1983). *Situational crime prevention: Its theoretical basis and practical scope. Crime and justice, An annual review of research* (Vol. 4). Chicago: University of Chicago Press.

Clarke, R. (2001). Rational choice. In R. Paternoster & R. Bachman (Eds.), *Explaining crime and criminals.* Los Angeles: Roxbury.

Clarke, R., & Cornish, D. (2001). Rational choice. In R. Paternoster & R. Bachman (Eds.), *Explaining crime and criminals.* Los Angeles: Roxbury.

Clarke, R., & Felson, M. (1993). *Routine activity and rational choice.* London: Transaction.

Clear, T., Hardyman, P., Stout, B., Lucken, K., & Dammer, H. (2000). A value of religion in prison: An inmate perspective. *Journal of Contemporary Criminal Justice, 16*(1), 53–74.

Cleare, A., & Bond, A. (1997). Does central serotonergic function correlate inversely with aggression? A study using D-fenfluramine in healthy subjects. *Psychiatry Research, 69,* 89–95.

Cleveland, H., Wiebe, R., van den Oord, E., & Rowe, D. (2000). Behavior problems among children from different family structures: The influence of genetic self-selection. *Child Development, 71,* 733–751.

Clinard, M., & Yeager, P. (2005). *Corporate crime.* Edison, NJ: Transaction.

Cloward, R., & Ohlin, L. (1960). *Delinquency and opportunity: A theory of delinquent gangs.* New York: The Free Press.

Coccaro, E., Bergeman, C., Kavoussi, R., & Seroczynski, A. (1997). Heritability of aggression and irritability: A twin study of the Buss-Durkee aggression scales in adult male subjects. *Biological Psychiatry, 41,* 273–284.

Coccaro, E., Berman, M., Kavoussi, R., & Hauger, R. (1996). Relationship of prolactin response to d-fenfluramine to behavioral and questionnaire assessments of aggression in personality-disordered men. *Biological Psychiatry, 40,* 157–164.

Cochran, J., Wood, P., & Arneklev, B. (1994). Is the religiosity-delinquency relationship spurious? A test of arousal and social control theories. *The Journal of Research in Crime and Delinquency, 31*(1), 92–112.

Cohen, A. (1955). *Delinquent boys: The culture of the gang.* New York: The Free Press.

Cohen, B., & Zeira, R. (1999). Social control, delinquency, and victimization among kibbutz adolescents. *International Journal of Offender Therapy and Comparative Criminology, 43*(4), 503–513.

Cohen, L. (1997). The cynic's guide to human nature and crime control: Why it hardly matters which theory you use ... *Politics & the Life Sciences, 16*(1), 23–25.

Cohen, L., & Felson, M. (1979). Social change in crime rate trends: A routine activity approach. *American Sociological Review, 44,* 588–608.

Cohen, L., & Land, K. (1987). Age, structure, and crime: Symmetry versus asymmetry and the projection of crime rates through the 1990s. *American Sociological Review, 52,* 170–183.

Cohen, L., Felson, M., & Land, K. (1980). Property crime rates in the United States: A macrodynamic analysis, 1947–1977; with ex ante forecasts for the mid-1980's. *American Journal of Sociology, 86,* 90–118.

Coleman, J. (1998). *The criminal elite* (4th ed.). New York: St. Martin's Press.

Collins, J., & Schmidt, F. (1993). Personality, integrity, and white collar crime: A construct validity study. *Personnel Psychology, 46*(2), 295–312.

Collins, P. (2000). Gender, black feminism, and black political economy. *Annals of the American Academy of Political and Social Science, 568,* 41–53.

Collins, W., Maccoby, E., Steinberg, L., Heatherington, M., & Bornstein, M. (2000). Contemporary research on parenting: The case for nature and nurture. *American Psychologist, 55,* 218–232.

Comings, D. (1997). Genetic aspects of childhood behavioral disorders. *Child Psychiatry and Human Development, 27*(3), 139–150.

Comings, D., Gade-Andavolu, R., Gonzalez, N., Wu, S., Muhleman, D., Chen C., et al. (2001). The additive effect of neurotransmitter genes in pathological gambling. *Clinical Genetics, 60*(X), 107–116.

Conger, R., & Simons, R. (1997). Life-course contingencies in the development of adolescent antisocial behavior: A Matching Law approach. In T. Thornberry (Ed.), *Developmental theories of crime and delinquency.* New Brunswick, NJ: Transaction.

Connor, J., Young, R., Lawford, B., Ritchie, T., & Noble, E. (2002). D2 dopamine receptor (DRD2) polymorphism is associated with severity of alcohol dependence. *European Psychiatry, 17*(X), 17–23.

Constantino, J., Morris, J., & Murphy, D. (1997). CSF 5-HIAA and family history of antisocial personality disorder in newborns. *American Journal of Psychiatry, 154*(12): 410–415.

Cook, E., Stein, M., Krasowski, M., Cox, N., Olkan, O., & Kieffer, J., et al. (1995). Association of attention deficit disorder and the dopamine transporter gene. *American Journal of Human Genetics, 56:* 993–998.

Cook, P. (2006). The deterrent effects of California's Proposition 8. *Criminology & Public Policy, 5*(3), 413–416.

Costello, B. (1997). On the logical adequacy of cultural deviance theories. *Theoretical Criminology, 1,* 403–428.

Costello, B., & Vowell, P. (1999). Testing control theory and differential association: A reanalysis of the Richmond Youth Project data. *Criminology, 37*(4), 742–815.

Coupe, T., & Blake, L. (2006). Daylight and darkness targeting strategies and the risks of being seen at residential burglaries. *Criminology, 44*(2), 431–464.

Courtet, P., Baud, P., Abbar, M., Boulenger, J., Castelnau, D., Mouthon, D., et al. (2001). Association between violent suicidal behavior and the low activity allele of the serotonin transporter gene. *Molecular Psychiatry, 6*(3), 338–341.

Covington, J., & Taylor, R. (1991). Fear of crime in urban residential neighborhoods: Implications of between- and within-neighborhood sources for current models. *The Sociological Quarterly, 32*(2), 231–49.

Covington, W., Jr. (1997). *Systems theory applied to television station management in the competitive marketplace.* Lanham, MD: University Press of America.

Cramer, F. (1993). *Chaos and order: The complex structure of living systems.* New York: VCH.

Cressey, D. (1960). Epidemiology and individual conduct. *Pacific Sociological Review, 3,* 47–58.

Crime-Times. (1995). 1:4, 6.

Crime-Times. (1997). 3:1(1).

Crime-Times. (1997). 3:1(3), 6.

Crime-Times. (1997). 3:3(2).

Crime-Times. (1998). 4:1(1).

Crime-Times. (2001). 7(4), 1.

Crime-Times. (2001). 7(4), 8.

Crockett, M., Clark, L., Tabibnia, G., Lieberman, M., & Robbins, T. (2008). Serotonin modulates behavioral reactions to unfairness. *Science, 320*(X), 1739.

Cromwell, P. (1995). *In their own words.* Los Angeles: Roxbury.

Cromwell, P., Olson, J., & Avary, D. (1991). *Breaking and entering: An ethnographic analysis of burglary.* Newbury Park, CA: Sage.

Crossman, L. (1995). *Factors which predict hostility toward women: Implications for counseling.* Paper presented at the annual meeting of the American Educational Research Association, San Francisco, CA.

Cui, M., Donnellan, M., & Conger, R. (2007). Reciprocal influences between parents' marital problems and adolescent internalizing and externalizing behavior. *Developmental Psychology, 43*(6), 1544–1552.

Cullen, F., & Wright, J. (1997). Liberating the anomie-strain paradigms: Implications from social-support theory. In N. Passas & R. Agnew (Eds.), *The future of anomie theory.* Boston: Northeastern University Press.

Cullen, F., Cavender, G., Maakestad, W., & Benson, M. (2006). *Corporate crime under attack: The fight to criminalize business violence.* Cincinnati, OH: Anderson, p. 25.

Cullen, F., Gendreau, P., Jarjoura, G., & Wright, J. (1997). Crime and the bell curve: Lessons from intelligent criminology. *Crime and Delinquency, 43*(4), 387–411.

Curran, D., & Renzetti, C. (1994). *Theories of crime.* Boston: Allyn & Bacon.

Currie, E. (1997). Market crime and community: Toward a mid-range theory of post-industrial violence. *Theoretical Criminology, 1,* 147–172.

Cushman, P. (1974). Relationship between narcotic addiction and crime. *Federal Probation, 38,* 38–43.

D'Alessio, S., & Stolzenberg, L. (1990). A crime of convenience: The environment and convenience store robbery. *Environment and Behavior, 22*(2), 255–271.

d'Orban, P. (1976). Barbiturate abuse. *Journal of Medical Ethics, 2,* 63–67.

Dabbs, J. (1995). Quoted in *Crime-Times, 1*(3), 2.

Dabbs, J., & Hargrove, M. (1997). Age, testosterone, and behavior among female prison inmates. *Psychosomatic Medicine, 59,* 477–480.

Dabbs, J., Carr, T., Frady, R., & Riad, J. (1995). Testosterone, crime, and misbehavior among 692 male prison inmates. *Personality and Individual Differences, 18*(5): 627–633.

Damasio, A. (2000). A neural basis for sociopathy. *Archives of General Psychiatry, 57*(2): 128–129.

Damasio, A., Tranel, Da., & Damasio, H. (1990). Individuals with sociopathic behavior caused by frontal damage fail to respond automatically to social stimuli. *Behavioral Brain Research, 41*(2): 81–94.

Davidson, R., Putnam, K., & Larson, C. (2000). Dysfunction in the neural circuitry of emotion regulation—A possible prelude to violence. *Science, 289*(5479), 591–594.

Davis, S. (1991). An overview: Are mentally ill people really more dangerous? *Social Work, 36*(2), 174–180.

Davison, E. (1996). An ecological analysis of crime in a mid-sized Southern city: Tests of routine activity and social disorganization approaches. *Disserta-*

tion Abstracts International, A: The Humanities and Social Sciences, 56(11), 4562-A.

Day, N., Richardson, G., Goldschmidt, L., & Cornelius, M. (2000). Effects of prenatal tobacco exposure on preschoolers' behavior. *Journal of Developmental and Behavioral Pediatrics, 21*(3), 180–188.

De Coster, S., & Kort-Butler, L. (2006). How general Is general strain theory? *Journal of Research in Crime & Delinquency, 43*(4), 297–325.

De Cristofaro, J., & LaGamma, E. (1995). Prenatal exposure to opiates. *Mental Retardation and Developmental Disabilities Research Reviews, 1*(3), 177–182.

Deckel, A., & Hesselbrock, V. (1995). Behavioral and cognitive measurements predict scores on the MAST: A 3-year prospective study. *Clinical and Experimental Research, 19*(2), 476–481.

DeFrance, J., Hymel, C., Trachtenberg, M., Ginsberg, L., Schweitzer, F., Estes, S., et al. (1997). Enhancement of attention processing by Kantroll (TM) in healthy humans: A pilot study. *Clinical Electroencephalography, 28*(2), 68–75.

DeFronzo, J. (1996). Welfare and burglary. *Crime and Delinquency, 42*(2): 223–230.

Delgado, R., & Stefancic, J. (2001). *Critical race theory: An introduction.* New York: New York University Press.

Delisi, M., Beaver, K., Wright, J., & Vaughan, M. (2008). The etiology of criminal onset: The enduring salience of nature and nurture. *Journal of Criminal Justice, 36*(3), 217–223.

DeMott, K. (1999). Personality disorders may be genetic. *Clinical Psychiatry News, 27*(12), 27.

Demuth, S., & Brown, S. (2004). Family structure, family processes, and adolescent delinquency: The significance of parental of parental absence versus parental gender. *Journal of Research in Crime & Delinquency, 41*(1), 58–81.

Dennet, D. (1993). *Consciousness explained.* New York: Penguin.

Denno, D. (1990). *Biology and violence.* New York: Cambridge University Press.

Depue, R., & Collins, P. (1999). Neurobiology of the structure of personality: Dopamine, facilitation of incentive motivation, and extraversion. *Behavioral and Brain Sciences, 22*, 491–569.

Dinan, T. (1996). Serotonin: Current understanding and the way forward. *International Clinical Psychopharmacology, 11*(1), 19–21.

Ditton, P. (1999). Mental health and treatment of inmates and probationers. Available: *www.ojp.gov/bjs/pub/ascii/mhtip.txt.*

Doherty, E. (2006). Self-control, social bonds, and desistance: A test of life-course interdependence. *Criminology, 44*(4), 807–833.

Donker, A., Smeenk, W., Van Der Laan, P., & Verhulst, F. (2003). Individual stability of antisocial behavior from childhood to adulthood: Testing the stability postulate of Moffitt's developmental theory. *Criminology, 41*(3), 593–609.

Dowling, J. (1998). *Creating mind: How the brain works.* New York: W.W. Norton and Company.

Downs, A. (1995). *Corporate executions: The ugly truth about layoffs—How corporate greed is shattering lives, companies, and communities.* New York: American Management Association.

Drapela, L. (2005). Does dropping out of high school cause deviant behavior? An analysis of the national education longitudinal study. *Deviant Behavior, 26*(1), 47–62.

Durkheim, E. (1893). *De la Division du Travail Social.* Paris: F. Alcan.

Durkheim, E. (1897). *Le Suicide.* Paris: F. Alcan.

Durkin, J. (1996). *Living groups: Group psychotherapy and general systems theory.* New York: Brunner/Mazel.

Eck, J. (1994). *Drug markets and drug places: A case-control study of the spatial structure of illicit drug dealing.* Doctoral dissertation, University of Maryland.

Eck, J., & Weisburd, D. (1995). *Crime and place.* Monsey, NY: Criminal Justice Press.

Einstadter, W., & Henry, S. (1995). *Criminological theory: An analysis of its underlying assumptions.* Fort Worth, TX: Harcourt Brace.

Einstadter, W., & Henry, S. (2006). *Criminological theory: An analysis of its underlying assumptions* (2nd Ed.). Lanham, MD: Rowman & Littlefield.

Elander, J., Rutter, M., Simonoff, E., & Pickles, A. (1997). Explanations for apparent late onset criminality in a high-risk sample of children followed up in adult life. *British Journal of Criminology, 40*(3), 497–509.

Ellingswood, E. (1971). Assault and homicide associated with amphetamine use. *American Journal of Psychiatry, 127,* 90–95.

Elliott, D. (1994). Serious violent offenders: Onset, development course, and termination—The American Society of Criminology 1993 Presidential Address. *Criminology, 32,* 1–21.

Elliott, D., Huizinga, D., & Ageton, S. (1985). *Explaining delinquency and drug use.* Beverly Hills, CA: Sage.

Elliott, D., Wilson, W., Huizinga, D., Sampson, R., Elliott, A., & Rankin, B. (1996). The effects of neighborhood disadvantage on adolescent development. *Journal of Research in Crime and Delinquency, 33,* 389–426.

Ellis, L. (1987). Criminal behavior and r/K selection: An extension of gene-based evolutionary theory. *Deviant Behavior, 8,* 149–176.

Ellis, L. (1988). The victimful-victimless crime distinction, and seven universal demographic correlates of victimful criminal behavior. *Personality and Individual Differences, 9,* 525–548.

Ellis, L. (1991). A synthesized(biosocial) theory of rape. *Journal of Consulting and Clinical Psychology, 59,* 631–642.

Ellis, L. (1991). Monoamine oxidase and criminality: Identifying an apparent biological marker for antisocial behavior. *Journal of Research in Crime and Delinquency, 28*(X), 227–251.

Ellis, L. (1996). Arousal theory and the religiosity-criminality relationship. In P. Cordella & L. Siegel (Eds.), *Readings in contemporary criminological theory.* Boston: Northeastern University Press.

Ellis, L. (1998). Neo-Darwinian theories of violent criminality and antisocial behavior: Photographic evidence from nonhuman animals and a review of the literature. *Aggression and Violent Behavior, 3,* 61–110.

Ellis, L., & Nyborg, H. (1992). Racial/ethnic variations in male testosterone levels: A probable contributor to group differences in health. *Steroids, 57,* 72–75.

Ellis, L., & Walsh, A. (1997). Gene-based evolutionary theories in criminology. *Criminology, 35,* 229–276.

Ellis, L., & Walsh, A. (2000). *Criminology: A global perspective.* Boston: Allyn & Bacon. *Merriam-Webster's Collegiate Dictionary* (2001). Retrieved from *www.m-w.com.*

Ellwanger, S. (2007). Strain, attribution, and traffic delinquency among young drivers. *Crime & Delinquency, 53*(4), 523–551.

Endler, N., & Magnusson, D. (1976). Toward an interactional psychology of personality. *Psychological Bulletin, 83,* 956–974.

Engel, R., & Calnon, J. (2004). Examining the influence of drivers' characteristics during traffic stops with police: Results from a national survey. *Justice Quarterly, 21,* 49–90.

England, M. & Wakely, J. (1991). *A colour atlas of the brain and spinal cord:* London: Wolfe Publishing.

Erikson, K. (1962). Notes on the sociology of deviance. *Social Problems, 9,* 311.

Erman, D., & Lundman, R. (2001). *Corporate and governmental deviance: Problems of organizational behavior in contemporary society* (6th Edition). New York: Oxford University Press.

Evans, R. (2001). Examining the informal sanctioning of deviance in a chat room culture. *Deviant Behavior, 22*(3), 195–210.

Evans, T., Cullen, F., Burton, V., Jr., Dunaway, R., & Benson, M. (1997). The social consequences of self-control: Testing the general theory of crime. *Criminology, 35*(3), 475–504.

Evans, T., Cullen, F., Dunaway, R., & Burton, V., Jr. (1995). Religion and crime reexamined: The impact of religion, secular controls, and social ecology on adult criminality. *Criminology, 33*(2), 195.

Eysenck, H. (1964). *Crime and personality.* London: Routledge & Kegan Paul.

Eysenck, H. (1977). *Crime and personality.* St. Albans, England: Paladin.

Ezinga, M., Weerman, F., Westenberg, P., & Bijleveld, C. (2008). Early adolescence and delinquency: Levels of psychosocial development and self-control as an explanation of misbehaviour and delinquency. *Psychology, Crime & Law, 14*(4), 339–356.

Faraone, S., Doyle, A., Mick, E., & Biederman, J. (2001). Meta-analysis of the association between the 7-repeat allele of the dopamine D4 receptor gene and attention deficit hyperactivity disorder. *American Journal of Psychiatry, 158*(X), 1052–1057.

Farrington, D. (1988). Psychobiological factors in the explanation and reduction of delinquency. *Today's Delinquent, 7,* 44–46.

Farrington, D. (1989). Early predictors of adolescent aggression and adult violence. *Victims of Violence, 4,* 79–100.

Farrington, D. (1993). Childhood origins of teenage antisocial behaviour and adult social dysfunction. *Journal of the Royal Society of Medicine, 86,* 13–17.

Farrington, D. (1994). Early developmental prevention of juvenile delinquency. *Criminal Behavior and Mental Health, 4*(3), 209–227.

Farrington, D. (1995). The development of offending and antisocial behaviour from childhood: Key findings from the Cambridge study in delinquent development. *Journal of Child Psychology, 360,* 929–963.

Farrington, D. (1996). The explanation and prevention of youthful offending. In J.

Farrington, D. (1997). Nurturant crime prevention strategies are also needed in the United Kingdom. *Politics & the Life Sciences, 16*(1), 26–27.

Farrington, D., & Junger, M. (Eds.). (1995). *Criminal Behavior and Mental Health, 5*(4). Special Issue.

Farrington, D., & West, D. (1995). Effects of marriage, separation, and children on offending by adult males. In Z. Blau & J. Hagan (Eds.), *Current perspectives on aging and the life cycle: Vol. 4. Delinquency and disrepute in the life course.* Greenwich, CT: JAI.

Farrington, D., Ohlin, L., & Wilson, J. (1986). *Understanding and controlling crime.* New York: Springer-Verlag.

Fattah, E. (1993). The rational choice/opportunity perspectives as a vehicle for integrating criminological and victimological theories. In R. Clarke & M. Felson (Eds.), *Routine activity and rational choice. Advances in criminological theory* (Vol. 5). New Brunswick, NJ: Transaction Publishers.

Faust, F. (1995). Series of personal communications. Tallahassee: Florida State University.

Fava, M., Davidson, K., Alpert, J., Nierenberg, A., Worthington, J., O'Sullivan, R., & Rosenbaum, J. (1996). Hostility changes following antidepressant treatment: Relationship to stress and negative thinking. *Journal of Psychiatric Research, 30*(6), 459–467.

Fava, M., Vuolo, R., Wright, E., Nierenberg, A., Alpert, J., & Rosenbaum, J. (2000). Fenfluramine challenge in unipolar depression with and without anger attacks. *Psychiatry Research, 94*, 9–18.

Feldman, H., Agar, M., & Beschner, G. (1979). *Angel dust: An ethnographic study of PCP users.* Lexington, MA: Lexington Books.

Felson, M. (1983). Ecology of crime. In S. Kadish (Ed.), *Encyclopedia of crime and justice.* New York: Free Press.

Felson, M. (1986). Linking the criminal choices, routine activities, informal control, and criminal outcomes. In D. Cornish & R. Clarke (Eds.), *The reasoning criminal: Rational choice perspectives on offending.* New York: Springer-Verlag.

Felson, M. (1987). Routine activities and crime prevention in the developing metropolis. *Criminology, 25*(4), 911–931.

Felson, M. (1994). *Crime and everyday life: Insights and implications for society.* Thousand Oaks, CA: Pine Forge Press.

Felson, M. (1995). Those who discourage crime. In J. Eck & D. Weisburd (Eds.), *Crime and place.* Monsey, NY: Criminal Justice Press.

Felson, R., & Staff, J. (2006). Explaining the academic performance-delinquency relationship. *Criminology, 44*(2), 299–320.

Ferguson, C. (2009). Genetic contributions to antisocial personality and behavior (APB): A meta-analytic review (1996–2006) from an evolutionary perspective. *Journal of Social Psychology.* Forthcoming.

Fergusson, D., & Horwood, L. (1995). Early disruptive behavior, IQ, and later school achievement and delinquent behavior. *Journal of Abnormal Child Psychology, 23*, 183–199.

Fergusson, D., Woodward, L., & Horwood, J. (1998). Maternal smoking during pregnancy and psychiatric adjustment in late adolescence. *Archives of General Psychiatry, 55*, 721–727.

Ferrell, J. (1997). Youth, crime, and cultural space. *Social Justice, 24*(4), 21–38.

Ferrell, J. (1998). Freight train graffiti: Subculture, crime, dislocation. *Justice Quarterly, 15*(4), 587–608.

Field, T., Scafidi, F., Pickens, R., Prodromidis, M., Pelaez-Nogueras, M., Torquati, J., et al. (1998). Poly-drug using adolescent mothers and their infants receiving early intervention. *Adolescence, 33*(129), 117–143.

Figlio, R., Hakim, S., & Rengert, G. (1986). *Metropolitan crime patterns.* Monsey, NY: Criminal Justice Press.

Finestone, H. (1967). Narcotics and criminality. *Law and Contemporary Problems, 22,* 60–85.

Fishbein, D. (1990). Biological perspectives in criminology. *Criminology, 28,* 27–72.

Fishbein, D. (1998). *How can neurobiological research inform prevention strategies?* Paper presented at the annual meeting of the American Society of Criminology, Las Vegas, NV.

Fishbein, D. (2001). *Biobehavioral perspectives in criminology.* Belmont, CA: Wadsworth.

Fishbein, D., & Pease, S. (1996). *The dynamics of drug abuse.* Boston: Allyn & Bacon.

Fishbein, D., & Thatcher, R. (1982). *Nutritional and electrophysiological indices of maladaptive behavior.* Paper presented at the MIT Conference on Research Strategies for Assessing the Behavioral Effects and Nutrients, Boston, MA.

Fisher, S., & Greenberg, R. (1977). *The scientific credibility of Freud's theories and therapy.* New York: Basic Books.

Fitzgerald, M.,(1985). *Neuroanatomy basic and applied.* London: Bailliere Tindall.

Foglia, J. (2000). Adding an explicit focus on cognition to criminological theory. In D.

Fowles, R., & Merva, M. (1996). Wage inequality and criminal activity: An extreme bounds analysis for the United States, 1975–1990. *Criminology, 34,* 163–182.

Frank, N., & Lynch, M. (1992). *Corporate crime, corporate violence.* New York: Harrow & Heston.

Frank, R. (1994). Talent and the winner-take-all society. *American Prospect, 17,* 99.

Franzek, E., Sprangers, N., Janssesn, A., Van Duijn, V., & Van De Wetering, B. (2008). Prenatal exposure to the 1944–45 Dutch 'hunger winter' and addiction later in life. *Addiction, 103*(X), 433–438.

Freeman, R. (1991). Crime and unemployment. In J. Wilson (Ed.), *Crime and public policy.* San Francisco: ICS Press.

Freisthler, B., Lascala, E., Gruenewald, P., & Treno, A. (2005). An examination of drug activity: Effects of neighborhood social organization on the development of drug distribution systems. *Substance Use & Misuse, 40*(5), 671–686.

Fried, P., Watkinson, B., & Gray, R. (1998). Differential effects on cognitive functioning in 9- to 12-year-olds prenatally exposed to cigarettes and marihuana. *Neurotoxicology and Teratology, 20*(3), 293–306.

Friedrichs, D. (1996). *Trusted criminals: White collar crime in contemporary society* (2nd Ed.) Belmont, CA: Wadsworth.

Friedrichs, D. (2006). *Trusted criminals: White collar crime in contemporary society* (3rd Ed.). Belmont, CA: Wadsworth.

Froggio, G., & Agnew, R. (2007). The relationship between crime and "objective" versus "subjective" strains. *Journal of Criminal Justice, 35*(1), 81–87.

Frye, V., & Wilt, S. (2001). Femicide and social disorganization. *Violence Against Women, 7*(3), 335–351.

Gaines, L., & Kraska, P. (1997). *Drugs, crime, and justice.* Prospect Heights, IL: Waveland Press.

Gale Encyclopedia of Psychology. (2001). Retrieved from *www.gale.com.*

Ganem, N., & Agnew, R. (2007). Parenthood and adult criminal offending: The importance of relationship quality. *Journal of Criminal Justice, 35*(6), 630–643.

Gardner, D., Lucas, P., & Cowdry, R. (1990). CSF metabolites in borderline personality disorder compared with normal controls. *Biological Psychiatry, 28*(X), 247–254.

Garofalo, J. (1987). Reassessing the lifestyle model of criminal victimization. In M.

Gates, L., & Rohe, W. (1987). Fear and reactions to crime: A revised model. *Urban Affairs Quarterly, 22,* 425–453.

Geiss, G. (2000). On the absence of self-control as the basis for a general theory of crime: A critique. *Theoretical Criminology, 4*(1), 35–53.

Gendreau, P., Little, T., & Goggin, C. (1996). A meta-analysis of the predictors of adult offender recidivism: What works! *Criminology, 34,* 575–607.

Gerson, L., & Preston, D. (1979). Alcohol consumption and the incidence of violent crime. *Journal of Studies on Alcohol, 40,* 307–312.

Gerstein, L., & Briggs, J. (1993). Psychological and sociological discriminants of violent and nonviolent serious juvenile offenders. *Journal of Addictions and Offender Counseling, 14*(1), 2–13.

Gartrell, J., & Marquez, S. (1995). The spurious relationship between IQ and social behavior: Ethnic abuse, gender ignorance, and confounded education. *The Alberta Journal of Educational Research, 41*(3), 277–282.

REFERENCES

Gharajedaghi, J. (1999). *Systems thinking: Managing chaos and complexity: A platform for designing business architecture.* Burlington, MA: Butterworth-Heinemann.

Giancola, P. (1995). Evidence for dorsolateral and orbital prefrontal cortical involvement in the expression of aggressive behavior. *Aggressive Behavior, 21,* 431–450.

Giancola, P. (2000). Neuropsychological functioning and antisocial behavior: Implications for etiology and prevention. In D. Fishbein (Ed.), *The science, treatment, and prevention of antisocial behaviors.* Kingston, NJ: Civic Research Institute.

Gibbs, J. (1975). *Crime, punishment, and deterrence.* New York: Elsevier.

Gibson, C., & Tibbetts, S. (1999). *Maternal cigarette smoking during pregnancy and early onset of criminal offending in an urban African-American birth cohort.* Paper presented at the annual meeting of the American Society of Criminology, Washington, DC.

Giedd, J., Blumenthal, J., Jeffries, N., Castellanos, F., Liu, H., Zijenbos, A., et al. (1999). Brain development during childhood and adolescence: A longitudinal MRI study. *Nature Neuroscience, 2,* 861–863.

Gilligan, C. (1982). *In a different voice. Psychological theory and women's development.* Cambridge, MA: Harvard University Press.

Giordano, P., Longmore, M., Schroder, R., & Seffrin, P. (2008). A life-course perspective on spirituality and desistance from crime. *Criminology, 46*(1), 99–132.

Glaser, D. (1956). Criminality theories and behavioral images. *American Journal of Sociology, 61,* 433–444.

Glaser, D. (1971). *Social deviance.* Chicago: Markham.

Glaser, D. (1974). Interlocking dualities in drug use, drug control, and crime. In J. Inciardi & C. Chambers (Eds.), *Drugs and the criminal justice system.* Beverly Hills, CA: Sage.

Glaser, D. (2000). Child abuse and neglect and the brain—A review. *Journal of Child Psychology and Psychiatry, 41,* 97–116.

Glassner, B., & Loughlin, J. (1987). *Drugs in adolescent worlds: Burnouts to straights.* New York: St. Martin's Press.

Glees, P. (1988). *The human brain.* New York: Cambridge University Press.

Glueck, S., & Glueck, E. (1950). *Unraveling juvenile delinquency.* New York: Commonwealth Fund.

Goetting, A. (1994). The parenting-crime connection. *Journal of Primary Prevention, 14*(3), 169–186.

Goffman, E. (1971). *Relations in public: Micro studies of the public order.* New York: Harper & Row.

Goldberg, E. (2001). Quote from *Crime-Times, 7*(4), 8.

Golden, M. (1997). *Heroic defeats: The politics of job loss.* New York: Cambridge University Press.

Goldschmidt, L., Day, N., & Richardson, G. (2000). Effects of prenatal marijuana exposure on child behavior problems at age 10. *Neurotoxicology and Teratology, 22*(3), 325–336.

Goldstein, A. (1994). *The ecology of aggression.* New York: Plenum Press.

Goldstein, P. (1979). *Prostitution and drugs.* Lexington, MA: D.C. Heath.

Goldstein, P. (1998). The drugs/violence nexus: A tripartite conceptual framework. In J. Inciardi & K. McElrath (Eds.), *The American drug scene: An anthology.* Los Angeles: Roxbury.

Goldstein, P., & Duchaine, N. (1980). *Daily criminal activities of street drug users.* Paper presented at the annual meeting of the American Society of Criminology, Toronto, Canada.

Golomb, B. (1998). Cholesterol and violence: Is there a connection? *Annals of Internal Medicine, 128,* 478–487.

Goodman, R. (1995). The relationship between normal variation in IQ and common childhood psychopathology: A clinical study. *European Child and Adolescent Psychiatry, 4*(3).

Gordon, D. (1996). *Fat and mean: The corporate squeeze of working Americans and the myth of managerial "downsizing".* New York: Martin Kessler Books.

Gordon, J. (2001). School delinquency in secondary school-aged children in Barbados: An examination of the influence of family, school, and peers. *Dissertation Abstracts International, A: The Humanities and Social Sciences, 61*(8), 3360-A.

Gordon, R. (1976). Prevalence: The rare datum in delinquency measurement and its implications for the theory of delinquency. In M. Klein (Ed.), *The juvenile justice system.* Beverly Hills, CA: Sage Publications.

Gordon, R. (1987). SES versus IQ in the race-IQ-delinquency model. *International Journal of Sociology and Social Policy, 7*(3), 30–96.

Gottfredson, D. (1999). *Exploring criminal justice: An introduction.* Los Angeles: Roxbury.

Gottfredson, D., McNeil, R., & Gottfredson, G. (1991). Social area influences on delinquency: A multilevel analysis. *Journal of Research in Crime and Delinquency, 28,* 197–226.

Gottfredson, L. (1997). Intelligence and social policy. *Intelligence, 24,* 1–320.

Gottfredson, M. (1984). *Victims of crime: The dimensions of risk.* Home Office Research Study No. 81. London: Her Majesty's Stationary Office.

Gottfredson, M., & Hirschi, T. (1990). *A general theory of crime.* Stanford, CA: Stanford University Press.

Gottfredson, M., & Hirschi, T. (1993). Commentary: Testing the general theory of crime. *Journal of Research in Crime and Delinquency, 30*(1), 47–54.

Gottfredson, M., & Hirschi, T. (Eds.), *Positive criminology.* Newbury Park, CA: Sage.

Gould, L. (1974). Crime and the addict: Beyond common sense. In J. Inciardi & K. McElrath (Eds.), *The American drug scene: An anthology.* Los Angeles: Roxbury.

Goyer, P., Andreason, P., Semple, W., Clayton, A., King, A., Compton-Toth, B., et al. (1994). Positron-emission tomography and personality disorders. *Neuropsychopharmacology, 10,* 21–28.

Graeff, F., Guimaraes, F., De Andrade, T., & Deakin, J. (1996). Role of 5-HT in stress, anxiety, and depression. *Pharmacology and Biochemistry of Behavior, 54*(1), 129–141.

Grasmick, H., Tittle, C., Bursik, R., Jr., & Arneklev, B. (1993). Testing the core empirical implications of Gottfredson and Hirschi's general theory of crime. *The Journal of Research in Crime and Delinquency, 30*(1), 5–29.

Greenberg, D. (1999). The weak strength of social control theory. *Crime and Delinquency, 45*(1), 66–81.

Greenberg, S., & Adler, F. (1974). Crime and addiction: An empirical analysis of the literature, 1920–1973. *Contemporary Drug Problems, 3,* 221–270.

Greene, J., & Taylor, R. (1988). Community-based policing and foot patrol: Issues of theory and evaluation. In J. Greene & S. Mastrofski (Eds.), *Community policing: Rhetoric or reality?* New York: Praeger.

Greenfield, S. (1996). *The human mind explained.* New York: Henry Holt.

Griffin, K., Botvin, G., Scheier, L., Diaz, T., & Miller, N. (2000). Parenting practices as predictors of substance use, delinquency, and aggression among urban minority youth: Moderating effects of family structure and gender. *Psychology of Addictive Behaviors, 14*(2), 174–184.

Gross, S., And Barnes, K. (2002). Road word: Racial profiling and drug interdiction on the highways. *Michigan Law Review, 101*(3), 653.

Grusky, D. (2008). *Social stratification: Class, race, and gender in sociological perspective.* Jackson, TN: Westview.

Guay, J., Ouimet, M., & Proulx, J. (2005). On intelligence and crime: A comparison of incarcerated sex offenders and non-sexual violent criminals. *International Journal of Law and Psychiatry, 28*(X), 405–417.

Gunnar, M. (1996). *Quality of care and the buffering of stress physiology: Its potential in protecting the developing human brain.* Minneapolis: University of Minnesota Institute of Child Development.

Guo, G., Roettger, M., & Cai, T. (2008). The integration of genetic propensities into social-control models of delinquency and violence among male youths. *American Sociological Review, 73*(4), 543–568.

Guo, G., Roettger, M., & Shih, J. (2007). Contributions of the DAT1 and DRD2 genes to serious and violent delinquency among adolescents and young adults. *Human Genetics, 121*(X), 125–136.

Haapanen, R., Britton, L., & Croisdale, T. (2007). Persistent criminality and career length. *Crime & Delinquency, 53*(1), 133–155.

Haapasalo, J., & Pokela, E. (1999). Child-rearing and child abuse antecedents of criminality. *Aggression and Violent Behavior, 4*(1), 107–127.

Haapasalo, J., & Virtanen, T. (1999). Paths between childhood emotional and other maltreatment and psychiatric problems in criminal offenders. *Journal of Emotional Abuse, 1*(4), 15–35.

Haberstick, B., Smolen, A., & Hewitt, J. (2006). Family-based association test of the 5HTTLPR and aggressive behavior in a general population sample of children. *Biological Psychiatry, 59*(X), 836–843.

Hagan, J. (1989). *Structural criminology.* New Brunswick, NJ: Rutgers University Press.

Hagan, J. (1993). The social embeddedness of crime and unemployment. *Criminology, 31*(4): 465–491.

Hagan, J. (1994). *Crime and disrepute.* Thousand Oaks, CA: Pine Forge Press.

Hagan, J., & Coleman, J. (2001). Returning captives of the American war on drugs: Issues of community and family reentry. *Crime and Delinquency, 47*(3), 352–367.

Hagan, J., & McCarthy, B. (1997). Intergenerational sanction sequences and trajectories of street-crime amplification. In I. Gotlib & B. Wheaton (Eds.), *Stress and adversity over the life course: Trajectories and turning points.* New York: Cambridge University Press.

Hagan, J., & Peterson, R. (1994). Criminal inequality in America. In J. Hagan & R. Peterson (Eds.), *Inequality and crime.* Stanford, CA: Stanford University Press.

Hagan, J., & Peterson, R. (1995). *Crime and inequality.* Stanford, CA: Stanford University Press.

Hagan, J., Hefler, G., Classen, G., Boehnke, K., & Merkens, H. (1998). Subterranean sources of subcultural delinquency beyond the American dream. *Criminology, 36*(2), 309–341.

Halperin, J., Newcorn, J., Kopstein, I., McKay, K., Schwaltz, S., Siever, L., et al. (1994). Serotonergic function in aggressive and nonaggressive boys with ADHD. *American Journal of Psychiatry, 151*(2), 682–689.

Hamazaki, T., Sawazaki, S., Itomura, M., Asoka, E., Nagao, Y., Nishimura, N., et al. (1996). The effect of docosahexaenoic acid on aggression in young adults: A placebo-controlled double-blind study. *Journal of Clinical Investigation, 97,* 1129–1133.

Hamid, A. (1998). *Drugs in America: Sociology, economics, and politics.* Newbury Park, CA: Sage.

Hansen, E., & Breivik, G. (2001). Sensation seeking as a predictor of positive and negative risk behaviour among adolescents. *Personality and Individual Differences, 30*(4), 627–640.

Hanson, R., & Morton-Bourgon, K. (2005). The characteristics of persistent sexual offenders: A meta-analysis of recidivism studies. *Journal of Consulting and Clinical Psychology, 73*(6), 1154–1163.

Hardman, P., & Morton, D. (1992). The link between developmental dyslexia, ADD, and chemical dependency. *Environmental Medicine, 8*(3): 61–72.

Hare, R. (1993). *Without conscience: The disturbing world of the psychopaths among us.* New York: Pocket Books.

Hare, R. (1996). Psychopathy: A clinical construct whose time has come. *Criminal Justice and Behavior, 23,* 25–54.

Hare, R. (1999). Psychopathy as a risk factor for violence. *Psychiatric Quarterly, 70*(3), 181–197.

Hare, R. (2000). Quoted in *Crime-Times, 6*(3), 6.

Harlow, J. (1848). Passage of an iron rod through the head. *Boston Medical and Surgical Journal, 39,* 389–393.

Harrigan, J. (2000). *Empty dreams, empty pockets: Class and bias in American politics.* New York: Addison-Wesley Longman.

Harris, D. (1999). The stories, the statistics, and the law: Why "driving while black" matters. *Minnesota Law Review, 84,* 265–326.

Harris, J. (1998). *The nurture assumption: Why children turn out the way they do.* New York: The Free Press.

Harvey, J., & Kosofsky, B. (1998). *Cocaine: Effects on the developing brain.* New York: New York Academy of Sciences.

Hawkes, W., & Hornbostel, L. (1996). Effects of dietary selenium on mood in healthy men living in a metabolic research unit. *Biological Psychiatry, 39*(2), 121–128.

Hawkins, J. (1996). *Delinquency and crime: Current theories.* New York: Cambridge University Press.

Hay, C., & Forrest, W. (2008). Self-control theory and the concept of opportunity: The case for a more systematic union. *Criminology, 46*(4), 1039–1072.

Haynie, D., & Osgood, D. (2005). Reconsidering peers and delinquency: How do peers matter? *Social Forces, 84*(2), 1109–1130.

Hazlett, E., Dawson, M., Buchsbaum, M., & Nuechterlein, K. (1993). Reduced regional brain glucose metabolism assessed by PET in electrodermal nonresponder schizophrenics: A pilot study. *Journal of Abnormal Psychology, 102,* 39–46.

Heck, C., & Walsh, A. (2000). The effects of maltreatment and family structure on minor and serious delinquency. *International Journal of Offender Therapy & Comparative Criminology, 44*(2), 178–193.

Heide, K., & Solomon, E. (2006). Biology, childhood trauma, and murder: Rethinking justice. *International Journal of Law & Psychiatry, 29*(3), 220–233.

Heimer, K. (1996). Gender, interaction, and delinquency: Testing a theory of differential social control. *Social Psychology Quarterly, 59,* 39–61.

Heimer, K., & Matsueda, R. (1994). Role-taking, role commitment, and delinquency: A theory of differential social control. *American Sociological Review, 59,* 365–390.

Helland, E., & Tabarrok, A. (2008). Does three strikes deter? A non-parametric estimation. *Journal of Human Resources, 22,* 309–330.

Henry, B., Caspi, A., Moffitt, T., & Silva, P. (1996). Temperamental and family predictions of violent and nonviolent criminal convictions: Age 3 to age 18. *Developmental Psychology, 32,* 614–623.

Henry, S., & Lanier, M. (2001). *What is crime? Controversies over the nature of crime and what to do about it.* Lanham, MD: Rowman & Littlefield.

Henry, S., & Milovanovic, D. (1996). *Constitutive criminology: Beyond postmodernism.* London: Sage.

Herman, A., Philbeck, J., Vasilopoulos, N., & Depetrillo, P. (2003). Serotonin transporter promoter polymorphism and differences in alcohol consumption behaviour in a college student population. *Alcohol and Alcoholism, 38*(X), 446–449.

Herrnstein, R. (1995). Criminogenic traits. In J. Wilson & J. Petersilia (Eds.), *Crime.* San Francisco: Institute for Contemporary Studies Press.

Herrnstein, R., & Murray, C. (1994). *The bell curve: Intelligence and class structure in American life.* New York: Free Press.

Hibbeln, J., & Salem, N., Jr. (1995). Dietary polyunsaturated fatty acids and depression: When cholesterol does not satisfy. *American Journal of Clinical Nutrition, 62*(1), 1–9.

Hibbeln, J., Linnoila, M., Umhau, J., Rawlings, R., George, D., & Salem, N., Jr. (1998). Essential fatty acids predict metabolites of serotonin and dopamine in cerebrospinal fluid among healthy control subjects, and early- and late-onset alcoholics. *Biological Psychiatry, 44*(4), 235–242.

Hibbeln, J., Umhau, J., Linnoila, M., George, D., Ragan, P., Shoaf, S., et al. (1998). A replication study of violent and nonviolent subjects: Cerebrospinal fluid metabolites of serotonin and dopamine are predicted by plasma essential fatty acids. *Biological Psychiatry, 44*(4), 243–249.

Hickey, E. (1991). *Serial murderers and their victims.* Pacific Grove, CA: Brooks/Cole.

Higgins, G., & Tewksbury, R. (2006). Sex and self-control theory: The measures and causal model may be different. *Youth & Society, 37*(4), 479–503.

Higley, J., Mehlman, P., Higley, S., Fernald, B., Vickers, J., Lindell, S., et al. (1996). Excessive mortality in young free-ranging male nonhuman primates with low cerebrospinal fluid 5-hydroxyindoleacetic acid concentrations. *Archives of General Psychiatry, 53:* 537–543.

Hill, S., De Bellis, M., Keshavan, M., Lowers, L., Shen, S., Hall, J., & Pitts, T. (2001). Right amygdala volume in adolescent and young adult offspring from families at high risk for developing alcoholism. *Biological Psychiatry, 49*(11), 894–905.

Hindelang, M. (1978). Race and involvement in common law personal crimes. *American Sociological Review, 49,* 93–109.

Hindelang, M., Gottfredson, M., & Garofalo, J. (1978). *Victims of personal crime: An empirical foundation for a theory of personal victimization.* Cambridge, MA: Ballinger.

Hindelang, M., Hirschi, T., & Weis, J. (1981). *Measuring delinquency.* Beverly Hills, CA: Sage.

Hipp, J. (2007). Block, tract, and levels of aggregation: Neighborhood structure and crime and disorder as a case in point. *American Sociological Review, 72*(5), 659–680.

Hirschi, T. (1969). *Causes of delinquency.* Berkeley: University of California Press.

Hirschi, T., & Gottfredson, M. (2001). Self-control theory. In R. Paternoster & R. Bachman (Eds.), *Explaining crime and criminals.* Los Angeles: Roxbury.

Hirschi, T., & Hindelang, M. (1977). Intelligence and delinquency: A revisionist review. *American Sociological Review, 42,* 572–587.

Hodgins, S., Lapalme, M., & Toupin, J. (1999). Criminal activities and substance use of patients with major affective disorders and schizophrenia: A 2-year follow-up. *Journal of Affective Disorders, 55*(2–3), 187–202.

Hodgins, S., Mednick, S., Brennan, P., Schulsinger, F., & Engberg, M. (1996). Mental disorder and crime: Evidence from a Danish birth cohort. *Archives of General Psychiatry, 53,* 489–495.

Hoffman, J. (2003). A contextual analysis of differential association, social control, and strain theories of delinquency. *Social Forces, 81*(3), 753–785.

Hoffman, J., & Miller, A. (1998). A latent variable analysis of general strain theory. *Journal of Quantitative Criminology, 14*(1), 83–110.

Hoffman, J., & Su, S. (1997). The conditional effects of stress on delinquency and drug use: A strain theory assessment of sex differences. *The Journal of Research in Crime and Delinquency, 34*(1), 46–78.

Holmes, C. (1992). *Recognizing brain dysfunction.* Brandon, VT: Clinical Psychology Publishing.

Holmes, M. (2000). Minority threat and police brutality: Determinants of civil rights criminal complaints in U.S. municipalities. *Criminology, 38*(2), 343–367.

Holtfreter, K., Reisig, M., & Pratt, T. (2008). Low self-control, routine activities, and fraud victimization. *Criminology, 46*(1), 189–220.

Horner, B., & Scheibe, K. (1997). Prevalence and implications of attention-deficit hyperactivity disorder among adolescents in treatment for substance abuse. *Journal of the American Academy of Child and Adolescent Psychiatry, 36*(1), 30–36.

Horney, J., Osgood, D., & Marshall, I. (1995). Criminal careers in the short-term: Intra-individual variability in crime and its relation to local life circumstances. *American Sociological Review, 60,* 655–673.

Horowitz, I. (1993). *The decomposition of sociology.* New York: Oxford University Press.

Hough, M. (1987). Offenders' choice of targets: Findings from victim surveys. *Journal of Quantitative Criminology, 3*(4), 355–370.

Howell, J. (1997). Improving the balance between child development and juvenile punishment in a comprehensive ... *Politics & the Life Sciences, 16*(1), 28–31.

Hoyt, H. (1943). The structure of American cities in the post-war era. *American Journal of Sociology, 48,* 475–492.

Hsieh, C., & Pugh, M. (1993). Poverty, income inequality, and violent crime: A meta-analysis of recent aggregate data studies. *Criminal Justice Review, 18*(2), 182–202.

Hubbard, D., & Pratt, T. (2002). A meta-analysis of the predictors of delinquency among girls. *Journal of Offender Rehabilitation, 34*(3), 1–13.

Hudziak, J., Rudiger, L., Neale, M., Heath, A., & Todd, R. (2000). A twin study of inattentive, aggressive, and anxious/depressed behaviors. *Journal of the American Academy of Child and Adolescent Psychiatry, 39,* 469–476.

Huizinga, D., Weiher, A., Menard, S., Espiritu, R., & Esbensen, F. (1998). *Some not so boring findings from the Denver Youth Survey.* Paper presented at the annual meeting of the American Society of Criminology, Las Vegas, NV.

Human Genome Management Information System. (2001). *Genomics and its impact on medicine and society: A 2001 primer.* Retrieved from *http://www.ornl.gov/hgmis/publicat/ primer2001/index.html.*

Hung-En Sung, H. (2003). Differential impact of deterrence vs rehabilitation as drug interventions on recidivism after 36 months. *Journal of Offender Rehabilitation, 37*(3/4), 95–108.

Hunter, A. (1978). *Symbols of incivility.* Paper presented at the annual meeting of the American Society of Criminology, Reno, NV.

Inciardi, J., & Chambers, C. (1972). Unreported criminal involvement of narcotic addicts. *Journal of Drug Issues, 2*(2), 57–64.

Inciardi, J., & McElrath, M. (1998). *The American drug scene: An anthology.* Los Angeles: Roxbury.

Jackson, T. (1957). Social disorganization and stake in conformity: Complementary factors in the predatory behavior of hoodlums. *Journal of Criminal Law, Criminology and Police Science, 48*, 12–17.

Jacobs, S. (1994). Social control of sexual assault by physicians and lawyers within the professional relationship: Criminal and disciplinary sanctions. *American Journal of Criminal Justice, 19*(1), 43–60.

Jacobsen, J. (2007). *The economics of gender.* New York: Wiley-Blackwell.

Jacobson, M., & Schardt, D. (1999). *Diet, ADHD, and behavior: A quarter-century review.* Washington, DC: Center for Science in the Public Interest.

Jaffee, S., Caspi, A., Moffitt, T., Polo-Tomás, M., & Taylor, A. (2007). Individual, family, and neighborhood factors distinguish resilient from non-resilient maltreated children: A cumulative stressors model. *Child Abuse & Neglect, 31*(3), 231–253.

Jang, S. (1999). Age-varying effects of family, school, and peers on delinquency: A multilevel modeling test of interactional theory. *Criminology, 37*(3), 643–685.

Jang, S. (2007). Gender differences in strain, negative emotions, and coping behaviors: A general strain theory approach. *Justice Quarterly, 24*(3), 523–553.

Jang, S., & Smith, C. (1997). A test of reciprocal causal relationships among parental supervision, affective ties, and delinquency. *Journal of Research in Crime and Delinquency, 34*(3), 307–336.

Jeffery, C. (1965). Criminal behavior and learning theory. *Journal of Criminal Law, Criminology, and Police Science, 56*, 294–300.

Jeffery, C. (1990). *Criminology: An interdisciplinary approach.* Englewood Cliffs, CA: Prentice-Hall.

Jeffery, C. (1996). *Mental health and crime prevention: A public health model.* Paper presented at the International Crime Prevention Practitioners Conference, Antwerp, Belgium.

Jeffery, C. (1998a). Criminology and criminal law: Science versus policy and the interaction of science and law. In W. Laufer & F. Adler (Eds.), *Advances in criminological theory* (Vol. 8.) New Brunswick, NJ: Transaction.

Jeffery, C. (1998b). *The prevention of juvenile violence.* Paper presented at the annual meeting of the Academy of Criminal Justice Sciences, Albuquerque, NM.

Jeffery, C., & Zahm, D. (1993). Crime prevention through environmental design, opportunity theory, and rational choice models. In R. Clarke & M. Felson (Eds.), *Routine activity and rational choice. Advances in criminological theory* (Vol. 5). New Brunswick, NJ: Transaction Publishers.

Jensen, A. (1969). How much can we boost IQ and scholastic achievement? *Harvard Educational Review, 39,* 1–123.

Jensen, A. (1998). *The g factor.* Westport, CT: Praeger.

Jensen, G. (1996). Comment on Chamlin and Cochran. *Criminology, 34*(1), 129–131.

Jensen, G., & Thompson, K. (1990). What's class got to do with it? A further examination of power-control theory. *American Journal of Sociology, 95,* 1009–1023.

Jensen, J., Lindgren, M., Meurling, A., Ingvar, D., & Levander, S. (1999). Dyslexia among Swedish prison inmates in relation to neuropsychology and personality. *Journal of the International Neuropsychological Society, 5*(5), 452–461.

Johnson, A. (2006). *Privilege, power, and difference* (2nd Ed.). New York: McGraw Hill.

Johnson, B., Goldstein, P., Preble, E., Schmeidler, J., Lipton, D., Sprunt, B., & Miller, T. (1985). *Taking care of business: The economics of crime by heroin abusers.* Lexington, MA: Lexington Books.

Jones, G., Zammit, S., Norton, N., Hamshere, M., Jones, S., Miham, C., Sanders, R., Mccarthy, G., Jones, L., Cardno, A., Gray, M., Murphy, K., & Owen, M. (2001). Aggressive behaviour in patients with schizophrenia is associated with catechol-O-methyltransferase genotype. *British Journal of Psychiatry, 179*(X), 351–355.

Junger, M., & Marshall, I. (1997). The interethnic generalizability of social control theory: An empirical test. *The Journal of Research in Crime and Delinquency, 34*(1), 79–112.

Junger, M., & Tremblay, R. (1999). Self-control, accidents, and crime. *Criminal Justice and Behavior, 26*(4), 485–501.

Kagan, J., Reznick, S., & Snidman, N. (1987). The physiology and psychology of behavioral inhibition in children. *Child Development, 58,* 1459–1473.

Kammen, W., & Maughan, B. (1993). Developmental pathways in disruptive child behavior. *Developmental Psychopathology, 5,* 103–133.

Kampov-Polevoy, A., Garbutt, J., & Janowsky, D. (1999). Association between preference for sweets and excessive alcohol intake: A review of animal and human studies. *Alcohol & Alcoholism, 34*(3), 386–395.

Kampov-Polevoy, A., Garbutt, J., & Jonowsky, D. (1997). Evidence of preference for a high-concentration sucrose solution in alcoholic men. *American Journal of Psychiatry, 154*(2), 269–270.

Kampov-Polevoy, A., Garbutt, J., Davis, C., & Jonowsky, D. (1998). Preference for higher sugar concentration and tridimensional personality questionnaire scores in alcoholic and nonalcoholic men. *Alcoholism: Clinical and Experimental Research, 22*(3), 610–614.

Kandel, E. (1991). *Biology, violence, and antisocial personality.* Durham, NH: New Hampshire University.

Kappeler, V., Blumberg, M., & Potter, G. (2000). *The mythology of crime and criminal justice* (3rd ed.). Prospect Heights, IL: Waveland Press.

Kapuscinski, C., Braithwaite, J., & Chapman, B. (1998). Unemployment and crime: Toward resolving the paradox. *Journal of Quantitative Criminology, 14*(3), 215–243.

Karp, D. (2001). Harm and repair: Observing restorative justice in Vermont. *Justice Quarterly, 18*(4), 727–757.

Katz, J. (1995). *Seductions of crime: Moral and sensual attractions in doing evil.* New York: Basic Books.

Katz, R. (2000). Explaining girls' and women's crime and desistance in the context of their victimization experiences: A developmental test of revised strain theory and the life course perspective. *Violence Against Women, 6*(6), 633–660.

Kawachi, I., Kennedy, B., & Wilkinson, R. (1999). Crime: Social disorganization and relative deprivation. *Social Science and Medicine, 48*(6), 719–731.

Kelley, B., Loeber, R., Keenan, K., & DeLamatre, M. (1997). *Developmental athways in boys' disruptive and delinquent behavior* (Juvenile Justice Bulletin). Washington, DC: OJJDP, U.S. Department of Justice.

Kelley, T. (1997). *An integrated systems approach to screening for brain dysfunction in delinquent offenders.* Master's thesis, Florida State University, Tallahassee.

Kelley, T., & Nute, D. (2000). *An integrated systems theory of crime.* Paper presented at the annual meeting of the American Society of Criminology, San Diego, CA.

Kempf, K. (1993). The empirical status of Hirschi's control theory. In F. Adler & W. Laufer (Eds.), *New directions in criminological theory: Advances in criminological theory* (Vol.4). New Brunswick, NJ: Transaction Press.

Kendler, K., & Prescott, C. (2006). *Genes, environment, and psychopathology: Understanding the causes of psychiatric and substance use disorders.* New York: The Guilford Press.

Kennedy, L., & Baron, S. (1993). Routine activities and a subculture of violence. A study of violence on the street. *Journal of Research in Crime and Delinquency, 30*(1), 88–112.

Kennedy, L., & Forde, D. (1990a). Risky lifestyles and dangerous results: Routine activities and exposure to crime. *Sociology and Social Research: An International Journal, 74*(4), 208–211.

Kennedy, L., & Forde, D. (1990b). Routine activities and crime: An analysis of victimization in Canada. *Criminology, 28*(1), 137–152.

Kennedy, R. (1997). *Race, crime, and the law.* New York: Vintage.

Kessler, D., & Levitt, S. (1999). Using sentence enhancements to distinguish between deterrence and incapacitation. *Journal of Law and Economics, 42,* 343–363.

Kiehl, K., Smith, A., Hare, R., Mendrek, A., Forster, B., Brink, J., & Liddle, P. (2001). Limbic abnormalities in affective processing by criminal psychopaths as revealed by functional magnetic resonance imaging. *Biological Psychiatry, 50*(X), 677–684.

Kierkus, C., & Baer, D. (2002). A social control explanation of the relationship between family structure and delinquent behaviour. *Canadian Journal of Criminology, 44*(4), 425–458.

Kim-Cohen, J., Caspi, A., Taylor, A., Williams, B., Newcombe, R., Craig, I., Moffitt, T. (2006). MAOA, maltreatment, and gene-environment interaction predicting children's mental health: New evidence and a meta-analysis. *Molecular Psychiatry, 11*(X), 903–913.

Klein, K., Forehand, R., Armistead, L., & Long, P. (1997). Delinquency during the transition to early adulthood: Family and parenting predictors from early adolescence. *Adolescence, 32*(125), 61–80.

Klepper, S., & Nagin, D. (1989). The deterrent effect of the perceived certainty and severity of punishment revisited. *Criminology, 27,* 721–746.

Klir, G. (1972). *Trends in general systems theory.* New York: Wiley.

Kochanska, M. (1991). Socialization and temperament in the development of guilt and conscience. *Child Development, 62,* 1379–1392.

Konner, M., & Kunz, A. (1990). Under the influence. *Omni, 12*(4), 62–66.

Kornhauser, R. (1978). *Social sources of delinquency.* Chicago: University of Chicago Press.

Kotler, M., Barak, P., Cohen, H., Averbuch, I., Grinshpoon, A., Gritsenko, I., Nemanov, L., & Ebstein, R. (1999). Homicidal behavior in schizophrenia associated with a genetic polymorphism determining low COMT activity. American Journal of Medical Genetics, 88(X), 628–633.

Kotulak, R. (1996). *Inside the brain: Revolutionary discoveries of how the mind works.* Kansas City, MO: Andrews McMeel.

Kovandzic, T., Sloan Iii, J., & Vieraitis, L. (2004). "Striking out" as crime reduction policy: The impact of "three strikes" laws on crime rates in U.S. cities. *Justice Quarterly, 21,* 207–239.

Kozel, N., Dupont, R., & Brown, D. (1972). A study of narcotic involvement in an offender population. *International Journal of the Addictions, 7,* 443–450.

Kramer, J. (1976). From demon to ally—How mythology has and may yet alter national drug policy. *Journal of Drug Issues, 6,* 390–406.

Kraska, P. (1990). The unmentionable alternative: The need for, and the argument against the decriminalization of drug laws. In R. Weisheit (Ed.), *Drugs, crime, and the criminal justice system.* Cincinnati, OH: Anderson.

Kruesi, M., Rapoport, J., Hamburger, S., Hibbs, E., & Potter, W. (1990). Cerebrospinal fluid monoamine metabolites, aggression and impulsivity in disruptive behavior disorders of children and adolescents. *Archives of General Psychiatry, 47*(X), 419–426.

Kruttschnitt, C., Uggen, C., & Shelton, K. (2000). Predictors of desistance among sex offenders: The interaction of formal and informal social controls. *Justice Quarterly, 17*(1), 61–88.

Kubrin, C. (2003). Structural covariates of homicide rates: Does type of homicide matter?. *Journal of Research in Crime & Delinquency, 40*(2), 139–170.

Kubrin, C., & Herting, J. (2003). Neighborhood correlates of homicide trends: An analysis using growth-curve modeling. *Sociological Quarterly, 44*(3), 329–350.

Kubrin, C., & Wadsworth, T. (2003). Identifying the structural correlates of African American killings. *Homicide Studies, 7*(1), 3–35.

Kubrin, C., & Weitzer, R. (2003). New directions in social disorganization theory. *Journal of Research in Crime & Delinquency, 40*(4), 374–402.

Kuhn, A. (1974). *The logic of social systems.* San Francisco: Jossey-Bass.

Kuhn, A. (1975). *Unified social science: A system-based introduction.* Homewood, CA: Dorsey Press.

Kumpfer, K., & Alvarado, R. (1998). *Effective family strengthening interventions.* Bulletin. Washington, DC: U.S. Department of Justice, Office of Justice Programs, Office of Juvenile Justice and Delinquency Prevention.

Kumpfer, K., & Alvarado, R. (1998, November). Effective family strengthening interventions. *OJJDP: Juvenile Justice Bulletin.*

Kurlychek, M., Brame, R., & Bushway, S. (2007). Enduring risk? Old criminal records and predictions of future criminal involvement. *Crime & Delinquency, 53*(1), 64–83.

Kushnick, L., & Jennings, L. (1999). *A new introduction to poverty: The role of race, power, and politics.* New York: New York University Press.

Laasko, M., Vaurio, O., Koivisto, E., Savolainen, L., Eronen, M., Aronen, H., et al. (2001). Psychopathy and the posterior hippocampus. *Behavioural Brain Research, 118*(2), 187–193.

Lachman, H., Nolan, K., Mohr, P., Saito, T., & Volavka, J. (1998). Association between catechol O-methyltransferase genotype and violence in schizophrenia and schizoaffective disorder. *American Journal of Psychiatry, 155*(X), 835–837.

LaFree, G., & Kick, E. (1986). Cross-national effects of development, distributional, and demographic variables on crime: A review and analysis. *International Annals of Criminology, 24*, 213–236.

LaGrange, T., & Silverman, R. (1999). Low self-control and opportunity: Testing the general theory of crime as an explanation for gender differences in delinquency. *Criminology, 37*(1), 41–73.

Lahey, B., & Loeber, R. (1994). Framework for a developmental model of oppositional defiant disorder and conduct disorder. In D. Routh (Ed.), *Disruptive behavior disorders in childhood*. New York: Plenum Press.

Lamberth, J. (1997). Report of John Lamberth, Ph.D. American Civil Liberties Union. etrieved May 5, 2006 from *http://www.aclu.org/court/lamberth.html*.

Land, K. (1997). Containing social disorder and involving the public in nurturant strategies: Feasible and cost ... *Politics & the Life Sciences, 16*(1), 31–33.

Land, K., Cantor, D., & Russell, S. (1995). Unemployment and crime rate fluctuations in the post-World War II United States. In J. Hagan & R. Peterson (Eds.), *Crime and inequality*. Stanford, CA: Stanford University Press.

Land, K., McCall, P., & Cohen, L. (1990). Structural covariates of homicide rates: Are there any invariances across time and space. *American Journal of Sociology, 95*, 922–963.

Landrigan, P., & Todd, A. (1999). Direct measurement of lead in bone: A promising biomarker. *Journal of the American Medical Association, 271*(3), 239–240.

Landrigan, P., Claudio, L., Markowitz, S., Berkowitz, G., Brenner, B., Romero, H., et al. (1999). Pesticides and inner-city children: Exposures, risks, and prevention. *Environmental Health Perspectives, 107*(3), 431–437.

Lane, J., & Meeker, J. (2000). Subcultural diversity and the fear of crime and gangs. *Crime and Delinquency, 46*(4), 497–521.

Langan, P., Greenfeld, L., Smith, S., Durose, M., & Levin, D. (2001). Contacts between the police and the public: Findings from the 1999 National Survey (No. NCJ184957). Washington, DC: Bureau of Justice Statistics, U.S. Department of Justice.

Langton, L., & Piquero, N. (2007). Can general strain theory explain white-collar crime? A preliminary investigation of the relationship between strain and select white-collar offenses. *Journal of Criminal Justice, 35*(1), 1–15.

Langton, L., Piquero, N., & Hollinger, R. (2006). An empirical test of the relationship between employee theft and low self-control. *Deviant Behavior, 27*(5), 537–565.

Lanier, M., & Henry, S. (1998). *Essential Criminology.* Boulder, CO: Westview Press.

Lanza-Kaduce, L., & Greenleaf, R. (2000). Age and race deference reversals: Extending Turk on police-citizen conflict. *The Journal of Research in Crime and Delinquency, 37*(2), 221–236.

Lappalainen, J., Long, J., Eggert, M., Ozaki, N., Robin, R., Brown, G., et al. (1998). Linkage of antisocial alcoholism to the serotonin 5-HT1B receptor gene in 2 populations. *Archives of General Psychiatry, 55,* 989–994.

Larzelere, R., & Patterson, G. (1990). Paternal management: Mediator of the effect of socioeconomic status on early delinquency. *Criminology, 28,* 301–323.

Laszlo, E. (1996). *The systems view of the world: A holistic vision for our time.* New York: G. Braziller.

Latimore, T., Tittle, C., & Grasmick, H. (2006). Childrearing, self-control, and crime: Additional evidence. *Sociological Inquiry, 76*(3), 343–371.

Laub, J. (1983). Urbanism, race, and crime. *Journal of Research in Crime and Delinquency, 20,* 183–198.

Laub, J., Sampson, R., & Allen, L. (2001). Toward a theory of age-graded informal social control. In R. Paternoster & R. Bachman (Eds.), *Explaining crime and criminals.* Los Angeles: Roxbury.

LeBeau, J., & Corcoran, W. (1990). Changes in calls for police service with changes in routine activities and the arrival and passage of weather fronts. *Journal of Quantitative Criminology, 6,* 269–291.

LeBeau, J., & Coulson, R. (1996). Routine activities and the spatial-temporal variation of calls for police service: The experience of opposites on the quality of life spectrum. *Police Studies, 19*(4), 1–14.

Lee, N. (1995). Culture conflict and crime in Alaskan native villages. *Journal of Criminal Justice, 23*(2): 177–189.

Lee, R., & Coccaro, E. (2001). The neuropsychopharmacology of criminality and aggression. *Canadian Journal of Psychiatry, 46,* 35–44.

Leeper-Piquero, N., & Sealock, M. (2000). Generalizing general strain theory: An examination of an offending population. *Justice Quarterly, 17*(3), 449–484.

Lemert, E. (1951). *Social pathology.* New York: McGraw-Hill.

Leonard, K., & Decker, S. (1994). The theory of social control: Does it apply to the very young? *Journal of Criminal Justice, 22*(2), 89–107.

Lersch, K. (1999). Social learning theory and academic dishonesty. *International Journal of Comparative and Applied Criminal Justice, 23*(1–2), 103–114.

Levine, D. (1993). Survival of the synapses. *The Sciences, 33,* 46–52.

Levitan, I., & Kaczmarek, L. (1991). *The neuron: Cell and molecular biology.* New York: Oxford University Press.

Levitt, S. (1997). A skeptical but sympathetic appraisal for nurturant crime-control policies. *Politics & the Life Sciences, 16*(1), 34–36.

Levitt, S. (1997). Using electoral cycles in police hiring to estimate the effects of police on crime. *American Economic Review, 87,* 270–290.

Levitt, S. (2004). Understanding why crime fell in the 1990s: Four factors that explain the decline and six that do not. *Journal of Economic Perspectives, 18,* 163–190.

Levy, F., Hay, D., McStephen, M., Wood, C., & Waldman, I. (1997). Attention-deficit hyperactivity disorder: A category or a continuum? Genetic analysis of a large-scale twin study. *Journal of the American Academy of Child and Adolescent Psychiatry, 36,* 737–744.

Lewin, K. (1935). *A dynamic theory of personality.* New York: McGraw-Hill.

Lewis, D., & Maxfield, M. (1980). Fear in the neighborhoods: An investigation of the impact of crime. *Journal of Research in Crime and Delinquency, 17,* 60–89.

Lewis, D., & Salem, G. (1981). Community crime prevention: An analysis of a developing strategy. *Crime and Delinquency, 27,* 405–421.

Lewis, D., & Salem, G. (1986). *Fear of crime: Incivility and the production of a social problem.* New Brunswick, NJ: Transaction.

Liao, D., Hong, C., Shih, H., & Tsai, S. (2004). Possible association between serotonin transporter promoter region polymorphism and extremely violent crime in Chinese males. *Neuropsychobiology, 50*(X), 284–287.

Lidberg, L., Tuck, J., Asberg, M., Scalia-Tomba, G., & Bertilsson, L. (1985). Homicide, suicide, and CSF 5-HIAA. *Acta Psychiatrica Scandinavica, 71*(X), 230–236.

Lilly, J., Cullen, F., & Ball, R. (1995). *Criminological theory: Context and consequences.* Thousand Oaks, CA: Sage.

Lilly, J.R., Cullen, F., & BALL, R. (2007). *Criminological theory: Context and consequences.* Thousand Oaks, CA: Sage.

Limson, R., Goldman, D., Roy, A., Lamparski, D., Ravitz, B., Adinoff, B., & Linnoila, M. (1991). Personality and cerebrospinal fluid monoamine metabolites in alcoholics and controls. *Archives of General Psychiatry, 48*(X), 437–441.

Lin, G. (1991). Maternal fetal folate transfer: Effect of ethanol and dietary folate deficiency. *Alcohol, 8*(3), 169–172.

Lindqvist, P., & Allebeck, P. (1990). Schizophrenia and crime: A longitudinal follow-up of 644 schizophrenics in Stockholm. *British Journal of Psychiatry, 157,* 345–350.

Lindsell-Roberts, S. (1994). *Loony laws and silly statutes.* New York: Sterling Publications.

Link, B., Andrews, H., & Cullen, F. (1992). The violent and illegal behavior of mental patients reconsidered. *American Sociological Review, 57,* 275–292.

Linnoila, M., Virkkunen, M., Schwannian, M., Nuutila, A., Rimon, R., & Goodwin, F. (1983). Low cerebrospinal fluid 5-hydroxyindoleacetic acid concentration differentiates impulsive from non-impulsive violent behavior. *Life Sciences, 33*(X), 2609–2614.

Lipsitt, D., Buka, S., & Lipsitt, L. (1990). Early intelligence scores and subsequent behavior. *American Journal of Family Therapy, 18,* 197–208.

Liska, A., Krohn, M., & Messner, S. (1989). Strategies and requisites for theoretical integration in the study of crime and deviance. In A. Liska, M. Krohn, & S. Messner (Eds.), *Theoretical integration in the study of deviance and crime: Problems and prospects.* Albany, NY: SUNY Press.

Liska, K. (2000). *Drugs and the human body* (6th ed.). New York: Macmillan.

Liu, J., Raine, A., Venables, P., & Mednick, S. (2004). Malnutrition at age 3 years and externalizing behavior problems at ages 8, 11, and 17 years. *American Journal of Psychiatry, 161*(11), 2005–2013.

Lo, C., Kim, Y., & Church, W. (2008). The effects of victimization on drug use: A multilevel analysis. *Substance Use & Misuse, 43*(10), 1340–1361.

Lochner, L. (2007). Individual perceptions of the criminal justice system. *American Economic Review, 97,* 444–460.

Lodhi, A., & Tilly, C. (1973). Urbanization, crime, and collective violence in nineteenth century France. *American Journal of Sociology, 79,* 297–318.

Loeber, R. & Stouthamer-Loeber, M. (1986). Family factors as correlates and predictors of juvenile conduct problems and delinquency. In M. Tonry & N. Morris (Eds.), *Crime and justice: An annual review of research.* Chicago: University of Chicago Press.

Loeber, R. (1990). Development and risk factors of juvenile antisocial behavior and delinquency. *Clinical Psychology Review, 10,* 1–41.

Loeber, R., & LeBlanc, M. (1991). Toward a developmental criminology. In M. Tonry & N. Morris (Eds.), *Crime and justice.* Chicago: The University of Chicago Press.

Loeber, R., & Stouthamer-Loeber, M. (1998). Development of aggressions and violence. Some common misconceptions and controversies. *American Psychologist, 53,* 242–259.

Loeber, R., Wung, P., Keenan, K., Giroux, B., Stouthamer-Loeber, M., van. Longshore, D., Turner, S., & Stein, J. (1996). Self-control in a criminal sample: An examination of construct validity. *Criminology, 34,* 209–228.

Lotz, R., & Lee, L. (1999). Sociability, school experience, and delinquency. *Youth and Society, 31*(2), 199–223.

Love, S. (2006). Illicit sexual behavior: A test of self-control theory. *Deviant Behavior, 27*(5), 505–536.

Lowenkamp, C., Cullen, F., & Pratt, T. (2003). Replicating Sampson and Groves' test of social disorganization theory: Revisiting a criminological classic. *Journal of Research in Crime & Delinquency, 40*(4), 351–373.

Lubinski, D. (2000). Scientific and social significance of assessing individual differences: "Sinking shafts a few critical points." *Annual Review of Psychology, 51,* 405–444.

Lucas, A., Morley, R., & Cole, T. (1998). Randomised trial of early diet in preterm babies and later intelligence quotient. *British Medical Journal, 317,* 1481–1487.

Lucas, S., Sexton, M., & Langenberg, P. (1996). Relationship between blood lead and nutritional factors in preschool children: A cross-cultural study. *Pediatrics, 97*(1), 74–79.

Ludwig, V. (1976). *General system theory: Foundations, development, applications.* New York: G. Braziller.

Luiselli, J., Arons, M., Marchese, N., Potoczny-Gray, A., & Rossi, E. (2000). Incidence of law-violating behavior in a community sample of children and adolescents with traumatic brain injury. *International Journal of Offender Therapy and Comparative Criminology, 44*(6), 647–656.

Lundman, R. (2004). Driver race, ethnicity, and gender and citizen reports of vehicle searches by police and vehicle search hits: Towards a triangulated scholarly understanding. *Journal of Criminal Law & Criminology, 94,* 309–349.

Lundman, R., & Kaufman, R. (2003). Driving while black: Effects of race, ethnicity, and gender on citizen self-reports of traffic stops and police encounters. *Criminology, 41*(1), 195–220.

Lurigio, A. (2001). Effective services for parolees with mental illnesses. *Crime and Delinquency, 47*(3), 446–461.

Lykken, D. (1995). *The antisocial personalities.* Hillsdale, NJ: Lawrence Erlbaum.

Lykken, D. (1996). Psychopathy, sociopathy, and crime. *Society, 34*(1), 29–39.

Lykken, D. (1997). Incompetent parenting: Its causes and cures. *Child Psychiatry & Human Development, 27*(3), 129–137.

Lykken, D. (2000). The causes and costs of crime and a controversial cure. *Journal of Personality, 68*(3), 559–605.

Lyman, D., Leukefeld, C., & Clayton, R. (2003). The contribution of personality to the overlap between *antisocial behavior* and substance use/misuse. *Aggressive Behavior, 29*(4), 316–331.

Lynam, D. (1996). Early identification of chronic offenders: Who is the fledgling psychopath? *Psychological Bulletin, 120*(2), 209–234.

Lynam, D., Moffitt, T., & Stouthamer-Loeber, M. (1993). Explaining the relation between IQ and delinquency: Class, race, test motivation, school failure, or self-control? *Journal of Abnormal Psychology, 102*(2), 187–196.

Lynam, M., & Potter, G. (1998). *Drugs in society.* Cincinnati, OH: Anderson.

Lynch, M. (2000). J. Phillippe Rushton on crime: An examination and critique of the explanation of crime and race. *Social Pathology, 6*(3), 228–244.

Lynch, M., & Stretesky, P. (2001). Radical criminology. In R. Paternoster & R. Bachman (Eds.), *Explaining crime and criminals.* Los Angeles: Roxbury.

Lynn, R. (1996). Dysgenics: Genetic deterioration in modern populations. Wesport, CT: Greenwood Press.

Lyons, C. (2007). Community (dis)organization and racially motivated crime. *American Journal of Sociology, 113*(3), 815–863.

Lyons, M. (1996). A twin study of self-reported criminal behavior. In Ciba Foundation (Ed.), *Genetics of criminal and antisocial behavior.* Chichester, NY: Wiley.

Machelak, R. (1997). Darwinizing crime control policies: Additional recommendations. *Politics & the Life Sciences, 16*(1), 36–37.

Mackey, W. (1997). Single-parent families contribute to violent crime. In K. Swisher (Ed.), *Single-parent families.* San Diego, CA: Greenhaven Press.

MacLean, P. (1990). *The triune brain in evolution: Role in paleocerebral functions.* New York: Plenum.

Macmillian, R., Mcmorris, B., & Kruttschnitt, C. (2004). Linked lives: *Stability* and change in maternal circumstances and trajectories of a*ntisocial* behavior in children. *Child Development, 75*(1), 205–220.

Maguire, M., & Bennett, T. (1982). *Burglary in a dwelling.* London: Heinemann.

Mak, A. (1994). Parental neglect and overprotection as risk factors in delinquency. *Australian Journal of Psychology, 46*(2), 107–111.

Mann, J., Mcbride, P., Anderson, G., & Mieczkowski, T. (1992). Platelet and whole blood serotonin content in depressed patients: Correlations with acute and life-time psychopathology. *Biological Psychiatry, 32*(X), 243–257.

Manuck, S., Flory, J., McCaffery, J., Matthews, K., Mann, J., & Muldoon, M. (1998). Aggression, impulsivity, and central nervous system serotonergic responsivity in a nonpatient sample. *Neuropsychopharmacology, 19*(4), 287–299.

Marcus, B. (2004). Self-control in the general theory of crime: Theoretical implications of a measurement problem. *Theoretical Criminology, 8*(1), 33–55.

Marenin, O. (1994). *The coming shift to complexifying theory (and policy)*. Paper presented at the annual meeting of the American Society of Criminology, Miami, FL.

Marenin, O., & Reisig, M. (1995). "A general theory of crime" and patterns of crime in Nigeria: An exploration of methodological assumptions. *Journal of Criminal Justice, 23*(6), 501–518.

Markowitz, F., Bellair, P., Liska, A., & Liu, J. (2001). Extending social disorganization theory: Modeling the relationships between cohesion, disorder, and fear. *Criminology, 39*(2), 293–320.

Marlowe, M., Stellern, J., Moon, C., & Errera, J. (1985). Main and interaction effects of metallic toxins on aggressive classroom behavior. *Aggressive Behavior, 11*, 41–48.

Martin, R. (2000). Anomie, spirituality, and crime. *Journal of Contemporary Criminal Justice, 16*(1), 75–98.

Martin, R., Mutchnick, R., & Austin, W. (1990). *Criminological thought: Pioneers past and present*. New York: Macmillan.

Marvell, T., & Moody. C. (1996). Specification problems, police levels and crime rates. *Criminology, 34*, 609–646.

Mason, D., & Frick, P. (1994). The heritability of antisocial behavior: A meta-analysis of twin and adoption studies. *Journal of Psychopathology & Behavioral Assessment, 16*(X), 301–323.

Massey, J., Krohn, M., & Bonati, L. (1989). Property crime and the routine activities of individuals. *Journal of Research in Crime and Delinquency, 26*(4), 378–400.

Masters, R. (1997). *Environmental pollution, toxic chemicals, crime and disease*. Retrieved from *www.dartmouth.edu/~rmasters*.

Masters, R., Hone, B., & Doshi, A. (1997). Environmental pollution, neurotoxicity, and criminal violence. In J. Rose (Ed.), *Environmental toxicology*. Basingstoke, England: Gordon & Breach.

Mathias, R. (1996). *The basics of brain imaging*. Retrieved from *www.nida.nih.gov/Nida_Notes/NNVol11N5/Basics.html*.

Matsueda, R. (1982). Testing control theory and differential association. *American Sociological Review, 47*, 489–504.

Matsueda, R. (1988). The current state of differential association theory. *Crime & Delinquency, 34*(3), 277–306.

Matsueda, R. (1992). Reflected appraisals, parental labeling and delinquency: Specifying a symbolic interactionist theory. *American Journal of Sociology, 97*, 1577–1611.

Matsueda, R. (2001). Labeling theory: Historical roots, implications, and recent developments. In R. Paternoster & R. Bachman (Eds.), *Explaining crime and criminals*. Los Angeles: Roxbury.

Matsueda, R., & Anderson, K. (1998). The dynamics of delinquent peers and delinquent behavior. *Criminology, 36*(2), 269–308.

Matsueda, R., & Heimer, K. (1988). Race, family structure, and delinquency. *American Sociological Review, 52*, 826–840.

Matsueda, R., Kreager, D., & Huizinga, D. (2006). Deterring delinquents: A rational choice model of theft and violence. *American Sociological Review, 71*, 95–122.

Matthews, K., Flory, J., Muldoon, M., & Manuck, S. (2000). Does socioeconomic status relate to central serotonergic responsivity in healthy adults? *Psychosomatic Medicine, 62*, 231–237.

Matthews, S., & Agnew, R. (2008). Extending deterrence theory. *Journal of Research in Crime & Delinquency, 45*(2), 91–118.

Matza, D. (1964). *Delinquency and drift*. New York: John Wiley.

Matza, D. (1969). *Becoming deviant*. Englewood Cliffs, NJ: Prentice-Hall.

Maughan, B., Taylor, A., Caspi, A., & Moffitt, T. (2004). Prenatal smoking and early childhood conduct problems: Testing genetic and environmental explanations of the association. *Archives of General Psychiatry, 61*(X), 836–843.

Maume, M., Ousey, G., & Beaver, K. (2005). Cutting the grass: A reexamination of the link between marital attachment, delinquent peers and desistance from marijuana use. *Journal of Quantitative Criminology, 21*(1), 27–53.

Maxfield, M. (1984). The limits of vulnerability in explaining fear of crime: A comparative neighborhood analysis. *Journal of Research in Crime and Delinquency, 21*, 233–250.

Maxfield, M. (1987). *Incivilities and fear of crime in England and Wales, and the United States: A comparative analysis*. Paper presented at the annual meeting of the American Society of Criminology, Montreal, Canada.

Maxwell, G., & Morris, A. (2001). Putting restorative justice into practice for adult offenders. *The Howard Journal of Criminal Justice, 40*(1), 55–69.

Mazerolle, P., & Maahs, J. (2000). General strain and delinquency: An alternative examination of conditioning. *Justice Quarterly, 17*(4), 753–778.

Mazerolle, P., & Piquero, A. (1997). Violent responses to strain: An examination of conditioning influences. *Violence and Victims, 12*(4), 323–343.

Mazerolle, P., & Piquero, A. (1998). Linking exposure to strain with anger: An investigation of deviant adaptations. *Journal of Criminal Justice, 26*(3), 195–211.

Mazur, A., & Booth, A. (1998). Testosterone and dominance in men. *Behavioral and Brain Sciences, 21*, 353–397.

Mazur, A., & Michalek, J. (1998). Marriage, divorce, and male testosterone. *Social Forces, 77*(1), 315–328.

McAdam, D. (2000). *Demonology.* Retrieved from *www.djmcadam.com/demons.htm.*

McBurnett, K., Lahey, B., Rathouz, P., & Loeber, R. (2000). Low salivary cortisol and persistent aggression in boys referred for disruptive behavior. *Archives of General Psychiatry, 57*(1), 38–43.

McBurnett, K., Lahey, B., Rathouz, P., & Loeber, R. (2000). Low salivary cortisol and persistent aggression in boys referred for disruptive behavior. *Archives of General Psychiatry, 57*(X), 38–43.

McCaghy, C., Capron, T., & Jamieson, J. (2000). *Deviant behavior* (5th ed.). Boston: Allyn & Bacon.

McCall, L. (2001). *Complex inequality: Gender, class and race in the new economy.* New York: Routledge.

McCall, P., Parker, K., & Macdonald, J. (2007). The dynamic relationship between homicide rates and social, economic, and political factors from 1970 to 2000. *Social Science Research, 37*, 3, 721–735.

McCarthy, B., Felmlee, D., & Hagan, J. (2004). Girl friends are better Gender, friends, and crime among school and street youth. *Criminology, 42*(4), 805–835.

McCarthy, B., Hagan, J., & Woodward, T. (1999). In the company of women: Structure and agency in a revised power-control theory of gender and delinquency. *Criminology, 37*(4), 761–788.

McCord, J. (1991). Family relationships, juvenile delinquency, and adult criminality. *Criminology, 29*(3), 397.

McCord, J. (2000). Developmental trajectories and intentional actions. *Journal of Quantitative Criminology, 16*(2), 237–253.

McCord, J. (2001). Forging criminals in the family. In S. White (Ed.), *Handbook of youth and justice: The Plenum series in crime and justice.* New York: Kluwer Academic/Plenum Publishers.

McCrae, R., Costa, P., Ostendorf, F., Angleitner, A., Hrebickova, M., Avia, M., et al. (2000). Nature over nurture: Temperament, personality, and life span development.

McDonald, L. (1982). Theory and evidence of rising crime in the nineteenth century. *British Journal of Sociology, 33*, 404–420.

McEwen, B., & Krahn, D. (1999). *The response to stress.* Retrieved from *www.naturalhealthweb. com/articles/McEwen.html.*

McGloin, J., Pratt, T., & Maahs, J. (2004). Rethinking the IQ-delinquency relationship: A longitudinal analysis of multiple theoretical models. *Justice Quarterly, 21*(3), 603–635.

McGue, M. (1994). Why developmental psychology should find room for behavior genetics. In C. Nelson (Ed.), *Threats to optimal development: Integrating biological, psychological, and social risk factors.* Hillsdale, NJ: Lawrence Erlbaum.

McGue, M., Bacon, S., & Lykken, D. (1993). Personality stability and change in early adulthood: A behavioral genetic analysis. *Developmental Psychology, 29,* 96–109.

McGue, M., Bouchard, T., Iacono, W., & Lykken, D. (1993). Behavioral genetics of cognitive ability: A lifespan perspective. In R. Plomin & G. McClearn (Eds.), *Nature, nurture, and psychology.* Washington, DC: American Psychological Association.

McGuffin, P., & Thapar, A. (1997). Genetic basis of bad behaviour in adolescents. *Lancet, 350,* 411–412.

McLoyd, V. (1990). The impact of economic hardship on black families and children: Psychological distress, parenting, and socio-emotional development. *Child Development, 61,* 311–346.

Mealey, L. (1995). The sociobiology of sociopathy: An integrated evolutionary model. *Behavioral and Brain Sciences, 18,* 523–559.

Mealey, L. (1997). An evolutionary, but not stable strategy for crime control. *Politics & the Life Sciences, 16*(1), 38–39.

Mears, D., Ploeger, M., & Warr, M. (1998). Explaining the gender gap in delinquency: Peer influence and moral evaluations of behavior. *The Journal of Research in Crime and Delinquency, 35*(3), 251–266.

Mednick, S., & Christiansen, K. (1977). *Biosocial bases of criminal behavior.* New York: Gardner Press.

Mednick, S., Gabrielli, W., & Hutchings, B. (1984). Genetic influences on criminal convictions: Evidence from an adoption cohort. *Science, 224*(X), 891–894.

Meehan A.J. & Ponder, M.C. (2002). Race and place: The ecology of racial profiling African American motorists. *Justice Quarterly, 19,* 399–430.

Meis, P., Goldenberg, R., Mercer, B., Moawad, A., Das, A., McNellis, D., et al. (1995). The preterm prediction study: Significance of vaginal infections. *American Journal of Obstetrics and Gynecology, 173*(4): 1231–1235.

Menard, S. (1995). A developmental test of Mertonian anomie theory. *The Journal of Research in Crime and Delinquency, 32*(2): 136–174.

Menard, S., & Elliott, D. (1994). Delinquent bonding, moral beliefs, and illegal behavior: A three wave-panel model. *Justice Quarterly, 11,* 173–188.

Menard, S., & Huizinga, D. (2001). Repeat victimization in a high-risk neighborhood sample of adolescents. *Youth and Society, 32*(4), 447–472.

Merriam-Webster's Collegiate Dictionary (2008). Entry for "group." Retrieved December 8, 2008 from *http://www.merriam-webster.com/dictionary/group*.

Merriam-Webster's Collegiate Dictionary (2008). Entry for "organization." Retrieved December 8, 2008 from *http://www.merriam-webster.com/dictionary/organization*.

Merriam-Webster's Collegiate Dictionary (2009). Entry for "culpable." Retrieved January 8, 2009 from *http://www.merriam-webster.com/dictionary/culpable*.

Merry, S. (1981). Defensible space undefended: Social factors in crime prevention through environmental design. *Urban Affairs Quarterly, 16,* 397–422.

Merton, R. (1938). *Social theory and social structure.* New York: Free Press.

Merton, R. (1968). *Social theory and social structure.* Glencoe, IL: The Free Press.

Merton, R. (1995). Opportunity structure: The emergence, diffusion, and differentiation as sociological concept, 1930s–1950s. In F. Adler & W. Laufer (Eds.), *Advances in criminological theory: The legacy of anomie theory (Vol. 6).* New Brunswick, NJ: Transaction.

Messerschmidt, J. (1997). *Crime as structured action: Gender, race, class and crime in the making.* Thousand Oaks, CA: Sage.

Messerschmidt, J. (2000). *Nine lives: Adolescent masculinities, the body, and violence.* Boulder, CO: Westview Press.

Messner, S., & Rosenfeld, R. (1994). *Crime and the American dream.* Belmont, CA: Wadsworth.

Messner, S., & Rosenfeld, R. (1997). Political restraint of the market and levels of criminal homicide: A cross-national application of institutional anomie theory. *Social Forces, 75,* 1393–1416.

Messner, S., & Rosenfeld, R. (2001). An institutional anomie theory of crime. In R. Paternoster & R. Bachman (Eds.), *Explaining crime and criminals.* Los Angeles: Roxbury.

Messner, S., & Tardiff, K. (1985). The social ecology of urban homicide: An application of the routine activity approach. *Criminology, 23,* 241–267.

Messner, S., & Tardiff, K. (1986). Economic inequality and levels of homicide: An analysis of urban neighborhoods. *Criminology, 24,* 297–316.

Messner, S., Krohn, M., & Liska, A. (1989). *Theoretical integration in the study of deviance and crime: Problems and prospects.* Albany, NY: SUNY Press.

Michalowski, R., & Kramer, R. (2006). *State-corporate crime: Wrongdoing at the intersection of business and government.* Camden, NJ: Rutgers.

Miethe, T., & McDowall, D. (1993). Contextual effects in models of criminal victimization. *Social Forces, 71,* 741–759.

Miethe, T., & Meier, R. (1994). *Crime and its social context: Toward an integrated theory of offenders, victims, and situations.* Albany, NY: SUNY Press.

Miethe, T., Lu, H., & Reese, E. (2000). Reintegrative shaming and recidivism risks in drug courts: Explanations for some unexpected findings. *Crime and Delinquency, 46*(4), 522–541.

Miethe, T., Stafford, M., & Long, J. (1987). Social differentiation in criminal victimization: A test of routine activities/lifestyle theories. *American Sociological Review, 52,* 184–194.

Miles, D., & Carey, G. (1997). Genetic and environmental architecture of human aggression. *Journal of Personality & Social Psychology, 72*(X), 207–217.

Miller, J. (1968). *The nature of living systems: An exposition of the basic concepts in general systems theory.* Washington, DC: Academy for Educational Development.

Miller, J. (1978). *Living systems.* New York: McGraw-Hill.

Miller, J. (1997). African American males in the criminal justice system. *Phi Delta Kappan,* June: 22–30.

Miller, J., & Cohen, A. (1997). On the demise and morrow of subculture theories of crime and delinquency. *Journal of Crime & Justice, 20*(2): 167–178.

Miller, J.M., Schreck, C, & Tewksbury, R. (2006). *Criminological theory: A brief introduction* (2nd Ed.). Upper Saddle River, NJ: Prentice Hall.

Miller, T., Cohen, M., & Wiersema, B. (1997). *Victim costs and consequences: A new look.* Washington, DC: U.S. Department of Justice, Office of Justice Programs, National Institute of Justice.

Miller, W. (1958). Lower class culture as a generating milieu of gang delinquency. *Journal of Social Issues, 14,* 5–19.

Mirsky, A., & Siegel, A. (1994). The neurobiology of violence and aggression. In A. Reiss, Jr., K. Miczek, & J. Roth (Eds.), *Violence: Biobehavioral influences* (2: pp. 59–172). Washington, DC: National Academy Press.

Modestin, J., Hug, A., & Ammann, R. (1997). Criminal behavior in males with affective disorders. *Journal of Affective Disorders, 42,* 29–38.

Moffitt, T. (1990). The neuropsychology of juvenile delinquency. In N. Morris & M. Tonry (Eds.), *Crime and justice.* Chicago: University of Chicago Press.

Moffitt, T. (1990). The neuropsychology of juvenile delinquency: A critical review. In M. Tonry & N. Morris (Eds.), *Crime and justice: An annual review of research* (pp. 99–169). Chicago: University of Chicago.

Moffitt, T. (1993). Adolescence-limited and life-course-persistent antisocial behavior: A developmental taxonomy. *Psychology Review, 100*(4), 674–701.

Moffitt, T. (1996). The neuropsychology of conduct disorder. In P. Cordella & L. Siegel (Eds.), *Readings in contemporary criminological theory.* Boston: Northeastern University Press.

Moffitt, T. (2005). The new look of behavioral genetics in developmental psychopathology: Gene-environment interplay in antisocial behaviors. *Psychological Bulletin, 131*(X), 533–554.

Moffitt, T., & Silva, P. (1988). IQ and delinquency: A direct test of the differential detection hypothesis. *Journal of Abnormal Psychology, 97*(X), 330–333.

Moffitt, T., & Silva, P. (1988). IQ and delinquency: A test of the differential detection hypothesis. *Behavior Genetics, 23*, 519–524.

Moffitt, T., Brammer, G., Caspi, A., Fawcett, J., Raleigh, M., Yuwiler, A., & Silva, P. (1998). Whole blood serotonin relates to violence in an epidemiological study. *Biological Psychiatry, 43*(6), 446–457.

Moffitt, T., Caspi, A., Fawcett, P., Brammer, G., Raleigh, M., Yuwiler, A., & Silva, P. (1997). Whole blood serotonin and family background relate to male violence. In A. Raine, P. Brennan, D. Farrington, & S. Mednick (Eds.), *Biosocial bases of violence.* New York: Plenum Press.

Moffitt, T., Caspi, A., Silva, P., & Stouthamer-Loeber, M. (1995). Individual differences in personality and intelligence are linked to crime: Cross-context evidence from nations, neighborhoods, genders, races, and age-cohorts. *Current Perspectives on Aging and the Life Cycle, 4*, 1–34.

Moir, A., & Jessel, D. (1995). *A mind to crime.* London: Michael Joseph.

Mokhiber, R. (2007). Twenty things you should know about corporate crime. Retrieved September 21, 2007 from *http://www.commondreams.org/archive/2007/06/13/1859/.*

Mokhiber, R., & Weissman, R. (1999). *Corporate predators: The hunt for megaprofits and the attack on democracy.* Monroe, ME: Common Courage Press.

Monahan, J. (1997). Mental illness and violent crime. *Alternatives to Incarceration, 3*(3), 20–22.

Moolchan, E., & Robinson, M. (2001). Behavioral and neural consequences of prenatal exposure to nicotine. *Journal of the American Academy of Child & Adolescent Psychiatry, 40*(6), 630–641.

Moon, B., Blurton, D., & Mccluskey, J. (2008). General strain theory and delinquency. *Crime & Delinquency, 54*(4), 582–613.

Moore, M. (1996). *Downsize this!* New York: Crown Publishers.

Moore, T., Scarpa, A., & Raine, A. (2002). A meta-analysis of serotonin metabolite 5-HIAA and antisocial behavior. *Aggressive Behavior, 28*(X), 299–316.

Morgan-Sharp, E. (1999). The administration of justice based on gender and race. In R. Muraskin & A. Roberts (Eds.). *Visions for change: Crime and justice in the 21st century* (2nd Ed.). Upper Saddle River, NJ: Prentice Hall.

Moriarty, L., & Williams, J. (1996). Examining the relationship between routine activities theory and social disorganization: An analysis of property crime victimization. *American Journal of Criminal Justice, 21*(1), 43–59.

Morizot, J., & Blanc, M. (2007). Behavioral, self, and social control predictors of desistance from crime. *Journal of Contemporary Criminal Justice, 23*(1), 50–71.

Morley, K., & Hall, W. (2003). Is there a genetic susceptibility to engage in criminal acts? *Trends and Issues in Crime and Justice, 263*(X), 1–6.

Mosher, C. (2001). Predicting drug arrest rates: Conflict and social disorganization perspectives. *Crime and Delinquency, 47*(1), 84–104.

Muhajarine, N. (1996). *Psychosocial, sociodemographic, and biomedical predictors of prenatal risk behaviour.* Doctoral dissertation, University of Saskatchewan, Saskatoon, Canada.

Mumola, C. (1999). *Substance abuse and treatment, state and federal prisoners, 1997* (Bureau of Justice Statistics Special Report). Washington, DC: U.S. Department of Justice.

Murphy, K., & Harris, N. (2007). Shaming, shame and recidivism: A tests of reintegrative shaming theory in the white-collar crime context. *British Journal of Criminology, 47*(6), 900–917.

Murray, C. (1995). The physical environment. In J. Wilson & J. Petersilia (Eds.), *Crime.* San Francisco: ICS.

Murray, H. (1938). *Explorations in personality.* New York: Oxford University Press.

Mutzell, S. (1994). Mortality, suicide, social maladjustment and criminality among male alcoholic parents and men from the general population and their offspring. *International Journal of Adolescence and Youth, 4*(3–4), 305–328.

Myers, S., & Ellis, J. (1992). IQ discrepancies among impulsive and non-impulsive inmates. *Social Behavior and Personality, 20*(3), 213–217.

Nagin, D. (1978). General deterrence: A review of the empirical evidence. In A. Blumstein, J. Cohen, & D. Nagin (Eds.), *Deterrence and incapacitation: Estimating the effects of criminal sanctions on crime rates.* Washington, DC: National Academy Press.

Nagin, D. (2008). Thoughts on the broader implications of the "miracle of the cells." *Criminology & Public Policy, 7*(1), 37–42.

Nagin, D., & Farrington, D. (1992). The stability of criminal potential from childhood to adulthood. *Criminology, 30,* 235–260.

Nagin, D., & Paternoster, R. (1991). On the relationship of past and future participation in delinquency. *Criminology, 29,* 163–190.

Nagin, D., & Paternoster, R. (1993). Enduring individual differences and rational choice theories of crime. *Law & Society Review, 24,* 467–496.

NAMI. (2002). Mental illness. Retrieved from *www.nami.org.*

National Cancer Institute. (1997). Quoted in *Crime-Times, 4*(1), 2.

National Institute On Media And The Family (2008). Children and media violence. Retrieved December 21, 2008 from *http://www.mediafamily.org/facts/facts_vlent.shtml.*

Needleman, H. (2000). Lead exposure linked to delinquency. Paper presented at the joint meetings of the American Academy of Pediatrics and Pediatric Academic Societies. Boston, MA.

Needleman, H., Riess, J., Tobin, M., Biesecker, G., & Greenhouse, J. (1996). Bone lead levels and delinquent behavior. *Journal of the American Medical Association, 275*(5), 363–369.

Needleman, H., Schell, A., Bellinger, D., Leviton, A., & Allred, E. (1990). The long-term effects of exposure to low doses of lead in childhood: An 11-year follow-up report. *New England Journal of Medicine, 322*(2): 83–88.

Nehig, A., & Debry, G. (1994). Potential teratogenic and neurodevelopmental consequences of coffee and caffeine exposure: A review of human and animal data. *Neurotoxicology and Teratology, 16*(6), 531–543.

Neisser, U., Boodoo, G., Bouchard, T., Boykin, A., Brody, N., & Ceci, S. (1996). Intelligence: Known and unknowns. *The American Psychologist, 51*(2), 77–101.

Neugebauer, R., Hoek, H., & Susser, E. (1999). Prenatal exposure to wartime famine and development of antisocial personality disorder in early adulthood. *Journal of the American Medical Association, 282*(5), 455–462.

Neuman, W., & Berger, R. (1988). Competing perspectives on cross-national crime: An evaluation of theory and evidence. *Sociological Quarterly, 29*(2), 281–313.

Nevin, R. (2000). How lead exposure relates to temporal changes in IQ, violent crime, and unwed pregnancy. *Environmental Research, 83*(1), 1–22.

New York Times(1996). *The New York Times special report: The downsizing of America.* New York: Times Books.

New, A., Gelernter, J., Kranzler, H., Coccaro, E., & Siever, L. (1998). Serotonin transporter protein gene polymorphism and personality measures in African American and European American subjects. *American Journal of Psychiatry, 155*(10), 1332–1338.

New, A., Trestman, R., Mitropoulou, V., Benishay, D., Coccaro, E., Silverman, J., & Siever, L. (1997). Serotonergic function and self-injurious behavior in personality disorder patients. *Psychiatry Research, 69*, 17–26.

Newson, J., Newson, E., & Adams, M. (1993). The social origins of delinquency. *Criminal Behavior and Mental Health, 3*(1), 19–29.

Nigg, J., & Huang-Pollock, S. (2003). An early-onset model of the role of executive functions and intelligence in conduct disorder. In B. Lahey, T. Moffitt, & A. Caspi (Eds.), *Causes of conduct disorder and juvenile delinquency* (pp. 227–253). New York: The Guilford Press.

Nihei, M., Desmond, N., McGlothan, J., Kuhlmann, A., & Guilarte, T. (2000). N-methyl-D-aspartate receptor subunit changes are associated with lead-induced deficits of long-term potentiation and spatial learning. *Neuroscience, 99*(2), 233–242.

Noble, K., Norman, M., & Farah, M. (2005). Neurocognitive correlates of socioeconomic status in kindergarten children. *Developmental Science, 8*(X), 74–87.

Nofziger, S., & Kurtz, D. (2005). Violent lives: A lifestyle model linking exposure to violence to juvenile violent offending. *Journal of Research in Crime & Delinquency, 42*(1), 3–26.

Nolan, K., Volavka, J., Lachman, H., & Saito, T. (2000). An association between a polymorphism of the tryptophan hydroxylase gene and aggression in schizophrenia and schizoaffective disorder. *Psychiatry Genetics, 10*(3), 109–115.

Nomiya, D., Miller, A., & Hoffman, J. (2000). Urbanization and rural depletion in modern Japan: An analysis of crime and suicide patterns. *International Journal of Comparative and Applied Criminal Justice, 24*(1–2), 1–18.

Nurco, D., Kinlock, T., & Hanlon, T. (1998). The drugs-crime connection. In J. Inciardi & K. McElrath (Eds.), *The American drug scene: An anthology.* Los Angeles: Roxbury.

Nye, F. (1958). *Family relationships and delinquent behavior.* New York: John Wiley.

O'Connor, T., Deater-Deckard, K., Fulker, D., Rutter, M., & Plomin, R. (1998). Genotype-environment correlations in late childhood and early adolescence: Antisocial behavioral problems and coercive parenting. *Developmental Psychology, 34*, 970–981.

O'Keane, V., Loloney, E., O'Neil, H., O'Connor, A., Smith, C., & Dinam, T. (1992). Blunted prolactin responses to d-fenfluramine challenge in sociopathy: Evidence for subsensitivity of central serotonergic function. *British Journal of Psychiatry, 160*, 643–646.

Obradovic, J., Pardini, D., Long, J., & Loeber, R. (2007). Measuring interpersonal callousness in boys from childhood to adolescence: An examination of longitudinal Invariance and temporal stability. *Journal of Clinical Child & Adolescent Psychology, 36*(3), 276–292.

Office of National Drug Control Policy. (2000). *Drug facts.* Retrieved from *www.whitehousedrugpolicy.gov/.*

Oh, J. (2005). Social disorganizations and crime rates in U.S. central cities: Toward an explanation of urban economic change. *Social Science Journal, 42*(4), 569–582.

Oleson, J. (1997). *Rebel angels: Patterns of offending in intellectual elites.* Paper presented at the annual meeting of the American Society of Criminology, Chicago.

Omi, M, & Winant, H. (1994). *Racial formation in the United States: From the 1960s to the 1990s* (2nd Ed.). New York: Routledge.

Orlebeke, J., Knol, D., & Verhulst, F. (1997). Increase in child behavior problems resulting from maternal smoking during pregnancy. *Archives of Environmental Health, 52*(4), 317–321.

Ortega, S., Corzine, J., Burnett, D., & Poyer, T. (1992). Modernization, age structure, and regional context: A cross-national study of crime. *Sociological Spectrum, 12,* 257–277.

Ortega, T., Andres, P., Lopez-Sobaler, A., Ortega, A., Redondo, R., Jimenez, A., & Jimenez, L. (1994). The role of folates in the diverse biochemical processes that control mental function. *Nutrition and Hospitalization, 9*(4), 251–256.

Ortiz, J., & Raine, A. (2004). Heart rate level and antisocial behavior in children and adolescents: A meta-analysis. *Journal of the American Academy of Child and Adolescent Psychiatry, 43*(2), 154–162.

Osgood, D. (1998). *Interdisciplinary integration: Building criminology by stealing from our friends.* Paper presented at the annual meeting of the American Society of Criminology, Las Vegas, NV.

Osgood, D., & Anderson, A. (2004). Unstructured socializing and rates of delinquency. *Criminology, 42*(3), 519–549.

Osgood, D., & Chambers, J. (2000). Social disorganization outside the metropolis: An analysis of rural youth violence. *Criminology, 38*(1), 81–115.

Osgood, D., Wilson, J., O'Malley, P., Bachman, J., & Johnston, L. (1996). Routine activities and individual deviant behavior. *American Sociological Review, 61,* 635–655.

Pajer, K., Gardner, W., Rubin, R., Perel, J., & Neal, S. (2001). Decreased cortisol levels in adolescent girls with conduct disorder. *Archives of General Psychiatry, 58*(X), 297–302.

Palermo, G., Gumz, E., & Liska, F. (1992). Mental illness and criminal behavior revisited. *International Journal of Offender Therapy and Comparative Criminology, 36*(1), 53–61.

Pallone, N. (1991). *Mental disorders among prisoners.* New Brunswick, NJ: Transaction.

Pallone, N., & Hennessy, J. (1993). Tinderbox criminal violence: Impulsivity, risk-taking, and the phenomenology of rational choice. In R. Clarke & M. Felson (Eds.), *Routine activity and rational choice.* New Brunswick, NJ: Transaction.

Panzarella-Tse, C., & McMahon, P. (1991, April). *Defensive attribution: A reexamination distinguishing between behavioral and characterlogical blame.* Paper presented at the meeting of the Eastern Psychological Association, New York.

Pardini, D., Loeber, R., & Stouthamer-Loeber, M. (2005). Developmental shifts in parent and peer influences on boys' beliefs about delinquent behavior. *Journal of Research on Adolescence, 15*(3), 299–323.

Park, N., Beom, L., Bolland, J., Vazsonyi, A., And Fei, S. (2008). Early adolescent pathways of antisocial behaviors in poor, inner-city neighborhoods. *Journal of Early Adolescence, 28*(2), 185–205.

Park, R. (1915). The city: Suggestions for the investigation of human behavior in the urban environment. *American Journal of Sociology, 20,* 577–612.

Park, R. (1952). *Human communities.* Glencoe, IL: The Free Press.

Passas, N. (1994). Privatization and corruption in Romania. *Crime, Law, and Social Change, 21A,* 375–379.

Passas, N. (2000). Global anomie, dysnomie, and economic crime: Hidden consequences of neoliberalism and globalization in Russia and around the world. *Social Justice, 27*(2), 16–44.

Patchin, J., Huebner, B., Mccluskey, J., Varano, S., & Bynum, T. (2006). Exposure to community violence and childhood delinquency. *Crime & Delinquency, 52*(2), 307–332.

Pate, A., Wycoff, M., Skogan, W., & Sherman, L. (1986). *The effects of police fear reduction strategies: A summary of findings from Houston and Newark.* Washington, DC: Police Foundation.

Paternoster, R. (1987). The deterrent effect of the perceived certainty and severity of punishment: A review of the evidence and issues. *Justice Quarterly, 4,* 173–217.

Paternoster, R., & Bachman, R. (2001). *Explaining crime and criminals.* Los Angeles: Roxbury.

Paternoster, R., & Brame, R. (1997). Multiple routes to delinquency? A test of developmental and general theories of crime. *Criminology, 35,* 49–84.

Paternoster, R., & Brame, R. (2000). On the association among self-control, crime, and analogous behaviors. *Criminology, 38*(3), 971–982.

Paternoster, R., & Iovanni, L. (1989). The labeling perspective and delinquency: An elaboration of the theory and assessment of the evidence. *Justice Quarterly, 6,* 359–394.

Paternoster, R., & Mazerolle, P. (1994). General strain theory and delinquency: A replication and extension. *Journal of Research in Crime and Delinquency, 31*(3), 235–263.

Paternoster, R., Brame, R., Bachman, R., & Sherman, L. (1997). Do fair procedures matter? The effect of procedural justice on spouse assault. *Law and Society Review, 31,* 163–204.

Patrick, C. (1994). Emotions and psychopathy: Startling new insights. *Psychophysiology, 31,* 319–330.

Patterson, B. (1991). Poverty, income inequality, and community crime rates. *Criminology, 29*(4): 755–776.

Patterson, G. (1999). A proposal relating a theory of delinquency to societal rates of juvenile crime: Putting Humpty Dumpty together again. In M. Cox & J. Brooks-Gunn (Eds.), *Conflict and cohesion in families: Causes and consequences (the Advances in Family Research series)*. Mahwah, NJ: Lawrence Erlbaum Associates.

Patterson, G., Crosby, G., & Vuchinich, S. (1992). Predicting risk for early police arrest. *Journal of Quantitative Criminology, 8*, 335–355.

Patterson, G., DeBaryshe, B., & Ramsey, E. (1989). Developmental perspective on antisocial behavior. *American Psychologist, 44*(2), 329–335.

Patterson, G., Reid, J., & Dishion, T. (1991). *Antisocial boys.* Eugene, OR: Castalia.

Patterson, R. (1995). Criminality among women: A review of the literature. *Journal of Offender Rehabiliation, 22*(3–4), 33–53.

Payne, A., & Salotti, S. (2007). A comparative analysis of social learning and social control theories in the prediction of college crime. *Deviant Behavior, 28*(6), 553–573.

Pearson, D. (2000). Minority health. In R. Lauer & J. Lauer (Eds.), *Troubled times: Readings in social problems.* Los Angeles: Roxbury.

Pennington, B., & Bennetto, L. (1993). Main effects or transactions in the neuropsychology of conduct disorder? Commentary on "The neuropsychology of conduct disorder." *Development and Psychopathology, 5*, 153–164.

Perrone, D., Sullivan, C., Pratt, T., & Margaryan, S. (2004). Parental efficacy: Self-control, and delinquency: A test of a general theory of crime on a nationally representative sample of youth. *International Journal of Offender Therapy & Comparative Criminology, 48*(3), 298–312.

Perry, B., & Polk, D. (1997). Personality similarity in twins reared apart and together. In J. Osofsky (Ed.), *Children in a violent society.* New York: Guillford Press.

Perry, B., & Pollard, R. (1998). Homeostasis, stress, trauma, and adaptation: A neurodevelopmental view of childhood trauma. *Child and Adolescent Psychiatric Clinics of America, 7*, 33–51.

Persson, A., Kerr, M., & Stattin, H. (2007). Staying in or moving away from structured activities: Explanations involving parents and peers. *Developmental Psychology, 43*(1), 197–207.

Peruche, B., & Plant, E. (2006). The correlates of law enforcement officers' automatic and controlled race-based responses to criminal suspects. *Basic & Applied Social Psychology, 28*(2), 193–199.

Petee, T., & Kowalski, G. (1993). Modeling rural violent crime rates: A test of social disorganization theory. *Sociological Focus, 26*(1), 87–89.

Petee, T., Kowalski, G., & Duffield, D. (1994). Crime, social disorganization, and social structure: A research note on the use of interurban ecological models. *American Journal of Criminal Justice, 19*(1), 117–132.

Peter, T., Lagrange, T., & Silverman, R. (2003). Investigating the interdependence of strain and self-control. *Canadian Journal of Criminology & Criminal Justice, 45*(4), 431–464.

Petrocelli, M., Piquero, A., & Smith, M. (2003). Conflict theory and racial profiling: An empirical analysis of police traffic stop data. *Journal of Criminal Justice, 31*(1), 1.

Petterson, T. (1991). Religion and criminality: Structural relationships between church involvement and crime rates in contemporary Sweden. *Journal for the Scientific Study of Religion, 30*(3), 279–291.

Petty, F., Davis, L., Kabel, D., & Kramer, G. (1996). Serotonin dysfunction disorders: A behavioral neurochemistry perspective. *Journal of Clinical Psychiatry, 57*(8), 11–16.

Phillips, D., Henderson, G., & Schenker, S. (1989). Pathogenesis of fetal alcohol syndrome: Overview with emphasis on the possible role of nutrition. *Alcohol, Health and Research World, 13*(3), 219–227.

Phillips, S., Erkanli, A., Keeler, G., Costello, E., & Angold, A. (2006). Disentangling the risks: Parent criminal justice involvement and children's exposure to family risks. *Criminology & Public Policy, 5*(4), 677–702.

Pihl, R., & Bruce, K. (1995). Cognitive impairment in children of alcoholics. *Alcohol, Health and Research World, 19*, 142–147.

Pinchot, R. (1994). *The brain*. New York: Torstar Books.

Pine, D., Coplan, J., Wasserman, G., Miller, L., Fried, J., Davies, M., et al. (1997). Neuroendocrine response to fenfluramine challenge to boys. Associations with aggressive behavior and adverse rearing. *Archives of General Psychiatry, 54*, 839–846.

Pine, D., Wasserman, G., Coplan, J., Fried, J., Huang, Y., Kassir, S., et al. (1996). Platelet serotonin 2A (5-Ht2A) receptor characteristics and parenting factors for boys at risk for delinquency: A preliminary report. *American Journal of Psychiatry, 153*(4), 538–544.

Piquero, A., & Bouffard, J. (2007). Something old, something new: A preliminary investigation of Hirschi's redefined self-control. *Justice Quarterly, 24*(1), 1–27.

Piquero, A., & Mazerolle, P. (2001). *Life-course criminology: Contemporary and classic readings*. Belmont, CA: Wadsworth.

Piquero, A., & Rosay, A. (1998). The reliability and validity of Grasmick et al.'s self-control scale: A comment on Longshore et al. *Criminology, 36*(1), 157–173.

Piquero, A., & Tibbetts, S. (1996). Specifying the direct and indirect effects of low self-control and situational factors in offenders' decision making: Toward a more complete model of rational offending. *Justice Quarterly, 13*(3), 481–510.

Piquero, A., & Tibbetts, S. (2001). *Rational choice and criminal behavior: Recent research and future challenges.* New York: Routledge.

Piquero, A., MacIntosh, R., & Hickman, M. (2000). Does self-control affect survey response? Applying exploratory, confirmatory, and item response theory analysis to Grasmick et al.'s self-control scale. *Criminology, 38*(3), 897–929.

Piquero, A., Moffitt, T., & Wright, B. (2007). Self-control and criminal career dimensions. *Journal of Contemporary Criminal Justice, 23*(1), 72–89.

Piquero, N., Carmichael, S., & Piquero, A. (2008). Assessing the perceived seriousness of white-collar and street crimes. *Crime & Delinquency, 54*(2), 291–312.

Plemin, R., & Petrill, S. (1997). Genetics and intelligence: What's new? *Intelligence, 24*, 53–77.

Pliszka, S., Rogeness, G., Renner, P., Sherman, J., & Broussard, T. (1988). Plasma neurochemistry in juvenile offenders. *Journal of the American Academy of Child and Adolescent Psychiatry, 27*(X), 588–594.

Pogarsky, G. (2007). Deterrence and individuals differences among convicted offenders. *Journal of Quantitative Criminology, 23*, 9–74.

Pogarsky, G., Kim, K., & Paternoster, R. (2005). Perceptual change in the national youth survey: lessons for deterrence theory and offender decision-making. *Justice Quarterly, 22*(1), 1–29.

Polakowski, M. (1994). Linking self- and social control with deviance: Illuminating the structure underlying a general theory of crime and its relation to deviant activity. *Journal of Quantitative Criminology, 10*(1), 41–78.

Pope, C. (1979). Race and crime revisited. *Crime and Delinquency, 25*(3), 347–357.

Pope, C., Lovell, R., & Hsia, H. (2001). Disproportionate minority confinement: A review of the research literature from 1989 through 2001. Available: *http://ojjdp.ncjrs.org/dmc/pdf/dmc89_01.PDF.*

Popenoe, D. (1993). American family decline, 1960–1990: Evidence from the 1980s. *Journal of Marriage and the Family, 55*, 527–542.

Porter, W., Jaeger, J., & Carlson, I. (1999). Endocrine, immune, and behavioral effects of aldicarb (carbamate), atrazine (triazine), and nitrate (fertilizer) mixtures at groundwater concentrations. *Toxicology and Industrial Health, 15*(1–2), 133–150.

Pratt, T., & Cullen, F. (2000). The empirical status of Gottfredson and Hirschi's general theory of crime: A meta-analysis. *Criminology, 38*(3), 931–964.

Pratt, T., & Cullen, F. (2000). The empirical status of Gottfredson and Hirschi's general theory of crime: A meta-analysis. *Criminology, 38*(X), 931–964.

Pratt, T., & Lowenkamp, C. (2002). Conflict theory, economic conditions, and homicide: A time-series analysis. *Homicide Studies, 6*(1), 61–83.

Pratt, T., Cullen, F., Blevins, K., Daigle, L., & Madensen, T. (2006). The empirical status of deterrence theory: A meta-analysis. In F. Cullen, J. P. Wright, & K.

Pratt, T., Cullen, F., Blevins, K., Daigle, L., & Unnever, J. (2002). The relationship of attention deficit hyperactivity disorder to crime and delinquency: A meta-analysis. *International Journal of Police Science and Management, 4*(4), 344–360.

Preble, E., & Casey, J. (1969). Taking care of business: The heroin user's life in the streets. *International Journal of Addictions,* 4(1): 1–24.

Prescott, C., & Kendler, K. (1999). Genetic and environmental contributions to alcohol abuse and dependence in a population-based sample of male twins. *American Journal of Psychiatry, 156*(1), 34–40.

Prins, H. (2001). Mental disorders and violent crime. *Prison Services Journal, 136,* 2–5.

Pruitt, D. (1998). *Your child: What every parent needs to know: What's normal, what's not, and when to seek help. Emotional, behavioral and cognitive development from infancy through preadolescence.* New York: HarperCollins.

Quay, H. (1985). Intelligence. In H. Quay (Ed.), *Handbook of juvenile delinquency.* New York: Wiley.

Raine, A. (1993). *The psychopathology of crime: Criminal behavior as a clinical disorder.* San Diego, CA: Academic Press.

Raine, A. (1997). Antisocial behavior and psychophysiology: A biosocial perspective and a prefrontal dysfunction hypothesis. In D. Stoff, J. Breiling, & J. Maser (Eds.), *Handbook of antisocial behavior.* New York: John Wiley.

Raine, A., Brennan, P., & Mednick, S. (1994). Birth complications combined with early maternal rejection at age 1 year predispose to violent crime at age 18 years. *Archives of General Psychiatry, 51,* 984–988.

Raine, A., Brennan, P., Farrington, D., & Mednick, S. (1997). *Biosocial bases of violence.* New York: Plenum Press.

Raine, A., Buchsbaum, M., & LaCasse, L. (1997). Brain abnormalities in murderers indicated by positron emission tomography. *Biological Psychiatry, 42,* 495–508.

Raine, A., Buchsbaum, M., & Lacasse, L. (1997). Brain abnormalities in murderers indicated by positron emission tomography. *Biological Psychiatry, 42*(X), 495–508.

Raine, A., Buchsbaum, M., Stanley, J., Lottenberg, S., Abel, L., & Stoddard, J. (1994). Selective reductions in prefrontal glucose metabolism in murderers. *Biological Psychiatry, 36,* 365–373.

Raine, A., Buchsbaum, M., Stanley, J., Lottenberg, S., Abel, L., & Stoddard, J. (1994). Selective reductions in prefrontal glucose metabolism in murderers. *Biological Psychiatry, 36*(X), 365–373.

Raine, A., Ishikawa, S., Arce, E., Lencz, T., Knuth, K., Bihrle, S., Lacasse, L., & Colletti, P. (2004). Hippocampal structural asymmetry in unsuccessful psychopaths. *Biological Psychiatry, 55*(X), 185–191.

Raine, A., Lencz, T., Bihrle, S., LaCasse, L., & Colletti, P. (2000). Reduced prefrontal gray matter volume and reduced autonomic activity in antisocial personality disorder. *Archives of General Psychiatry, 57*(2), 119–127.

Raine, A., Lencz, T., Bihrle, S., Lacasse, L., & Colletti, P. (2000). Reduced prefrontal gray matter volume and reduced autonomic activity in antisocial personality disorder. *Archives of General Psychiatry, 57*(X), 119–127.

Raine, A., Lencz, T., Taylor, K., Hellige, J., Bihrle, S., Lacasse, L., Lee, M., Ishikawa, S., & Colletti, P. (2003). Corpus callosum abnormalities in psychopathic antisocial individuals. *Archives of General Psychiatry, 60*(X), 1134–1142.

Raine, A., Meloy, J., Bihrle, S., Stoddard, J., Lacasse, L., & Buchsbaum, M. (1998). Reduced prefrontal and increased subcortical brain functioning assessed using positron emission tomography in predatory and affective murderers. *Behavioral Sciences and the Law, 16*(X), 319–332.

Raine, A., Reynolds, C., Venables, P., Mednick, S., & Farrington, D. (1998). Fearlessness, stimulation-seeking, and large body size at age 3 years as early predispositions to childhood aggression at age 11 years. *Archives of General Psychiatry, 55*(8), 745–751.

Raine, A., Venables, P., & Mednick, S. (1997). Low resting heart rate at age 3 years predisposes to aggression at age 11 years: Evidence from the Mauritius Child Health Project. *Journal of the American Academy of Child and Adolescent Psychiatry, 36*(10), 1457–1464.

Raine, A., Venables, P., & Williams, M. (1990a). Autonomic orienting responses in 15-years-old male subjects and criminal behavior at age 24. *American Journal of Psychiatry, 147*(7), 933–937.

Raine, A., Venables, P., & Williams, M. (1990b). Relationships between central and autonomic measures of arousal at age 15 years and criminality at age 24 years. *Archives of General Psychiatry, 47*, 1003–1007.

Raine, A., Venables, P., & Williams, M. (1995). High autonomic arousal and electrodermal orienting at age 15 years as protective factors against criminal behavior at age 29 years. *American Journal of Psychiatry, 152*(11), 1595–1600.

Raine, A., Venables, P., & Williams, M. (1996). Better autonomic conditioning and faster electrodermal half-recovery time at age 15 years as possible protective factors against crime at age 29 years. *Developmental Psychology, 32*(4), 624–630.

Raloff, J. (1995). Gene appears to alter lead's toxicity. *Science News, 147:* 151.

Raphael, S. (2006). The deterrent effects of California's Proposition 8: Weighing the evidence. *Criminology & Public Policy, 5*(3), 471–478.

Rasanen, P., Hakko, H., Isohanni, M., Hodgins, S., Jarvelin, M., & Tiihonen, J. (1999). Maternal smoking during pregnancy and risk of criminal behavior among adult male offspring in the Northern Finland 1966 birth cohort. *American Journal of Psychiatry, 156*(6), 857–862.

Rasmussen, K., Storsaeter, O., & Levander, S. (1999). Personality disorders, psychopathy, and crime in a Norwegian prison population. *International Journal of Law and Psychiatry, 22*(1), 91–97.

Rasmussen, P., & Gillberg, C. (2000). Natural outcome of ADHD with developmental coordination disorder at age 22 years: A controlled, longitudinal, community-based study. *Journal of the American Academy of Child and Adolescent Psychiatry, 39*(11), 1424–1431.

Ratchford, M., & Beaver, K. (2009). Neuropsychological deficits, low self-control, and delinquent involvement: Toward a biosocial explanation of delinquency. *Criminal Justice and Behavior, 36*(2), 147–160.

Rebellon, C. (2006). Do adolescents engage in delinquency to attract the social attention of peers? *Journal of Research in Crime & Delinquency, 43*(4), 387–411.

Rebellon, C., & Van Gundy, K. (2005). Can control theory explain the link between parental physical abuse and delinquency? A longitudinal analysis. *Journal of Research in Crime & Delinquency, 42*(3), 247–274.

Reckless, W. (1961). A new theory of delinquency and crime. *Federal Probation, 25,* 42–46.

Reed, M., & Rose, D. (1998). Doing what Simple Simon says?: Estimating the underlying causal structures of delinquent associations, attitudes, and serious theft. *Criminal Justice and Behavior, 25*(2), 240–274.

Regnerus, M. (2002). Friends' influence on adolescent theft and minor delinquency: A developmental test of peer-reported effects. *Social Science Research, 31*(4), 681–705.

Reiman, J. (1998). *The rich get richer and the poor get prison* (5th ed.). Boston: Allyn & Bacon.

Reiman, J. (2006). *The rich get richer and the poor get prison* (8th Ed.).Boston, MA: Allyn & Bacon.

Reisig, M., & Cancino, J. (2004). Incivilities in nonmetropolitan communities: The effects of structural constraints, social conditions, and crime. *Journal of Criminal Justice, 32*(1), 15–29.

Reiss, A. (1951). Delinquency as the failure of personal and social controls. *American Sociological Review, 16,* 196–207.

Reiss, A. (1985). *Policing a city's central district: The Oakland story.* Washington, DC: U.S. Department of Justice, National Institute of Justice.

Reiss, A. (1986). Co-offender influences on criminal careers. In A. Blumstein, J. Roth, & C. Visher (Eds.), *Criminal careers and "career criminals"* (Vol. II). Washington, DC: National Academy Press.

Reiss, A., & Ross, J. (1993). *Understanding and preventing violence.* Washington, DC: National Academy Press.

Reiss, A., & Tonry, M. (1986). *Communities and crime.* Chicago: University of Chicago Press.

Reiss, A., Abrams, M., Singer, H., Ross, J., & Bencla, M. (1996). Brain development, gender, and IQ in children: A volumetric imaging study. *Brain, 119,* 1763–1774.

Rengert, G., & Wasilchick, J. (1985). *Suburban burglary: A time and place for everything.* Springfield, IL: Charles C. Thomas.

Reppetto, T. (1974). *Residential crime.* Cambridge, MA: Ballinger.

Retz, W., Retz-Junginger, P., Supprian, T., Thome, J., & Rosler, M. (2004). Association of serotonin transporter promoter gene polymorphism with violence: Relation with personality disorder, impulsivity, and childhood ADHD psychopathology. *Behavioral Sciences and the Law, 22*(X), 415–425.

Rhee, S., & Waldman, I. (2002). Genetic and environmental influences on antisocial behavior: A meta-analysis of twin and adoption studies. *Psychological Bulletin, 128*(X), 490–529.

Rice, K., & Smith, W. (2002). Socioecological models of automotive theft: Integrating routine activity and social disorganization approaches. *Journal of Research in Crime & Delinquency, 39*(3), 304–336.

Richardson, A. (2006). *They are what you feed them: How food can improve your child's behaviour, mood and learning.* Hammersmith, London: Harper Thorsons.

Richardson, W. (2000). Criminal behavior fueled by attention deficit hyperactivity disorder and addiction. In D. Fishbein (Ed.), *The science, treatment, and prevention of antisocial behaviors: Application to the criminal justice system.* Kingston, NJ: Civic Research Institute.

Richerson, P. (1997). Culture and human "nature." *Politics & the Life Sciences, 16*(1), 40–42.

Riley, D. (1987). Time and crime: The link between teenager lifestyle and delinquency. *Journal of Quantitative Criminology, 3*(4), 339–354.

Rinne, T., Westenberg, H., den Boer, J., & van den Oord, B. (2000). Serotonergic blunting to metachlorophenylpiperazine (m-CPP) highly correlates with sustained childhood abuse in impulsive and autoaggressive female borderline patients. *Biological Psychiatry, 47,* 548–556.

Risemberg, H. (1989). Fetal neglect and abuse. *New York State Journal of Medicine, 89*(3), 148–151.

Roach, K. (2000). Changing punishment at the turn of the century: Restorative justice on the rise. *Canadian Journal of Criminology, 42*(3), 249–280.

Robinson, M. (1997). *Ecology and crime: Lifestyles, routine activities, and residential burglary victimization.* Doctoral dissertation, Florida State University, Tallahassee.

Robinson, M. (1998). A look at the relationship between high aesthetics/low incivilities, criminal victimization & perceptions of risk. *Journal of Security Administration, 21*(2), 19–32.

Robinson, M. (1998). Accessible targets, but not advisable ones: The role of accessibility in student apartment burglary. *Journal of Security Administration, 21*(1), 28–43.

Robinson, M. (1998). *Its all in your head: Integrating neurological factors into criminological theory.* Paper presented at the annual meeting of the American Society of Criminology, Las Vegas, NV.

Robinson, M. (1998). Tobacco: The greatest crime in world history? *The Critical Criminologist, 8*(3), 20–22.

Robinson, M. (1999). Lifestyles, routine activities, and residential burglary victimization. *Journal of Crime and Justice, 22*(1), 27–56.

Robinson, M. (1999). The theoretical development of Crime Prevention Through Environmental Design (CPTED). *Advances in Criminological Theory, 8,* 427–462.

Robinson, M. (2001). Crime prevention through environmental design in elementary and secondary schools. In D. Robinson (Ed.), *Police and crime prevention.* Upper Saddle River, NJ: Prentice-Hall.

Robinson, M. (2002). *Justice blind? Ideals and realities of American criminal justice.* Upper Saddle River, NJ: Prentice-Hall.

Robinson, M. (2003). Peter Knight (Ed.). Eugenics. In *Encyclopedia of American Conspiracy Theories.* Santa Barbara, CA: ABC-CLIO.

Robinson, M. (2008). *Death nation: The experts explain American capital punishment.* Upper Saddle River, NJ: Prentice Hall.

Robinson, M., & del Carmen, A. (1999). Downsizing, corporate security, and loss prevention. *Security Journal, 12*(2), 27–37.

Robinson, M., & Kelley, T. (1998). *The use of neurological cues by probation officers to assess brain dysfunction in offenders.* Paper presented at the annual meeting of the Academy of Criminal Justice Sciences. Albuquerque, NM.

Robinson, M., & Kelley, T. (2000). The identification of neurological correlates of brain dysfunction in offenders by probation officers. In D. Fishbein

(Ed.), *The science, treatment, and prevention of antisocial behaviors.* Kingston, NJ: Civic Research Institute.

Robinson, M., & Murphy, D. (2008). *Greed is good: Maximization and elite deviance in America.* Landham, MA: Rowman and Littlefield.

Robinson, W. (1950). Ecological correlations and the behavior of individuals. *American Sociological Review, 15,* 351–357.

Roche, D. (2006). Dimensions of restorative justice. *Journal of Social Issues, 62*(2), 217–238.

Rock, P., & Holdaway, S. (1998). Thinking about criminology: Facts are bits of biography. In S. Holdaway & P. Rock (Eds.), *Thinking about criminology.* Toronto: University of Toronto Press.

Roebuck, T., Mattson, S., & Riley, E. (1999). Behavioral and psychosocial profiles of alcohol-exposed children. *Clinical and Experimental Research, 23*(6), 1070–1076.

Rohe, W., & Burby, R. (1988). Fear of crime in public housing. *Environment and Behavior, 20,* 700–720.

Rolison, G. (1993). Toward an integrated theory of female criminality and incarceration. In B. Fletcher, L. Shaver, et al. (Eds.), *Women prisoners: A forgotten population.* Westport, CT: Praeger Publishers/ Greenwood Publishing Group.

Rollin, J. (1997). The social ecology of crime in Saginaw, Michigan. *Dissertation Abstracts International, A: The Humanities and Social Sciences, 58*(2), 0591-A.

Romero, E., Gomez-Fraguela, J., Luengo, M., & Sobral, J. (2003). The self-control construct in the general theory of crime: An investigation in terms of personality psychology. *Psychology, Crime & Law, 9*(1), 61–86.

Romero, M. (2006). Racial profiling and immigration law enforcement: Rounding up of usual suspects in the Latino community. *Critical Sociology, 32*(2/3), 447–473.

Roncek, D., & Maier, P. (1991). Bars, blocks, and crimes revisited: Linking the theory of routine activities to the empiricism of "hot spots." *Criminology, 29*(4), 725–753.

Rosay, A. (2000). Narrowing the causes of criminal and analogous behaviors from self-control to risk-seeking and impulsivity. *Dissertation Abstracts International, A: The Humanities and Social Sciences, 61*(1), 376-A.

Rose, D., & Clear, T. (1998). Incarceration, social capital, and crime: Implications for social disorganization theory. *Criminology, 36*(3), 441–479.

Rosenbaum, J., & Prinsky, L. (1991). The presumption of influence: Recent responses to popular music subcultures. *Crime and Delinquency, 37*(4), 528–535.

Rosenfeld, R., & Messner, S. (1998). *Beyond the criminal justice system: Anomie, institutional vitality, and crime in the United States.* Paper presented at the annual meeting of the American Sociological Association. San Francisco.

Rosoff, S., Pontell, H., & Tillman, R. (1998). *Profit without honor: White-collar crime and the looting of America.* Upper Saddle River, NJ: Prentice-Hall.

Rosoff, S., Pontell, H., & Tillman, R. (2002). *Profit without honor: White-collar crime and the looting of America* (2nd ed.). Upper Saddle River, NJ: Prentice-Hall.

Rosoff, S., Pontell, H., & Tillman, R. (2006). *Profit without honor: White-collar crime and the looting of America* (4th Ed). Upper Saddle River, NJ: Prentice Hall.

Ross, L. (1996). The relationship between religion, self-esteem, and delinquency. *Journal of Crime and Justice, 19*(2), 195–214.

Rothbart, M., & Ahadi, S. (1994). Temperament and the development of personality. *Journal of Abnormal Psychology, 103,* 55–66.

Rothbart, M., Ahadi, S., & Evans, D. (2000). Temperament and personality: Origins and outcomes. *Journal of Personality and Social Psychology, 78,* 122–135.

Rotton, J., & Cohn, E. (2004). Outdoor temperature, climate control, and criminal assault. *Environment & Behavior, 36*(2), 276–306.

Rountree, P., & Warner, B. (1999). Social ties and crime: Is the relationship gendered? *Criminology, 37*(4), 789–813.

Rountree, P., Land, K., & Miethe, T. (1994). Macro-micro integration in the study of victimization: A hierarchical logistic analysis across Seattle neighborhoods. *Criminology, 32,* 387–414.

Rowe, D. (1992). Three shocks to socialization research. *Behavioral and Brain Sciences, 14,* 401–402.

Rowe, D. (1994). *The limits of family influence: Genes, experience, and behavior.* New York: Guilford Press.

Rowe, D. (1996). An adaptive strategy theory of crime and delinquency. In J. Hawkins (Ed.), *Delinquency and crime: Current theories.* New York: Cambridge University Press.

Rowe, D. (2002). *Biology and crime.* Los Angeles, CA: Roxbury.

Rowe, D., Stever, C., Chase, D., Sherman, S., Abramowitz, A., & Waldman, I. (2001). Two dopamine receptor genes related to reports of childhood retrospective inattention and conduct disorder symptoms. *Molecular Psychiatry, 6*(X), 429–433.

Ruden, R. (1997). *The craving brain: The biobalance approach to controlling addictions.* New York: Harper Collins.

Ruden, R., & Byalick, M. (1997). *The craving brain: The biobalance approach to controlling addictions.* New York: Harper Collins.

Ruff, H., Bijur, P., Markowitz, M., Ma, Y., & Rosen, J. (1993). Declining blood lead levels and cognitive changes in moderately lead-poisoned children. *Journal of the American Medical Association, 269*(13): 1641–1646.

Rujesco, D., Giegling, I., Gietl, A., Hartmann, A., & Möller, H. (2003). A functional single nucleotide polymorphism (V158M) in the COMT gene is associated with aggressive personality traits. *Biological Psychiatry, 54*(X), 34–39.

Rutter, M., & Giller, H. (1983). *Juvenile delinquency: Trends and perspectives.* New York: Penguin Books.

Ryan, J. (2006). Dependent youth in juvenile justice: Do positive peer culture programs work for victims of child maltreatment? *Research on Social Work Practice, 16*(5), 511–519.

Saegert, S., & Winkel, G. (2004, December). Crime, social capital, and community participation. *American Journal of Community Psychology, 34*(3/4), 219–233.

Sampson, R. (1985). Race and criminal violence: A demographically disaggregated analysis of urban homicide. *Crime & Delinquency, 31*, 47–82.

Sampson, R. (1987). Does an intact family reduce burglary risk for its neighbors? *Sociology and Social Research, 71*, 204–207.

Sampson, R. (1995). The community. In J. Wilson & J. Petersilia (Eds.), *Crime.* San Francisco: ICS Press.

Sampson, R. (1999). Techniques of research neutralization. *Theoretical Criminology, 3*, 438–451.

Sampson, R. (2000). A neighborhood-level perspective on social change and the social control of adolescent delinquency. In L. Crockett & R. Silbereisen (Eds.), *Negotiating adolescence in times of social change.* New York: Cambridge University Press.

Sampson, R., & Groves, B. (1989). Community structure and crime: Testing social disorganization theory. *American Journal of Sociology, 94*, 774–802.

Sampson, R., & Laub, J. (1993). *Crime in the making: Pathways and turning points through life.* Cambridge, MA: Harvard University Press.

Sampson, R., & Laub, J. (1997). A life course theory of cumulative disadvantage and the stability of delinquency. In T. Thornberry (Ed.), *Developmental theories of crime and delinquency: Advances in criminological theory* (Vol. 7). New Brunswick, NJ: Transaction.

Sampson, R., & Laub, J. (1999). Crime and deviance over the lifecourse: The salience of adult social bonds. In F. Scarpitti & A. Nielsen (Eds.), *Crime and criminals: Contemporary and classical readings in criminology.* Los Angeles: Roxbury Press.

Sampson, R., & Raudenbush, S. (1999). Systematic observation of public places: A new look at disorder in urban neighborhoods. *American Journal of Sociology, 105*(3), 603–651.

Sampson, R., & Raudenbush, S. (2001). Disorder in urban neighborhoods: Does it lead to crime? *National Institute of Justice Research in Brief.* February.

Sampson, R., & Wilson, W. (1994). Toward a theory of race, crime, and urban inequality. In J. Hagan & R. Peterson (Eds.), *Inequality and crime.* Stanford, CA: Stanford University Press.

Sampson, R., & Wilson, W. (2000). Toward a theory of race, crime, and urban inequality. In S. Cooper (Ed.), *Criminology.* Madison, WI: Coursewise.

Sampson, R., & Wooldredge, J. (1987). Linking the micro- and macro-level dimensions of lifestyle-routine activity and opportunity models of predatory victimization. *Journal of Quantitative Criminology, 3*(4), 371–393.

Sampson, R., Raudenbush, S., & Earls, F. (1997). Neighborhoods and violent crime: A multi-level study of collective efficacy. *Science, 277,* 398–462.

Samuelson, L., & Hartnagel, T. (1995). Crime and social control among high school dropouts. *Journal of Crime and Justice, 18*(1); 129–165.

Sanchez-Martin, J., Fano, E., Ahedo, L., Cardas, J., Brain, P., & Azpiroz, A. (2000). Relating testosterone levels and free play social behavior in male and female preschool children. *Psychoneuroendocrinology, 25*(8), 773–783.

Sanson, A., Smart, D., Prior, M., & Oberklaid, F. (1993). Precursors of hyperactivity and aggression. *Journal of the American Academy of Child and Adolescent Psychiatry, 32,* 1207–1216.

Saradhi, P. (2001). *Biophysical processes in living systems.* Enfield, NH: Science Publishers.

Saugstad, L. (1997). Optimal foetal growth in the reduction of learning and behaviour disorder and prevention of sudden infant death syndrome (SIDS) after the first month. *International Journal of Psychophysiology, 27*(2), 107–121.

Savage, J., & Vila, B. (1997). Lagged effects of nurturance on crime: A cross-national comparison. *Studies on Crime & Crime Prevention, 6*(1), 101–120.

Savage, J., & Vila, B. (2001). Changes in child welfare and subsequent crime rates trends: Evaluating the lagged nurturance hypothesis. *Journal of Applied Developmental Psychology.*

Savolainen, J. (2000). Inequality, welfare state, and homicide: Further support for the institutional anomie theory. *Criminology, 38*(4), 1021–1042.

Scarpa, A., Raine, A., Venables, P., & Mednick, S. (1997). Heart rate and skin conductance in behaviorally inhibited Mauritian children. *Journal of Abnormal Psychology, 106*(2), 182–190.

Scarr, H. (1973). *Patterns of burglary.* Washington, DC: U.S. Department of Justice.

Schafer, J., Carter, D., Katz-Bannister, A., & Wells, W. (2006). Decision making in traffic stop encounters: A multivariate analysis of police behavior. *Police Quarterly, 9*(2), 184–209.

Schatzman, M. (1975). Cocaine and the drug problem. *Journal of Psychedelic Drugs, 7*(1), 7–17.

Schmidt, L., Fox, N., Rubin, K., Hu, S., & Hamer, D. (2002). Molecular genetics of shyness and aggression in preschoolers. *Personality and Individual Differences, 33*(X), 227–238.

Schoenthaler, S. (1991). Abstracts of early papers on the effects of vitamin and mineral supplementation on IQ and behavior. *Personality and Individual Differences, 12*(4), 335–341.

Schoenthaler, S., & Bier, I. (1999). Vitamin-mineral intake and intelligence: A macrolevel analysis of randomized controlled trials. *Journal of Alternative and Complementary Medicine, 5*(2), 125–134.

Schoenthaler, S., & Bier, I. (2000). The effect of vitamin-mineral supplementation on juvenile delinquency among American schoolchildren: A randomized, double-blind placebo-controlled trial. *Journal of Alternative and Complementary Medicine, 6*(1), 7–17.

Schoenthaler, S., Amos, S., Eysenck, J., Peritz, E., & Yudkin, J. (1993). Controlled trial of vitamin-mineral supplementation: Effects on intelligence and performance. *Personality and Individual Differences, 12*(4): 19–29.

Schoenthaler, S., Bier, I., Young, K., Nichols, D., & Jansenns, S. (2000). The effect of vitamin-mineral supplementation on the intelligence of American school children: A randomized, double-blind placebo-controlled trial. *Journal of Alternative and Complementary Medicine, 6*(1), 19–29.

Schoepfer, A., & Piquero, A. (2006). Self-control, moral beliefs, and criminal activity. *Deviant Behavior, 27*(1), 51–71.

Scholl, T., Hediger, M., Schall, J., Khoo, C., & Fischer, R. (1996). Dietary and serum folate: Their influence on the outcome of pregnancy. *American Journal of Clinical Nutrition, 63*: 520–525.

Schor, E. (1999). *Caring for your school age child: Ages 5–12.* New York: Bantam Books.

Schreck, C., & Fisher, B. (2004). Specifying the influence of family and peers on violent victimization. *Journal of Interpersonal Violence, 19*(9), 1021–1041.

Schuckit, M., & Smith, T. (1996). An 8-year follow up of 450 sons of alcoholic and control subjects. *Archives of General Psychiatry, 53*(3): 202–210.

Schur, E. (1971). *Radical nonintervention: Rethinking the delinquency problem.* Englewood Cliffs, NJ: Prentice-Hall.

Schwab, J., Gray-Ice, H., & Prentice, F. (2000). *Family functioning: The general living systems research model.* New York: Kluwer Academic/Plenum Publishers.

Schwartz, I., Rendon, J., & Hsieh, C. (1994). Is child maltreatment a leading cause of delinquency? *Child Welfare, 73*(5), 639–655.

Sellin, T. (1938). *Culture conflict and crime.* New York: Social Science Research Council.

Sguin, J., Pihl, R., Harden, P., Tremblay, R., & Boulerice, B. (1995). Cognitive and neuropsychological characteristics of physically aggressive boys. *Journal of Abnormal Psychology, 104*(4), 614–624.

Shaw, C., & McKay, H. (1929). *Juvenile delinquency and urban areas.* Chicago: University of Chicago Press.

Shaw, C., & McKay, H. (1942). *Juvenile delinquency and urban areas* (5th ed.). Chicago: University of Chicago Press.

Shaw, C., & McKay, H. (1972). *Juvenile delinquency and urban areas* (12th ed.). Chicago: University of Chicago Press.

Shelden, R. (2001). *Controlling the dangerous classes: A critical introduction to the history of criminal justice.* Boston: Allyn & Bacon.

Sherman, D., Lacono, W., & McGue, M. (1997). Attention-deficit hyperactivity disorder dimensions: A twin study of inattention and impulsivity-hyperactivity. *Journal of the American Academy of Child and Adolescent Psychiatry, 36*(6), 745–753.

Sherman, L. (1993). Defiance, deterrence, and irrelevance: A theory of the criminal sanction. *Journal of Research in Crime and Delinquency, 30,* 445–473.

Sherman, L. (1995). Hot spots of crime and criminal careers of place. In J. Eck & D. Weisburd (Eds.), *Crime and place.* Monsey, NY: Criminal Justice Press.

Sherman, L., & Rogan, L. (1995). Deterrent effects of police raids on crack houses: A randomized, controlled experiment. *Justice Quarterly, 12*(4), 755–781.

Sherman, L., & Weisburd, D. (1995). General deterrent effects of police patrol in crime "hot spots": A randomized, controlled trial. *Justice Quarterly, 12*(4), 625–648.

Sherman, L., Gartin, P., & Buerger, M. (1989). Hot spots of predatory crime: Routine activities and the criminology of place. *Criminology, 27*(1), 27–55.

Sherman, L., Gottfredson, D., MacKenzie, D., Eck, J., Reuter, P., & Bushway, S. (1997). *Preventing crime: What works, what doesn't, what's promising.* A report to the United States Congress, prepared for the National Institute of Justice. Retrieved from *www.ncjrs.org/ works/.*

Sherman, L., Smith, D., Schmidt, J., & Rogan, D. (1992). Crime, punishment, and stake in conformity: Legal and informal control of domestic violence. *American Sociological Review, 57*(5), 680–690.

Shoemaker, D. (1996). *Theories of delinquency* (3rd ed.). New York: Oxford University Press.

Shore, P. (1996). *Culture in mind: Cognition, culture, and the problem of meaning.* New York: Oxford University Press.

Shore, R. (1997). *Rethinking the brain: New insights into early development.* New York: Families and Work Institute.

Shover, N., & Wright, J. (2000). *Crimes of privilege: Readings in white-collar crime.* New York: Oxford University Press.

Siegel, D. (1999). *The developing mind: How relationships and the brain interact to shape who we are.* New York: The Guilford Press.

Siegel, L. (1995). *Criminology* (5th ed.). Minneapolis/St. Paul, MN: West.

Siegel, L. (2001). *Criminology* (7th ed.). Belmont, CA: Wadsworth.

Siennick, S., & Staff, J. (2008). Explaining the education deficits of delinquent youths. *Criminology, 46*(3), 609–635.

Sigurdsson, J., & Gudjonsson, G. (1996). Psychological characteristics of juvenile alcohol and drug users. *Journal of Adolescence, 19*(2), 121–126.

Silver, E. (1999). Violence and mental illness from a social disorganization perspective: An analysis of individual and community risk factors. *Dissertation Abstracts International, A: The Humanities and Social Sciences, 60*(6), 2236-A.

Silver, E., & Miller, L. (2004). Sources of informal social control in Chicago neighborhoods. *Criminology, 42*(3), 551–583.

Simeon, D., Stanley, B., Frances, A., Mann, J., Winchel, R., & Stanley, M. (1992). Self-mutilation in personality disorders: Psychological and biological correlates. *American Journal of Psychiatry, 149*(X), 221–226.

Simon, D. (2002). *Elite deviance* (7th ed.). Boston: Allyn & Bacon.

Simon, D. (2007). *Elite deviance* (9th Ed). Boston, MA: Allyn & Bacon.

Simon, D., & Eitzen, D. (1993). *Elite deviance* (4th ed.). Needham Heights, MA: Allyn & Bacon.

Simon, D., & Hagan, F. (1999). *White-collar deviance.* Needham Heights, MA: Allyn & Bacon.

Simons, R. (1978). The meaning of the IQ-delinquency relationship. *American Sociological Review, 43,* 268–270.

Simons, R., Chao, W., Conger, R., & Elder, G. (2001). Quality of parenting as mediator of the effect of childhood defiance on adolescent friendship choices and delinquency: A growth curve analysis. *Journal of Marriage & the Family, 63*(1), 63–79.

Simons, R., Johnson, C., Conger, R., & Elder, G., Jr. (1998). A test of latent trait versus life-course perspectives on the stability of adolescent antisocial behavior. *Criminology, 36*(2), 217–243.

Simons, R., Simons, L., & Wallace, L. (2004). *Families, delinquency, and crime: Linking society's most basic institutions to antisocial behavior.* Los Angeles, CA: Roxbury.

Simons, R., Stewart, E., Gordon, L., Conger, R., & Elder Jr., G. (2002). A test of life-course explanations for stability and change in antisocial behavior from adolescence to young adulthood. *Criminology, 40*(2), 401–434.

Simons, R., Wu, C., Conger, R., & Lorenz, F. (1994). Two routes to delinquency: Differences between early and late starters in the impact of parenting and deviant peers. *Criminology, 32*(2), 247–275.

Singh, V. (1991). The underclass in the United States: Some correlates of economic change. *Sociological Inquiry, 61,* 505–521.

Sitren, A., & Applegate, B. (2007). Testing the deterrent effects of personal and vicarious experience with punishment and punishment avoidance. *Deviant Behavior, 28*(1), 29–55.

Skinner, W., & Fream, A. (1997). A social learning theory analysis of computer crime among college students. *Journal of Research in Crime and Delinquency, 34*(4), 495–518.

Skogan, W. (1981). On attitudes and behaviors. In D. Lewis (Ed.), *Reactions to crime.* Beverly Hills, CA: Sage.

Skogan, W. (1986). Fear of crime and neighborhood change. In A. Reiss & M. Tonry (Eds.), *Communities and crime.* Chicago: University of Chicago Press.

Skogan, W. (1990). *Disorder and decline.* Berkeley: University of California Press.

Skogan, W. (1991). *Disorder and decline.* New York: Free Press.

Skogan, W. (1995). Crime and the racial fears of white Americans. *Annals of the American Academy of Political and Social Science, 539,* 59–71.

Skogan, W., & Maxfield, M. (1981). *Coping with crime: Individual and neighborhood reactions.* Beverly Hills, CA: Sage.

Skolnick, J. (1966). *Justice without trial: Law enforcement in a democratic society.* New York: Wiley.

Slocum, L., Simpson, S., & Smith, D. (2005). Strained lives and crime: Examining intra-individual variation in strain and offending in a sample of incarcerated women. *Criminology, 43*(4), 1067–1110.

Slutske, W., Eisen, S., Xian, H., True, W., Lyons, M., Goldberg, J., & Tsuang, M. (2001). A twin study of the association between pathological gambling and antisocial personality disorder. *Journal of Abnormal Psychology, 110*(2), 297–308.

Slutske, W., Heath, A., Dinwiddie, S., Madden, P., Bucholz, K., Dunne, M., et al. (1997). Modeling genetic and environmental influences in the etiology of conduct disorder: A study of 2,682 adult twin pairs. *Journal of Abnormal Psychology, 106*(2), 266–279.

Smith, C., & Thornberry, T. (1995). The relationship between childhood mal-treatment and adolescent involvement in delinquency. *Criminology, 33*(4), 451–481.

Smith, D., Leve, L., & Chamberlain, P. (2006). Adolescent girls' offending and health-risking sexual behavior: The predictive role of trauma. *Child Maltreatment, 11*(4), 346–353.

Smith, K., Fairburn, C., & Cowen, P. (1997). Relapse of depression after rapid depletion of tryptophan. *Lancet, 349*(9056), 915–919.

Smith, M. (2001). Alternatives to incarceration: What future for "public safety" and "restorative justice" in community corrections? *Corrections Forum, 10*(4), 35–41.

Smith, R. (1995). *Racism in the post-civil rights era: Now you see it, now you don't.* Albany: State University of New York Press.

Smith-Cunnien, S., & Parilla, P. (2001). Restorative justice in the criminal justice curriculum. *Journal of Criminal Justice Education, 12*(2), 385–403.

Society for Neuroscience. (1996). *Brain briefings.* Retrieved from *www.sfn.org/briefings.*

Soderstrom, H., Tullberg, M., & Wikkels, C. (2000). Reduced regional cerebral blood flow in non-psychotic violent offenders. *Psychiatry Research, 98,* 29–41.

Soler, H., Vinayak, P., & Quadagno, D. (2000). Biosocial aspects of domestic violence. *Psychoneuroendocrinology, 25*(7), 721–739.

Soloff, P., Meltzer, C., Greer, P., Constantine, D., & Kelly, T. (2000). A fenfluramine-activated FDG-PET study of borderline personality disorder. *Biological Psychiatry, 47,* 540–547.

Sood, B., Delaney-Black, V., Covington, C., Nordstrom-Klee, B., Ager, J., Templin, T., Janisse, J., Martier, S., & Sokol, R. (2001). Prenatal alcohol exposure and childhood behavior at age 6 to 7 years: I. Dose-response effect. *Pediatrics, 108*(2), e34.

Sowell, E., Thompson, P., Holmes, C., Jernigan, T., & Toga, A. (1999). In vivo evidence for post-adolescent brain maturation in frontal and striatal regions. *Nature Neuroscience, 2,* 859–861.

Spano, R., & Nagy, S. (2005). Social guardianship and social isolation: An application and extension of lifestyle/routine activities theory to rural adolescents. *Rural Sociology, 70*(3), 414–437.

Spano, R., Freilich, J., & Bolland, J. (2008). Gang membership, gun carrying, and employment: Applying routine activities theory to explain violent victimization among inner city, minority youth living in extreme poverty. *Justice Quarterly, 25*(2), 381–410.

Spitz, M., & Shi, H. (1998). Case control study of the D2 dopamine receptor gene and smoking status in lung cancer patients. *Journal of the National Cancer Institute, 90*(5), 358–363.

Sprich, S., Biederman, J., Crawford, M., Mundy, E., & Faraone, S. (2000). Adoptive and biological families of children and adolescents with ADHD. *Journal of the American Academy of Child and Adolescent Psychiatry, 39*(11).

Stalenheim, E., Eriksson, E., von Knorring, L., & Wide, L. (1998). Testosterone as a biological marker in psychopathy and alcoholism. *Psychiatry Research, 77*(2), 79–88.

Stanley, B., Molcho, A., Stanley, M., Winchel, R., Gameroff, M., Parsons, B., & Mann, J. (2000). Association of aggressive behavior with altered serotonergic function in patients who are not suicidal. *American Journal of Psychiatry, 157,* 609–614.

Stattin, H., & Klackenberg-Larsson, I. (1993). Early language and intelligence development and their relationship to future criminal behavior. *Journal of Abnormal Psychology, 102*(3), 369–378.

Steegmans, P., Fekkes, D., Hoes, A., Bak, A., van der Does, E., & Grobbee, D. (1996). Low serum cholesterol concentration and serotonin metabolism in men. *British Medical Journal, 312*(7025): 221.

Stein, D., Trestman, R., & Mitropoulou, V. (1996). Impulsivity and serotonergic function in compulsive personality disorder. *Journal of Neuropsychiatry, 8,* 393–398.

Steinberg, R. (1995). *In search of the human mind.* Orlando, FL: Harcourt Brace.

Sterman, J. (2000). *Business dynamics: Systems thinking and modeling for a complex world.* Boston: Irwin/McGraw-Hill.

Steury, E. (1993). Criminal defendants with psychiatric impairment: Prevalence, probabilities and rates. *Journal of Criminal Law and Criminology, 84,* 354–374.

Steury, E., & Choinski, M. (1995). "Normal" crimes and mental disorder: A two-group comparison of deadly and dangerous felonies. *International Journal of Law and Psychiatry, 18*(2), 183–207.

Stevens, L., Zentall, S., Abate, M., Kuczek, T., & Burgess, J. (1995). Omega-3 fatty acids in boys with behavior, learning, and health problems. *Physiology and Behavior 59,* 915–920.

Stevens, L., Zentall, S., Deck, J., Abate, M., Watkins, B., Lipp, S., & Burgess, J. (1995). Essential fatty acid metabolism in boys with attention deficit hyperactivity disorder. *American Journal of Clinical Nutrition, 62*(4), 761–768.

Stevenson, J., & Goodman, R. (2001). Association between behavior at age 3 years and adult criminality. *British Journal of Psychiatry, 179,* 197–202.

Stewart, E., Elifson, K., & Sterk, C. (2004). Integrating the general theory of crime into an explanation of violent victimization among female offenders. *Justice Quarterly, 21*(1), 159–181.

Stewart, E., Simons, R., Conger, R., & Scaramella, L. (2002). Beyond the interactional relationship between delinquency and parenting practices: The contribution of legal sanctions. *Journal of Research in Crime & Delinquency, 39*(1), 36–59.

Stiles, B., Liu, X., & Kaplan, H. (2000). Relative deprivation and deviant adaptations: The mediating effects of negative self-feelings. *Journal of Research in Crime and Delinquency, 37*(1), 64–90.

Stinchcombe, A. (1968). *Constructing social theories.* New York: Harcourt, Brace & World.

Stokes, P. (1995). The potential role of excessive cortisol induced by HPA hyperfunction in the pathogenesis of depression. *European Neuropsychopharmacology, 5,* 77–82.

Straus, M., & Mouradian, V. (1998). Impulsive corporal punishment by mothers and antisocial behavior and impulsiveness of children. *Behavioral Sciences and the Law, 16*(3), 353–374.

Streeten, D. (2001). *The general organization of the autonomic nervous system.* Retrieved from *www.ndrf.org/ans.htm.*

Strom, K., & Macdonald, J. (2007). The influence of social and economic disadvantage on racial patterns in youth homicide over time. *Homicide Studies, 11*(1), 50–69.

Strous, R., Bark, N., Parsia, S., Volavka, J., & Lachman, H. (1997). Analysis of a functional catechol-O-methyltransferase gene polymorphism in schizophrenia: Evidence for association with aggressive and antisocial behavior. *Psychiatry Research, 69*(X), 71–77.

Stylianou, S. (2002). The relationship between elements and manifestations of low self-control in a general theory of crime: two comments and a test. *Deviant Behavior, 23*(6), 531–557.

Sullivan, G., & Spritzer, K. (1997). The criminalization of persons with serious mental illness living in rural areas. *Journal of Rural Health, 13*(1), 6–13.

Survey of Inmates in State and Federal Correctional Facilities. (1997). Summary retrieved from *www.ojp.usdoj.gov/bjs/abstract/satsfp97.htm.*

Sutherland, E. (1924). *Principles of criminology* Chicago: Lippincott.

Sutherland, E. (1939). *Principles of criminology* (3rd ed.). Philadelphia: J. B. Lippincott.

Sutherland, E. (1947). *Principles of criminology* (4th ed.). Philadelphia: Lippincott.

Sutherland, E. (1977a). Is "white-collar crime" crime? In G. Geis & R. Meier (Eds.), *White-collar crime: Offenses in business, politics, and the professions*. New York: The Free Press.

Sutherland, E. (1977b). White-collar criminality. In G. Geis & R. Meier (Eds.), *White-collar crime: Offenses in business, politics, and the professions*. New York: The Free Press.

Sutherland, E., & Cressey, D. (1974). *Criminology* (9th ed.). Philadelphia: Lippincott.

Swezey, R. (1973). Estimating drugs crime relationships. *International Journal of the Addictions, 8,* 701–721.

Tannenbaum, F. (1938). *Crime and the community*. Boston: Ginn.

Tarde, G. (1968). *Penal philosophy*. Montclair, NJ: Patterson Smith. (Original work published 1890).

Tarter, R., Mezzich, A., Hsieh, Y., & Parks, S. (1995). Cognitive capacity in female adolescent substance abusers. *Drug and Alcohol Dependence, 39,* 15–21.

Taylor, E., Chadwick, O., Heptinstall, E., & Danckaerts, M. (1996). Hyperactivity and conduct problems as risk factors for adolescent development. *Journal of the American Academy of Child and Adolescent Psychiatry, 35*(9), 1213–1226.

Taylor, I., Walton, P., & Young, J. (1974). *The new criminology: For a social theory of deviance*. New York: Harper & Row.

Taylor, L. (1993). The role of offender profiling in classifying rapists: Implications for counseling. *Counseling Psychology Quarterly, 6*(4), 325–349.

Taylor, M., & Nee, C. (1988). The role of cues in simulated residential burglary. *British Journal of Criminology, 28,* 396–401.

Taylor, R. (1996). Neighborhood responses to disorder and local attachments: The systemic model of attachment, social disorganization, and neighborhood use value. *Sociological Forum, 11*(1), 41–74.

Taylor, R. (1997). Social order and disorder of street blocks and neighborhoods: Ecology, microecology, and the systemic model of social disorganization. *The Journal of Research in Crime and Delinquency, 34*(1), 113–155.

Taylor, R. (2001). The ecology of crime, fear, and delinquency: Social disorganization versus social efficacy. In R. Paternoster & R. Bachman (Eds.), *Explaining crime and criminals*. Los Angeles: Roxbury.

Taylor, R., & Harrell, A. (1996). *Physical environment and crime* (National Institute of Justice Research Report). Washington, DC: U.S. Department of Justice.

Taylor, R., Shumaker, S., & Gottfredson, S. (1985). Neighborhood level links between physical features and local sentiments, deterioration, fear of crime and confidence. *Journal of Architectural Planning and Research, 21,* 261–275.

Taylor, T., Freng, A., Esbensen, F., & Peterson, D. (2008). Youth gang membership and serious violent victimization: The importance of lifestyles and routine activities. *Journal of Interpersonal Violence, 23*(10), 1441–1464.

Teicher, M., Ito, Y., Glod, C., Schiffer, F., & Gelbard, H. (1997). Early abuse, limbic system dysfunction, and borderline personality disorder. In J. Osofsky (Ed.), *Children in a violent society.* New York: Guilford Press.

Tennes, K., & Kreye, M. (1985). Children's adrenocortical responses to classroom activities and tests in elementary school. *Psychosomatic Medicine, 47*(X), 451–460.

Tennes, K., Kreye, M., Avitable, N., & Wells, R. (1986). Behavioral correlates of excreted catecholamines and cortisol in second-grade children. *Journal of the American Academy of Child and Adolescent Psychiatry, 25*(X), 764–770.

Terpstra, D., Rozell, E., & Robinson, R. (1993). The influence of personality and demographic variables on ethical decisions related to insider trading. *The Journal of Psychology, 127*(4), 375–389.

Thaxton, S., & Agnew, R. (2004). The nonlinear effects of parental and teacher attachment on delinquency: Disentangling strain from social control explanations. *Justice Quarterly, 21*(4), 763–791.

Thomas, J., Garrison, M., Slawecki, C., Ehlers, C., & Riley, E. (2000). Nicotine exposure during the neonatal brain growth spurt produces hyperactivity in preweaning rats. *Neurotoxicity and Teratology, 22*(5), 695–701.

Thomas, T., & Znaniecki, F. (1958). *The Polish peasant in Europe and America.* New York: Dover Publications.

Thompson, C., & Fisher, B. (1996). Predicting household victimization utilizing a multi-level routine activity approach. *Journal of Crime and Justice, 19*(2), 49–66.

Thornberry, T. (1987). Toward an interactional theory of delinquency. *Criminology, 25*, 863–887.

Thornberry, T. (1997). Introduction. Some advantages of developmental and life-course perspectives for the study of crime and delinquency. In T. Thornberry (Ed.), *Developmental theories of crime and delinquency.* New Brunswick, NJ: Transaction.

Thornberry, T., Krohn, M., Lizotte, A., Smith, C., & Perter, P. (1998). *Taking stock: An overview of the findings from the Rochester Youth Development Study.* Paper presented at the annual meeting of the American Society of Criminology, Las Vegas, NV.

Thornberry, T., Lizotte, A., Krohn, M., Farnworth, M., & Jang, S. (1994). Delinquent peers, beliefs, and delinquent behavior: A longitudinal test of interactional theory. *Criminology, 32*(1), 47–83.

Tiffany, W., & Ketchel, J. (1979). Psychological deterrence in robberies of banks and its application to other institutions. In J. Kramer (Ed.), *The role of behavioral sciences in physical security.* National Bureau of Standards, Gaithersburg, MD.

Tinklenberg, J. (1973). Alcohol and violence. In P. Bourne (Ed.), *Alcoholism: Progress in research and treatment.* New York: Academic Press.

Titterington, V., Vollum, S., & Diamond, P. (2003). Neighborhoods and homicide. *Homicide Studies, 7*(3), 263–288.

Tittle, C. (1995). *Control balance: Toward a general theory of deviance.* Oxford: Westview Press.

Tittle, C. (1997). *The limits of theoretical integration.* Paper presented at the annual meeting of the American Society of Criminology, Chicago.

Tittle, C. (2001). Control balance. In R. Paternoster & R. Bachman (Eds.), *Explaining crime and criminals.* Los Angeles: Roxbury.

Tittle, C., & Botchkovar, E. (2005). The generality and hegemony of self-control theory: A comparison of Russian and US adults. *Social Science Research, 34*(4), 703–731.

Tittle, C., & Meier, R. (1990). Specifying the SES/delinquency relationship. *Criminology, 28,* 271–299.

Tittle, C., & Paternoster, R. (2000). *Social deviance and crime: An organizational and theoretical approach.* Los Angeles, CA: Roxbury.

Tittle, C., Ward, D., & Grasmick, H. (2003). Self-control and crime/deviance: Cognitive vs. behavioral measures. *Journal of Quantitative Criminology, 19*(4), 333–365.

Toby, J. (1957). Social disorganization and state in conformity. *Journal of Criminal Law, Criminology, and Police Science, 48:* 12–17.

Tomaskovic-Devey, D., Wright, C., Czaja, R., & Miller, K. (2006). Self-reports of police speeding stops by race: Results from the North Carolina reverse record check survey. *Journal of Quantitative Criminology, 22*(4), 279–297.

Tonry, M. (1995). *Malign neglect: Race, crime, and punishment in America.* New York: Oxford University Press.

Tonry, M., & Farrington, D. (1995). *Building a safer society.* Chicago: University of Chicago Press.

Tonry, M., Ohlin, L., & Farrington, D. (1991). *Human development and criminal behavior.* New York: Springer-Verlag.

Tori, C., & Emavardhana, T. (1998). The psychology of Thai delinquent youth: A study of self-perception, ego defenses, and personality traits. *International Journal of Offender Therapy and Comparative Criminology, 42*(4), 305–318.

Torrey, E. (1994). Violent behavior by individuals with serious mental illness. *Innovations & Research in Clinical Services, Community Support, and Rehabilitation, 3*(3), 5–17.

Torrey, E., Steiber, J., Ezekiel, J., Wolfe, S., Sharftein, J., Noble, J., & Flynn, L. (1992). *Criminalizing the seriously mentally ill: The abuse of jails as mental hospitals.* Washington, DC: National Alliance for the Mentally Ill and the Public Citizens Health Research Group.

Toy, C. (1992). Coming out to play: Reasons to join and participate in Asian gangs. *Journal of Gang Research, 1*(1), 13–29.

Tranel, D., & Damasio, H. (1994). Neuroanatomical correlates of electrodermal skin conductance responses. *Psychophysiology, 31*, 427–438.

Tremblay, R., Pihl, R., Vitaro, F., & Dobkin, P. (1994). Predicting early onset of male antisocial behavior from preschool behavior. *Archives of General Psychiatry, 51*, 732–739.

Tremblay, R., Vitaro, F., Bertrand, L., LeBlanc, M., Beauchesne, H., Boileau, H., & David, L. (1992). Parent and child training to prevent early onset of delinquency: A Montreal Longitudinal Experimental Study. In J. McCrod & R. Tremblay (Eds.), *Preventing antisocial behavior.* New York: Guillford.

Tsamis, V. (1998). *Developmental sociology: The empirical mapping of early child development.* Paper presented at the International Sociological Association, Warsaw, Poland.

Tseloni, A., Wittebrood, K., Farrell, G., & Pease, K. (2004). Burglary victimization in England and Wales, the United States, and the Netherlands: A cross-national comparative test of routine activities and lifestyle theories. *British Journal of Criminology, 44*(1), 66–91.

Tu, J., Shafey, H., & VanDewetering, C. (1994). Iron deficiency in two adolescents with conduct, dysthymic, and movement disorders. *Canadian Journal of Psychiatry, 39*,.

Tunnell, K. (1994). *Choosing crime: The criminal calculus of property offenders.* Chicago: Nelson-Hall.

Turner, M., Piquero, A., & Pratt, T. (2005). The school context as a source of self-control. *Journal of Criminal Justice, 33*(4), 327–339.

Tuthill, R. (1996). Hair lead levels related to children's classroom attention-deficit behavior. *Archives of Environmental Health, 51*(3), 214–220.

Tyler, T. (2006). Restorative justice and procedural justice: Dealing with rule breaking. *Journal of Social Issues, 62*(2), 307–326.

U.S. Census (2008). Income, poverty, and health insurance coverage in the United States: 2007. Retrieved January 13, 2009 from: *http://www.census.gov/prod/2008pubs/p60-235.pdf.*

U.S. Department of Energy. (1992). *Primer on molecular genetics.* Washington, DC: U.S. Department of Energy. Office of Energy Research.

U.S. Department of Energy. (2001). *Primer on molecular genetics.* Retrieved from *http://www.ornl.gov/hgmis/publicat/primer/intro.html.*

Udry, J. (1990). Biosocial models of adolescent problem behaviors. *Social Biology, 37,* 1–10.

Unis, A., Cook, E., Vincent, J., Gjerde, D., Perry, B., Mason, C., & Mitchell, J. (1997). Platelet serotonin measures in adolescents with conduct disorder. *Biological Psychiatry, 42*(7): 553–559.

Unnever, J., Cullen, F., & Pratt, T. (2003). Parental management, ADHD, and delinquent involvement: Reassessing Gottfredson and Hirschi's general theory. *Justice Quarterly, 20*(3), 471–500.

Valdez, A. (2001). Biker gangs: Crime on wheels. *Police, 25*(1), 46–48.

Van Brunschot, E., & Branningan, A. (1995). IQ and crime: Dull behavior and/or misspecified theory? *The Alberta Journal of Educational Research, 41*(3), 316–321.

van den Oord, E., Boomsma, D., & Verhulst, F. (1994). A study of problem behaviors in 10- to 15-year-old biologically related and unrelated international adoptees. *Behavior Genetics, 24*(3): 193–205.

Van Goozen, S. (2005). Hormones and the developmental origins of aggression. In R. Tremblay, W. Hartup, & J. Archer (Eds.), *Developmental origins of aggression* (pp. 281–306). New York: The Guilford Press.

van Goozen, S., Matthys, W., Cohen-Kettenis, P., Thijssen, J., & van Engeland, H. (1998). Adrenal androgens and aggression in conduct disorder prepubertal boys and normal controls. *Biological Psychiatry, 43*(2), 156–158.

Van Wyk, J., Benson, M., & Harris, D. (2000). A test of strain and self-control theories: Occupational crime in nursing homes. *Journal of Crime & Justice, 23*(2), 27–44.

Van Wyk, J., Benson, M., Fox, G., & Demaris, A. (2003). Detangling individual-, partner-, and community-level correlates of partner violence. *Crime & Delinquency, 49*(3), 412–438.

Vargha-Khadem, F., Cowan, J., & Mishkin, M. (2000). *Sociopathic behaviour after early damage to prefrontal cortex.* Paper presented at the annual meeting of the Society for Neuroscience.

Vastag, B. (1998). Smoke this: Genetics research begins to uncloud who gets hooked. *Journal of the National Cancer Institute, 90*(17), 1254–1255.

Vazsonyi, A., & Crosswhite, J. (2004). A test of Gottfredson and Hirschi's general theory of crime in African American Adolescents. *Journal of Research in Crime & Delinquency, 41*(4), 407–432.

Veysey, B., & Messner, S. (1999). Further testing of social disorganization theory: An elaboration of Sampson and Groves's "community structure and crime." *The Journal of Research in Crime and Delinquency, 36*(2), 156–174.

Vieraitis, L. (2000). Income inequality, poverty, and violent crime: A review of the empirical evidence. *Social Pathology, 6*(1), 24–45.

Vila, B. (1994). A general paradigm for understanding criminal behavior: Extending evolutionary ecological theory. *Criminology, 32*, 311–360.

Vila, B. (1997). Human nature and crime control: Improving the feasibility of nurturant crime control strategies. *Politics & the Life Sciences, 16*(1), 3–21.

Vila, B. (1997). Human nature and crime control: Improving the feasibility of nurturant strategies. *Politics and the Life Sciences, 16*, 3–21.

Virkkunen, M. (1985). Urinary free cortisol secretion in habitually violent offenders. *Acta Psychiatrica Scandinavia, 72*(1), 40–44.

Virkkunen, M., & Linnoila, M. (1990). Serotonin in early onset, male alcoholics with violent behaviour. *Annals of Medicine, 22*, 327–331.

Virkkunen, M., Goldman, D., & Linnoila, M. (1996). Serotonin in alcoholic violent offenders. In G. Bock & J. Goode (Eds.), *Genetics of criminal and antisocial behavior.* Chichester, England: John Wiley.

Virkkunen, M., Rawlings, R., Tokola, R., Poland, R., Guidotta, A., Nemeroff, C., et al. (1994). Suicidality and 5-HIAA concentration associated with a tryptophan hydroxylase polymorphism. *Archives of General Psychiatry, 51*, 20–27.

Virkunnen, M. (1974). Alcohol as a factor precipitating aggression and conflict behavior leading to homicide. *British Journal of the Addictions, 69*, 149–154.

Volavka, J. (1995). *Neurobiology of violence.* Washington, DC: American Psychiatric Press.

Volavka, J., Bilder, R., & Nolan, K. (2004). Catecholamines and aggression: The role of COMT and MAO polymorphisms. *Annals of the New York Academy of Sciences, 1036*(X), 393–398.

Volavka, J., Czobor, P., Goodwin, D., Gabrielli, W., & Penick, W. (1996). The electroencephalogram after alcohol administration in high-risk men and the development of alcohol use disorders 10 years later: Preliminary findings. *Archives of General Psychiatry, 53*(3), 258–263.

Vold, G. (1958). *Theoretical criminology.* New York: Oxford University Press.

Vold, G. (1979). *Theoretical criminology* (2nd ed.). New York: Oxford University Press.

Vold, G., Bernard, T., & Snipes, J. (1998). *Theoretical criminology* (4th ed.). New York: Oxford University Press.

Voss, H., & Petersen, D. (1971). *Ecology, crime and delinquency.* New York: Merideth.

Wakschlag, L., Pickett, K., Cook, E., Benowitz, N.,& Leventhal, B. (2002). Maternal smoking during pregnancy and severe antisocial behavior in offspring: A review. *American Journal of Public Health, 92*(6), 966–974.

Waldo, G., & Dinitz, S. (1967). Personality attributes of the criminal: An analysis of research studies, 1950–1965. *Journal of Research in Crime and Delinquency, 4*(2), 185–202.

Walker, S. (1998). *Sense and nonsense about crime and drugs.* Belmont, CA: Wadsworth.

Walker, S., III, Fisher, A., & Gaerin, D. (1997). *Relationship of childhood behavioral symptoms, prescription stimulant use, and adolescent and young adult drug abuse.* La Jolla: California Neuropsychiatric Institute.

Walker, S., Spohn, C., & Delone, M. (2000). *The color of justice: Race, ethnicity, and crime in America.* Belmont, CA: Wadsworth.

Waller, I., & Okihiro, N. (1978). *Burglary and the public: A victimological approach to crime justice.* Paper presented at the annual meeting of the American Society of Criminology, Reno, NV.

Walsh, A. (2000). Behavior genetics and anomie/strain theory. *Criminology, 38,* 1075–1107.

Walsh, A. (2002). *Biosocial criminology: Introduction and integration.* Cincinnati, OH: Anderson Publishing.

Walsh, A. (2009). *Biology and criminology: The biosocial synthesis.* New York: Routledge.

Walsh, A. (2009). Crazy by design: A biosocial approach to the age-crime curve." In A.

Walsh, A., & Beaver, K. (2007). *Criminology: An interdisciplinary approach.* Thousand Oaks, CA: Sage,.

Walsh, A., & Beaver, K. (2009). *Biosocial criminology: New directions in theory and research.* New York: Routledge.

Walsh, A., & Ellis, L. (1997). The neurobiology of nurturance, evolutionary expectations, and crime control. *Politics & the Life Sciences, 16*(1), 42–44.

Walsh, A., & Ellis, L. (1999). Political ideology and American criminologists' explanations for criminal behavior. *The Criminologist, 24*(6), 1–27.

Walsh, D. (1980). *Break-ins: Burglary from private houses.* London: Constable.

Walsh, E., Buchanan, A., & FAHY, T. (2002). Violence and schizophrenia: Examining the evidence. *British Journal of Psychiatry, 180*(X), 490–495.

Walters, G., & White, T. (1989). Heredity and crime: Bad genes or bad research. *Criminology, 27,* 455–486.

Wand, G., Mangold, D., El Deiry, S., McCaul, M., & Hoover, D. (1998). Family history of alcoholism and hypothalamic opioidergic activity. *Archives of General Psychiatry, 55*(12), 1114–1119.

Wand, G., Mangold, D., el Deitry, S., McCaul, M., & Hoover, D. (1998). Family history of alcoholism and hypothalamic opioidergic activity. *Archives of General Psychiatry, 55*(12): 1114–1119.

Wang, F., & Arnold, M. (2008). Localized income inequality, concentrated disadvantage and homicide. *Applied Geography, 28*(4), 259–270.

Ward, N. (1997). Assessment of chemical factors in relation to child hyperactivity. *Journal of Nutritional and Environmental Medicine, 7,* 333.

Warner, B., & Fowler, S. (2003). Strain and violence: Testing a general strain theory model of community violence. *Journal of Criminal Justice, 31*(6), 511–521.

Warner, B., & Pierce, G. (1993). Reexamining social disorganization theory using calls to the police as a measure of crime. *Criminology, 31*(4), 493–517.

Warner, B., & Rountree, P. (1997). Local social ties in a community and crime model: Questioning the systemic nature of informal social control. *Social Problems, 44*(4), 520–536.

Warner-Rogers, J., Taylor, A., Taylor, E., & Sandberg, S. (2000). Inattentive behavior in childhood. *Journal of Learning Disabilities, 33*(6), 520–537.

Warr, M. (1990). Dangerous situations: Social context and fear of victimization. *Social Forces, 68,* 891–907.

Warr, M. (1993). Age, peers, and delinquency. *Criminology, 31*(1), 17–40.

Warr, M. (1996). Organization and instigation in delinquent groups. *Criminology, 34,* 11–37.

Warr, M. (1998). Life-course transitions and desistance from crime. *Criminology, 36*(2), 183–216.

Warr, M. (2001). The social origins of crime: Edwin Sutherland and the theory of differential association. In R. Paternoster & R. Bachman (Eds.), *Explaining crime and criminals.* Los Angeles: Roxbury.

Warr, M., & Stafford, M. (1983). Fear of victimization: A look at the proximate causes. *Social Forces, 61,* 1033–1043.

Warren, P., Tomaskovic-Devey, D., Smith, W., Zingraff, M., & Mason, M. (2006). Driving while black: Bias processes and racial disparity in police stops. *Criminology, 44*(3), 709–738.

Watkins, C. (1999). Social control of the drinking driver. *Journal of Crime and Justice, 22*(2), 225–230.

Weaver, G., & Wootton, R. (1992). The use of the MMPI special scales in the assessment of delinquent personality. *Adolescence, 27*(107), 545–554.

Webtser, C., Doob, A., & Zimring, F. (2006). Proposition 8 and crime rates in California: The case of the disappearing deterrent. *Criminology & Public Policy, 5*(3), 417–448.

Weigel, R., Hessing, D., & Elffers, H. (1999). Egoism: Measurement and implications for deviance. *Psychology, Crime and Law, 5*(4), 349–378.

Weil, A. (1998). Why people take drugs. In J. Inciardi & K. McElrath (Eds.), *The American drug scene: An anthology.* Los Angeles: Roxbury.

Weintraub, K., & Gold, M. (1991). Monitoring and delinquency. *Criminal Behavior and Mental Health, 1*(3), 268–281.

Weisburd, D., & Schlegel, K. (1992). Returning to the mainstream: Reflections on past and future white-collar crime study. In K. Schlegel & D. Weisburd (Eds.), *White-collar crime reconsidered.* Boston: Northeastern University Press.

Weisburd, D., Enat, T., & Kowalski, M. (2008). The miracle of the cells: An experimental study of interventions to increase payment of court-ordered financial obligations. *Criminology & Public Policy, 7*(1), 5–8.

Weiss, B. (1997). Pesticides as a source of developmental disabilities. *Mental Retardation and Developmental Disabilities Research Reviews, 3,* 246–256.

Weissman, M., Warner, V., Wickramaratne, P., & Kandel, D. (1999). Maternal smoking during pregnancy and psychopathology in offspring followed to adulthood. *Journal of the American Academy of Child and Adolescent Psychiatry, 38*(7), 892–899.

Welsh, W., Stokes, R., & Greene, J. (2000). A macro-level model of school disorder. *Journal of Research in Crime and Delinquency, 37*(3), 243–283.

Werbach, M. (1995). Nutritional influences on aggressive behavior. *Journal of Orthomolecular Medicine, 7*(1). Available: *www.healthy.net/library/journals/ortho/issue7.1/Jom-mw1.htm.*

Wessely, S. (1997). The epidemiology of crime, violence, and schizophrenia. *The British Journal of Psychiatry, 170*(32), 8–11.

Westergaard, G., Suomi, S., Higley, J., & Mehlman, P. (1999). CSF 5-HIAA and aggression in female macaque monkeys: Species and interindividual differences. *Psychopharmacology, 146:* 440–446.

Westview Press.

White, G. (1999). Crime and the decline of manufacturing, 1970–1990. *Justice Quarterly, 16*(1), 81–97.

Whitehead, A. (1925). *Science and the modern world.* New York: MacMillan.

Widom, C. (1989). Does violence beget violence? A critical examination of the literature. *Psychological Bulletin, 106,* 3–28.

Widom, C. (2000). Childhood victimization: Early adversity, later psychopathology. *National Institute of Justice Journal,* January.

Widom, C., & Maxfield, M. (2001, February). An update on the "cycle of violence." *National Institute of Justice Research in Brief.*

Wiebe, R. (2003). Reconciling psychopathy and low self-control. *Justice Quarterly, 20*(2), 297–336.

Wiebe, R. (2006). Using an expanded measure of self-control to predict delinquency. *Psychology, Crime & Law, 12*(5), 519–536.

Wiesner, M., & Capaldi, D. (2003). Relations of childhood and adolescent factors to offending trajectories of young men. *Journal of Research in Crime & Delinquency, 40*(3), 231–262.

Wikstroem, P. (1998). Communities and crime. In M. Tonry (Ed.), *The handbook of crime and punishment*. New York: Oxford University Press.

Wikstroem, P., & Loeber, R. (2000). Do disadvantaged neighborhoods cause well-adjusted children to become adolescent delinquents? A study of male juvenile serious offending, individual risk and protective factors and neighborhood context. *Criminology, 38*, 1109–1142.

Wilens, T., Biederman, J., Mick, E., Faraone, S., & Spencer, T. (1997). Attention deficit hyperactivity disorder (ADHD) is associated with early onset substance use disorders. *Journal of Nervous and Mental Disease, 185*(8), 475–482.

Willatts, P., Forsyth, J., DiModugno, M., Varma, S., & Colvin, M. (1998). Effect of long-chain polyunsaturated fatty acids in infant formula on problem solving at 10 months of age. *Lancet, 352*(9129), 688–691.

Williams, F., & McShane, M. (1994). *Criminological theory* (2nd ed.). Englewood Cliffs, NJ: Prentice-Hall.

Williams, L., Clinton, L., Winfree, L., & Clark, R. (1992). Family ties, parental discipline, and delinquency: A study of youthful misbehavior by parochial high school students. *Sociological Spectrum, 12*(4), 381–401.

Wilson, J. (1968). The urban unease: Community vs. city. *The Public Interest, 12*, 25–39.

Wilson, J., & Herrnstein, R. (1985). *Crime and human nature*. New York: Simon & Schuster.

Wilson, J., & Kelling, G. (1982). Broken windows: The police and neighborhood safety. *The Atlantic Monthly*, (March): 29–38.

Wilson, W. (1987). *The truly disadvantaged: The inner city, the underclass, and public policy*. Chicago: University of Chicago Press.

Winchester, F., & Jackson, H. (1982). *Residential burglary: The limits of prevention* (Home Office Research Study 74). London: Her Majesty's Stationary Office.

Winfree Jr., L., Taylor, T., He, N., & Esbensen, F. (2006). Self-control and variability over time: multivariate results using a 5-year, multisite panel of youths. *Crime & Delinquency, 52*(2), 253–286.

Witt, R., Clarke, A., & Fielding, N. (1999). Crime and economic activity: A panel data approach. *The British Journal of Criminology, 39*(3), 391–400.

Woermann, F., van Elst, L., Koepp, M., Free, S., Thompson, P., Trimble, M., & Duncan, J. (2000). Reduction of frontal neocortical grey matter associated with affective aggression in patients with temporal lobe epilepsy: An objective voxel by voxel analysis of automatically segmented MRI. *Journal of Neurology, Neurosurgery, and Psychiatry, 68*(2), 162–169.

Wolf, Y. (1997). A balanced paradigm of crime control: Programmatic and methodological considerations. *Politics & the Life Sciences, 16*(2), 313–314.

Wolman, W., & Colamosca, A. (1997). *The Judas economy: The triumph of capital and the betrayal of work.* Reading, PA: Addison-Wesley.

Wood, P., Cochran, J., Pfefferbaum, B., & Arneklev, B. (1995). Sensation-seeking and delinquent substance use: An extension of learning theory. *Journal of Drug Issues, 25*(1), 173–193.

Wood, P., Gove, W., Wilson, J., & Cochran, J. (1997). Nonsocial reinforcement and habitual criminal conduct: An extension of learning theory. *Criminology, 35*(2), 335–366.

Wood, P., Pfefferbaum, B., & Arneklev, B. (1993). Risk-taking and self-control: Social psychological correlates of delinquency. *Journal of Crime and Justice, 16*, 111–130.

Wright, B., Caspi, A., Moffitt, T., & Paternoster, R. (2004). Does the perceived risk of punishment deter criminally-prone individuals? Rational choice, self-control, and crime. *Journal of Research in Crime and Delinquency, 41*, 180–213.

Wright, B., Caspi, A., Moffitt, T., & Silva, P. (1999). Low self-control, social bonds, and crime: Social causation, social selection or both? *Criminology, 37*(3), 479–514.

Wright, J. (2009). Inconvenient truths: Science, race, and crime. In A. Walsh, & K. Beaver (2009). *Biosocial criminology: New directions in theory and research.* New York: Routledge.

Wright, J., & Beaver, K. (2005). Do parents matter in creating self-control in their children? A genetically informed test of Gottfredson and Hirschi's theory of low self-control. *Criminology, 43*(4), 1169–1202.

Wright, J., & Beaver, K. (2005). Do parents matter in creating self-control in their children? A genetically informed test of Gottfredson and Hirschi's theory of low self-control. *Criminology 43*(4), 1169–1202.

Wright, J., & Rossi, P. (1983). *Armed and considered dangerous: A survey of felons and their firearms.* Hawthorne, NY: Aldine de Guyer.

Wright, J., Beaver, K., Delisi, M., Vaughan, M., Boivert, D., & Vaske, J. (2008). Lombroso's legacy: The miseducation of criminologists. *Journal of Criminal Justice Education, 19*(3), 325–338.

Wright, J., Boisvert, D., Dietrich, K., & Ris, M. D. (2009). The ghost in the machine and criminal behavior: Criminology for the 21st century. In A.

Walsh, & K. Beaver (2009). *Biosocial criminology: New directions in theory and research*. New York: Routledge.

Wright, J., Cullen, F., Agnew, R., & Brezina, T. (2001). "The root of all evil?": An exploratory study of money and delinquent involvement. *Justice Quarterly, 18*(2), 239–268.

Wright, J., Dietrich, K., Ris, M., Hornung, R., Wessel, S., Lanphear, B., Ho, M., & Rae, M. (2008). Association of prenatal and childhood blood lead concentrations with criminal arrests in early adulthood. *PLoS, 5*(5), 0732–0740.

Wright, J., Tibbetts, S., & Daigle, L. (2008). *Criminals in the making: Criminality across the life course*. Thousand Oaks, CA: Sage.

Wright, R., & Decker, S. (1994). *Burglars on the job: Streetlife and residential break-ins*. Boston: Northeastern University Press.

Wurtman, R. (1995). Quoted in *Crime-Times, 1*, (1–2), 1.

Xie, M., & Mcdowall, D. (2008). The effects of residential turnover on household victimization. *Criminology, 46*(3), 539–575.

Yang, Y., Raine, A., Lencz, T., Bihrle, S., Lacasse, L., & Colletti, P. (2005). Volume reduction in prefrontal gray matter in unsuccessful criminal psychopaths. *Biological Psychiatry, 57*(X), 1103–1108.

Yaralian, P., & Raine, A. (2001). Psychophysiology and brain dysfunction. In R. Paternoster & R. Bachman (Eds.), *Explaining crime and criminals*. Los Angeles: Roxbury.

Yeudall, L. (1977). Neuropsychological assessments in forensic disorders. *Canada's Mental Health, 25*(2), 7–14.

Yinger, J. (1994). *Ethnicity: Source of strength? Source of conflict*. Albany: State University of New York Press.

Yochelson, S., & Samenow, S. (1976). *The criminal personality*. New York: Jason Aronson.

Young, S., Stallings, M., Corley, R., Krauter, K., & Hewitt, J. (2000). Genetic and environmental influences on behavioral disinhibition. *American Journal of Medical Genetics, 96*, 684–695.

Yu, M. (2001). *Environmental toxicology: Impacts of environmental toxicants on living systems*. Boca Raton, FL: Lewis Publishers.

Yudofsky, S., Silver, J., & Schneider, S. (1987). Pharmacologic treatment of aggression. *Psychiatric Annals, 17*(X), 397–407.

Zametkin, A., Nordahl, T., Gross, M., King, A., Semple, W., Rumsey, J., et al. (1990). Cerebral glucose metabolism in adults with hyperactivity of childhood onset. *New England Journal of Medicine, 323*(1), 1361–1366.

Zeifman, D., & Hazan, C. (1997). Attachment: The bond in pair-bonds. In J. Simpson & D. Kenrick (Eds.), *Evolutionary social psychology*. Mahwah, NJ: Lawrence Erlbaum.

Zhang, L., & Messner, S. (2000). The effects of alternative measures of delinquent peers on self-reported delinquency. *The Journal of Research in Crime and Delinquency, 37*(3), 323–337.

Zimbardo, P. (1992). Quoted by the Canadian Centre for Missing Children. Retrieved from *www.victimsofviolence.on.ca/research292.html*.

Zimring, F. (1997). The doom of a good intention. *Politics & the Life Sciences, 16*(1), 44–45.

Zuckerman, M. (1987). A critical look at three arousal constructs in personality theories: Optimal levels of arousal, strength of the nervous system, and sensitivities to signals of reward and punishment. In J. Strelau & H. Eysenck (Eds.), *Personality dimensions and arousal: Perspectives on individual differences*. New York: Plenum Press.

Zuckerman, M. (1990). The psychophysiology of sensation-seeking. *Journal of Personality, 58*, 314–345.

Index

Pages with tables or illustrations are indicated in **bold** font.